S0-BRS-381

Minding Women:
Reshaping the
Educational Realm

Edited by

CHRISTINE A. WOYSHNER

and

HOLLY S. GELFOND

Reprint Series No. 30

Harvard Educational Review

371,822
m663

Copyright © 1998 by President and Fellows of Harvard College

All rights reserved. No part of this publication may be reproduced or transmitted in any form or by any means, electronic or mechanical, including photocopy, recording, or any information storage and retrieval systems, without permission in writing from the publisher.

Library of Congress Catalog Card Number 97-77122

ISBN 0-916690-32-6

Harvard Educational Review
Gutman Library Suite 349
6 Appian Way
Cambridge, MA 02138

Cover Design: Alyssa Morris
Cover Drawing: Kevin Parker
Editorial Production: Dody Riggs
Typesetting: Sheila Walsh

This book is dedicated to Cathryn and Amy Pye,
and Victoria and Hannah Woyshner.

May your wisdom, compassion, and courage
guide your journey from girlhood to womanhood.

Contents

Foreword

JANIE VICTORIA WARD

For most of this century, the traditional academic and research community tacitly ignored women; to them we didn't exist, didn't contribute, and didn't matter. Fortunately, despite our invisibility, we believed otherwise. During the past two decades we set about remedying such falsehoods and asserting the validity of our own truth claims. The articles, essays, poems, and research reports presented in *Minding Women: Reshaping the Educational Realm* map a trajectory of research on women. They chronicle the forces of feminist resistance to the prevailing dominant discourse that excludes women from research and scholarship, and in so doing call forth the voices of women and girls — unveiling our lives, our work, and the sensibilities we bring to our reflections upon who we are and what we do.

Moving from silence to voice, the authors in *Minding Women* reflect women's shift from the periphery to the center of intellectual inquiry. In establishing a research agenda that is more reflective of and attuned to women's realities and perspectives, researchers in many disciplines have been transforming theory production with a powerful momentum. As women's membership in the research community grows more diverse nationally and internationally, new interests emerge to capture our attention and expand the parameters around which future discussions will unfold. Outside the academy, the critical attention to women's lives has been similarly influential, most notably in supporting and expanding our understanding of a wide range of important issues from public policy (the feminization of poverty) to law (reproductive rights) and medicine (women's health).

Over the past twenty years, as scholarship and research became more responsive to and reflective of *some* women, other women, failing to see themselves represented once again, unleashed their own critique of the feminist critique. Over time, and largely through the application of feminist pedagogies such as hearing from and listening to women, voices of opposition were heard in a second wave of resistance led by women of color, poor and working-class women, lesbians, and other historically marginalized women. These women, "the outsiders within," dismayed by what they perceived as the routine disregard afforded them in the newly emerging theories of womanhood, warned their predominately White, socially privileged sister researchers against creating an exclusionary feminism, and called for all feminist scholars to seriously attend to the intersections of race, class, and cultural differences within gender. We gain from these readings an appreciation of the progressive evolution of woman-centered theory production and the critical influence of social position vis-à-vis theory construction.

Historically, we began by identifying and explaining the nature and function of women's oppression, the powerful ways in which sexism and racism fundamentally shape women's lives. We are finding, however, that the enterprise of minding women takes us on introspective journeys that are at once both personal and political. In our attempt to locate ourselves within the multiple, often overlapping narratives of women's lives, increasing numbers of researchers are turning their gaze inward, critically examining the processes by which we come to know and value who we are and what we do. Some women, particularly those of us whose marginalized identities and experiences disallow our race and gender subjectivities from aligning with the dominant discourse, will consciously engage in oppositional, counter-conversations of resistance. And as we struggle against external forces of race, gender, and class oppression, we will also turn our gaze inward in order to root out the oppressor within, that is, the self-hatred that comes from the internalization of pejorative beliefs about disenfranchised women and families. In turn, White women will look inward and confront their own privilege and the ways in which it can both blind and bind, thus obstructing honest theory construction. We will refuse to participate in theoretical constructions of women that do not take into account and accordingly reflect the truth of our lives.

Minding Women reminds us of our stories of resistance and liberation — of women rising up from being hidden, ignored, and silenced, fighting back from having their truth claims devalued and undermined. These are hard-won battles of women's self-determination, and the range of women's experiences — in history, education, and social activism — elicits pride in our power. I hope that the writings in this book, and particularly the essays, stories, and poems of the younger women, strengthen a desire to fight on.

Introduction

Minding Women: Reshaping the Educational Realm captures the influential scholarship of the 1970s, 1980s, and 1990s that insisted that researchers and practitioners *mind* — pay attention to, give heed, and be concerned with — the development and education of girls and women. With her 1977 *Harvard Educational Review* article "In a Different Voice," Carol Gilligan challenged the academic community to respond to her call that women and girls be understood on their own terms. Gilligan's scholarship redefined many facets of educational research and practice, changing the framework for thinking about moral development — about justice, care, love, and the nature of human relationships. As such, her work has influenced a myriad of disciplines related to education — including moral development, psychology, teacher education, pedagogy, and the history of women in education — and inspired a broad array of fields less directly related to education, such as gender studies, philosophy, medicine, and law. In essence, Gilligan's groundbreaking article marked the beginning of a process that has redefined the educational realm. Since Gilligan's research was first published, many researchers have followed suit and broadened the scholarship to include previously unheard voices, such as those of girls and women of color, and of people of various ethnicities, races, and sexual preferences.

As women in the fields of education and psychology, we have chosen to edit a book devoted to girls and women in education in order to acknowledge the significant developments in scholarship that have taken place during our own lifetimes. *Minding Women* is about how this scholarship has influenced the understanding of girls and women. By incorporating this new research, the field of education has been transformed: this research not only helps us to better understand the experiences of girls and women, but also leads us to question and reconstruct basic assumptions that have guided and formed education as we know it in such areas as pedagogy, curriculum, and psychological and social development.

In the interest of sharing our hopes and questions with others, *Minding Women* is our offering to educators, psychologists, historians, and other researchers and practitioners interested in girls' and women's education. We believe that the selections in *Minding Women* have a timelessness that transcends the eras in which they were written and that they will continue to influence educational research and practice into the next century. Other current events cause us to reflect on the progress that has been made that affects research in this arena. For instance, the creation of a Chair of Gender Studies at our own university to be held by Carol Gilligan demonstrates a public acknowledgment by Harvard University of the importance of this work in the past and a commitment to continuing this research in the future. This Chair will serve as a permanent and salient symbol to encourage and inspire future scholars. We hope that this volume will also inspire others to continue research in this diverse, vital, and ever-changing area.

The chapters of *Minding Women* are organized thematically into five sections: Classics; Feminist Pedagogy; Girls and Young Women; History; and Identity. Each section highlights pioneering articles within that area. The articles in each section are arranged in the order in which they originally appeared in the *Harvard Educational Review*. This format is meant to reflect the evolution of girls' and women's struggles in education. Some of the questions that have guided us and shaped this volume are: How has the research on girls' and women's development evolved over the past twenty years? How have new understandings of girls' and women's development influenced the educational realm? What is a feminist pedagogy and how can it be implemented? What are the experiences of women in the past and what can we learn from these experiences? What are the complexities and conundrums of a woman's identity as she explores the intersections of her experiences as a person of color, or as an Indigenous American lesbian, a gay or bisexual youth? How do a woman's multiple identities intersect with her role as researcher, teacher, writer, growing girl?

Part One, "Classics," features two works by Carol Gilligan: "In a Different Voice: Women's Conceptions of Self and Morality" and "Woman's Place in Man's Life Cycle." In "In a Different Voice," Gilligan interviews women about their decisions to have or not have an abortion. She brings to the foreground women's conceptions of morality — responsibility to others, connectedness, care, and compassion — and juxtaposes these frameworks against traditional theories of moral development that highlight conceptions of morality based on justice and rights. In "Woman's Place in Man's Life Cycle," Gilligan critiques theories of psychological development that emphasize separation and autonomy as the primary goal of development. Drawing on literary and psychological sources, Gilligan argues that such theories, by ignoring intimacy and relationship, reflect a bias that originates in conceptions and patriarchal ideals of men's lives, and thus obfuscates women's psychological growth and development.

In her classic article, "Excluding Women from the Educational Realm," Jane Roland Martin examines the exclusion of women in the field of the philosophy of education: "Although throughout history women have reared and taught the young and have themselves been educated, they are excluded both as the subjects and objects of educational thought" (p. 60). Martin concludes that by addressing questions regarding women's activities and values such as child-rearing and nurturance, the field of the philosophy of education would be transformed.

In Part Two, "Feminist Pedagogy," Marilyn Schuster and Susan Van Dyne analyze the process of integrating women into the liberal arts curriculum. In "Placing Women in the Liberal Arts: Stages of Curriculum Transformation," they suggest that teachers move through a variety of stages — noting important women who are absent from the curriculum, identifying significant contributions made by women, discussing why women often are not in leadership roles, discussing women on their own terms — resulting in a more "balanced" curriculum.

Eva Young and Mariwilda Padilla, in "Mujeres Unidas en Acción: A Popular Education Process," describe feminist pedagogy at work in a nonprofit, community-based agency in Dorchester, Massachusetts. The authors highlight the agency's educational program for Spanish-speaking women, a program that strengthens literacy in their native language, thus fostering these women's process of second-language acquisition as well as their ability to become organizers and leaders within their own community. We conclude this section with Kathleen Weiler's critique of Paulo Freire's work, "Freire and a Feminist Pedagogy of Difference." Weiler questions Freire's notion that all who experience oppression and/or liberation do so in the same manner. By integrating the complexity of feminist pedagogy with Freire's vision, Weiler addresses the specificity of women's lives by suggesting the importance of personal experience as a source of knowledge, questioning the authority of the teacher, and exploring the perspectives of people of different races, classes, and ethnicities.

"Girls and Young Women," the title of Part Three, opens with "Chronicles" — selections presenting the voices of six young women. The topics these women describe include their experiences of rape, of coming to terms with their sexuality, and of moving from a private to public school as an African American. They also reflect on the nature of relationships and the way women are represented in pop culture. Michelle Fine, in "Sexuality, Schooling, and Adolescent Females: The Missing Discourse of Desire," challenges the implementation, and lack thereof, of sex education in schools. Fine argues that despite substantial evidence of the success of school-based sex education programs, few public schools actually provide such programs, and those that do fail to do so in a way that fosters the full development of a sexual self. In "Voice, Play, and a Practice of Ordinary Courage in Girls' and Women's Lives," Annie Rogers explores how girls often lose the courage to speak their minds and hearts as they enter adolescence. Rogers asks, "What is a practice of courage in relationships that makes it possible for women and girls . . . to stay with one another, rather than abandoning one another at the edge of difficult and vital truths?" (p. 211). Rogers suggests that by accessing girls' inner lives through voice, play, and a "poetics of research" grounded in feminist epistemologies, we may create a way to sustain the development of courage in girls throughout their adolescence and beyond.

We contrast Michelle Fine's focus on developing girls' positive sexual identities by acknowledging their sexual desires with Nan Stein's chapter, "Sexual Harassment in School: The Public Performance of Gendered Violence." Stein argues that adult intervention by teachers and parents is needed to curtail and prevent sexual harassment in the schools. Stein presents numerous cases of sexual harassment of both girls and boys in schools, and advocates for a curriculum that heightens awareness of these issues. Stein also describes cases in which students filed lawsuits with the Office of Civil Rights, and how the varied responses of the courts and faculty sent mixed messages to students and adults about how to conceptualize, judge, and respond to sexual harassment.

Part Four, "History," begins with William Ayers's contribution, "'We Who Believe in Freedom Cannot Rest Until It's Done': Two Dauntless Women of the Civil Rights Movement and the Education of a People." Ayers reviews biographies of activist educators Ella Baker and Septima Clark, highlighting the contributions of these two African American women to educational history. Commenting that they were not widely known outside of the movement, Ayers points out that we all need to know their stories because such knowledge "inspires us with what can be done and instructs us on what is yet to be done" (p. 258). Linda Eisenmann, in "Reconsidering a Classic: Assessing the History of Women's Higher Education a Dozen Years after Barbara Solomon," examines the role and impact of Barbara Solomon's now classic 1985 text, *In the Company of Educated Women*. Eisenmann reflects on Solomon's influence on the field of women's educational history, and shows how current historical research — such as the study of normal schools and academies — grew out of Solomon's work. Yet Eisenmann critiques Solomon for placing too much emphasis on women's access to higher education, thereby ignoring the importance of wider historical and educational influences such as economics, women's occupational choices, and the treatment of women in society at large. Eisenmann assesses the important contributions made by Solomon and urges future research to focus on areas beyond the limits defined by Solomon's book.

Linda Perkins explores the lives of Black women at prestigious colleges in "The African American Female Elite: The Early History of African American Women in the Seven Sister Colleges, 1880–1960." Perkins outlines the historical experiences of African American women who attended the Seven Sister colleges from the institutions' founding to the civil rights era of the 1960s. Perkins illustrates how the Seven Sisters mirrored the views of the larger society in terms of race, and how issues of discrimination in admissions, housing, and financial aid in these institutions were influenced by and had an influence on the overall African American struggle for full participatory citizenship. In "The Hidden Half: A History of Native American Women's Education," Deirdre Almeida surveys the educational experiences of indigenous women and girls in the United States, covering both Native women's traditional learning and their education in formal, Western-based settings. Almeida demonstrates how traditional education for Native American women was, and still is, connected to the political power of Native American women within their communities. She shows how Western-based education and government control have been used to destroy the traditional power of Native American women. Almeida presents the voices of Native American women who have resisted the breakdown of this power and have used education to reclaim and protect it. Part Four concludes with a contemplation of historiography in Kathleen Weiler's "Reflections on Writing a History of Women Teachers." Weiler reflects on the writing of her book *Country Schoolwomen,* and on some of the most salient issues currently under debate among feminist scholars. She offers her insights into the process of uncovering the lives of women of the past through oral history and document analysis in light of questions about the nature of knowledge, the influence of language in the social construction of gender, and the importance of considering the conditions under which testimony is given.

In Part Five, "Identity," Alex Wilson examines "How We Find Ourselves: Identity Development and Two Spirit People." Wilson challenges traditional separations of sexual and racial identity, and examines identity development from an Indigenous American woman's perspective. This perspective, according to Wilson, holds that sexuality and the experience of culture and community are inseparable. Following this, she argues for a reconstruction of identity development models to embrace such perspectives. Sofia Villenas, in "The Colonizer/Colonized Chicana Ethnographer: Identity, Marginalization, and Co-optation in the Field," examines her complicity in her own colonization and marginalization as a researcher in the field of ethnography. Reflecting on her work in a rural North Carolina Latino community, she questions the position of dominant-culture ethnographers and recognizes her own role as a border-crosser. In "Learning in the Dark: How Assumptions of Whiteness Shape Classroom Knowledge," Frances Maher and Mary Kay Thompson Tetreault interrogate their own assumptions of Whiteness in their book, *The Feminist Classroom.* Maher and Tetreault revisit how assumptions of Whiteness — that being White is "normal," the invisibility and pervasiveness of White privilege, and how academic frameworks used in the classroom are based on White perspectives — shape the construction of knowledge in the classroom. Maher and Tetreault also question their previously held assumptions of being White feminist allies, recognizing it as a social position of privilege over women of color. Stacey Lee, in "The Road to College: Hmong American Women's Pursuit of Higher Education," presents her findings from interviews with a group of Hmong American women who are pursuing or have completed higher education in the United States. Lee argues that the focus on cultural differences as the sole explanation for the low educational participation and achievement among Hmong American women ignores the existence of economic, racial, and other structural barriers to their educational persistence and success. These women's stories illustrate that cultural transformation is neither a smooth nor unambiguous process.

As valuable a contribution as this collection of articles may be, we still feel that the process of learning about women and girls of all races, ethnicities, and classes — their ways of knowing, learning, resisting, developing, relating, and teaching — has just begun. As the evolution of the study of girls and.

women continues, it reflects the ever-changing awareness of the diversity within society at large and the educational realm specifically. Our vision here, and for the future of the *Harvard Educational Review*, is to build on the progress achieved in this arena over the past several decades in order to address the still urgent issues faced by girls and women as they learn, develop, and achieve their dreams.

CHRISTINE A. WOYSHNER
HOLLY S. GELFOND
Harvard Graduate School of Education

PART ONE

Classics

In a Different Voice:
Women's Conceptions of Self and of Morality

CAROL GILLIGAN

In this chapter, which is as relevant today as it was twenty years ago, Carol Gilligan reminds educators and researchers to scrutinize not only the underlying assumptions of theories of developmental psychology, but also the model of adulthood toward which they point. Gilligan examines the limitations of several theories, most notably Kohlberg's stage theory of moral development, and concludes that developmental theory has not given adequate expression to the concerns and experiences of women. Through a review of psychological and literary sources, she illustrates the feminine construction of reality. Then, from her own research data — including interviews with women contemplating abortion — she derives an alternative sequence for the development of women's moral judgments. Finally, Gilligan argues for an expanded conception of adulthood that would result from the integration of the "feminine voice" into developmental theory.

The arc of developmental theory leads from infantile dependence to adult autonomy, tracing a path characterized by an increasing differentiation of self from other and a progressive freeing of thought from contextual constraints. The vision of Luther, journeying from the rejection of a self defined by others to the assertive boldness of "Here I stand" and the image of Plato's allegorical man in the cave, separating at last the shadows from the sun, have taken powerful hold on the psychological understanding of what constitutes development. Thus, the individual, meeting fully the developmental challenges of adolescence as set for him by Piaget, Erikson, and Kohlberg, thinks formally, proceeding from theory to fact, and defines both the self and the moral autonomously, that is, apart from the identification and conventions that had comprised the particulars of his childhood world. So equipped, he is presumed ready to live as an adult, to

Harvard Educational Review Vol. 47 No. 4 November 1977, 481–517

love and work in a way that is both intimate and generative, to develop an ethical sense of caring and a genital mode of relating in which giving and taking fuse in the ultimate reconciliation of the tension between self and other.

Yet the men whose theories have largely informed this understanding of development have all been plagued by the same problem, the problem of women, whose sexuality remains more diffuse, whose perception of self is so much more tenaciously embedded in relationships with others, and whose moral dilemmas hold them in a mode of judgment that is insistently contextual. The solution has been to consider women as either deviant or deficient in their development.

That there is a discrepancy between concepts of womanhood and adulthood is nowhere more clearly evident than in the series of studies on sex-role stereotypes reported by Broverman, Vogel, Broverman, Clarkson, and Rosenkrantz (1972). The repeated finding of these studies is that the qualities deemed necessary for adulthood — the capacity for autonomous thinking, clear decisionmaking, and responsible action — are those associated with masculinity but considered undesirable as attributes of the feminine self. The stereotypes suggest a splitting of love and work that relegates the expressive capacities requisite for the former to women while the instrumental abilities necessary for the latter reside in the masculine domain. Yet, looked at from a different perspective, these stereotypes reflect a conception of adulthood that is itself out of balance, favoring the separateness of the individual self over its connection to others and leaning more toward an autonomous life of work than toward the interdependence of love and care.

This difference in point of view is the subject of this chapter, which seeks to identify in the feminine experience and construction of social reality a distinctive voice, recognizable in the different perspective it brings to bear on the construction and resolution of moral problems. The first section begins with the repeated observation of difference in women's concepts of self and of morality. This difference is identified in previous psychological descriptions of women's moral judgments and described as it again appears in current research data. Examples drawn from interviews with women in and around a university community are used to illustrate the characteristics of the feminine voice. The relational bias in women's thinking that has, in the past, been seen to compromise their moral judgment and impede their development now begins to emerge in a new developmental light. Instead of being seen as a developmental deficiency, this bias appears to reflect a different social and moral understanding.

This alternative conception is enlarged in the second section through consideration of research interviews with women facing the moral dilemma of whether to continue or abort a pregnancy. Since the research design allowed women to define as well as resolve the moral problem, developmental distinctions could be derived directly from the categories of women's thought. The responses of women to structured interview questions regarding the pregnancy decision formed the basis for describing a developmental sequence that traces progressive differentiations in their understanding and judgment of conflicts between self and other. While the sequence of women's moral development follows the three-level progression of all social developmental theory, from an egocentric through a societal to a universal perspective, this progression takes place within a distinct moral conception. This conception differs from that derived by Kohlberg from his all-male longitudinal research data.

This difference then becomes the basis in the third section for challenging the current assessment of women's moral judgment at the same time that it brings to bear a new perspective on developmental assessment in general. The inclusion in the overall conception of development of those categories derived from the study of women's moral judgment enlarges developmental understanding, enabling it to encompass better the thinking of both sexes. This is particularly true with respect to the construction and resolution of the dilemmas of adult life. Since the conception of adulthood retrospectively shapes the theoretical understanding of the development that precedes it, the changes in that conception that follow from the more central inclusion of women's judgments recast developmental understanding and lead to a reconsideration of the substance of social and moral development.

Characteristics of the Feminine Voice

The revolutionary contribution of Piaget's work is the experimental confirmation and refinement of Kant's assertion that knowledge is actively constructed rather than passively received. Time, space, self, and other, as well as the categories of developmental theory, all arise out of the active interchange between the individual and the physical and social world in which he lives and of which he strives to make sense. The development of cognition is the process of reappropriating reality at progressively more complex levels of apprehension, as the structures of thinking expand to encompass the increasing richness and intricacy of experience.

Moral development, in the work of Piaget and Kohlberg, refers specifically to the expanding conception of the social world as it is reflected in the understanding and resolution of the inevitable conflicts that arise in the relations between self and others. The moral judgment is a statement of priority, an attempt at rational resolution in a situation where, from a different point of view, the choice itself seems to do violence to justice.

Kohlberg (1969), in his extension of the early work of Piaget, discovered six stages of moral judgment, which he claimed formed an invariant sequence, each successive stage representing a more adequate construction of the moral problem, which in turn provides the basis for its more just resolution. The stages divide into three levels, each of which denotes a significant expansion of the moral point of view from an egocentric through a societal to a universal ethical conception. With this expansion in perspective comes the capacity to free moral judgment from the individual needs and social conventions with which it had earlier been confused and anchor it instead in principles of justice that are universal in application. These principles provide criteria upon which both individual and societal claims can be impartially assessed. In Kohlberg's view, at the highest stages of development morality is freed from both psychological and historical constraints, and the individual can judge independently of his own particular needs and of the values of those around him.

That the moral sensibility of women differs from that of men was noted by Freud (1925/1961) in the following by now well-quoted statement:

> I cannot evade the notion (though I hesitate to give it expression) that for women the level of what is ethically normal is different from what it is in man. Their superego is never so inexorable, so impersonal, so independent of its emotional origins as we require it to be in men. Character-traits which critics of every epoch have brought up against women — that they show less sense of justice than men, that they are less ready to submit to the great exigencies of life, that they are more often influenced in their judgments by feelings of affection or hostility — all these would be amply accounted for by the modification in the formation of their super-ego which we have inferred above. (pp. 257–258)

While Freud's explanation lies in the deviation of female from male development around the construction and resolution of the Oedipal problem, the same observations about the nature of morality in women emerge from the work of Piaget and Kohlberg. Piaget (1932/1965), in his study of the rules of children's games, observed that, in the games they played, girls were "less explicit about agreement [than boys] and less concerned with legal elaboration" (p. 93). In contrast to the boys' interest in the codification of rules, the girls adopted a more pragmatic attitude, regarding "a rule as good so long as the game repays it" (p. 83). As a result, in comparison to boys, girls were found to be "more tolerant and more easily reconciled to innovations" (p. 52).

Kohlberg (1971) also identifies a strong interpersonal bias in the moral judgments of women, which leads them to be considered as typically at the third of his six-stage developmental sequence. At that stage, the good is identified with "what pleases or helps others and is approved of by them" (p. 164). This mode of judgment is conventional in its conformity to generally held notions of the good but also psychological in its concern with intention and consequence as the basis for judging the morality of action.

That women fall largely into this level of moral judgment is hardly surprising when we read from the Broverman et al. (1972) list that prominent among the twelve attributes considered to be desirable for women are tact, gentleness, awareness of the feelings of others, strong need for security, and easy expression of tender feelings. And yet, herein lies the paradox, for the very traits that have traditionally defined the "goodness" of women, their care for and sensitivity to the needs of others, are those that mark them as deficient in moral development. The infusion of feeling into their judgments keeps them from developing a more independent and abstract ethical con-

6

ception in which concern for others derives from principles of justice rather than from compassion and care. Kohlberg, however, is less pessimistic than Freud in his assessment, for he sees the development of women as extending beyond the interpersonal level, following the same path toward independent, principled judgment that he discovered in the research on men from which his stages were derived. In Kohlberg's view, women's development will proceed beyond Stage Three when they are challenged to solve moral problems that require them to see beyond the relationships that have in the past generally bound their moral experience.

What then do women say when asked to construct the moral domain; how do we identify the characteristically "feminine" voice? A Radcliffe undergraduate, responding to the question, "If you had to say what morality meant to you, how would you sum it up?" replies:

> When I think of the word morality, I think of obligations. I usually think of it as conflicts between personal desires and social things, social considerations, or personal desires of yourself versus personal desires of another person or people or whatever. Morality is that whole realm of how you decide these conflicts. A moral person is one who would decide, like by placing themselves more often than not as equals, a truly moral person would always consider another person as their equal . . . in a situation of social interactions, something is morally wrong where the individual ends up screwing a lot of people. And it is morally right when everyone comes out better off.[1]

Yet when asked if she can think of someone whom she would consider a genuinely moral person, she replies, "Well, immediately I think of Albert Schweitzer because he has obviously given his life to help others." Obligation and sacrifice override the ideal of equality, setting up a basic contradiction in her thinking.

Another undergraduate responds to the question, "What does it mean to say something is morally right or wrong?" by also speaking first of responsibilities and obligations:

> Just that it has to do with responsibilities and obligations and values, mainly values. . . . In my life situation I relate morality with interpersonal relationships that have to do with respect for the other person and myself. [Why respect other people?] Because they have a consciousness or feelings that can be hurt, an awareness that can be hurt.

The concern about hurting others persists as a major theme in the responses of two other Radcliffe students:

> [Why be moral?] Millions of people have to live together peacefully. I personally don't want to hurt other people. That's a real criterion, a main criterion for me. It underlies my sense of justice. It isn't nice to inflict pain. I empathize with anyone in pain. Not hurting others is important in my own private morals. Years ago, I would have jumped out of a window not to hurt my boyfriend. That

---

[1] The Radcliffe women whose responses are cited were interviewed as part of a pilot study on undergraduate moral development conducted by the author in 1970.

was pathological. Even today though, I want approval and love and I don't want enemies. Maybe that's why there is morality — so people can win approval, love and friendship.

My main moral principle is not hurting other people as long as you aren't going against your own conscience and as long as you remain true to yourself. . . . There are many moral issues such as abortion, the draft, killing, stealing, monogamy, etc. If something is a controversial issue like these, then I always say it is up to the individual. The individual has to decide and then follow his own conscience. There are no moral absolutes. . . . Laws are pragmatic instruments, but they are not absolutes. A viable society can't make exceptions all the time, but I would personally. . . . I'm afraid I'm heading for some big crisis with my boyfriend someday, and someone will get hurt, and he'll get more hurt than I will. I feel an obligation to not hurt him, but also an obligation to not lie. I don't know if it is possible to not lie and not hurt.

The common thread that runs through these statements, the wish not to hurt others and the hope that in morality lies a way of solving conflicts so that no one will get hurt, is striking in that it is independently introduced by each of the four women as the most specific item in their response to a most general question. The moral person is one who helps others; goodness is service, meeting one's obligations and responsibilities to others, if possible, without sacrificing oneself. While the first of the four women ends by denying the conflict she initially introduced, the last woman anticipates a conflict between remaining true to herself and adhering to her principle of not hurting others. The dilemma that would test the limits of this judgment would be one where helping others is seen to be at the price of hurting the self.

The reticence about taking stands on "controversial issues," the willingness to "make exceptions all the time" expressed in the final example above, is echoed repeatedly by other Radcliffe students, as in the following two examples:

I never feel that I can condemn anyone else. I have a very relativistic position. The basic idea that I cling to is the sanctity of human life. I am inhibited about impressing my beliefs on others.

I could never argue that my belief on a moral question is anything that another person should accept. I don't believe in absolutes. . . . If there is an absolute for moral decisions, it is human life.

Or as a thirty-one-year-old Wellesley graduate says, in explaining why she would find it difficult to steal a drug to save her own life despite her belief that it would be right to steal for another: "It's just very hard to defend yourself against the rules. I mean, we live by consensus, and you take an action simply for yourself, by yourself, there's no consensus there, and that is relatively indefensible in this society now."

What begins to emerge is a sense of vulnerability that impedes these women from taking a stand, what George Eliot (1860/1965) regards as the girl's "susceptibility" to adverse judgments of others, which stems from her lack of power and consequent inability to do something in the world. While relativism in men, the unwillingness to make moral judgments that Kohlberg and Kramer (1969) and Kohlberg and Gilligan (1971) have associated with the adolescent crisis of identity and belief, takes the form of calling into question the concept of morality itself, the women's reluctance to judge stems rather from their uncertainty about their right to make moral statements or, perhaps, the price for them that such judgment seems to entail. This contrast echoes that made by Matina Horner (1972), who differentiated the ideological fear of success expressed by men from the personal conflicts about succeeding that riddled the women's responses to stories of competitive achievement.

> Most of the men who responded with the expectation of negative consequences because of success were not concerned about their masculinity but were instead likely to have expressed existential concerns about finding a "non-materialistic happiness and satisfaction in life." These concerns, which reflect changing attitudes toward traditional kinds of success or achievement in our society, played little, if any, part in the female stories. Most of the women who were high in fear of success imagery continued to be concerned about the discrepancy between success in the situation described and feminine identity. (pp. 163–164)

When women feel excluded from direct participation in society, they see themselves as subject to a consensus or judgment made and enforced by the men on whose protection and support they depend and by whose names they are known. A divorced middle-aged woman, mother of adolescent daughters, resident of a sophisticated university community, tells the story as follows:

> As a woman, I feel I never understood that I was a person, that I can make decisions and I have a right to make decisions. I always felt that that belonged to my father or my husband in some way or church which was always represented by a male clergyman. They were the three men in my life: father, husband, and clergyman, and they had much more to say about what I should or shouldn't do. They were really authority figures which I accepted. I didn't rebel against that. It only has lately occurred to me that I never even rebelled against it, and my girls are much more conscious of this, not in the militant sense, but just in the recognizing sense. . . . . I still let things happen to me rather than make them happen, than to make choices, although I know all about choices. I know the procedures and the steps and all. [Do you have any clues about why this might be true?] Well, I think in one sense, there is less responsibility involved. Because if you make a dumb decision, you have to take the rap. If it happens to you, well, you can complain about it. I think that if you don't grow up feeling that you ever had any choices, you don't either have the sense that you have emotional responsibility. With this sense of choice comes this sense of responsibility.

The essence of the moral decision is the exercise of choice and the willingness to accept responsibility for that choice. To the extent that women perceive themselves as having no choice, they correspondingly excuse themselves from the responsibility that decision entails. Childlike in the vulnerability of their dependence and consequent fear of abandonment, they claim to wish only to please but in return for their goodness they expect to be loved and cared for. This, then, is an "altruism" always at risk, for it presupposes an innocence constantly in danger of being compromised by an awareness of the trade-off that has been made. Asked to describe herself, a Radcliffe senior responds:

> I have heard of the onion skin theory. I see myself as an onion, as a block of different layers, the external layers for people that I don't know that well, the agreeable, the social, and as you go inward there are more sides for people I know that I show. I am not sure about the innermost, whether there is a core, or whether I have just picked up everything as I was growing up, these different influences. I think I have a neutral attitude towards myself, but I do think in terms of good and bad. . . . Good — I try to be considerate and thoughtful of other people and I try to be fair in situations and be tolerant. I use the words but I try and work them out practically. . . . Bad things — I am not sure if they are bad, if they are altruistic or I am doing them basically for approval of other people. [Which things are these?] The values I have when I try to act them out. They deal mostly with interpersonal type relations. . . . If I were doing it for approval, it would be a very tenuous thing. If I didn't get the right feedback, there might go all my values.

Ibsen's play, *A Doll's House* (1879/1965), depicts the explosion of just such a world through the eruption of a moral dilemma that calls into question the notion of goodness that lies at its center. Nora, the "squirrel wife," living with her husband as she had lived with her father, puts into action this conception of goodness as sacrifice and, with the best of intentions, takes the law into her own hands. The crisis that ensues, most painfully for her in the repudiation of that goodness by the very person who was its recipient and beneficiary, causes her to reject the suicide that she had initially seen as its ultimate expression and chose instead to seek new and firmer answers to the adolescent questions of identity and belief.

The availability of choice and with it the onus of responsibility has now invaded the most private sector of the woman's domain and threatens a similar explosion. For centuries, women's sexuality anchored them in passivity, in a receptive rather than active stance, where the events of conception and childbirth could be controlled only by a withholding in which their own sexual needs were either denied or sacrificed. That such a sacrifice entailed a cost to their intelligence as well was seen by Freud (1908/1959) when he tied the "undoubted intellectual inferiority of so many women" to "the inhibition of thought necessitated by sexual suppression" (p. 199). The strategies of withholding and denial that women have employed in the politics of sexual relations appear similar to their evasion or withholding of judgment in the moral realm. The hesitance expressed in the previous examples to claim one's sexuality, bespeaks a self uncertain of its strength, unwilling to deal with consequence, and thus avoiding confrontation.

Thus women have traditionally deferred to the judgment of men, although often while intimating a sensibility of their own which is at variance with that judgment. Maggie Tulliver, in *The Mill on the Floss* (Eliot, 1860/1965) responds to the accusations that ensue from the discovery of her secretly continued relationship with Phillip Wakeham by acceding to her brother's moral judgment while at the same time asserting a different set of standards by which she attests her own superiority:

> I don't want to defend myself. . . . I know I've been wrong — often continually. But yet, sometimes when I have done wrong, it has been because I have feelings that you would be the better for if you had them. If *you* were in fault ever, if you had done anything very wrong, I should be sorry for the pain it brought you; I should not want punishment to be heaped on you. (p. 188)

An eloquent defense, Kohlberg would argue, of a Stage Three moral position, an assertion of the age-old split between thinking and feeling, justice and mercy, that underlies many of the clichés and stereotypes concerning the difference between the sexes. But considered from another point of view, it is a moment of confrontation, replacing a former evasion, between two modes of judging, two differing constructions of the moral domain — one traditionally associated with masculinity and the public world of social power, the other with femininity and the privacy of domestic interchange. While the developmental ordering of these two points of view has been to consider the masculine as the more adequate and thus as replacing the feminine as the individual moves toward higher stages, their reconciliation remains unclear.

The Development of Women's Moral Judgment

Recent evidence for a divergence in moral development between men and women comes from the research of Haan (Note 1) and Holstein (1976) whose findings lead them to question the possibility of a "sex-related bias" in Kohlberg's scoring system. This system is based on Kohlberg's six-stage description of moral development. Kohlberg's stages divide into three levels, which he designates as preconventional, conventional, and postconventional, thus denoting the major shifts in moral perspective around a center of moral understanding that equates justice with the maintenance of existing social systems. While the preconventional conception of justice is based on the needs of the self, the conventional judgment derives from an understanding of society. This understanding is in turn superseded by a postconventional or principled conception of justice where the good is formulated in universal terms. The quarrel with Kohlberg's stage scoring does not pertain to the structural differentiation of his levels but rather to questions of stage and sequence. Kohlberg's stages begin with an obedience and punishment orientation (Stage One), and go from there in invariant order to instrumental hedonism (Stage Two), interpersonal concordance (Stage Three), law and order (Stage Four), social contract (Stage Five), and universal ethical principles (Stage Six).

The bias that Haan and Holstein question in this scoring system has to do with the subordination of the interpersonal to the societal definition of the good in the transition from Stage Three to Stage Four. This is the transition that has repeatedly been found to be problematic for women. In 1969, Kohlberg and Kramer identified Stage Three as the characteristic mode of women's moral judgments, claiming that, since women's lives were interpersonally based, this stage was not only "functional" for them but also adequate for resolving the moral conflicts that they faced. Turiel (1973) reported that while girls reached Stage Three sooner than did boys, their judgments tended to remain at that stage while the boys' development continued further along Kohlberg's scale. Gilligan, Kohlberg, Lerner, and Belenky (1971) found a similar association between sex and moral-judgment stage in a study of high-school students, with the girls' responses being scored predominantly at Stage Three while the boys' responses were more often scored at Stage Four.

This repeated finding of developmental inferiority in women may, however, have more to do with the standard by which development has been measured than with the quality of women's thinking per se. Haan's data (Note 1) on the Berkeley Free Speech Movement and Holstein's (1976) three-year longitudinal study of adolescents and their parents indicate that the moral judgments of women differ from those of men in the greater extent to which women's judgments are tied to feelings of empathy and compassion and are concerned more with the resolution of "real-life" as opposed to hypothetical dilemmas (Note 1, p. 34). However, as long as the categories by which development is assessed are derived within a male perspective from male research data, divergence from the masculine standard can be seen only as a failure of development. As a result, the thinking of women is often classified with that of children. The systematic exclusion from consideration of alternative criteria that might better encompass the development of women indicates not only the limitations of a theory framed by men and validated by research samples disproportionately male and adolescent but also the effects of the diffidence prevalent among women, their reluctance to speak publicly in their own voice, given the constraints imposed on them by the politics of differential power between the sexes.

In order to go beyond the question, "How much like men do women think, how capable are they of engaging in the abstract and hypothetical construction of reality?" it is necessary to identify and define in formal terms developmental criteria that encompass the categories of women's thinking. Such criteria would include the progressive differentiations, comprehensiveness, and adequacy that characterize higher-stage resolution of the "more frequently occurring, real-life moral dilemmas of interpersonal, empathic, fellow-feeling concerns" (Haan, Note 1, p. 34), which have long been the center of women's moral judgments and experience. To ascertain whether the feminine construction of the moral domain relies on a language different from that of men, but one which deserves equal credence in the definition of what constitutes development, it is necessary first to find the places where women have the power to choose and thus are willing to speak in their own voice.

When birth control and abortion provide women with effective means for controlling their fertility, the dilemma of choice enters the center of women's lives. Then the relationships that have traditionally defined women's identities and framed their moral judgments no longer flow inevitably from their reproductive capacity but become matters of decision over which they have control. Released from the passivity and reticence of a sexuality that binds them in dependence, it becomes possible for women to question with Freud what it is that they want and to assert their own answers to that question. However, while society may affirm publicly the woman's right to choose for herself, the exercise of such choice brings her privately into conflict with the conventions of femininity, particularly the moral equation of goodness with self-sacrifice. While independent assertion in judgment and action is considered the hallmark of adulthood and constitutes as well the standard of masculine development, it is rather in their care and concern for others that women have both judged themselves and been judged.

The conflict between self and other thus constitutes the central moral problem for women, posing a dilemma whose resolution requires a reconciliation between femininity and adulthood. In the absence of such a reconciliation, the moral problem cannot be resolved. The "good woman" masks assertion in evasion, denying responsibility by claiming only to meet the needs of others, while the "bad woman" forgoes or renounces the commitments that bind her in self-deception and betrayal. It is precisely this dilemma — the conflict between compassion and autonomy, between virtue and power — which the feminine voice struggles to resolve in its effort to reclaim the self and to solve the moral problems in such a way that no one is hurt.

When a woman considers whether to continue or abort a pregnancy, she contemplates a decision that affects both self and others and engages directly the critical moral issue of hurting. Since the choice is ultimately hers and therefore one for which she is responsible, it raises precisely those questions of judgment that have been most problematic for women. Now she is asked whether she wishes to interrupt that stream of life which has for centuries immersed her in the passivity of dependence while at the same time imposing on her the responsibility for care. Thus the abortion decision brings to the core of feminine apprehension, to what Joan Didion (1972) calls "the irreconcilable difference of it — that sense of living one's deepest life underwater, that dark involvement with blood and birth and death" (p. 14), the adult questions of responsibility and choice.

How women deal with such choices has been the subject of my research, designed to clarify, through considering the ways in which women construct and resolve the abortion decision, the nature and development of women's moral judgment. Twenty-nine women, diverse in age, race, and social class, were referred by abortion and pregnancy counseling services and participated in the study for a variety of reasons. Some came to gain further clarification with respect to a decision about which they were in conflict, some in response to a counselor's concern about repeated abortions, and others out of an interest in and/or willingness to contribute to ongoing research. Although the pregnancies occurred under a variety of circumstances in the lives of these women, certain commonalities could be discerned. The adolescents often failed to use birth control because they denied or discredited their capacity to bear children. Some of the older women attributed the pregnancy to the omission of contraceptive measures in circumstances where intercourse had not been anticipated. Since the pregnancies often coincided with efforts on the part of the women to end a relationship, they may be seen as a manifestation of ambivalence or as a way of putting the relationship to the ultimate test of commitment. For these women, the pregnancy appeared to be a way of testing truth, making the baby an ally in the search for male support and protection or, that failing, a companion victim of his rejection. There were, finally, some women who became pregnant either as a result of a failure of birth control or intentionally as part of a joint decision that later was reconsidered. Of the twenty-nine women, four decided to have the baby, one miscarried, twenty-one chose abortion, and three remained in doubt about the decision.

In the initial part of the interview, the women were asked to discuss the decision that confronted them: how they were dealing with it, the alternatives they were considering, their reasons for and against each option, the people involved, the conflicts entailed, and the ways in which making this decision affected their self concepts and their relationships with others. Then, in the second part of the interview, moral judgment was assessed in the hypothetical mode by presenting for resolution three of Kohlberg's standard research dilemmas.

While the structural progression from a preconventional through a conventional to a postconventional moral perspective can readily be discerned in the women's responses to both actual and hypothetical dilemmas, the conventions that shape women's moral judgments differ from those that apply to men. The construction of the abortion dilemma, in particular, reveals the existence of a distinct moral language whose evolution informs the sequence of women's development. This is the language of selfishness and responsibility, which defines the moral problem as one of obligation to exercise care and avoid hurt. The infliction of hurt is considered selfish and immoral in its reflection of unconcern, while the expression of care is seen as the fulfillment of moral responsibility. The reiterative use of the language of selfishness and responsibility and the underlying moral orientation it reflects sets the women apart from the men whom Kohlberg studied and may be seen as the critical reason for their failure to develop within the constraints of his system.

In the developmental sequence that follows, women's moral judgments proceed from an initial focus on the self as the *first level* to the discovery, in the transition to the *second level,* of the concept of responsibility as the basis for a new equilibrium between self and others. The elaboration of this con-

14

cept of responsibility and its fusion with a maternal concept of morality, which seeks to ensure protection for the dependent and unequal, characterizes the *second level* of judgment. At this level the good is equated with caring for others. However, when the conventions of feminine goodness legitimize only others as the recipients of moral care, the logical inequality between self and other and the psychological violence that it engenders create the disequilibrium that initiates the *second* transition. The relationship between self and others is then reconsidered in an effort to sort out the confusion between conformity and care inherent in the conventional definition of feminine goodness and to establish a new equilibrium, which dissipates the tension between selfishness and responsibility. At the *third level,* the self becomes the arbiter of an independent judgment that now subsumes both conventions and individual needs under the moral principle of nonviolence. Judgment remains psychological in its concern with the intention and consequences of action, but it now becomes universal in its condemnation of exploitation and hurt.

Level 1: Orientation to Individual Survival

In its initial and simplest construction, the abortion decision centers on the self. The concern is pragmatic, and the issue is individual survival. At this level, "should" is undifferentiated from "would," and others influence the decision only through their power to affect its consequences. An eighteen-year-old, asked what she thought when she found herself pregnant, replies: "I really didn't think anything except that I didn't want it. [Why was that?] I didn't want it, I wasn't ready for it, and next year will be my last year and I want to go to school."

Asked if there was a right decision, she says, "There is no right decision. [Why?] I didn't want it." For her the question of right decision would emerge only if her own needs were in conflict; then she would have to decide which needs should take precedence. This was the dilemma of another eighteen-year-old, who saw having a baby as a way of increasing her freedom by providing "the perfect chance to get married and move away from home," but also as restricting her freedom "to do a lot of things."

At this first level, the self, which is the sole object of concern, is constrained by lack of power; the wish "to do a lot of things" is constantly belied by the limitations of what, in fact, is being done. Relationships are, for the most part, disappointing: "The only thing you are ever going to get out of going with a guy is to get hurt." As a result, women may in some instances deliberately choose isolation to protect themselves against hurt. When asked how she would describe herself to herself, a nineteen-year-old, who held herself responsible for the accidental death of a younger brother, answers as follows:

> I really don't know. I never thought about it. I don't know. I know basically the outline of a character. I am very independent. I don't really want to have

to ask anybody for anything and I am a loner in life. I prefer to be by myself than around anybody else. I manage to keep my friends at a limited number with the point that I have very few friends. I don't know what else there is. I am a loner and I enjoy it. Here today and gone tomorrow.

The primacy of the concern with survival is explicitly acknowledged by a sixteen-year-old delinquent in response to Kohlberg's Heinz dilemma, which asks if it is right for a desperate husband to steal an outrageously overpriced drug to save the life of his dying wife:

> I think survival is one of the first things in life and that people fight for. I think it is the most important thing, more important than stealing. Stealing might be wrong, but if you have to steal to survive yourself or even kill, that is what you should do. . . . Preservation of oneself, I think, is the most important thing; it comes before anything in life.

The First Transition: From Selfishness to Responsibility

In the transition which follows and criticizes this level of judgment, the words selfishness and responsibility first appear. Their reference initially is to the self in a redefinition of the self-interest which has thus far served as the basis for judgment. The transitional issue is one of attachment or connection to others. The pregnancy catches up the issue not only by representing an immediate, literal connection, but also by affirming, in the most concrete and physical way, the capacity to assume adult feminine roles. However, while having a baby seems at first to offer respite from the loneliness of adolescence and to solve conflicts over dependence and independence, in reality the continuation of an adolescent pregnancy generally compounds these problems, increasing social isolation and precluding further steps toward independence.

To be a mother in the societal as well as the physical sense requires the assumption of parental responsibility for the care and protection of a child. However, in order to be able to care for another, one must first be able to care responsibly for oneself. The growth from childhood to adulthood, conceived as a move from selfishness to responsibility, is articulated explicitly in these terms by a seventeen-year-old who describes her response to her pregnancy as follows:

> I started feeling really good about being pregnant instead of feeling really bad, because I wasn't looking at the situation realistically. I was looking at it from my own sort of selfish needs because I was lonely and felt lonely and stuff. . . . Things weren't really going good for me, so I was looking at it that I could have a baby that I could take care of or something that was part of me, and that made me feel good . . . but I wasn't looking at the realistic side . . . about the responsibility I would have to take on . . . I came to this decision that I was going to have an abortion [because] I realized how much responsibility goes with having a child. Like you have to be there, you can't be out of the house all the time which is one thing I like to do . . . and I decided that I have to take on responsibility for myself and I have to work out a lot of things.

16

Stating her former mode of judgment, the wish to have a baby as a way of combating loneliness and feeling connected, she now criticizes that judgment as both "selfish" and "unrealistic." The contradiction between wishes for a baby and for the freedom to be "out of the house all the time" — that is, for connection and also for independence — is resolved in terms of a new priority, as the criterion for judgment changes. The dilemma now assumes moral definition as the emergent conflict between wish and necessity is seen as a disparity between "would" and "should." In this construction the "selfishness" of willful decision is counterposed to the "responsibility" of moral choice:

> What I want to do is to have the baby, but what I feel I should do which is what I need to do, is have an abortion right now, because sometimes what you want isn't right. Sometimes what is necessary comes before what you want, because it might not always lead to the right thing.

While the pregnancy itself confirms femininity — "I started feeling really good: it sort of made me feel, like being pregnant, I started feeling like a woman" — the abortion decision becomes an opportunity for the adult exercise of responsible choice.

> [How would you describe yourself to yourself?] I am looking at myself differently in the way that I have had a really heavy decision put upon me, and I have never really had too many hard decisions in my life, and I have made it. It has taken some responsibility to do this. I have changed in that way, that I have made a hard decision. And that has been good. Because before, I would not have looked at it realistically, in my opinion. I would have gone by what I wanted to do, and I wanted it, and even if it wasn't right. So I see myself as I'm becoming more mature in ways of making decisions and taking care of myself, doing something for myself. I think it is going to help me in other ways, if I have other decisions to make put upon me, which would take some responsibility. And I would know that I could make them.

In the epiphany of this cognitive reconstruction, the old becomes transformed in terms of the new. The wish to "do something for myself" remains, but the terms of its fulfillment change as the decision affirms both femininity and adulthood in its integration of responsibility and care. Morality, says another adolescent, "is the way you think about yourself . . . sooner or later you have to make up your mind to start taking care of yourself. Abortion, if you do it for the right reasons, is helping yourself to start over and do different things."

Since this transition signals an enhancement in self-worth, it requires a conception of self which includes the possibility for doing "the right thing," the ability to see in oneself the potential for social acceptance. When such confidence is seriously in doubt, the transitional questions may be raised but development is impeded. The failure to make this first transition, despite an understanding of the issues involved, is illustrated by a woman in her late twenties. Her struggle with the conflict between selfishness and responsibility pervades but fails to resolve her dilemma of whether or not to have a third abortion.

I think you have to think about the people who are involved, including yourself. You have responsibilities to yourself . . . and to make a right, whatever that is, decision in this depends on your knowledge and awareness of the responsibilities that you have and whether you can survive with a child and what it will do to your relationship with the father or how it will affect him emotionally.

Rejecting the idea of selling the baby and making "a lot of money in a black market kind of thing . . . because mostly I operate on principles and it would just rub me the wrong way to think I would be selling my own child," she struggles with a concept of responsibility which repeatedly turns back on the question of her own survival. Transition seems blocked by a self-image which is insistently contradictory:

[How would you describe yourself to yourself?] I see myself as impulsive, practical — that is a contradiction — and moral and amoral, a contradiction. Actually the only thing that is consistent and not contradictory is the fact that I am very lazy which everyone has always told me is really a symptom of something else which I have never been able to put my finger on exactly. It has taken me a long time to like myself. In fact there are times when I don't, which I think is healthy to a point and sometimes I think I like myself too much and I probably evade myself too much, which avoids responsibility to myself and to other people who like me. I am pretty unfaithful to myself . . . I have a hard time even thinking that I am a human being, simply because so much rotten stuff goes on and people are so crummy and insensitive.

Seeing herself as avoiding responsibility, she can find no basis upon which to resolve the pregnancy dilemma. Instead, her inability to arrive at any clear sense of decision only contributes further to her overall sense of failure. Criticizing her parents for having betrayed her during adolescence by coercing her to have an abortion she did not want, she now betrays herself and criticizes that as well. In this light, it is less surprising that she considered selling her child, since she felt herself to have, in effect, been sold by her parents for the sake for maintaining their social status.

The Second Level: Goodness as Self-Sacrifice

The transition from selfishness to responsibility is a move toward social participation. Whereas at the first level, morality is seen as a matter of sanctions imposed by a society of which one is more subject than citizen, at the second level, moral judgment comes to rely on shared norms and expectations. The woman at this level validates her claim to social membership through the adoption of societal values. Consensual judgment becomes paramount and goodness the overriding concern as survival is now seen to depend on acceptance by others.

Here the conventional feminine voice emerges with great clarity, defining the self and proclaiming its worth on the basis of the ability to care for and protect others. The woman now constructs the world perfused with the assumptions about feminine goodness reflected in the stereotypes of the Broverman et al. (1972) studies. There the attributes considered desirable for women all presume an other, a recipient of the "tact, gentleness and easy expression of feeling" which allow the woman to respond sensitively while evoking in return the care which meets her own "very strong need for security" (p. 63). The strength of this position lies in its capacity for caring; its limitation is the restriction it imposes on direct expression. Both qualities are elucidated by a nineteen-year-old who contrasts her reluctance to criticize with her boyfriend's straightforwardness:

> I never want to hurt anyone, and I tell them in a very nice way, and I have respect for their own opinions, and they can do the things the way that they want, and he usually tells people right off the bat. . . . He does a lot of things out in public which I do in private. . . . it is better, the other [his way], but I just could never do it.

While her judgment clearly exists, it is not expressed, at least not in public. Concern for the feelings of others imposes a deference which she nevertheless criticizes in an awareness that, under the name of consideration, a vulnerability and a duplicity are concealed.

At the second level of judgment, it is specifically over the issue of hurting that conflict arises with respect to the abortion decision. When no option exists that can be construed as being in the best interest of everyone, when responsibilities conflict and decision entails the sacrifice of somebody's needs, then the woman confronts the seemingly impossible task of choosing the victim. A nineteen-year-old, fearing the consequences for herself of a second abortion but facing the opposition of both her family and her lover to the continuation of the pregnancy, describes the dilemma as follows:

> I don't know what choices are open to me; it is either to have it or the abortion; these are the choices open to me. It is just that either way I don't . . . I think what confuses me is it is a choice of either hurting myself or hurting other people around me. What is more important? If there could be a happy medium, it would be fine, but there isn't. It is either hurting someone on this side or hurting myself.

While the feminine identification of goodness with self-sacrifice seems clearly to dictate the "right" resolution of this dilemma, the stakes may be high for the woman herself, and the sacrifice of the fetus, in any event, compromises the altruism of an abortion motivated by a concern for others. Since femininity itself is in conflict in an abortion intended as an expression of love and care, this is a resolution which readily explodes in its own contradiction.

"I don't think anyone should have to choose between two things that they love," says a twenty-five-year-old woman who assumed responsibility not only for her lover, but also for his wife and children in having an abortion she did not want:

> I just wanted the child and I really don't believe in abortions. Who can say when life begins. I think that life begins at conception and . . . I felt like there were changes happening in my body and I felt very protective . . . [but] I felt

a responsibility, my responsibility if anything ever happened to her [his wife]. He made me feel that I had to make a choice and there was only one choice to make and that was to have an abortion and I could always have children another time and he made me feel if I didn't have it that it would drive us apart.

The abortion decision was, in her mind, a choice not to choose with respect to the pregnancy — "That was my choice, I had to do it." Instead, it was a decision to subordinate the pregnancy to the continuation of a relationship that she saw as encompassing her life — "Since I met him, he has been my life. I do everything for him; my life sort of revolves around him." Since she wanted to have the baby and also to continue the relationship, either choice could be construed as selfish. Furthermore, since both alternatives entailed hurting someone, neither could be considered moral. Faced with a decision which, in her own terms, was untenable, she sought to avoid responsibility for the choice she made, construing the decision as a sacrifice of her own needs to those of her lover. However, this public sacrifice in the name of responsibility engendered a private resentment that erupted in anger, compromising the very relationship that it had been intended to sustain.

> Afterwards we went through a bad time because I hate to say it and I was wrong, but I blamed him. I gave in to him. But when it came down to it, I made the decision. I could have said, "I am going to have this child whether you want me to or not," and I just didn't do it.

Pregnant again by the same man, she recognizes in retrospect that the choice in fact had been hers, as she returns once again to what now appears to have been missed opportunity for growth. Seeking, this time, to make rather than abdicate the decision, she sees the issue as one of "strength" as she struggles to free herself from the powerlessness of her own dependence:

> I think that right now I think of myself as someone who can become a lot stronger. Because of the circumstances, I just go along like with the tide. I never really had anything of my own before . . . [this time] I hope to come on strong and make a big decision, whether it is right or wrong.

Because the morality of self-sacrifice had justified the previous abortion, she now must suspend that judgment if she is to claim her own voice and accept responsibility for choice.

She thereby calls into question the underlying assumption of Level Two, which leads the woman to consider herself responsible for the action of others, while holding others responsible for the choices she makes. This notion of reciprocity, backwards in its assumptions about control, disguises assertion as response. By reversing responsibility, it generates a series of indirect actions, which leave everyone feeling manipulated and betrayed. The logic of this position is confused in that the morality of mutual care is embedded in the psychology of dependence. Assertion becomes personally dangerous in its risk of criticism and abandonment, as well as potentially immoral in its power to hurt. This confusion is captured by Kohlberg's

(1969) definition of Stage Three moral judgment, which joins the need for approval with the wish to care for and help others.

When thus caught between the passivity of dependence and the activity of care, the woman becomes suspended in an immobility of both judgment and action. "If I were drowning, I couldn't reach out a hand to save myself, so unwilling am I to set myself up against fate" (p. 7), begins the central character of Margaret Drabble's novel, *The Waterfall* (1971), in an effort to absolve herself of responsibility as she at the same time relinquishes control. Facing the same moral conflict which George Eliot depicted in *The Mill on the Floss,* Drabble's heroine proceeds to relive Maggie Tulliver's dilemma but turns inward in her search for the way in which to retell that story. What is initially suspended and then called into question is the judgment which "had in the past made it seem better to renounce myself than them" (Drabble, p. 50).

The Second Transition: From Goodness to Truth

The second transition begins with the reconsideration of the relationship between self and other, as the woman starts to scrutinize the logic of self-sacrifice in the service of a morality of care. In the interview data, this transition is announced by the reappearance of the word selfish. Retrieving the judgmental initiative, the woman begins to ask whether it is selfish or responsible, moral or immoral, to include her own needs within the compass of her care and concern. This question leads her to reexamine the concept of responsibility, juxtaposing the outward concern with what other people think with a new inner judgment.

In separating the voice of the self from those of others, the woman asks if it is possible to be responsible to herself as well as to others and thus to reconcile the disparity between hurt and care. The exercise of such responsibility, however, requires a new kind of judgment whose first demand is for honesty. To be responsible, it is necessary first to acknowledge what it is that one is doing. The criterion for judgment thus shifts from "goodness" to "truth" as the morality of action comes to be assessed not on the basis of its appearance in the eyes of others, but in terms of the realities of its intention and consequence.

A twenty-four-year-old married Catholic woman, pregnant again two months following the birth of her first child, identifies her dilemma as one of choice: "You have to now decide; because it is now available, you have to make a decision. And if it wasn't available, there was no choice open; you just do what you have to do." In the absence of legal abortion, a morality of self-sacrifice was necessary in order to insure protection and care for the dependent child. However, when such sacrifice becomes optional, the entire problem is recast.

The abortion decision is framed by this woman first in terms of her responsibility to others: having a second child at this time would be contrary to medical advice and would strain both the emotional and financial resources of the family. However, there is, she says, a third reason for having an abortion, "sort of an emotional reason. I don't know if it is selfish or not, but it would really be tying myself down and right now I am not ready to be tied down with two."

Against this combination of selfish and responsible reasons for abortion is her Catholic belief that

> . . . it is taking a life, and it is. Even though it is not formed, it is the potential, and to me it is still taking a life. But I have to think of mine, my son's and my husband's, to think about, and at first I think that I thought it was for selfish reasons, but it is not. I believe that too, some of it is selfish. I don't want another one right now; I am not ready for it.

The dilemma arises over the issue of justification for taking a life: "I can't cover it over, because I believe this and if I do try to cover it over, I know that I am going to be in a mess. It will be denying what I am really doing." Asking "Am I doing the right thing; is it moral?," she counterposes to her belief against abortion her concern with the consequences of continuing the pregnancy. While concluding that "I can't be so morally strict as to hurt three other people with a decision just because of my moral beliefs," the issue of goodness still remains critical to her resolution of the dilemma:

> The moral factor is there. To me it is taking a life, and I am going to take that upon myself, that decision upon myself and I have feelings about it, and talked to a priest . . . but he said it is there and it will be from now on, and it is up to the person if they can live with the idea and still believe they are good.

The criteria for goodness, however, move inward as the ability to have an abortion and still consider herself good comes to hinge on the issue of selfishness with which she struggles to come to terms. Asked if acting morally is acting according to what is best for the self or whether it is a matter of self-sacrifice, she replies:

> I don't know if I really understand the question. . . . Like in my situation where I want to have the abortion and if I didn't it would be self-sacrificing, I am really in the middle of both those ways . . . but I think that my morality is strong and if these reasons — financial, physical reality and also for the whole family involved — were not here, that I wouldn't have to do it, and then it would be a self-sacrifice.

The importance of clarifying her own participation in the decision is evident in her attempt to ascertain her feelings in order to determine whether or not she was "putting them under" in deciding to end the pregnancy. Whereas in the first transition, from selfishness to responsibility, women made lists in order to bring to their consideration needs other than their own, now, in the second transition, it is the needs of the self which have to be deliberately uncovered. Confronting the reality of her own wish for an abortion, she now must deal with the problem of selfishness and the qualification that she feels it imposes on the "goodness" of her decision. The primacy of this concern is apparent in her description of herself:

> I think in a way I am selfish for one thing, and very emotional, very . . . and I think that I am a very real person and an understanding person and I can handle life situations fairly well, so I am basing a lot of it on my ability to do the things that I feel are right and best for me and whoever I am involved with. I think I was very fair to myself about the decision, and I really think that I have been truthful, not hiding anything, bringing out all the feelings involved. I feel it is a good decision and an honest one, a real decision.

Thus she strives to encompass the needs of both self and others, to be responsible to others and thus to be "good" but also to be responsible to herself and thus to be "honest" and "real."

While from one point of view, attention to one's own needs is considered selfish, when looked at from a different perspective, it is a matter of honesty and fairness. This is the essence of the transitional shift toward a new conception of goodness which turns inward in an acknowledgment of the self and an acceptance of responsibility for decision. While outward justification, the concern with "good reasons," remains critical for this particular woman: "I still think abortion is wrong, and it will be unless the situation can justify what you are doing." But the search for justification has produced a change in her thinking, "not drastically, but a little bit." She realizes that in continuing the pregnancy she would punish not only herself but also her husband, toward whom she had begun to feel "turned off and irritated." This leads her to consider the consequences self-sacrifice can have both for the self and for others. "God," she says, "can punish, but He can also forgive." What remains in question is whether her claim to forgiveness is compromised by a decision that not only meets the needs of others but that also is "right and best for me."

The concern with selfishness and its equation with immorality recur in an interview with another Catholic woman whose arrival for an abortion was punctuated by the statement, "I have always thought abortion was a fancy word for murder." Initially explaining this murder as one of lesser degree — "I am doing it because I have to do it. I am not doing it the least bit because I want to," she judges it "not quite as bad. You can rationalize that it is not quite the same." Since "keeping the child for lots and lots of reasons was just sort of impractical and out," she considers her options to be either abortion or adoption. However, having previously given up one child for adoption, she says: "I knew that psychologically there was no way that I could hack another adoption. It took me about four-and-a-half years to get my head on straight; there was just no way I was going to go through it again." The decision thus reduces in her eyes to a choice between murdering the fetus or damaging herself. The choice is further complicated by the fact that by continuing the pregnancy she would hurt not only herself but also her parents, with whom she lived. In the face of these manifold moral contradictions, the psychological demand for honesty that arises in counseling finally allows decision:

> On my own, I was doing it not so much for myself: I was doing it for my parents. I was doing it because the doctor told me to do it, but I had never resolved in

my mind that I was doing it for me. Because it goes right back to the fact that I never believed in abortions. . . . Actually, I had to sit down and admit, no, I really don't want to go the mother route now. I honestly don't feel that I want to be a mother, and that is not really such a bad thing to say after all. But that is not how I felt up until talking to Maureen [her counselor]. It was just a horrible way to feel, so I just wasn't going to feel it, and I just blocked it right out.

As long as her consideration remains "moral," abortion can be justified only as an act of sacrifice, a submission to necessity where the absence of choice precludes responsibility. In this way, she can avoid self-condemnation, since, "When you get into moral stuff then you are getting into self-respect and that stuff, and at least if I do something that I feel is morally wrong, then I tend to lose some of my self-respect as a person." Her evasion of responsibility, critical to maintaining the innocence necessary for self-respect, contradicts the reality of her own participation in the abortion decision. The dishonesty in her plea of victimization creates the conflict that generates the need for a more inclusive understanding. She must now resolve the emerging contradiction in her thinking between two uses of the term right: "I am saying that abortion is morally wrong, but the situation is right, and I am going to do it. But the thing is that eventually they are going to have to go together, and I am going to have to put them together somehow." Asked how this could be done, she replies:

> I would have to change morally wrong to morally right. [How?] I have no idea. I don't think you can take something that you feel is morally wrong because the situation makes it right and put the two together. They are not together, they are opposite. They don't go together. Something is wrong, but all of a sudden because you are doing it, it is right.

This discrepancy recalls a similar conflict she faced over the question of euthanasia, also considered by her to be morally wrong until she "took care of a couple of patients who had flat EEGs and saw the job that it was doing on their families." Recalling that experience, she says:

> You really don't know your black and whites until you really get into them and are being confronted with it. If you stop and think about my feelings on euthanasia until I got into it, and then my feelings about abortion until I got into it, I thought both of them were murder. Right and wrong and no middle but there is a gray.

In discovering the gray and questioning the moral judgments which formerly she considered to be absolute, she confronts the moral crisis of the second transition. Now the conventions which in the past had guided her moral judgment become subject to a new criticism, as she questions not only the justification for hurting others in the name of morality but also the "rightness" of hurting herself. However, to sustain such criticism in the face of conventions that equate goodness with self-sacrifice, the woman must verify her capacity for independent judgment and the legitimacy of her own point of view.

Once again transition hinges on self-concept. When uncertainty about her own worth prevents a woman from claiming equality, self-assertion falls prey to the old criticism of selfishness. Then the morality that condones self-destruction in the name of responsible care is not repudiated as inadequate but rather is abandoned in the face of its threat to survival. Moral obligation, rather than expanding to include the self, is rejected completely as the failure of conventional reciprocity leaves the woman unwilling any longer to protect others at what is now seen to be her own expense. In the absence of morality, survival, however "selfish" or "immoral," returns as the paramount concern.

A musician in her late twenties illustrates this transitional impasse. Having led an independent life which centered on her work, she considered herself "fairly strong-willed, fairly in control, fairly rational and objective" until she became involved in an intense love affair and discovered in her capacity to love "an entirely new dimension" in herself. Admitting in retrospect to "tremendous naiveté and idealism," she had entertained "some vague ideas that some day I would like a child to concretize our relationship . . . having always associated having a child with all the creative aspects of my life." Abjuring, with her lover, the use of contraceptives because, "as the relationship was sort of an ideal relationship in our minds, we liked the idea of not using foreign objects or anything artificial," she saw herself as having relinquished control, becoming instead "just simply vague and allowing events to just carry me along." Just as she began in her own thinking to confront "the realities of that situation" — the possibility of pregnancy and the fact that her lover was married — she found herself pregnant. "Caught" between her wish to end a relationship that "seemed more and more defeating" and her wish for a baby, which "would be a connection that would last a long time," she is paralyzed by her inability to resolve the dilemma which her ambivalence creates.

The pregnancy poses a conflict between her "moral" belief that "once a certain life has begun, it shouldn't be stopped artificially" and her "amazing" discovery that to have the baby she would "need much more [support] than I thought." Despite her moral conviction that she "should" have the child, she doubts that she could psychologically deal with "having the child alone and taking the responsibility for it." Thus a conflict erupts between what she considers to be her moral obligation to protect life and her inability to do so under the circumstances of this pregnancy. Seeing it as "my decision and my responsibility for making the decision whether to have or have not the child," she struggles to find a viable basis on which to resolve the dilemma.

Capable of arguing either for or against abortion "with a philosophical logic," she says, on the one hand, that in an overpopulated world one should have children only under ideal conditions for care but, on the other, that one should end a life only when it is impossible to sustain it. She describes her impasse in response to the question of whether there is a difference between what she wants to do and what she thinks she should do:

Yes, and there always has. I have always been confronted with that precise situation in a lot of my choices, and I have been trying to figure out what are the things that make me believe that these are things I should do as opposed to what I feel I want to do. [In this situation?] It is not that clear cut. I both want the child and feel I should have it, and I also think I should have the abortion and want it, but I would say it is my stronger feeling, and that I don't have enough confidence in my work yet and that is really where it is all hinged, I think . . . [the abortion] would solve the problem and I know I can't handle the pregnancy.

Characterizing this solution as "emotional and pragmatic" and attributing it to her lack of confidence in her work, she contrasts it with the "better thought out and more logical and more correct" resolution of her lover who thinks that she should have the child and raise it without either his presence or financial support. Confronted with this reflected image of herself as ultimately giving and good, as self-sustaining in her own creativity and thus able to meet the needs of others while imposing no demands of her own in return, she questions not the image itself but her own adequacy in filling it. Concluding that she is not yet capable of doing so, she is reduced in her own eyes to what she sees as a selfish and highly compromised fight

for my survival. But in one way or another, I am going to suffer. Maybe I am going to suffer mentally and emotionally having the abortion, or I would suffer what I think is possibly something worse. So I suppose it is the lesser of two evils. I think it is a matter of choosing which one I know that I can survive through. It is really. I think it is selfish, I suppose, because it does have to do with that. I just realized that. I guess it does have to do with whether I would survive or not. [Why is this selfish?] Well, you know, it is. Because I am concerned with my survival first, as opposed to the survival of the relationship or the survival of the child, another human being . . . I guess I am setting priorities, and I guess I am setting my needs to survive first. . . . I guess I see it in negative terms a lot . . . but I do think of other positive things; that I am still going to have some life left, maybe. I don't know.

In the face of this failure of reciprocity of care, in the disappointment of abandonment where connection was sought, survival is seen to hinge on her work which is "where I derive the meaning of what I am. That's the known factor." While uncertainty about her work makes this survival precarious, the choice for abortion is also distressing in that she considers it to be "highly introverted — that in this one respect, having an abortion would be going a step backward; going outside to love someone else and having a child would be a step forward." The sense of retrenchment that the severing of connection signifies is apparent in her anticipation of the cost which abortion would entail:

Probably what I will do is I will cut off my feelings, and when they will return or what would happen to them after that, I don't know. So that I don't feel anything at all, and I would probably just be very cold and go through it very coldly. . . . The more you do that to yourself, the more difficult it becomes to love again or to trust again or to feel again. . . . Each time I move away from that, it becomes easier, not more difficult, but easier to avoid committing myself to a relationship. And I am really concerned about cutting off that whole feeling aspect.

Caught between selfishness and responsibility, unable to find in the circumstances of this choice a way of caring which does not at the same time destroy, she confronts a dilemma which reduces to a conflict between morality and survival. Adulthood and femininity fly apart in the failure of this attempt at integration as the choice to work becomes a decision not only to renounce this particular relationship and child but also to obliterate the vulnerability that love and care engender.

The Third Level: The Morality of Nonviolence

In contrast, a twenty-five-year-old woman, facing a similar disappointment, finds a way to reconcile the initially disparate concepts of selfishness and responsibility through a transformed understanding of self and a corresponding redefinition of morality. Examining the assumptions underlying the conventions of feminine self-abnegation and moral self-sacrifice, she comes to reject these conventions as immoral in their power to hurt. By elevating nonviolence — the injunction against hurting — to a principle governing all moral judgment and action, she is able to assert a moral equality between self and other. Care then becomes a universal obligation, the self-chosen ethic of a postconventional judgment that reconstructs the dilemma in a way that allows the assumption of responsibility for choice.

In this woman's life, the current pregnancy brings to the surface the unfinished business of an earlier pregnancy and of the relationship in which both pregnancies occurred. The first pregnancy was discovered after her lover had left and was terminated by an abortion experienced as a purging expression of her anger at having been rejected. Remembering the abortion only as a relief, she nevertheless describes that time in her life as one in which she "hit rock bottom." Having hoped then to "take control of my life," she instead resumed the relationship when the man reappeared. Now, two years later, having once again "left my diaphragm in the drawer," she again becomes pregnant. Although initially "ecstatic" at the news, her elation dissipates when her lover tells her that he will leave if she chooses to have the child. Under these circumstances, she considers a second abortion but is unable to keep the repeated appointments she makes because of her reluctance to accept the responsibility for that choice. While the first abortion seemed an "honest mistake," she says that a second child would make her feel "like a walking slaughter-house." Since she would need financial support to raise the child, her initial strategy was to take the matter to "the welfare people" in the hope that they would refuse to provide the necessary funds and thus resolve her dilemma:

> In that way, you know, the responsibility would be off my shoulders, and I could say, it's not my fault, you know, the state denied me the money that I would

need to do it. But it turned out that it was possible to do it, and so I was, you know, right back where I started. And I had an appointment for an abortion, and I kept calling and cancelling it and then remaking the appointment and cancelling it, and I just couldn't make up my mind.

Confronting the need to choose between the two evils of hurting herself or ending the incipient life of the child, she finds, in a reconstruction of the dilemma itself, a basis for a new priority that allows decision. In doing so, she comes to see the conflict as arising from a faulty construction of reality. Her thinking recapitulates the developmental sequence, as she considers but rejects as inadequate the components of earlier-stage resolutions. An expanded conception of responsibility now reshapes moral judgment and guides resolution of the dilemma, whose pros and cons she considers as follows:

Well, the pros for having the baby are all the admiration that you would get from, you know, being a single woman, alone, martyr, struggling, having the adoring love of this beautiful Gerber baby . . . just more of a home life than I have had in a long time, and that basically was it, which is pretty fantasyland; it is not very realistic. . . . Cons against having the baby: it was going to hasten what is looking to be the inevitable end of the relationship with the man I am presently with. . . . I was going to have to go on welfare, my parents were going to hate me for the rest of my life, I was going to lose a really good job that I have, I would lose a lot of independence . . . solitude . . . and I would have to be put in a position of asking help from a lot of people a lot of the time. Cons against having the abortion is having to face up to the guilt . . . and pros for having the abortion are I would be able to handle my deteriorating relation with S. with a lot more capability and a lot more responsibility for him and for myself . . . and I would not have to go through the realization that for the next twenty-five years of my life I would be punishing myself for being foolish enough to get pregnant again and forcing myself to bring up a kid just because I did this. Having to face the guilt of a second abortion seemed like, not exactly, well, exactly the lesser of the two evils but also the one that would pay off for me personally in the long run because by looking at why I am pregnant again and subsequently have decided to have a second abortion, I have to face up to some things about myself.

Although she doesn't "feel good about having a second abortion," she nevertheless concludes,

I would not be doing myself or the child or the world any kind of favor having this child. . . . I don't need to pay off my imaginary debts to the world through this child, and I don't think that it is right to bring a child into the world and use it for that purpose.

Asked to describe herself, she indicates how closely her transformed moral understanding is tied to a changing self-concept:

I have been thinking about that a lot lately, and it comes up different than what my usual subconscious perception of myself is. Usually paying off some sort of debt, going around serving people who are not really worthy of my attentions because somewhere in my life I think I got the impression that my needs are really secondary to other people's, and that if I feel, if I make any demands on other people to fulfill my needs, I'd feel guilty for it and submerge my own in favor of other people's, which later backfires on me, and I feel a great deal of resentment for other people that I am doing things for, which causes friction and the eventual deterioration of the relationship. And then I start all over again. How would I describe myself to myself? Pretty frustrated and a lot angrier than I admit, a lot more aggressive than I admit.

Reflecting on the virtues which comprise the conventional definition of the feminine self, a definition which she hears articulated in her mother's voice, she says, "I am beginning to think that all these virtues are really not getting me anywhere. I have begun to notice." Tied to this recognition is an acknowledgment of her power and worth, both previously excluded from the image she projected:

I am suddenly beginning to realize that the things that I like to do, the things I am interested in, and the things that I believe and the kind of person I am is not so bad that I have to constantly be sitting on the shelf and letting it gather dust. I am a lot more worthwhile than what my past actions have led other people to believe.

Her notion of a "good person," which previously was limited to her mother's example of hard work, patience and self-sacrifice, now changes to include the value that she herself places on directness and honesty. Although she believes that this new self-assertion will lead her "to feel a lot better about myself," she recognizes that it will also expose her to criticism:

Other people may say, "Boy, she's aggressive, and I don't like that," but at least, you know, they will know that they don't like that. They are not going to say, "I like the way she manipulates herself to fit right around me." . . . What I want to do is just be a more self-determined person and a more singular person.

While within her old framework abortion had seemed a way of "copping out" instead of being a "responsible person [who] pays for his mistakes and pays and pays and is always there when she says she will be there and even when she doesn't say she will be there is there," now, her "conception of what I think is right for myself and my conception of self-worth is changing." She can consider this emergent self "also a good person," as her concept of goodness expands to encompass "the feeling of self-worth; you are not going to sell yourself short and you are not going to make yourself do things that, you know, are really stupid and that you don't want to do." This reorientation centers on the awareness that:

I have a responsibility to myself, and you know, for once I am beginning to realize that that really matters to me . . . instead of doing what I want for myself and feeling guilty over how selfish I am, you realize that that is a very usual way for people to live . . . doing what you want to do because you feel that your wants and your needs are important, if to no one else, then to you, and that's reason enough to do something that you want to do.

Once obligation extends to include the self as well as others, the disparity between selfishness and responsibility is reconciled. Although the conflict between self and other remains, the moral problem is restructured in an awareness that the occurrence of the dilemma itself precludes non-violent resolution. The abortion decision is now seen to be a "serious" choice affecting both self and others: "This is a life that I have taken, a conscious decision to terminate, and that is just very heavy, a very heavy thing." While accepting the necessity of abortion as a highly compromised resolution, she turns her attention to the pregnancy itself, which she now considers to denote a failure of responsibility, a failure to care for and protect both self and other.

As in the first transition, although now in different terms, the conflict precipitated by the pregnancy catches up the issues critical to development. These issues now concern the worth of the self in relation to others, the claiming of the power to choose, and the acceptance of responsibility for choice. By provoking a confrontation with these issues, the crisis can become "a very auspicious time; you can use the pregnancy as sort of a learning, teeing-off point, which makes it useful in a way." This possibility for growth inherent in a crisis which allows confrontation with a construction of reality whose acceptance previously had impeded development was first identified by Coles (1964) in his study of the children of Little Rock. This same sense of possibility is expressed by the women who see, in their resolution of the abortion dilemma, a reconstructed understanding which creates the opportunity for "a new beginning," a chance "to take control of my life."

For this woman, the first step in taking control was to end the relationship in which she had considered herself "reduced to a nonentity," but to do so in a responsible way. Recognizing hurt as the inevitable concomitant of rejection, she strives to minimize that hurt "by dealing with [his] needs as best I can without compromising my own . . . that's a big point for me, because the thing in my life to this point has been always compromising, and I am not willing to do that any more." Instead, she seeks to act in a "decent, human kind of way . . . one that leaves maybe a slightly shook but not totally destroyed person." Thus the "nonentity" confronts her power to destroy which formerly had impeded any assertion, as she consider the possibility for a new kind of action that leaves both self and other intact.

The moral concern remains a concern with hurting as she considers Kohlberg's Heinz dilemma in terms of the question, "who is going to be hurt more, the druggist who loses some money or the person who loses their life?" The right to property and right to life are weighed not in the abstract, in terms of their logical priority, but rather in the particular, in terms of the actual consequences that the violation of these rights would have in the lives of the people involved. Thinking remains contextual and admixed with feelings of care, as the moral imperative to avoid hurt begins to be informed by a psychological understanding of the meaning of nonviolence.

Thus, release from the intimidation of inequality finally allows the expression of a judgment that previously had been withheld. What women then enunciate is not a new morality, but a moral conception disentangled from the constraints that formerly had confused its perception and impeded its articulation. The willingness to express and take responsibility for judgment stems from the recognition of the psychological and moral necessity for an equation of worth between self and other. Responsibility for care then includes both self and other, and the obligation not to hurt, freed from conventional constraints, is reconstructed as a universal guide to moral choice.

The reality of hurt centers the judgment of a twenty-nine-year-old woman, married and the mother of a preschool child, as she struggles with the dilemma posed by a second pregnancy whose timing conflicts with her completion of an advanced degree. Saying that "I cannot deliberately do something that is bad or would hurt another person because I can't live with having done that," she nevertheless confronts a situation in which hurt has become inevitable. Seeking that solution which would best protect both herself and others, she indicates, in her definition of morality, the ineluctable sense of connection which infuses and colors all of her thinking:

> [Morality is] doing what is appropriate and what is just within your circumstances, but ideally it is not going to affect — I was going to say, ideally it wouldn't negatively affect another person, but that is ridiculous, because decisions are always going to affect another person. But you see, what I am trying to say is that it is the person that is the center of the decision making, of that decision making about what's right and what's wrong.

The person who is the center of this decisionmaking begins by denying, but then goes on to acknowledge, the conflicting nature both of her own needs and of her various responsibilities. Seeing the pregnancy as a manifestation of the inner conflict between her wish, on the one hand, "to be a college president" and, on the other, "to be making pottery and flowers and having kids and staying at home," she struggles with contradiction between femininity and adulthood. Considering abortion as the "better" choice — because "in the end, meaning this time next year or this time two weeks from now, it will be less of a personal strain on us individually and on us as a family for me not to be pregnant at this time," she concludes that the decision has

> got to be, first of all, something that the woman can live with — a decision that the woman can live with, one way or another, or at least try to live with, and that it be based on where she is at and other people, significant people in her life, are at.

At the beginning of the interview she had presented the dilemma in its conventional feminine construction, as a conflict between her own wish to have a baby and the wish of others for her to complete her education. On the basis of this construction she deemed it "selfish" to continue the pregnancy because it was something "I want to do." However, as she begins to examine her thinking, she comes to abandon as false this conceptualization of the problem, acknowledging the truth of her own internal conflict and elaborating the tension which she feels between her femininity and the adulthood of her work life. She describes herself as "going in two directions" and values that part of herself which is "incredibly compassionate and sensitive" — her capacity to recognize and meet, often with anticipation, the needs of others. Seeing her "compassion" as "something I don't want to lose" she regards it as endangered by her pursuit of professional advancement. Thus the self-deception of her initial presentation, its attempt to sustain the fiction of her own innocence, stems from her fear that to say that *she* does not want to have another baby at this time would be

> an acknowledgment to me that I am an ambitious person and that I want to have power and responsibility for others and that I want to live a life that extends from 9 to 5 every day and into the evenings and on weekends, because that is what the power and responsibility means. It means that my family would necessarily come second . . . there would be such an incredible conflict about which is tops, and I don't want that for myself.

Asked about her concept of "an ambitious person" she says that to be ambitious means to be

> power hungry [and] insensitive. [Why insensitive?] Because people are stomped on in the process. A person on the way up stomps on people, whether it is family or other colleagues or clientele, on the way up. [Inevitably?] Not always, but I have seen it so often in my limited years of working that it is scary to me. It is scary because I don't want to change like that.

Because the acquisition of adult power is seen to entail the loss of feminine sensitivity and compassion, the conflict between femininity and adulthood becomes construed as a moral problem. The discovery of the principle of nonviolence begins to direct attention to the moral dilemma itself and initiates the search for a resolution that can encompass both femininity and adulthood.

Developmental Theory Reconsidered

The developmental conception delineated at the outset, which has so consistently found the development of women to be either aberrant or incomplete, has been limited insofar as it has been predominantly a male conception, giving lip-service, a place on the chart, to the interdependence of intimacy and care but constantly stressing, at their expense, the importance and value of autonomous judgment and action. To admit to this conception the truth of the feminine perspective is to recognize for both sexes the central importance in adult life of the connection between self and other, the universality of the need for compassion and care. The concept of the separate self and of the moral principle uncompromised by the constraints of reality is an adolescent ideal, the elaborately wrought philosophy of a Stephen Daedalus, whose flight we know to be in jeopardy. Erikson (1964), in contrasting the ideological morality of the adolescent with the ethics of adult care, attempts to grapple with this problem of integration, but is impeded by the limitations of his own previous developmental conception. When his developmental stages chart a path where the sole precursor to the intimacy of adult relationships is the trust established in infancy and all intervening experience is marked only as steps toward greater independence, then separation itself becomes the model and the measure of growth. The observation that for women, identity has as much to do with connection as with separation led Erikson into trouble largely because of his failure to integrate this insight into the mainstream of his developmental theory (Erikson, 1968).

The morality of responsibility which women describe stands apart from the morality of rights which underlies Kohlberg's conception of the highest stages of moral judgment. Kohlberg (Note 3) sees the progression toward these stages as resulting from the generalization of the self-centered adolescent rejection of societal morality into a principled conception of individual natural rights. To illustrate this progression, he cites as an example of integrated Stage Five judgment, "possibly moving to Stage Six," the following response of a twenty-five-year-old subject from his male longitudinal sample:

> [What does the word morality mean to you?] Nobody in the world knows the answer. I think it is recognizing the right of the individual, the rights of other individuals, not interfering with those rights. Act as fairly as you would have them treat you. I think it is basically to preserve the human being's right to existence. I think that is the most important. Secondly, the human being's right to do as he pleases, again without interfering with somebody else's rights. (p. 29)

Another version of the same conception is evident in the following interview response of a male college senior whose moral judgment also was scored by Kohlberg (Note 4) as at Stage Five or Six:

> [Morality] is a prescription, it is a thing to follow, and the idea of having a concept of morality is to try to figure out what it is that people can do in order to make life with each other livable, make for a kind of balance, a kind of equilibrium, a harmony in which everybody feels he has a place and an equal share in things, and it's doing that — doing that is kind of contributing to a state of affairs that go beyond the individual in the absence of which, the individual has no chance for self-fulfillment of any kind. Fairness; morality is kind of essential, it seems to me, for creating the kind of environment, interaction between people, that is prerequisite to this fulfillment of most individual goals and so on. If you want other people to not interfere with your pursuit of whatever you are into, you have to play the game.

In contrast, a woman in her late twenties responds to a similar question by defining a morality not of rights but of responsibility:

> [What makes something a moral issue?] Some sense of trying to uncover a right path in which to live, and always in my mind is that the world is full of real and recognizable trouble, and is it heading for some sort of doom and is it right to bring children into this world when we currently have an overpopulation problem, and is it right to spend money on a pair of shoes when I have a

pair of shoes and other people are shoeless. . . . It is part of a self-critical view, part of saying, how am I spending my time and in what sense am I working? I think I have a real drive to, I have a real maternal drive to take care of someone. To take care of my mother, to take care of children, to take care of other people's children, to take care of my own children, to take care of the world. I think that goes back to your other question, and when I am dealing with moral issues, I am sort of saying to myself constantly, are you taking care of all the things that you think are important and in what ways are you wasting yourself and wasting those issues?

While the postconventional nature of this woman's perspective seems clear, her judgments of Kohlberg's hypothetical moral dilemmas do not meet his criteria for scoring at the principled level. Kohlberg regards this as a disparity between normative and metaethical judgments which he sees as indicative of the transition between conventional and principled thinking. From another perspective, however, this judgment represents a different moral conception, disentangled from societal conventions and raised to the principled level. In this conception, moral judgment is oriented toward issues of responsibility. The way in which the responsibility orientation guides moral decision at the postconventional level is described by the following woman in her thirties:

[Is there a right way to make moral decisions?] The only way I know is to try to be as awake as possible, to try to know the range of what you feel, to try to consider all that's involved, to be as aware as you can be to what's going on, as conscious as you can of where you're walking. [Are there principles that guide you?] The principle would have something to do with responsibility, responsibility and caring about yourself and others. . . . But it's not that on the one hand you choose to be responsible. That's why there's not just a principle that once you take hold of you settle — the principle put into practice here is still going to leave you with conflict.

The moral imperative that emerges repeatedly in the women's interviews is an injunction to care, a responsibility to discern and alleviate the "real and recognizable trouble" of this world. For the men Kohlberg studied, the moral imperative appeared rather as an injunction to respect the rights of others and thus to protect from interference the right to life and self-fulfillment. Women's insistence on care is at first self-critical rather than self-protective, while men initially conceive obligation to others negatively in terms of non-interference. Development for both sexes then would seem to entail an integration of rights and responsibilities through the discovery of the complementarity of these disparate views. For the women I have studied, this integration between rights and responsibilities appears to take place through a principled understanding of equity and reciprocity. This understanding tempers the self-destructive potential of a self-critical morality by asserting the equal right of all persons to care. For the men in Kohlberg's sample as well as for those in a longitudinal study of Harvard undergraduates (Gilligan & Murphy, Note 5) it appears to be the recognition through experience of the need for a more active responsibility in taking care that corrects the potential indifference of a morality of noninterference and turns attention from the logic to the consequences of choice. In the development of a post-conventional ethic understanding, women come to see the violence generated by inequitable relationships, while men come to realize the limitations of a conception of justice blinded to the real inequities of human life.

Kohlberg's dilemmas, in the hypothetical abstraction of their presentation, divest the moral actors from the history and psychology of their individual lives and separate the moral problem from the social contingencies of its possible occurrence. In doing so, the dilemmas are useful for the distillation and refinement of the "objective principles of justice" toward which Kohlberg's stages arrive. However, the reconstruction of the dilemma in its contextual particularity allows the understanding of cause and consequence which engages the compassion and tolerance considered by previous theorists to qualify the feminine sense of justice. Only when substance is given to the skeletal lives of hypothetical people is it possible to consider the social injustices which their moral problems may reflect and to imagine the individual suffering their occurrence may signify or their resolution engender.

The proclivity of women to reconstruct hypothetical dilemmas in terms of the real, to request or supply the information missing about the nature of the people and the places where they live, shifts their judgment away from the hierarchical ordering of principles and the formal procedures of decision making that are critical for scoring at Kohlberg's highest stages. This insistence on the particular signifies an orientation to the dilemma and to moral problems in general that differs from any of Kohlberg's stage descriptions. Given the constraints of Kohlberg's system and the biases in his research sample, this different orientation can only be construed as a failure in development. While several of the women in the research sample clearly articulated what Kohlberg regarded as a postconventional metaethical position, none of them were considered by Kohlberg to be principled in their normative moral judgments pointed toward an identification of the violence inherent in the dilemma itself which was seen to compromise the justice of any of its possible resolutions. This construction of the dilemma led the women to recast the moral judgment from a consideration of the good to a choice between evils.

The woman whose judgment of the abortion dilemma concluded the developmental sequence presented in the preceding section saw Kohlberg's Heinz dilemma in these terms and judged Heinz's action in terms of a choice between selfishness and sacrifice. For Heinz to steal the drug, given the circumstances of his life (which she inferred from his inability to pay two thousand dollars), he would have "to do something which is not in his best interest, in that he is going to get sent away, and that is a supreme sacrifice, a sacrifice which I would say a person truly in love might be willing to make." However, not to steal the drug "would be selfish on his part . . . he would just have to feel guilty about not allowing her a chance to live longer." Heinz's decision to steal is considered not in terms of the logical priority of life over property which justifies its rightness, but rather in terms of the actual consequences that stealing would have for a man of limited means and little social power.

Considered in the light of its probable outcomes — his wife dead, or Heinz in jail, brutalized by the violence of that experience and his life compromised by a record of felony — the dilemma itself changes. Its resolution has less to do with the relative weight of life and property in an abstract moral conception than with the collision it has produced between two lives, formerly conjoined but now in opposition, where the continuation of one life can now occur only at the expense of the other. Given this construction, it becomes clear why consideration revolves around the issue of sacrifice and why guilt becomes the inevitable concomitant of either resolution.

> Demonstrating the reticence noted in the first section about making moral judgments, this woman explains her reluctance to judge in terms of her belief that everybody's existence is so different that I kind of say to myself, that might be something that I wouldn't do, but I can't say that it is right or wrong for that person. I can only deal with what is appropriate for me to do when I am faced with specific problems.

Asked if she would apply to others her own injunction against hurting, she says:

> See, I can't say that it is wrong. I can't say that it is right or that it's wrong because I don't know what the person did that the other person did something to hurt him . . . so it is not right that the person got hurt, but it is right that the person who just lost the job has got to get that anger up and out. It doesn't put any bread on his table, but it is released. I don't mean to be copping out. I really am trying to see how to answer these questions for you.

Her difficulty in answering Kohlberg's questions, her sense of strain with the construction which they impose on the dilemma, stems from their divergence from her own frame of reference:

> I don't even think I use the words right and wrong anymore, and I know I don't use the word moral, because I am not sure I know what it means. . . . We are talking about an unjust society, we are talking about a whole lot of things that are not right, that are truly wrong, to use the word that I don't use very often, and I have no control to change that. If I could change it, I certainly would, but I can only make my small contribution from day to day, and if I don't intentionally hurt somebody, that is my contribution to a better society. And so a chunk of that contribution is also not to pass judgment on other people, particularly when I don't know the circumstances of why they are doing certain things.

The reluctance to judge remains a reluctance to hurt, but one that stems now not from a sense of personal vulnerability but rather from a recognition of the limitations of judgment itself. The deference of the conventional feminine perspective can thus be seen to continue at the postconventional level, not as moral relativism but rather as part of a reconstructed moral understanding. Moral judgment is renounced in an awareness of the psychological and social determinism of all human behavior at the same time as moral concern is reaffirmed in recognition of the reality of human pain and suffering.

> I have a real thing about hurting people and always have, and that gets a little complicated at times, because, for example, you don't want to hurt your child. I don't want to hurt my child but if I don't hurt her sometimes, then that's hurting her more, you see, and so that was a terrible dilemma for me.

Moral dilemmas are terrible in that they entail hurt; she sees Heinz's decision as "the result of anguish, who am I hurting, why do I have to hurt them." While the morality of Heinz's theft is not in question, given the circumstances which necessitated it, what is at issue is his willingness to substitute himself for his wife and become, in her stead, the victim of exploitation by a society which breeds and legitimizes the druggist's irresponsibility and whose injustice is thus manifest in the very occurrence of the dilemma.

The same sense that the wrong questions are being asked is evident in the response of another woman who justified Heinz's action on a similar basis, saying "I don't think that exploitation should really be a right." When women begin to make direct moral statements, the issues they repeatedly address are those of exploitation and hurt. In doing so, they raise the issue of nonviolence in precisely the same psychological context that brought Erikson (1969) to pause in his consideration of the truth of Gandhi's life.

In the pivotal letter, around which the judgment of his book turns, Erikson confronts the contradiction between the philosophy of nonviolence that informed Gandhi's dealing with the British and the psychology of violence that marred his relationships with his family and with the children of the ashram. It was this contradiction, Erikson confesses,

> which almost brought *me* to the point where I felt unable to continue writing *this* book because I seemed to sense the presence of a kind of untruth in the very protestation of truth; of something unclean when all the words spelled out an unreal purity; and, above all, of displaced violence where nonviolence was the professed issue. (p. 231)

In an effort to untangle the relationship between the spiritual truth of Satyagraha and the truth of his own psychoanalytic understanding, Erikson reminds Gandhi that "Truth, you once said, 'excludes the use of violence because man is not capable of knowing the absolute truth and therefore is not competent to punish'" (p. 241). The affinity between Satyagraha and psychoanalysis lies in their shared commitment to seeing life as an "experiment in truth," in their being

> somehow joined in a universal "therapeutics," committed to a Hippocratic principle that one can test truth (or the healing power inherent in a sick situation) only by action which avoids harm — or better, by action which maximizes mutuality and minimizes the violence caused by unilateral coercion or threat. (p. 247)

Erikson takes Gandhi to task for his failure to acknowledge the relativity of truth. This failure is manifest in the coercion of Gandhi's claim to exclusive possession of the truth, his "unwillingness to learn from *anybody anything* except what was approved by the 'inner voice'" (p. 236). This claim led Gandhi, in the guise of love, to impose his truth on others without awareness or regard for the extent to which he thereby did violence to their integrity.

The moral dilemma, arising inevitably out of a conflict of truths, is by definition a "sick situation" in that its either/or formulation leaves no room for an outcome that does not do violence. The resolution of such dilemmas, however, lies not in the self-deception of rationalized violence — "I was" said Gandhi, "a cruelly kind husband. I regarded myself as her teacher and so harassed her out of my blind love for her" (p. 233) — but rather in the replacement of the underlying antagonism with a mutuality of respect and care.

Gandhi, whom Kohlberg has mentioned as exemplifying Stage Six moral judgment and whom Erikson sought as a model of an adult ethical sensibility, instead is criticized by a judgment that refuses to look away from or condone the infliction of harm. In denying the validity of his wife's reluctance to open her home to strangers and in his blindness to the different reality of adolescent sexuality and temptation, Gandhi compromised in his everyday life the ethic of nonviolence to which in principle and in public he was so steadfastly committed.

The blind willingness to sacrifice people to truth, however, has always been the danger of an ethics abstracted from life. This willingness links Gandhi to the biblical Abraham, who prepared to sacrifice the life of his son in order to demonstrate the integrity and supremacy of his faith. Both men, in the limitations of their fatherhood, stand in implicit contrast to the woman who comes before Solomon and verifies her motherhood by relinquishing truth in order to save the life of her child. It is the ethics of an adulthood that has become principled at the expense of care that Erikson comes to criticize in his assessment of Gandhi's life.

This same criticism is dramatized explicitly as a contrast between the sexes in *The Merchant of Venice* (1598/1912), where Shakespeare goes through an extraordinary complication of sexual identity (dressing a male actor as a female character who in turn poses as a male judge) in order to bring into the masculine citadel of justice the feminine plea for mercy. The limitation of the contractual conception of justice is illustrated through the absurdity of its literal execution, while the "need to make exceptions all the time" is demonstrated contrapuntally in the matter of the rings. Portia, in calling for mercy, argues for that resolution in which no one is hurt, and as the men are forgiven for their failure to keep both their rings and their word, Antonio in turn forgoes his "right" to ruin Shylock.

The research findings that have been reported in this chapter suggest that women impose a distinctive construction on moral problems, seeing moral dilemmas in terms of conflicting responsibilities. This construction was found to develop through a sequence of three levels and two transitions, each level representing a more complex understanding of the relationship between self and other and each transition involving a critical reinterpretation of the moral conflict between selfishness and responsibility. The development of women's moral judgment appears to proceed from an initial concern with survival, to a focus on goodness, and finally to a principled understanding of nonviolence as the most adequate guide to the just resolution of moral conflicts.

In counterposing to Kohlberg's longitudinal research on the development of hypothetical moral judgment in men a cross-sectional study of women's responses to actual dilemmas of moral conflict and choice, this essay precludes the possibility of generalization in either direction and leaves to further research the task of sorting out the different variables of occasion and sex. Longitudinal studies of women's moral judgments are necessary in order to validate the claims of stage and sequence presented here. Similarly, the contrast drawn between the moral judgments of men and women awaits for its confirmation a more systematic comparison of the responses of both sexes. Kohlberg's research on moral development has confounded the variables of age, sex, type of decision, and type of dilemma by presenting a single configuration (the responses of adolescent males to hypothetical dilemmas of conflicting rights) as the basis for a universal stage sequence. This paper underscores the need for systematic treatment of these variables and points toward their study as a critical task for future moral development research.

For the present, my aim has been to demonstrate the centrality of the concepts of responsibility and care in women's constructions of the moral domain, to indicate the close tie in women's thinking between conceptions of the self and conceptions of morality, and, finally, to argue the need for an expanded developmental theory that would include, rather than rule out from developmental consideration, the difference in the feminine voice. Such an inclusion seems essential, not only for explaining the development of women but also for understanding in both sexes the characteristics and precursors of an adult moral conception.

Reference Notes

1. Haan, N. *Activism as moral protest: Moral judgments of hypothetical dilemmas and an actual situation of civil disobedience.* Unpublished manuscript, University of California at Berkeley, 1971.
2. Turiel, E. *A comparative analysis of moral knowledge and moral judgment in males and females.* Unpublished manuscript, Harvard University, 1973.
3. Kohlberg, L. *Continuities and discontinuities in childhood and adult moral development revisited.* Unpublished paper, Harvard University, 1973.
4. Kohlberg, L. Personal communication, August 1976.
5. Gilligan, C., & Murphy, M. *The philosopher and the "dilemma of the fact": Moral development in late adolescence and adulthood.* Unpublished manuscript, Harvard University, 1977.

References

Broverman, I., Vogel, S., Broverman, D., Clarkson, F., & Rosenkrantz, P. (1972). Sex-role stereo-types: A current appraisal. *Journal of Social Issues, 28,* 59–78.

Coles, R. (1964). *Children of crisis.* Boston: Little, Brown.

Didion, J. (1972, July 30). The women's movement. *New York Times Book Review,* pp. 1–2, 14.

Drabble, M. (1969). *The waterfall.* Hammondsworth, Eng.: Penguin Books.

Eliot, G. (1965). *The mill on the floss.* New York: New American Library. (Original work published 1860)

Erikson, E. H. (1964). *Insight and responsibility.* New York: W. W. Norton.

Erikson, E. H. (1968). *Identity: Youth and crisis.* New York: W. W. Norton.

Erikson, E. H. (1969). *Gandhi's truth.* New York: W. W. Norton.

Freud, S. (1959). "Civilized" sexual morality and modern nervous illness. In J. Strachey (Ed.), *The standard edition of the complete psychological works of Sigmund Freud* (vol. 9). London: Hogarth Press. (Original work published 1908)

Freud, S. (1961). Some psychical consequences of the anatomical distinction between the sexes. In J. Strachey (Ed.), *The standard edition of the complete psychological works of Sigmund Freud* (vol. 19). London: Hogarth Press. (Original work published 1925)

Gilligan, C., Kohlberg, L., Lerner, J., & Belenky, M. (1971). Moral reasoning about sexual dilemmas: The development of an interview and scoring system. *Technical Report of the President's Commission on Obscenity and Pornography* (vol. 1) [415 060-137]. Washington, DC: U.S. Government Printing Office.

Haan, N. (1975). Hypothetical and actual moral reasoning in a situation of civil disobedience. *Journal of Personality and Social Psychology, 32,* 255–270.

Holstein, C. (1976). Development of moral judgment: A longitudinal study of males and females. *Child Development, 47,* 51–61.

Horner, M. (1972). Toward an understanding of achievement-related conflicts in women. *Journal of Social Issues, 29,* 157–174.

Ibsen, H. (1965). A doll's house. In *Ibsen plays.* Hammondsworth, Eng.: Penguin Books. (Original work published 1879)

Kohlberg, L. (1971). From is to ought: How to commit the naturalistic fallacy and get away with it in the study of moral development. In T. Mischel (Ed.), *Cognitive development and epistemology.* New York: Academic Press.

Kohlberg, L., & Gilligan, C. (1971). The adolescent as a philosopher: The discovery of the self in a postconventional world. *Daedalus, 100,* 1051–1056.

Kohlberg, L., & Kramer, R. (1969). Continuities and discontinuities in childhood and adult moral development. *Human Development, 12,* 93–120.

Piaget, J. (1965). *The moral judgment of the child.* New York: Free Press. (Original work published 1932)

Shakespeare, W. (1912). The merchant of Venice. In *The comedies of Shakespeare.* London: Oxford University Press. (Original work published 1598)

The research reported here was partially supported by a grant from the Spencer Foundation. I wish to thank Mary Belenky for her collaboration and colleagueship in the abortion decision study and Michael Murphy for his comments and help in preparing this manuscript.

Woman's Place
in Man's Life Cycle

CAROL GILLIGAN

In this chapter, Carol Gilligan continues the work that would lead to her ground-breaking book, In a Different Voice. *Gilligan draws on literary and psychological sources to document the way in which theories of the life cycle, by taking for their model the lives of men, have failed to account for the experiences of women. Arguing that this bias has promoted a concern with autonomy and achievement at the expense of attachment and intimacy, she suggests that systematic attention to women's lives, in both theory and research, will allow an integration of these concerns into a more balanced conception of human development.*

In the second act of *The Cherry Orchard*, Lopakhin, the young merchant, describes his life of hard work and success. Failing to convince Madame Ranevskaya to cut down the cherry orchard to save her estate, he will go on, in the next act, to buy it himself. He is the self-made man, who, in purchasing "the estate where grandfather and father were slaves," seeks to eradicate the "awkward, unhappy life" of the past, replacing the cherry orchard with summer cottages where coming generations "will see a new life" (Act III). Elaborating this developmental vision, he describes the image of man that underlies and supports this activity: "At times when I can't go to sleep, I think: Lord, thou gavest us immense forests, unbounded fields and the widest horizons, and living in the midst of them we should indeed be giants.". At which point, Madame Ranevskaya interrupts him, saying, "You feel the need for giants — They are good only in fairy tales, anywhere else they only frighten us" (Act II).

Conceptions of the life cycle represent attempts to order and make coherent the unfolding experiences and perceptions, the changing wishes and realities of everyday life. But the truth of such conceptions depends in part on the position of the observer. The brief excerpt from Chekhov's play (1904/1956) suggests that when the observer is a woman, the truth may be

Harvard Educational Review Vol. 49 No. 4 November 1979, 431–446

of a different sort. This discrepancy in judgment between men and women is the center of my consideration.

This essay traces the extent to which psychological theories of human development, theories that have informed both educational philosophy and classroom practice, have enshrined a view of human life similar to Lopakhin's while dismissing the ironic commentary in which Chekhov embeds this view. The specific issue I address is that of sex differences, and my focus is on the observation and assessment of sex differences by life-cycle theorists. In talking about sex differences, however, I risk the criticism which such generalization invariably invites. As Virginia Woolf said, when embarking on a similar endeavor: "When a subject is highly controversial — and any question about sex is that — one cannot hope to tell the truth. One can only show how one came to hold whatever opinion one does hold" (1929, p. 4).

At a time when efforts are being made to eradicate discrimination between the sexes in the search for equality and justice, the differences between the sexes are being rediscovered in the social sciences. This discovery occurs when theories formerly considered to be sexually neutral in their scientific objectivity are found instead to reflect a consistent observational and evaluative bias. Then the presumed neutrality of science, like that of language itself, gives way to the recognition that the categories of knowledge are human constructions. The fascination with point of view and the corresponding recognition of the relativity of truth that has informed the fiction of the twentieth century begin to infuse our scientific understanding as well when we begin to notice how accustomed we have become to seeing life through men's eyes.

A recent discovery of this sort pertains to the apparently innocent classic by Strunk and White (1959), *The Elements of Style*. The Supreme Court ruling on the subject of discrimination in classroom texts led one teacher of English to notice that the elementary rules of English usage were being taught through examples which counterposed the birth of Napoleon, the writings of Coleridge, and statements such as, "He was an interesting talker, a man who had traveled all over the world and lived in half a dozen countries" (p. 7) with "Well, Susan, this is a fine mess you are in" (p. 3) or, less drastically, "He saw a woman, accompanied by two children, walking slowly down the road" (p. 8).

Psychological theorists have fallen as innocently as Strunk and White into the same observational bias. Implicitly adopting the male life as the norm, they have tried to fashion women out of a masculine cloth. It all goes back, of course, to Adam and Eve, a story which shows, among other things, that, if you make a woman out of a man you are bound to get into trouble. In the life cycle, as in the Garden of Eden, it is the woman who has been the deviant.

The penchant of developmental theorists to project a masculine image, and one that appears frightening to women, goes back at least to Freud (1905/1961), who built his theory of psychosexual development around the experiences of the male child that culminate in the Oedipus complex. In the 1920s, Freud struggled to resolve the contradictions posed for his theory by the different configuration of female sexuality and the different dynamics of the young girl's early family relationships. After trying to fit women into his masculine conception, seeing them as envying that which they missed, he came instead to acknowledge, in the strength and persistence of women's pre-Oedipal attachments to their mothers, a developmental difference. However, he considered this difference in women's development to be responsible for what he saw as women's developmental failure.

Deprived by nature of the impetus for a clear-cut Oedipus resolution, women's superego, the heir to the Oedipus complex, consequently was compromised. It was never, Freud observed, "so inexorable, so impersonal, so independent of its emotional origins as we require it to be in men" (1925/1961, p. 257). From this observation of difference, "that for women the level of what is ethically normal is different from what it is in men" (p. 257), Freud concluded that "women have less sense of justice than men, that they are less ready to submit to the great exigencies of life, that they are more often influenced in their judgments by feelings of affection and hostility" (pp. 257–258).

Chodorow (1974, 1978) addresses this evaluative bias in the assessment of sex differences in her attempt to account for "the reproduction within each generation of certain general and nearly universal differences that characterize masculine and feminine personality and roles" (1974, p. 43). Writing from a psychoanalytic perspective, she attributes these continuing differences between the sexes not to anatomy but rather to "the fact that women, universally, are largely responsible for early child care and for (at least) later female socialization" (1974, p. 43). Because this early social environment differs for and is experienced differently by male and female children, basic sex differences recur in personality development. As a result, "in any given society, feminine personality comes to define itself in relation and connection to other people more than masculine personality does. (In psychoanalytic terms, women are less individuated than men; they have more flexible ego boundaries.)" (1974, p. 44).

In her analysis, Chodorow relies primarily on Stoller's research on the development of gender identity and gender-identity disturbances. Stoller's work indicates that male and female identity, the unchanging core of personality formation, is "with rare exception firmly and irreversibly established for both sexes by the time a child is around three" (Chodorow, 1978, p. 150). Given that for both sexes the primary caretaker in the first three years of life is typically female, the interpersonal dynamics of gender identity formation are different for boys and girls. Female identity formation takes place in a context of ongoing relationship as "mothers tend to experience their daughters as more like, and continuous with, themselves. Correspondingly, girls tend to remain part of the dyadic primary mother-child relationship itself. This means that a girl continues to experience herself as involved in issues of merging and separation, and in an attachment characterized by primary identification and the fusion of identification and object choice" (1978, p. 166).

In contrast, "mothers experience their sons as a male opposite" and, as a result, "boys are more likely to have been pushed out of the preoedipal relationship and to have had to curtail their primary love and sense of empathic tie with their mother" (1978, p. 166). Consequently, boys' development entails a "more emphatic individuation and a more defensive firming of ego boundaries." For boys, but not for girls, "issues of differentiation have become intertwined with sexual issues" (1978, p. 167).

Thus Chodorow refutes the masculine bias of psychoanalytic theory, claiming that the existence of sex differences in the early experiences of individuation and relationship "does not mean that women have 'weaker ego boundaries' than men or are more prone to psychosis" (1978, p. 167). What it means instead is that "the earliest mode of individuation, the primary construction of the ego and its inner object-world, the earliest conflicts and the earliest unconscious definitions of self, the earliest threats to individuation, and the earliest anxieties which call up defenses, all differ for boys and girls because of differences in the character of the early mother-child relationship for each" (1978, p. 167). Because of these differences, "girls emerge from this period with a basis for 'empathy' built into their primary definition of self in a way that boys do not" (1978, p. 167). Chodorow thus replaces Freud's negative and derivative description of female psychology with a more positive and direct account of her own:

> Girls emerge with a stronger basis for experiencing another's needs and feelings as one's own (or of thinking that one is so experiencing another's needs and feelings). Furthermore, girls do not define themselves in terms of the denial of preoedipal relational modes to the same extent as do boys. Therefore, regression to these modes tends not to feel as much a basic threat to their ego. From very early, then, because they are parented by a person of the same gender . . . girls come to experience themselves as less differentiated than boys, as more continuous with and related to the external object-world, and as differently oriented to their inner object-world as well. (1978, p. 167)

Consequently, "issues of dependency, in particular, are handled and experienced differently by men and women" (Chodorow, 1974, p. 44). For boys and men, separation and individuation are critically tied to gender identity since separation from the mother is essential for the development of masculinity. "For girls and women, by contrast, issues of femininity or feminine identity are not problematic in the same way" (1974, p. 44); they do not depend on the achievement of separation from the mother or on the progress of individuation. Since, in Chodorow's analysis, masculinity is defined through separation while femininity is defined through attachment, male gender identity will be threatened by intimacy while female gender identity will be threatened by individuation. Thus males will tend to have difficulty with relationships while females will tend to have problems with separation. The quality of embeddedness in social interaction and personal relationships that characterizes women's lives in contrast to men's, however, becomes not only a descriptive difference but also a developmental liability when the milestones of childhood and adolescent development are described by markers of increasing separation. Then women's failure to separate becomes by definition a failure to develop.

The sex differences in personality formation that Chodorow delineates in her analysis of early childhood relationships as well as the bias she points out in the evaluation of these differences, reappear in the middle childhood years in the studies of children's games. Children's games have been considered by Mead (1934) and Piaget (1932/1965) as the crucible of social development during the school years. In games children learn to take the role of the other and come to see themselves through another's eyes. In games they learn respect for rules and come to understand the ways rules can be made and changed.

Lever (1976), considering the peer group to be the agent of socialization during the elementary school years and play to be a major activity of socialization at that time, set out to discover whether there were sex differences in the games that children play. Studying 181 fifth-grade, white, middle-class, Connecticut children, ages 10 and 11, she observed the organization and structure of their playtime activities. She watched the children as they played during the school recess, lunch, and in physical education class, and, in addition, kept diaries of their accounts as to how they spent their out-of-school time.

From this study, Lever reports the following sex differences: boys play more out of doors than girls do; boys more often play in large and age-heterogeneous groups; they play competitive games more often than girls do, and their games last longer than girls' games (Lever, 1976). The last is in some ways the most interesting finding. Boys' games appeared to last longer not only because they required a higher level of skill and were thus less likely to become boring, but also because when disputes arose in the course of a game, the boys were able to resolve the disputes more effectively than the girls: "During the course of this study, boys were seen quarrelling all the time, but not once was a game terminated because of a quarrel and no game was interrupted for more than seven minutes. In the gravest debates, the final word was always to 'repeat the play,' generally followed by a chorus of 'cheater's proof'" (1976, p. 482). In fact, it seemed that the boys enjoyed the legal debates as much as they did the game itself, and even marginal players of lesser size or skill participated equally in these recurrent squabbles. In contrast, the eruption of disputes among girls tended to end the game.

Thus Lever extends and corroborates the observations reported by Piaget (1932/1965) in his naturalistic study of the rules of the game, where he found boys becoming increasingly fascinated with the legal elaboration of rules and the development of fair procedures for adjudicating conflicts, a fascination that, he noted, did not hold for girls. Girls, Piaget observed, had a more "pragmatic" attitude toward rules, "regarding a rule as good as long as the game repaid it" (1932/1965, p. 83). As a result, he considered girls to be more tolerant in their attitudes toward rules, more willing to make exceptions, and more easily reconciled to innovations. However, and presumably as a result, he concluded that the legal sense which he considered essential to moral development "is far less developed in little girls than in boys" (1932/1965, p. 77).

This same bias that led Piaget to equate male development with child development also colors Lever's work. The assumption that shapes her discussion of results is that the male model is the better one. It seems, in any case, more adaptive since as Lever points out it fits the requirements Riesman (1961) describes for success in modern corporate life. In contrast, the sensitivity and care for the feelings of others that girls develop through their primarily dyadic play relationships have little market value and can even impede professional success. Lever clearly implies that, given the realities of adult life, if a girl does not want to be dependent on men, she will have to learn to play like a boy.

Since Piaget argues that children learn the respect for rules necessary for moral development by playing rule-bound games, and Kohlberg (1971) adds that these lessons are most effectively learned through the opportunities for role-taking that arise in the course of resolving disputes, the moral lessons inherent in girls' play appear to be fewer than for boys. Traditional girls' games like jump rope and hopscotch are turn-taking games where competition is indirect in that one person's success does not necessarily signify another's failure. Consequently, disputes requiring adjudication are less likely to occur. In fact, most of the girls whom Lever interviewed claimed that when a quarrel broke out, they ended the game. Rather than elaborating a system of rules for resolving disputes, girls directed their efforts instead toward sustaining affective ties.

Lever concludes that from the games they play boys learn both independence and the organizational skills necessary for coordinating the activities of large and diverse groups of people. By participating in controlled and socially approved competitive situations, they learn to deal with competition in a relatively forthright manner — to play with their enemies and compete with their friends, all in accordance with the rules of the game. In contrast, girls' play tends to occur in smaller, more intimate groups, often the best-friend dyad, and in private places. This play replicates the social pattern of primary human relationships in that its organization is more cooperative and points less toward learning to take the role of the generalized other than it does toward the development of the empathy and sensitivity necessary for taking the role of the particular other.

Chodorow's analysis of sex differences in personality formation in early childhood is thus extended by Lever's observations of sex differences in the play activities of middle childhood. Together these accounts suggest that boys and girls arrive at puberty with a different interpersonal orientation and a different range of social experiences. While Sullivan (1953), tracing the sequence of male development, posits the experience of a close same-sex friendship in preadolescence as necessary for the subsequent integration of sexuality and intimacy, no corresponding account is available to describe girls' development at this critical juncture. Instead, since adolescence is considered a crucial time for separation and individuation, the period of "the second individuation process" (Blos, 1967), it has been in adolescence that female development has appeared most divergent and thus most problematic.

"Puberty," Freud said, "which brings about so great an accession of libido in boys, marked in girls by a fresh wave of repression" (1905/1961, p. 220) necessary for the transformation of the young girl's "masculine sexuality" into the "specifically feminine" sexuality of her adulthood. Freud posits this transformation on the girl's acknowledgement and acceptance of "the fact of her castration." In his account puberty brings for girls a new awareness of "the wound to her narcissism" and leads her to develop, "like a scar, a sense of inferiority" (Freud, 1925/1961, p. 253). Since adolescence is, in Erikson's expansion of Freud's psychoanalytic account, the time when the ego takes on an identity which confirms the individual in relation to society, the girl arrives at this juncture in development either psychologically at risk or with a different agenda.

The problem that female adolescence presents for psychologists of human development is apparent in Erikson's account. Erikson (1950) charts eight stages of psychosocial development in which adolescence is the fifth. The task of this stage is to forge a coherent sense of self, to verify an identity that can span the discontinuity of puberty and make possible the adult capacity to love and to work. The preparation for the successful resolution of the adolescent identity crisis is delineated in Erikson's description of the preceding four stages. If in infancy the initial crisis of trust vs. mistrust generates enough hope to sustain the child through the arduous life cycle that lies ahead, the task at hand clearly becomes one of individuation. Erikson's second stage centers on the crisis of autonomy versus shame and doubt, the walking child's emerging sense of separateness and agency. From there, development goes on to the crisis of initiative versus guilt, successful resolution of which represents a further move in the direction of autonomy. Next, following the inevitable disappointment of the magical wishes of the oedipal period, the child realizes with respect to his parents that to beat them he must first join them and learn to do what they do so well. Thus in the middle childhood years, development comes to hinge on the crisis of industry versus inferiority, as the demonstration of competence becomes critical to the child's developing self-esteem. This is the time when children strive to learn and master the technology of their culture in order to recognize themselves and be recognized as capable of becoming adults. Next comes adolescence, the celebration of the autonomous, initiating, industrious self through the forging of an identity based on an ideology that can support and justify adult commitments. But about whom is Erikson talking?

Once again it turns out to be the male child — the coming generation of men like George Bernard Shaw, William James, Martin Luther, and Mahatma Gandhi — who provide Erikson with his most vivid illustrations. For the woman, Erikson (1968) says, the sequence is a bit different. She holds her identity in abeyance as she prepares to attract the man by whose name she will be known, by whose status she will be defined, the man who will rescue her from emptiness and loneliness by filling "the inner space" (Erikson, 1968). While for men, identity precedes intimacy and generativity in the optimal cycle of human separation and attachment, for women these tasks seem instead to be fused. Intimacy precedes, or rather goes along with, identity as the female comes to know herself as she is known, through her relationships with others.

Two things are essential to note at this point. The first is that, despite Erikson's observation of sex differences, his chart of life-cycle stages remains unchanged: identity continues to precede intimacy as the male diagonal continues to define his life-cycle conception. The second is that in the male life cycle there is little preparation for the intimacy of the first adult stage. Only the initial stage of trust versus mistrust suggests the type of mutuality that Erikson means by intimacy and generativity and Freud by genitality: the rest is separateness, with the result that development itself comes to be identified with separation and attachments appear as developmental impediments, as we have repeatedly found to be the case in the assessment of women.

Erikson's description of male identity as forged in relation to the world and of female identity as awakened in a relationship of intimacy with another person, however controversial, is hardly new. In Bettelheim's discussion of fairy tales in *The Uses of Enchantment* (1976) an identical portrayal appears. While Bettelheim argues, in refutation of those critics who see in fairy tales a sexist literature, that opposite models exist and could readily be found, nevertheless the ones upon which he focuses his discussion of adolescence conform to the pattern we have begun to observe.

The dynamics of male adolescence are illustrated archetypically by the conflict between father and son in "The Three Languages" (Bettelheim, 1976). Here a son, considered hopelessly stupid by his father, is given one last chance at education and sent for a year to study with a famous master. But when he returns, all he has learned is "what the dogs bark" (1976, p. 97). After two further attempts of this sort, the father gives up in disgust and orders his servants to take the child into the forest and kill him. The servants, however, those perpetual rescuers of disowned and abandoned children, take pity on the child and decide simply to leave him in the forest. From there, his wanderings take him to a land beset by furious dogs whose barking permits nobody to rest and who periodically devour one of the inhabitants. Now it turns out that our hero has learned just the right thing: he can talk with the dogs and is able to quiet them, thus restoring peace to the land. The other knowledge he acquires serves him equally well, and he emerges triumphant from his adolescent confrontation with his father, a giant of the life-cycle conception.

In contrast, the dynamics of female adolescence are depicted through the telling of a very different story. In the world of the fairy tale, the girl's first bleeding is followed by a period of intense passivity in which nothing seems to be happening. Yet in the deep sleep of Snow White and Sleeping Beauty, Bettelheim sees that inner concentration which he considers to be the necessary counterpart to the activity of adventure. The adolescent heroines awaken from their sleep not to conquer the world but to marry the prince. Their feminine identity is inwardly and interpersonally defined. As in Erikson's observation, for women, identity and intimacy are more intricately conjoined. The sex differences depicted in the world of the fairy tales, like the fantasy of the woman warrior in Maxine Hong Kingston's (1977) recent autobiographical novel (which in turn echoes the old stories of Troilus and Cressida and Tancred and Chlorinda) indicate repeatedly that active adventure is a male activity, and if women are to embark on such endeavors, they must at least dress like men.

These observations about sex difference support the conclusion reached by McClelland that "sex role turns out to be one of the most important determinants of human behavior. Psychologists have found sex differences in their studies from the moment they started doing empirical research" (1975, p. 81). But since it is difficult to say "different" without saying "better" or "worse," and since there is a tendency to construct a single scale of measurement, and since that scale has been derived and standardized on the basis of men's observations and interpretations of research data predominantly or exclusively drawn from studies of males, psychologists have tended, in McClelland's words, "to regard male behavior as the 'norm' and female behavior as some kind of deviation from that norm" (1975, p. 81). Thus when women do not conform to the standards of psychological expectation, the conclusion has generally been that something is wrong with the women.

What Horner (1972) found to be wrong with women was the anxiety they showed about competitive achievement. From the beginning, research on human motivation using the Thematic Apperception Test (TAT) was plagued by evidence of sex differences which appeared to confuse and complicate data analysis. The TAT presents for interpretation an ambiguous cue — a picture about which a story is to be written or a brief story stem to be completed. Such stories in reflecting projective imagination are considered to reveal the ways in which people construe what they perceive — that is, the concepts and interpretations they bring to their experience and thus presumably the kind of sense that they make of their lives. Prior to Horner's work, it was clear that women made a different kind of sense than men of situations of competitive achievement, that in some way they saw the situation differently or the situation aroused in them some different response.

On the basis of his studies of men, McClelland (1961) had divided the concept of achievement motivation into what appeared to be its two logical components, a motive to approach success ("hope success") and a motive to avoid failure ("fear failure"). When Horner (1972) began to analyze the problematic projective data on female achievement motivation, she identified as a third category the unlikely motivation to avoid success ("fear success"). Women appeared to have a problem with competitive achievement, and that problem seemed, in Horner's interpretation, to emanate from a perceived conflict between femininity and success, the dilemma of the female adolescent who struggles to integrate her feminine aspirations and the identifications of her early childhood with the more masculine competence she has acquired at school. Thus Horner reports, "When success is likely or possible, threatened by the negative consequences they expect to follow success, young women become anxious and their positive achievement strivings become thwarted" (1972, p. 171). She concludes that this fear exists because for most women, the anticipation of success in competitive achievement activity, especially against men, produced anticipation of certain negative consequences, for example, threat of social rejection and loss of femininity."

It is, however, possible to view such conflicts about success in a different light. Sassen (forthcoming), on the basis of her reanalysis of the data presented in Horner's thesis, suggests that the conflicts expressed by the women might instead indicate "a heightened perception of the 'other side' of competitive success, that is, the great emotional costs of success achieved through competition, or an understanding which, while confused, indicates an awareness that something is rotten in the state in which success is defined as having better grades than everyone else" (Sassen, forthcoming). Sassen points out that Horner found success anxiety to be present in women only when achievement was directly competitive, that is, where one person's success was at the expense of another's failure.

From Horner's examples of fear of success, it is impossible to differentiate between neurotic or realistic anxiety about the consequences of achievement, the questioning of conventional definitions of success, or the discovery of personal goals other than conventional success. The construction of the problem posed by success as a problem of identity and ideology that appears in Horner's illustrations, if taken at face value rather than assumed to be derivative, suggests Erikson's distinction between a conventional and neohumanist identity, or, in cognitive terms, the distinction between a conventional and postconventional thought (Loevinger, 1970; Inhelder & Piaget, 1958; Kohlberg, 1971; Perry, 1968).

In his elaboration of the identity crisis, Erikson discusses the life of George Bernard Shaw to illustrate the young person's sense of being co-opted prematurely by success in a career he cannot wholeheartedly endorse. Shaw at seventy, reflecting upon his life, describes his crisis at the age of twenty as one caused not by lack of success or the absence of recognition, but by too much of both:

> I made good in spite of myself, and found, to my dismay, that Business, instead of expelling me as the worthless imposter I was, was fastening upon me with no intention of letting me go. Behold me, therefore, in my twentieth year, with a business training, in an occupation which I detested as cordially as any sane person lets himself detest anything he cannot escape from. In March, 1876, I broke loose. (Erikson, 1968, p. 143)

At which point Shaw settled down to study and to write as he pleased. Hardly interpreted as evidence of developmental difficulty, of neurotic anxiety about achievement and competition, Shaw's refusal suggested to Erikson, "the extraordinary workings of an extraordinary personality coming to the fore" (1968, p. 144).

We might on these grounds begin to ask not why women have conflicts about succeeding but why men show such readiness to adopt and celebrate a rather narrow vision of success. Remembering Piaget's observation, corroborated by Lever, that boys in their games are concerned more with rules while girls are more concerned with relationships, often at the expense of the game itself; remembering also that, in Chodorow's analysis, men's social orientation is positional and women's orientation is personal, we begin to understand why, when Anne becomes John in Horner's tale of competitive success and the stories are written by men, fear of success tends to disappear. John is considered by other men to have played by the rules and won. He has the *right* to feel good about his success. Confirmed in his sense of his own identity as separate from those who, compared to him, are less competent, his positional sense of self is affirmed. For Anne, it is possible that the position she could obtain by being at the top of her medical school class may not, in fact, be what she wants.

"It is obvious," Virginia Woolf said, "that the values of women differ very often from the values which have been made by the other sex" (1929, p. 76). Yet, she adds, it is the masculine values that prevail. As a result, women come to question the "normality" of their feelings and to alter their judgments in deference to the opinion of others. In the nineteenth-century novels written by women, Woolf sees at work "a mind slightly pulled from the straight, altering its clear vision in the anger and confusion of deference to external authority" (1929, p. 77). The same deference that Woolf identifies in nineteenth-century fiction can be seen as well in the judgments of twentieth-century women. Women's reluctance to make moral judgments, the difficulty they experience in finding or speaking publicly in their own voice, emerge repeatedly in the form of qualification and self-doubt, in intimations of a divided judgment, a public and private assessment which are fundamentally at odds (Gilligan, 1977).

Yet the deference and confusion that Woolf criticizes in women derive from the values she sees as their strength. Women's deference is rooted not only in their social circumstances but also in the substance of their moral concern. Sensitivity to the needs of others and the assumption of responsibility for taking care lead women to attend to voices other than their own and to include in their judgment other points of view. Women's moral weakness, manifest in an apparent diffusion and confusion of judgment, is thus inseparable from women's moral strength, an overriding concern with relationships and responsibilities. The reluctance to judge can itself be indicative of the same care and concern for others that infuses the psychology of women's development and is responsible for what is characteristically seen as problematic in its nature.

Thus women not only define themselves in a context of human relationship but also judge themselves in terms of their ability to care. Woman's place in man's life cycle has been that of nurturer, caretaker, and helpmate, the weaver of those networks of relationships on which she in turn relies. While women have thus taken care of men, however, men have in their theories of psychological development tended either to assume or devalue that care. The focus on individuation and individual achievement that has dominated the description of child and adolescent development has recently been extended to the depiction of adult development as well. Levinson in his study, *The Seasons of a Man's Life* (1978), elaborates a view of adult development in which relationships are portrayed as a means to an end of individual achievement and success. In the crucial relationships of early adulthood, the "Mentor" and the "Special Woman" are defined by the role they play in facilitating the man's realization of his "Dream." Along similar lines Vaillant (1977), in his study of men, considers altruism a defense, characteristic of mature ego functioning and associated with successful "adaptation to life," but conceived as derivative rather than primary in contrast to Chodorow's analysis, in which empathy is considered "built-in" to the woman's primary definition of self.

The discovery now being celebrated by men in mid-life of the importance of intimacy, relationships, and care is something that women have known from the beginning. However, because that knowledge has been considered "intuitive" or "instinctive," a function of anatomy coupled with destiny, psychologists have neglected to describe its development. In my research, I have found that women's moral development centers on the elaboration of that knowledge. Women's moral development thus delineates a critical line of psychological development whose importance for both sexes becomes apparent in the intergenerational framework of a life-cycle perspective. While the subject of moral development provides the final illustration of the reiterative pattern in the observation and assessment of sex differences in the literature on human development, it also indicates more particularly why the nature and significance of women's development has for so long been obscured and considered shrouded in mystery.

The criticism that Freud (1961) makes of women's sense of justice, seeing it as compromised in its refusal of blind impartiality, reappears not only in the work of Piaget (1934) but also in that of Kohlberg (1958). While girls are an aside in Piaget's account of *The Moral Judgment of the Child* (1934), an odd curiosity to whom he devotes four brief entries in an index that omits "boys" altogether because "the child" is assumed to be male, in Kohlberg's research on moral development, females simply do not exist. Kohlberg's six stages that describe the development of moral judgment from childhood to adulthood were derived empirically from a longitudinal study of eighty-four boys from the United States. While Kohlberg (1973) claims universality for his stage sequence and considers his conception of justice as fairness to have been naturalistically derived, those groups not included in his original sample rarely reach his higher stages (Edwards, 1975; Gilligan, 1977). Prominent among those found to be deficient in moral development when measured by Kohlberg's scale are women whose judgments on his scale seemed to exemplify the third stage in his six-stage sequence. At this stage morality is conceived in terms of relationships, and goodness is equated with helping and pleasing others. This concept of goodness was considered by Kohlberg and Kramer (1969) to be functional in the lives of mature women insofar as those lives took place in the home and thus were relationally bound. Only if women were to go out of the house to enter the arena of male activity would they realize the inadequacy of their Stage Three perspective and progress like men toward higher stages where morality is societally or universally defined in accordance with a conception of justice as fairness.

In this version of human development, however, a particular conception of maturity is assumed, based on the study of men's lives and reflecting the importance of individuation in their development. When one begins instead with women and derives developmental constructs from their lives, then a different conception of development emerges, the expansion and elaboration of which can also be traced through stages that comprise a developmental sequence. In Loevinger's (1966) test for measuring ego development that was drawn from studies of females, fifteen of the thirty-six sentence stems to complete begin with the subject of human relationships (for example, "Raising a family. . . ; If my mother. . . ; Being with other people. . . ; When I am with a man. . . ; When a child won't join in group activities. . . .") (Loevinger & Wessler, 1970, p. 141). Thus ego development is described and measured by Loevinger through conception of relationships as well as by the concept of identity that measures the progress of individuation.

Research on moral judgment has shown that when the categories of women's thinking are examined in detail (Gilligan, 1977) the outline of a moral conception different from that described by Freud, Piaget, or Kohlberg begins to emerge and to inform a different description of moral development. In this conception, the moral problem is seen to arise from conflicting responsibilities rather than from competing rights and to require for its resolution a mode of thinking that is contextual and inductive rather than formal and abstract.

This conception of morality as fundamentally concerned with the capacity for understanding and care also develops through a structural progression of increasing differentiation and integration. This progression witnesses the shift from an egocentric through a societal to the universal moral perspective that Kohlberg described in his research on men, but it does so in different terms. The shift in women's judgment from an egocentric to a conventional to a principled ethical understanding is articulated through their use of a distinct moral language, in which the terms "selfishness" and "responsibility" define the moral problem as one of care. Moral development then consists of the progressive reconstruction of this understanding toward a more adequate conception of care.

The concern with caring centers moral development around the progressive differentiation and integration that characterize the evolution of the understanding of relationships just as the conception of fairness delineates the progressive differentiation and balancing of individual rights. Within the responsibility orientation, the infliction of hurt is the center of moral concern and is considered immoral whether or not it can otherwise be construed as fair or unfair. The reiterative use of the language of selfishness and responsibility to define the moral problem as a problem of care sets women apart from the men whom Kohlberg studied and from whose thinking he derived his six stages. This different construction of the moral problem by women may be seen as the critical reason for their failure to develop within the constraints of Kohlberg's system.

Regarding all constructions of responsibility as evidence of a conventional moral understanding, Kohlberg defines the highest stages of moral development as deriving from a reflective understanding of human rights. That the morality of rights differs from the morality of responsibility in its emphasis on separation rather than attachment, in its consideration of the individual rather than the relationship as primary, is illustrated by two quotations that exemplify these different orientations. The first comes from a twenty-five-year-old man who participated in Kohlberg's longitudinal study. The quotation itself is cited by Kohlberg to illustrate the principled conception of morality that he scores as "integrated [Stage] Five judgment, possibly moving to Stage Six."

> [What does the word morality mean to you?] Nobody in the world knows the answer. I think it is recognizing the right of the individual, the rights of other individuals, not interfering with those rights. Act as fairly as you would have them treat you. I think it is basically to preserve the human being's right to existence. I think that is the most important. Secondly, the human being's right to do as he pleases, again without interfering with somebody else's rights.

> [How have your views on morality changed since the last interview?] I think I am more aware of an individual's rights now. I used to be looking at it strictly from my point of view, just for me. Now I think I am more aware of what the individual has a right to. (Note 1, p. 29)

"Clearly," Kohlberg states,

> these responses represent attainment of the third level of moral theory. Moving to a perspective outside of that of his society, he identifies morality with justice (fairness, rights, the Golden Rule), with recognition of the rights of others as these are defined naturally or intrinsically. The human's right to do as he pleases without interfering with somebody else's rights is a formula defining rights prior to social legislation and opinion which defines what society may expect rather than being defined by it. (Note 1, pp. 29–30)

The second quotation comes from my interview with a woman, also twenty-five years old and at the time of the interview a third-year student at Harvard Law School. She described her conception of morality as follows:

> [Is there really some correct solution to moral problems or is everybody's opinion equally right?] No, I don't think everybody's opinion is equally right. I think that in some situations . . . there may be opinions that are equally valid and one could conscientiously adopt one of several courses of action. But there are other situations which I think there are right and wrong answers, that sort

of inhere in the nature of existence, of all individuals here who need to live with each other to live. We need to depend on each other and hopefully it is not only a physical need but a need of fulfillment in ourselves, that a person's life is enriched by cooperating with other people and striving to live in harmony with everybody else, and to that end, there are right and wrong, there are things which promote that end and that move away from it, and in that way, it is possible to choose in certain cases among different courses of action, that obviously promote or harm that goal.

[Is there a time in the past when you would have thought about these things differently?] Oh, yah. I think that I went through a time when I thought that things were pretty relative, that I can't tell you what to do and you can't tell me what to do, because you've got your conscience and I've got mine. . . .

[When was that?] When I was in high school, I guess that it just sort of dawned on me that my own ideas changed and because my own judgment changed, I felt I couldn't judge another person's judgment . . . but now I think even when it is only the person himself who is going to be affected, I say it is wrong to the extent it doesn't cohere with what I know about human nature and what I know about you, and just from what I think is true about the operation of the universe I could say I think you are making a mistake.

[What led you to change, do you think?] Just seeing more of life, just recognizing that there are an awful lot of things that are common among people . . . there are certain things that you come to learn promote a better life and better relationships and more personal fulfillment than other things that in general tend to do the opposite and the things that promote these things, you would call morally right.

These responses also represent a reflective reconstruction of morality following a period of relativistic questioning and doubt, but the reconstruction of moral understanding is based not on the primacy and universality of individual rights, but rather on what she herself describes as a "very strong sense of being responsible to the world." Within this construction, the moral dilemma changes from how to exercise one's rights without interfering with the rights of others to how "to lead a moral life which includes obligations to myself and my family and people in general." The problem then becomes one of limiting responsibilities without abandoning moral concern. When asked to describe herself, this woman says that she values

having other people that I am tied to and also having people that I am responsible to. I have a very strong sense of being responsible to the world, that I can't just live for my enjoyment, but just the fact of being in the world gives me an obligation to do what I can to make the world a better place to live in, no matter how small a scale that may be on.

Thus while Kohlberg's subject worries about people interfering with one another's rights, this woman worries about "the possibility of omission, of your not helping others when you could help them."

The issue this law student raises is addressed by Loevinger's fifth "autonomous" stage of ego development. The terms of its resolution lie in achieving partial autonomy from an excessive sense of responsibility by recognizing that other people have responsibility for their own destiny (Loevinger, 1968). The autonomous stage in Loevinger's account witnesses a relinquishing of moral dichotomies and their replacement with "a feeling for the complexity and multifaceted character of real people and real situations" (1970, p. 6).

Whereas the rights conception of morality that informs Kohlberg's principled level [Stages Five and Six] is geared to arriving at an objectively fair or just resolution to the moral dilemmas to which "all rational men can agree" (Kohlberg, 1976), the responsibility conception focuses instead on the limitations of any particular resolution and describes the conflicts that remain. This limitation of moral judgment and choice is described by a woman in her thirties when she says that her guiding principle in making moral decisions has to do with "responsibility and caring about yourself and others, not just a principle that once you take hold of, you settle [the moral problem]. The principle put into practice is still going to leave you with conflict."

Given the substance and orientation of these women's judgments, it becomes clear why a morality of rights and noninterference may appear to women as frightening in its potential justification of indifference and unconcern. At the same time, however, it also becomes clear why, from a male perspective, women's judgments appear inconclusive and diffuse, given their insistent contextual relativism. Women's moral judgments thus elucidate the pattern that we have observed in the differences between the sexes, but provide an alternative conception of maturity by which these differences can be developmentally considered. The psychology of women that has consistently been described as distinctive in its greater orientation toward relationships of interdependence implies a more contextual mode of judgment and a different moral understanding. Given the differences in women's conceptions of self and morality, it is not surprising that women bring to the life cycle a different point of view and that they order human experience in terms of different priorities.

The myth of Demeter and Persephone, which McClelland cites as exemplifying the feminine attitude toward power, was associated with the Eleusinian Mysteries celebrated in ancient Greece for over two thousand years (1975, p. 96). As told in the Homeric *Hymn to Demeter* (1971), the story of Persephone indicates the strengths of "interdependence, building up resources and giving" (McClelland, 1975, p. 96) that McClelland found in his research on power motivation to characterize the mature feminine style. Although, McClelland says, "it is fashionable to conclude that no one knows what went on in the Mysteries, it is known that they were probably the most important religious ceremonies, even partly on the historical record, which were organized by and for women, especially at the onset before men by means of the cult of Dionysus began to take them over" (1975, p. 96). Thus McClelland regards the myth as "a special presentation of feminine psychology" (1975). It is, as well, a life-cycle story par excellence.

Persephone, the daughter of Demeter, while out playing in the meadows with her girl friends, sees a beautiful narcissus which she runs to pick. As she does so, the earth opens and she is snatched away by Pluto, who takes her to his underworld kingdom. Demeter, goddess of the earth, so mourns the loss of her daughter that she refuses to allow anything to grow. The crops that sustain life on earth shrivel and dry up, killing men and animals alike, until Zeus takes pity on man's suffering and persuades his brother to return Persephone to her mother. But before she leaves, Persephone eats some pomegranate seeds which ensure that she will spend six months of every year in the underworld.

The elusive mystery of women's development lies in its recognition of the continuing importance of attachment in the human life cycle. Woman's place in man's life cycle has been to protect this recognition while the developmental litany intones the celebration of separation, autonomy, individuation, and natural rights. The myth of Persephone speaks directly to the distortion in this view by reminding us that narcissism leads to death, that the fertility of the earth is in some mysterious way tied to the continuation of the mother-daughter relationship, and that the life cycle itself arises from an alternation between the world of women and that of men. My intention in this essay has been to suggest that only when life-cycle theorists equally divide their attention and begin to live with women as they have lived with men will their vision encompass the experience of both sexes and their theories become correspondingly more fertile.

Reference Note

1. Kohlberg, L. *Continuities and discontinuities in childhood and adult moral development revisited.* Unpublished manuscript, Harvard University, 1973.

References

Bettelheim, B. (1976). *The uses of enchantment.* New York: Knopf.

Blos, P. (1967). The second individuation process of adolescence. In A. Freud (Ed.), *The psychoanalytic study of the child* (vol. 22). New York: International Universities Press.

Chekhov, A. (1956). *The cherry orchard.* (S. Young, Trans.). New York: Modern Library. (Original work published 1904)

Chodorow, N. (1974). Family structure and feminine personality. In M. Rosaldo & L. Lamphere (Eds.), *Women, culture and society.* Stanford, CA: Stanford University Press.

Chodorow, N. (1978). *The reproduction of mothering.* Berkeley: University of California Press.

Edwards, C. P. (1975). Societal complexity and moral development: A Kenyan study. *Ethos, 3,* 505–527.

Erikson, E. (1968). *Identity: Youth and crisis.* New York: Norton.

Freud, S. (1961). Female sexuality. In J. Strachey (Ed.), *The standard edition of the complete psychological works of Sigmund Freud* (vol. 21). London: Hogarth Press. (Original work published 1931)

Freud, S. (1961). Some psychical consequences of the anatomical distinction between the sexes. In J. Strachey (Ed.), *The standard edition of the complete psychological works of Sigmund Freud* (vol. 19). London: Hogarth Press. (Original work published 1925)

Freud, S. (1961). Three essays on sexuality. In J. Strachey (Ed.), *The standard edition of the complete psychological works of Sigmund Freud* (vol. 7). London: Hogarth Press. (Original work published 1905.)

Gilligan, C. (1977). In a different voice: Women's conceptions of the self and of morality. *Harvard Educational Review, 47*, 481–517.

The Homeric Hymn. (1971). (C. Boer, Trans.). Chicago: Swallow Press.

Horner, M. (1972). Toward an understanding of achievement-related conflicts in women. *Journal of Social Issues, 28*(2), 157–174.

Inhelder, B., & Piaget, J. (1958). *The growth of logical thinking from childhood to adolescence.* New York: Basic Books.

Kingston, M. H. (1977). *The woman warrior.* New York: Vintage Books.

Kohlberg, L., & Kramer, R. (1969). Continuities and discontinuities in childhood and adult moral development. *Human Development, 12*, 93–120.

Kohlberg, L. (1971). From is to ought: How to commit the naturalistic fallacy and get away with it in the study of moral development. In T. Mischel (Ed.), *Cognitive development and epistemology.* New York: Academic Press.

Lever, J. (1976). Sex differences in the games children play. *Social Problems, 23*, 478–487.

Levinson, D. (1978). *The seasons of a man's life.* New York: Knopf.

Loevinger, J., & Wessler, R. (1970). *The meaning and measurement of ego development.* San Francisco: Jossey-Bass.

McClelland, D. (1961). *The achieving society.* New York: Van Nostrand.

McClelland, D. (1975). *Power: The inner experience.* New York: Irvington.

Mead, G. H. (1934). *Mind, self and society.* Chicago: University of Chicago Press.

Perry, W. (1968). *Forms of intellectual and ethical development in the college years.* New York: Holt, Rinehart & Winston.

Piaget, J. (1965). *The moral judgment of the child.* New York: Free Press. (Original work published 1932)

Riesman, D. (1961). *The lonely crowd.* New Haven: Yale University Press.

Sassen, G. (1980). Success-anxiety in women: A constructivist theory of its sources and it significance. *Harvard Educational Review, 50*, 13–24.

Strunk, W., & White, E. B. (1959). *The elements of style.* New York: Macmillan.

Sullivan, H. S. (1953). *The interpersonal theory of psychiatry.* New York: Norton.

Vaillant, G. (1977). *Adaptation to life.* Boston: Little, Brown.

Woolf, V. (1929). *A room of one's own.* New York: Harcourt, Brace & World.

Excluding Women from the Educational Realm

JANE ROLAND MARTIN

Jane Roland Martin examines the exclusion of women from the philosophy of education, both as writers about education and as objects of educational study and thought. She traces the history of this exclusion from a misunderstanding of the writings of Plato, Rousseau, and Pestalozzi on the education of women, and builds a comprehensive critique of the concepts of education. Martin proposes a possible reconstruction of the field of philosophy of education to include women, and describes the benefits of such a needed undertaking.

In recent years a literature has developed which documents the ways in which intellectual disciplines such as history and psychology, literature and the fine arts, sociology and biology are biased according to sex. The feminist criticism contained in this literature reveals that the disciplines fall short of the ideal of epistemological equality, that is, equality of representation and treatment of women in academic knowledge itself — for example, in scientific theories, historical narratives, and literary interpretations. The disciplines exclude women from their subject matter; they distort the female according to the male image of her; and they deny the feminine by forcing women into a masculine mold. While certain aspects of philosophy have been subjected to feminist scrutiny,[1] the status of women in the subject matter of philosophy of education has not yet been studied. This is unfortunate, for philosophy of education has more than theoretical significance; in dealing with prescriptive questions of education which touch all our lives, it has great practical significance. Furthermore, as a consequence of state teacher certification requirements and the fact that public school teaching is primarily a women's occupation, a large proportion of philosophy of education students are women. It is important to understand, there-

Harvard Educational Review Vol. 52 No. 2 May 1982, 133–148

fore, that, although throughout history women have reared and taught the young and have themselves been educated, they are excluded both as the subjects and objects of educational thought from the standard texts and anthologies: as subjects, their philosophical works on education are ignored; as objects, works by men about their education and also their role as educators of the young are largely neglected. Moreover, the very definition of education and the educational realm adopted implicitly by the standard texts, and made explicit by contemporary analytic philosophers of education, excludes women.

Invisible Women

In an earlier issue of this journal I argued that the common interpretation of Rousseau's educational thought cannot explain what he has to say about the education of Sophie, the prototype of woman.[2] Rather than admit to the inadequacy of the accepted interpretation, the standard texts either ignore Rousseau's account of the education of Sophie or treat it as an aberration in his thought.

Rousseau's account of the education of girls and women is no aberration; on the contrary, it is integral to his philosophy of education. Nor is Plato's account of the education of women in Book V of the *Republic* an aberration; yet a number of the standard texts and anthologies omit all references to Book V. Others neither anthologize nor comment on those sections containing Plato's proposal that both males and females can be rulers of the Just State and that all those who are suited to rule should, regardless of sex, be given the same education.[3] Moreover, the texts which mention Plato's views on the education of women do so in passing or with significant distortion.[4]

A study done by Christine Pierce has shown that translators and commentators have consistently misinterpreted Book V of Plato's *Republic;* they have been unable to comprehend that such a great philosopher sanctioned the equality of the sexes.[5] Few writers of the standard texts in the history of educational philosophy seem able to grasp this either. Other scholars, for example John Dewey and Thomas Henry Huxley, have also treated women's education seriously.[6] Nonetheless, only one standard text lists girls and women in its index.[7] The others do not perceive sex or gender to be an educational category, even though many of the philosophers whose thought constitutes their subject matter did.

The standard texts have also ignored what philosophers of education have said about the educative role of women as mothers. In his classic pedagogical work, *Leonard and Gertrude,* Johann Heinrich Pestalozzi presents Gertrude neither — to use his biographer's words — "as the sweetheart of some man nor, in the first place, as the wife of her husband but as the mother of her child."[8] As such, Pestalozzi presents her as the model of the good educator. When the nobleman Arner and his aide visit Cotton Meyer in Gertrude's village, Meyer describes Gertrude as one who understands how to establish schools which stand in close connection with the life of the home, instead of in contradiction to it.[9] They visit Gertrude and closely observe her teaching methods. Arner's aide is so impressed by Gertrude that he resolves to become the village schoolmaster. When he finally opens a school, it is based on principles of education extracted from Gertrude's practice.

Pestalozzi is not discussed in as many of the standard texts as are Plato and Rousseau. Insofar as the texts do include his thought, however, they scarcely acknowledge that he thinks Gertrude's character and activities "set the example for a new order."[10] Pestalozzi's insight that mothers are educators of their children and that we can learn from their methods has been largely ignored in educational philosophy.

Just as the exclusion of women as objects of educational thought by historians of educational philosophy is easily seen from a glance at the indexes of the standard texts, their exclusion as subjects is evident from a glance at the tables of contents in which the works of women philosophers of education have been overlooked. The one exception is Maria Montessori, whose work is discussed at length by Robert Rusk.[11] However, she is neither mentioned nor anthologized in the other texts I have surveyed, including Robert Ulich's massive anthology, *Three Thousand Years of Educational Wisdom*.

Montessori's claim to inclusion in the standard texts and anthologies is apparent, for her philosophical works on the education of children are widely known. She is not, however, the only woman in history to have developed a systematic theory of education. Many women have been particularly concerned with the education of their own sex. For example, in *A Vindication of the Rights of Woman*, Mary Wollstonecraft challenged Rousseau's theory of the education of girls and developed her own theory.[12] Wollstonecraft, in turn, was influenced by the writings on education and society of Catherine Macaulay, in particular her *Letters on Education*.[13] In numerous books and articles Catharine Beecher set forth a philosophy of education of girls and women which presents interesting contrasts to Wollstonecraft's;[14] and the utopian novel *Herland*, written by Charlotte Perkins Gilman, rests on a well-developed educational philosophy for women.[15]

While Montessori's work was certainly familiar to the authors and editors of the standard texts and anthologies, it is doubtful that Macaulay, Wollstonecraft, Beecher, and Gilman were even known to these men, let alone that they were perceived as educational philosophers. It is possible to cite them here because feminist research in the last decade has uncovered the lives and works of many women who have thought systematically about education. The works of these women must be studied and their significance determined before one can be sure that they should be included in the standard texts and anthologies. This analytic and evaluative endeavor remains to be done.

It should not be supposed, however, that all the men whose educational thought has been preserved for us by the standard texts are of the stature of Plato and Rousseau or that all the works represented in the anthologies are as important as the *Republic* and *Emile*. On the contrary, a reader of these books will find writings of considerable educational significance by otherwise unknown thinkers, and writings of questionable educational value by some of the great figures of Western philosophy. Thus, while criteria do have to be satisfied before Macaulay, Wollstonecraft, Beecher, Gilman, and others are given a place in the history of educational thought, they cannot in fairness be excluded simply for being regarded as less profound thinkers than Plato.

The question remains whether the women cited here can be excluded because their overriding interest is the education of their own sex. In view of the fate of Sophie, Gertrude, and Plato's female guardians as objects of educational thought, one can only assume that, had the works of these women been known to exist, they also would have been ignored by the standard texts and anthologies of the field. From the standpoint of the history of educational thought, women thinkers are in double jeopardy: they are penalized for their interest in the education of their own sex because that topic falls outside the field; and, as the case of Montessori makes clear, those who have written about education in general are penalized simply for being women.

Defining the Educational Realm

Lorenne Clark has shown that, from the standpoint of political theory, women, children, and the family dwell in the "ontological basement," outside and underneath the political structure.[14] This apolitical status is due not to historical accident or necessity but to arbitrary definition. The reproductive processes of society — processes in which Clark includes creation and birth and the rearing of children to "more or less independence" — are by fiat excluded from the political domain, which is defined in relation to the public world of productive processes. Since the subject matter of political theory is politics, and since reproductive processes have been traditionally assigned to women and have taken place within the family, it follows that women and the family are excluded from the very subject matter of the discipline.

The analogy between political theory and educational philosophy is striking. Despite the fact that the reproductive processes of society, broadly understood, are largely devoted to childrearing and include the transmission of skills, beliefs, feelings, emotions, values, and even world views, they are not considered to belong to the educational realm. Thus, education, like politics, is defined in relation to the productive processes of society, and the status of women and the family are "a-educational" as well as apolitical. It is not surprising, then, that Pestalozzi's insight about Gertrude is overlooked by historians of educational philosophy; for in performing her maternal role, Gertrude participates in reproductive processes which are by definition excluded from the educational domain. If Gertrude is outside the educational realm, so is Sophie, for the training Rousseau intends for her aims at fitting her to be a good wife and mother, that is, to carry on the reproductive processes of society.[17] Yet, the exclusion of these processes from education does not in itself entail the exclusion of training *for* them; people could be prepared to carry on reproductive processes through bona fide educational activities even if the processes themselves are outside of education. However, since educational philosophy defines its subject matter only in terms of productive processes, even this preparation is excluded.

We can see the boundaries of the educational realm in the distinction commonly made between liberal and vocational education. Vocational education is clearly intended to prepare people to carry on the productive processes of society.[18] Liberal education, on the other hand, is not seen as preparation for carrying on its reproductive processes. Even though disagreements abound over which intellectual disciplines are proper to liberal education and the way they are to be organized, no one conceives of liberal education as education in childrearing and family life. The distinction between liberal and vocational education corresponds not to a distinction between the two kinds of societal processes but to one between head and hand *within* productive processes. Liberal education is thus preparation for carrying on processes involving the production and consumption of ideas, while vocational education is preparation for processes involving manual labor.

Historians of educational philosophy have no more interest in Sophie than they do in Gertrude, for Rousseau places Sophie in the home and tailors her education to the role he assigns her there. Indeed, educational philosophy has no ready vocabulary to describe the kind of education Rousseau designs for Sophie. It is not a liberal education, for she will learn coquetry and modesty and skill in lacemaking, not science, history, literature, or rational thinking.[19] Like vocational education, her training has narrow and clearly specified ends. Yet vocational education programs prepare their graduates to enter the job market, whereas Sophie's education is designed to keep her out of that arena.[20]

Philosophy of education has no ready classification for the training Rousseau would provide women because it falls outside the educational domain. However, there is a classification for the training Plato would provide the women guardians of his Just State. For Plato, ruling is a matter of knowing the Good, which involves using one's reason to grasp the most abstract, theoretical knowledge possible. Thus, the education he prescribes for the guardian class is a type of liberal education — one which greatly influences educational thought and practice even today. How, then, are we to explain that historians of educational philosophy ignore Plato's theory of the education of women? In a field which excludes the reproductive processes of society from its subject matter and identifies women with these processes, Plato's theory is an anomaly. Plato places women in the public world and prescribes for them an education for the productive processes of society. Although their education falls squarely within the educational realm as defined by the field and can be readily classified, the fact that *women* are to receive this education is lost to view. The position of women in the history of educational philosophy is not an enviable one. Excluded from its subject matter insofar as they are commonly tied by theory to the reproductive processes of society, women are denied recognition even when a particular theory such as Plato's detaches their lives and their education from childrearing and the family.

The Analytic Paradigm: Peters's Concept of Education

Contemporary philosophical analysis has made explicit the boundaries of the educational realm assumed by the standard texts in the history of educational philosophy. In *Ethics and Education*, R. S. Peters writes that education is something "we consciously contrive for ourselves or for others" and that "it implies that something worthwhile is being or has been intentionally transmitted in a morally acceptable manner."[21] Peters distinguishes between two senses of the word "education." As an activity, education must fulfill three conditions — intentionality, voluntariness, and comprehension — for it involves the *intentional* transmission of something worthwhile, an element of *voluntariness* on the part of the learner, and some *comprehension* by the learner both of what is being learned and of the standards the learner is expected to attain.[22] As an achievement, education involves also the acquisition of knowledge, understanding, and cognitive perspectives.[23]

The analytic literature in philosophy of education is filled with discussions of Peters's concept of education, and at various points in his career he has elaborated upon and defended it.[24] Over the years he has come to acknowledge that there are two concepts of education: one encompassing "any process of childrearing, bringing up, instructing, etc.," and the other encompassing only those processes directed toward the development of an educated person.[25] Peters considers only the second, narrower concept to have philosophical significance. He has analyzed this concept in one work after another and has traced its implications in his book, *The Logic of Education*. This narrow concept is the basis not only for his own philosophical investigations of education but also for those of his many collaborators, students, and readers.

Peters is no insignificant figure in the philosophy of education. Indeed, his concept of education, which excludes the reproductive processes of society, defines the domain of the now-dominant school of philosophy of education — analytic philosophy of education.[26] Peters has given analytic philosophy of education a research paradigm which defines the types of problems, approaches, and solutions for the field only in terms of the productive processes of society. Thus from its standpoint, when Gertrude teaches her children, she is frequently not engaged in the activity of education. While a good deal of what she does fulfills Peters's condition of intentionality, and although she always acts in a morally acceptable manner, there are many occasions on which the children fail to meet the condition of voluntariness.

At times, however, the children are voluntary learners, as when the neighbor children implore Gertrude to teach them spinning:

> "Can you spin?" she asked.
>
> "No," they answered.
>
> "Then you must learn, my dears. My children wouldn't sell their knowledge of it at any price, and are happy enough on Saturday, when they each get their few kreutzers. The year is long, my dears, and if we earn something every week, at the end of the year there is a lot of money, without our knowing how we came by it."
>
> "Oh, please teach us!" implored the children, nestling close to the good woman.
>
> "Willingly," Gertrude replied, "come every day if you like, and you will soon learn."[27]

However, with her own children Gertrude constantly instills manners and proper conduct without their permission:

> "What business was it of yours to tell the Bailiff day before yesterday, that you knew Arner would come soon? Suppose your father had not wished him to know that he knew it, and your chattering had brought him into trouble?"
>
> "I should be very sorry, mother. But neither of you said a word about its being a secret."
>
> "Very well, I will tell your father when he comes home, whenever we are talking together, we must take care to add after each sentence: 'Lizzie may tell that to the neighbors, and talk about it at the well; but this she must not mention outside the house.' So then you will know precisely what you may chatter about."
>
> "O mother, forgive me! That was not what I meant."
>
> Gertrude talked similarly with all the other children about their faults, even saying to little Peggy: "You mustn't be so impatient for your soup, or I shall make you wait longer another time, and give it to one of the others."[28]

There are numerous questions about the transmission of values by the family which philosophy of education could answer: What does "transmit" mean in this context? Which values ought to be transmitted by the family? Should the values transmitted by the family be reinforced by schools or should they be challenged? Do schools have the right to challenge them? Yet as its subject matter is presently defined, philosophy of education cannot ask them, for they are questions about the reproductive processes of society which are inappropriate to raise, let alone to answer.

From the standpoint of contemporary analytic philosophy of education. Gertrude's educational activities and those of mothers in general are irrelevant. Indeed, any account of mothering is considered outside the field. For example, Sara Ruddick's recent innovative account of maternal thought, which gives insights into a kind of thinking associated with the reproductive processes of society, has no more place in the field than Pestalozzi's insights about Gertrude in her capacity as mother.[29]

The kind of maternal thought Ruddick describes and Gertrude embodies is the kind Sophie must exhibit if she is to perform well the traditional female role Rousseau assigned her. As Ruddick makes clear, however, "maternal" is a social, not a biological category: although maternal thought arises out of childrearing practices, men as well as women express it in various ways of working and caring for others.[30] Thus it is something Sophie must learn, not something she is born with. Notice, however, when Sophie learns maternal skills from her mother and in raising her own children, this learning will also fall outside the educational realm. It will lack Peters's voluntariness and intentionality and will be part of the childrearing processes he would have philosophers of education ignore. In sum, the definition of education used by analytic philosophers today excludes the teaching, the training, and the socialization of children for which women throughout history have had prime responsibility.[31]

The Analytic Paradigm:
Hirst's Concept of Liberal Education

Yet Sophie's learning would not be admitted to the educational realm even if it were designed in such a way that it met Peters's criteria of an educational process. It would still include unacceptable goals and content. According to Peters, the goal of education is the development of the educated person, who does not simply possess knowledge, but has some understanding of principles for organizing facts and of the "reason why" of things. The educated person's knowledge is not inert, but characterizes the person's way of looking at things and involves "the kind of commitment that comes from getting on the inside of a form of thought and awareness." This involves caring about the standards of evidence implicit in science or the canons of proof inherent in mathematics and possessing cognitive perspective.[32] At the center of Peters's account of education and the educated person is the notion of initiation into worthwhile activities, the impersonal cognitive content and procedures of which are "enshrined in *public traditions*."[33] Mathematics, science, history, literature, philosophy: these are the activities into which Peters's educated person is initiated. That person is one who has had, and has profited from, a liberal education of the sort outlined by Peters's colleague Paul Hirst in his essay, "Liberal Education and the Nature of Knowledge":

> First, sufficient immersion in the concepts, logic and criteria of the discipline for a person to come to know the distinctive way in which it "works" by pursuing these in particular cases; and then sufficient generalization of these over the whole range of the discipline so that his experience begins to be widely structured in this distinctive manner. It is this coming to look at things in a certain way that is being aimed at, not the ability to work out in minute particulars all the details that can be in fact discerned. It is the ability to recognise empirical assertions or aesthetic judgments for what they are, and to know the kind of considerations on which their validity will depend, that matters.[34]

If Peters's educated person is not in fact Hirst's liberally educated person, he or she is certainly the identical twin.

Hirst's analysis of liberal education has for some time been the accepted one in the field of philosophy of education.[35] In his view, liberal education consists of an initiation into what he takes to be the seven forms of knowledge.[36] Although in his later writings he carefully denies that these forms are themselves intellectual disciplines, it is safe to conclude that his liberally educated people will acquire the conceptual schemes and cognitive perspectives they are supposed to have through a study of mathematics, physical sciences, history, the human sciences, religion, literature and fine arts, and philosophy. These disciplines will not necessarily be studied separately; an interdisciplinary curriculum is compatible with Hirst's analysis. But it is nonetheless their subject matter, their conceptual apparatus, their standards of proof and adequate evidence that must be acquired if the ideal liberal education is to be realized.

In one way or another, then, the intellectual disciplines constitute the content of Peters's curriculum for the educated person. Since the things Rousseau would have Sophie learn — modesty, attentiveness, reserve, sewing, embroidery, lacemaking, keeping house, serving as hostess, bringing up children — are not part of these disciplines and are not enshrined in public traditions, they fall outside the curriculum of the educated person. But this is to say that they fall outside of education itself for, as we have seen, education, in Peters's analysis, is necessarily directed to the development of the educated person. Just as Rousseau's curriculum for Sophie is excluded from the educational realm, curricula in Beecher's domestic economy, Ruddick's maternal thinking, and Nancy Chodorow's mothering capacities would also be excluded.[37] Given the analyses of the concepts of education, the educated person, and liberal education which are accepted in general outline by the field of philosophy of education, no curriculum preparing people for the reproductive processes can belong to a realm which is reserved for the ways of thinking, acting, and feeling involved in *public* traditions. Since girls and women are the ones who traditionally have carried on the reproductive processes of society, it is *their* activities of teaching and learning and *their* curriculum which are excluded from the educational realm. Sophie and Gertrude are as irrelevant to analytic philosophers of education as they are to the writers of texts in the history of educational philosophy.

The Analytic Paradigm:
The Rationality Theory of Teaching

I have said that Gertrude teaches her children even though analytic philosophers of education would say she is not educating them. Yet according to Peters, only a fraction of what Gertrude does could be called "teaching." This is because the concept of teaching is so closely linked to the concept of education that, in ruling out so many of Gertrude's activities as instances of education, Peters's analysis also rules them out as instances of teaching.

But quite apart from Peters's criteria, Gertrude fails to qualify as a teacher according to the accepted analysis of the concept of teaching. Perhaps the best brief statement of this analysis — what I have elsewhere called the rationality theory of teaching[38] — is found in a little known essay by Israel Scheffler. Beliefs, Scheffler says,

> can be acquired through mere unthinking contact, propaganda, indoctrination, or brainwashing. Teaching, by contrast, engages the mind, no matter what the subject matter. The teacher is prepared to *explain,* that is, to acknowledge the student's right to ask for reasons and his concomitant right to exercise his judgment on the merits of the case. Teaching is, in this standard sense, an initiation into open rational discussion.[39]

In this passage Scheffler harks back to the original account of teaching he gave in his earlier book *The Language of Education* where he states that to teach "is at some points at least to submit oneself to the understanding and independent judgment of the pupil, to his demand for reasons, to his sense of what constitutes an adequate explanation." And he adds:

> Teaching involves further that, if we try to get the students to believe that such and such is the case, we try also to get him to believe it for reasons that, within the limits of his capacity to grasp, are *our* reasons. Teaching, in this way, requires us to reveal our reasons to the student and, by so doing, to submit them to his evaluation and criticism.[40]

Scheffler is not the only contemporary philosopher of education who has emphasized connections between teaching and rationality. Numerous colleagues and critics in the field have elaborated upon and modified his analysis of teaching, and others have arrived independently at conclusions similar to his.[41] The relevant point for the present inquiry is that, according to this analysis of the concept of teaching, the learner's rationality must be acknowledged in two ways: the manner in which the teacher proceeds and the type of learning to be achieved. Thus, the rationality theory holds that to be teaching one must expose one's reasons to the learner so that the learner can evaluate them, and also that one's aim must be that the learner also have reasons, and attain a level of learning involving understanding.

On some occasions Gertrude does approximate the conception of teaching which the rationality theory embodies. When she tries to get her children to learn that virtue must be its own reward, she cautions them to give away their bread quietly so that no one may see them and reveals to them her reason that "people needn't think you want to show off your generosity."[42] When one son asks her to give him a mouthful of bread for himself since he is giving his portion away, she refuses to do so. He asks for her reason and receives the reply: "So that you needn't imagine we are only to think of the poor after our own hunger is satisfied."[43] Yet one is left wondering what Gertrude would say and do if her children ever questioned the values she instills in them. One suspects that she would quickly resort to appeals to authority, a move of which the rationality theory would not approve.

Consider now the occasion on which Gertrude attempts to transmit her values to some neglected children by washing them, combing their hair, dressing them with care, and scrubbing their house. She neither gives reasons for the values of cleanliness and order in which she so firmly believes nor tries to *acknowledge the rationality* of the children in other ways.[44] And on another occasion when Gertrude invites these children to pray with her own children, and then accompanies them to their house with a "cheery parting, bidding them to come again soon,"[45] the intention is that they acquire good habits, but the mode of acquisition is quite divorced from the giving of explanations and the evaluation of reasons. Gertrude expected that through her kindness, good example, and the efficacy of unconscious imitation, these derelict children will adopt her values. She does not seem to care whether they understand the habits and values they are adopting or have proper backing for the associated beliefs they are acquiring.

It must be made clear, however, that the rationality theory does not function as an account of *good* teaching. It is not meant to be prescriptive; rather its function is to tell us what *constitutes* or *counts as* teaching. If Gertrude's actions do not meet its twofold requirement of rationality in the manner in which the teacher proceeds and in the type of learning to be achieved, adherents of the theory will not judge her teaching to be deficient; they will judge her not to be teaching at all. They will do so, moreover, no matter how reasonable or appropriate her actions may be. That Gertrude's actions are appropriate, given the value she places on cleanliness and godliness, the age of the neighbor children, and their condition, will be evident to readers who know young children. However, the rationality theory is not concerned that teaching be a rational activity in the ordinary sense that the actions constituting it be suited to the ends envisioned. Its sole concern is that the learner's reason be taken into account. Thus there are many contexts in which an activity meeting the requirements of the rationality theory of teaching will not be rational from the standpoint of the demands of the particular context.

In the process of bringing new infants to the point of independence, parents often do things which fit the rationality theory's criteria of teaching. Yet most of the teaching and learning which takes place in relation to the reproductive processes of society do not fit these criteria.[46] Values are transmitted, sex roles are internalized, character traits are developed, skills are acquired, and moral schemes and world views are set in place. Yet, if the teacher's reasons are not revealed or the learner's rationality is not acknowledged, the rationality theory denies the labels of "teacher" and "learner" to the parties involved.

The analysis of teaching which occupies a central position in philosophy of education today embodies a Socratic conception of both teaching and learning. The give and take of Socrates and his friends philosophizing in the marketplace, the Oxford tutor and his tutee, the graduate seminar: these are the intuitively clear cases of teaching and learning on which the analytic paradigm is based. Gertrude teaching her children a song to sing to their father when he returns home or the neighbors to count as they are spinning and sewing, Marmee helping Jo to curb her temper, Mrs. Garth making little Lotty learn her place — the activities and processes of childrearing which have traditionally belonged to women as mothers are at best considered to be peripheral cases of teaching and learning and are more likely not to qualify under these headings at all.[47]

A Servant of Patriarchal Policy

In defining education and the questions that can be asked about it, the analyses of contemporary philosophy of education make women and their activities and experiences invisible. The question naturally arises whether this matters. As long as women can enter the educational realm in practice — as they can and do today — what difference does it make that educational philosophy does not acknowledge gender as a bona fide educational category? As long as Plato and Rousseau discussed the education of girls and women in major works and Pestalozzi recognized the ability of mothers to teach, what difference does it make that the texts in the history of educational philosophy ignore their accounts and that the paradigms of analytic philosophy of education do not apply to Sophie, Gertrude, or women in general?

It matters for many reasons. When the experience of women is neither reflected nor interpreted in the texts and anthologies of the history of educational philosophy, women are given no opportunity to understand and evaluate the range of ideals — from Plato's guardians to Sophie and Gertrude — which the great thinkers of the past have held for them. When Wollstonecraft and Montessori are ignored in these texts, students of both sexes are denied contact with the great female minds of the past; indeed, they are denied the knowledge that women have ever thought seriously and systematically about education. What is more important is that, when the works of women are excluded from texts and anthologies, the message that women are not capable of significant philosophical reflection is transmitted.

By placing women outside the educational realm or else making them invisible within it, the contemporary paradigms of philosophy of education also contribute to the devaluation of women. Peters's conviction that only the narrow sense of education is worthy of philosophical inquiry keeps us from perceiving the teaching which takes place in child-rearing as a serious, significant undertaking; it makes women's traditional activities appear trivial and banal. Similarly, in defining teaching in terms of a very narrow conception of rationality — the giving and understanding of reasons — the rationality theory of teaching makes the educational activities of mothers, and by implication mothers themselves, appear nonrational, if not downright irrational.

In a report on recent contributions to philosophy of education, Scheffler protested that philosophy is not a handmaiden of policy. "Its function is not to facilitate policy," he said, "but rather to enlighten it by pressing its traditional questions of value, virtue, veracity, and validity."[48] Yet by its very definition of its subject matter, philosophy of education facilitates patriarchal policy; for in making females invisible, philosophy of education helps maintain the inequality of the sexes. It reinforces the impression that girls and women are not important human beings and that the activities they have traditionally performed in carrying on the reproductive processes of society are not worthwhile. Furthermore, philosophy's traditional questions of value, virtue, veracity, and validity cannot be asked about the education of females because females are unseen in the educational realm. Thus the enlightenment that philosophy is capable of giving is denied to policies which directly affect girls and women.

I do not know if philosophy can ever be as divorced from policy as Scheffler would have it. But as long as there is no epistemological equality for women in philosophy of education, that discipline will serve patriarchal policy, albeit unintentionally. For when the activities and experiences of females are excluded from the educational realm, those of males provide our norms. Thus, the qualities Socrates displays in his philosophical conversations with his male companions in the marketplace are built into our very definition of teaching even as the ones Gertrude displays in her interactions with her children are overlooked. Similarly, the traditional male activities of science and mathematics, history and philosophy are built into the curriculum of the educated person even as activities traditionally assigned to females are ignored.

Do not misunderstand: I am not suggesting that the curriculum Rousseau prescribed for Sophie should become the norm or that cooking and sewing should be placed on a par with science and history. An education for coquetry and guile is not good for either sex; and, while there is nothing wrong with both sexes learning how to cook and sew, I am not advocating that these skills be incorporated into the liberal curriculum. Nor am I endorsing Pestalozzi's claim that Gertrude's particular mode of teaching should be a model for all to emulate. My point is, rather, that when the activities and experiences traditionally associated with women are excluded from the educational realm and when that realm is defined in terms of male activities and experiences, then these become the educational norms for all human beings.

It has been shown that psychological theories of development have difficulty incorporating findings about females because they are derived from male data.[49] It should now be clear that the paradigms of analytic philosophy of education are also based on male data. The examples which generate the rationality theory of teaching, Peters's concept of education and the educated person, and Hirst's theory of liberal education all derive from male experience. The response of the psychologists to the difficulty presented them by female data is to impose on their female subjects a masculine mold. The response of philosophers of education to female data is similar: Gertrude's teaching is at best defective; education for carrying on the reproductive processes of society is at best illiberal. Thus, the male norms which are implicit in the concepts and theories of philosophy of education today devalue women, and thereby serve patriarchal policy. But this is only part of the story. A corollary of this devaluation of women is that men are denied an education for carrying out the reproductive processes of society. In this way, the traditional sexual division of labor is supported.

Reconstituting the Educational Realm

The exclusion of women from the educational realm harms not only women; the field of philosophy of education itself is adversely affected. As the example of Rousseau's *Emile* illustrates, interpretations of works by major educational thinkers in which the education of both males and females is discussed will be deficient when they are based solely on material concerned with males. My discussion of the rationality theory of teaching — a theory which is quite implausible as an account of the teaching of young children — makes clear that analyses of concepts are likely to be inadequate when the cases which inform them and against which they are tested are derived solely from male experience. Furthermore, when gender is not seen to be a relevant educational category, important questions are begged.

When the educational realm embodies only male norms, it is inevitable that any women participating in it will be forced into a masculine mold. The question of whether such a mold is desirable for females needs to be asked, but it cannot be asked so long as philosophers of education assume that gender is a difference which makes no difference.[50] The question of whether the mold is desirable for males also needs to be asked; yet when our educational concepts and ideals are defined in male terms, we do not think to inquire into their validity for males themselves.

Perhaps the most important concern is that, when the educational realm makes women invisible, philosophy of education cannot provide an adequate answer to the question of what constitutes an educated person. Elsewhere I have argued at some length that Hirst's account of liberal education is seriously deficient — it presupposes a divorce of mind from body, thought from action, and reason from feeling and emotion — and that, since Peters's educated person is for all intents and purposes Hirst's liberally educated person, Peters's conception should be rejected.[51] Simply put, it is far too narrow to serve as an ideal which guides the educational enterprise and to which value is attached: it provides at best an ideal of an educated *mind,* not of an educated *person,* although, to the extent that its concerns are strictly cognitive, even in this sense it leaves much to be desired.

An adequate ideal of the educated person must join thought to action, and reason to feeling and emotion. As I pointed out in an earlier section, however, liberal education is designed to prepare people to carry on the productive processes of society, in particular those involving the production and consumption of ideas. Thus Peters's educated person is intended to inhabit a world in which feelings and emotions such as caring, compassion, empathy, and nurturance have no legitimate role to play. To incorporate these into a conception of the educated person would be to introduce traits which were not merely irrelevant to the desired end, but very likely incompatible with it.

Peters's conception of the educated person is untenable, yet the remedy for its narrow intellectualism is unavailable to philosophers of education as long as the criteria for what falls within the educational realm mirrors the distinction between the productive and the reproductive processes of society. An adequate conception of the educated person must join together what Peters and Hirst have torn asunder: mind and body; thought and action; and reason, feeling, and emotion. To do this the educational realm must be reconstituted to include the reproductive processes of society.

It is important to understand that the exclusion of both women and the reproductive processes of society from the educational realm by philosophy of education is a consequence of the structure of the discipline and not simply due to an oversight which is easily corrected. Thus, philosophical inquiry into the nature of those processes or into the education of women cannot simply be grafted onto philosophy of education as presently constituted. On the contrary, the very subject matter of the field must be redefined.

Such a redefinition ought to be welcomed by practitioners in the field, for there is every reason to believe that it will ultimately enrich the discipline. As the experiences and activities which have traditionally belonged to women come to be included in the educational realm, a host of challenging and important issues and problems will arise. When philosophy of education investigates questions about childrearing and the transmission of values, when it develops accounts of gender education to inform its theories of liberal education, when it explores the forms of thinking, feeling, and acting associated with childrearing, marriage, and the family, when the concept of coeducation and concepts such as mothering and nurturance become subjects for philosophical analysis, philosophy of education will be invigorated.

New questions can be asked when the educational realm is reconstituted, and old questions can be given more adequate answers. When Gertrude, Sophie, and Plato's female guardians are taken seriously by historians of educational thought and when Rousseau's philosophy of education is counterbalanced by those of Wollstonecraft, Beecher, and Gilman, the theories of the great historical figures will be better understood. When analyses of the concept of teaching take childrearing activities to be central, insight into that prime educational process will be increased. When the activities of family living and childrearing fall within the range of worthwhile activities, theories of curriculum will be more complete.

It is of course impossible to know now the precise contours of a reconstituted educational realm, let alone to foresee the exact ways in which the inclusion of women and the reproductive processes of society will enrich the discipline of philosophy of education. Yet the need for a redefinition of its subject matter is imperative if philosophy of education is to cease serving patriarchal policy. The promise of enrichment is real.

Notes

1. See Kathryn Pyne Parsons, "Moral Revolution," in *The Prism of Sex*, ed. Julia A. Sherman and Evelyn Torton Beck (Madison: University of Wisconsin Press, 1979), pp. 189–227; and Lawrence Blum, "Kant's and Hegel's Moral Rationalism: A Feminist Perspective," *Canadian Journal of Philosophy*, forthcoming.

2. Jane Roland Martin, "Sophie and Emile: A Case Study of Sex Bias in the History of Educational Thought," *Harvard Educational Review*, 51 (1981), 357–372.

3. See Robert Ulich, ed., *Three Thousand Years of Educational Wisdom* (Cambridge, MA: Harvard Univ. Press, 1948) and his *History of Educational Thought* (New York: American Book, 1945); Robert S. Brumbaugh and Nathaniel M. Lawrence, *Philosophers on Education: Six Essays on the Foundations of Western Thought* (Boston: Houghton Mifflin, 1963): Paul Nash, Andreas M. Kazemias, and Henry J. Perkinson, eds., *The Educated Man: Studies in the History of Educational Thought* (New York: Wiley, 1965); Kingsley Price, *Education and Philosophical Thought*, 2nd ed. (Boston: Allyn & Bacon, 1967); Paul Nash, comp., *Models of Man: Explorations in the Western Educational Tradition* (New York: Wiley, 1968); and Steven M. Cahn, comp., *The Philosophical Foundations of Education* (New York: Harper & Row, 1970).

4. For example, although Brumbaugh and Lawrence call Plato "the great educational revolutionist of his time" in part because of his "insistence on the equality of women" (*Philosophers on Education*, p. 38), they say not another word about that insistence. Robert S. Rusk, who presents Plato's position on the education of women in some detail in his anthology, is apparently so distressed by it that he says what any reader of the *Republic* knows to be false, namely, "Plato can only secure the unity of the state *at the cost of sacrificing all differences*" (*The Doctrines of the Great Educators*, rev. 3rd ed. [New York: St. Martin's, 1965], pp. 28–29, emphasis added). Nash comments that Plato's model of the educated person applies "only to those rare men *and rarer women* who are capable of understanding the underlying harmony of the universe," (*Models of Man*, p. 9 emphasis added) without acknowledging that Plato himself never makes a comparative judgment of the ability of males and females in his Just State to grasp The Good.

5. Christine Pierce, "Equality: *Republic* V," *The Monist*, 57 (1973), 1–11.

6. See, for example, John Dewey, "Is Coeducation Injurious to Girls?," *Ladies' Home Journal*, 28 (1911), pp. 60–61: Thomas Henry Huxley, "Emancipation — Black and White," *Lay Sermons, Addresses, and Reviews* (New York: Appleton, 1870: rpt. in Nash, *Models of Man*, pp. 285–288).

7. Nash, *Models of Man*.

8. Kate Silber, *Pestalozzi* (New York: Schocken Books, 1965), p. 42.

9. John Heinrich Pestalozzi, *Leonard and Gertrude*, trans. Eva Channing (Boston: Heath, 1885), ch. 22.

10. Silber, *Pestalozzi*, p. 42.

11. Rusk, *The Doctrines*, ch. 12.

12. Mary Wollstonecraft, *A Vindication of the Rights of Woman* (New York: Norton, 1967); see also Mary Wollstonecraft Godwin, *Thoughts on the Education of Daughters* (Clifton, NJ: Kelley, 1972).

13. *Letters on Education*, ed. Gina Luria (New York: Garland, 1974). For discussion of Macaulay's life and works, see Florence S. Boos, "Catherine Macaulay's *Letters on Education* (1790): An

Early Feminist Polemic," *University of Michigan Papers in Women's Studies*, 2 (1976), 64–78; Florence Boos and William Boos, "Catherine Macaulay: Historian and Political Reformer," *International Journal of Women's Studies*, 3 (1980), 49–65.

14. For a list of Beecher's published works, see Kathryn Kish Sklar, *Catharine Beecher: A Study in American Domesticity* (New York: Norton, 1973).

15. Charlotte Perkins Gilman, *Herland* (New York: Pantheon Books, 1979).

16. "The Rights of Women: The Theory and Practice of the Ideology of Male Supremacy," in *Contemporary Issues in Political Philosophy*, ed. William R. Shea and John King-Farlow (New York: Science History Publications, 1976), pp. 49–65.

17. See Susan Moller Okin, *Women in Western Political Thought* (Princeton: Princeton University Press, 1979), ch. 6; Lynda Lange, "Rousseau: Women and the General Will," in *The Sexism of Social and Political Theory*, ed. Lorenne M. G. Clark and Lynda Lange (Toronto: University of Toronto Press, 1979), pp. 41–52; and Martin, "Sophie and Emile."

18. See Marvin Lazerson and W. Norton Grubb, eds., *American Education and Vocationalism* (New York: Teachers College Press, 1974).

19. Rousseau, ch. 5. For the account of liberal education which dominates the thinking of philosophers of education today see Paul H. Hirst, "Liberal Education and the Nature of Knowledge," in *Philosophical Analysis and Education*, ed. Reginald D. Archambault (London: Routledge & Kegan Paul, 1965), pp. 113–138; rpt. in Paul H. Hirst, *Knowledge and the Curriculum* (London: Routledge & Kegan Paul, 1974). Page references will be to this volume.

20. I recognize that I have omitted from this discussion all reference to home economics education. Briefly, home economics education has historically been classified as vocational education (see Lazerson and Grubb). However, in the form which is relevant to the present discussion, namely, the preparation of women for their place in the home, it lacks the distinguishing mark of other vocational studies in that it is not intended as training for jobs in the marketplace. Furthermore, contemporary philosophy of education has seldom, if ever, recognized its existence.

21. R. S. Peters, *Ethics and Education* (Glenview, IL: Scott, Foresman, 1967), pp. 2, 3.

22. Peters, *Ethics and Education*, p. 17.

23. Peters, *Ethics and Education*, p. 27.

24. See R. S. Peters, "What is an Educational Process?," in *The Concept of Education*, ed. R. S. Peters (London: Routledge & Kegan Paul, 1967); Paul H. Hirst and R. S. Peters, *The Logic of Education* (London: Routledge & Kegan Paul, 1970); R. S. Peters, "Education and the Educated Man," in *A Critique of Current Educational Aims*, ed. R. F. Dearden, Paul H. Hirst, and R. S. Peters (London: Routledge & Kegan Paul, 1972); R. S. Peters, J. Woods, and W. H. Dray, "Aims of Education — A Conceptual Inquiry," in *The Philosophy of Education*, ed. R. S. Peters (London: Oxford Univ. Press, 1973).

25. See, for example, Peters, "Education and the Educated Man," p. 8.

26. In this section and the ones to follow I will only be discussing paradigms of analytic philosophy of education. There are other schools within philosophy of education, but this one dominates the field today as the recent N.S.S.E. Yearbook, *Philosophy and Education*, testifies (ed. Jonas Soltis [Chicago: The National Society for the Study of Education, 1981]).

27. Pestalozzi, *Leonard and Gertrude*, pp. 87–88.

28. Pestalozzi, *Leonard and Gertrude*, p. 44.

29. Sara Ruddick, "Maternal Thinking," *Feminist Studies*, 6 (1980), 342–367.

30. Ruddick, "Maternal Thinking," p. 346.

31. I do not mean to suggest that these activities have been in the past or are now carried on exclusively by women. On the contrary, both men and women have engaged in them and do now. Our culture assigns women responsibility for them, however.

32. Peters, *Ethics and Education*, p. 8ff.

33. R. S. Peters, *Education as Initiation* (London: Evans Brothers, 1964), p. 35, emphasis added.

34. Hirst, "Liberal Education," p. 47.

35. For an extended critique of Hirst's analysis in this respect, see Jane Roland Martin, "Needed: A New Paradigm for Liberal Education," in *Philosophy and Education* pp. 37–59.

36. In Hirst, "Liberal Education," p. 46. Hirst listed the seven as: mathematics, physical sciences, human sciences, history, religion, literature and fine arts, and philosophy.

37. See Ruddick, "Maternal Thinking"; Nancy Chodorow, *The Reproduction of Mothering* (Berkeley: University of California Press, 1978); and Catharine M. Beecher, *Suggestions Respecting Improvements in Education* (Hartford, CT: Packard & Butler, 1829).

38. Jane Roland Martin, *Explaining, Understanding, and Teaching* (New York: McGraw-Hill, 1970), ch. 5.

39. "Concepts of Education: Reflections on the Current Scene," in Israel Scheffler, *Reason and Teaching* (Indianapolis: Bobbs-Merrill, 1973), p. 62.

40. Israel Scheffler, *The Language of Education* (Springfield, IL: Thomas, 1960), p. 57.

41. See, for example, Thomas F. Green, "A Topology of the Teaching Concept," *Studies in Philosophy and Education, 3* (1964–65), 284–319; and his "Teaching, Acting, and Behaving," *Harvard Educational Review, 34* (1964), 507–524.

42. Pestalozzi, *Leonard and Gertrude,* p. 55.

43. Pestalozzi, *Leonard and Gertrude,* p. 54.

44. Pestalozzi, *Leonard and Gertrude,* p. 87.

45. Pestalozzi, *Leonard and Gertrude,* pp. 88–89.

46. Philosophy of education is not alone in placing Gertrude and the mothers she represents in the "ontological basement." In ch. 2 of *Worlds Apart* (New York: Basic Books, 1978), Sara Lawrence Lightfoot discusses mothers and teachers but never acknowledges that mothers *qua* mothers teach.

47. These examples of mother-teachers are taken from Louisa May Alcott, *Little Women* (Boston: Little, Brown, 1936); and George Eliot, *Middlemarch* (Boston: Houghton Mifflin, 1956).

48. "Philosophy of Education: Some Recent Contributions," *Harvard Educational Review, 50* (1980), 402–406.

49. See Carol Gilligan, "In a Different Voice: Women's Conceptions of Self and Morality," *Harvard Educational Review, 47* (1977), 481–517; Carol Gilligan, "Woman's Place in Man's Life Cycle," *Harvard Educational Review, 49* (1979), 431–446.

50. Jane Roland Martin, "Sex Equality and Education," in *"Femininity," "Masculinity," and "Androgyny": A Modern Philosophical Discussion,* ed. Mary Vetterling-Braggin (Totowa, NJ: Littlefield, Adams, 1982).

51. Jane Roland Martin, "Needed: A Paradigm for Liberal Education"; "The Ideal of the Educated Person," *Educational Theory, 31* (1981), 97–110.

This essay was written while I was a fellow at the Mary Ingraham Bunting Institute, Radcliffe College. I wish to thank Naomi Chazan, Anne Costain, Ann Diller, Carol Gilligan, Diane Margolis, Michael Martin, Beatrice Nelson, and Janet Farrell Smith for helpful comments on the original draft.

PART TWO

Feminist Pedagogy

Placing Women
in the Liberal Arts:
Stages of Curriculum Transformation

MARILYN R. SCHUSTER
SUSAN VAN DYNE

Research on women has created a new body of knowledge that is reshaping our understanding of the traditional curriculum. The scholarship about women's experience produced in the last three decades has entered the curriculum primarily through women's studies courses. But what happens next? Over the past two decades, informed administrators and women's studies teachers have attempted to transform traditional courses throughout the curriculum. In this chapter, Marilyn Schuster and Susan Van Dyne present a paradigm of how teachers and students experience the process of curricular change. Their analysis suggests that teachers may move through a sequence of stages and try a variety of strategies in order to represent women and minorities, and thus a fuller range of human experience, in their courses.

Curricular Change in the Twenty-First Century:
Why Women?

For the first time in history, women represent the majority of the college population. Moreover, a growing percentage of women undergraduates — nearly 20 percent in some institutions — are older returning students. The women we educate will organize their adult lives in substantially different patterns than in the past. Census statistics have already recorded the demise of the traditional nuclear family: fewer than 20 percent of the U.S. population are in households in which both parents and two or more children are living together; only 7 percent live in families in which the wife or mother does not work outside the home. In 1980, over 50 percent of mothers with

Harvard Educational Review Vol. 54 No. 4 November 1984, 413–428

preschool children had full- or part-time employment. With the life expectancy for American women now over seventy, most women can anticipate forty years of work in their adult years, even if they spend ten years exclusively in childrearing.

At the same time that postgraduate expectations of women are shifting, the ethnic characteristics of the youth cohort, or the pool of potential college applicants among traditional-age students, are changing dramatically. By 1990, groups currently designated as minorities in the educational system will represent 30 percent of the youth cohort nationwide. In Texas and California, 45 percent of the public high school graduates will be members of minority groups in 1990; in New York, the estimate is 32 percent, in New Jersey, 28 percent.[1] These statistics demand that we do more to prepare our women and men students for adult lives in a multicultural world in which work will not be a choice but an economic necessity.

Administrators are more likely than most faculties to acknowledge that maintaining or returning to the core curricula and distribution requirements of the past will no longer adequately serve the student population we must educate for the twenty-first century.[2] Nonetheless, transforming institutional structures in order to incorporate scholarship on women and non-white cultural groups effectively is a particularly difficult task at this historical moment. External and internal forces have created a context of crisis in American higher education that imperils progressive change. Budget cuts, retrenchment, a steady-state faculty, a shrinking pool of applicants, the vocationalism of women and men students — narrowing opportunities in the 1980s have put many faculty members on the defensive, making them more protective of their own special interests at the very moment that interdepartmental cooperation and a broader, institutional vision are called for.[3]

Scholarship on Women: Redefining the Core Curriculum

The scholarship about women's experience produced in the last two decades has entered the curriculum primarily through women's studies courses. More recently the intellectual implications of this substantial body of research have led informed administrators and experienced women's studies teachers to undertake a transformation of courses throughout the curriculum. The multicultural, interdisciplinary perspective that feminist scholarship has produced in concert with black studies reveals that the gaps and distortions in a curriculum that is predominantly white, male, Western, and heterosexist in its assumptions are large-scale and pervasive. Informed by work in black and ethnic studies, the study of women, in the words of Peggy McIntosh of the Wellesley Center for Research on Women, "makes visible many men who were not previously featured in the curriculum. In fact, about nine-tenths of the world's population suddenly become visible when one takes the emphasis off the public lives of white Western men . . . and includes those who, for reasons of sex, race, class, or national or religious background, were defined as lower-caste."[4] Since the late 1970s, over fifty programs nationwide at a variety of institutions have begun to develop strategies to reeducate established teachers, to incorporate material on women and minority groups into traditional courses, and, in doing so, to restore quality and responsibility at the core of the liberal arts.[5]

We propose here a description of the curriculum change process engendered by these recognitions. Our observations grow out of our experience as codirectors of the Smith College curriculum transformation project, now in its fourth year of implementation, and our participation in the National Consulting Program of the Wellesley College Center for Research on Women. Designing, leading, and evaluating faculty seminars is central to our work on our campus and in our consulting at other institutions. Comparing the outcomes of projects developed in institutions with marked differences in size, student populations, human and budgetary resources, and political climates has enabled us to identify important commonalities. Our observations are corroborated by other feminist teachers, researchers, and administrators around the country.[6]

What is surprising, given the depth and extent of the scholarship and the commitment of women's studies teachers to share their findings with colleagues, is the relative reluctance of many faculty members to learn about the study of women. In the last twenty years, more information has been gathered about women's experience than has ever been available before. Like the growth of computer science, the explosion of research on women's experience is a key factor reshaping American education in the final two decades of the twentieth century. The adaptability of the computer to all areas of the curriculum and its transforming effect on what and how we learn is widely recognized by administrators. The need for computer literacy has already spurred faculty retraining programs on nearly every campus and has been identified in many institutions' core education requirements. The impact of scholarship about women throughout all academic disciplines, and on our pedagogy has been steadily growing and may have an even more profound effect than the computer revolution on how we understand human experience, how we organize knowledge, and how we teach our students. As a faculty member observed, "Trying to add material about women to a conventional course is like adding the fact that the world is round to a course based on the assumption that the world is flat." Just as the impact of computer technology can no longer be confined to the math department, the understanding of women's experience in every culture cannot be restricted to separate women's studies courses; it has become crucially important to every course in the liberal arts.

Faculty Development: Redefining Competence

Research on women not only has created a new body of knowledge but is reshaping our understanding of the traditional curriculum, including the conceptualization of periods in history, genres in literature, the role of the "private" or "domestic" sphere in politics, and the choice, design, and interpretation of scientific research questions. Yet, by and large, most faculties are not professionally current in this important scholarship and pass on an incomplete version of human history in their courses. The translation of this information and perspective into classroom practice cannot be accomplished merely by good will. Some teachers experience more psychological resistance to understanding women than to learning about computers. They recognize that without becoming a computer scientist it is nonetheless important to understand the implication of the computer for their own research and teaching; it is a cultural and intellectual phenomenon that cannot be ignored. Yet many teachers continue to think that feminist research and "women's issues" can be taken care of by specialized groups and, therefore, have no direct bearing on their own courses. Because the computer is a product of science, it is not as politically charged a subject of study as is feminist scholarship, the product of a social movement. The example of computer literacy programs and writing-across-the-curriculum projects for faculty has demonstrated that institutions need to make long-term commitments to faculty education and offer substantial incentives and collegial guidance to enable teachers to gain access to new learning. The same kind of programs are needed to help faculty members catch up in the scholarship on women and to incorporate these insights into courses in every academic field.

If we have learned anything from the last five years' efforts to transform the curriculum to include the experience of women and subordinate cultural groups, it is that we are engaged in a long-term process. While our goals are clear — to be inclusive, to see and respect differences, to recognize political motives in the structures of our knowledge — the results, in terms of concrete products, are still unfinished. The descriptions we offer colleagues are as much statements of what we must strive for as they are demonstrations of what we have accomplished. Nevertheless, because of the importance of the scholarship on women that has accumulated in almost every discipline, our vision of a representative curriculum is no longer merely negative. We no longer need to define curriculum in terms of what it must overcome or avoid — racism, sexism or class bias; the promotion of exclusively male-centered values; the proclivity for making female students feel invisible in the classroom.

In gaining commitment to these goals from administrators and teachers, we need to counter their impatience for the finished product, their understandably urgent demand for the transformed syllabus, the fully integrated textbook, the inclusive general education requirements, and the truly liberal core curriculum. The shape and substance of these changes become clearer as we understand more about the process. The curriculum, like education itself, is hardly static, and our eagerness to have closure, to touch actual products, should not make us forget that because knowledge is historical we will need to revise the curriculum again and again.

We have tried to describe the process of undertaking curriculum change because we have learned through our consulting work that individual teachers, planning groups, and institutions may move through the process faster, with less chance of being derailed in their efforts, if they can anticipate the potential roadblocks. While no descriptive or theoretical account can substitute for actual engagement in the task, we have found that an intellectual overview can be a key strategy to help those participating in the change process identify sources of resistance in others and in themselves.

Sources of Resistance: Invisible Paradigms

Women's studies has enabled us to see what we have come to call the "invisible paradigms" of the academic system and the larger cultural context that marginalize or trivialize the lives of women, of blacks and ethnic minorities, and of those outside the dominant class or culture. Invisible paradigms are the skeletons in the closet of even the most liberal institutions. They are, to use another image to make the invisible visible, the infrastructure of our academic system: the internalized assumptions, the network of unspoken agreements, the implicit contracts that all the participants in the process of higher education have agreed to, usually unconsciously, in order to bring about learning. This infrastructure has worked so long and has supported the commerce of higher education so effectively that we no longer see it, notice its presence, or, most importantly, name it for the determining force that it is. Not surprisingly, these invisible paradigms are organized around power (who has it and how we are allowed access to it) and around values (among available choices, what is important and what is best). In our analysis of the curriculum change process, we have tried to bring as many of these to light as possible.

Inevitably, invisible paradigms are related to ideology. The more coherent an ideology and the better it serves the interests of those who benefit from the status quo, the less visible these paradigms will be to those who perpetuate them. Because a feminist transformation of the curriculum is often opposed on the grounds that it is ideological, we would like to define how we understand this often volatile term. It is helpful to us to regard ideology as a dynamic system of values and priorities, conscious and unconscious, by which men and women organize their actions and expectations, and explain their choices.[8] If the reigning ideology of higher education in the past has been pervasively male-defined, the practice and theory of black studies and women's studies prove that it is not inevitable and that other ideologies are possible. In her keynote address to the 1981 Wingspread Conference, Florence Howe contrasts the types of political choices that education implies.

> In the broadest context of that word, teaching is a political act: some person is choosing, for whatever reasons, to teach a set of values, ideas, assumptions, and pieces of information, and in so doing, to omit other[s]. . . . If all those choices form a pattern excluding half the human race, that is a political act

one can hardly help noticing. . . . To include women with seriousness and vision, and with some attention to the perspective of women as a hitherto subordinate group, is simply another kind of political act.

In a university whose goal is that abstraction called truth, no political act ought ideally to be excluded, if it might shed light on the ultimate goal. And the study of half the human race — the political act we call women's studies — cannot be excluded without obvious consequences to the search for truth.[9]

Charting the Change Process

We produce something more dramatic than a ripple effect when we introduce women as subjects of study on a syllabus, when we take seriously the needs and authority of women students, and when we undertake the faculty development necessary to do both successfully. Outlining the evolution of efforts to effect curriculum change reveals many parallels with the directions of scholarship on women over the last twenty years. The insights from that research have altered the content of many academic disciplines.[10] Accumulation of these new data, in turn, generates new questions about the nature of women's experience and that of other groups not currently represented on the traditional syllabus. As a result of the important landmarks in this scholarship, and because of the examples of curriculum change projects across the country, we can begin to identify the interactions between research questions and classroom practice that stimulate the transformation of the curriculum.

Our description suggests that teachers move through a sequence of stages, trying a variety of strategies in order to represent women and minorities adequately in their courses.[11] Yet we would like to acknowledge at the outset that these stages have fluid boundaries and that individuals may not experience them as a strictly linear progression. Of course, it is unlikely that different groups of teachers within a single institution will be moving through the same stages at the same time. Our emphasis in organizing the description as a series of stages is to illustrate that certain phenomena are often associated, that raising a particular set of questions leads to similar kinds of curricular outcomes. Even more important, the more fully we understand the commitments that lead teachers to ask these questions, the more able we are to motivate continued growth among our colleagues.

Table 1 highlights the major characteristics of the six stages in our description of the change process. We have attempted to identify for each stage the operative perspective for seeing women's experience, the questions raised about women in order to reconstruct the syllabus, the incentives that motivate faculty and govern their intellectual inquiry and teaching, the means or strategies used to represent women on the syllabus, and the curricular outcomes, including the types of courses typically generated at each stage, and the changes in the student's role in her or his education. In

84

TABLE 1   *Stages of Curriculum Change*

Stages	Questions	Incentives	Means	Outcome
Absence of women not noted	Who are the truly great thinkers/ actors in history?	Maintaining "standards of excellence"	Back to basics	Pre-1960's exclusionary core curriculum Student as "vessel"
Search for missing women	Who are the great women – the female Shakespeares, Napoleons, Darwins?	Affirmative action/com-pensatory	Add on to existing data within conventional paradigms	"Exceptional" women on male syllabus Student's needs recognized
Women as disadvan-taged, sub-ordinate group	Why are there so few women leaders? Why are women's roles devalued?	Anger/social justice	Protest existing paradigms but within perspective of dominant group	"Images of women" courses "Women in politics" Women's Studies begins Links with ethnic, cross-cultural studies
Women studied on own terms	What was/is women's experi-ence? What are dif-ferences among women? (attention to race, class, cul-tural difference)	Intellectual	Outside existing paradigms; develop insider's perspective	Women-focused courses Interdisciplinary courses Student values own experience
Women as challenge to disciplines	How valid are cur-rent definitions of historical periods, greatness, norms for behavior? How must our questions change to account for women's experi-ence, diversity, differ-ence?	Epistemology	Testing the paradigms Gender as category of analysis	Beginnings of integration Theory courses Student collaborates in learning
Trans-formed, "balanced" curriculum	How can women's and men's exper-ience be understood together? How do class and race intersect with gender?	Inclusive vision of human expe-rience based on difference, di-versity, not sameness, gen-eralization	Transform the paradigms	Reconceptualized, inclusive core Transformed introductory courses Empowering of student

analyzing the sources of resistance to change at each level, we have focused on the obstacles for the teacher and for the student. Our observations are derived from listening to teachers involved in faculty development projects and to those who drop out or refuse to join them.

Stage 1: Invisible Women

The absence of women from the curriculum is simply not noticed in some institutions. Although this phenomenon was much more common in past decades, it is hardly rare today. In fact, it may be the most harmful outcome of the recent push for curricular "coherence" that moves many faculties in the mid-1980s to reconsider a central core of required courses as the heart of a liberal education. To the extent that their search for coherence is nostalgic, faculties may simply reproduce the old orders and alleged civilities of their own undergraduate education rather than undertake a revision of the curriculum that reflects the state of current knowledge.[12] The wish to teach a curriculum in which the experiences of women and of nonwhite cultures are entirely absent is not, of course, perceived as regressive or exclusionary by its supporters. Teachers arrested at this stage often claim the existence of indisputable "standards of excellence" and their moral as well as intellectual responsibility to maintain them. Excellence, in their definition, implies greatness; the expectation is that we will all know and recognize greatness when we are exposed to it. The questions posed at this stage in structuring a syllabus focus on the incomparable individual: Who are the truly great thinkers, or writers, or actors in history? These questions assume criteria of greatness that transcend specific cultures and historical periods; teachers who argue for these standards acknowledge no relativity in their judgments, nor any ideological context surrounding them.

If these values are reminiscent of Matthew Arnold and his father, the most recent incarnation of these values was also influenced by the specific historical and social circumstances following World War II. The core curriculum many of us grew up on, Rhoda Dorsey of Goucher College reminds us, was designed for the predominantly male population returning to college on the G.I. Bill.[13] What was regarded as essential knowledge was substantially shaped by both the producers and primary consumers of that education — the dramatic influx of male Ph.D.s who began teaching, even at women's colleges, in the 1950s, along with the return of male students in great numbers to the college classroom. The current popularity of plans to return to an essentially exclusionary definition of knowledge lies in the simplicity of the appeal. "Back to basics" is a rallying cry that rejects the last two decades of curriculum change as frivolous. Proponents of the old core would dismiss the proliferation of women's studies and the diversification of ethnic and cultural studies as confusing fragmentation, and would disparage the grudging place made in the academy for student-centered learning as a misguided notion of "relevance." Serious students need sterner stuff, which is usually equated with the subjects, and often the very books, these teachers themselves studied twenty or forty years ago. This definition distrusts education as process and prefers fixed principles of value and judgment and supposedly timeless products.

Not surprisingly, teachers who want to provide the "truly great" or "the best that has been thought and known" tend to conceive of their students as waiting vessels. Although the female (or male) student's passivity in this kind of curriculum is often very real, the professor does not imagine himself as exercising power in determining what is valued or regarded as "best," and would probably never agree that his choices on the syllabus or in the classroom are political or gendered. More likely, this type of teacher sees himself as the vehicle for transmitting knowledge that is imagined to be immutable and apolitical. Many male professors do not notice the absence of women from the curriculum. When a system of priorities, a set of values, or a syllabus serves a group's interests, or at least does not constrain them, members of that group find it very difficult to become aware of the inadequacies of these designs. The number of female professors who still see no inequity or omissions in the male-defined curriculum is more startling, and serves to underscore dramatically how thoroughly women students may be deceived into believing traditional curricular values are congruent with their interests.

How can this stage — in which the experience of women is omitted from the definition of essential knowledge — be maintained or returned to now given twenty years of scholarship on women, the growth of women's studies programs, and the steadily rising proportion of women students in every classroom throughout higher education? Ironically, women students themselves may unwittingly collude in its perpetuation. When no representation of women's experience appears in the curriculum, a woman student is encouraged to believe the "generic man" includes her. With no basis for comparison, she may erroneously assume that male-derived definitions of "the good, the true, and the beautiful" actually describe her own experience. Student resistance to this male-centered curriculum is surprisingly low; the profound reaction to its omissions occurs, for women, only after graduation.[14]

Stage 2: Search for the Missing Women

Because most colleges pride themselves as much on a liberal learning environment as on their mission to conserve wisdom, committed teachers in Stage 1 may be moved to raise questions about adding women to the curriculum because they become aware of the needs of women students. The conviction that a woman student needs role models may prompt the teacher to begin a search for the women missing from the curriculum. Interestingly, the number of bright women students who must be present in the classroom in order to raise these questions is disproportionately large compared to the number that are believed to constitute an adequate representation on the syllabus.

The search for women figures good enough to be included on the syllabus may be well-meaning, but it risks being short-lived because of the way that questions are raised at this stage: Who are the great women? Who are the female Shakespeares, Napoleons, Darwins? The missing women are assumed to resemble the men who are already present in the traditional curriculum; the criteria by which greatness or excellence is defined remain unexamined. A few women turn up when the syllabus is revised with these expectations, but they exist in isolation from each other, apparent anomalies within their gender.

These "women worthies" who do appear are usually actors in the public sphere — queens, martyrs, suffragists, female novelists with male pseudonyms — women whose outstanding characteristic is their similarity to men. Adding these women to the existing order on the syllabus gives students the distorted sense that women have participated only occasionally in the production of history and culture, or expressed themselves only eccentrically in their writing or behavior. The courses that emerge at this stage of attempted curriculum transformation show women's experience as the "special case" of the larger topic, which is still considered ungendered.

The fair-minded faculty member whose search for worthwhile women to study is guided by resemblances to the established male examples may find less than he or she hoped for. Most women's histories, recovered in such a search, will not measure up to those of the preeminent male model: as writers, their production will seem "minor" in form or scope; as political activists, their participation in the sweep of history will seem sporadic; as representatives of a culture, their significance will seem subordinate or muted; as biological or moral beings, their condition will appear derivative or flawed. It is important to notice that the "minor status" of most women, considered from this perspective in the change process, is typically attributed to an individual fault or inadequacy, a personal inability to achieve prominence, genius, or "universal" value. If only Emily Dickinson had written longer poems or Jane Austen broader novels, or if only that reformer could have championed more than her specifically female causes: these are the reasons we often hear at this stage for not devoting more days of the semester to women's experience. In other words, the more women's experience and production have differed from men's, the less they will seem worth including in a survey of knowledge structured by male norms. The very differences that could illuminate the study of both genders bar the admission of all but a few women to the traditional syllabus.

The motivation of teachers at this stage is usually a liberal desire for equity within the status quo. Faculty members may become stuck here for some of the same reasons that they find it difficult to do affirmative action hiring. All other things being equal, when a teacher decides whether to choose a familiar male figure or to introduce a new female figure who may be equally relevant or important to the topic on the syllabus, it is less trouble to choose the man. The context of the established syllabus, like the context of the established department, makes it extremely unlikely that the token woman will seem equal to the same things or equal in the same way.

The danger of regression is significant. To return to the familiar on the syllabus seems less problematic to some teachers than to include "minor" figures, they may say, "just to have some women." Teachers may experience an apparent conflict between their intellectual responsibility to reach the best or most important material in their field and their moral responsibility to include a representative number of women and minorities on the syllabus.

Stage 3: Women as a Subordinate Group

How can teachers overcome this anxiety? The solution, demonstrated in the scholarship on women in every discipline, has been to look beyond the individual and to begin a structural analysis of the experience of women and nonwhite cultural groups. The types of questions raised at this stage shift dramatically from the terms available in the structure of conventional syllabi. Instead of looking only at outcomes — the actions, production, or expression of individual women — the typical questions that move teachers into the next stage of the curriculum change process look for causes: Why are there so few women leaders? Why are women's traditional roles (or forms of expression) devalued?

These questions are often provoked by the frustrating search for the missing women. Rather than opting out of the transformation endeavor because of the initially disappointing results, concerned faculty members find themselves moved by extra-academic concerns. Women teachers identify their duty to raise such questions for their women and men students in order to enable them to seek social justice. Women and men teachers also begin redefining their intellectual responsibility. Rather than a narrowly defined responsibility to a disciplinary canon of great works or great acts, they broaden their inquiry to encompass the historical and cultural context as the means for understanding the results they found at Stage 2. Such a comprehensive understanding of what constitutes their legitimate subject matter is liberating, yet it may create new sources of anxiety. As teachers begin a program of interdisciplinary reading and teaching, they often express doubts about their ability to judge work in fields outside their own specialty.

Both teachers and students often report that they feel angry when they discuss the new questions of Stage 3. The classroom heats up because the material introduced about women begins to make visible the "invisible paradigms" upon which the old syllabi rest. The multiple structures of the culture that define women as a disadvantaged or subordinate group begin to emerge. Understandably, women students in late adolescence regard the news that their opportunities may be in any way limited as extremely unwelcome; likewise, young male students are uncomfortable with the possibility that male-defined cultural values or systems are unfair. Because most young women and young men have relatively little experience in the adult work world, and because both groups are relatively unconscious of their gender socialization, they are skeptical of a structural analysis that suggests their behavior is either constrained (female) or culpable (male).[15] Predictably, student resistance to courses that focus on a structural analysis of gender asymmetry is quite high. Students, rather than faculty, are most likely to take flight at this stage in the change process. For women students especially, the temptation is great to dissociate themselves from the disadvantages they perceive as defining women as a group. As protection, they may cling to a faith in an "individual solution," and believe that their merit or worth will be sufficient to overcome the disability of gender. Another reaction may be that such a picture of social reality may be "historically" true but is irrelevant to their own futures. Contemporary women students, whether or not they represent a "post-feminist" generation, may believe that the equality of aspirations they express will be matched by an equality of opportunities as a result of the women's movement. Rather than be mobilized to examine the persistent and pervasive gender inequalities that remain and work to change them as their teachers might have hoped, these students, both male and female, may deny the problem exists.

Despite the difficulties of this stage, we cannot afford to forget the valuable truths about women's experience, relative to men's, that were learned here. The early years of women's studies generated many important courses that examined the representation of women as a subordinate group. In literature, such courses might have examined "images of women" in the novels of the established canon of male authors, and identified stereotypes such as the "virgin" and the "whore," the "earth mother" or "castrating bitch." In the social sciences, they may have studied gender roles in the family and society, or differential participation in the paid labor force. A common denominator among these courses is that they were conceived in a spirit of protest against the gender arrangements that shaped women's experience to their disadvantage. Their insights have enabled us to see the paradigms that govern not only our social behavior, but also the assignment of values and the criteria for judgment that lead to a male-dominated syllabus. The first wave of women's studies courses brought women as a group (rather than as isolated individuals) onto the syllabus, yet the most striking characteristic of the analysis was the oppression of women.

Stage 4: Women Studied on Their Own Terms

Fortunately, the history of women's studies and of black studies offers proven strategies for overcoming both the anger and the disbelief of Stage 3. The example of black studies gave women's studies another perspective that has made the kind of curriculum transformation we are currently envisioning a possibility. We have learned from black studies that only from the narrow perspective of the dominant group within a North American context was slavery the most salient feature of black experience. To study black experience in its own terms, it was necessary to step outside the paradigms of the dominant group, and outside the framework of the androcentric, white, Western syllabus, and attempt to adopt an "insider's perspective." What became visible was the range and diversity of black experience, both within and beyond the North American context, including forms of resistance to oppression and various sources and strategies for exercising power. Rather than focusing on cultural subordination, the evolution of black studies demonstrated that the multicultural realities of black experience — African, Afro-American, Afro-Caribbean, for example — could be articulated on their own terms. As Johnnella Butler, chair of Afro-American Studies at Smith College, has said, black studies has enriched our definitions of culture and ethnicity and complicated the question of what is American.[16]

The second major movement in women's studies courses and in feminist scholarship, especially in the humanities and the social sciences, has been to delineate the character of women's experience as women themselves have expressed it. This stage is crucial to successful transformation of traditional courses because only through developing women-focused courses do we discover the data we need to draw a full picture of human experience. This stage takes as its premise the eye-opening declaration of Gerda Lerner that "to document the experience of women would mean documenting all of history: they have always been of it, in it, and making it . . . half, at least, of the world's experience has been theirs, half of the world's work and much of its products."[17] Rather than disappointment, disbelief, or anger, the participants in this stage of the change process, teachers and students alike, experience a liberating intellectual excitement, a sense of expanding possibilities.

For teachers, whole new fields of inquiry are opened; new areas for research, publication, and professional renewal become available. The compelling motivation most frequently described by teachers who have entered this stage is a voracious intellectual appetite: What was and is women's experience, known as a subject rather than object? What are the differences among women, such as race, class, and culture, that have contributed to their identities? This stage produces the careful cross-cultural comparisons that complicate the questions we ask about the dimensions of women's experience and that enable us to avoid inaccurate generalizations about "all women" derived from a limited sample.

Women students are attracted to the new material and new perspective because this stage of curriculum development can provide informed access to their own experience, and the means for valuing what they have lived. When we develop courses that focus on the actual experience of ordinary women, we often find illuminating patterns emerge that allow us to understand the politics of domestic life; the artistic characteristics of noncanonical forms (such as letters and journals) or of collective or folk forms (such as quilts). Just as a female student may be inspired by the example of the extraordinary women, the "women worthies" studied in Stage 2, she learns to reflect more self-consciously on her own daily behavior and her choices for self-expression by studying the wealth of "nontraditional" materials made visible in Stage 4.

Stage 5: Women as a Challenge to the Disciplines

What we learn in Stage 4 is too important to keep to ourselves or to study with only a limited group of self-selected students in women-focused courses. The accumulation of data gathered from the insider's perspective causes us to question in profound ways the frameworks that organize our traditional courses: How valid are current definitions of historical periods, standards of greatness or excellence, norms for behavior? How must the organizing questions of each academic discipline change to account for the diversity of gender, race, and class? Teachers who have spent some time developing women-focused courses or who have read extensively in the scholarship on women are the most likely to undertake a thorough form of curriculum transformation: they test the paradigms that have conventionally organized knowledge on the syllabus to exclude or marginalize women and other subordinate groups. In personal terms, the move from women-focused study to transformation of the conventional curriculum is inevitable because, as teachers, most of us inhabit both worlds and must necessarily question how what we learned by studying women bears on the other courses we usually teach in our departments. In institutional terms, the movement from women's studies to integrating or transforming the core curriculum is rarely seen as a natural or welcome outgrowth. When faculty members who have enjoyed a Stage 1 curriculum for most of their professional lives are asked the questions typical of Stage 5, they often feel that their own credentials, as well as the worth and integrity of their academic discipline, are in doubt. In questioning the paradigms we use to perceive, analyze, and organize experience, we are pointedly asking not only what we know but how we came to know it, and consequently the intellectual investment on both sides of the debate may be higher here than at earlier points in the process of change. Even those who are willing to admit the validity of the feminist critique of the disciplines (that periodization in history does not mark the significant changes in women's estates, that canons of great art and literature are derived from and reinforce male practice as most valuable, that the scientific method defines objectivity in androcentric rather than gender-neutral terms) may resist the deconstruction of their own discipline.[18] Underneath all the wide variety of expressions of resistance is a residual fear of loss — a reluctance to give up what had seemed most stable, efficient, authoritative, transcendent of contexts, and free of ideological or personal values — in short, a fear that feminist criticism means a loss of subject matter and methodology without a compensating gain. If the current systems are flawed, we often hear, they at least serve us better than no system at all. When feminists can offer us a workable alternative, then we'll consider reconceiving the total design of the syllabus.

In 1980 Catherine Stimpson, the editor of *SIGNS*, a journal of interdisciplinary feminist research, characterized the first five years of *SIGNS's* publications as "the deconstruction of error" and identified the next major task as "the reconstruction of theory."[19] Yet the very tools that allowed us to document the errors have already provided the strategies for an alternative construction of the syllabus. To allay the fears of wholesale loss and to demonstrate that feminist theory has moved beyond merely offering a critique, those engaged in curriculum transformation need to be explicit about the ways that gender as a category of analysis enriches and illuminates traditional subjects, including the experience of elite, white men. Using gender, race, and class as primary categories of analysis will transform our perspective on familiar data and concepts as well as reveal new material to be studied.

How is this possible? All of the earlier stages of feminist analysis and curriculum change have highlighted the operation of gender as a principle for exclusion or subordination of material on the syllabus. Although the conventional syllabus is purported to be gender-neutral or gender-free, we now recognize that it is inevitably and pervasively gendered. Recognizing the gendered nature of all texts allows us to recuperate material that, in our earlier anger, seemed corrupt or false and teach it in a new light. Having uncovered the error that most material on the conventional syllabus is derived from male experience and is erroneously generalized to represent the human condition, we might, nonetheless, agree that these are helpful descriptions of what it means to be male and of a certain race and class at a certain moment in history. This stage unequivocally means a loss of old certainties, but the gains are the recovery of meaningful historical and social context, the discovery of previously invisible dimensions of the old subjects, and access to instruments of analysis (gender, race, and class as significant variables) that expose strata of formerly suppressed material.

Stage 6: The Transformed Curriculum

What are the paradigms that would make it possible to understand women's and men's experiences together? What would a curriculum that offers an inclusive vision of human experience and that attends as carefully to difference and genuine pluralism as to sameness and generalization actually look like? Although we possess the tools of analysis that allow us to conceive of such an education, we cannot, as yet, point to any institution that has entered the millennium. What will exist there depends on the recognition that any paradigm is historical and that no one framework is likely to serve for all time. This stage promotes process rather than immutable products and fixed principles.

Our descriptions so far resemble an ideal frame of mind or a hypothetical state more than they promise a syllabus we could distribute to classes next term. Perhaps the greatest danger at this stage is the impatience for a concrete product. Administrators and teachers who are persuaded that the curriculum could be improved by more equitable representation of gender, race, and class often underestimate the time it will take. Lerner suggests that if patriarchy has held sway for over 2000 years, we should not be surprised if, in a discipline like history, it takes several dozen women scholars fully funded for the length of most grants to even imagine the categories that would have to change in order to bring this curriculum into being.[20] While the goal of a Stage 6 curriculum is often readily assented to, the means may seem too costly or cumbersome. Many well-meaning college presidents and deans wish to move directly from Stage 1 to Stage 6 without an allocation of resources and an enduring, clear commitment to women-focused study. There is a temptation to believe that the promised land can be attained without passing through the difficult terrain of women's studies. Some curriculum change projects risk foundering because "good intentions," especially among administrators who want to sponsor programs that will be perceived as apolitical, are substituted for the expertise developed by those who have taught and contributed to the scholarship on women. It would be an intellectual mistake of monumental proportions to believe that we can do without or bypass women-focused study in the name of the "greater good" of the transformed or "gender-balanced" curriculum. The vital work of Stage 4, studying women on their own terms, generates the transformative questions that stimulate the change process, as well as provides the data and alternative paradigms that inform the whole continuum of curriculum transformation we have described.

We would like to propose some of the elements that would characterize a transformed course. We have intentionally included the teacher's and student's relationship to the changed subject matter and to each other as crucial ingredients. A transformed course would:

- be self-conscious about *methodology* — use gender as a category of analysis, no matter what is on the syllabus (even if all males);
- present changed content in a *changed context* — awareness of all knowledge as historical and socially constructed, not immutable;
- develop an *interdisciplinary perspective* — the language of discourse, assumptions of a field, and analytical methods are made visible by contrast with other fields
- pay meaningful attention to intersections of *race, class, and cultural differences within gender* — avoid universalizing beyond data;
- study new subjects in their *own terms* — not merely as other, alien, non-normative, non-Western — encourage a true *pluralism;*
- *test paradigms* rather than merely "add on" women figures or issues — incorporate analyses of gender, race, and class by a thorough reorganization of available knowledge;
- make the student's experience and learning process part of the explicit content of the course — reaffirm the transcendent goals of the course;
- and recognize that, because *culture reproduces itself in the classroom,* the more conscious we are of this phenomenon, the more likely we are to turn it to our advantage in teaching the transformed course.

Notes

1. Harold L. Hodgkinson, *Guess Who's Coming to College: Your Students in 1990* (Washington, DC: National Institute of Independent Colleges and Universities, 1983). The report is also excerpted in *Academe, 69,* No. 1 (1983), 13–20.
2. *Liberal Education and the New Scholarship on Women: Issues and Constraints in Institutional Change,* Report of the Wingspread Conference for college and university presidents, October 1981 (Washington, DC: Association of American Colleges, 1982).
3. Among articles that document these related trends are Lee Hansen, "'Bottoming Out?' The Annual Report on the Economic Status of the Profession, 1983–84," *Academe, 70,* No. 3 (1984), 3–10; Robert Jacobson, "A.A.U.P.'s Leader Assays Decline in Faculty Morale, Governance," *Chronicle of Higher Education,* December 27 1984, pp. 15, 17; Hazard S. Adams, "How Departments Commit Suicide," in *Professors 83,* ed. Richard Brod and Phyllis Franklin (New York: MLA, 1983), pp. 29–35.
4. Peggy McIntosh, "The Study of Women: Implications for Reconstructing the Liberal Arts Disciplines," *Forum for Liberal Education, 4,* No. 1 (1981), 1–3.
5. See *Directory of Projects: Transforming the Liberal Arts Curriculum through Incorporation of the New Scholarship on Women,* comps. Barbara Kneubuhl and Peggy McIntosh (Wellesley, MA: Wellesley College Center for Research on Women), an annual directory. For reports on the progress of exemplary projects, see these special issues: *Forum for Liberal Education, 4,* No. 1 (1981) and *Forum for Liberal Education, 6,* No. 5 (1984). For discussions on the implications of scholarship on women to the liberal arts curriculum, see these special issues: *Change,* April 1982; *Women's Studies Quarterly, 10,* No. 1 (1982); and *Academe, 69,* No. 5 (1983).
6. Peggy McIntosh, *Interactive Phases of Curricular Re-vision: A Feminist Perspective,* Working Paper No. 124 (Wellesley, MA: Wellesley College Center for Research on Women, 1983); Elizabeth Arch and Susan Kirschner, "Transformation of the Curriculum: Problems of Conception and Deception," *Women's Studies International Forum, 7,* No. 3 (1984), 149–151; and "Faculty Development: Models for Institutional Change," Sec. 2 in *Women's Place in the Academy: Transforming the Liberal Arts Curriculum,* ed. Marilyn Schuster and Susan Van Dyne (Totowa, NJ: Rowman & Allanheld, in press).
7. Janice Monk, associate director of the Southwest Institute for Research on Women (SIROW), in personal communication.
8. We are indebted to Mary Poovey's definition of ideology in her "*Persuasion* and the Powers of Love," in *The Representation of Women in Fiction,* ed. Carolyn Heilbrun and Margaret Higonnet (Baltimore: Johns Hopkins University Press, 1983), p. 178, n. 2.
9. Howe, in *Liberal Education and the New Scholarship on Women,* pp. 5–21; rpt. "Feminist Scholarship: The Extent of the Revolution," in *Change,* April 1982, pp. 12–20.
10. For essays analyzing the transformative effect of research on women on the disciplines, see our "Selected Bibliography for Integrating Research on Women's Experience in the Liberal Arts Curriculum," included in our *Women's Place in the Academy.* See also Elizabeth Abel and Edward K. Abel, eds., *The SIGNS Reader: Women, Gender, and Scholarship* (Chicago: University of Chicago Press, 1983); Elizabeth Langland and Walter Grove, eds., *A Feminist Perspective in the Academy: The Difference It Makes* (Chicago: University of Chicago Press, 1983); Paul Lauter, ed., *Reconstructing American Literature: Courses and Critiques* (Old Westbury, NY: Feminist Press, 1983); Julia A. Sherman and Evelyn T. Beck, eds., *The Prism of Sex: Essays in the Sociology of Knowledge* (Madison: University of Wisconsin Press, 1979); Dale Spender, ed., *Men's Studies Modified: The Impact of Feminism on the Academic Disciplines* (Elmsford, NY: Pergamon Press, 1981); and the Working Papers Series of the Wellesley College Center for Research on Women, a list of which is available from the Center.
11. See Gerda Lerner, "Placing Women in History: Definitions and Challenges," in *The Majority Finds Its Past: Placing Women in History* (London: Oxford University Press, 1979); McIntosh, *Interactive Phases of Curricular Re-Vision;* and Arch and Kirschner, "Transformation of Curriculum."

12. For examples of essays that express a longing for old "certainties" and a rejection of the insights of new scholarship, see Arnold Beichman, "Is Higher Education in the Dark Ages?" *New York Times Magazine,* November 6, 1983, pp. 46–90; and L. Steven Zwerling, "A New Mission for Continuing Education: Teaching the Skills of the Liberal Arts," *Chronicle of Higher Education,* March 28, 1984, p. 80.

13. Dorsey in remarks at the opening panel of college presidents at the Skidmore College Conference, *Towards Equitable Education for Women and Men: Models from the Last Decade,* Saratoga Springs, New York, March 11, 1983.

14. Countless letters from our former students over the last fifteen years confirm this phenomenon. Other women's studies teachers and scholars report this postgraduate awakening in their lives, and feminist scholarship of the last two decades often includes such an account of the author's education. See, for example, Howe, "Feminist Scholarship," pp. 12–20.

15. Of course, some students have always worked, and students at public institutions are more likely than the privileged, mostly white population of elite schools to know firsthand about gender inequalities in the workplace. Such experiences may ready them for a feminist structural analysis or only reinforce their sense that these pervasive inequalities are "natural."

16. Johnnella Butler, "Complicating the Question: Black Studies and Women Studies," in *Women's Place in the Academy.*

17. Gerda Lerner, *The Female Experience: An American Documentary* (Indianapolis: Bobbs-Merrill, 1977), p. xxi.

18. See, for example, Peggy McIntosh, "Warning: The New Scholarship on Women May Be Hazardous to Your Ego," *Women's Studies Quarterly,* 10 (1982), 29–31.

19. Catherine Stimpson, "The Scholarship About Women: The State of the Art," *Annals of Scholarship,* 1 (1980), 2–14.

20. Lerner, in a comment made at the Wingspread Conference.

This essay is adapted from a chapter in the authors' book, *Women's Place in the Academy: Transforming the Liberal Arts Curriculum,* published in February 1985 by Rowman & Allanheld.

Mujeres Unidas en Acción:
A Popular Education Process

EVA YOUNG
MARIWILDA PADILLA

Eva Young and Mariwilda Padilla present a challenging and touching example of the practice of feminist pedagogy: the struggle of a group of Latinas in Dorchester, Massachusetts, to educate themselves. The authors provide a description of Mujeres Unidas en Acción, Inc. — a nonprofit community-based agency offering educational programs to low-income Latinas — in terms of its development and structure, and take an in-depth look at one of its educational components, the Spanish program. Young and Padilla illustrate the core and spirit of the agency by providing concrete examples of its participatory approach through which the voices of all its members are heard and validated at all levels of functioning and by including testimonies of the program participants. The authors reflect on the agency's philosophical stance, by discussing the connection between the daily lives of these women and the teaching and learning practices experienced at Mujeres Unidas. They pay particular attention to the social, political, and economic context from which the women come and in which they live.

Mujeres Unidas en Acción (Women United in Action) is a nonprofit community-based agency offering educational programs to low-income Latina women living in Dorchester, Massachusetts. All of the women attending Mujeres's programs are outside the United States's social, political, and economic mainstream, because we live in poverty.[1] In addition, we contend that institutionalized racism and other forms of oppression, such

[1] Recent research literature shows that, in general, Puerto Ricans in the United States suffer from lack of economic resources. Rodríguez (1989) cites studies which indicate that "the economic situation of Puerto Ricans in the United States has worsened with time" (p. 36). She writes:

Tienda and Jensen (1986), in their analysis of the 5% decennial census data (1960–80), found Puerto Ricans in the states to be the only group to experience a drop in real family income between 1970 and 1980 and to show a steadily increasing concentration in the lowest income

Harvard Educational Review Vol. 60 No. 1 February 1990, 1–17

as sexism, classism, and discrimination, can be understood as other causes that keep Latina women outside the mainstream.[2] We believe that our lack of education is rooted in a system that perpetuates exclusion and provides no options for people who are not privileged. Therefore, at Mujeres we are working for change by creating opportunities and developing educational programs that generate our advancement as women, and particularly as women of color.

Mujeres is based upon the right and the control we believe each woman should have over her own education. Its processes guarantee and institutionalize active participation in the agency's administrative, academic, and social development. We like to think of Mujeres Unidas en Acción as a "social incubator" through which Latina women have the opportunity and access to develop their skills in community organization, development, and leadership. We believe that a safe environment in which all people are committed to sharing skills and supporting each other will enable women to advance.

This article provides an overview of our agency, as well as an in-depth description of one of its educational components, the Spanish program. Specifically, we focus on the agency's origins, its current structure, and its educational activities. The discussion of administrative and educational phi-

---

quartile (other groups compared were Blacks, Mexicans, other Hispanics, and Native Americans). . . . Bean and Tienda (1988) also found Puerto Ricans to have declining economic well-being, as measured by falling labor force participation, high unemployment, poverty, and declines in real family income. (p. 47)

In addition, women in particular fall consistently into the low economic end of the scale. Rodríguez (1989) mentions a study done by Darity and Myers (1987) which found that Puerto Rican female-headed households were among the poorest families. A study done by the Hispanic Office for Planning and Education (HOPE) and the Massachusetts Institute of Technology (MIT) in 1987 states that

Half of all Hispanic families with children under 18 are supported by single mothers. This family structure has important implications for the prevalence of poverty among families as well as for the strategies to promote full employment for Hispanics. When families are supported by a sole earner, especially women, they are much more likely to be poor. For single-parent families to survive above the poverty level, it becomes even more crucial for the bread-winner to gain access to higher wage jobs. (Borges, Vázquez-Fuentes, & Kluver, 1987, p. 36)

This study also states that "in Massachusetts, current Assistance for Families with Dependent Children benefits (usually the only option for unemployed single mothers) are approximately 30 percent below the poverty level" (p. 13). As the statewide Massachusetts Commission for Hispanic Affairs stated in 1986, "The availability of services sought by single-parent households, such as daycare, after-school programs or counseling is crucial to the well-being of Hispanic families" (p. 33). According to a survey commissioned by the Boston Redevelopment Authority (BRA) in 1985, females made up 63 percent of all Hispanics. The 1980 census shows that 52 percent of Hispanics in Boston had no high school diploma. These figures suggest that there is a disproportionate number of women who have been kept outside the mainstream.

[2] There is some literature that has dealt with the racial experience of Puerto Ricans in the United States. For example, Rodríguez (1989) states:

As Puerto Ricans entered into "the America dilemma" (Myrdal, 1944) two facts about the racial order were quite clear. One was that the context in which Puerto Ricans stepped offered only two paths — one to the White World and one to the not-White world. Choice of path was dependent on racial classification according to U.S. standards. Use of these standards divided the group, negated the cultural existence of Puerto Ricans, and ignored their expectations that they be treated, irrespective of race, as a culturally intact group. The other quite obvious fact about the race order was that those Americans who were White were socioeconomically better off. (p. 56) losophies illustrates how they are put into practice. We also give examples of the agency's participatory approach — the active participation of Mujeres members in all educational and administrative decisionmaking processes — and its educational objectives — creating a critical vision of society and developing literary skills in the native language to reinforce the process of second-language acquisition.

A Holistic View of Mujeres

Mujeres Unidas en Acción began in 1979 as a pilot project under the auspices of a nonprofit community agency called WeCan. The agency's principal mission was to develop programs to rehabilitate vacant lots and abandoned buildings, advocate for low-income housing, and organize the residents of twenty-two blocks around Codman Square in Dorchester, Massachusetts.[3]

During the winter of 1979, while teaching residents how to set up insulation material, a WeCan volunteer discovered that a great number of Latinas did not know how to speak English. The volunteer noticed major differences between native English speakers and the Spanish-speaking women who had lived in the United States for years. These women clearly seemed left behind. The majority, from Puerto Rico, were also low-income, unmarried mothers with little or no education in their native language. Faced with this great need for education, WeCan volunteers organized a program to teach English as a second language (ESL) in a local church basement. The purpose of the ESL program, called Mujeres Latinas de Dorchester (Latina Women of Dorchester), was to include the Latinas in WeCan community activities.[4]

Through the use of a participatory approach,[5] various community affairs activities were developed. Originally, there were two volunteer teachers and one child-care worker offering services. The Latina women's enthusiastic response to the English program was unexpected, and in less than a year the number of women attending classes grew from eight to twenty. Initially, teachers were using the same beginning English curriculum for students with widely different skills. Students who were illiterate received extra help. Also, once a week the agency offered remedial courses in reading, conversational English, and writing. During initial stages the agency's growth accelerated

[3] The state census of 1985 showed the following percentages for Hispanics in the following areas in and around Dorchester: North Dorchester, 13 percent Hispanics of a population of 26,005; South Dorchester, 7 percent of a total population of 16,373; Roxbury, 13 percent of a total population of 58,475; and Mattapan, 6 percent of a total population of 40,395.

[4] To this date there are very few written documents that trace the specific growth of the agency. Currently, Mujeres is dedicated to documenting the early growth and development of the agency through oral histories.

[5] Our participatory approach means that women are given the opportunity and are encouraged to express their opinions and ideas at all levels of the agency. For example, classroom curriculum is developed around students' needs as articulated by them. For women who have never before been asked to express an opinion, doing so and being respected for it makes them active participants and is empowering. Providing learning experiences that promote critical thinking skills allows women to make decisions about their own lives and take a more active and assertive role in them.

in a variety of ways. As the number of women attending classes increased, the number and range of classes were no longer sufficient to meet diverse student needs, and so the agency reached beyond its original goal, expanding from only providing ESL classes to providing a wide range of support services.

We believe that Mujeres's accelerated growth is due to our unique and innovative approach to supporting and helping low-income Latinas in their struggle to become active members of society. The agency's fiscal conduit, WeCan, disappeared in 1981 due to federal government budget cuts. In 1982, when the center was able to incorporate itself as a nonprofit agency to serve the community of low-income Latinas, the name was changed to Mujeres Unidas en Acción, Inc. At Mujeres, all services are free. Funds come from the City of Boston, private foundations, corporations, and community fund-raising activities.

The mission of Mujeres Unidas is to provide opportunities for low-income women to participate in and take control of their education and use it as a liberating tool. This is evident in each and every component of Mujeres Unidas's programs. Today Mujeres Unidas offers services to over one hundred women and thirty-five children aged one to five. At present, we are unable to accommodate all of the women who are interested in our services. All services, including emotional counseling and academic and technical education, are participant-based. We offer four levels of ESL: beginner; intermediate; advanced intermediate; and advanced English. This last course is offered in collaboration with Bunker Hill Community College and allows students to earn four college-level credits of ESL. In addition, Mujeres Unidas offers a preparatory course for the Graduate Equivalency Diploma (GED), and a literacy course, both of which are taught in Spanish. These educational programs have become the pillar of our participatory process.

Recently, we began to offer job and educational counseling, sponsored by the Gateway Cities Program.[6] Since the agency's formation, students have initiated support groups in accordance with their needs. In this way, they share experiences and help each other. Support groups include individual and group emotional counseling, and an alcoholism and substance-abuse support group. In 1987, a meditation group was initiated because a student, Nora Zuñiga, expressed a need to have a space for meditation. In her own words: "humans need food not only for the body but also for the soul." After a year, these students decided to merge with the alcoholism and substance-abuse group. This group, called *compañeras* (sisterhood), meets once a week and is open to all women from the community. It was formed by a recovering alcoholic who studied at Mujeres, and is the first of its kind in Massachusetts for Latinas.

---

[6] The Gateway Cities Program is a local aid initiative, created in fiscal year 1987 by a legislative State order. Gateway Cities funds have helped municipalities and local community groups provide services in such areas as immigration assistance, housing, economic development, interpreter and translation services, specialized education, and municipal access programs. As of fiscal year 1989, however, the Gateway Cities program funds were not renewed due to budget cuts.

In January 1989, as part of a pilot project in collaboration with Boston's Department of Public Health (DPH), one of the agency's counselors began to develop a support group for battered women. Created by Latinas for low-income Latina women, it will be unique in Massachusetts. The idea for organizing this support group came from a student who had attended a workshop at Mujeres in the fall of 1988, given by Dr. Elba Crespo from the Prevention of Family Violence Unit for DPH. Other women also expressed concern about dealing with domestic violence or not wanting to confront it.

Two other types of programs, forums and minicourses, further illustrate how the participatory approach is put into practice. Since its beginning, Mujeres Unidas has sponsored a community issues forum every Friday; ideas come from student suggestions. After these ideas are developed into topics, students select them in a meeting early in the semester. Guest speakers are subsequently invited to address them.

In response to many students who wanted to learn more practical skills, Mujeres Unidas started a series of minicourses this past winter. Tina Cueva, the outreach worker and a graduate of Mujeres Unidas's program, affirms that "when we learn something practical, it gives us a sense of achievement. After we finish this first step, we look at the next one with greater ease." Practical minicourses are offered in areas such as typing, citizenship, and driving. Nine students have already passed the written part of the driving exam and are preparing to take the practical exam. During the spring semester four students studied to take the citizenship exam. Two women took the test and passed, and one has been sworn in as a U.S. citizen. The other two continue to study, and plan to take the test soon. Six other students are enrolled in the typing courses.

A childcare program supports Mujeres's students through their years at the center. Under the supervision of two teachers, both former graduates of our ESL program, children gather from Monday to Friday in an environment where learning experiences are shared, while their mothers are attending classes. This is the first time that many of the children have been separated from their mothers and are not under the care of other family members. Although this can be a difficult experience for them, we have found that as time passes, especially because their mothers are close by, the experience becomes a positive one. After a while, children willingly let go of their mothers' hands to walk into their own childcare room. It has also been positive because any time there is a childcare activity, attendance is great. Of thirty-five children enrolled in childcare, twenty-five children and their mothers participate in practically all of the activities organized for special days. Since one of the teachers is from the Cape Verde Islands, the children learn Cape Verdean Creole in addition to Spanish and English. We think that first-hand experience with different languages is valuable for the children's development of vocabulary and for their appreciation of language diversity.

The participatory approach is also practiced in the agency's administrative structure. Mujeres has chosen to function as a collective since its origin. It is composed of the ten Mujeres Unidas staff workers. In addition, student representatives are elected to this body at the beginning of each semester. The student representatives serve as liaisons between students and the collective. They are responsible for raising issues that are relevant to the students. Through their participation in bimonthly collective meetings, they are an integral part of the decisionmaking process. The meetings are open to all students and volunteers; everyone's opinions and ideas are welcomed and discussed.

The collective's major responsibilities are: 1) to develop programs based on the needs expressed by the student population; 2) to make recommendations about expanding the program; 3) to develop long- and short-term plans; and 4) to discuss topics related to the Latina community, particularly those affecting low-income Latinas.

Volunteers, although welcome, usually do not attend collective meetings, because the majority serve on a part-time basis or conduct home visits on weekends. The volunteers are primarily Anglo, middle-class, educated women who want to learn more about the Latina community, develop their teaching skills, and support efforts for the advancement of other women. The responsibility of the volunteers is to support students who are unable to register because of a lack of space, or who need special attention or additional instruction. Specifically, they meet with students one-on-one or in small groups, providing citizenship classes and tutorials in participants' homes and at the agency in subjects such as math, English, and understanding cultural differences. There is also a volunteer representative on the staff, who is responsible for bringing volunteers' ideas to the collective meeting discussions.

In the collective we see and treat each other as equals, despite our cultural, class, social, and educational differences. Of course, in the group's dynamics, differences are periodically observed, depending upon the topic being discussed. Nevertheless, these differences are seen as necessary and positive for the development of equal community participation. During our collective meetings we respect and take into consideration the different levels and types of knowledge each has on a given issue. As Tina Cueva, the outreach worker, says, "the fact that we don't have a boss inspires each one of us to develop ideas, and to be innovative, instead of just waiting for someone to tell us what to do."

It would be impossible to talk about social transformation — particularly in the case of the Latina, who has historically been raised to be a mother, daughter, sister, or wife — without including radical changes in the power structure to validate her own voice.[7] One structure which may oppress many women is the hierarchically organized family. In many low-income families, the male figure, when present, is the one who represents authority, giving

---

[7] Social transformation in this context refers to a transformed society in which people can see themselves in control of their lives, having the access, the options, and the opportunities to develop skills and as being able to control their destinies. And one in which people can see themselves as members of a collective process in which diversity in race, culture, language, gender and sexual orientation is respected and tolerated.

orders and making the decisions. Some of our students, for example, have been forbidden by their husbands, partners, or lovers to continue their education (since learning English is considered to be enough), or to participate in other activities sponsored by the agency. Other students need to fulfill certain obligations, such as food preparation and ensuring that the home is cleaned, before they can participate in any activity outside the home. In many such households the mother is the sole provider for the emotional needs and social upbringing of the children. This situation is oppressive because these women are kept from pursuing other options, such as furthering their education or pursuing other interests.

Radical changes are needed both inside and outside of the woman. Internally, women need to identify their own feelings of oppression and gain the strength to confront them. Externally, stereotypical roles need to be confronted; the roots of gender roles need to be discussed openly and addressed in a way that gives equal responsibility to men and women. Women need freedom to work and study, to change the traditional roles of mother, daughter, sister, and emotional supporter. We believe that for these roles to be changed, society must reinvest resources in our educational processes and our social structures. Socialization based on gender roles needs to be questioned, critically analyzed, and changed. For example, a more equitable sharing of responsibility for childrearing would require, among other things, reassessing job priorities and schedules, creating childcare centers, and achieving parity in salaries for males and females.

It would be absurd to maintain a hierarchical system in an organization such as Mujeres Unidas, because that would perpetuate the present social oppression women face. The decision for Mujeres to be a collective grew out of an urgent need to provide women, particularly low-income women, with the space to express their opinions freely. The participatory approach allows Mujeres to function in an environment where the importance of the collective process minimizes the risk of one person taking on all of the power.

The dynamics of development for the dispossessed must include practical and immediate action to validate our voices —to appreciate, understand, and learn from what each woman experiences, thinks, and speaks. At Mujeres Unidas, workers and students learn the value of their own words. They learn to be assertive in what they are trying to express. One example of this is the review process for Mujeres's Personnel Manual, which began in June 1987, when we realized that the manual needed revision. Policies for maternity leave, temporary workers, and other issues of current concern to staff were not included in the old manual. In June of 1988, Mujeres Unidas, with technical assistance from the Boston Women's Fund, began revising the personnel manual. A typical revision process, in which the agency's director reviews the manual, makes necessary changes, and then sends a memorandum to workers and the Board of Directors[8] for approval, was not used because this

---

[8] The Board of Directors is formed by former Assistance for Families with Dependent Children (AFDC) recipients, current AFDC recipients who are students at Mujeres, graduates of Mujeres, and professional Latina women.

approach worked against the participatorial principles of the agency. Instead, we created a committee composed of members of the collective and students. The process of developing the personnel manual took about six months. Each article, amendment, and phrase was read and reread until all of the workers and students present at the meetings understood, analyzed, criticized, and expanded the content, so that it was based on their own experiences. The collective's members and students joined efforts to produce something in common. The different skills of each of the participants converged to create a new personnel manual. We consider this a concrete example of education functioning as a liberating tool. While we recognize that the extenuating efforts, time commitments, and slow pace of the process can be cumbersome and sometimes overburdening, we feel that the results are worthwhile. At present the personnel manual is at the Board of Directors for their approval.

The Board of Directors of Mujeres Unidas is an essential component of the agency's structure. It has several different functions. The first is to be its legal representative, in accordance with regulations governing nonprofit organizations. At the same time, our Board maintains a system of checks and balances. The Board of Directors is composed of 40 percent professional women and 60 percent low-income Latinas. This duality in composition means that Board members necessarily have the responsibility of educating themselves. The professional women learn from the community women's experiences, struggles, and survival. Simultaneously, the women from the community learn from the professional women the skills needed to become active members, not only of the Board of Directors, but of other decision-making structures as well. For example, when the position of secretary of the Board was vacant, Nelly, a newly arrived immigrant from Puerto Rico who had become involved with Mujeres's Board, was nominated by her peers to fill it. Nelly brings to the Board firsthand knowledge of single parenting and experience with the challenges faced by an immigrant learning a new language. In turn, the Board can help Nelly develop the skills to become a good secretary. Before committing herself, Nelly asked to see a job description and other information necessary for performing her job well. She stated, "I need to know really well what my responsibilities are." This is one way Board members exchange ideas, resources, and skills.

Board members also participate in Mujeres Unidas's working committees. These were created to organize the daily work needed to operate a community-based agency; they also involve students, staff, and Board members in collaboration for learning diverse skills. There are three working committees: Evaluation, Planning, and Personnel; Fund-Raising and Special Events; and the Development, Maintenance, and Dissemination of the Board of Directors' Information.

The formation of these committees represents another part of our liberating process, providing an additional forum for our students to develop their creative ideas, critical thinking, and leadership skills, and become active in the structure and functioning of the agency. Working committees comprise at least two members and meet approximately every three months, depending on the particular situation. The committees have organized a variety of activities, including selling food at lunchtime for fund-raising; publishing a booklet on AIDS and safe sex for mothers; and the Community Unity Festival, a day of celebration and solidarity in Roxbury and Dorchester for communities of color.

We believe that the success of Mujeres Unidas is demonstrated by the large number of women who come to register for our programs. At the end of the most recent Spring cycle, eighty-four students had already registered for the current Fall-Winter cycle. We get at least two or three phone calls a week asking for information about our courses. For our five-week Summer cycle, in which we offer two classes instead of our usual four, we could only register twenty-four students; an additional twenty-nine students were placed on a waiting list due to a lack of available space. Furthermore, we can see success in the number of Mujeres graduates who are now either working or in college or technical schools. After our incorporation in 1982, we began graduating students in the fiscal year of 1983–1984. Since 1983, sixty-five out of ninety-five students have graduated from the Advanced ESL class, and twenty-eight out of a group of thirty-five have obtained their GED. One student from the ESL program has obtained a B.A. in Economics from the University of Massachusetts, Boston. She is currently a member of the Board of Directors. Another student finished Mujeres's ESL program in 1986 and obtained certification in Word Processing at the Humphrey Occupational Center of the Boston Public Schools. She also finished Advanced English at Bunker Hill Community College and is currently enrolled in the School of Management at the University of Massachusetts, Boston. Most of our students would never have thought it possible to continue their education at a local university; Mujeres has opened the door to the future for many of them.

One of the reasons for our success has been our ability to recognize, identify, and overcome the barriers faced by Latinas in their struggle for self-development. These barriers are often deeply rooted in Latino culture. The Latina immigrant not only confronts the difficulties of a competitive, individualistic society in the United States, which oppresses her in a variety of ways; she also brings her own internalized marks of oppression. The roles of the obedient woman and mother, as well as other cultural stereotypes, are handicaps to the liberation process. Specifically, many women who come to Mujeres want only to learn English; they do not want to deal with other issues and problems at home. Their participation in class discussions allows them to realize that the problems each of them may face at home or in their lives are not theirs alone. For example, many women experienced problems with health-care providers. They learn that problems often have the same roots — lack of education, lack of job opportunities, racism, discrimination — and that the solutions can only be found collectively. The role of the obedient woman, who follows orders and does not think critically, interferes with the search for self. In fact, many come to Mujeres precisely because they want to change and improve their status as women in order to be better role models for their children.

One of the educational components at Mujeres, the Spanish program, has attempted to sensitively explore these barriers. In this program the women have begun to identify problems, thus obtaining control over their education and, ultimately, over their lives.

An In-Depth Look at the Spanish Program

In one Spanish class we were working with photographs of Latino working families doing different household chores. The family structure varied in each; some showed mothers and children, others had both the parents and children. The *compañeras* wrote about the contents of the photographs. Each person read her work aloud. Later, we commented on what we had written, and compared the families in the pictures to our own families. Maria, Carmen, and Brunilda, all single mothers — like the women in some of the photographs — responded to the question: "Does this family look like yours?" by agreeing that these families were very similar to their own. Juanita, also a single mother, holding a picture of a mother, father, and their children, said, "Yes, this family looks like mine, but in my family the only thing that is missing is the father of my children, but I'm that too."

There are so many Latina women like Juanita, who have the responsibility of raising a family alone. It is difficult to raise healthy human beings capable of leading productive lives —teaching them good values, giving them proper support, being a good role model for their socialization, financially maintaining the home — while playing the role of both mother and father. Eighty percent of the women who participate in Mujeres's Spanish Educational Program are single mothers.[9] While some of these women have been in the United States for as short a time as two or three months and others have been here for as long as twenty-five years, the majority have lived in the States for a total of ten years. The women in this program mainly come from Puerto Rico and the Dominican Republic, although we have had students from Guatemala, El Salvador, and the Cape Verde Islands. Their level of education varies. Some have never been to school, others have completed three to four years of elementary schooling; still others have completed some years of high school. But none have studied beyond high school. All of them receive public assistance. This description clearly demonstrates this group's lack of economic resources. The reasons that these women give for wanting to strive for a good education and claim their right to a better life include insufficient economic resources, lack of a support system, low level of formal education, and the necessity to be a good mother. Matilde, a forty-one-year-old Puerto

---

[9] By "single mothers" we mean women heads of household with children raising a family by themselves without the presence of a paternal figure.

Rican woman, expressed her feelings this way: "I left school because I had to help my family. But I have to start depending on myself, finish high school in order to get a good job and take stock in my self-worth without constantly waiting for help from Welfare."

The Spanish Program is based on the following four premises: 1) education is a universal right; 2) it is necessary to strengthen the native language in order to facilitate the acquisition of a second language; 3) there is a lack of educational resources for low-income families in Latin American countries; and 4) there are few educational opportunities in the United States for low-income Latinas. At Mujeres, education is a right, and not a privilege. With this in mind, the collective started an educational program in Spanish. In this way Mujeres Unidas is contributing to the quality of Latina women's lives.

In order to bridge the gap between these women's lack of education and their adaptation to a new culture and language, Mujeres provides literacy courses in their native language, Spanish. We believe that in order to promote learning a foreign language, it is necessary to master basic reading and writing skills in one's own language (Cummins, 1981). If such skills are not developed, it is difficult to learn another language beyond the acquisition of some listening comprehension and oral communication skills. Furthermore, to approach a complete education, one should at least learn to read and write in one's native language. The need to develop literacy skills in the native language was evident in the women's verbal testimonies of their lives, and the oral dialogues done in ESL classes.

Program participants range in age from twenty to fifty-eight, with an average age of thirty-four. Almost all are heads of household. Primarily because of social conditions in their countries, most of these women — as mentioned earlier — suffer from a lack of formal schooling. Their economic and social development corresponds to that found in some Third World countries, where the possibility of an education is rare, if not nonexistent.[10] Our own personal experiences as Latina women from lower- and lower-middle-class backgrounds have shown us that the educational resources available in our countries are highly limited for the poor. In the Dominican Republic, for example, 33 percent of the population is illiterate, and 40 percent of the labor force is unemployed (Hilsum, 1983). Although Hilsum does not indicate specifically what percentage of women are illiterate, these data suggest that access to social resources such as education and employment is scarce for the poor, including poor women. Indeed, one of the reasons Hilsum offers for these high percentages is the poverty of the country: "A lot of

[10] Philip Berryman (1987) states: "Today Latin America is in its worst economic crisis since the 1930s. Servicing the foreign debt ($360 billion) consumes 40 percent of the continent's exports. In some countries, such as Peru, living standards have fallen back to the levels of twenty years ago. Latin America produces less food per capita than it did forty years ago. . . ." (p. 183). He bases his data on the work of Morris David Morris (1979). Information on the economic conditions in Latin America can also be found in: *North American Congress on Latin America (NACLA), 22*(4), (July-August, 1988); *Mujeres Adelante, 9* (October-December, 1986).

people cannot go to school because they must work from a very young age to help their families attain the basic needs of food, housing, and clothing."[11]

Think for a moment of what life is like for a single woman, with two or more children, who emigrates from her native country to raise her family in the United States. Latin American countries are exploited countries, where a lack of resources for poor people and — in many cases — war combine to force people to emigrate to find better living conditions, a stable income, and adequate health services for their children. Women participating in the Spanish Program often give these as their reasons for coming to the United States. The historical realities of poverty, migration, and war in Latin America serve as evidence in the testimonies of these women. For example, the migration of Puerto Ricans fleeing poverty throughout the 1920s, 1940s, and 1950s has been well documented (see López, 1980; Maldonado-Denis, 1970; Nieves-Falcón, 1971; Rodríguez, 1989). Currently, the migration of Dominicans to cities in Massachusetts is primarily a result of the poverty and lack of educational opportunities in their country. The presence of war in Central America has caused women to emigrate into the United States (see Mental Health Committee, 1989; Organización Panamericana de la Salud, 1988). In addition, the women have described some of the personal conditions that motivated them to look for new horizons in the United States. Many of these women emigrated in order to flee from personal problems and psychological and physical abuse by their husbands or partners.

Seven current participants in the Spanish Literacy course were forced to leave school when they were younger. In the patriarchal societies of their Latin American countries, especially in low socioeconomic groups, learning to add, subtract, read, and write is still believed to be sufficient education. Once they are educated at that level, young women must stay home to help support the rest of the family. Carmen, a forty-eight-year-old Puerto Rican woman and a pre-GED student, states, "My father took me out of school as soon as I learned to read and write a little. According to him that was all I needed to learn since I had to help my mother with the housework and take care of my little brothers and sisters." Society has forced women to take on the responsibilities of home and family; this is true not only in Latin American countries, but even in those, like Puerto Rico, that are more industrialized. Carmen's testimony reflects current realities: even though women may be part of the labor force, society still imposes on them the additional role of housewife. This is what is known as *doble carga* (double work). Women

---

[11] Hilsum (1983) explains that in the Dominican Republic, government credit, irrigation, and desalination schemes are directed almost exclusively into export crops. For example, research undertaken by Women of the South in 1980 showed that 9 percent of the cattle from the region was eaten elsewhere, as was 80 percent of the fish, 92 percent of the bananas, and 80 percent of the grapefruit and kidney beans. She states: "As the men tramp the region looking for work, the women often are left to support and bring up the children. When women manage to find work, it is usually as small traders, domestic servants, or farm laborers. They fight a never-ending battle against poor housing, lack of sanitation, ill health and malnutrition" (p. 116).

must work outside the home to support their families in addition to doing all the housework. Society limits the educational opportunities of women, and does not recognize the value of their roles. Thus, we can say that women's lack of education is closely tied to social factors.

Marcia Rivera-Quintero, a Puerto Rican feminist, writes that

> The home constituted the center of activity for women given that the biological reproductive functions developed there. The duties that peasant women carried out, set the basis for generalization and hegemony of the conceptualization of housework as women's work. The production and biological reproduction of the human species were closely linked processes and the former was subordinated to the patriarchal family. (1980, p. 13)

Even though Quintero's study examined the lives of women at the beginning of this century, it remains relevant today, chiefly because industrialization in Puerto Rico is situated in the capital and coastal towns — the areas of highest economic value. Therefore, the benefits of industrialization — such as job opportunities, modernization, and more education — did not, and in many cases still have not, reached rural areas of the island, particularly the center.

For many of our students the home environment has provided the only means of socialization. Since they do not have jobs, they do not have the opportunity to leave the house regularly. If they have children, they do not have money for childcare or for public transportation. At Mujeres, we face this reality daily. Because of these limitations and the scarce resources available, the need for these women to be educated is vital. We believe that if women are educated, they increase their opportunities to find decent jobs, which will improve their financial situation and better their living conditions. At Mujeres, women have the chance and the space to socialize by exchanging concerns, ideas, and realities with other women and, therefore, to discover new things that can improve their lives.

Finally, we would like to point out that the scarcity of educational opportunities for many of these women in the United States makes our Spanish Program indispensable. In 1980 women made up 52 percent of the Latino population in Massachusetts, and women single heads of household made up 19.4 percent of the Latino population in the United States.[12] We want to note that many low-income Latinas who are single heads of household are not counted in the population census because they are undocumented in this country. The crucial need for education becomes even more striking when we add that only 43 percent of Latinas in the nation have completed high school.[13] The testimonies of women at Mujeres link the high dropout rate to language barriers and the quality of the education they received in the United States.[14]

---

[12] Data from the 1980 population census, projections for 1985.

[13] Data from the 1980 population census.

[14] The quality of education received by minority groups in the United States has been questioned in recent literature (see, for example, Rodríguez, 1989).

The Spanish Program has two components: the Literacy Program (pre-GED) and the course for preparation for the GED exam. Mujeres Unidas's literacy program has been named pre-GED because it prepares students to develop basic skills in reading, writing, and arithmetic. Mastery of these skills is required for the GED. Nearly 90 percent of the women enter directly into the GED course because they already have these skills. Ideally, when women finish the pre-GED course they will move on into the GED program. In fact in the summer of 1989 we had our first student, Georgina Cruz, move from the pre-GED to the GED course.

Our experience with the program has shown us that learning to read and write is a slow process for adult women, many of whom have not had previous experience in an educational program. Thus, we have built into the program the time and space for the women to adapt to and feel at ease in a new environment, an environment with different responsibilities from those of their households. The program's final objectives are to prepare women to obtain their high school diplomas and pursue higher education. We encourage them to work on their English reading and writing skills so that fluency in both Spanish and English is developed and strengthened.

The Spanish program began in September, 1987, and so far, twenty women have obtained their high school diplomas. Currently, 28 women are enrolled in the Spanish courses: 11 Dominicans, 15 Puerto Ricans, 1 Guatemalan, and 1 Cape Verdean. Included in this total are two former GED students who are now paid tutors for the Spanish program and are currently students in the ESL program. By allowing graduates of the program to stay on as tutors, we feel we are encouraging the women's participation in their own educational process.

Students actively participate in the development of curriculum based on their learning needs. The curriculum is open to the integration of topics and themes the students deem necessary. For example, if a student feels the need to have information about an issue, she will express this need to the group, which then decides how to address this in the discussion. Some of the topics suggested include: domestic violence, rape, machismo, racism, child psychology, welfare benefits, adolescent problems, menopause, drugs, AIDS, and historical facts about their respective countries. In practice, it is a very informal process, based on the principle that education should go beyond what is dictated in books.

We believe that effective education is one which generates meaningful change — for example, changing the roles imposed by society on women. Specific examples of social roles imposed by society are the tripartite role of women in society (mother, wife, and housewife) and stereotypes of women's behavior, such as submissiveness and obedience. We realize that women are oppressed as a consequence of the imposition of such roles. The existence of these beliefs in patriarchal societies of Third World countries, as well as in societies of industrialized countries such as the United States, makes us affirm the need for social change which will allow us, as women, to transform our roles. We understand that education is one of the means by which we can achieve meaningful change in women's history and the history of society. Based on this, the Spanish program utilizes a methodology that springs from the pedagogical philosophy of Brazilian educator Paulo Freire. The program is based on four beliefs: that we must develop a process to understand oppression; that learning language is more than learning grammatical rules; that reading the word is reading the world; and that education is action.

First, we understand that in order to achieve social changes there must be a liberating process that allows us to recognize our condition as oppressed women (Freire, 1971). To engage in such a process we need to have a clear understanding of our native language (Cummins, 1981). We confront the question: How can we begin to liberate ourselves in a language that we do not understand?

Second, using Freire's conceptualization of oppression, we believe that understanding a language goes beyond familiarity with grammatical forms of that language. That is to say, grammatical rules are only one part of any language system; such rules are subject to a communicative context. Language is communication. Through it we can express what and how we feel and think, and we facilitate social interrelationships among people. In this view, words are seen as important, not because of their grammatical characteristics, but because of the meanings and world visions they reflect. Therefore, words are not detached from reality, but rather, the reality is signified by the words.

When we learn to use our language critically we gain a deeper understanding of our reality. Thus, we not only educate ourselves with respect to the text we study, but also with respect to its context. For instance, if we are discussing the word *educación* (education), not only do we learn to write it, but also to understand its significance in terms of the influence it can have on our own lives. The text is a word, *educación*, with its grammatical form, spelling, and any identifying accent rules. The context is understanding what education means for us. Education could be a way of understanding and reacting to the social and political environment, or of identifying and understanding oppressive structures and obtaining control over ourselves and our lives.

To put this methodology into practice we use popular theater techniques as learning tools. These techniques are adapted from the work of the French director, Auguste Boalt, who incorporates Freire's pedagogical theory into theater as a means of social education. Good results can be achieved working with Latino people through theater, because culturally we are very expressive, frequently using body language to communicate. There is no teacher in the theater forum, although students can volunteer to serve as facilitators for a specific session. There is also no philosophy of instruction per se, other than the desire to look for solutions to certain problems.

Theater forum is one of our most successful resources, a vehicle for presenting alternative solutions to enacted situations. First, a theme is suggested and a drama created to present it. The drama is performed, utilizing both language and physical expression. An anti-model, or a response to a negative or unacceptable aspect of the situation being performed, is then chosen by the participants. Those watching the action interrupt it when they feel that there is a disagreement between their own interpretation of the event and what is being presented. In order to present their alternative they must in turn become actresses, replacing the person whose message they disagree with. Through verbal and physical expression they present their alternative solutions. At the end there is an open discussion with all the participants to stimulate a critical view of the theme presented.

An activity during Mujeres's AIDS education month will serve to illustrate this process. The Spanish and ESL classes met for a theater forum session. After completing a values-clarification exercise in which myths and realities about AIDS were discussed, the students developed a theater piece on a situation involving AIDS. One situation concerned a mother who found that her son was gay and at a very high risk of getting or being exposed to the disease. Two women played the roles of the mother and the son. The woman playing the mother was told by the facilitator to be the anti-model — a mother who cannot accept the homosexuality of her son. The situation was presented in a conversation between the mother and the son that developed into an argument. The son wanted to be accepted as a homosexual, and as a homosexual at risk of getting AIDS. The mother blamed him for all that was happening in their lives. At some point during the situation one of the students in the audience watching stopped the action and took on the role of the mother herself. In her performance, she tried to be more open to her son's problems and to look for professional help, thus suggesting an alternative.

At the beginning of each semester we carry out an exercise of theater forum, using the meaning of education in the lives of the participants as a theme. This is how we try to recognize the importance and influence that education might have on us. Another session of theater forum serves to illustrate this point. This time the situation was about a woman sent to Mujeres to study by a local Welfare office. The woman was very reluctant to do it, because education had no meaning to her at that time; she was content with watching soap operas on television — the anti-model. Different students stopped the action to provide alternatives to the anti-model by talking about what education meant to them. Some of their ideas, as they presented them in the theater forum, were that education was a way to improve the qualities of their lives by providing them and their children with more opportunities for development and growth, enabling them to face the world as active participants.

The impact that this nontraditional teaching approach has had is amazing; according to these students, expanding their reality in new and refreshing ways has led them to become more involved in their own educational process. Expanding their reality is very important for the women who attend our program, given the limited socialization to which they have been subjected. One participant states:

> Mujeres Unidas and its Spanish program have opened up doors for my future. Not only do I learn specific subject matters, but I also have learned a lot about the realities of the world around me and how to face the world better. I've grown tremendously as a human being.
>
> — *Genoveva, Puerto Rican mother of two*

Third, we believe that reading a word is reading reality. When women understand the meaning of a word and the impact that meaning may have in their lives, they understand a reality which in one way or another is linked to the role they are playing in society. Thus, conditions are created to stimulate critical thinking of the historical moment in which we are living. This is how we begin to become conscious of the reality we live in as Latinas in this country.

We need to understand that we are cultural beings and that we respond to the cultural patterns we have internalized. When women have a clear understanding of these patterns, they reassert their own culture; who they are, and the goals they wish to achieve for their own growth, become clearer. This process makes it easier to question the assumptions of other cultures as well. North American culture has standards very different from those of Latino cultures. Our experience as Latina women tells us that if we understand where we come from we will know better where we are going.

The final objective of liberation pedagogy is action. Once we know who we are and where we come from, we can better confront North American culture and change patterns of women's oppression in this country. When knowledge leads to action, social change is achieved, because "one makes one's presence known." An example of taking action comes from Carmen Torres, a student of the GED class who participated as Mujeres's spokeswoman in a rally for the Gateways City Program in March of 1989. She spoke to the members of the Gateways Advisory Council about the problems that low-income Latina women face in getting an education in this country. She stated: "We do not have money to afford daycare services so we can go to school. We really need programs like this [Gateways] to have the chance to contribute in a better way to the future." Clearly, she is articulating her concerns and the concerns of other women in similar situations. She brought an issue to a governing body to let them know that issues facing Latina women need to be addressed. We feel that women's experiences in class discussions, participation in theater forums, and other activities at Mujeres that allow women to speak, serve as a practice arena for speaking their voice in society in general.

Implementation of this methodology presents us with certain disadvantages. In many cases, for example, fear of the challenge that comes along with knowledge of an oppressive reality is hard to overcome. The learning process is often slow because it requires full participation of the students in their educational process. Despite these difficulties, we reaffirm the effectiveness of this method, reflected in student work and achievement. At the present time, all the *compañeras* in the GED class who have taken the exam have passed it with very high scores.

The learning process has been one in which mutual support between student and teacher is essential to success. The communication and solidarity developed by women in the class, at the root of the participatory process, helped overcome fears one by one, such as fear of the challenge, fear of coming to school after being an adult, fear of the unknown, fear of power, fear of failure, fear of not being able to learn to read and write, fear of speaking another language, and fear of being rejected.

Also, it is important to mention that the students' attendance and retention has been astounding; the women who were able to get here stayed here. Of the few who have left, most keep in constant contact with Mujeres Unidas, and the ones who do not keep in touch often return. One student states:

> I was a student at Mujeres from 1984–1986. I finished the level 4 ESL class and I had to move on. What I learned at Mujeres was the most important learning I have done in my life. After leaving Mujeres I went to Puerto Rico for two years. . . . I believe now that I lost a lot of time there. On returning to the United States I was feeling very frustrated and when I asked for my treasured school I found out that they were offering GED preparation and I immediately signed up. Now I feel so much happier with the hope that I am reaching my fulfillment.
>
> — *Carmen Fortis, mother of three*

We cannot overlook the impact of the Spanish program at an individual level, where women are raising their consciousness as oppressed people and are realizing the importance of education in their native language. The impact can also be seen at the community level, with the creation of new leaders. One example of this is Mujeres's support group, *compañeras*. As mentioned earlier, this group was formed thanks to the initiative of a student who is at present a recovering alcoholic. She has an incredible will to move forward in her life, as the formation of the support group reflects. She has just received her high school equivalency degree after taking the GED course at Mujeres. The program's impact is also manifested at a societal level in the form of student action, for example, in uniting to demand rights at a local or national rally. Another example of students taking action occurred during "AIDS Month," when, after presenting a video on AIDS, one student from the GED class and another student from the pre-GED class suggested showing the video to their husbands and partners in order to educate the men on AIDS prevention. We see these kinds of actions as contributing to the transformation of society and the creation of history.

One way of measuring success is to document what the students accomplish once they have graduated. One of the program's students published two of her poems in the book, *Need I Say More*, published by the Adult Literacy Resource Institute in Boston (Spring, 1988). Another student received an award from the Boston Public Schools for her work in the struggle to maintain bilingual programs in certain high schools. Both carried out their work in their native language, Spanish.

In one way or another, in spite of economic, societal, political, and familial barriers, all the women involved in the development of Mujeres Unidas are committed to social change. When you acknowledge the tremendous necessity for changing the present power structures which perpetuate racism, the patriarchal system, sexism, and homophobia, and you acknowledge the economic and political oppression of certain parts of society, you begin to understand the depth of the commitment the women have made toward taking action in order to achieve social change. We believe that in order to take action, it is necessary to continue discovering our truth, our language, and our word. With these discoveries we can then challenge the existing forces of oppression and institutionalize change. At Mujeres Unidas, change has been institutionalized through painstaking educational activities and an innovative administration; here everyone learns from each other.

Freire and a
Feminist Pedagogy
of Difference

KATHLEEN WEILER

In this chapter, Kathleen Weiler presents a feminist critique that challenges tradi-
tional Western knowledge systems. As an educator, Weiler is interested in the im-
plications of this critique for both the theory and practice of education. She begins
with a discussion of the liberatory pedagogy of Paulo Freire and the profound
importance of his work. She then questions Freire's assumptions of a single kind
of experience of oppression and his abstract goals for liberation. A feminist peda-
gogy, she claims, offers a more complex vision of liberatory pedagogy. Weiler traces
the growth of feminist epistemology from the early consciousness-raising groups to
current women's studies programs. She identifies three ways that a feminist peda-
gogy, while reflecting critically on Freire's ideas, also builds on and enriches his
pedagogy: in its questioning of the role and authority of the teacher; in its recog-
nition of the importance of personal experience as a source of knowledge; and in
its exploration of the perspectives of people of different races, classes, and cultures.

We are living in a period of profound challenges to traditional Western epistemology and political theory. These challenges, couched in the language of postmodernist theory and in postcolonialist critiques, reflect the rapid transformation of the economic and political structure of the world order: the impact of transnational capital; the ever more comprehensive integration of resources, labor, and markets; the pervasiveness of media and consumer images. This interdependent world system is based on the exploitation of oppressed groups, but the system at the same time calls forth oppositional cultural forms that give voice to the conditions of these groups. White male bourgeois dominance is being challenged by people of color, women, and other oppressed groups, who assert the validity of their own knowledge and demand social justice and equality in numerous political

Harvard Educational Review Vol. 61 No. 4 November 1991, 449–474

and cultural struggles. In the intellectual sphere, this shifting world system has led to a shattering of Western metanarratives and to the variety of stances of postmodernist and cultural-identity theory. A major theoretical challenge to traditional Western knowledge systems is emerging from feminist theory, which has been increasingly influenced by postmodernist and cultural-identity theory. Feminist theory, like other contemporary approaches, validates difference, challenges universal claims to truth, and seeks to create social transformation in a world of shifting and uncertain meanings.

In education, these profound shifts are evident on two levels: first, at the level of practice, as excluded and formerly silenced groups challenge dominant approaches to learning and to definitions of knowledge; and second, at the level of theory, as modernist claims to universal truth are called into question.[1] These challenges to accepted truths have been raised not only to the institutions and theories that defend the status quo, but also to the critical or liberatory pedagogies that emerged in the 1960s and 1970s. Feminist educational critics, like other theorists influenced by postmodernism and theories of difference, want to retain the vision of social justice and transformation that underlies liberatory pedagogies, but they find that their claims to universal truths and their assumptions of a collective experience of oppression do not adequately address the realities of their own confusing and often tension-filled classrooms. This consciousness of the inadequacy of classical liberatory pedagogies has been particularly true for feminist educators, who are acutely aware of the continuing force of sexism and patriarchal structures and of the power of race, sexual preference, physical ability, and age to divide teachers from students and students from one another.

Paulo Freire is without question the most influential theorist of critical or liberatory education. His theories have profoundly influenced literacy programs throughout the world and what has come to be called critical pedagogy in the United States. His theoretical works, particularly *Pedagogy of the Oppressed*, provide classic statements of liberatory or critical pedagogy based on universal claims of truth.[2] Feminist pedagogy as it has developed in the United States provides a historically situated example of a critical pedagogy in practice. Feminist conceptions of education are similar to Freire's pedagogy in a variety of ways, and feminist educators often cite Freire as the educational theorist who comes closest to the approach and goals of feminist pedagogy.[3] Both feminist pedagogy as it is usually defined and Freirean pedagogy rest upon visions of social transformation; underlying both are certain common assumptions concerning oppression, consciousness, and historical change. Both pedagogies assert the existence of oppression in people's material conditions of existence and as a part of consciousness; both rest on a view of consciousness as more than a sum of dominating discourses, but as containing within it a critical capacity — what Antonio Gramsci called "good sense"; and both thus see human beings as subjects and actors in history and hold a strong commitment to justice and a vision of a better world and of the potential for liberation.[4] These ideals have powerfully influenced teachers and students in a wide range of educational settings, both formal and informal.

But in action, the goals of liberation or opposition to oppression have not always been easy to understand or achieve. As universal goals, these ideals do not address the specificity of people's lives; they do not directly analyze the contradictions between conflicting oppressed groups or the ways in which a single individual can experience oppression in one sphere while being privileged or oppressive in another. Feminist and Freirean teachers are in many ways engaged in what Teresa de Lauretis has called "shifting the ground of signs," challenging accepted meanings and relationships that occur at what she calls "political or more often micropolitical" levels, groupings that "produce no texts as such, but by shifting the 'ground' of a given sign . . . effectively intervene upon codes of perception as well as ideological codes."[5] But in attempting to challenge dominant values and to "shift the ground of signs," feminist and Freirean teachers raise conflicts for themselves and for their students, who also are historically situated and whose own subjectivities are often contradictory and in process. These conflicts have become increasingly clear as both Freirean and feminist pedagogies are put into practice. Attempting to implement these pedagogies without acknowledging the conflict not only of divided consciousness — what Audre Lorde calls "the oppressor within us" — but also the conflicts among groups trying to work together to name and struggle against oppression — among teachers and students in classrooms, or among political groups working for change in very specific areas — can lead to anger, frustration, and a retreat to safer or more traditional approaches.[6] The numerous accounts of the tensions of trying to put liberatory pedagogies into practice demonstrate the need to reexamine the assumptions of the classic texts of liberatory pedagogy and to consider the various issues that have arisen in attempts at critical and liberatory classroom practice.[7]

As a White feminist writing and teaching from the traditions of both critical pedagogy and feminist theory, these issues are of particular concern to me. In this article, I examine and critique the classic liberatory pedagogy of Paulo Freire, particularly as it is presented in *Pedagogy of the Oppressed*, his most famous and influential text. I then examine the development and practice of feminist pedagogy, which emerged in a particular historical and political moment in the United States, and which, as a situated pedagogy, provides an example of some of the difficulties of putting these ideals into practice and suggests at the same time some possible theoretical and practical directions for liberatory pedagogies in general. I argue that an exploration of the conflicts and concerns that have arisen for feminist teachers attempting to put into practice their versions of a feminist pedagogy can help enrich and re-envision Freirean goals of liberation and social progress. This emerging pedagogy does not reject the goals of justice — the end of oppression, and liberation — but frames them more specifically in the context of historically defined struggles and calls for the articulation of interests and identity on the part of teacher and theorist as well as student. This approach questions whether the oppressed cannot act also as oppressors and challenges the idea of a commonality of oppression. It raises questions about common experience as a source of knowledge, the pedagogical authority of the teacher, and the nature of political and pedagogical struggle.

The Pedagogy of Paulo Freire

Freire's pedagogy developed in particular historical and political circumstances of neocolonialism and imperialism. As is well known, Freire's methods developed originally from his work with peasants in Brazil and later in Chile and Guinea-Bissau.[8] Freire's thought thus needs to be understood in the context of the political and economic situation of the developing world. In Freire's initial formulation, oppression was conceived in class terms and education was viewed in the context of peasants' and working people's revolutionary struggles. Equally influential in Freire's thought and pedagogy were the influence of radical Christian thought and the revolutionary role of liberation theology in Latin America. As is true for other radical Christians in Latin America, Freire's personal knowledge of extreme poverty and suffering challenged his deeply felt Christian faith grounded in the ethical teachings of Jesus in the Gospels. Freire's pedagogy is thus founded on a moral imperative to side with the oppressed that emerges from both his Christian faith and his knowledge and experience of suffering in the society in which he grew up and lived. Freire has repeatedly stated that his pedagogical method cannot simply be transferred to other settings, but that each historical site requires the development of a pedagogy appropriate to that setting. In his most recent work, he has also addressed sexism and racism as systems of oppression that must be considered as seriously as class oppression.[9] Nonetheless, Freire is frequently read without consideration for the context of the specific settings in which his work developed and without these qualifications in mind. His most commonly read text still is his first book to be published in English, *Pedagogy of the Oppressed*. In this classic text, Freire presents the epistemological basis for his pedagogy and discusses the concepts of oppression, conscientization, and dialogue that are at the heart of his pedagogical project, but as he enacted it in settings in the developing world and as it has been appropriated by radical teachers in other settings.

Freire organizes his approach to liberatory pedagogy in terms of a dualism between the oppressed and the oppressors and between humanization and dehumanization. This organization of thoughts in terms of opposing forces reflects Freire's own experiences of literacy work with the poor in Brazil, a situation in which the lines between oppressor and oppressed were clear. For Freire, humanization is the goal of liberation; it has not yet been achieved, nor can it be achieved so long as the oppressors oppress the oppressed. That is, liberation and humanization will not occur if the roles of oppressor and oppressed are simply reversed. If humanization is to be realized, new relationships among human beings must be created:

> Because it is a distortion of being more fully human, sooner or later being less human leads the oppressed to struggle against those who made them so. In order for this struggle to have meaning, the oppressed must not, in seeking to regain their humanity (which is a way to create it), become in turn oppressors of the oppressors, but rather restorers of the humanity of both.[10]

The struggle against oppression leading to humanization is thus utopian and visionary. As Freire says elsewhere, "To be utopian is not to be merely idealistic or impractical but rather to engage in denunciation and annunciation."[11] By denunciation, Freire refers to the naming and analysis of existing structures of oppression; by annunciation, he means the creation of new forms of relationships and being in the world as a result of mutual struggle against oppression. Thus Freire presents a theoretical justification for a pedagogy that aims to critique existing forms of oppression and to transform the world, thereby creating new ways of being, or humanization.

Radical educators throughout the world have used *Pedagogy of the Oppressed* as the theoretical justification for their work. As an eloquent and impassioned statement of the need for and possibility of change through reading the world and the word, there is no comparable contemporary text.[12] But when we look at *Pedagogy of the Oppressed* from the perspective of recent feminist theory and pedagogy, certain problems arise that may reflect the difficulties that have sometimes arisen when Freire's ideas are enacted in specific settings. The challenges of recent feminist theory do not imply the rejection of Freire's goals for what he calls a pedagogy for liberation; feminists certainly share Freire's emphasis on seeing human beings as the subjects and not the objects of history. A critical feminist rereading of Freire, however, points to ways in which the project of Freirean pedagogy, like that of feminist pedagogy, may be enriched and re-envisioned.

From a feminist perspective, *Pedagogy of the Oppressed* is striking in its use of the male referent, a usage that was universal when the book was written in the 1960s.[13] Much more troublesome, however, is the abstract quality of terms such as humanization, which do not address the particular meanings imbued by men and women, Black and White, or other groups. The assumption of *Pedagogy of the Oppressed* is that in struggling against oppression, the oppressed will move toward true humanity. But this leaves unaddressed the forms of oppression experienced by different actors, the possibility of struggles among people oppressed differently by different groups — what Cameron McCarthy calls "nonsynchrony of oppression."[14] This assumption also presents humanization as a universal, without considering the various definitions this term may bring forth from people of different groups. When Freire speaks of the oppressed needing to fight the tendency to become "sub-oppressors," he means that the oppressed have only the pattern of oppression before them as a way of being in a position other than the one they are in. As Freire writes, "Their ideal is to be men; but for them, to be men is to be oppressors. This is their model of humanity."[15] What is troubling here is not that "men" is used for human beings, but that the model of oppressor implied here is based on the immediate oppressor of men — in this case, bosses over peasants or workers. What is not addressed is the possibility of simultaneous contradictory positions of oppression and dominance: the man oppressed by his boss could at the same time oppress his wife, for example, or the White woman oppressed by sexism could exploit the Black woman. By framing this discussion in such abstract terms, Freire slides over the contradictions and tensions within social settings in which overlapping forms of oppression exist.

This usage of "the oppressed" in the abstract also raises difficulties in Freire's use of experience as the means of acquiring a radical literacy, "reading the world and the word." At the heart of Freire's pedagogy is the insistence that all people are subjects and knowers of the world. Their political literacy will emerge from their reading of the world — that is, their own experience. This reading will lead to collective knowledge and action. But what if that experience is divided? What if different truths are discovered in reading the world from different positions? For Freire, education as the practice of freedom "denies that men are abstract, isolated, independent, and unattached to the world. . . . Authentic reflection considers neither abstract man nor the world without men, but men in their relations with the world."[16] But implicit in this vision is the assumption that, when the oppressed perceive themselves in relation to the world, they will act together collectively to transform the world and to move toward their own humanization. The nature of their perception of the world and their oppression is implicitly assumed to be uniform for all the oppressed. The possibility of a contradictory experience of oppression among the oppressed is absent. As Freire says:

> Accordingly, the point of departure must always be with men in the "here and now," which constitutes the situation within which they are submerged, from which they emerge, and in which they intervene. Only by starting from this situation — which determines their perception of it — can they begin to move.[17]

The assumption again is that the oppressed, these men, are submerged in a common situation of oppression, and that their shared knowledge of that oppression will lead them to collective action.

Central to Freire's pedagogy is the practice of conscientization; that is, coming to a consciousness of oppression and a commitment to end that oppression. Conscientization is based on this common experience of oppression. Through this reading of the world, the oppressed will come to knowledge. The role of the teacher in this process is to instigate a dialogue between teacher and student, based on their common ability to know the world and to act as subjects in the world. But the question of the authority and power of the teacher, particularly those forms of power based on the teacher's subject position as raced, classed, gendered, and so on, is not addressed by Freire. There is, again, the assumption that the teacher is "on the same side" as the oppressed, and that as teachers and students engage together in a dialogue about the world, they will uncover together the same reality, the same oppression, and the same liberation. In *Pedagogy of the Oppressed*, the teacher is presented as a generic man whose interests will be with the oppressed as they mutually discover the mechanisms of oppression. The subjectivity of the Freirean teacher is, in this sense, what Gayatri Chakravorty Spivak refers to as "transparent."[18] In fact, of course, teachers are not abstract; they are women or men of particular races, classes, ages, abilities, and so on. The teacher will be seen and heard by students not as an abstraction, but as a particular person with a certain defined history and relationship to the world. In a later book, Freire argues that the teacher has to assume authority, but must do so without becoming authoritarian. In this recognition of the teacher's authority, Freire acknowledges the difference between teacher and students:

> The educator continues to be different from the students, but, and now for me this is the central question, the difference between them, if the teacher is democratic, if his or her political dream is a *liberating* one, is that he or she cannot permit the necessary difference between the teacher and the students to become "antagonistic."[19]

In this passage, Freire acknowledges the power of the teacher by virtue of the structural role of "teacher" within a hierarchical institution and, under the best of circumstances, by virtue of the teacher's greater experience and knowledge. But Freire does not go on to investigate what the other sources of "antagonism" in the classroom might be. However much he provides a valuable guide to the use of authority by the liberatory teacher, he never addresses the question of other forms of power held by the teacher by virtue of race, gender, or class that may lead to antagonisms. Without naming these sources of tension, it is difficult to address or build upon them to challenge existing structures of power and subjectivities. Without recognizing more clearly the implicit power and limitations of the position of teacher, calls for a collective liberation or for opposition to oppression slide over the surface of the tensions that may emerge among teachers and students as subjects with conflicting interests and histories and with different kinds of knowledge and power. A number of questions are thus left unaddressed in *Pedagogy of the Oppressed:* How are we to situate ourselves in relation to the struggle of others? How are we to address our own contradictory positions as oppressors and oppressed? Where are we to look for liberation when our collective "reading of the world" reveals contradictory and conflicting experiences and struggles? The Freirean vision of the oppressed as undifferentiated and as the source of unitary political action, the transparency of the subjectivity of the Freirean teacher, and the claims of universal goals of liberation and social transformation fail to provide the answers to these questions.

Calling into question the universal and abstract claims of *Pedagogy of the Oppressed* is certainly not to argue that Freire's pedagogy should be rejected or discarded. The ethical stance of Freire in terms of praxis and his articulation of people's worth and ability to know and change the world are an essential basis for radical pedagogies in opposition to oppression. Freire's thought illuminates the central question of political action in a world increasingly without universals. Freire, like liberation theologians such as Sharon Welch, positions himself on the side of the oppressed; he claims the moral imperative to act in the world. As Peter McLaren has commented in reference to Freire's political stand, "The task of liberating others from their suffering may not emerge from some transcendental fiat, yet it nevertheless compels us to affirm our humanity in solidarity with victims."[20] But in order better to seek the affirmation of our own humanity and to seek to end suffering and oppression, I am arguing for a more situated theory of oppression and subjectivity, and for the need to consider the contradictions of such universal claims of truth or process.

In the next section of this chapter, I explore feminist pedagogy as an example of a situated pedagogy of liberation. Like Freirean pedagogy, feminist pedagogy is based on assumptions of the power of consciousness raising, the existence of oppression and the possibility of ending it, and the desire for social transformation. But in its historical development, feminist pedagogy has revealed the shortcomings that emerge in the attempt to enact a pedagogy that assumes a universal experience and abstract goals. In the attempt of feminist pedagogy to address these issues, a more complex vision of a liberatory pedagogy is being developed and explored.

Feminist Pedagogy, Consciousness Raising, and Women's Liberation

Feminist pedagogy in colleges and universities has developed in conjunction with the growth of women's studies and what is inclusively called "the new scholarship on women." These developments within universities — the institutionalization of women's studies as programs and departments and the challenge to existing canons and disciplines by the new scholarship on women and by feminist theory — are reflected in the classroom teaching methods that have come to be loosely termed feminist pedagogy. Defining exactly what feminist pedagogy means in practice, however, is difficult. It is easier to describe the various methods used in specific women's studies courses and included by feminist teachers claiming the term feminist pedagogy than it is to provide a coherent definition.[21] But common to the claims of feminist teachers is the goal of providing students with the skills to continue political work as feminists after they have left the university. Nancy Schniedewind makes a similar claim for what she calls "feminist process," which she characterizes as "both a feminist vision of equalitarian personal relations and societal forms and the confidence and skills to make their knowledge and vision functional in the world."[22]

The pedagogy of feminist teachers is based on certain assumptions about knowledge, power, and political action that can be traced beyond the academy to the political activism of the women's movement in the 1960s. This same commitment to social change through the transformative potential of education underlay Freire's pedagogy in Brazil during the same period. Women's studies at the university level have since come to encompass a wide variety of political stances and theoretical approaches. Socialist feminism, liberal feminism, radical feminism, and postmodern feminism all view issues from their different perspectives. Nonetheless, feminist pedagogy continues to echo the struggles of its origins and to retain a vision of social activism. Virtually all women's studies courses and programs at least partially reflect this critical, oppositional, and activist stance, even within programs now established and integrated into the bureaucratic structures of university life. As Linda Gordon points out:

> Women's studies did not arise accidentally, as the product of someone's good idea, but was created by a social movement for women's liberation with a sharp critique of the whole structure of society. By its very existence, women's studies constitutes a critique of the university and the body of knowledge it imparts.[23]

Despite tensions and splits within feminism at a theoretical level and in the context of women's studies programs in universities, the political commitment of women's liberation that Gordon refers to continues to shape feminist pedagogy. Thus, like Freirean pedagogy, feminist pedagogy is grounded in a vision of social change. And, like Freirean pedagogy, feminist pedagogy rests on truth claims of the primacy of experience and consciousness that are grounded in historically situated social change movements. Key to understanding the methods and epistemological claims of feminist pedagogy is an understanding of its origins in more grassroots political activity, particularly in the consciousness-raising groups of the women's liberation movement of the late 1960s and early 1970s.

Women's consciousness-raising groups began to form more or less spontaneously in northeastern and western U.S. cities in late 1967 among White women who had been active in the civil rights and new left movements.[24] In a fascinating parallel to the rise of the women's suffrage movement out of the abolitionist movement in the mid-nineteenth century, these activist and politically committed women came to apply the universal demands for equality and justice of the civil rights movement to their own situation as women.[25] While public actions such as the Miss America protest of 1968, mass meetings, and conferences were organized in this early period, the unique organizational basis for the women's liberation movement was grounded in the small groups of women who came together for what came to be known as consciousness raising. Early consciousness-raising groups, based on friendship and common political commitment, focused on the discussion of shared experiences of sexuality, work, family, and participation in the male-dominated left political movement. Consciousness raising focused on collective political change rather than on individual therapy. The groups were unstructured and local — they could be formed anywhere and did not follow formal guidelines — but they used the same sorts of methods because these methods addressed common problems. One woman remembers the first meeting of what became her consciousness-raising group:

> The flood broke loose gradually and then more swiftly. We talked about our families, our mothers, our fathers, our siblings; we talked about our men; we talked about school; we talked about "the movement" (which meant new left men). For hours we talked and unburdened our souls and left feeling high and planning to meet again the following week.[26]

Perhaps the clearest summary of consciousness raising from this period can be found in Kathie Sarachild's essay, "Consciousness Raising: A Radical Weapon."[27] In this article, Sarachild, a veteran of the civil rights movement in the South and a member of Redstockings, one of the earliest and most influential women's groups, presents an account that is both descriptive and proscriptive.[28] She makes it clear that consciousness raising arose spontaneously among small groups of women and that she is describing and summarizing a collective process that can be used by other groups of women. Fundamental to Sarachild's description of consciousness raising is its grounding in the need for political action. She describes the emergence of the method of consciousness raising among a group of women who considered themselves radicals in the sense of demanding fundamental changes in society. As Sarachild comments:

> We were interested in getting to the roots of problems in society. You might say we wanted to pull up weeds in the garden by their roots, not just pick off the leaves at the top to make things look good momentarily. Women's liberation was started by women who considered themselves radicals in this sense.[29]

A second fundamental aspect of consciousness raising is the reliance on experience and feeling. According to Sarachild, the focus on examining women's own experience came from a profound distrust of accepted authority and truth. These claims about what was valuable and true tended to be accepting of existing assumptions about women's "inherent nature" and "proper place." In order to call those truths into question (truths we might now call hegemonic and that Foucault, for example, would tie to structures of power), women had nowhere to turn except to their own experience. Sarachild describes the process in her group:

> In the end the group decided to raise its consciousness by studying women's lives by topics like childhood, jobs, motherhood, etc. We'd do any outside reading we wanted to and thought was important. But our starting point for discussion, as well as our test of the accuracy of what any of the books said, would be the actual experience we had in these areas.[30]

The last aspect of consciousness raising was a common sharing of experience in a collective, leaderless group. As Michele Russell points out, this sharing is similar to the practice of "testifying" in the Black church, and depends upon openness and trust in the group.[31] The assumption underlying this sharing of stories was the existence of commonality among women; as Sarachild puts it, "we made the assumption, an assumption basic to consciousness raising, that most women were like ourselves — not different."[32]

The model for consciousness raising among the Redstockings, as with other early groups, came from the experiences of many of the women as organizers in the civil rights movement in the South. Sarachild, for instance, cites the example of the Student Nonviolent Coordinating Committee, and quotes Stokely Carmichael when she argues for the need for people to organize in order to understand their own conditions of existence and to fight their own struggles. Other sources cited by Sarachild include the nineteenth-century suffragist Ernestine Rose, Mao Zedong, Malcolm X, and the practice of "speaking bitterness" in the Chinese revolution described by William Hinton in *Fanshen*.[33] Both the example of the civil rights movement and the revolutionary tradition of the male writers that provided the model for early consciousness raising supported women's commitment to political action and social change.[34] As Sarachild comments:

> We would be the first to dare to say and do the undareable, what women really felt and wanted. The first job now was to raise awareness and understanding, our own and others — awareness that would prompt people to organize and to act on a mass scale.[35]

Thus consciousness raising shared the assumptions of earlier revolutionary traditions: that understanding and theoretical analysis were the first steps to revolutionary change, and that neither was adequate alone; theory and practice were intertwined as praxis. As Sarachild puts it, "Consciousness raising was seen as both a method for arriving at the truth and a means for action and organizing."[36] What was original in consciousness raising, however, was its emphasis on experience and feeling as the guide to theoretical understanding, an approach that reflected the realities of women's socially defined subjectivities and the conditions of their lives. Irene Peslikis, another member of Redstockings, wrote, "When we think of what it is that politicizes people it is not so much books or ideas but experience."[37]

While Sarachild and other early feminists influenced by a left political tradition explored the creation of theory grounded in women's feelings and experiences, they never lost the commitment to social transformation.[38] In their subsequent history, however, consciousness raising and feminist pedagogy did not always retain this political commitment to action. As the women's movement expanded to reach wider groups of women, consciousness raising tended to lose its commitment to revolutionary change. This trend seems to have been particularly true as the women's movement affected women with a less radical perspective and with little previous political involvement. Without a vision of collective action and social transformation, consciousness raising held the possibility of what Berenice Fisher calls "a diversion of energies into an exploration of feelings and 'private' concerns to the detriment of political activism."[39] The lack of structure and the local natures of consciousness-raising groups only reinforced these tendencies toward a focus on individual rather than collective change. The one site in which the tradition of consciousness raising did find institutional expression was in academia, in the growth of women's studies courses and programs stimulated by the new scholarship on women. The founders of these early courses and programs tended to be politically committed feminists who themselves had experienced consciousness raising and who, like Freire, assumed that education could and should be a means of social change.

The first women's studies courses, reflecting the growth of the women's movement in what has come to be called the second wave of feminism, were taught in the late 1960s.[40] In 1970, Paul Lauter and Florence Howe founded The Feminist Press, an important outlet for publishing early feminist scholarship and recovering lost texts by women writers.[41] In 1977, the founding of the National Women's Studies Association provided a national organization, a journal, and yearly conferences that gave feminists inside and outside of academia a forum to exchange ideas and experiences. By the late 1980s, respected journals such as *Signs* and *Feminist Studies* were well established, and women's studies programs and courses were widespread (if not always enthusiastically supported by administrations) in colleges and universities.[42] At the same time, feminist research and theory — what has come to be called "the new scholarship on women" — put forth a profound challenge to traditional disciplines.[43] The growth of women's studies programs and feminist scholarship thus provided an institutional framework and theoretical underpinning for feminist pedagogy, the attempt to express feminist values and goals in the classroom. But while feminist scholarship has presented fundamental challenges to traditional androcentric knowledge, the attempt to create a new pedagogy modeled on consciousness raising has not been as successful or coherent a project. Serious challenges to the goal of political transformation through the experience of feminist learning have been raised in the attempt to create a feminist pedagogy in the academy. The difficulties and contradictions that have emerged in the attempt to create a feminist pedagogy in traditional institutions like universities raise serious questions for all liberatory pedagogies and echo some of the problems raised by the unitary and universal approach of *Pedagogy of the Oppressed*. But in engaging these questions, feminist pedagogy suggests new directions that can enrich Freirean pedagogies of liberation.

Feminist pedagogy has raised three areas of concern that are particularly useful in considering the ways in which Freirean and other liberatory pedagogies can be enriched and expanded. The first of these concerns the role and authority of the teacher; the second addresses the epistemological question of the source of the claims for knowledge and truth in personal experience and feeling; the last, emerging from challenges by women of color and postmodernist feminist theorists, raises the question of difference. Their challenges have led to a shattering of the unproblematic and unitary category "woman," as well as of an assumption of the inevitable unity of "women."

Instead, feminist theorists have increasingly emphasized the importance of recognizing difference as a central category of feminist pedagogy. The unstated assumption of a universal experience of "being a woman" was exploded by the critiques of postmodern feminists and by the growing assertion of lesbians and women of color that the universal category "woman" in fact meant "White, heterosexual, middle-class woman," even when used by White, heterosexual, socialist feminists, or women veterans of the civil rights movement who were committed to class or race struggles.[44] These theoretical challenges to the unity of both "woman" and "women" have in turn called into question the authority of women as teachers and students in the classroom, the epistemological value of both feeling and experience, and the nature of political strategies for enacting feminist goals of social change. I turn next to an exploration of these key issues of authority, experience, feeling, and difference within feminist pedagogy and theory.

The Role and Authority of the Teacher

In many respects, the feminist vision of the teacher's authority echoes that Freirean image of the teacher who is a joint learner with students and who holds authority by virtue of greater knowledge and experience. But as we have seen, Freire fails to address the various forms of power held by teachers depending on their race, gender, and the historical and institutional settings in which they work. In the Freirean account, they are in this sense "transparent." In the actual practice of feminist pedagogy, the central issues of difference, positionality, and the need to recognize the implications of subjectivity or identity for teachers and students have become central. Moreover, the question of authority in institutional settings makes problematic the possibility of achieving the collective and nonhierarchical vision of early consciousness-raising groups within university classrooms. The basic elements of early consciousness-raising groups — an emphasis on feeling, experience, and sharing, and a suspicion of hierarchy and authority — continue to influence feminist pedagogy in academic settings. But the institutionalized nature of women's studies in the hierarchical and bureaucratic structure of academia creates tensions that run counter to the original commitment to praxis in consciousness-raising groups. Early consciousness-raising groups were homogeneous, antagonistic to authority, and had a commitment to political change that had directly emerged from the civil rights and new left movements. Feminist pedagogy within academic classrooms addresses heterogeneous groups of students within a competitive and individualistic culture in which the teacher holds institutional power and responsibility (even if she may want to reject that power).[45] As bell hooks comments, "The academic setting, the academic discourse [we] work in, is not a known site for truthtelling."[46] The very success of feminist scholarship has meant the development of a rich theoretical tradition with deep divisions and opposing goals and methods.[47] Thus the source of the teacher's authority as a "woman" who can call upon a "common woman's knowledge" is called into question; at the same time the feminist teacher is "given" authority by virtue of her role within the hierarchical structure of the university.

The question of authority in feminist pedagogy seems to be centered around two different conceptions. The first refers to the institutionally imposed authority of the teacher within a hierarchical university structure. The teacher in this role must give grades, is evaluated by administrators and colleagues in terms of expertise in a body of knowledge, and is expected to take responsibility for meeting the goals of an academic course as it is understood within the wider university. This hierarchical structure is clearly in opposition to the collective goals of a common women's movement and is miles from the early structureless consciousness-raising groups in which each woman was an expert on her own life. Not only does the university structure impose this model of institutional authority, but students themselves expect it. As Barbara Hillyer Davis comments: "The institutional pressure to [impart knowledge] is reinforced by the students' well-socialized behavior. If I will tell them 'what I want,' they will deliver it. They are exasperated with my efforts to depart from the role of dispenser of wisdom."[48] Feminist educators have attempted to address this tension between their ideals of collective education and the demands of the university by a variety of expedients: group assignments and grades, contracts for grades, pass/fail courses, and such techniques as self-revelation and the articulation of the dynamics of the classroom.[49]

Another aspect of institutionalized authority, however, is the need for women to *claim* authority in a society that denies it to them. As Culley and Portuges have pointed out, the authority and power of the woman feminist teacher is already in question from many of her students precisely because she is a woman:

> As women, our own position is precarious, and the power we are supposed to exercise is given grudgingly, if at all. For our own students, for ourselves, and for our superiors, we are not clearly "us" or "them." The facts of class, of race, of ethnicity, of sexual preference — as well as gender — may cut across the neat divisions of teacher/student.[50]

Thus the issue of institutional authority raises the contradictions of trying to achieve a democratic and collective ideal in a hierarchical institution, but it also raises the question of the meaning of authority for feminist teachers, whose right to speak or to hold power is itself under attack in a patriarchal (and racist, homophobic, classist, and so on) society. The question of asserting authority and power is a central concern to feminists precisely because as women they have been taught that taking power is inappropriate. From this perspective, the feminist teacher's acceptance of authority becomes in itself liberating to her and to her students. It becomes a claim to authority in terms of her own value as a scholar and a teacher in a patriarchal society that structurally denies or questions that authority as it is manifest in the organization and bureaucracy of the university. Women students, after all, are socialized to be deferential, and both men and women students are taught to accept male authority. It is instructive for students to see women assert authority. But this use of authority will lead to positive social change only if those teachers are working also to empower students in a Freirean sense.[51] As Susan Stanford Friedman argues:

> What I and other women have needed is a theory of feminist pedagogy consistent with our needs as women operating at the fringes of patriarchal space. As we attempt to move on to academic turf culturally defined as male, we need a theory that first recognizes the androcentric denial of *all* authority to women and, second, points out a way for us to speak with an authentic voice not based on tyranny.[52]

These concerns lead to a conception of authority and power in a positive sense, both in terms of women asserting authority as women, and in terms of valuing intellectual work and the creation of theory as a means of understanding and, thus, of changing the world.

The authority of the intellectual raises issues for feminists in the academy that are similar to those faced by other democratic and collective political movements, such as those described by Freire. There is a contradiction between the idea of a women's movement including all women and a group of what Berenice Fisher calls "advanced women."[53] Feminists who question the whole tradition of androcentric thought are deeply suspicious of women who take a position of "experts" who can translate and interpret other women's experiences. Fisher articulates these tensions well:

> Who are intellectuals in relation to the women's movement? . . . Are intellectuals sorts of leaders, sage guides, women who give voice to or clarify a broader urge toward social change? Is intellectual work essentially elitist, a matter of mere privilege to think, to write, to create? Is it simply a patriarchal mode of gaining and maintaining power, a way of negating women's everyday experience, a means of separating some women from the rest of the "community?"[54]

Fisher argues that feminist intellectuals are struggling with these questions in their scholarship, teaching, and roles within the universities and the wider women's movement. She does not reject the authority of the feminist intellectual, but she also does not deny the need to address and clarify these contradictions. She, like Charlotte Bunch, is an embodiment of this attempt to accept both the authority and responsibility of the feminist intellectual who is creating theory.

In terms of feminist pedagogy, the authority of the feminist teacher as intellectual and theorist finds expression in the goal of making students themselves theorists of their own lives by interrogating and analyzing their own experience. In an approach very similar to Freire's concept of conscientization, this strategy moves beyond the naming or sharing of experience to the creation of a critical understanding of the forces that have shaped that experience. This theorizing is antithetical to traditional views of women. As Bunch points out, traditionally women are supposed to worry about mundane survival problems, to brood about fate, and to fantasize in a personal manner. We are not meant to think analytically about society, to question the ways things are, to consider how things could be different. Such thinking involves an active, not a passive, relationship to the world.[55]

Thus feminist educators like Fisher and Bunch accept their authority as intellectuals and theorists, but they consciously attempt to construct their pedagogy to recognize and encourage the capacity of their students to theorize and to recognize their own power.[56] This is a conception of authority not in the institutional terms of a bureaucratized university system, but rather an attempt to claim the authority of theorist and guide for students who are themselves potential theorists.

Feminist concerns about the authority of the feminist teacher address questions of classroom practice and theory ignored by Freire — in his formulation of the teacher and student as two "knowers" of the world, and in his assertion that the liberatory teacher should acknowledge and claim authority but not authoritarianism. The feminist exploration of authority is much richer and addresses more directly the contradictions between goals of collectivity and hierarchies of knowledge. Feminist teachers are much more conscious of the power of various subject positions than is represented in Freire's "transparent" liberatory teacher. An acknowledgment of the realities of conflict and tensions based on contradictory political goals, as well as of the meaning of historically experienced oppression for both teachers and students, leads to a pedagogy that respects difference not just as significant for students, but for teachers as well.

Personal Experience as a Source of Knowledge and Truth

As feminists explore the relationship of authority, theory, and political action, they raise questions about the categories and claims for truth underlying both consciousness raising and feminist pedagogy. These claims rest on categories of experience and feeling as guides to theoretical understanding and political change. Basic to the Freirean method of conscientization is the belief in the ability of all people to be knowers and to read both the word and the world. In Freirean pedagogy, it is through the interrogation of their own experiences that the oppressed will come to an understanding of their own power as knowers and creators of the world; this knowledge will contribute to the transformation of their world. In consciousness-raising groups and in feminist pedagogy in the university, a similar reliance on experience and feeling has been fundamental to the development of a feminist knowledge of the world that can be the basis for social change. Underlying both Freirean and early feminist pedagogy is an assumption of a common experience as the basis for political analysis and action. Both experience and feeling were central to consciousness raising and remain central to feminist pedagogy in academia; they are claimed as a kind of "inner knowing," shaped by society but at the same time containing an oppositional quality. Feeling is looked to as a guide to a deeper truth than that of abstract rationality. Experience, which is interpreted through ideologically constructed categories, also can be the basis for an opposition to dominant schemes of truth if what is experienced runs counter to what is set forth and accepted as "true." Feminist educators, beginning with women in the early consciousness-raising groups, have explored both experience and feeling as sources of knowledge, and both deserve closer examination.

In many ways, feeling or emotion has been seen traditionally as a source of women's knowledge about the world. As we have seen, in the early consciousness-raising groups, feelings were looked to as the source of a "true" knowledge of the world for women living in a society that denied the value of their perceptions. Feelings or emotions were seen as a way of testing accepted claims of what is universally true about human nature or, specifically, about women. Claims such as Freud's theory of penis envy, for example, were challenged by women first because these theoretical descriptions of women's psychology did not match women's own feelings about their lives. As feminist pedagogy has developed, with a continued emphasis on the function of feelings as a guide to knowledge about the world, emotions have been seen as links between a kind of inner truth or inner self and the outer world — including ideology, culture, and other discourses of power.[57] However, as feminist educators have explored the uses of feeling or emotion as a source of knowledge, several difficulties have become clear. First of all, there is a danger that the expression of strong emotion can be simply cathartic and can deflect the need for action to address the underlying causes of that emotion. Moreover, it is not clear how to distinguish among a wide range of emotions as the source of political action. At a more theoretical level, there are contradictions involved in claiming that the emotions are a source for knowledge and at the same time arguing that they are manipulated and shaped by dominant discourses. Both consciousness-raising groups and feminist theorists have asserted the social construction of feelings and their manipulation by the dominant culture; at the same time, they look to feelings as a source of truth. Berenice Fisher points to the contradiction implicit in these claims:

> In theoretical terms, we cannot simultaneously claim that all feelings are socially conditioned and that some feelings are "true." We would be more consistent to acknowledge that society only partly shapes our emotions, leaving an opening where we can challenge and change the responses to which we have been socialized. That opening enables the consciousness-raising process to take place and gives us the space in which to reflect on the new emotional responses that our process evokes.[58]

In this formulation, Fisher seems to be arguing for a kind of Gramscian "good sense," a locus of knowing in the self that is grounded in feeling as a guide to theoretical understanding. Feelings thus are viewed as a kind of cognition — a source of knowledge.

Perhaps the most eloquent argument for feelings as a source of oppositional knowledge is found in the work of Audre Lorde. Lorde, a Black lesbian feminist theorist and poet, writes from the specificity of her own socially defined and shaped life. For her, feeling is the source of poetry, a means of knowing that challenges White, Western, androcentric epistemologies. She specifically ties her own feelings as a Black woman to a non-Western way of knowing. She writes:

> As we come more into touch with our own ancient, non-European consciousness of living as a situation to be experienced and interacted with, we learn more and more to cherish our feelings, to respect those hidden sources of power from where true knowledge and, therefore, lasting action comes.[59]

Lorde is acutely aware of the ways in which the dominant society shapes our sense of who we are and what we feel. As she points out, "Within living structures defined by profit, by linear power, by institutional dehumanization, our feelings were not meant to survive."[60] Moreover, Lorde is conscious of the oppressor within us: "For we have, built into all of us, old blueprints of expectation and response, old structures of oppression, and these must be altered at the same time as we alter the living conditions which are the result of those structures."[61] But although Lorde does not deny what she calls "the oppressor within," she retains a belief in the power of deeper feeling to challenge the dominant definitions of truth and to point the way to an analysis that can lead to an alternative vision:

> As we begin to recognize our deepest feelings, we begin to give up, of necessity, being satisfied with suffering and self-negation, and with the numbness which so often seems like their only alternative in society. Our acts against oppression become integral with self, motivated and empowered from within.[62]

For Lorde, then, feelings are a guide to analysis and to action. While they are shaped by society and are socially constructed in that sense, Lorde insists on a deeper reality of feeling closer in touch with what it means to be human. This formulation echoes the Freirean vision of humanization as a new way of being in the world other than as oppressor and oppressed. Both Freire and Lorde retain a Utopian faith in the possibility that human beings can create new ways of being in the world out of collective struggle and a human capacity to feel. Lorde terms this the power of the erotic; she speaks of the erotic as "a measure between the beginnings of our sense of self and the chaos of our strongest feelings," a resource "firmly rooted in the power of our unexpressed or unrecognized feeling."[63] Because the erotic can challenge the dominant, it has been denied as a source of power and knowledge. But for Lorde, the power of the erotic provides the basis for visionary social change.

In her exploration of feelings and of the erotic as a source of knowledge about the world, Lorde does not reject analysis and rationality. But she questions the depth of critical understanding of those forces that shape our lives that can be achieved using only the rational and abstract methods of analysis given to us by dominant ideology. In Foucault's terms, she is seeking a perspective from which to interrogate dominant regimes of truth; central to her argument is the claim that an analysis framed solely in the terms of accepted discourse cannot get to the root of structures of power. That is what her well-known phrase, "The Master's Tools Will Never Dismantle the Master's House," implies. As she argues:

> Rationality is not unnecessary. It serves the chaos of knowledge. It serves feeling. It serves to get from this place to that place. But if you don't honor those places, then the road is meaningless. Too often, that's what happens with the worship of rationality and that circular, academic analytic thinking. But ultimately, I don't see feel/think as a dichotomy. I see them as a choice of ways and combinations.[64]

Lorde's discussion of feeling and the erotic as a source of power and knowledge is based on the assumption that human beings have the capacity to feel and know, and can engage in self-critique; people are not completely shaped by dominant discourse. The oppressor may be within us, but Lorde insists that we also have the capacity to challenge our own ways of feeling and knowing. When tied to a recognition of positionality, this validation of feeling can be used to develop powerful sources of politically focused feminist education.

For Lorde and Fisher, this kind of knowing through an exploration of feeling and emotion requires collective inquiry and constant reevaluation. It is a contingent and positioned claim to truth. Similar complexities arise in the use of experience as the basis for feminist political action. Looking to experience as the source of knowledge and the focus of feminist learning is perhaps the most fundamental tenet of feminist pedagogy. This is similar to the Freirean call to "read the world" to seek the generative themes that codify power relationships and social structures. The sharing of women's experiences was the touchstone of early consciousness-raising groups and continues to be a fundamental method of feminist pedagogy. That women need to examine what they have experienced and lived in concrete ways, in their own bodies, is a materialistic conception of experience. In an early essay, Adrienne Rich pointed to this materiality of experience: "To think like a woman in a man's world means . . . remembering that every mind resides in a body; remaining accountable to the female bodies in which we live; constantly retesting given hypotheses against lived experience."[65] As became clear quite early in the women's movement, claims about experience as a source of women's knowledge rested on certain assumptions about commonalities in women's lives. Women were conceived of as a unitary and relatively undifferentiated group. Sarachild, for example, spoke of devising "new theories which . . . reflect the actual experience and feelings and necessities of women."[66] Underlying this approach was the assumption of a common woman's experience, one reflecting the world of the White, middle-class, heterosexual women of the early feminist movement. But as the critiques of lesbians, women of color, and postmodernist feminist theorists have made clear, there is no single woman's experience to be revealed. Both experience and feeling thus have been called into question as the source of an unproblematic knowledge of the world that will lead to praxis. As Diana Fuss comments: "'female experience' is never as unified, as knowable, as universal, and as stable as we presume it to be."[67]

Challenges to the concept of a unitary women's experience by both women of color and by postmodern critics has not meant the abandonment of experience as a source of knowledge for feminist teachers. Of course experience, like feeling, is socially constructed in the sense that we can only understand it and speak about it in ideas and terms that are part of an existing ideology and language. But in a stance similar to that of Lorde in her use of the erotic, feminist teachers have explored the ways in which women have experienced the material world through their bodies. This self-examination of lived experience is then used as a source of knowledge that can illuminate the social processes and ideology that shape us. As Fuss suggests, "Such a position permits the introduction of narratives of lived experience into the classroom while at the same time challenging us to examine collectively the central role social and historical practices play in shaping and producing these narratives."[68] One example of this approach is found in the work of Frigga Haug and the group of German feminists of which she is a part.[69] Haug and this group use what they call collective memory work to explore their feelings about their own bodies in order to uncover the social construction of their selves:

> Our collective empirical work set itself the high-flown task of identifying the ways in which individuals construct themselves into existing structures, and are thereby themselves formed; the way in which they reconstruct social structures; the points at which change is possible, the points where our chains chafe most, the point where accommodations have been made.[70]

This collective exploration of "the point where . . . chains chafe most" recalls the Freirean culture circles, in which peasants would take such examples as their personal experiences with the landlord as the starting point for their education or conscientization. Basic to their approach is a belief in reflection and a rejection of a view of people as "fixed, given, unchangeable." By working collectively on "memory work," a sharing and comparison of their own lives, Haug and her group hope to uncover the workings of hegemonic ideology in their own subjectivities. Another example of such collective work can be found in the Jamaican women's theater group, Sistren. Founded in 1977, Sistren is a collaborative theater group made up of working-class Jamaican women who create and write plays based on a collaborative exploration of their own experiences. The life histories of the women of Sistren have been collected in *Lionheart Girl: Life Stories of Jamaican Women*. In the compilation of this book, the Sistren collective used the same process of the collective sharing and analysis of experience that is the basis for their theater work. As the company's director Honor Ford-Smith writes:

> We began meeting collectively at first. Starting with our childhood, we made drawings of images based on such themes as where we had grown up, symbols

of oppression in our lives, our relationships with men, our experience with race and the kind of work we had done.[71]

For Haug and her group, the Sistren collective, the early consciousness-raising groups, and the Freirean culture circles, collective sharing of experience is the source of knowledge of the forces that have shaped and continue to shape them. But their recognition of the shifting meaning of experience as it is explored through memory insists on the profoundly social and political nature of who we are.

The Question of Difference

Both women of color writing from a perspective of cultural feminism and postmodernist feminist theorists converge in their critique of the concept of a universal "women's experience." While the idea of a unitary and universal category "woman" has been challenged by women of color for its racist assumptions, it has also been challenged by recent analyses of feminist theorists influenced by postmodernism, who point to the social construction of subjectivity and who emphasize the "unstable" nature of the self. Postmodernist feminist critics such as Chris Weedon have argued that socially given identities such as "woman" are "precarious, contradictory, and in process, constantly being reconstituted in discourse each time we speak."[72] This kind of analysis considers the ways in which "the subject" is not an object; that is, not fixed in a static social structure, but constantly being created, actively creating the self, and struggling for new ways of being in the world through new forms of discourse or new forms of social relationships. Such analysis calls for a recognition of the positionality of each person in any discussion of what can be known from experience. This calling into question the permanence of subjectivities is what Jane Flax refers to as the "unstable self."[73] If we view individual selves as being constructed and negotiated, then we can begin to consider what exactly those forces are in which individuals shape themselves and by which they are shaped. The category of "woman" is itself challenged as it is seen more and more as a part of a symbolic system of ideology. Donna Haraway calls all such claims of identity into question:

> With the hard-won recognition of their social and historical constitution, gender, race, and class cannot provide the basis for belief in "essential" unity: There is nothing about being "female" that naturally binds women. There is not even such a state as "being" female, itself a highly complex category constructed in contested sexual discourses and other social practices. Gender, race, or class consciousness is an achievement forced on us by the terrible historical experience of the contradictory social realities of patriarchy, colonialism, and capitalism.[74]

These analyses support the challenges to assumptions of an essential and universal nature of women and women's experience that have come from lesbian critics and women of color.[75]

Both women of color and lesbian critics have pointed to the complexity of socially given identities. Black women and other women of color raise challenges to the assumption that the sharing of experience will create solidarity and a theoretical understanding based upon a common women's standpoint. Lesbian feminists, both White and of color, point to the destructive nature of homophobia and what Adrienne Rich has called compulsory heterosexuality. As is true of White, heterosexual, feminist educators, these theorists base their analysis upon their own experiences, but those experiences reveal not only the workings of sexism, but of racism, homophobia, and class oppression as well. This complex perspective underlies the Combahee River Collective Statement, a position paper written by a group of African American feminists in Boston in the 1970s. This statement makes clear what a grounded theory of experience means for women whose value is denied by the dominant society in numerous ways. The women in the Combahee River Collective argue that "the most profound and potentially most radical politics come directly out of our own identity, as opposed to working to end somebody else's oppression."[76] For African American women, an investigation of the shaping of their own identities reveals the ways in which sexism and racism are interlocking forms of oppression:

> As children we realized that we were different from boys and that we were treated differently. For example, we were told in the same breath to be quiet both for the sake of being "ladylike" and to make us less objectionable in the eyes of white people. As we grew older we became aware of the threat of physical and sexual abuse from men. However, we had no way of conceptualizing what was so apparent to us, what we *knew* was really happening.[77]

When African American teachers like Michele Russell or Barbara Omolade describe their feminist pedagogy, they ground that pedagogy in an investigation of experience in material terms. As Russell describes her teaching of an introductory Black Studies class for women at Wayne County Community College in Detroit: "We have an hour together. . . . The first topic of conversation — among themselves and with me — is what they went through just to make it in the door, on time. That, in itself becomes a lesson."[78] And Omolade points out in her discussion of her teaching at Medgar Evers College in New York, a college whose students are largely African American women:

> No one can teach students to "see," but an instructor is responsible for providing the coherent ordering of information and content. The classroom process is one of information-sharing in which students learn to generalize their particular life experiences within a community of fellow intellectuals.[79]

Thus the pedagogy of Russell and Omolade is grounded in experience as a source of knowledge in a particularly materialistic way; the knowledge generated reveals the overlapping forms of oppression lived by women of color in this society.

The investigation of the experiences of women of color, lesbian women, women whose very being challenges existing racial, sexual, heterosexual, and class dominance, leads to a knowledge of the world that both acknowledges differences and points to the need for an "integrated analysis and practice based upon the fact that the major systems of oppression are interlocking."[80] The turning to experience thus reveals not a universal and common women's essence, but, rather, deep divisions in what different women have experienced, and in the kinds of knowledge they discover when they examine their own experience. The recognition of the differences among women raises serious challenges to feminist pedagogy by calling into question the authority of the teacher/theorist, raising feelings of guilt and shame, and revealing tensions among students as well as between teacher and students. In classes of African American women taught by African American teachers, the sharing of experience can lead to the same sense of commonality and sharing that was true of early consciousness-raising groups. But in settings in which students come from different positions of privilege or oppression, the sharing of experience raises conflicts rather than building solidarity. In these circumstances, the collective exploration of experience leads not to a common knowledge and solidarity based on sameness, but to the tensions of an articulation of difference. Such exploration raises again the problems left unaddressed by Freirean pedagogy: the overlapping and multiple forms of oppression revealed in "reading the world" of experience.

Conclusion

Both Freirean and feminist pedagogies are based on political commitment and identification with subordinate and oppressed groups; both seek justice and empowerment. Freire sets out these goals of liberation and social and political transformation as universal claims, without exploring his own privileged position or existing conflicts among oppressed groups themselves. Writing from within a tradition of Western modernism, his theory rests on a belief of transcendent and universal truth. But feminist theory influenced by postmodernist thought and by the writings of women of color challenges the underlying assumptions of these universal claims. Feminist theorists in particular argue that it is essential to recognize, as Julie Mitchell comments, that we cannot "live as human subjects without in some sense taking on a history."[81] The recognition of our own histories means the necessity of articulating our own subjectivities and our own interests as we try to interpret and critique the social world. This stance rejects the universalizing tendency of much "malestream" thought, and insists on recognizing the power and privilege of who we are. As Biddy Martin and Chandra Mohanty comment:

> The claim to a lack of identity or positionality is itself based on privilege, on the refusal to accept responsibility for one's implication in actual historical or social relations, or a denial that positionalities exist or that they matter, the denial of one's own personal history and the claim to a total separation from it.[82]

Fundamental to recent feminist theory is a questioning of the concept of a coherent subject moving through history with a single essential identity. Instead, feminist theorists are developing a concept of the constant creation and negotiation of selves within structures of ideology and material constraints.[83] This line of theoretical analysis calls into question assumptions of the common interests of the oppressed, whether conceived of as women or peasants; it challenges the use of such universal terms as oppression and liberation without locating these claims in a concrete historical or social context. The challenges of recent feminist theory and, in particular, the writings of feminists of color point to the need to articulate and claim a particular historical and social identity, to locate ourselves, and to build coalitions from a recognition of the partial knowledges of our own constructed identities. Recognizing the standpoint of subjects as shaped by their experience of class, race, gender, or other socially defined identities has powerful implications for pedagogy, in that it emphasizes the need to make conscious the subject positions not only of students but of teachers as well. These lines of theoretical analysis have implications for the ways in which we can understand pedagogy as contested, as a site of discourse among subjects, teachers, and students whose identities are, as Weedon puts it, contradictory and in process. The theoretical formulation of the "unstable self," the complexity of subjectivities, what Giroux calls "multi-layered subjects," and the need to position ourselves in relation to our own histories raise important issues for liberatory pedagogies. If all people's identities are recognized in their full historical and social complexity as subject positions that are in process, based on knowledges that are partial and that reflect deep and conflicting differences, how can we theorize what a liberatory pedagogy actively struggling against different forms of oppression may look like? How can we build upon the rich and complex analysis of feminist theory and pedagogy to work toward a Freirean vision of social justice and liberation?

In the complexity of issues raised by feminist pedagogy, we can begin to acknowledge the reality of tensions that result from different histories, from privilege, oppression, and power as they are lived by teachers and students in classrooms. To recognize these tensions and differences does not mean abandonment of the goals of social justice and empowerment, but it does make clear the need to recognize contingent and situated claims and to acknowledge our own histories and selves in process. One significant area of feminist work has been grounded in the collective analysis of experience and emotion, as exemplified by the work of Haug and her group in Germany or by the Jamaican women's theater group, Sistren. In many respects, these projects look back to consciousness raising, but with a more developed theory of ideology and an acute consciousness of difference. As Berenice Fisher argues, a collective inquiry "requires the slow unfolding of layers of experience, both the contradictory experiences of a given woman and the conflicting experiences of different women."[84] Another approach builds on what Bernice Reagon calls the need for coalition building, a recognition and validation of difference. This is similar to what has come to be known as identity politics, exemplified in what Minnie Bruce Pratt is seeking in her discussion of trying to come to terms with her own identity as a privileged Southern White woman.[85] Martin and Mohanty speak of this as a sense of "home," a recognition of the difficulties of coming to terms with privilege or oppression, of the benefits of being an oppressor, or of the rage of being oppressed.[86] This is a validation of both difference and conflict, but also an attempt to build coalitions around common goals rather than a denial of differences.[87] It is clear that this kind of pedagogy and exploration of experiences in a society in which privilege and oppression are lived is risky and filled with pain. Such a pedagogy suggests a more complex realization of the Freirean vision of the collective conscientization and struggle against oppression, one which acknowledges difference and conflict, but which, like Freire's vision, rests on a belief in the human capacity to feel, to know, and to change.

Notes

1. See as representative Henry Giroux, ed., *Postmodernism, Feminism and Cultural Politics* (Albany: State University of New York Press, 1991); Cleo Cherryholmes, *Power and Criticism: Poststructural Investigations in Education* (New York: Teachers College Press, 1988); Henry Giroux and Roger Simon, eds., *Popular Culture, Schooling and Everyday Life* (Westport, CT: Bergin & Garvey, 1989); Deborah Britzman, *Practice Makes Practice* (Albany: State University of New York Press, 1991); Patti Lather, *Getting Smart: Feminist Research and Pedagogy With/in the Postmodern* (New York: Routledge, 1991).
2. Paulo Freire, *Pedagogy of the Oppressed* (New York: Herder & Herder, 1971), p. 28.
3. Margo Culley and Catherine Portuges, "Introduction," in *Gendered Subjects* (Boston: Routledge & Kegan Paul, 1985). For comparisons of Freirean and feminist pedagogy, see also Frances Maher, "Classroom Pedagogy and the New Scholarship on Women," in *Gendered Subjects*, pp. 29–48, and "Toward a Richer Theory of Feminist Pedagogy: A Comparison of 'Liberation' and 'Gender' Models for Teaching and Learning," *Journal of Education, 169,* No. 3 (1987), 91–100.
4. Antonio Gramsci, *Selections from the Prison Notebooks* (New York: International Publishers, 1971).
5. Teresa de Lauretis, *Alice Doesn't: Feminism, Semiotics, Cinema* (Bloomington: Indiana University Press, 1984), p. 178.
6. Audre Lorde, *Sister Outsider* (Trumansburg, NY: The Crossing Press, 1984).
7. See, for example, Elizabeth Ellsworth, "Why Doesn't This Feel Empowering? Working through the Repressive Myths of Critical Pedagogy," *Harvard Educational Review, 59* (1989), 297–324; Ann Berlak, "Teaching for Outrage and Empathy in the Liberal Arts," *Educational Foundations, 3,* No. 2 (1989), 69–94; Deborah Britzman, "Decentering Discourses in Teacher Education: Or, the Unleashing of Unpopular Things," in *What Schools Can Do: Critical Pedagogy and Practice,* ed. Candace Mitchell and Kathleen Weiler (Albany: State University of New York Press, 1992).
8. Freire's method of codifications and generative themes have been discussed frequently. Perhaps the best introduction to these concrete methods can be found in Paulo Freire, *Education for Critical Consciousness* (New York: Seabury,1973).
9. See, for example, Paulo Freire, *The Politics of Education* (Westport, CT: Bergin & Garvey, 1985); Paulo Freire and Donaldo Macedo, *Literacy: Reading the Word and the World* (Westport, CT: Bergin & Garvey, 1987); Paulo Freire and Ira Shor, *A Pedagogy For Liberation* (London: Macmillan, 1987); Myles Horton and Paulo Freire, *We Make*

the Road by Walking: Conversations on Education and Social Change, ed. Brenda Bell, John Gaventa, and John Peters (Philadelphia: Temple University Press, 1990).

10. Freire, *Pedagogy of the Oppressed*, p. 28.

11. Paulo Freire, "The Adult Literacy Process as Cultural Action for Freedom," in *The Politics of Education*, p. 57.

12. Freire and Macedo, *Literacy: Reading the Word and the World*.

13. See Simone de Beauvoir, *The Second Sex* (New York: Knopf, 1953), for a more striking use of the male referent.

14. Cameron McCarthy, "Rethinking Liberal and Radical Perspectives on Racial Inequality in Schooling: Making the Case for Nonsynchrony," *Harvard Educational Review, 58* (1988), 265–280.

15. Freire, *Pedagogy of the Oppressed*, p. 30.

16. Freire, *Pedagogy of the Oppressed*, p. 69.

17. Freire, *Pedagogy of the Oppressed*, p. 73.

18. Gayatri Chakravorty Spivak, "Can the Subaltern Speak?," in *Marxism and the Interpretation of Culture*, ed. Cary Nelson and Lawrence Grossberg (Urbana: University of Illinois Press, 1988), pp. 271–313.

19. Freire and Shor, *A Pedagogy for Liberation*, p. 93.

20. Peter McLaren, "Postmodernity and the Death of Politics: A Brazilian Reprieve," *Educational Theory, 36* (1986), p. 399.

21. When definitions of feminist pedagogy are attempted, they sometimes tend toward generalization and such a broad inclusiveness as to be of dubious usefulness. For example, Carolyn Shrewsbury characterizes feminist pedagogy as follows:

> It does not automatically preclude any technique or approach. It does indicate the relationship that specific techniques have to educational goals. It is not limited to any specific subject matter but it does include a reflexive element that increases the feminist scholarship component involved in the teaching/learning of any subject matter. It has close ties with other liberatory pedagogies, but it cannot be subsumed under other pedagogical approaches. It is transformative, helping us revision the educational enterprise. But it can also be phased into a traditional teaching approach or another alternative pedagogical approach. (Shrewsbury, "What Is Feminist Pedagogy?," *Women's Studies Quarterly, 15,* Nos. 3–4 [1987], p. 12)

Certain descriptions of feminist pedagogy show the influence of group dynamics and interactionist approaches. See, for example, Nancy Schniedewind, "Feminist Values: Guidelines for Teaching Methodology in Women's Studies," *Radical Teacher, 18,* 25–28. Methods used by feminist teachers include cooperation, shared leadership, and democratic process. Feminist teachers describe such techniques as keeping journals, soliciting students' responses to readings and to the classroom dynamics of a course, the use of role playing and theater games, the use of self-revelation on the part of the teacher, building leadership skills among students by requiring them to teach parts of a course, and contracting for grades. For accounts of classroom practice, see the articles in the special issue on feminist pedagogy of *Women's Studies Quarterly, 15,* Nos. 3–4 (1987); Culley and Portuges, *Gendered Subjects;* Charlotte Bunch and Sandra Pollack, eds., *Learning Our Way* (Trumansburg, NY: Crossing Press, 1983); Gloria Hull, Patricia Bell Scott, and Barbara Smith, ed., *But Some of Us Are Brave* (Old Westbury, NY: Feminist Press, 1982); and numerous articles in *Women's Studies Newsletter* and *Radical Teacher*.

22. Nancy Schniedewind, "Teaching Feminist Process," *Women's Studies Quarterly, 15,* Nos. 3–4 (1987), p. 29.

23. Linda Gordon, "A Socialist View of Women's Studies: A Reply to the Editorial, Volume 1, Number 1," *Signs, 1* (1975), p. 559.

24. A discussion of the relationship of the early women's liberation movement to the civil rights movement and the new left can be found in Sara Evans, *Personal Politics* (New York: Vintage Press, 1980). Based on extensive interviews as well as pamphlets and private documents, Evans shows the origins of both political goals and methods in

the earlier male-dominated movement, particularly the model of Black student organizers and the Black church in the South.

25. While mid-nineteenth-century suffragists developed their ideas of human equality and justice through the abolitionist movement, by the late nineteenth century, White suffragists often demonstrated racist attitudes and employed racist strategies in their campaigns for suffrage. This offers another instructive parallel to the White feminist movement of the 1960s. Here, once again, feminist claims emerged out of an anti-racist struggle for civil rights, but later too often took up the universalizing stance that the experiences and issues of White women represented the lives of all women. See bell hooks, *Ain't I a Woman?* (Boston: South End Press, 1981) and *Feminist Theory from Margin to Center* (Boston: South End Press, 1984) for powerful discussions of these issues.

26. Nancy Hawley as quoted in Evans, *Personal Politics,* p. 205.

27. Kathie Sarachild, "Consciousness Raising: A Radical Weapon," in *Feminist Revolution,* ed. Redstockings (New York: Random House, 1975).

28. Redstockings included a number of women who were influential in the women's movement; Shulamith Firestone, Rosalyn Baxandall, Ellen Willis, and Robin Morgan were among a number of other significant feminist writers and activists who participated.

29. Sarachild, "Consciousness Raising," p. 144.

30. Sarachild, "Consciousness Raising," p. 145.

31. Michele Russell, "Black-Eyed Blues Connection: From the Inside Out," in Bunch and Pollack, *Learning Our Way,* pp. 272–284.

32. Sarachild, "Consciousness Raising," p. 147.

33. William Hinton, *Fanshen* (New York: Vintage Books, 1966).

34. See Berenice Fisher, "Guilt and Shame in the Women's Movement: The Radical Ideal of Political Action and Its Meaning for Feminist Intellectuals," *Feminist Studies, 10* (1984), 185–212, for an extended discussion of the impact of the methods and goals of the civil rights movement on consciousness raising and the early women's liberation movement.

35. Sarachild, "Consciousness Raising," p. 145.

36. Sarachild, "Consciousness Raising," p. 147.

37. Irene Peslikis, "Resistances to Consciousness," in *Sisterhood Is Powerful,* ed. Robin Morgan (New York: Vintage Books, 1970), p. 339.

38. See, for example, Kathy McAfee and Myrna Wood, "Bread and Roses," in *Voices from Women's Liberation,* ed. Leslie Tanner (New York: New American Library, 1970) for an early socialist feminist analysis of the need to connect the women's movement with the class struggle.

39. Berenice Fisher, "What is Feminist Pedagogy?," *Radical Teacher, 18,* 20–25. See also bell hooks, "on self-recovery," in *talking back: thinking feminist, thinking black* (Boston: South End Press, 1989).

40. Marilyn Boxer, "For and about Women: The Theory and Practice of Women's Studies in the United States," in *Reconstructing the Academy: Women's Education and Women's Studies,* ed. Elizabeth Minnich, Jean O'Barr, and Rachel Rosenfeld (Chicago: University of Chicago Press, 1988), p. 71.

41. See Florence Howe, *Myths of Coeducation* (Bloomington: University of Indiana Press, 1984), for a collection of essays documenting this period.

42. Boxer estimates there were over 300 programs and 30,000 courses in women's studies given in 1982. See "For and about Women," p. 70.

43. The literature of feminist challenges to specific disciplines is by now immense. For general discussions of the impact of the new scholarship on women, see Ellen DuBois, Gail Kelly, Elizabeth Kennedy, Carolyn Korsmeyer, and Lillian Robinson, eds., *Feminist Scholarship: Kindling in the Groves of Academe* (Urbana: University of Illinois Press, 1985), and Christie Farnhum, ed., *The Impact of Feminist Research in the Academy* (Bloomington: Indiana University Press, 1987).

44. See, for example, Diana Fuss, *Essentially Speaking* (New York: Routledge, 1989); hooks, *talking back;* Britzman, *Practice Makes Practice.*

45. Susan Stanford Friedman, "Authority in the Feminist Classroom: A Contradiction in Terms?" in Culley and Portuges, *Gendered Subjects,* 203–208.

46. hooks, *talking back,* p. 29.

47. See Alison Jaggar, *Feminist Politics and Human Nature* (Sussex, Eng.: Harvester Press, 1983), for an excellent discussion of these perspectives.

48. Barbara Hillyer Davis, "Teaching the Feminist Minority," in Bunch and Pollack, *Learning Our Way,* p. 91.

49. See, for example, Evelyn Torton Beck, "Self-disclosure and the Commitment to Social Change," *Women's Studies International Forum,* 6 (1983), 159–164.

50. Margo Culley and Catherine Portuges, "The Politics of Nurturance," in *Gendered Subjects,* p. 12. See also Margo Culley, "Anger and Authority in the Introductory Women's Studies Classroom," in *Gendered Subjects,* pp. 209–217.

51. See Davis, "Teaching the Feminist Minority," for a thoughtful discussion of the contradictory pressures on the feminist teacher both to nurture and challenge women students.

52. Friedman, "Authority in the Feminist Classroom," p. 207.

53. Fisher, "What is Feminist Pedagogy?" p. 22.

54. Fisher, "Guilt and Shame in the Women's Movement," p. 202.

55. Charlotte Bunch, "Not by Degrees: Feminist Theory and Education," in Bunch and Pollack, *Learning Our Way,* p. 156.

56. See Berenice Fisher, "Professing Feminism: Feminist Academics and the Women's Movement," *Psychology of Women Quarterly,* 7 (1982), 55–69, for a thoughtful discussion of the difficulties of retaining an activist stance for feminists in the academy.

57. See Arlie Russell Hochschild, *The Managed Heart* (Berkeley: University of California Press, 1983), for a discussion of the social construction of emotions in contemporary society. Hochschild argues that emotion is a "biologically given sense . . . and a means by which we know about our relation to the world" (p. 219). At the same time she investigates the ways in which the emotions themselves are manipulated and constructed.

58. Berenice Fisher, "The Heart Has Its Reasons: Feeling, Thinking, and Community Building in Feminist Education," *Women's Studies Quarterly,* 15, Nos. 3–4 (1987), 48.

59. Lorde, *Sister Outsider,* p. 37.

60. Lorde, *Sister Outsider,* p. 34.

61. Lorde, *Sister Outsider,* p. 123.

62. Lorde, *Sister Outsider,* p. 58.

63. Lorde, *Sister Outsider,* p. 53.

64. Lorde, *Sister Outsider,* p. 100.

65. Adrienne Rich, "Taking Women Students Seriously," in *On Lies, Secrets, and Silence,* ed. Adrienne Rich (New York: W. W. Norton, 1979), p. 243.

66. Sarachild, "Consciousness Raising," p. 148.

67. Fuss, *Essentially Speaking,* p. 114.

68. Fuss, *Essentially Speaking,* p. 118.

69. Frigga Haug, *Female Sexualization* (London: Verso Press, 1987).

70. Haug, *Female Sexualization,* p. 41.

71. Sistren Collective with Honor Ford-Smith, *Lionheart Girl: Life Stories of Jamaican Women* (London: Woman's Press, 1986), p. 15.

72. Chris Weedon, *Feminist Practice and Poststructuralist Theory* (Oxford: Basil Blackwell, 1987), p. 33.

73. Jane Flax, "Postmodernism and Gender Relations in Feminist Theory," *Signs, 12* (1987), 621–643.

74. Donna Haraway, "A Manifesto for Cyborgs," *Socialist Review, 80* (1985), 72.

75. As representative, see Johnella Butler, "Toward a Pedagogy of Everywoman's Studies," in Culley and Portuges, *Gendered Subjects;* hooks, *talking back;* Hull, Scott, and Smith, *But Some of Us Are Brave;* Gloria Joseph and Jill Lewis, *Common Differences: Conflicts in Black and White Perspectives* (New York: Anchor Books, 1981); Chierrie Moraga and Gloria Anzaldua, eds., *This Bridge Called My Back* (Watertown, MA: Persephone Press, 1981); Barbara Omolade, "A Black Feminist Pedagogy," *Women's Studies Quarterly, 15,* Nos. 3–4 (1987), 32–40; Russell, "Black-Eyed Blues Connection," pp. 272–284; Elizabeth Spellman, "Combatting the Marginalization of Black Women in the Classroom," in Culley and Portuges, *Gendered Subjects,* pp. 240–244.

76. Combahee River Collective, "Combahee River Collective River Statement," in *Home Girls,* ed. Barbara Smith (New York: Kitchen Table — Women of Color Press, 1983), p. 275.

77. Combahee River Collective, "Combahee River Collective Statement," p. 274.

78. Russell, "Black-Eyed Blues Connection," p. 155.

79. Omolade, "A Black Feminist Pedagogy," p. 39.

80. Combahee River Collective, "Combahee River Collective Statement," p. 272.

81. Juliet Mitchell, *Women: The Longest Revolution* (New York: Pantheon Books, 1984).

82. Biddy Martin and Chandra Mohanty, "Feminist Politics: What's Home Got to Do With It?" in *Feminist Studies/ Critical Studies,* ed. Teresa de Lauretis (Bloomington: University of Indiana Press, 1986), p. 208.

83. See, for example, Flax, "Postmodernism and Gender Relations in Feminist Theory"; Sandra Harding, *The Science Question in Feminism* (Ithaca: University of Cornell Press, 1986); Dorothy Smith, *The Everyday World as Problematic* (Boston: Northeastern University Press, 1987); Haraway, "A Manifesto for Cyborgs," *Socialist Review, 80* (1985), 64–107; Nancy Hartsock, *Money, Sex, and Power* (New York: Longman, 1983); Mary O'Brien, *The Politics of Reproduction* (Boston: Routledge & Kegan Paul, 1981); Irene Diamond and Lee Quinby, eds., *Feminism and Foucault* (Boston: Northeastern University Press, 1988); Linda Alcoff, "Cultural Feminism versus Post Structuralism: The Identity Crisis in Feminist Theory," *Signs, 13* (1988), 405–437; Special Issue on Feminism and Deconstruction, *Feminist Studies, 14,* No. 1 (1988); Judith Butler, *Gender Trouble* (New York: Routledge, 1990); Linda Nicholson, ed., *Feminism/Postmodernism* (New York: Routledge, 1990).

84. Fisher, "The Heart Has Its Reasons," p. 49.

85. Minnie Bruce Pratt, "Identity: Skin Blood Heart," in *Yours in Struggle,* ed. Elly Bulkin, Minnie Bruce Pratt, and Barbara Smith (Brooklyn, NY: Long Hand Press, 1984).

86. Martin and Mohanty, "What's Home Got to Do With It?"

87. Bernice Reagon, "Coalition Politics: Turning the Century," in Smith, *Home Girls,* pp. 356–369.

PART THREE

Girls and Young Women

Chronicles

In this chapter, the voices of several young women are juxtaposed in their writings on various issues covering diverse interests and concerns in young women's lives: education, violence, rape, family, and sexuality. It is our hope that the voices of these young women will illustrate for the reader a sampling of important topics that concern girls and young women, and the courage they find to write about them. The selections, written within the last ten years, highlight the need for continued study of girls' development, for more and better educational programs and opportunities for girls and women, and the need to educate both young men and women on the perils of violence.

Untitled

KARI LARSEN

In the poem below, Kari Larsen expresses the pain and sense of loss felt by a child whose country has been ravaged by war. Kari was born in Vietnam sometime in 1971. In the fall of 1973, her village was destroyed. Only a few small children survived the attack; Kari, then known as "Hang," was among them. She was adopted by her new family in 1974. Ms. Larsen searches for a remembrance of her heritage through a poetic vision of her birth mother and expresses her hope to be remembered in return.

> this is a poem to my birth mother
> whom I never knew
>
> whose sorrow filled Asian eyes,
> lovely golden brown complexion,
> and raven black hair
> are all a figment of my imagination;
> for I was too young then,
> to now recall your face
>
> I have felt your presence and love often
> and you will never be forgotten,

Harvard Educational Review Vol. 58 No. 3 August 1988, 331

I am a part of you
and I hope you haven't forgotten me

the Vietnam War, the war that separated us,
the war that killed millions
the war that left millions lonely and homeless

it's about you, mother,
about how I wondered
how you are
if you're content, sad, or lonely

I wish that I had a memory of you
a memory of you and I together
so I write this poem to you,
my birth mother whom I never knew

A Black Student's Reflection on Public and Private Schools

IMANI PERRY

My name is Imani Perry. I am a fifteen-year-old Black female who has experienced both private and public education. These experiences have led me to believe there are significant differences between the two types of education that deserve to be acknowledged and resolved by society as a whole.

After ten years in private schools I made the decision to attend a public school. I left because I felt isolated as a person of color. I yearned to have a large, strong Black community be a part of my development. I believed that I would find such a community in the public high school of my city, which is a fairly urban school with approximately 2,600 students, 20 percent of whom are Black.

Despite the fact that I had never been in a traditional public school environment, when I decided to go to one I had certain expectations about the teaching. I assumed that the teaching philosophy would be similar to that of the private schools I had attended. I expected that any teaching differences that did exist would be limited to less sophisticated reading, or a less intense work load. As I quickly learned, the differences were more substantial.

I believe the differences I found in the teaching between the private and public schools that I attended would best be illustrated by several examples of what I encountered. My initial realization of this difference began with an argument I had with a math teacher over a point value on a test. I felt that he should give partial credit for problems with computational errors rather than procedural errors, or conceptual misunderstanding. I presented

Harvard Educational Review Vol. 58 No. 3 August 1988, 332–336

this point to the math teacher, who responded by saying math is computation and the theories and concepts of math are only used to compute. I was astonished by this statement. Coming from a school where the teachers' stated goal for freshman math was to begin to teach you how to become a "theoretical mathematician," my entire perception of math was different. Perhaps that emphasis on theoretical math was also extreme; nevertheless, I believe that a good math teacher believes that computation in math should be used to assist in the organization of theories. Computation is a necessary but not sufficient step toward math knowledge. I felt this teacher was probably the product of schooling that did not emphasize the artistic qualities of math. While I could sympathize with his position, I felt that all I loved about math — new ideas, discussing unproved theorems, and developing personal procedures — was being ignored. I withdrew from this course only to find the ideological differences emerged again in my advanced English class at the public school, particularly in essay writing.

In this class, once we wrote a paper — mind you, with no assistance from the teacher — the process ended. We did not discuss papers, receive constructive criticism, or improve them through rewriting. Despite the fact that there was no proofreading assistance offered, 10 percent of the grade was taken off for sentence errors. It seemed as if the teacher assumed we no longer needed to continue developing our writing skills.

In my last school, which had an abundance of excellent essayists, my English teacher would give a detailed description of what he felt about each paper. At points where he felt one deserved praise or criticism, he would make comments in the margin. He would not neglect to correct punctuation errors — such as commas instead of semicolons — but these errors were not the sole criteria for our grades, especially if the writing was good. The emphasis was upon improving intellectual and organizational skills to raise the quality of the writing.

These examples illustrate my belief that my learning environment had changed from a place where thought and theory were emphasized to a place where form and precision were emphasized. The teaching system at the public school appears to assume that at some point in our education, learning and thinking are no longer important. Schooling in this situation becomes devoted to making things look correct. This is in sharp contrast to my private schools, where proper form was something I learned was necessary, but secondary in importance to the content and organization of what is produced.

Because of this difference in the concept of teaching and learning, there is also a difference in what and who teachers consider intelligent. The teaching at the public school has less to do with thinking and processing ideas, and more to do with precision and detail in appearance. Therefore, students who are considered intelligent by the public school faculty possess different skills than those at the private schools I have attended. In the public school a student is considered intelligent if he or she is well-behaved and hard working. The ability to grasp a subject in its entirety — from theory to practice — is not valued.

For example, in the fall of 1987 there was an academic contest, where my school was competing against other public schools. All the teachers I encountered were very enthusiastic about it. The students who were selected to participate were raised on a pedestal. These students, most of whom were clean-cut and apparently straight-laced, were to serve as our models of very intelligent students. They were drilled in formulas, book plots, and other information for several days a week. It seemed as if the teachers were not concerned with whether the students digested the depth of these subjects and resources as long as the students completed all the reading, memorized the facts, and could repeat the information. The contest was more a demonstration of a memory function than anything else. In my opinion there is nothing wrong with such a contest, but it should be recognized for what it is and is not. One thing it is not is a true measure of knowledge and ability. This was never recognized by the school.

Another example of how a different view of intelligence is manifested in this public school is the school's view of two students whom I know. I will identify them as Student A and Student B. Student B is an intellectual. She reads, is analytical in her discussions and is knowledgeable. Student A is very precise with his homework, answers the patronizing questions the teachers ask ("What color was the horse?" "Black with a white spot!" "Correct!"), and is very "all-American" in behavior and appearance. Student A is considered more intelligent at this public school because he displays skills that are considered signs of intelligence at this school. The intelligence criteria at this school are more related to superficial qualities such as appearance, knowing facts, etc., rather than the intellectual qualities that student B possesses. Student B displays an ability to learn and write in creative and analytical formats. I left a school where the criterion for intelligence was the student's thought process resulting from the information, for a school where the information was the measure of intelligence.

In reflecting on schooling it is important to realize that all people, including teachers, have biases based on the physical appearances of other people. On the train most people are more likely to sit next to the clean-shaven Harvard freshman than next to the Mohawked, multiple-earringed punk-rocker. In teachers, however, these biases should diminish as they begin to know a student. Unfortunately, in the public school there is an absence of teacher-student contact. Because of this lack of contact there are no criteria by which intelligence can be determined, besides grades, appearance, and behavior. As I mentioned before, the grading system at this school often reflects one's ability to memorize and not one's thinking and analytical abilities. Moreover, since people are biased in their acceptance of different appearances, students who look different are judged differently. The only way they can make up for this difference is to be "well behaved," and, as I will mention later, the definition of well-behaved is arbitrary.

All these issues I have discussed have very negative effects for students from minority groups, more specifically the Black and Hispanic youths who make up a large percentage of most urban schools. It is those Black and

Hispanic students who retain strong cultural characteristics in their personalities who are most negatively affected by teachers' emphasis on behavior,
appearance, and respect for authority.

Public schools' emphasis on the teaching of form merely trains students
for low-powered or menial jobs that do not require analytical thought. It is
evident when most students are discussing what they intend to be that their
goals are most often focused toward areas and professions about which they
have some idea or knowledge. If in class you've never spoken about how
language and colloquialisms are reflections of the society you are studying,
you definitely will not be thinking of being a linguist. And if you are only
asked to type a paper summarizing the book, rather than writing an analysis
of it, the primary skill shown is typing. This should not be the main skill
which is emphasized.

The neglect of intellectual development also occurs in higher-level classes,
but at least the resources, books, etc., available to students are not altogether
lacking in intellectual value. Occasionally these resources will have depth
and content, be philosophical, or insightful. But in lower-level classes, where
minority students are most often found and where bad textbooks are used
without outside resources, the reading has less content, and the point of
reading is to perfect reading skills, not to broaden thinking skills or gain
knowledge of how the subject is currently affecting us. It is often not possible
to broaden your thinking skills or knowledge with the books used in lower-
level classes, which are more often stripped of any content. In an upper-level
class, if you have a parent who wants you to know the subject in depth, and
to think about it, it is possible to do that detached from the school environment, because the subject matter may have content, or have some meaning
beyond the words. My high-level sophomore English class read *Moby Dick* as
an outside reading. We didn't discuss the symbolism or religious qualities of
it, but I am aware of them because I read critical essays and discussed them
with my mother. If one is reading a book which has been stripped of meaningful content, it is not helpful to do outside research because it is lacking
in meaning.

Many students from minority groups are being trained only in form and
not in creative ways of thinking. This I believe causes disenchantment among
students. Upper-class students are not as affected, because of their social
class, and their "social responsibility" to be achievers. This is especially true
of upper-class students in a public school whose social-class peers are in
private schools. But instead of striving to be true leaders, they quickly learn
how to be good students by being well-behaved. What well-behaved means is
always taking the teacher's word as absolute truth and never questioning the
teacher's authority. This definition of well-behaved is of course culturally
based and can be in opposition to cultures of Black and Hispanic students.

In Black and Hispanic cultures, respect and obedience come and develop
with the relationship. Rather than being automatic, respect must be earned.
For example, one will occasionally hear a Black child say to a stranger, "You
can't tell me what to do, you're not my mother." But at the same time, often

one will see Black kids following the orders and rules of an adult friend of the family, whom they would under no circumstances disrespect. In addition, in Black and Hispanic cultures it appears that adult and child cultures are more integrated than those of other ethnic groups. For example, parties in the Hispanic community will often have an age range from toddler to elderly. Children are often present in the conversation and socializing of adults and are not treated as separate, as they may be in other cultures.

When this relationship is not made between teacher and student, it is not an acceptable educational situation, because the Black and Hispanic students are now expected to respect someone in a different manner than their culture has socialized them to. Often students are not aware of the fact that the demands being placed on them by the relationship conflict with those of their culture. They then show signs of what a teacher views as a lack of the respect that he/she deserves. The student might feel it is just a sign that they do not know the teacher and have no obligation to him or her. Many times I have seen a dumbstruck student of color sent to detention; when asked what he or she did, the student will seriously say that he or she has no idea; perhaps that he or she sucked his or her teeth in dismay, or something of that sort.

Black and Hispanic students have less of a chance at building strong relationships with any teachers because their appearance and behavior may be considered offensive to the middle-class white teachers. These students show signs of what white teachers, and some teachers of color, consider disrespect, and they do not get the nurturing relationships that develop respect and dedication. They are considered less intelligent, as can be seen in the proportion of Blacks and Hispanics in lower-level as opposed to upper-level classes. There is less of a teacher-student contact with "underachievers," because they are guided into peer tutoring programs. Perhaps this is understandable, because the teachers have less of a vested interest in the achievement of students that are not of their community, or have less of an idea of how to educate them. Public school teachers are no longer part of the same community as the majority of their students. The sad part of the situation is that many students believe that this type of teaching is what academic learning is all about. They have not had the opportunity to experience alternative ways of teaching and learning. From my experience in public school, it appears that many minority students will never be recognized as capable of analytical and critical thinking.

In the beginning of this article I spoke about my decision to leave my private school because of feeling isolated. After three months at a large urban public school I found myself equally isolated — intellectually as well as racially. My thinking process has gradually affected my opinions and character. I am in upper-level classes in which there are barely any kids of color, except Asians. Black and Hispanic students have been filtered down into lower-level classes. Most of the students I meet are kind, interesting people whom I like and respect. However, because the environment of the school is one in which ideas are not valued or fostered, I find it difficult to discuss issues with them, because my thoughtfulness has flourished, while others have been denied an opportunity to explore their intellectual development. I am now at a point of deciding which isolation is worse, cultural/racial or intellectual-opinion-based and slightly racial. This is a decision many Black students who have attended private schools at some time are wrestling to make, a decision that will affect their development, knowledge, and viewpoint of education, and their relationships to educators — those supposed possessors of greater knowledge than themselves.

Afterword: Since the writing of this article I have returned to a private school with the feeling that one's educational development is too much to sacrifice. I now attend a private high school with a strong unified Black community, as well as academic merit. Even though I did not remain at the urban public school, I valued my experience there, mostly because through it I learned one of the most blatant forms of oppression and inequity for lower-class students in American society, and I appreciate the opportunities with which I have been blessed.

A Dream Guy, a Nightmare Experience

ANONYMOUS

I'm lying on the floor, in a dark room, unable to move. Then I see him, standing over me, laughing. I try to move, but I'm paralyzed. He gets closer and closer and right when he's about to kiss me, I wake up, screaming. After that I'm too upset to go back to sleep, so I sit up and cry all night.

My nightmares aren't as vivid as before, but they're there. Just when I think it's finally over, the memories come back to haunt me. I keep thinking that maybe I could have done something to prevent it. Maybe if I hadn't been such a sucker for a happy ending. Maybe if I had thought ahead. Maybe . . . Maybe . . .

I Was 13

He didn't go to the same schools but he lived in the neighborhood, and was always hanging around. I used to see him in the morning, before school. He was about 16, kind of tall, with short, dark hair, and the most beautiful grey eyes I've ever seen. He'd say "hi" when he saw me and even though I didn't really know him, I started to like him. Occasionally, I'd stop and talk to him — nothing too personal. We talked about the movies we'd seen, music and stuff like that. I began to look forward to our little talks, and was disappointed when I didn't see him around the school. I was 13 at the time.

Reprinted with permission from *New Youth Connections*, copyright © 1994 by Youth Communication. For more information, write to Youth Communication, 144 W. 27th St., Suite 8-R, New York, NY 10001.

Harvard Educational Review Vol. 65 No. 2 Summer 1995, 258–261

One day, after school, he was waiting for me. I was with my friend Charlene. We were talking outside the school and I pretended that I didn't see him. He kept trying to get my attention, but I pretended not to notice. I don't know why — maybe I didn't want Charlene to know I had a crush on him.

He Carried My Books

When I said goodbye to my friend, I walked slowly to the end of my block. "Hello," he called out to me. I turned, slowly, and smiled at him. "Hi, Eric," I said shyly. "Where are you going?" he asked. I told him I was going to the train station. He asked if he could walk me there, and, being the lovesick puppy that I was, I said, "Sure."

He carried my books and we talked all the way to the train station. When we arrived, he asked if he could have my phone number. I was so excited that I gave it to him without any hesitation.

He called that night. We talked for at least two hours. He told me that he lived with his aunt and his brother. He said he'd been wanting to talk to me for a while, that he liked me and wanted to get together sometime. That phone call made me the happiest person in the world. After I got off the phone with him, I called some of my friends and told them. Being liked by a guy made me feel important.

A Small Kiss

The next time I saw him, he walked me to the train station again, and we talked some more. Then he kissed me goodbye. It was just a small kiss, but it made me feel wonderful. I was convinced he was a great guy.

He called me again that night. We talked for a while, and just as I hoped, he "popped the question."

"Yes! I'll go out with you!" I half screamed. For the rest of the night, I was practically floating in mid-air, I was so happy. "Somebody loves me," I thought.

We were "boyfriend and girlfriend" for a grand total of five days. He called me and we saw each other throughout the week. Then after school on Friday, he was waiting for me in our usual meeting place, on the corner by the schoolyard. He said he wanted to take me someplace special that afternoon. I was thrilled. I thought maybe we would go to the movies or something. "But first," he said, "we have to stop by my house for a minute."

It was a pretty big apartment, but it looked like it hadn't been cleaned in years. He brought me into the kitchen and got a glass of water. Then we went into the living room and sat on a sofa with the stuffing coming out of it. He told me to leave my books on the floor. Then he turned on the television and shut off all the lights and said, "We'll go in a minute. I'm tired. I want to rest for a second. Sit down with me." So, I did.

This Doesn't Feel Right

We sat in the darkness and watched TV for a while. I asked him where his aunt and his brother were. He stared at me with those eyes and replied, "out" plain and simple. He was acting kind of weird, but I didn't want to say anything because I thought he might get mad or something. He took my hand and started to kiss me. At first it was kind of nice. But then he started getting too aggressive, putting his hands in places they didn't belong.

I remember thinking to myself, "This doesn't feel right. What's he doing?" I started getting scared and told him to stop. But he didn't. I tried pushing him away, but I was too small. He was a lot bigger than me. He forced himself on top of me and pulled my pants down. No matter how much I struggled, he wouldn't let up. He held me down by the shoulders and raped me. I was crying and screaming, "No! Stop! Please stop!" But he wouldn't. Exhausted from crying and trying to get him off me, I stared into the blackness, tears sliding off of my cheeks.

It all happened very fast. As soon as I could, I fixed my pants, tried to wipe the tears away, and got the hell out of there. I walked the eight blocks to the train station and waited for the train in a daze. I kept telling myself that it didn't really happen, that it couldn't really happen — not to me.

The Trip Home

On the train this guy pressed up against me and tried to talk to me. I just turned around and walked through to the other car. Then I caught this girl looking at me, like she knew. I gave her a really ugly stare and she looked away, embarrassed.

When I finally made it home, the first thing I did was jump in the shower. I washed my entire body, but I just couldn't seem to feel clean. I dried myself off and put on some clean clothes. Then I looked at the clothes I was wearing at the time it happened. I noticed blood on my pants and shirt. I had a small cut on my chest and my legs were scraped up — I guess from struggling. I took the clothes, balled them up and put them in a plastic bag. I carried them to the incinerator and threw them out. Then I went into my room, lay down on my bed and cried. Thank God my mother wasn't home.

I didn't want to think about it, but I couldn't help it. I'll never forget the look he gave me afterwards. It was like he was proud of what he had done. Then something else popped into my mind: What if I get pregnant? I closed my eyes and tried to block the thought. (Thankfully, I wasn't, but I was really scared for a while.)

Playing Sick Seemed the Only Escape

I saw him once more afterwards when I went to the store with Charlene one day after school. I was getting some juice and, while I was walking up to the counter to pay for it, he and two of his friends came into the store. My heart raced and I dropped the bottle. It smashed on the floor, but I didn't hear it. Charlene grabbed me and pulled me out of there. She knew something was wrong, but she kept her mouth shut. I didn't leave my house for a few weeks after that. I was afraid I might see him again. I was staying home more and more. Playing sick seemed to be the only escape.

One day, my best friend was over at my house, and I decided to tell her. I just couldn't keep this horrible secret inside of me any longer. "Kate, I need to tell you something," I said. I took a deep breath and sat down. "Kate," I tried to go slowly, but the words raced out of my mouth. "I was going out with this guy and I thought he was really nice but he wasn't. Kate, you're my best friend and I want you to help me. I was raped."

Kate just stared at me, in shock. Then the expression on her face changed to one of disbelief. "Well," she said, "How do you know if he really raped you?" I couldn't believe it. My best friend, doubting me, almost accusing me of lying. Things between us were never the same from then on. I can't say that I hate her, because I don't. I just don't talk to her — about anything.

Telling Someone — Getting Help

Eventually, I told some friends and a few adults. I am happy to say that all of them really helped me. They always listened when I needed to talk, anytime. Even if it was 3:30 in the morning, and I had trouble sleeping, I could call them up and they'd help me get through it. Now I really regret not speaking to anyone sooner.

It happened almost three years ago, but I still think about it as though it were yesterday. I have to stop asking myself if it was my fault, if I "asked for it." It wasn't my fault, I didn't ask for it. I had no control over the situation. The only thing I did wrong was wait so long to get help.

Rape is a horrible thing, I know that now. You have to be aware. You have to be careful. It can happen to anyone. And yes, you can be raped by someone you know. One minute you're watching TV, riding along in a car, getting help with homework. The next minute you're fighting to get away, gasping for breath, staring off into the blackness. If it does happen to you, remember, it's not your fault. Tell someone fast. Get help. It'll really make a difference later on.

Women Are Under a Rap Attack

YELENA DYNNIKOV

Free expression is great as long as someone's got something to say. Censorship is wrong if it prevents people from voicing their opinions on political

Reprinted with permission from *New Youth Connections*, copyright © 1994 by Youth Communication. For more information, write to Youth Communication, 144 W. 27th St., Suite 8-R, New York, NY 10001.

Harvard Educational Review Vol. 65 No. 2 Summer 1995, 271–273

and social issues. Discussions of topics like sexual preference, animal rights, and whether or not abortion should be legal are examples of what should not be censored. When you stand up for what you believe in and tell people about it, you're making an important statement. It is your right under the First Amendment of the Constitution to do so. In cases like these, censorship is not acceptable and cannot be tolerated.

But I have to admit there are times when I think censorship just might be a good idea. Like when I hear music that is insulting and degrading to women. Free expression receives a slap in the face when so-called "artists" use their First Amendment rights to demean women and send the message that we're all "stupid tramps."

Rappers or Cave Men?

A good example is "A B-tch Iz a B-tch" by NWA. This rap is just an endless stream of curses and threats of violence against women. And Awesome Dre is anything but awesome in his rap, "Sex Fiend." He seems to think that having sex with any girl he sees is his right: "Don't have to have permission 'cause I'm Awesome Dre." He believes women were created for the sole purpose of satisfying a man. I think he needs to change his name. How about Stone Age Dre, the caveman rapper?

When I hear songs like these, my jaw hardens and I shake with anger. I remember my first reaction to hearing Ice-T rap, "You know you want to do it too . . . you say you don't but I know you do." Fear rose up inside me. Are there really men out there who feel this way? "We both want it. Don't make it tough girl," Ice-T continued.

I pressed the "stop" button on my Walkman to reassure myself that it could be stopped. That I could shut him up. But as silence filled the air, I questioned my action. What did I shut up — Ice-T or my Walkman? When guys on the street start following you and hassling you because they think you're good for only one thing, how do you shut them up? There's no stop button to use on them.

Degrading Stereotypes

So many rap songs follow the same pattern — they create negative stereotypes of women and then use those stereotypes to legitimize treating women like dirt. It's an endless cycle. Women are first degraded and lowered: "Are you that funky, dirty, money-hungry, scandalous stuck-up, hairpiece wearing b-itch? Yup, you probably are!" ["A B-tch Iz a B-tch" by NWA] The girl's personality and credibility is lowered to that of a carrot stick.

These rappers never want to get to know the women they pursue. In fact, they proudly admit that they're only after one thing. "Kickin' conversation, ain't talkin' down nothing. When all that's really on your mind is what? Let's get butt naked and f—k." ["GIRLS, L.G.B.N.A.F." by Ice-T] And if a woman doesn't leap at the chance, she is immediately branded a b-tch. "When you say 'hi,' she don't say 'hi.' Are you the kind that think you're so damn fly? B-tch, eat sh-t and die!" ["A B-tch Iz a B-tch" by NWA]

We're Not Sex Toys

These raps suggest that women are plastic dummies with no brains, no ambitions, no personalities, and no feelings. They are portrayed by the "artists" as purely shallow sex toys. A girl's only function is to please the guy and after that she's discarded.

By now, you may be thinking, "What is she so worked up about? It's only music." It's because I think music is the only form of communication that really reaches a person. It steals the breath. It speaks to the heart. It moves the soul. It speaks even when no words are added and when accompanied by words, music can move boulders. It can also crash boulders if misused.

I hear lots of teens say that just because you hear something in a song does not mean that you'll go out and do it. Although that may be true, one cannot deny that music can affect and influence a person subconsciously.

Let's say a guy is out with a girl and wants to have sex with her but she says "No," but another part of him is hearing Ice-T sing, "You say you don't want it but I know you do." A whole crew of rappers has hammered into his head the idea that you don't have to take what the girl says seriously, that having sex with who you want, when you want, is a guy's right. And anyway, deep down she really wants it, no matter what she says. The line between fantasy and reality may get confused. Some guys might start to think that saying "No" is just another way of saying "Convince me." But it's not. A guy who doesn't listen when a woman says "no" is a rapist.

Let's Boycott

I think some of these songs put women in real danger (in addition to being ignorant and offensive). I wish they could be censored but I doubt that will happen. But there are things that can be done. Look at what happened with Ice-T's song "Cop Killer." Whether or not you agree with the people who were offended by that song, you have to admit that they were effective — they got it taken off the album. If enough people complained against songs that are threatening to women, maybe we could get some of those taken off the air.

Refusing to buy and support those tapes is a way of fighting the stereotype of women they are putting out. If you hear an offensive song on the radio that hurts you personally, act on it. Call up the radio stations that play it and tell them that they have lost a listener because of that particular song. Write to the record company that produced it and tell them why you refuse to buy their records. A campaign like this can work if we make it work!

The Phone Call

JOY CAIRES

When I look into our photo albums, I often wonder at the innocence and trust apparent in my old photographs. How is it that the baby I was has become the person I am now? It almost seems pointless to ask. Looking at the dozens of photographs, I take note of what I look like: I have my father's hands and his smile, I have the broad powerful frame of both my parents. We are so alike, yet so different. Our similarities are only on the surface, and I think my parents may wonder where this daughter of theirs has come from. I can almost note to the day when I began to diverge from the path they expected of me, or rather, when they noticed that I was headed somewhere they could not follow. I was expected, like my brothers before me, to go to college where I would meet someone (of the opposite gender) to marry. However, by the time I was fifteen, I had realized that I would not be following in my brothers' footsteps, and at this point my parents began to notice that I was not communicating my hopes for the future.

Both my brothers moved away when I was little, and my mom, dad, younger sister, and I live in separate worlds, spheres actually, that occasionally intersect but rarely meet for long. Part of this is due to my independence; I resent asking for anything and rarely do, even when I desperately need help or advice. They did not understand my world, my path, and I did not want them to. Therefore, when I was thirteen I began to withdraw from my parents, stopped talking to them much, except about silly superficial things, like, "How was your day?" "Fine." That was my reply to nearly every question, except for the big one; the question that seemed to tear my entire world apart.

It was my junior year, and I had just turned sixteen in August. School had been in session for a couple of months, and, in general, my life was miserable. Everyone seemed on my back. My relationship with my parents became worse as I began to withdraw more and more. I was trying to drown myself in work in order to keep out of my head. I didn't mind the stress. As long as I didn't have to deal with myself I was okay. Then, as I was passing by the administration office between classes, the school secretary gave me a message. "Your Mom wants you to call, she says it's important." I didn't really think much about the message. I just figured that she wanted me to run to the store or go to the pharmacy, so when I got a chance I went over to the phone in the office. Standing there staring at the spare, white phone, I suddenly got a strange feeling that this was really not a phone call that I wanted to make. The phone seemed to stare up at me threateningly. I steeled my nerves; it was just a phone call — no reason to worry. Slowly I reached for the phone and dialed. The ring of the phone was unnaturally loud, breaking the silence.

Harvard Educational Review Vol. 66 No. 2 Summer 1996, 175–177

"Hello."

A slightly out of breath voice picked up on the other line.

"Hi Mom, it's me. They said you wanted me to call."

"I went into your room today." At that moment I wanted to sink into the brown carpet beneath me. Every square inch of my being longed to run as far away from that phone as possible. My hand clenched the bone-white receiver in a painful grip and I clung to the edge of the desk like a sailor clinging to a life raft. With that brief statement, I knew that what I had been trying to hide for so long was out. She knew. There was nothing I could do about it. Through my own carelessness I would never be able to face my parents again.

I keep journals obsessively. They help me organize my feelings. They are an outlet for everything I cannot say to anyone. With those words I knew that mom had done the unthinkable: she had read my thoughts. I glanced at the clock; "Mom, I have math. I really have to go. Please."

"No, I need to know something; when I went into your room to open your curtain, I found something, and I need to know if it's true." Her words were choppy and pained. Slowly I spoke.

"What?" The room seemed to be getting smaller, and my breath quickened as I clenched my fist and felt my fingernails dig into my palm. Everything seemed to spin about me as she read my own words back to me verbatim. I could vividly remember writing that page in my journal and at that moment I regretted ever laying pen to paper, ever living, ever breathing, ever thinking.

"It says here 'I'm a lesbian' and I want to know if that's true."

I released the breath that had turned stale in my lungs. Shakily, I spoke into the receiver.

"Mom, I have class, I have to go." What could I say? I clenched my fist harder, rocking back and forth in my shoes.

"No, I need to know. No matter what I still love you." I could almost hear the tears in her voice and I, too, was close to the edge.

"No . . . Mom, I have to go, I'm on the school phone." I felt my voice grow firm as I struggled to regain control.

"Then why did you write it?"

"Mom, I have to go." Then, for the first time in my life, I hung up on her. Conversation over. Picking up my books I rushed out of the room, her words echoing again and again throughout my head, driving out thought of all else. As I looked out at the brilliant blue sky I felt so small, and the world outside seemed so big. It was a beautiful view that left no escape. I knew that I could not hide forever, and the rest of my life stretched out before me — a new era.

The next few weeks were hard on all of us as my mom searched for a concrete reason for my lesbianism. I was grounded for several months and sent to a psychiatrist in hopes that I would change. Because I was not prepared to come out to my parents, I was unable to explain to my mother that my sexuality was not anybody's fault. Several of our discussions dissolved into screaming matches as she accused me of tearing our family apart. My dad, on the other hand, pretended nothing had happened and refused to even say the word "lesbian." My parents did not want me to tell my sister or brothers, and I agreed because I was not ready to deal with their reactions.

Since the initial day of my mom's discovery, we've talked a lot, and now, more than a year and a half later, my mom still has difficulty accepting my sexuality. But, coming to terms with being out to my parents has taught me to respect the strength it takes to be myself when so many stand against me. Gradually I have learned to love and respect myself for the strengths I have. I never want to have to hide again.

Maybe someday my mom will be able to see me as my friends do: opinionated, verbose, feminist, bookworm, writer, philosopher, actress, and idealist who also happens to have a crush on Melissa Etheridge. Maybe someday she will realize that my lesbianism is just one part of a very complex whole — something that has contributed to my identity and broadened my horizons. Whether or not "someday" ever comes, I know that I have the strength to continue to be who I am. So, on the first day of the fall semester, listen for my contagious laugh and look for the rainbows I wear with pride.

Returned Letters

RACHEL LIBERATORE

This essay discusses an event that occurred after a friend's father returned nine months' worth of letters I had sent her, along with his note that she had attempted suicide and run away. As a result of this, I ended up coming to terms with the consequences of my silences, and my desire to live in a way that was beautiful and more real, because I could. I've changed my friend's name in this essay.

It's late autumn. I'm sitting in the orange leaves on the steps near the auditorium. Sitting down the steps from me, two girls hold each other. One of them is crying. The bell rings for lunch, but as they linger one girl says, "No matter how much our families hate us forever and ever, we'll be fine." I'm close to crying from the intensity of their words, their closeness, and the belief that someday I could be in the arms of a woman saying the same thing.

My thoughts revolve around Chrisy, whose hair is the same color as the leaves, wondering where she ran away to when she fled her small, homophobic town. A week earlier I had arrived home from swim practice to find a box of letters and postcards on my bed — my correspondence with Chrisy — a sixteen-year-old girl who lived in the Midwest. We had met through Alyson Publications' pen-pal exchange program for young gay, lesbian, and bisexual people, and we devoted a large portion of our letters to our feelings for women, and the implications of living with those feelings. The box gaped

Harvard Educational Review Vol. 66 No. 2 Summer 1996, 189–191

open from its resting place in the center of the pastel comforter on my unfixed bed, the top flap of the box addressed to my parents. Knowing they might have read my confessions brought an immediate terror that transformed into anger when I saw the scrawled note on top. It said: "I am sending the enclosed for your information. Chrisy has run away after attempting suicide six weeks ago. I wish you luck."

My sister had intervened and my parents hadn't read the letters, but my secret had surfaced. Walking the dog that night past plots of desert land and water ravines, on a stretch that showed the city lights extending from the mountains out to the horizon, I felt angry and powerless.

I couldn't live the gay aspects of my life as some sort of hidden and underground game anymore. For the first time I felt ready to tell my story, and knew I needed to tell Chrisy's story, too, not because the world lacked stories, but because it lacked the stories I really cared about.

First, I decided to have the terrifying "I'm not straight" talk with my parents. I felt angry at Chrisy's father for sending back all my letters, as if to purge his life of all the tangible evidence of his daughter's lesbianism. When Chrisy told her parents she considered herself a lesbian, they assured her those feelings must be "just a phase" and they asked her to please not tell everyone and his brother. My friend Rebecca's parents took her bisexuality as casual news that didn't affect them enough to acknowledge it. I primarily feared that, like my friends' parents, mine would not take me seriously.

I chose a Sunday night for the talk, after we returned home from dinner at my grandparents'. I entered my parents' room and sat on their bed with my dog. I petted her for courage and began talking, crying a little, but surviving. I explained that Chrisy's father sent them these letters because he realized how much secrets hurt families. This was an assumption, but one I preferred to believe and share over my other paranoid theory that he wanted to take his anger out by hurting another family. It shouldn't hurt, but in most families finding out a son or daughter is bisexual or gay does hurt, and he knew that, too. At one point my mother said, "I don't even want to think about this," and I said, "I want you to think about this because I have to think about it every day."

It bothered me that neither of my parents expressed surprise, since they told me they'd never talked to each other about who I could be. At that point I realized they weren't as liberal as I thought they were. My mother had lesbian and gay friends, and constantly talked about gay issues, yet I got the feeling she regarded those issues as not possibly touching us. This hurt, because I had a great idealism about my family and I wanted to believe we could be visionary.

I recently read a short story where this girl comes out to her parents and has a difficult time dealing with their inability to talk about it. She says, "I don't want to have to do this alone." My returned letters made me realize that it's close to impossible to "do this alone."

Chrisy shared visions and bravery, and an identity that amazed me. I thought this bravery meant she'd be okay in spite of the hostilities she faced, but it wasn't enough for her. She gave me the impression she'd do what she needed to survive. Chrisy wanted deeply to feel high on life, and she found some beautiful ways to do it. Once she snuck away to a lesbian coffee shop, making eye contact with most of the women there, which she described as "the biggest high." Listening to the passionate music of Melissa Etheridge and playing Etheridge's music on her guitar in the Illinois fields also made her high.

In her second letter she expressed the desire to "come out" during her senior year of high school, so she could take a woman to the prom. I marveled that she believed she could wait that long; silence hurts too much after awhile. By her third letter, she wrote about telling various friends about her feelings for women, and discovering that only a handful gave their support. In the months before her suicide attempt, she struggled to feel valid as part of the only openly gay couple in her school.

In an adult world, I see people as having more perspective. It's like the lyrics from a song by Dar Williams, "I'm older now, I know the gradual rise and fall of a daily victory." Pain and joy become a more familiar pattern. But to younger people, emotions matter as if the world depended upon them, or hinged upon them. In a teenage world, where the pain and joy of every experience is magnified and words have the potential to create or destroy the world, Chrisy described the lowest of all lows in an untitled poem. She didn't name it, she said, because she couldn't think of a label that would give it justice:

> I watch,
> Alone in its likeness
> Stranded with its fear and shame
> Surrounded by others
> Trying to hide concern
> Only then with laughter and disgust
> Striving to be known.
> I listen
> To hear the cries from within.
> To be set free

In the silent world of her poem, one familiar to most bisexual and gay teenagers, only vague hints from a few of your classmates save you from complete alienation. You note others' glances and subtle clues, hoping you're not alone. You want a place where you don't have to lie anymore, living under people's false assumptions. The more friends I have, the more I have to face how many young people suffer from feeling that it's not okay to pursue romantic relationships with people they feel drawn to.

I don't know how to contact Chrisy, how to connect with her world and stop worrying. Her letters mentioned friends by first name only, so I can't write them, and her father's scrawled note, "I wish you good luck," seemed rather final. Someone tore the return address off the envelope of the last letter I sent her; I hope she brought the address with her, wherever she went.

Sexuality, Schooling, and Adolescent Females:

The Missing Discourse of Desire

MICHELLE FINE

Michelle Fine argues in this chapter that the anti-sex rhetoric surrounding sex education and school-based health clinics does little to enhance the development of sexual responsibility and subjectivity in adolescents. Despite substantial evidence of the success of both school-based health clinics and access to sexuality education, the majority of public schools do not sanction or provide such information. According to Fine, female students, particularly low-income girls, suffer most from the inadequacies of present sex education policies. Current practices and language lead to increased experiences of victimization, teenage pregnancy, and increased drop-out rates. The author combines a thorough review of the literature with her research in public schools to make a compelling argument for "sexuality education" that fosters not only the full development of a sexual self, but also girls' overall development in the educational context.

Since late 1986, popular magazines and newspapers have printed steamy stories about education and sexuality. Whether the controversy surrounds sex education or school-based health clinics (SBHCs), public discourses of adolescent sexuality are represented forcefully by government officials, New Right spokespersons, educators, "the public," feminists, and health-care professionals. These stories offer the authority of "facts," insights into the political controversies, and access to un-acknowledged fears about sexuality (Foucault, 1980). Although the facts usually involve the adolescent female body, little has been heard from young women themselves.

This article examines these diverse perspectives on adolescent sexuality and, in addition, presents the views of a group of adolescent females. The article is informed by a study of numerous current sex education curricula, a year of negotiating for inclusion of lesbian and gay sexuality in a citywide

Harvard Educational Review Vol. 58 No. 1 February 1988, 29–53

sex education curriculum, and interviews and observations gathered in New York City sex education classrooms.[1] The analysis examines the desires, fears, and fantasies which give structure and shape to silences and voices concerning sex education and school-based health clinics in the 1980s.

Despite the attention devoted to teen sexuality, pregnancy, and parenting in this country, and despite the evidence of effective interventions and the wide-spread public support expressed for these interventions (Harris, 1985), the systematic implementation of sex education and SBHCs continues to be obstructed by the controversies surrounding them (Kantrowitz et al., 1987; Leo, 1986). Those who resist sex education or SBHCs often present their views as based on rationality and a concern for protecting the young. For such opponents, sex education raises questions of promoting promiscuity and immorality, and of undermining family values. Yet the language of the challenges suggests an effect substantially more profound and primitive. Gary Bauer, Undersecretary of Education in the U.S. Department of Education, for example, constructs an image of immorality littered by adolescent sexuality and drug abuse:

> There is ample impressionistic evidence to indicate that drug abuse and promiscuity are not independent behaviors. When inhibitions fall, they collapse across the board. When people of any age lose a sense of right and wrong, the loss is not selective. . . . [T]hey are all expressions of the same ethical vacuum among many teens. . . . (1986)

Even Surgeon General C. Everett Koop, a strong supporter of sex education, recently explained: "[W]e have to be as explicit as necessary. . . . You can't talk of the dangers of snake poisoning and not mention snakes" (quoted in Leo, 1986, p. 54). Such commonly used and often repeated metaphors associate adolescent sexuality with victimization and danger.

Yet public schools have rejected the task of sexual dialogue and critique, or what has been called "sexuality education." Within today's standard sex education curricula and many public school classrooms, we find: 1) the authorized suppression of a discourse of female sexual desire; 2) the promotion of a discourse of female sexual victimization; and 3) the explicit privileging of married heterosexuality over other practices of sexuality. One finds an unacknowledged social ambivalence about female sexuality which ideologically separates the female sexual agent, or subject, from her coun-

[1] The research reported in this article represents one component of a year-long ethnographic investigation of students and dropouts at a comprehensive public high school in New York City. Funded by the W. T. Grant Foundation, the research was designed to investigate how public urban high schools produce dropout rates in excess of 50 percent. The methods employed over the year included: in-school observations four days/week during the fall, and one to two days/week during the spring; regular (daily) attendance in a hygiene course for twelfth graders; an archival analysis of more than 1200 students who compose the 1978–79 cohort of incoming ninth graders; interviews with approximately 55 recent and long-term dropouts; analysis of fictional and autobiographical writings by students; a survey distributed to a subsample of the cohort population; and visits to proprietary schools, programs for Graduate Equivalency Diplomas, naval recruitment sites, and a public high school for pregnant and parenting teens. The methods and preliminary results of the ethnography are detailed in Fine (1986).

terpart, the female sexual victim. The adolescent woman of the 1980s is constructed as the latter. Educated primarily as the potential victim of male sexuality, she represents no subject in her own right. Young women continue to be taught to fear and defend in isolation from exploring desire, and in this context there is little possibility of their developing a critique of gender or sexual arrangements.

Prevailing Discourses of Female Sexuality inside Public Schools

> If the body is seen as endangered by uncontrollable forces, then presumably this is a society or social group which fears change — change which it perceived simultaneously as powerful and beyond its control. (Smith-Rosenberg, 1978, p. 229)

Public schools have historically been the site for identifying, civilizing, and containing that which is considered uncontrollable. While evidence of sexuality is everywhere within public high schools — in the halls, classrooms, bathrooms, lunchrooms, and the library — official sexuality education occurs sparsely: in social studies, biology, sex education, or inside the nurse's office. To understand how sexuality is managed inside schools, I examined the major discourses of sexuality which characterize the national debates over sex education and SBHCs. These discourses are then tracked as they weave through the curricula, classrooms, and halls of public high schools.

The first discourse, *sexuality as violence,* is clearly the most conservative, and equates adolescent heterosexuality with violence. At the 1986 American Dreams Symposium on education, Phyllis Schlafly commented: "Those courses on sex, abuse, incest, AIDS, they are all designed to terrorize our children. We should fight their existence, and stop putting terror in the hearts and minds of our youngsters." One aspect of this position, shared by women as politically distinct as Schlafly and the radical feminist lawyer Catherine MacKinnon (1983), views heterosexuality as essentially violent and coercive. In its full conservative form, proponents call for the elimination of sex education and clinics and urge complete reliance on the family to dictate appropriate values, mores, and behaviors.

Sexuality as violence presumes that there is a causal relationship between official silence about sexuality and a decrease in sexual activity — therefore, by not teaching about sexuality, adolescent sexual behavior will not occur. The irony, of course, lies in the empirical evidence. Fisher, Byrne, and White (1983) have documented sex-negative attitudes and contraceptive use to be negatively correlated. In their study, sex-negative attitudes do not discourage sexual activity, but they do discourage responsible use of contraception. Teens who believe sexual involvement is wrong deny responsibility for contraception. To accept responsibility would legitimate "bad" behavior. By contrast, Fisher et al. (1983) found that adolescents with sex-positive attitudes tend to be both more consistent and more positive about contraceptive use.

By not teaching about sexuality, or by teaching sex-negative attitudes, schools apparently will not forestall sexual activity, but may well discourage responsible contraception.

The second disclosure, *sexuality as victimization,* gathers a much greater following. Female adolescent sexuality is represented as a moment of victimization in which the dangers of heterosexuality for adolescent women (and, more recently, of homosexuality for adolescent men) are prominent. While sex may not be depicted as inherently violent, young women (and today, men) learn of their vulnerability to potential male predators.

To avoid being victimized, females learn to defend themselves against disease, pregnancy, and "being used." The discourse of victimization supports sex education, including AIDS education, with parental consent. Suggested classroom activities emphasize "saying no," practicing abstinence, enumerating the social and emotional risks of sexual intimacy, and listing the possible diseases associated with sexual intimacy. The language, as well as the questions asked and not asked, represents females as the actual and potential victims of male desire. In exercises, role plays, and class discussions, girls practice resistance to trite lines, unwanted hands, opened buttons, and the surrender of other "bases" they are not prepared to yield. The discourses of violence and victimization both portray males as potential predators and females as victims. Three problematic assumptions underlie these two views:

- First, female subjectivity, including the desire to engage in sexual activity, is placed outside the prevailing conversation (Vance, 1984).
- Second, both arguments present female victimization as contingent upon unmarried heterosexual involvement — rather than inherent in existing gender, class, and racial arrangements (Rubin, 1984). While feminists have long fought for the legal and social acknowledgment of sexual violence against women, most have resisted the claim that female victimization hinges primarily upon sexual involvement with men. The full range of victimization of women — at work, at home, on the streets — has instead been uncovered. The language and emotion invested in these two discourses divert attention away from structures, arrangements, and relationships which oppress women in general, and low-income women and women of color in particular (Lorde, 1978).
- Third, the messages, while narrowly anti-sexual, nevertheless buttress traditional heterosexual arrangements. These views assume that as long as females avoid premarital sexual relations with men, victimization can be avoided. Ironically, however, protection from male victimization is available primarily through marriage — by coupling with a man. The paradoxical message teaches females to fear the very men who will ultimately protect them.

The third discourse, *sexuality as individual morality,* introduces explicit notions of sexual subjectivity for women. Although quite judgmental and moralistic, this discourse values women's sexual decisionmaking as long as the decisions made are for premarital abstinence. For example, Secretary of Education William Bennett urges schools to teach "morality literacy" and to educate towards "modesty," "chastity," and "abstinence" until marriage. The language of self-control and self-respect reminds students that sexual immorality breeds not only personal problems but also community tax burdens.

The debate over morality in sex education curricula marks a clear contradiction among educational conservatives over whether and how the state may intervene in the "privacy of families." Non-interventionists, including Schlafly and Onalee McGraw, argue that educators should not teach about sexuality at all. To do so is to take a particular moral position which subverts the family. Interventionists, including Koop, Bennett, and Bauer, argue that schools should teach about sexuality by focusing on "good values," but disagree about how. Koop proposes open discussion of sexuality and the use of condoms, while Bennett advocates "sexual restraint" ("Koop AIDS Stand Assailed," 1987). Sexuality in this discourse is posed as a test of self-control; individual restraint triumphs over social temptation. Pleasure and desire for women as sexual objects remain largely in the shadows, obscured from adolescent eyes.

The fourth discourse, a *discourse of desire,* remains a whisper inside the official work of U.S. public schools. If introduced at all, it is as an interruption of the ongoing conversation (Snitow, Stansell, & Thompson, 1983). The naming of desire, pleasure, or sexual entitlement, particularly for females, barely exists in the formal agenda of public schooling on sexuality. When spoken, it is tagged with reminders of "consequences" — emotional, physical, moral, reproductive, and/or financial (Freudenberg, 1987). A genuine discourse of desire would invite adolescents to explore what feels good and bad, desirable and undesirable, grounded in experiences, needs, and limits. Such a discourse would release females from a position of receptivity, enable an analysis of the dialectics of victimization and pleasure, and would pose female adolescents as subjects of sexuality, initiators as well as negotiators (Golden, 1984; Petchesky, 1984; Thompson, 1983).

In Sweden, where sex education has been offered in schools since the turn of the century, the State Commission on Sex Education recommends teaching students to "acquire a knowledge . . . [which] will equip them to experience sexual life as a source of happiness and joy in fellowship with other [people]" (Brown, 1983, p. 88). The teachers' handbook goes on, "The many young people who wish to wait [before initiating sexual activity] and those who have had early sexual relations should experience, in class, [the feeling] that they are understood and accepted" (p. 93). Compare this to an exercise suggested in a major U.S. metropolitan sex education curriculum: "Discuss and evaluate: things which may cause teenagers to engage in sexual relations before they are ready to assume the responsibility of marriage" (see Philadelphia School District, 1986; and New York City Board of Education, 1984).

A discourse of desire, though seldom explored in U.S. classrooms, does occur in less structured school situations. The following excerpts, taken from group and individual student interviews, demonstrate female adolescents' subjective experiences of body and desire as they begin to articulate notions of sexuality.

In some cases young women pose a critique of marriage:

> I'm still in love with Simon, but I'm seeing Jose. He's OK but he said, "Will you be my girl?" I hate that. It feels like they own you. Like I say to a girlfriend, "What's wrong? You look terrible!" and she says, "I'm married!" (Millie, a 16-year-old student from the Dominican Republic)

In other cases they offer stories of their own victimization:

> It's not like last year. Then I came to school regular. Now my old boyfriend, he waits for me in front of my building every morning and he fights with me. Threatens me, gettin' all bad. . . . I want to move out of my house and live 'cause he ain't gonna stop no way. (Sylvia, age 17, about to drop out of twelfth grade)

Some even speak of desire:

> I'm sorry I couldn't call you last night about the interview, but my boyfriend came back from [the] Navy and I wanted to spend the night with him, we don't get to see each other much. (Shandra, age 17, after a no-show for an interview)

In a context in which desire is not silenced, but acknowledged and discussed, conversations with adolescent women can, as seen here, educate through a dialectic of victimization and pleasure. Despite formal silencing, it would be misleading to suggest that talk of desire never emerges within public schools. Notwithstanding a political climate organized around the suppression of this conversation, some teachers and community advocates continue to struggle for an empowering sex education curriculum both in an out of the high school classroom.

Family life curricula and/or plans for a school-based health clinic have been carefully generated in many communities. Yet they continue to face loud and sometimes violent resistance by religious and community groups, often from outside the district lines (Boffey, 1987; "Chicago School Clinic," 1986; Dowd, 1986; Perlez, 1986a, 1986b; Rohter, 1985). In other communities, when curricula or clinics have been approved with little overt confrontation, monies for training are withheld. For example, in New York City in 1987, $1.7 million was initially requested to implement training on the Family Life education curriculum. As sex educators confronted community and religious groups, the inclusion of some topics as well as the language of others were continually negotiated. Ultimately, the Chancellor requested only $600,000 for training, a sum substantially inadequate to the task.[2]

In this political context many public school educators nevertheless continue to take personal and professional risks to create materials and foster classroom environments which speak fully to the sexual subjectivities of

---

[2] This information is derived from personal communications with former and present employees of major urban school districts who have chosen to remain anonymous.

young women and men. Some operate within the privacy of their classrooms, subverting the official curriculum and engaging students in critical discussion. Others advocate publicly for enriched curricula and training. A few have even requested that community-based advocates *not* agitate for official curricular change, so "we [teachers] can continue to do what we do in the classroom, with nobody looking over our shoulders. You make a big public deal of this, and it will blow open."[3] Within public school classrooms, it seems that female desire may indeed be addressed when educators act subversively. But in the typical sex education classroom, silence, and therefore distortion, surrounds female desire.

The blanketing of female sexual subjectivity in public school classrooms, in public discourse, and in bed will sound familiar to those who have read Luce Irigaray (1980) and Helene Cíxous (1981). These French feminists have argued that expressions of female voice, body, and sexuality are essentially inaudible when the dominant language and ways of viewing are male. Inside the hegemony of what they call The Law of the Father, female desire and pleasure can gain expression only in the terrain already charted by men (see also Burke, 1980). In the public school arena, this constriction of what is called sexuality allows girls one primary decision — to say yes or no — to a question not necessarily their own. A discourse of desire in which young women have a voice would be informed and generated out of their own socially constructed sexual meanings. It is to these expressions that we now turn.

The Bodies of Female Adolescents: Voices and Structured Silences

If four discourses can be distinguished among the many positions articulated by various "authorities," the sexual meanings voiced by female adolescents defy such classification. A discourse of desire, though absent in the "official" curriculum, is by no means missing from the lived experiences or commentaries of young women. This section introduces their sexual thoughts, concerns, and meanings, as represented by a group of Black and Latina female adolescents — students and dropouts from a public high school in New York City serving predominantly low-income youths. In my year at this comprehensive high school I had frequent opportunity to speak with adolescents and listen to them talk about sex. The comments reported derive from conversations between the young women and their teachers, among themselves, and with me, as researcher. During conversations, the young women talked freely about fears and, in the same breath, asked about passions. Their struggle to untangle issues of gender, power, and sexuality underscores the fact that, for them, notions of sexual negotiation cannot be separated from sacrifice and nurturance.

The adolescent female rarely reflects simply on sexuality. Her sense of sexuality is informed by peers, culture, religion, violence, history, passion,

[3] Personal communication.

authority, rebellion, body, past and future, and gender and racial relations of power (Espin, 1984; Omolade, 1983). The adolescent woman herself assumes a dual consciousness — at once taken with the excitement of actual/anticipated sexuality and consumed with anxiety and worry. While too few safe spaces exist for adolescent women's exploration of sexual subjectivities, there are all too many dangerous spots for their exploitation.

Whether in a classroom, on the street, at work, or at home, the adolescent female's sexuality is negotiated by, for, and despite the young woman herself. Patricia, a young Puerto Rican woman who worried about her younger sister, relates: "You see, I'm the love child and she's the one born because my mother was raped in Puerto Rico. Her father's in jail now, and she feels so bad about the whole thing so she acts bad." For Patricia, as for the many young women who have experienced and/or witnessed sexual violence, discussions of sexuality merge representations of passions with violence. Often the initiator of conversation among peers about virginity, orgasm, "getting off," and pleasure, Patricia mixed sexual talk freely with references to force and violence. She is a poignant narrator who illustrates, from the female adolescent's perspective, that sexual victimization and desire coexist (Benjamin, 1983).

Sharlene and Betty echo this braiding of danger and desire. Sharlene explained: "Boys always be trying to get into my panties," and Betty added: "I don't be needin' a man who won't give me no pleasure but take my money and expect me to take care of him." This powerful commentary on gender relations, voiced by Black adolescent females, was inseparable from their views of sexuality. To be a woman was to be strong, independent, and reliable — but not too independent for fear of scaring off a man.

Deidre continued this conversation, explicitly pitting male fragility against female strength: "Boys in my neighborhood ain't wrapped so tight. Got to be careful how you treat them. . . ." She reluctantly admitted that perhaps it is more important for Black males than females to attend college, "Girls and women, we're stronger, we take care of ourselves. But boys and men, if they don't get away from the neighborhood, they end up in jail, on drugs or dead . . . or wack [crazy]."

These young women spoke often of anger at males, while concurrently expressing a strong desire for male attention: "I dropped out 'cause I fell in love, and couldn't stop thinking of him." An equally compelling desire was to protect young males — particularly Black males — from a system which "makes them wack." Ever aware of the ways that institutional racism and the economy have affected Black males, these young women seek pleasure but also offer comfort. They often view self-protection as taking something away from young men. Lavanda offered a telling example: "If I ask him to use a condom, he won't feel like a man."

In order to understand the sexual subjectivities of young women more completely, educators need to reconstruct schooling as an empowering context in which we listen to and work with the meanings and experiences of gender and sexuality revealed by the adolescents themselves. When we refuse that responsibility, we prohibit an education which adolescents wholly need and deserve. My classroom observations suggest that such education is rare.

Ms. Rosen, a teacher of a sex education class, opened one session with a request: "You should talk to your mother or father about sex before you get involved." Nilda initiated what became an informal protest by a number of Latino students: "Not our parents! We tell them one little thing and they get crazy. My cousin got sent to Puerto Rico to live with her religious aunt, and my sister got beat 'cause my father thought she was with a boy." For these adolescents, a safe space for discussion, critique, and construction of sexualities was not something they found in their homes. Instead, they relied on school, the spot they chose for the safe exploration of sexualities.

The absence of safe spaces for exploring sexuality affects all adolescents. It was paradoxical to realize that perhaps the only students who had an in-school opportunity for critical sexual discussion in the comfort of peers were the few students who had organized the Gay and Lesbian Association (GALA) at the high school. While most lesbian, gay, or bisexual students were undoubtedly closeted, those few who were "out" claimed this public space for their display and for their sanctuary. Exchanging support when families and peers would offer little, GALA members worried that so few students were willing to come out, and that so many suffered the assaults of homophobia individually. The gay and lesbian rights movement had powerfully affected these youngsters, who were comfortable enough to support each other in a place not considered very safe — a public high school in which echoes of "faggot!" fill the halls.

In the absence of an education which explores and unearths danger and desire, sexuality education classes typically provide little opportunity for discussions beyond those constructed around superficial notions of male heterosexuality (see Kelly, 1986, for a counterexample). Male pleasure is taught, albeit as biology. Teens learn about "wet dreams" (as the onset of puberty for males), "erection" (as the preface to intercourse), and "ejaculation" (as the act of inseminating). Female pleasures and questions are far less often the topic of discussion. Few voices of female sexual agency can be heard. The language of victimization and its underlying concerns — "Say No," put a brake on his sexuality, don't encourage — ultimately deny young women the right to control their own sexuality by providing no access to a legitimate position of sexual subjectivity. Often conflicted about self-representation, adolescent females spend enormous amounts of time trying to "save it," "lose it," convince others that they have lost or saved it, or trying to be "discreet" instead of focusing their energies in ways that are sexually autonomous, responsible, and pleasurable. In classroom observations, girls who were heterosexually active rarely spoke, for fear of being ostracized (Fine, 1986). Those who were heterosexual virgins had the same worry. And most students who were gay, bisexual, or lesbian remained closeted, aware of the very real dangers of homophobia.

Occasionally, the difficult and pleasurable aspects of sexuality were discussed together, coming either as an interruption, or because an educational context was constructed. During a social studies class, for example, Catherine, the proud mother of two-year-old Tiffany, challenged an assumption underlying the class discussion — that teen motherhood devastates mother and child; "If I didn't get pregnant I would have continued on a downward path, going nowhere. They say teenage pregnancy is bad for you, but it was good for me. I know I can't mess around now, I got to worry about what's good for Tiffany and for me."

Another interruption came from Opal, a young Black student. Excerpts from her hygiene class follow.

Teacher: Let's talk about teenage pregnancy.

Opal: How come girls in the locker room say, "You a virgin?" and if you say "Yeah" they laugh and say "Ohh, you're a virgin. . . ." And some Black teenagers, I don't mean to be racial, when they get ready to tell their mothers they had sex, some break on them and some look funny. My friend told her mother and she broke all the dishes. She told her mother so she could get protection so she don't get pregnant.

Teacher: When my 13-year-old (relative) asked for birth control I was shocked and angry.

Portia: Mothers should help so she can get protection and not get pregnant or diseases. So you was wrong.

Teacher: Why not say "I'm thinking about having sex?"

Portia: You tell them after, not before, having sex but before pregnancy.

Teacher (now angry): Then it's a fait accompli and you expect my compassion? You have to take more responsibility.

Portia: I am! If you get pregnant after you told your mother and you got all the stuff and still get pregnant, you the fool. Take up hygiene and learn. Then it's my responsibility if I end up pregnant. . . .

> (Field Note, October 23, Hygiene Class)

Two days later, the discussion continued.

Teacher: What topics should we talk about in sex education?

Portia: Organs, how they work.

Opal: What's an orgasm?

[laughter]

Teacher: Sexual response, sensation all over the body. What's analogous to the male penis on the female?

Theo: Clitoris.

Teacher: Right, go home and look in the mirror.

Portia: She is too much!

Teacher: Why look in the mirror?

Elaine: It's yours.

Teacher: Why is it important to know what your body looks like?

Opal: You should like your body.

Teacher: You should know what it looks like when it's healthy, so you can recognize problems like vaginal warts.

(Field Note, October 25, Hygiene Class)

The discourse of desire, initiated by Opal but evident only as an interruption, faded rapidly into the discourse of disease — warning about the dangers of sexuality.

It was in the spring of that year that Opal showed up pregnant. Her hygiene teacher, who was extremely concerned and involved with her students, was also quite angry with Opal: "Who is going to take care of that baby, you or your mother? You know what it costs to buy diapers and milk and afford child care?"

Opal, in conversation with me, related, "I got to leave [school] 'cause even if they don't say it, them teachers got hate in their eyes when they look at my belly." In the absence of a way to talk about passion, pleasure, danger, and responsibility, this teacher fetishized the latter two, holding the former two hostage. Because adolescent females combine these experiences in their daily lives, the separation is false, judgmental, and ultimately not very educational.

Over the year in this high school, and in other public schools since, I have observed a systematic refusal to name issues, particularly issues that caused adults discomfort. Educators often projected their discomfort onto students in the guise of "protecting" them (Fine, 1987). An example of such silencing can be seen in a (now altered) policy of the school district of Philadelphia. In 1985 a student informed me, "We're not allowed to talk about abortion in our school." Assuming this was an overstatement, I asked an administrator at the District about this practice. She explained, "That's not quite right. If a student asks a question about abortion, the teacher can define abortion, she just can't discuss it." How can definition occur without discussion, exchange, conversation, or critique unless a subtext of silencing prevails (Greene, 1986; Noddings, 1986)?

Explicit silencing of abortion has since been lifted in Philadelphia. The revised curriculum now reads:

Options for unintended pregnancy:
- (a) adoption
- (b) foster care
- (c) single parenthood
- (d) teen marriage
- (e) abortion

A footnote is supposed to be added, however, to elaborate the negative consequences of abortion. In the social politics which surround public schools, such compromises are apparent across cities.

The New York City Family Life Education curriculum reads similarly (New York City Board of Education, 1984, p. 172):

> List: The possible options for an unintended pregnancy. What considerations should be given in the decision on the alternatives?
> - adoption
> - foster care
> - mother keeps baby
> - elective abortion
>
> Discuss:
> - religious viewpoints on abortion
> - present laws concerning abortion
> - current developments in prenatal diagnosis and their implication for abortion issues
> - why abortion should not be considered a contraceptive device
>
> List: The people or community services that could provide assistance in the event of an unintended pregnancy
>
> Invite: A speaker to discuss alternatives to abortion; for example, a social worker from the Department of Social Services to discuss foster care.

One must be suspicious when diverse views are sought only for abortion, and not for adoption, teen motherhood, or foster care. The call to silence is easily identified in current political and educational contexts (Fine, 1987; Foucault, 1980). The silence surrounding contraception and abortion options and diversity in sexual orientations denies adolescents information and sends the message that such conversations are taboo — at home, at church, and even at school.

In contrast to these "official curricula," which allow discussion and admission of desire only as an interruption, let us examine other situations in which young women were invited to analyze sexuality across categories of the body, the mind, the heart, and of course, gender politics.

Teen Choice, a voluntary counseling program held on-site by non-Board of Education social workers, offered an instance in which the complexities of pleasure and danger were invited, analyzed, and braided into discussions of sexuality. In a small group discussion, the counselor asked of the seven ninth graders, "What are the two functions of a penis?" One student responded, "To pee!" Another student offered the second function: "To eat!" which was followed by laughter and serious discussion. The conversation proceeded as the teacher asked, "Do all penises look alike?" The students explained, "No, they are all different colors!"

The freedom to express, beyond simple right and wrong answers, enabled these young women to offer what they knew with humor and delight. This discussion ended as one student insisted that if you "jump up and down a lot, the stuff will fall out of you and you won't get pregnant," to which the social worker answered with slight exasperation that millions of sperm would have to be released for such "expulsion" to work, and that of course, it wouldn't work. In this conversation one could hear what seemed like too much experience, too little information, and too few questions asked by the students. But the discussion, which was sex-segregated and guided by the experiences and questions of the students themselves (and the skills of the social worker), enabled easy movement between pleasure and danger, safety and desire, naiveté and knowledge, and victimization and entitlement.

What is evident, then, is that even in the absence of a discourse of desire, young women express their notions of sexuality and relate their experiences. Yet, "official" discourses of sexuality leave little room for such exploration. The authorized sexual discourses define what is safe, what is taboo, and what will be silenced. This discourse of sexuality mis-educates adolescent women. What results is a discourse of sexuality based on the male in search of desire and the female in search of protection. The open, coed sexuality discussions so many fought for in the 1970s have been appropriated as a forum for the primacy of male heterosexuality and the preservation of female victimization.

The Politics of Female Sexual Subjectivities

In 1912, an education committee explicitly argued that "scientific" sex education "should . . . keep sex consciousness and sex emotions at the minimum" (Leo, 1986). In the same era G. Stanley Hall proposed diversionary pursuits for adolescents, including hunting, music, and sports, "to reduce sex stress and tension . . . to short-circuit, transmute it and turn it on to develop the higher powers of men [sic]" (Hall, 1914, pp. 29, 30). In 1915 Orison Marden, author of *The Crime of Silence,* chastised educators, reformers, and public health specialists for their unwillingness to speak publicly about sexuality and for relying inappropriately on parents and peers, who were deemed too ignorant to provide sex instruction (Imber, 1984; Strong, 1972). And in 1921 radical sex educator Maurice Bigelow wrote:

> Now, most scientifically-trained women seem to agree that there are no corresponding phenomena in the early pubertal life of the normal young woman who has good health (corresponding to male masturbation). A limited number of mature women, some of them physicians, report having experienced in the pubertal years localized tumescence and other disturbances which made them definitely conscious of sexual instincts. However, it should be noted that most of these are known to have had a personal history including one or more such abnormalities such as dysmenorrhea, uterine displacement, pathological ovaries, leucorrhea, tuberculosis, masturbation, neurasthenia, nymphomania, or other disturbances which are sufficient to account for local sexual stimulation. In short such women are not normal. . . . (p. 179)

In the 1950s public school health classes separated girls from boys. Girls "learned about sex" by watching films of the accelerated development of breasts and hips, the flow of menstrual blood, and then the progression of venereal disease as a result of participation in out-of-wedlock heterosexual activity.

Thirty years and a much-debated sexual revolution later (Ehrenreich, Hess, & Jacobs, 1986), much has changed. Feminism, the Civil Rights Movement, the disability and gay rights movements, birth control, legal abortion with federal funding (won and then lost), and reproductive technologies are part of these changes (Weeks, 1985). Due both to the consequences of, and the backlashes against, these movements, students today do learn about sexuality — if typically through the representations of female sexuality as inadequacy or victimization, male homosexuality as a story of predator and prey, and male heterosexuality as desire.

Young women today know that female sexual subjectivity is at least not an inherent contradiction. Perhaps they even feel it is an entitlement. Yet when public schools resist acknowledging the fullness of female sexual subjectivities, they reproduce a profound social ambivalence which dichotomizes female heterosexuality (Espin, 1984; Golden, 1984; Omolade, 1983). This ambivalence surrounds a fragile cultural distinction between two forms of female sexuality: *consensual* sexuality, representing consent or choice in sexuality, and *coercive* sexuality, which represents force, victimization, and/or crime (Weeks, 1985).

During the 1980s, however, this distinction began to be challenged. It was acknowledged that gender-based power inequities shape, define, and construct experiences of sexuality. Notions of sexual consent and force, except in extreme circumstances, became complicated, no longer in simple opposition. The first problem concerned how to conceptualize power asymmetries and consensual sexuality. Could *consensual* female heterosexuality be said to exist within a context replete with structures, relationships, acts, and threats of female victimization (sexual, social, and economic) (MacKinnon, 1983)? How could we speak of "sexual preference" when sexual involvement outside of heterosexuality may seriously jeopardize one's social and/or economic well-being (Petchesky, 1984)? Diverse female sexual subjectivities emerge through, despite, and because of gender-based power assymetries. To imagine a female sexual self, free of and uncontaminated by power, was rendered naive (Foucault, 1980; Irigaray, 1980; Rubin, 1984).

The second problem involved the internal incoherence of the categories. Once assumed fully independent, the two began to blur as the varied practices of sexuality went public. At the intersection of these presumably parallel forms — coercive and consensual sexualities — lay "sexual" acts of violence and "violent" acts of sex. "Sexual" acts of violence, including marital rape, acquaintance rape, and sexual harassment, were historically considered consensual. A woman involved in a marriage, on a date, or working outside her home "naturally" risked receiving sexual attention; her consent was inferred from her presence. But today, in many states, this woman can sue her husband for such sexual acts of violence; in all states, she can prosecute a boss. What was once part of "domestic life" or "work" may, today, be criminal. On the other hand, "violent" acts of sex, including consensual sadomasochism and the use of violence-portraying pornography, were once considered inherently coercive for women (Benjamin, 1983; Rubin, 1984; Weeks, 1985). Female involvement in such sexual practices historically had been dismissed as nonconsensual. Today such romanticizing of a naive and moral "feminine sexuality" has been challenged as essentialist, and the assumption that such a feminine sexuality is "natural" to women has been shown to be false (Rubin, 1984).

Over the past decade, understandings of female sexual choice, consent, and coercion have grown richer and more complex. While questions about female subjectivities have become more interesting, the answers (for some) remain deceptively simple. Inside public schools, for example, female adolescents continue to be educated as though they were the potential *victims* of sexual (male) desire. By contrast, the ideological opposition represents only adult married women as fully consensual partners. The distinction of coercion and consent has been organized simply and respectively around age and marital status — which effectively resolves any complexity and/or ambivalence.

The ambivalence surrounding female heterosexuality places the victim and subject in opposition and derogates all women who represent female sexual subjectivities outside of marriage — prostitutes, lesbians, single mothers, women involved with multiple partners, and particularly, Black single mothers (Weitz, 1984). "Protected" from this derogation, the typical adolescent woman, as represented in sex education curricula, is without any sexual subjectivity. The discourse of victimization not only obscures the derogation, it also transforms socially distributed anxieties about female sexuality into acceptable, and even protective, talk.

The fact that schools implicitly organize sex education around a concern for female victimization is suspect, however, for two reasons. First, if female victims of male violence were truly a social concern, wouldn't the victims of rape, incest, and sexual harassment encounter social compassion, and not suspicion and blame? And second, if sex education were designed primarily to prevent victimization but not to prevent exploration of desire, wouldn't there be more discussions of both the pleasures and relatively fewer risks of disease or pregnancy associated with lesbian relationships and protected sexual intercourse, or of the risk-free pleasures of masturbation and fantasy? Public education's concern for the female victim is revealed as deceptively thin when real victims are discredited, and when nonvictimizing pleasures are silenced.

This unacknowledged social ambivalence about heterosexuality polarizes the debates over sex education and school-based health clinics. The anxiety effectively treats the female sexual victim as though she were a completely separate species from the female sexual subject. Yet the adolescent women quoted earlier in this text remind us that the female victim and subject coexist in every woman's body.

Toward a Discourse of Sexual Desire and Social Entitlement: In the Student Bodies of Public Schools

I have argued that silencing a discourse of desire buttresses the icon of woman-as-victim. In so doing, public schooling may actually disable young women in their negotiations as sexual subjects. Trained through and into positions of passivity and victimization, young women are currently educated away from positions of sexual self-interest.

If we re-situate the adolescent woman in a rich and empowering educational context, she develops a sense of self which is sexual as well as intellectual, social, and economic. In this section I invite readers to imagine such a context. The dialectic of desire and victimization — across spheres of labor, social relations, and sexuality — would then frame schooling. While many of the curricula and interventions discussed in this paper are imperfect, data on the effectiveness of what *is* available are nevertheless compelling. Studies of sex education curricula, SBHCs, classroom discussions, and ethnographies of life inside public high schools demonstrate that a sense of sexual and social entitlement for young women *can* be fostered within public schools.

Sex Education as Intellectual Empowerment

Harris and Yankelovich polls confirm that over 80 percent of American adults believe that students should be educated about sexuality within their public schools. Seventy-five percent believe that homosexuality and abortion should be included in the curriculum, with 40 percent of those surveyed by Yankelovich et al. (N = 1015) agreeing that 12-year-olds should be taught about oral and anal sex (see Leo, 1986; Harris, 1985).

While the public continues to debate the precise content of sex education, most parents approve and support sex education for their children. An Illinois program monitored parental requests to "opt out" and found that only 6 or 7 of 850 children were actually excused from sex education courses (Leo, 1986). In a California assessment, fewer than 2 percent of parents disallowed their children's participation. And in a longitudinal 5-year program in Connecticut, 7 of 2,500 students requested exemption from these classes (Scales, 1981). Resistance to sex education, while loud at the level of public rhetoric and conservative organizing, is both less vocal and less active within schools and parents' groups (Hottois & Milner, 1975; Scales, 1981).

Sex education courses are offered broadly, if not comprehensively, across the United States. In 1981, only 7 of 50 states actually had laws against such instruction, and only one state enforced a prohibition (Kirby & Scales, 1981). Surveying 179 urban school districts, Sonnenstein and Pittman (1984) found that 75 percent offered some sex education within senior and junior high schools, while 66 percent of the elementary schools offered sex education units. Most instruction was, however, limited to 10 hours or less, with content focused on anatomy. In his extensive review of sex education programs, Kirby (1985) concludes that less than 10 percent of all public school students are exposed to what might be considered comprehensive sex education courses.

The progress on AIDS education is more encouraging, and more complex (see Freudenberg, 1987), but cannot be adequately reviewed in this article. It is important to note, however, that a December 1986 report released by the U.S. Conference of Mayors documents that 54 percent of the 73 largest school districts and 25 state school agencies offer some form of AIDS education (Benedetto, 1987). Today, debates among federal officials — including Secretary of Education Bennett and Surgeon General Koop — and among educators question *when* and *what* to offer in AIDS education. The question is no longer *whether* such education should be promoted.

Not only has sex education been accepted as a function of public schooling, but it has survived empirical tests of effectiveness. Evaluation data demonstrate that sex education can increase contraceptive knowledge and use (Kirby, 1985; Public/Private Ventures, 1987). In terms of sexual activity (measured narrowly in terms of the onset or frequency of heterosexual intercourse), the evidence suggests that sex education does not instigate an earlier onset or increase of heterosexual intercourse (Zabin, Hirsch, Smith, Streett, & Hardy, 1986). The data for pregnancy rates appear to demonstrate no effect for exposure to sex education alone (see Dawson, 1986; Marsiglio & Mott, 1986; Kirby, 1985).

Sex education as constituted in these studies is not sufficient to diminish teen pregnancy rates. In all likelihood it would be naive to expect that sex education (especially if only ten hours in duration) would carry such a "long arm" of effectiveness. While the widespread problem of teen pregnancy must be attributed broadly to economic and social inequities (Jones et al., 1985), sex education remains necessary and sufficient to educate, demystify, and improve contraceptive knowledge and use. In conjunction with material opportunities for enhanced life options, it is believed that sex education and access to contraceptives and abortion can help to reduce the rate of unintended pregnancy among teens (Dryfoos, 1985a, 1985b; National Research Council, 1987).

School-Based Health Clinics: Sexual Empowerment

The public opinion and effectiveness for school-based health clinics are even more compelling than those for sex education. Thirty SBHCs provide on-site health care services to senior, and sometimes junior, high school students in more than 18 U.S. communities, with an additional 25 communities developing similar programs (Kirby, 1985). These clinics offer, at a minimum, health counseling, referrals, and follow-up examinations. Over 70 percent conduct pelvic examinations (Kirby, 1985), approximately 52 percent prescribe contraceptives, and 28 percent dispense contraceptives (Leo, 1986). None performs abortions, and few refer to abortions.

All SBHCs require some form of general parental notification and/or consent, and some charge a nominal fee for generic health services. Relative to private physicians, school-based health clinics and other family planning agencies are substantially more willing to provide contraceptive services to unmarried minors without specific parental consent (consent in this case referring explicitly to contraception). Only one percent of national Planned Parenthood affiliates require consent or notification, compared to 10 percent of public health department programs and 19 percent of hospitals (Torres & Forrest, 1985).

The consequences of consent provisions for abortion are substantial. Data from two states, Massachusetts and Minnesota, demonstrate that parental consent laws result in increased teenage pregnancies or increased numbers of out-of-state abortions. The Reproductive Freedom Project of the American Civil Liberties Union, in a report which examines the consequences of such consent provisions, details the impact of these statutes on teens, on their familial relationships, and ultimately, on their unwanted children (Reproductive Freedom Project, 1986). In an analysis of the impact of Minnesota's mandatory parental notification law from 1981 to 1985, this report documents over 7,000 pregnancies in teens aged 13–17, 3,500 of whom "went to state court to seek the right to confidential abortions, all at considerable personal cost." The report also notes that many of the pregnant teens did not petition the court, "although their entitlement and need for confidential abortions was as strong or more so than the teenagers who made it to court. . . . Only those minors who are old enough and wealthy enough or resourceful enough are actually able to use the court bypass option" (Reproductive Freedom Project, p. 4).

These consent provisions, with allowance for court bypass, not only increase the number of unwanted teenage pregnancies carried to term, but also extend the length of time required to secure an abortion, potentially endangering the life of the teenage woman, and increasing the costs of the abortion. The provisions may also jeopardize the physical and emotional well-being of some young women and their mothers, particularly when paternal consent is required and the pregnant teenager resides with a single mother. Finally, the consent provisions create a class-based health care system. Adolescents able to afford travel to a nearby state, or able to pay a private physician for a confidential abortion, have access to an abortion. Those unable to afford the travel, or those who are unable to contact a private physician, are likely to become teenage mothers (Reproductive Freedom Project, 1986).

In Minneapolis, during the time from 1980 to 1984 when the law was implemented, the birth rate for 15- to 17-year-olds increased 38.4 percent, while the birth rate of 18- and 19-year-olds — not affected by the law — rose only .3 percent (Reproductive Freedom Project, 1986). The state of Massachusetts passed a parental consent law which took effect in 1981. An analysis of the impact of that law concludes that ". . . the major impact of the Massachusetts parental consent law has been to send a monthly average of between 90 and 95 of the state's minors across state lines in search of an abortion. This number represents about one in every three minor abortion patients living in Massachusetts" (Cartoof & Klerman, 1986). These researchers, among others, write that parental consent laws could have more devastating effects in larger states, from which access to neighboring states would be more difficult.

The inequalities inherent in consent provisions and the dramatic consequences which result for young women are well recognized. For example, twenty-nine states and the District of Columbia now explicitly authorize minors to grant their own consent for receipt of contraceptive information and/or services, independent of parental knowledge or consent (see Melton & Russo, 1987, for full discussion; National Research Council, 1987; for a full analysis of the legal, emotional, and physical health problems attendant upon parental consent laws for abortion, see the Reproductive Freedom Project report). More recently, consent laws for abortion in Pennsylvania and California have been challenged as unconstitutional.

Public approval of SBHCs has been slow but consistent. In the 1986 Yankelovich survey, 84 percent of surveyed adults agree that these clinics should provide birth control information; 36 percent endorse dispensing of contraceptives to students (Leo, 1986). In 1985, Harris found that 67 percent of all respondents, including 76 percent of Blacks and 76 percent of Hispanics, agree that public schools should establish formal ties with family planning clinics for teens to learn about and obtain contraception (Harris, 1985). Mirroring the views of the general public, a national sample of school administrators polled by the Education Research Group indicated that more than 50 percent believe birth control should be offered in school-based clinics; 30 percent agree that parental permission should be sought, and 27 percent agree that contraceptives should be dispensed, even if parental consent is not forthcoming. The discouraging news is that 96 percent of these respondents indicate that their districts do not presently offer such services (Benedetto, 1987; Werner, 1987).

Research on the effectiveness of SBHCs is consistently persuasive. The three-year Johns Hopkins study of school-based health clinics (Zabin et al., 1986) found that schools in which SBHCs made referrals and dispensed contraceptives noted an increase in the percentage of "virgin" females visiting the program as well as an increase in contraceptive use. They also found a significant reduction in pregnancy rates: There was a 13 percent increase at experimental schools after 10 months, versus a 50 percent increase at control schools; after 28 months, pregnancy rates decreased 30 percent at experimental schools versus a 53 percent increase at control schools. Furthermore, by the second year, a substantial percentage of males visited the clinic (48 percent of males in experimental schools indicated that they "have ever been to a birth control clinic or to a physician about birth control," compared to 12 percent of males in control schools). Contrary to common belief, the schools in which clinics dispensed contraceptives showed a substantial postponement of first experience of heterosexual intercourse among high school students and an increase in the proportion of young women visiting the clinic prior to "first coitus."

Paralleling the Hopkins findings, the St. Paul Maternity and Infant Care Project (1985) found that pregnancy rates dropped substantially in schools with clinics, from 79 births/1,000 (1973) to 26 births/1,000 (1984). Teens who delivered and kept their infants had an 80 percent graduation rate, relative to approximately 50 percent of young mothers nationally. Those who stayed in school reported a 1.3 percent repeat birth rate, compared to 17 percent nationally. Over three years, pregnancy rates dropped by 40 percent. Twenty-five percent of young women in the school received some form of family planning and 87 percent of clients were continuing to use contraception at a 3-year follow-up. There were fewer obstetric complications; fewer babies were born at low birth weights; and prenatal visits to physicians increased relative to students in the control schools.

Predictions that school-based health clinics would advance the onset of sexual intimacy, heighten the degree of "promiscuity" and incidence of pregnancy, and hold females primarily responsible for sexuality were countered by the evidence. The onset of sexual intimacy was postponed, while contraception was used more reliably. Pregnancy rates substantially diminished and, over time, a large group of males began to view contraception as a shared responsibility.

It is worth restating here that females who received family planning counseling and/or contraception actually postponed the onset of heterosexual intercourse. I would argue that the availability of such services may enable females to feel they are sexual agents, entitled and therefore responsible, rather than at the constant and terrifying mercy of a young man's pressure to "give in" or of a parent's demands to "save yourself." With a sense of sexual agency and not necessarily urgency, teen girls may be less likely to use or be used by pregnancy (Petchesky, 1984).

Nontraditional Vocational Training: Social and Economic Entitlements

The literature reviewed suggests that sex education, access to contraception, and opportunities for enhanced life options, in combination (Dryfoos, 1985a, 1985b; Kirby, 1985; Select Committee on Children, Youth and Families, 1985), can significantly diminish the likelihood that a teenager will become pregnant, carry to term, and/or have a repeat pregnancy, and can increase the likelihood that she will stay in high school through graduation (National Research Council, 1987). Education toward entitlement — including a sense of sexual, economic, and social entitlement — may be sufficient to affect adolescent girls' views on sexuality, contraception, and abortion. By framing female subjectivity within the context of social entitlement, sex education would be organized around dialogue and critique, SBHCs would offer health services, options counseling, contraception, and abortion referrals, and the provision of real "life options" would include nontraditional vocational training programs and employment opportunities for adolescent females (Dryfoos, 1985a, 1985b).

In a nontraditional vocational training program in New York City designed for young women, many of whom are mothers, participants' attitudes toward contraception and abortion shifted once they acquired a set of vocational skills, a sense of social entitlement, and a sense of personal competence (Weinbaum, personal communication, 1986). The young women often began the program without strong academic skills or a sense of competence. At the start, they were more likely to express more negative sentiments about contraception and abortion than when they completed the program. One young woman, who initially held strong anti-abortion attitudes, learned that she was pregnant midway through her carpentry apprenticeship. She decided to abort, reasoning that now that she has a future, she can't risk losing it for another baby (Weinbaum, paraphrase of personal communication, 1986). A developing sense of social entitlement may have transformed this young woman's view of reproduction, sexuality, and self.

The Manpower Development Research Corporation (MDRC), in its evaluation of Project Redirection (Polit, Lahn, & Stevens, 1985) offers similar conclusions about a comprehensive vocational training and community-based mentor project for teen mothers and mothers-to-be. Low-income teens were enrolled in Project Redirection, a network of services designed to instill self-sufficiency, in which community women served as mentors. The program included training for what is called "employability," Individual Participation Plans, and peer group sessions. Data on education, employment, and pregnancy outcomes were collected at 12 and 24 months after enrollment. Two years after the program began, many newspapers headlined the program as a failure. The data actually indicated that at 12 months, the end of program involvement, Project Redirection women were significantly *less likely* to experience a repeat pregnancy than comparison women; *more likely* to be using contraception; *more likely* to be in school, to have completed school, or to be in the labor force; and twice as likely (20 percent versus 11 percent, respectively) to have earned a Graduate Equivalency Diploma. At 24 months, however, approximately one year out of the program, Project and comparison women were virtually indistinguishable. MDRC reported equivalent rates of repeat pregnancies, dropout, and unemployment.

The Project Redirection data demonstrate that sustained outcomes cannot be expected once programs have been withdrawn and participants confront the realities of a dismal economy and inadequate child care and social services. The data confirm, however, the effectiveness of comprehensive programs to reduce teen pregnancy rates and encourage study or work as long as the young women are actively engaged. Supply-side interventions — changing people but not structures or opportunities — which leave unchallenged an inhospitable and discriminating economy and a thoroughly impoverished child care/social welfare system are inherently doomed to long-term failure. When such programs fail, the social reading is that "these young women can't be helped." Blaming the victim obscures the fact that the current economy and social welfare arrangements need overhauling if the sustained educational, social, and psychological gains accrued by the Project Redirection participants are to be maintained.

In the absence of enhanced life options, low-income young women are likely to default to early and repeat motherhood as a source of perceived competence, significance, and pleasure. When life options are available, however, a sense of competence and "entitlement to better" may help to prevent second pregnancies, may help to encourage education, and, when available, the pursuit of meaningful work (Burt, Kimmich, Goldmuntz, & Sonnenstein, 1984).

Femininity May Be Hazardous to Her Health: The Absence of Entitlement

Growing evidence suggests that women who lack a sense of social or sexual entitlement, who hold traditional notions of what it means to be female — self-sacrificing and relatively passive — and who undervalue themselves, are disproportionately likely to find themselves with an unwanted pregnancy and to maintain it through to motherhood. While many young women who drop out, pregnant or not, are not at all traditional in these ways, but are quite feisty and are fueled with a sense of entitlement (Fine, 1986; Weinbaum, personal communication, 1987), it may also be the case that young women who do internalize such notions of "femininity" are disproportionately at risk for pregnancy and dropping out.

The Hispanic Policy Development Project reports that low-income female sophomores who, in 1980, expected to be married and/or to have a child by age 19 were disproportionately represented among nongraduates in 1984. Expectations of early marriage and childbearing correspond to dramatic increases (200 to 400 percent) in nongraduation rates for low-income adolescent women across racial and ethnic groups (Hispanic Policy Development Project, 1987). These indicators of traditional notions of womanhood bode poorly for female academic achievement.

The Children's Defense Fund (1986) recently published additional data which demonstrate that young women with poor basic skills are three times more likely to become teen parents than women with average or above-average basic skills. Those with poor or fair basic skills are four times more likely to have more than one child while a teen; 29 percent of women in the bottom skills quintile became mothers by age 18 versus 5 percent of young women in the top quintile. While academic skill problems must be placed in the context of alienating and problematic schools, and not viewed as inherent in these young women, those who fall in the bottom quintile may nevertheless be the least likely to feel entitled or in control of their lives. They may feel more vulnerable to male pressure or more willing to have a child as a means of feeling competent.

My own observations, derived from a year-long ethnographic study of a comprehensive public high school in New York City, further confirm some of these conclusions. Six months into the ethnography, new pregnancies began showing. I noticed that many of the girls who got pregnant and carried to term were not those whose bodies, dress, and manner evoked sensuality and experience. Rather, a number of the pregnant women were those who were quite passive and relatively quiet in their classes. One young woman, who granted me an interview anytime, washed the blackboard for her teacher, rarely spoke in class, and never disobeyed her mother, was pregnant by the spring of the school year (Fine, 1986).

Simple stereotypes, of course, betray the complexity of circumstances under which young women become pregnant and maintain their pregnancies. While U.S. rates of teenage sexual activity and age of "sexual initiation" approximate those of comparable developed countries, the teenage pregnancy, abortion, and childbearing rates in the United States are substantially higher. In the United States, teenagers under age fifteen are at least five times more likely to give birth than similarly aged teens in other industrialized nations (Jones et al., 1985; National Research Council, 1987). The national factors which correlate with low teenage birthrates include adolescent access to sex education and contraception, and relative equality in the distribution of wealth. Economic and structural conditions which support a class-stratified society, and which limit adolescent access to sexual information and contraception, contribute to inflated teenage pregnancy rates and birthrates.

This broad national context acknowledged, it might still be argued that within our country, traditional notions of what it means to be a woman—to remain subordinate, dependent, self-sacrificing, compliant, and ready to marry and/or bear children early—do little to empower women or enhance a sense of entitlement. This is not to say that teenage dropouts or mothers tend to be of any one type. Yet it may well be that the traditions and practices of "femininity" as commonly understood may be hazardous to the economic, social, educational, and sexual development of young women.

In summary, the historic silencing within public schools of conversations about sexuality, contraception, and abortion, as well as the absence of a discourse of desire—in the form of comprehensive sex education, school-based health clinics, and viable life options via vocational training and placement—all combine to exacerbate the vulnerability of young women whom schools, and the critics of sex education and SBHCs, claim to protect.

Conclusion

Adolescents are entitled to a discussion of desire instead of the anti-sex rhetoric which controls the controversies around sex education, SBHCs, and AIDS education. The absence of a discourse of desire, combined with the lack of analysis of the language of victimization, may actually retard the development of sexual subjectivity and responsibility in students. Those most "at risk" of victimization through pregnancy, disease, violence, or harassment

— all female students, low-income females in particular, and non-heterosexual males — are those most likely to be victimized by the absence of critical conversation in public schools. Public schools can no longer afford to maintain silence around a discourse of desire. This is not to say that the silencing of a discourse of desire is the primary root of sexual victimization, teen motherhood, and the concomitant poverty experienced by young and low-income females. Nor could it be responsibly argued that interventions initiated by public schools could ever be successful if separate from economic and social development. But it is important to understand that by providing education, counseling, contraception, and abortion referrals, as well as meaningful educational and vocational opportunities, public schools could play an essential role in the construction of the female subject — social and sexual.

And by not providing such an educational context, public schools contribute to the rendering of substantially different outcomes for male and female students, and for male and female dropouts (Fine, 1986). The absence of a thorough sex education curriculum, of school-based health clinics, of access to free and confidential contraceptive and abortion services, of exposure to information about the varieties of sexual pleasures and partners, and of involvement in sustained employment training programs may so jeopardize the educational and economic outcomes for female adolescents as to constitute sex discrimination. How can we ethically continue to withhold educational treatments we know to be effective for adolescent women?

Public schools constitute a sphere in which young women could be offered access to a language and experience of empowerment. In such contexts, "well-educated" young women could breathe life into positions of social critique and experience entitlement rather than victimization, autonomy rather than terror.

References

Bauer, G. (1986). *The family: Preserving America's future.* Washington, DC: U.S. Department of Education.

Benedetto, R. (1987, January 23). AIDS studies become part of curricula. *USA Today,* p. D1.

Benjamin, J. (1983). Master and slave: The fantasy of erotic domination. In A. Snitow, C. Stansell, & S. Thompson (Eds.), *Powers of desire* (pp. 280–299). New York: Monthly Review Press.

Bennett, W. (1987, July 3). Why Johnny can't abstain. *National Review,* pp. 36–38, 56.

Bigelow, M. (1921). *Sex-Education.* New York: Macmillan.

Boffey, P. (1987, February 27). Reagan to back AIDS plan urging youths to avoid sex. *New York Times,* p. A14.

Brown, P. (1983). The Swedish approach to sex education and adolescent pregnancy: Some impressions. *Family Planning Perspectives, 15*(2), 92–95.

Burke, C. (1980). Introduction to Luce Irigaray's "When our lips speak together." *Signs, 6,* 66–68.

Burt, M., Kimmich, M., Goldmuntz, J., & Sonnenstein, F. (1984). *Helping pregnant adolescents: Outcomes and costs of service delivery.* Final Report on the Evaluation of Adolescent Pregnancy Programs. Washington, DC: Urban Institute.

Cartoof, V., & Klerman, L. (1986). Parental consent for abortion: Impact of the Massachusetts law. *American Journal of Public Health, 76* 397–400.

Chicago school clinic is sued over birth control materials. (1986, October 16). *New York Times,* p. A24.

Children's Defense Fund. (1986). *Preventing adolescent pregnancy: What schools can do.* Washington, DC: Author.

Children's Defense Fund. (1987). *Adolescent pregnancy: An anatomy of a social problem in search of comprehensive solutions.* Washington, DC: Author.

Cíxous, H. (1981). Castration or decapitation? *Signs, 7,* 41–55.

Dawson, D. (1986). The effects of sex education on adolescent behavior. *Family Planning Perspectives, 18,* 162–170.

Dowd, M. (1986, April 16). Bid to update sex education confronts resistance in city. *New York Times,* p. A1.

Dryfoos, J. (1985a). A time for new thinking about teenage pregnancy. *American Journal of Public Health, 75,* 13–14.

Dryfoos, J. (1985b). School-based health clinics: A new approach to preventing adolescent pregnancy? *Family Planning Perspectives, 17*(2), 70–75.

Ehrenreich, B., Hess, E., & Jacobs, G. (1986). *Re-making love.* Garden City, NY: Anchor Press.

Espin, O. (1984). Cultural and historical influences on sexuality in Hispanic/Latina women: Implications for psychotherapy. In C. Vance (Ed.), *Pleasure and danger* (pp. 149–164). Boston: Routledge & Kegan Paul.

Fine, M. (1986). Why urban adolescents drop into and out of high school. *Teachers College Record, 87,* 393–409.

Fine, M. (1987). Silencing in public school. *Language Arts, 64,* 157–174.

Fisher, W., Byrne, D., & White, L. (1983). Emotional barriers to contraception. In D. Byrne & W. Fisher (Eds.), *Adolescents, sex, and contraception* (pp. 207–239). Hillsdale, NJ: Lawrence Erlbaum.

Foucault, M. (1980). *The history of sexuality* (Vol. 1). New York: Vintage Books.

Freudenberg, N. (1987). The politics of sex education. *HealthPAC Bulletin.* New York: HealthPAC.

Golden, C. (1984, March). *Diversity and variability in lesbian identities.* Paper presented at Lesbian Psychologies Conference of the Association of Women in Psychology.

Greene, M. (1986). In search of a critical pedagogy. *Harvard Educational Review, 56,* 427–441.

Hall, G. S. (1914). Education and the social hygiene movement. *Social Hygiene, 1* (1 December), 29–35.

Harris, L., and Associates. (1985). *Public attitudes about sex education, family planning and abortion in the United States.* New York: Author.

Hispanic Policy Development Project. (1987, Fall). *1980 high school sophomores from poverty backgrounds: Whites, Blacks, Hispanics look at school and adult responsibilities,* Vol. 1, No. 2, New York: Author.

Hottois, J., & Milner, N. (1975). *The sex education controversy.* Lexington, MA: Lexington Books.

Imber, M. (1984). Towards a theory of educational origins: The genesis of sex education. *Educational Theory, 34,* 275–286.

Irigaray, L. (1980). When our lips speak together. *Signs, 6,* 69.

Jones, E., Forrest, J., Goldman, N., Henshaw, S., Lincoln, R., Rosoff, J., Westoff, C., & Wulf, D. (1985). Teenage pregnancy in developed countries. *Family Planning Perspectives, 17*(1), 55–63.

Kantrowitz, B., Hager, M., Wingert, S., Carroll, G., Raine, G., Witherspoon, D., Huck, J., & Doherty, S. (1987, February 16). Kids and contraceptives. *Newsweek,* pp. 54–65.

Kelly, G. (1986). *Learning about sex.* Woodbury, NY: Barron's Educational Series.

Kirby, D. (1985). *School-based health clinics: An emerging approach to improving adolescent health and addressing teenage pregnancy.* Washington, DC: Center for Population Options.

Kirby, D., & Sales, P. (1981, April). An analysis of state guidelines for sex education instruction in public schools. *Family Relations,* pp. 229–237.

Koop, C. E. (1986). *Surgeon General's report on acquired immune deficiency syndrome.* Washington, DC: Office of the Surgeon General.

Koop's AIDS stand assailed. (1987, March 15). New York Times, p. A25.

Leo, J. (1986, November 24). Sex and schools. *Time,* pp. 54–63.

Lorde, A. (1980, August). *Uses of the erotic: The erotic as power.* Paper presented at the Fourth Berkshire Conference on the History of Women, Mt. Holyoke College, Holyoke, MA.

MacKinnon, C. (1983). Complicity: An introduction to Andrea Dworkin's "Abortion," Chapter 3, "Right-Wing Women." *Law and Inequality, 1,* 89–94.

Marsiglio, W., & Mott, F. (1986). The impact of sex education on sexual activity, contraceptive use and premarital pregnancy among American teenagers. *Family Planning Perspectives, 18*(4), 151–162.

Melton, S., & Russon, N. (1987). Adolescent abortion. *American Psychologist, 42,* 69–83.

National Research Council. (1987). *Risking the future: Adolescent sexuality, pregnancy and childbearing* (Vol. 1). Washington, DC: National Academy Press.

New York City Board of Education. (1984). *Family living curriculum including sex education. Grades K through 12.* New York City Board of Education, Division of Curriculum and Instruction.

Noddings, N. (1986). Fidelity in teaching, teacher education, and research for teaching. *Harvard Educational Review, 56,* 496–510.

Omolade, B. (1983). Hearts of darkness. In A. Snitow, C. Stansell, & S. Thompson (Eds)., *Powers of desire* (pp. 350–367). New York: Monthly Review Press.

Perlez, J. (1986a, June 24). On teaching about sex. *New York Times,* p. C1.

Perlez, J. (1986b, September 24). School chief to ask mandatory sex education. *New York Times,* p. A36.

Petchesky, R. (1984). *Abortion and women's choice.* New York: Longman.

Philadelphia School District. (1986). Sex education curriculum. Draft.

Polit, D., Kahn, J., & Stevens, D. (1985). *Final impacts from Project Redirection.* New York: Manpower Development Research Center.

Public/Private Ventures. (1987, April). *Summer training and education program.* Philadelphia: Author.

Reproductive Freedom Project. (1986). *Parental consent laws on abortion: Their catastrophic impact on teenagers.* New York: American Civil Liberties Union.

Rohter, L. (1985, October 29). School workers shown AIDS film. *New York Times,* p. B3.

Rubin, G. (1984). Thinking sex: Notes for a radical theory of the politics of sex. In C. Vance (Ed.), *Pleasure and danger* (pp. 267–319). Boston: Routledge & Kegan Paul.

St. Paul Maternity and Infant Care Project. (1985). *Health services project description.* St. Paul, MN: Author.

Scales, P. (1981). Sex education and the prevention of teenage pregnancy: An overview of policies and programs in the United States. In T. Ooms (Ed.), *Teenage pregnancy in a family context: Implications for policy* (pp. 213–253). Philadelphia: Temple University Press.

Schlafly, P. (1986). Presentation on women's issues. American Dreams Symposium, Indiana University of Pennsylvania.

Selected group to see original AIDS tape. (1987, January 29). *New York Times,* p. B4.

Smith-Rosenberg, C. (1978). Sex as symbol in Victorian purity: An ethnohistorical analysis of Jacksonian America. *American Journal of Sociology, 84,* 212–247.

Snitow, A., Stansell, C., & Thompson, S. (Eds.). (1983). *Powers of desire.* New York: Monthly Review Press.

Sonnenstein, F., & Pittman, K. (1984). The availability of sex education in large city school districts. *Family Planning Perspectives, 16*(1), 19–25.

Strong, B. (1972). Ideas of the early sex education movement in America, 1890–1920. *History of Education Quarterly, 12,* 129–161.

Thompson, S. (1983). Search for tomorrow: On feminism and the reconstruction of teen romance. In A. Snitow, C. Stansell, & S. Thompson (Eds.), *Powers of desire* (pp. 367–384). New York: Monthly Review Press.

Torres, A., & Forest, J. (1985). Family planning clinic services in the United States, 1983. *Family Planning Perspectives, 17*(1), 30–35.

Vance, C. (1984). *Pleasure and danger.* Boston: Routledge & Kegan Paul.

Weeks, J. (1985). *Sexuality and its discontents.* London: Routledge & Kegan Paul.

Weitz, R. (1984). What price independence? Social reactions to lesbians, spinsters, widows and nuns. In J. Freeman (Ed.), *Women: A feminist perspective* (3rd ed.). Palo Alto, CA: Mayfield.

Werner, L. (1987, November 14). U.S. report asserts administration halted liberal "anti-family agenda." *New York Times,* p. A12.

Zabin, L., Hirsch, M., Smith, E., Streett, R., & Hardy, J. (1986). Evaluation of a pregnancy prevention program for urban teenagers. *Family Planning Perspectives, 18*(3), 119–126.

Zelnick, M., & Kim, Y. (1982). Sex education and its association with teenage sexual activity, pregnancy and contraceptive use. *Family Planning Perspectives, 14*(3), 117–126.

This paper was originally developed during the Laurie Seminar on Women's Studies at Douglass College, Carol Gilligan, Chair, 1986. The ethnographic research was funded by the W. T. Grant Foundation. The author wishes to thank many individuals for thorough reading, comments, critique, and support: Nancy Barnes, Linda Brodkey, Richard Friend, Carol Gilligan, Henry Giroux, Carol Joffee, Rayna Rapp, David Surrey, and Sandy Weinbaum; additionally, Lori Cornish of Planned Parenthood in Philadelphia provided invaluable research assistance. These individuals bear no responsibility for the final document, but deserve many thanks for their willingness to pursue, unpack, and reconstruct the ideas with me.

Voice, Play, and a Practice of Ordinary Courage in Girls' and Women's Lives

ANNIE G. ROGERS

In this chapter, Annie Rogers explores the etymology of courage, linking the "ordinary courage" of eight- to twelve-year-old girls with an old meaning of the word: "to speak one's mind by telling all one's heart." She then observes how many girls use their ordinary courage as they reach adolescence. Her observation is embedded in a newly emerging psychology of women based on empirical studies of girls that have documented a striking loss of voice, of resiliency, and of self-confidence in girls as they enter early adolescence. These studies have identified adolescence as a time of particular vulnerability and risk in young women's psychological development, as it becomes increasingly dangerous for them to speak their minds truthfully within the context of cultural conspiracies to silence women's knowledge. In order to capture the girls' inner life of feeling, Rogers introduces a "poetics of research," a particular discourse grounded in feminist epistemology and methodology, as well as the voice-centered, relational practice of research she has helped to create.

Introduction: A Poetics of Research

> Artistic form is congruent with the dynamic forms of our direct sensuous life; works of art are projections of "felt life," as Henry James called it, into spatial, temporal, and poetic structures. They are images of feeling that formulate it for our conception. (Langer, 1942, p. 159)

The language of empirical "science," the language of formal propositions, of tests and proofs, Suzanne Langer (1942) tells us, cannot take the press or imprint of inner life, the life of feeling. To convey this life, the language of the arts is required. When the inner life, the "direct sensuous life" (Langer, 1942, p. 159), *is* the subject of empirical research, as it is in

Harvard Educational Review Vol. 63 No. 3 Fall 1993, 265–295

this article about courage, the form of research and of writing about research itself must become artistic. Writing in an artistic, subjective voice is not an impediment to theory building, but allows me to build theory and use theory to make suggestions for educational practice. In this article, I have created what I call a poetics of research, finding the "spatial, temporal, and poetic structures" (Langer, 1942, p. 159) necessary to convey what I have learned about courage in the lives of individual girls and women. The "poetics of research" I present here involves changing not only the voice of research, but also its practices. The particular practices of research I rely on through-out this article are drawn from an overlapping theoretical model much like Russian nesting dolls. Since this model guides my entire project, I will briefly explain it. At the broadest level, I am guided by feminist epistemology and methodology; then, nested in that framework is the voice-centered, rela-tional approach to research developed by the Harvard Project on Women's Psychology and Girls' Development; nested in that approach is the subjective model of writing for social scientists outlined by the sociologist Susan Krieger (1991); and, finally, nested within that subjective model is the last "doll," the philosophical poetics of Gaston Bachelard (1958/1969). While I cannot ex-plain the details of each part of this model within the scope of this paper, I will touch on each of its components.

Women scholars have criticized the portrayal of girls and women as objects of social construction, and have made efforts to correct research practices accordingly for nearly two decades, though this work is still relatively un-known (see Collins, 1989; Harding, 1987; Nielsen, 1990). Feminist episte-mology, a set of theories about the nature of knowledge, has challenged many tenets of classical androcentric epistemology. Women scholars have questioned those tests of legitimacy required of "knowledge" and of the "knower" that historically have been defined by men in Western patriarchal societies and cultures. Specifically, they have challenged the existence of abstract, objective, and universal truths, laws, or principles defined as "knowl-edge" and derived by a "knower" through male-defined practices of argu-mentation or experimentation. Feminist methodology is a theory or set of guidelines about how to conduct research in the face of disbelief in such an epistemology. A feminist methodologist, for example, rejects the belief that one can separate the "subjectivity" of the researcher from the "object" of her research and, in fact, creates research practices that close the inevitable distance between the researcher and the participants in the research (see also Cook & Fonow, 1990; Ladner, 1987). Feminist methodologists also reject the belief in universal laws or truths and seek out ways to limit the power of researchers to make global generalizations. Resisting the "objectification" of the research process, a feminist methodologist might criticize the omission of the researcher as a protagonist in the research, as well as its interpreter and author, and seek ways to include her or him as a "subjective" presence throughout the research process. These concerns guided me in the design of my research, particularly what I chose to define as legitimate "knowledge," as well as the ways in which I formed relationships in various contexts in the course of this research and the manner in which I have represented those relationships in this article.

More specifically, the practice of research I present is based on a voice-centered, relational approach to psychology and education pioneered by myself and other members of the Harvard Project on Women's Psychology and Girls' Development. This approach entails listening to girls and women as authorities about their own experiences and representing their voices in a written text, rather than replacing their words with psychological interpretations that cannot be questioned by the reader. Listening to girls and women in this way requires us to bring ourselves into relationship with another subjective voice, a real presence, a living girl or woman who may or may not be able to recognize herself in our descriptions of her. Knowing the power of making psychological interpretations, which includes our power to make ourselves invulnerable by revealing only the lives of others, my colleagues and I have tried to reveal our own lived experience in our work, so that our readers might understand the basis for our interpretations. A voice-centered, relational approach to research entails representing verbatim the voices of girls and women, including the voice of the researcher. The presence of two voices, two perspectives, which may or may not be in harmony or agreement, allows a reader room to agree or disagree with the researcher's interpretations. This voice-centered, relational way of conducting research, I believe, is vital to educational research and educational practice — because it reveals human differences and limits the power of the researchers' interpretations and generalizations.

To reveal myself in my work means to bring the self, the psyche, soul, mind, spirit — that peculiarly structured inner world that makes each of us who we are — directly into my work. This means that when I go into a school or community or clinical setting in the course of my research, I form relationships, expecting both to influence others and to be influenced and changed myself. If I participate in authentic relationships, how could this be otherwise? Moreover, like Susan Krieger (1991), who argues against the commonly held belief that the self is a "contaminant" in social science research (to be held out of research relationships and, even more critically, to be circumvented in making interpretations), I believe that the self is a researcher's finest and most valuable "touchstone" for making relationships and creating interpretations throughout the research process. Many common practices of ethnographic and interview research, however, are concerned with ways to keep track of or reflect upon one's social position and deeply held beliefs, with the goal of "bracketing" or "putting aside" what one knows as oneself. I think that these practices, particularly for women and others who have been marginalized in academic discourse, muffle one's voice, knowledge, and originality.

Another increasingly common practice among researchers, including feminist researchers, involves naming one's social location — one's gender, race or ethnicity, social class, and (sometimes) one's sexual orientation — and the social location of the research participants, and saying little more.

Such information has been withheld in social science research far too long, to the detriment of knowing anything at all about researchers or the participants in their research. But the naming of social locations in a given society or culture, though important information, does not begin to replace the details of subjective experience. The individual voices of researchers and participants reveal the complexity of inner life when it is not robbed of its own subjectivity.

Finally, the last Russian nesting doll of this model, the concept most central to this work, though clearly embedded or nested in other, larger practices and frameworks, is the concept of a "poetics" as defined by the French philosopher Gaston Bachelard (1958/1969). His poetics joins the mind with the soul, and the imagination with "dreaming consciousness," in the act of writing itself. The poetics he creates as a philosopher is meant to be a "reverberation," a "resonance," a "re-percussion" — of time, space, and memory — that arises in the reader in response to the imaginative speech of the writer. This particular poetics, a sensitivity and responsiveness to the emergent images and the associative logic of poetry, is central to the way I interpret and write about courage throughout this article.

In addition to presenting this nested theoretical model, the "poetics of research" that guides my work throughout this article, I want to describe briefly the contexts of my research, myself, and the girls and women who were participants in my research.

I went to many places over the course of five years (1987–1991) to learn about courage in the lives of girls and women. The different contexts of my research included several schools: a private girls' school, a coeducational public elementary school, and a small and innovative coeducational community school. It also included my clinical consulting room, a woman's oral history project, and an acting workshop for women and men from all over the world. I came to each of these places as a researcher, as a participant, or as a therapist, and quickly became a part of a community.

The voices of girls and women, including those of my colleagues and myself, that I draw upon in this article include the following groups:

1. Eighteen preadolescent and adolescent girls and three adult women who were involved in a longitudinal research study and pilot program to prevent pervasive losses of voice and knowledge among girls. I directed this project, entitled "Strengthening Healthy Resistance and Courage in Girls," for four years. We called the pilot program the "Theater, Writing, and Outing Club." The women who were part of this program were Carol Gilligan, principal investigator for the study, Normi Noel, a director and voice teacher from Boston's Shakespeare & Company, and myself. We are European American and European Canadian women, diverse with respect to sexual orientation and class, ranging in age from our thirties to our fifties. The girls we met with in two groups came from two different schools. One group of ten girls attended a coeducational public elementary school, the Tobin School in Cambridge, Massachusetts, and was diverse with respect to class, race,

ethnicity, and socioeconomic status. These girls were fourth and fifth graders with whom we met weekly after school for three years. The second group of eight girls attended a small, innovative coeducational community school, the Atrium School in Watertown, Massachusetts. This school, founded by Virginia Kahn and a group of interested parents, was designed to be responsive to the educational and emotional needs of elementary-aged children. They were all European American girls from the sixth-grade class. We met with them intensively for short periods over three summers.

2. Two girls I interviewed as participants in the Laurel-Harvard study, a longitudinal study of girls' development between the Harvard Project on Women's Psychology and Girls' Development and the Laurel School, a private girls' school in Cleveland, Ohio. This study was directed by Lyn Mikel Brown, with Carol Gilligan as the principal investigator. Eighty-six percent were European American girls, and 14 percent were girls of color, primarily from upper-middle-class homes.

3. One adolescent European American girl I have seen in my private psychotherapy practice.

4. Seven European American women, some of whom are immigrants to this country, ranging in age from thirty to eighty years old, from differing socioeconomic and ethnic groups, who came together to talk about their lives. These women formed the Intergenerational Women's Oral History Group at the Erikson Center in Cambridge, Massachusetts.[1]

5. Two women, diverse in nationality and sexual orientation, who were engaged in an intensive, month-long acting workshop for professional male and female actors from all over the world offered by Shakespeare & Company in Wellesley, Massachusetts.

Although the girls I present in this article attended both private and public schools and are diverse in ethnicity, race, and class, I have chosen to present detailed interviews with an Asian American girl and an African American girl to address the continuing silence of these girls' voices in the research literature on human development. I make no claim to generalize from my interviews with these two girls, nor from the larger studies I draw upon here, to the experiences of all girls and women. I have not set out to test hypotheses about human development here. The purpose of writing this article, rather, is to explore my theoretical understanding of girls' and women's development based on limited empirical studies and my efforts to prevent and treat psychological difficulties. The girls whose voices I bring into this article illustrate a pattern, a loss and regaining of courage. I hope my poetics of writing and research will be useful to educators, as well as to educational and psychological researchers, in understanding what these girls are saying.

I begin with an ordinary scene from girls' lives in school.

---

[1] The Intergenerational Program at the Erikson Center, directed by Dorothy Austin, is a program for vital elders, adults, teenagers, and children. It was designed and is run by resident artists, elders, and Center staff. I am a resident artist and have directed an ethnographic study of the project.

Play, Invention, and the Embodiment of Courage

And did you ever tell me
how your mother called you in from play
and from whom? To what? These atoms filmed by ordinary dust
that common life we each and all bent out of orbit from
to which we must return simply to say
this is where I came from
this is what I knew . . .
(Rich, 1981, p. 22)

On a Friday afternoon, I wait for a play to begin.[2] Eve, a slim eleven-year-old girl with straight brown hair pulled back in a ponytail, jumps up with a red plastic container and dumps shells along the edge of the audience, to indicate a "shoreline." Amy gets up and faces the audience, her black-and-white composition book in hand. The room grows quiet. Amy's red bangs touch her eyebrows. She begins, "Stories and poems about life on Plum Island." In a flash, Joan, Eve, and Rachel gather behind her. The girls hover in a circle, backs rounded as they lean in with extended arms. "I live on an island called Plum Island," Amy reads, and glances over at her "island." "I live next to the ocean," she continues, as the girls spin and scatter out, making the motion of waves with their bodies, leaning forward, pulling back. "I wake up to the sound of wind in the trees. In other islands you wake up to the sounds of birds." The girls begin to make gull sounds. The audience bursts into laughter.

I, too, am caught up in the girls' playful inventiveness in this drama that involves their entire bodies. Amy's voice comes clearly into the room. She takes me to the island, and in the school auditorium, the ocean breaks against a shoreline.

The play seems, at first glance, a bit silly, a delightful little piece, but nothing worth noting — in fact, one of the most ordinary experiences in children's lives. Yet, as I watch this scene, I am struck by a quality of boldness in the girls' play. Other girls come to mind: A ten-year-old sitting in the back seat of my car says, "I know all about lies. My house is wallpapered with lies," in a heated discussion about when it is not good to lie. A twelve-year-old girl, wary and sad, suddenly looks directly into my eyes and says, "My dad is really a violent man. You wouldn't know it meeting him on the street, but at home he just crushes my mother down like an aluminum can that you, that you would just step on."[3] I listen to girls' voices late in childhood, and I hear a natural courage, an edge into truth-telling that is potentially disruptive and troubling. But what do I mean by courage?

---

[2] The group I am observing here are sixth graders at the Atrium School, who are members of the Theater, Writing, and Outing Club for Girls, a program designed to strengthen and preserve girls' voices during a developmental period when their voices are clearest. The names presented in this text are all pseudonyms, with the exception of the names of the researchers.

[3] One of the girls was a member of the Tobin School Theater, Writing, and Outing Club group, and the other girl I saw in private practice.

I begin with the life history of the word courage, its etymology in the English language.[4] Courage came from the Latin word *cor*, meaning "heart," and from a common Romanic word, *aetaticum*, or "age." In its original English form, in 1051, courage meant "the heart of an age." Yet by 1300, courage had lost its association with age, and therefore with time and with development. Taken out of time, courage meant simply "heart." In 1300, courage was also linked very closely with speaking. One definition of courage was "to speak one's mind by telling all one's heart" (Simpson & Weiner, 1989, p. 1051). At this time, the definition of courage drew speaking into relation with mind and heart, intellect and love.

In the year 1386, Chaucer wrote, "And smale foules maken melodie . . . so pricketh hem nature in hir corages" in the Prologue to *The Canterbury Tales* (Baugh, 1963). In modern parlance, the music of small birds pricks the travelling pilgrims in their very natures, or hearts; that is, in "hir corages." Courage, then, meant "a responsive heart," as well as "a spirit or liveliness."

By 1490, however, courage was commonly used to mean "that quality of mind which shows itself in facing danger without fear or shrinking, bravery, boldness, valour" (Simpson & Weiner, 1989, p. 1051). At this point in time, courage became cut off from the heart, the seat of feelings. No longer embodied, courage was defined as a "quality of mind" revealed through the absence of fear. The verb forms "take courage" and "pluck up courage" came into common usage and were associated with the spoils of the warrior: stealing, pillaging, and sometimes rape.

One way to understand the etymology of courage is to consider its history as a series of losses. Over the course of five centuries, from 1051 to 1490, courage was cut off from its sources in time, in the heart, and in feelings. In other words, courage was slowly dissociated from what traditional Western culture considers "feminine" qualities, and came to mean "that quality of mind that shows itself in facing danger without fear or shrinking," a definition associated with the bravery and heroism of boys and men. The pattern of losses in the history of the word courage seems to reflect an increasing invisibility of girls' and women's courage in Western culture. This historical pattern interests me because it also seems to reflect losses girls experience as they come of age in contemporary times. Girls we have studied show a tendency to be vulnerable to certain psychological losses as they move from childhood into adolescence: the loss of clarity, of self-confidence, of voice itself (Brown, 1989; Brown & Gilligan, 1992; Rogers & Gilligan, 1989).

I sit in a small music room with Marcia — one of the participants in the Laurel-Harvard study — a thirteen-year-old European American eighth-grade girl wearing a plaid skirt and green sweater, her legs crossed. Dark, curly hair frames her face. I have come to interview her. I want to learn from Marcia about the lives of girls. She studies me in swift glances, her face closed, as I set up my tape recorder. During this interview I listen to the

---

[4] Judith Jordan has also written about courage, emphasizing "courage in connection" within the context of a relational practice of psychotherapy. See her paper, "Courage in Connection: Conflict, Compassion, Creativity" (1990).

cadence of Marcia's quick sentences, punctuated by the phrases: "I don't know" and "this doesn't make any sense." We hear these phrases sharply increase in our longitudinal interviews, marking a repression of knowledge as girls enter early adolescence (see also Brown & Gilligan, 1992). I feel Marcia slipping away from me; her confusion and the dismissal of her knowledge resonates with the voices of girls her age whom I have interviewed over several years. I begin to wonder if girls lose not only clarity, self-confidence, and voice — but also their courage — as they come of age in androcentric cultures.

But I remember Amy at eleven, her voice coming straight out into the room as she stood reading, and the three girls playing to one side of her. I remember these girls on the beach at Plum Island, where we took them one day — running and twirling in their strong little tadpole bodies, the sudden shifts in feelings — pleasure to impatience to anger and back to pleasure — how their voices carried these feelings easily on the wind. The historical, layered meanings of courage live in these girls' bodies. Courage — "the heart of an age," "to speak one's mind by telling all one's heart," to have a "responsive heart," as well as a "spirit or liveliness" and a quality of "boldness." I discover that by restoring the word courage to its original meanings, the ordinary experiences of the eight- to twelve-year-old girls I have observed and known suddenly become coherent to me.

From Ordinary to Transgressive Courage

Reading the bones, wetting a fingertip
to trace archaic characters, I feel
a breeze of silence flow up past my wrist,
icy. Can I speak here? The bones say I must.
(Ponsot, 1988, p. 72)

My observation about a loss of courage in the lives of girls is embedded in a newly emerging psychology of women based on empirical studies of girls. As a number of recent studies document, adolescence is a time of psychological risk and vulnerability for girls (see Ebata, 1987; Elder, Nguyen, & Caspi, 1985; Petersen, 1988; Petersen & Ebata, 1987). In particular, the move into adolescence affects girls' self-conceptions. Adolescence marks a sharp increase in episodes of depression (Rutter, 1986) and eating disorders among girls, and a sharp drop in self-esteem and self-confidence, at least in White and Latina girls (Block, 1990; Greenberg-Lake Analysis Group, 1991; Wellesley College Center for Research on Women, 1992). In addition, girls tend to lose ground in their assessments of their academic achievement and in their aspirations during adolescence. Girls begin to separate their feelings and intellectual experiences at this time (Debold, 1990), and to show a striking loss of intelligence and capacity to think critically, as measured by standardized tests (Bernardez, 1965; Burks et al., 1930; Hoffman, 1975; Lueptow,

1980). There is clearly a need to understand what is happening in the lives of girls inside and outside of schools, and why adolescence is a time of psychological distress and risk.

In their work together, Lyn Mikel Brown and Carol Gilligan (1992) provide an explanation for the appearance of psychological distress in girls' development. As late childhood falls into adolescence, many of the twelve- and thirteen-year-old girls at the Laurel School began to live under the "tyranny" of the "perfect girl," a mythological (but oh so real!) icon of the culture — the girl that everybody loves because she has no bad thoughts and feelings, but is always "kind" and "nice." Her power was so real to the girls themselves that they began to lose a full range of feelings, and seemed quite suddenly confused (see also Brown, 1991a). Brown and Gilligan (1993) describe one possible outcome of this struggle as a "series of dissociations girls must make between psyche and body, between self and relationship, between the inner world of thoughts and feelings and the outer world of public knowledge — if they are to enter, without disrupting, the world they live in as young women." Another possible outcome would be for girls to resist these disconnections, and in doing so to change the order of their relationships in the world. In calling attention to the costs of girls' dissociations, Brown and Gilligan also theoretically explain how the psychological problems that some girls experience during adolescence — eating disorders and depression — are rooted in the politics of girls' relationships (see also Gilligan, 1990a).

I come back to the observation of courage among younger girls.

What happens to the ordinary courage of these girls as their bodies begin to change, as nubs of breasts emerge and hips begin to form the contours of a woman's body? To tell a coherent story about even a single girl's development and the fate of her courage, I must enter another's psyche, take time to know another "self," someone like myself and also different from myself. But what concept of self can hold the embodied meanings of a girl's courage? I turn to Pamela Hadas, a poet who describes the "self" as "any true I in a story" (1987, p. 190). Similarly, the psychologist Lyn Mikel Brown (1989) sees a connection between the development of self and story as she describes girls' willingness to trust the authority of their own experience, at least until the edge of adolescence (1991b). Brown notices, however, that to speak with authority about one's own life, a girl must resist "the cultural story of female becoming" (1991b, p. 2).

I have begun to articulate a concept of self that is inseparable from courage, the determination to speak truthfully, with integrity, to tell a story that has not been welcomed in the world. What I mean by the "true I" is the self who describes her experience courageously, rendering a story in detailed transparency, voicing a full range of feelings.

Two girls and one woman come to my mind, come into the room, three voices, three muses, each with a story about her relationship with her mother. Together they illustrate one pattern in women's development: a move from "ordinary courage" to what I call "transgressive courage."

Helen — a fourth-grade European American girl from the Atrium School — is nine years old. She wears a green corduroy dress and white tights, her dark hair caught back in a barrette. She sits on a folding metal chair, swinging her feet, in a small room in her elementary school. It is early afternoon, just after lunchtime in her school day. She tells me about a time when her mother left the house after an argument with her father. "No one was doing anything about it, and so I knew where she was and I called her up, and asked why did you leave us like that? I told her to come home. I said, I am mad at you for leaving us. You can talk to Daddy now, . . . so please come home. And she did." In straightforward terms, Helen tells her mother what she thinks and feels, and effectively brings her home. She describes this phone exchange in the same matter-of-fact tone of voice she uses to tell me about playing croquet with her dog: "I usually win and she doesn't like that, but what can you expect?"

Karen — a depressed fourteen-year-old girl I have seen in my clinical practice — sits with one leg crossed over the other, fingering the edges of her grey sweatshirt, looking out of the window into the twilight. "I don't want to tell my mother a lot of things anymore," she begins:

> If I ever said to her, you know, why don't you fight back? I am really mad about you giving in to dad all the time, my mother would think she did something wrong and she would feel bad about it. I think she wants to think she knows a lot about my true feelings because she is afraid that if she doesn't, she will know she doesn't and she will be afraid that, you know, she's just not important in my life, we are just not as close anymore, which isn't true.

As if walking through a room where all the mirrors are hung crooked, I get dizzy trying to find my way through this statement. "But if you were to say that you are mad?" I ask. "Why should I make her life sadder by telling her, by saying that? I mean, she doesn't need to know, it is just better that she does not know all of me."

Karen's voice is uncertain, small, but her face is set, daring me to inquire any further. She looks away, and comes back to meet my eyes. Her sadness is immense.

Susan turns toward me, light brown hair falling away from her face. Susan, a woman in my Psychology of Women Seminar at Harvard, recalls a conversation with her mother when her father was hospitalized:

> My senses were trained to listen closely to the strain of voice, to hear the meaning of breath, to catch the deflections, to push gently. . . . My mother's voice is not coming from her body. She's struggling to make up answers that she thinks are acceptable for me to hear. She doesn't want me to worry. She doesn't want me to know that she is worried. . . . From years of training I know how to push the anger aside and gently press for more information.

I can read the signposts of Susan's knowledge, for she reads, as I read and decipher, a coded knowledge of relationships between women. This recognition swiftly passes back and forth between us.

As I listen to Helen, Karen, and Susan, I hear a struggle for courage in relationships in a society where speaking about what one knows as a girl or a woman is not simple. What was ordinary and natural questioning of her mother for nine-year-old Helen has become a dangerous set of questions for Karen at fourteen. Karen herself senses this and calls her unspoken questions "kind of like trespassing, you know, going where you are not supposed to go." And Susan, who secretly trespasses into forbidden knowledge about her mother's feelings, carries this unspeakable knowledge around like a bomb. Karen's and Susan's courage has become transgressive insofar as they have each dared to know what they are not supposed to know about their mothers and voiced their knowledge with me. Transgressive courage involves going beyond the strictures of forbidden knowledge of relationships, including cultural conspiracies of silence that surround women's knowledge.

These three muses represent not only individual girls and women I have spoken with and known variously as a clinician, teacher, and researcher; they also represent a broader pattern of girls' and women's development within a repressive culture. The loss of an ordinary, embodied courage — a "boldness, spirit and liveliness," the capacity to "speak one's mind by telling all one's heart" — is a loss many girls experience at the edge of adolescence, a loss that leaves in its wake unspeakable longing and rage, as well as a struggle for courage in relationships — the sense that speaking as a "true I" is transgressive and dangerous. What is unspeakable and unspoken in the public world then becomes a feminine "underground" (Gilligan, 1990b), a private world where the "unpaid-for education" of women takes place (Woolf, 1938/1966), where women's knowledge of relationships is buried or kept under wraps in any androcentric culture.

Listening to Narratives of Courage

I'm on my way running
I'm on my way running
Looking toward me is the edge of the world . . .
    (Traditional song for a young girl's puberty ceremony,
    Papago Tribe, cited in Reese, Wilkinson, & Koppelman, 1983, p. 1)

In order to understand a loss of ordinary courage in women's lives, I have had to go back to girls who have yet to experience such a loss. I listen to pre-adolescent girls speaking about themselves and their relationships and re-enter my questions about courage from the point of view of an "insider," a woman remembering her girlhood and the moments when, running ahead, "looking toward me is the edge of the world." As I listen to girls from different social classes and ethnic groups in various school settings within this culture, I know that there are things I do not hear or fully understand, there are lines I am not able to cross, and there are some questions I do not even think to ask.

In this section, I present the voices of two girls, an eleven-year-old African American girl, and a ten-year-old Asian American girl.[5] The girls come from middle- and upper-middle-class families. As an American woman of Irish ancestry who grew up in a lower-class home, I am different from these girls in two fundamental ways: 1) I have not been exposed to the racism that they and their families face every day in this society and culture; and 2) I grew up less privileged than they in terms of socioeconomic status. Because these realities are by no means simple, and because describing sociological differences without clearly understanding individual voices may be misleading, I present the girls' voices in some detail, so that any reader can agree with or reject my interpretations. I also include the ways that the girls spoke or behaved in other contexts wherever that might shed further light on my interpretations.

The method of analysis I use is based on the *Listener's Guide* (Brown et al., 1988; Brown & Gilligan, 1992; Rogers, Brown, & Tappan, 1994), a way of listening to girls in interview texts developed by members of the Harvard Project on Women's Psychology and Girls' Development. The method entails listening for multiple voices within a text through differing interpretive frameworks. Using this method, I have learned to become a "responsive" and "resisting" reader of interview texts, to hear girls speaking both against and within cultural prescriptions about their lives, reading between the gaps I feel between lived experience and the dominant culture's conventions of femininity (see Brown & Gilligan, 1990).

As I read to understand girls' narratives as stories about courage, I am not asking girls to agree or disagree with my concept of "ordinary courage." I developed this concept over a period of years in response to listening to many girls and women, and I am relying on the older definition of the word, as described earlier. In order to discern what I call ordinary courage — "the capacity to speak one's mind by telling all one's heart" — I listen to several voices with a single text in mind. I attend first to the "true I" speaking, that is, the self who describes her experience with a full range of feelings in detailed transparency. Then I listen again for the "feminine not spoken," that is, for a subtext of unspoken meanings or messages (see also Rogers, 1992). Finally, I piece together an interpretation of each girl's struggle for courage by turning to a text written by an older woman; a woman who shares each girl's race and class, as I do not share this experience or understanding with them. Often I hear a resonance between their voices, a haunting harmony, as if listening to singing. This way of listening opens into an acoustical space between girls' and women's voices, where I join as a third voice speaking about what I recall, what I know, and what I do not understand. The purpose of working this way is not to present a "final" or "true" or even classically "valid" interpretation of data. (Such a goal assumes that by employing certain strategies I could put aside all potential differences in inter-

---

[5] These girls were part of the Strengthening Healthy Resistance and Courage in Girls longitudinal study, but were not members of the Theater, Writing, and Outing Club.

pretation and come to the "right" interpretation.) I do not think this is possible. Therefore, by bringing together multiple voices — the voice of a girl telling a story about relationships, the voice of a woman like the girl drawn from literature, and my own voice as a researcher — I seek to highlight and hold differences in voice and in perspective alongside one another and, in so doing, not to override or overwrite any single voice.

Let me now introduce eleven-year-old LaTanya, a middle-class African American girl who attends a small community school. She is a lively, humorous girl, her voice clear and strong. Asked to tell a story about a relationship, she tells the following story about her father:

> Jokewise and things like that my dad's fun to be around. Like when we go down and get pizzas he likes to make me embarrassed. He says the greatest thing is watching daughters being embarrassed by their dads. So he had his slippers on and we went down to get pizza and I said, "I will go in and get it dad," and he said, "No, I'll come," and I said, "Please dad, stay in there," and he said, "No, I'm coming," and I gave him the money and said, "I'm going back to the car," and then he said, "No, come." So I came with him and we went in and got the pizzas and everything and we come back and he started dancing around in the street and really, really, he was dancing up and down and twirling around and I almost dropped the pizzas it was so funny. And we got in and he started, you know, accelerating (she makes accelerating noises) like that, and it was so funny, and so I was laughing and when we got back home and so he does lots of crazy things.

I read first for the narrative "I" of this story; focusing on the self statements in the text: "I said I will go in . . . I said please dad, stay in there . . . I gave him the money . . . [I] said I'm going back to the car . . . I came with him . . . I almost dropped the pizzas . . . I was laughing." LaTanya tells her interviewer about giving her father a series of commands, of protesting, then suddenly giving in and almost dropping the pizzas. I identify the self speaking here as a "true I" because she creates a drama of detailed transparency. As I listen to the tape of her interview, I can hear peals of laughter. As LaTanya tells about teetering between going and staying, she clearly enjoys being teased. In her story, she creates a dialogue or play that is fundamentally two-sided. If I listen for what LaTanya knows about relationships, how she considers her father through this story, here is how she describes him: "My dad's fun to be around. . . . he likes to make me embarrassed . . . he says the greatest thing is watching daughters being embarrassed by their dads . . . he had his slippers on . . . he said no, I'll come . . . he said, no, I'm coming . . . he said no, come . . . he started dancing . . . he was dancing up and down and twirling around . . . he started, you know, accelerating like that . . . he does lots of crazy things." As I listen to her, I get the impression that LaTanya knows her father as a man who plays with her and does not placate her, but who instead holds his own in this argument about his own silliness.

What is unspoken here? What questions are whispered between the lines of this funny little story? Of course, I cannot know with any certainty, as

LaTanya was not directly asked these questions. But, I have learned that there are commonly unspoken messages and questions in girls' stories that remain muffled, enfolded in silence. I listen between the lines of LaTanya's story about playing and teasing with her father from other sections of the interview in an attempt to understand her unspoken messages, questions, and silences. LaTanya tells a companion story about her fourteen-year-old sister and her father: "He makes her change clothes from skimpy stuff to clothes he likes better before she goes out [on dates], and he doesn't really listen to her like he does with me. . . . When they fight, they do that a lot these days, he usually wins. He wins with me too, but I mean, I can just tell, I can tell, that he really embarrasses her sometimes." I hear questions La-Tanya does not speak directly: Will my dad ever really embarrass me? For how long will he play with me as he does now, when I am eleven? For how long will I be able to hold my own in arguments with him, even when he "wins"?

In my attempt to understand LaTanya's story, I turn to a poem by Nikki Giovanni:

> a poem is pure energy
> horizontally contained
> between the mind of the reader
> of the poet and the ear of the reader
> if it does not sing discard the ear
> for poetry is song
> if it does not delight discard
> the heart for poetry is joy . . .
> (Giovanni, cited in Webber & Grumman, 1978, p. 192)

This poem, together with LaTanya's narrative, speaks to me about her ordinary, embodied courage, linking LaTanya with many other girls of this age. Eleven-year-old LaTanya tells a story about the possibility of listening too, listening in a relationship — and LaTanya's capacity to dwell in possibility, to live between the lines of argument and play with her father, *is* the poetry of her story. Her courage comes from her connection with a "true I" who understands her father's intentions and can argue playfully. In fact, LaTanya's capacity to play her part in this scene depends upon her seeing through her father — seeing that he wishes to tease her, make her embarrassed, and beyond this, sensing that his pleasure in the game revolves around her playing her part by giving him commands about what he may and may not do, by protesting what she will and will not do. LaTanya's story of how she plays in the street with her dad, almost dropping the pizzas, is Nikki Giovanni's poetry of song and delight.

In the next excerpt, I am interviewing a girl I have observed in the classroom, so that she knows who I am before I begin to interview her. Her voice plays against my voice in the following dialogue.

Meyee is ten years old and in the fourth grade in her small community school this year. She is a second-generation Chinese American girl with straight black hair, pulled back in a ponytail today. She has dark eyes that light up as she speaks and an easy smile. She sits on a small sofa in a cozy office in her private school, tugging on the ears of a stuffed Eeyore. We have been talking for about forty minutes, and are in the section of the interview protocol where I ask girls about relationships in which others were not listening to them.

"Can you tell me about a time when you felt you were not being listened to?" I ask her.

Meyee pauses, thinking this over. "When my mom and dad make decisions without consulting me and I feel like 'But mom, you never ask to hear me . . . But MOM!' It makes me really mad and I hate it and I feel that they are taking advantage of me just because I am younger."

"Can you tell me about a certain time?"

"I don't remember any, but I just feel it," she replies, looking off.

"When you say, 'they are taking advantage of me,' can you imagine that you might have a little bit of power?" I ask.

"Well, my parents consult me about my birthday, what kind of party would I like, what kind of cake would I like?" she says with a rising inflection. She tilts her head and raises one shoulder.

"So some decisions they might include you?"

"Not very often," she says wryly.

"Okay. When you are not being listened to, how do you get people to listen?"

"I shout," Meyee says, very matter of fact.

"Does that work?" I wonder out loud.

"Sometimes." Ruefully, she adds, "I also get sent to my room. But, oh well."

Meyee looks at me and grins conspiratorially. "I also do a very mean, practical joke on them. Like if my mom is talking to my dad, this is a good idea, I haven't done it yet, I could just go to one of the upper extensions, we have a ton of them [in our house], I could just go up and like burp, a real loud burp, and that would get their attention or something." We laugh.

"Do you think *that* would work?" I ask her.

"Maybe. It would get them very mad, but it would also get them to listen to me. And if they ask for an explanation, I'll tell them."

I begin by listening to the narrative "I," the self who responds to my questions. "I feel like, 'But mom, you never ask to hear me'. . . I hate it . . . I feel that they are taking advantage . . . I am younger . . . I don't remember . . . I just feel it . . . I shout . . . I also get sent to my room . . . I also do a very mean practical joke on them . . . I haven't done it yet . . . I could just go . . . I could just go up and like burp . . . I'll tell them." As I listen to the "I" clauses in this order, I hear a "true I," a girl who feels her thoughts and trusts her feelings, even when she doesn't have a memory of a particular incident. This ten-year-old girl speaking about herself also feels "taken advantage of" and not listened to, but cares enough, or has enough courage perhaps, to disrupt her family a bit on her own behalf — by shouting, or by planning "a very mean practical joke."

As I listen to what Meyee does not say, what she perhaps knows but doesn't say to me, I feel the edge of her daring. She calls a loud burp a "very mean practical joke." The joke and how "mean" it is depends, of course, on the disruptiveness of her act, on catching her parents off guard to get them to listen to her. She implies that this behavior may require an explanation: "If they ask me for an explanation, I'll tell them." But she has also spoken about making her parents angry, and about getting sent to her room. Meyee implies that her plan is risky, she may be punished for it. What remains unspoken is that she must continually gauge what she can and cannot do and say because she is, in fact, younger and relatively less powerful than her parents.

What Meyee can and cannot say aloud is affected, to some extent, by my questions and responses to her. They are the questions and responses of an adult woman who grew up as an Irish American girl in a family where she often felt powerless. I am also her interviewer here — and therefore more powerful than she is in this situation. When Meyee says, "They are taking advantage of me," I ask, "Can you imagine that you might have a little bit of power?" I wanted to align myself with her daring through that question, but perhaps I dismissed her feeling of powerlessness, not wanting to recall my own feelings. She tells me then that her parents consult her about her birthday. In a rising inflection she gives examples: "What kind of party would I like, what kind of cake would I like?" — as if to say, "Is this what you want me to say?" The back and forth dance of what can and cannot be spoken about we create together. When I ask, rather hopefully, "So some decisions they might include you?" she replies, "Not very often," bringing me back to her reality and to my questions about not being listened to.

I listen next to Nelly Wong, a Chinese American writer, and bring a fragment of one of her poems to Meyee's story, to my own questions about courage:

> When I was growing up, I was proud
> of my English, my grammar, my spelling
> fitting into the group of smart children
> smart Chinese children, fitting in,
> belonging, getting in line
> (Wong, cited in Reese et al., 1983, p. 171)

I have observed Meyee in her school, "fitting in, belonging, getting in line," yet I hear Meyee as a resistor of conventions. She does not fit the image of the "good girl" of a dominant White culture — she is too outspoken, too mischievous. And she does not fit the image of a "good Asian girl" either — she is too strong, too bold. "And if they ask for an explanation, I'll tell them," she says, thinking about her experiment with a "loud burp." But I wonder what she can tell her parents, her teachers, and me, her interviewer. It seems to me that Meyee's plan for the practical joke of a loud burp requires some foresight and courage; but if she is to continue to say what she knows aloud — to trust her own feelings and knowledge as a Chinese American girl growing into a woman in this culture and learning about herself and the world in our educational system — she will need much more foresight and courage. I wonder what she will know as a young woman, this girl of ten who is now so strong and brave.

In reading the interview transcripts of these two girls, LaTanya and Meyee, I noticed that I did not directly ask them about their experiences as African American and Asian American girls, as children who stand outside the dominant culture by virtue of both race and gender. In retrospect, I wish that I had asked this question, because I might have learned something critical about their different experiences of courage. I mark this gap in my knowledge and skill so that others might see the gap and wonder about it too.

The Recovery of Courage: Through Voice and Play

What is a practice of courage in relationships that makes it possible for women and girls, and for women of different generations, to stay with one another, rather than abandoning one another at the edge of difficult and vital truths? I think again of Amy, Helen, Meyee, and LaTanya, girls at ten and eleven — their ordinary courage, their outspokenness, and their insistence on real or authentic relationships. Living just at the edge of adolescence, these girls conducted profound experiments in relationships — experiments to sustain their courage. But to continue to do so is anything but easy. Adolescent girls and women who risk their truths in relationships risk a great deal. Courage may be in fact dangerous at times — when knowledge is new and fragile; when reaching out for a desired connection may lead to a painful repudiation; when speaking without any real possibility of being heard may lead to betrayal or abandonment. But the ways girls and women, and women of different generations, negotiate these difficult issues together mark the fate of female courage in families and schools, and in the culture at large.

The recovery of ordinary courage in women's lives is nothing short of extraordinary, because it depends upon finding a voice to speak what has been unspeakable. Often this process begins in a safe, playful, and challenging relational context among women or among women and girls together. Women of all ages then begin to remember and re-experience that lively and playful and knowing younger self that Emily Hancock calls "the girl within" (Hancock, 1989).

"Finding a voice" is not a metaphorical phrase, but a literal, psycho-physical finding of voice. The voice, played on breath and linked with real feelings, reveals the self — and is therefore vital to authentic contact and to the recovery of courage. Kristin Linklater, who has extensive experience training actors, describes in her book *Freeing the Natural Voice* (1976) a voice that carries every nuance of human thought, a voice connected with breath and with feelings: "The natural voice is transparent — revealing, not describing, inner impulses of emotion and thought, directly and spontaneously" (p. 2).

Linklater's "natural voice" is, in my terms, the voice of ordinary courage. Muscular tension, or any inhibition of the free flow of breath in the body, distorts this voice and protects us from being known. But when an adolescent girl or a woman begins to speak in a natural or transparent voice, bringing herself into relationships as a "true I," and living courageously in the sense of "speaking her mind by telling all her heart," she may be in danger. Within some contexts, women can expect to be heard only if they learn to "modulate" their voices. A loud or strong voice in a woman tends to be associated with rudeness, anger, and aggression. The effort to modulate the voice, to be quiet, involves going "off" one's voice. It is not unusual for adult women in Western cultures to sound somewhat "breathy," which results in a diminishment of clarity and power, as well as a narrowing of the full octave of pitches available for speaking. Perhaps once these physical changes have affected the voices of adolescent girls, it is easier for girls to adapt to living as women within men's knowledge and traditions—in our educational system and in our society.

The range of self-protective compromises — including the unconscious covering of voice — that diminishes a girl's courage and knowledge of herself, seems endless. Are these self-protective compromises really necessary, or might the ordinary, embodied courage of girls somehow remain intact? And if self-protective compromises at adolescence are unavoidable to girls in this culture, can ordinary courage be recovered later in life?

These questions became acute in my developmental and preventive work with girls and women in three different contexts: a) in the Theater, Writing, and Outing Club for Girls from the Atrium School conducted by myself, Carol Gilligan, and Normi Noel; b) in the Shakespeare & Company's month-long acting workshop in which I was a participant; and c) in the Intergenerational Women's Oral History Group at the Erikson Center, in which I was also a participant. In each of these settings, women and girls experienced ordinary courage — through voice and play. Three distinct but overlapping stories that emerged from the contexts described clarify the process of coming into courage for girls and women at different times in their development.

In the first instance, both the ease of calling forth the ordinary courage of preadolescent girls and the fragility of their courage became clear to me.

The members of the Theater, Writing, and Outing Club for Girls sit in a circle in an empty school auditorium. Eight eleven- and twelve-year-old girls have gathered with three women: Carol Gilligan; Normi Noel, a director and voice teacher from Boston's Shakespeare & Company; and myself. Normi is leading the group in theater exercises this rainy Wednesday morning. She tells us that to be actors first we must be entirely honest about our feelings, because our feelings will become the "stuff" of theater. We go around the group. Joan begins: "If I say my feelings, they will keep changing," observing at age twelve, just at the edge of adolescence, the fluidity of her own emotional life. We speak around this circle, each intent, without evaluations.

Then Normi introduces a game, "Stories: One-word-at-a-time." The girls want to create a story about witches. They will create the story word by word. Normi takes on the role of group "scribe." There is little or no time to think. Here is the story about "witches" composed on the spot:

> Witches. There are disgusting witches. Broomsticks.
> Bugs owls eat, like crawly insects. Witches tend to want
> everything. They tend to think of anything that you love.
> But they can magically transform into production hats. Eat
> chicken and never eat fried pickles. They are going home
> soon so that they can disguise themselves as rabbits with
> leaves. Feelings I feel: gross disgusting sick mad witches.
> Crazy women eat toilet paper and barbaric hair. They're
> very indigestous, overwhelming like antidisestablish-
> mentarianists, or weird people. Hair spray smells like
> witches' breath. Garbage smells like farts. Murals feel
> revolting, like cats and sardines. Anyway, people tend
> subconsciously to throw up.

Here is a story about forbidden feelings, a story about greed, love, disguise, disgust, and about what cannot be digested. It may also be read as a rather rude, banal story about witches told by eight young girls. But I listen to this story from another vantage point, from the point of view of a woman who listens for a story of courage. What is spoken and what is unspeakable in this story? What do girls know about women, when women are disguised as witches? I hear the girls naming an unspeakable longing and vulnerability in women: "Witches tend to want everything. They tend to think of anything that you love." I hear a struggle to see through disguise and not to be taken in by the mystifying ways women cover themselves: "They are going home soon to disguise themselves as rabbits with leaves." The girls touch on the subject of women's madness; their voices join in with a chorus of voices condemning women: "Feelings I feel: gross, disgusting, sick, mad, witches. Crazy women eat toilet paper and barbaric hair." The girls also actively resist female conventions of beauty: "Hair spray smells like witches' breath." In quick succession, "witches' breath" is associated with "garbage," "farts," and "cats and sardines." The girls reject the entire list, framing this line of associations with the phrases, "they're very indigestous" and "people tend subconsciously to throw up."

Listening to and watching the girls perform their story with these thoughts flying through my mind, I double over in laughter as they play out, in lively mimed movements, each phrase of their story, and "freeze" to hold their outrageous poses on Normi's command.

What Carol, Normi, and I are doing here seems quite simple. Through the avenue of play and theater, we call girls' voices out into the room, we listen to them and enjoy them, and we delight in their ordinary courage — played through their voices and physical poses. We hear ourselves through the girls' voices, ourselves speaking a bit more clearly and courageously. But what we are doing is also dangerous. When we perform this for the girls' mothers and teachers, for example, the bad feelings, all the madness and ugliness held in this fanciful story, go flat. The fragility of the girls' courage becomes apparent only when it disappears in front of this audience.

Yet I know that I could not stay with the girls' feelings and know the full range of my own responses without Normi and Carol, without all our conversations about how the girls affect each of us. Being with the girls brings to the surface my questions about courage, and their ordinary courage soaks into my body, straightens my spine. When Normi commutes from New York to work with us, she gets dizzy on the long train rides back and forth as she comes and goes from experiencing her own courage with girls and women in this way. For a few weeks after our summer session with these eleven- and twelve-year-old girls, I can look at Carol standing straight in one of her sundresses, her long hair falling in a different way, and I can tell that she is thinking of one particular girl who also stands that way. I ask her and find that I am correct. The girls connect with each of us beyond the time we spend with them — they come into our bodies, they enter our dreams, they join us on our train journeys, they speak to us when we sit down to write. Witches indeed!

We three, all adult women, remember ourselves vividly as girls in their presence. During this period of our work with the girls, Carol had recently returned from participating in a month-long acting workshop conducted by Shakespeare & Company. She had discovered, she told us, "the mechanism of dissociation in girls' voices at adolescence." What she learned was "the way girls dissociate is to stop breathing, hold their stomachs in, and in this way, girls cut off breath and feelings from their voices." I was intrigued by this idea, and still more intrigued as I watched Normi work with the eleven- and twelve-year-old girls in our Theater, Writing, and Outing Club. Normi noticed that "the girls' voices come straight out from the center of their faces." She added, "These little creatures naturally speak on their voices most of the time! Women do not do that." I did not know what the phrase "on their voices" really meant, but I wanted to find out because that phrase seemed intricately linked with ordinary courage.

In the second context, Shakespeare & Company's acting workshop, I came to understand this linkage between voice and courage more fully. "What am I doing here?" I ask myself, looking around the dim room, which gradually grows lighter. Of course I know. Encouraged by Carol and Normi, I have come to this acting workshop to explore the links between voice and courage, beginning with my voice and a search for my own courage.[6] The fear is familiar enough. I feel uncannily light-hearted, however. Restless, unable to sleep more than five hours the night before, I have returned to the place I began my voice class. I button my sweater up to my chin, remembering: The room lit up with lamps. Seven people, men and women, sitting in a semicircle of folding chairs at one end, my "basics" group. For me, unlike the others who are professional Shakespearean actors, this is my first voice class. Each

---

[6] Tina Packer, the director of the company, invited me to attend.

one has stood and performed one of Shakespeare's monologues or sonnets, but I have chosen to begin with a poem, one of my own (Rogers, 1990), not daring to start with Shakespeare.

"From the porch/ when dark/ stole the colors of childhood/ from the very sky . . ." I begin. "Where are you?" asks Kristin, my basics teacher.[7] "On the porch," I answer, as if this were a perfectly obvious place to begin. "No, no!" she says, striding toward me, her brown eyes sharp. "First you have to come into this room!" I look around thinking, "What could be simpler?" But it wasn't simple at all to come into my body in that room. Over the next thirty minutes, Kristin had me perform a "three-act play." "Here is how it goes," she said, "Act I: I am, Act II: here, Act III: in this room." Stomping on the carpet in bare feet, pounding the walls with my hands, whispering, shouting, I cajole and finally convince myself, Kristin, and my small audience of my presence in the room.

Kristin pulls one of the folding chairs out from the semicircle and places it backwards. "Sit," she says, "and begin your poem."

"From the porch/ when dark/ stole the colors of childhood from the very sky . . ." "What? What are the colors of childhood?" Kristin asks. "You know, feelings, ordinary things, play." "What are you feeling?" "Nothing in particular." She pulls me up from the chair and begins a clapping game, dancing around me in her grey high-top tennis shoes, in her black sweat suit with moons and stars, her short grey hair standing up on end. She sticks her tongue out at me and encourages me to give chase around the chair. Laughing, I chase her and sit again, and still laughing, begin —"From the porch/ when dark/ stole the colors of childhood from the very sky/ and I'd lost a shoe-box-full of/ myself . . ." "Of what? Not of things." "Of myself." "Say it again." "Of myself" I whisper. "Again." "Of myself" I say aloud, and feel the fresh loss of my whole lively self. "Go on." "The voices came./ They were in the loosening bud of my body/ they came like blue rain/ like angels from the dark." Kristin stands next to me, one hand on my belly. "Breathe," she says, as I stop breathing. "What did the voices say to you? Did you like them? Did they frighten you? What does blue rain feel like? Who were the angels? Where were you standing on the porch? How old were you? What were you seeing and hearing from the porch?" Her questions come into my body with each intake of breath.[8] Images, voices, feelings, the view from the back porch flood me, in my thirteen-year-old body. "Keep going," Kristin says softly. "They came from everywhere/ snowing down, they swirled and settled on a white wooden table . . ." Kristin pummels my chest, moves my arms up and down, "Just ignore me," she says, "I'm helping you." And she was! My words came clearly into the room. I heard myself saying, "They said: Go and lick

---

[7] Kristin Linklater is the Director of Training of this acting workshop. She is the author of *Freeing the Natural Voice* (1976), a widely used voice method, and has trained actors at theater companies and universities throughout the world.

[8] Linklater's voice and text work here is designed to bring an actor's feelings and life experiences to bear directly on his or her performance. The method of asking a rapid succession of questions in rhythm with the actor's breathing is called "Dropping-In," a way to get a text "into the body" pioneered by Packer, Linklater, and a core group of master teachers at Shakespeare & Company.

the white metal ice/ that tears ragged/ a layer of tongue . . ." "Like that? The voices just asked you like that?" Kristin says, incredulous. "Well no, they were a little meaner," I admitted. "Meaner? I bet they were downright sadistic!" She grabs me by the hand and takes me back to the couch at the far end of the room. She looks back at my basics group. "Don't move until you feel terrified. Then raise one finger," she instructs them. "Here, stand up here and try it again — to them." I stand in silence. Kristin shouts, "Off you go!" Caught off guard, I shout, "Go and lick the white metal ice/ that tears ragged/ a layer of tongue." I yell it over and over, my throat dry. At the other end of the room, no one budges. Kristin is up on the couch with me in a flash. "I want you to send them terror. I want you to make them want to get out of this room — fast," she whispers to me. Suddenly, my voice, filled with hatred and suppressed rage, comes from deep within my abdomen, from a place I've never heard before. "Go and lick the white metal ice/ that tears ragged/ a layer of tongue!" "Good. . . . Now go on," Kristin says, laughing. "I tried to hold them in my very hand;/ they evaporated, as if endangered things/ and my fingers lay/ as in a bell that lay above a clapper./ They rang out cracking from the sky/ like ink left in a blotter too long./ At day's end/ each one of them would make up/ for me/ the deepest crib/ of doubt/ black me in."

The white ceiling became a dark sky, filled with cold stars, then black — and the voices, once cut off from me, came back to me. My own voice came from within my body, resonated through the tiny bones of my face. My lips and arms tingled from the vibrations. And my small audience sat still, as if suspended in time. "Like that?" I asked, turning to Kristin, who had climbed down from the couch and was now grinning like the Cheshire Cat himself.

Reliving this work, I stood and looked out into the falling snow and felt wetness on my cheeks. My small voice, not so very small after all, lived in my body. I had struggled for understanding, for words, for voice itself, at the edge of the sofa, at the edge of the unspeakable — as a "true I." I wanted more of this, much more, for myself — and for other girls and women.

It is not coincidental that the poem I chose for my voice work reveals a story about a loss of voice so complete as to mean a loss of "myself" at age thirteen. "When dark stole the colors of childhood from the very sky . . ." ushers in a time of crisis in many girls' development when cultural darkness and psychological repression lead to a loss of ordinary courage. Once my own courage was endangered in this way, the "true I" became fragmented and "the voices came from everywhere." Carrying my dissociated hate and rage, they said, "Go and lick the white metal ice that tears ragged a layer of tongue." These voices echoed cultural messages to forget what I knew, to stop speaking. Yet, once these voices came back into my body, released on sound, their repression was no longer necessary. Courage seemed, at least momentarily, ordinary again.

Voice, played on breath in the body, is, I discovered, a powerful way for women to recover memory and courage. Kristin is a Scottish woman a generation older than I, and I experienced myself in the position of the daughter in this playful and powerful scene with her. The process of recovering ordinary courage involved crossing a full generation in relationship with a woman, and with travelling back in time through the psycho-physical experience of the voice work. I wondered about the intergenerational possibilities for extending this work. Was it critical to cross a generation in order for women to experience the recovery of memory and of courage? Was the structure of the voice work critical? How would elderly women experience themselves in a relational context with younger women?

I had the chance to explore some of these questions in a third context, a structured six-week-long Intergenerational Women's Oral History Group at the Erikson Center in Cambridge, Massachusetts. The group was created and facilitated by Vicki Magee and Lisa Sjostrom, who had joined me in writing a year-long ethnography at the Erikson Center (see Rogers, Fradin, Magee, & Sjostrom, 1992). I was invited to participate in this group, as well as to act as an advisor. We met weekly in a large sunny room with many windows. Sitting in a circle with teacups in hand, we were a group of seven women ranging in age from thirty to eighty. Each week we prepared to talk about a different topic or time period in our lives, guided by questions created by the two facilitators, who were also full participants in our conversations.

I arrived a little late at the Erikson Center one early spring day. The others had already gathered in the circle. The tape recorder picked up the overlapping voices and laughter of the group as we settled in. The topic of the week was adolescence. Some of us brought pictures and mementos to share. Nora pushed back a few grey wisps of hair, sat up straighter, and began:

> The worst moment of my adolescence was, I was probably twelve, and you see I was a tomboy. It was a matter of great pride that I could do anything my older brother could do, and my friends were tomboys too. After school, um, this was in the twenties, after school, we would change out of our dresses into what would nowadays be called shorts, but they were our bloomers and middies, and we'd put on our sneakers. I was a year younger than my friends, because I'd skipped first grade. And just about this time, a new girl moved into our neighborhood. She was not like us, she was from Boston . . . and she was kind of glamorous. All the time I was becoming more and more jealous of Emily, she was growing closer and closer to my best friend Faith. . . . We would be going to this tea-dance, that was the plan. I would, of course, come home and climb trees and ride my bike, going about what I'd always done with great determination, but Faith wasn't interested in doing these things any longer. She was too busy making plans with Emily for the tea dance. And one day everything just rolled up inside me in this great tremendous surge of anger, and I turned to Faith and I pounded her on the chest just as hard as I could. And then I ran home, crying. To have hurt my friend. She was totally bewildered by my attack. It was terrible. Somehow my mother seemed to know and to understand, I didn't expect that from her, but she didn't think it was so terrible, what I'd done. But everything just stopped. My whole world stopped. It was the end of everything. We didn't play after school. It was the end of an era.

Listening to the tape of this conversation, I hear, as Nora moves into the memory of herself at twelve, her voice shift and become more vibrant and full. Her voice drops down and catches the edge of her rage as she says, "And one day everything just rolled up inside me in this great tremendous surge of anger, and I turned to Faith and I pounded her on the chest just as hard as I could." There is no one present working with Nora to help her come onto her voice — this spontaneously happens as she enters the memory of herself at twelve. As she continues to speak, her voice becomes "transparent — revealing inner impulses of emotion and thought directly"; in other words, she comes onto Linklater's "natural voice" (p. 2).

When Nora continues and says, "But everything just stopped. My whole world stopped. It was the end of everything. We didn't play after school. It was the end of an era," her voice changes again. I hear her bewilderment and her sadness, also familiar to me, and to all of us in the room as we sit in rapt silence. I hear within her bewilderment the confusion of the girls I have listened to: "I don't know . . ." What can be known? What is understood? Nora says her mother knew and understood, "Somehow my mother seemed to know and to understand," yet this was not enough, because "everything just stopped." As I hear Nora's voice change, carrying every nuance of feeling so that we, her listeners, enter her story moment by moment with her, I hear the ordinary courage of the girls I have known. This quality of courage, "the capacity to speak one's mind by telling all one's heart," comes into her body and into her voice at eighty as she lives within the memory of herself at twelve.

What is the relational context in which this happened? The context is intergenerational, and it is with women that Nora chooses to tell this story. I have known Nora and been with her in a community setting for nine months — making music, doing artwork, cooking, talking, eating, and planning the program of our activities together.[9] I was drawn to Nora initially when I discovered that she was an impossible tease, playful and quick. That playful and courageous girl clearly lived just below the surface and could be quite easily called out to play with me.

As we continued to talk about our adolescence in the group that day, the familiar pattern emerged: each of us entered a time of loss during adolescence, loss of voice and of self, and each of us in different ways struggled hard to hold onto ourselves and harder still to remember and live within our resistance and our courage as women. In our thirties and forties and sixties and eighties, this was clearly an ongoing, life-long struggle.

Nora and the conversation about her story stay with me. What is the practice of relationships that might sustain girls' courage and help women to recover those memories of themselves as courageous girls? Could a practice of courage come into schools, where women and girls might join together most readily? And with what implications for girls' development and education, for women's knowledge, creativity, and power?

---

[9] Nora is a member of the staff. I am a resident artist and have directed an ethnographic study of the project.

Looking Back — Toward a Practice of Courage

You're beside me at the window,
Shivering sympathetically. Together
we go over the details. Each telling begins
my education again. I want to know
nothing less than I know . . .
(Mazur, 1986, p. 16)

The "we" of this poem becomes you and I — you, the reader of this article, I, its author — looking back through the window of the text toward a practice of courage among girls and women. Together we go over the details.

When courage is linked to one of its oldest meanings in the English language, "to speak one's mind by telling all one's heart," the embodied or ordinary courage of eight- to twelve-year-old girls becomes readily visible and audible. Yet the courage of girls has been rendered all but nonexistent over the centuries as the word came to signify the bravery and heroic valor of men, so that neither men nor women were likely to discern the courage of girls. This cultural loss is reflected by a developmental loss of ordinary courage that occurs in many girls' lives in early adolescence.

At this time in their development, some girls begin to forget the ordinary courage they experienced in relationships as children. In early adolescence, these girls invent a "cover story" and a "cover girl" to go with their stories — the girl who has no bad thoughts or feelings, but who is always nice and kind (see Brown, 1989; Brown & Gilligan, 1992). At this time in their lives, these girls speak about feeling abandoned or betrayed by women and stop saying what they really think and feel. Girls who give up authentic relationships try to sustain an anemic shadow of these relationships in the service of becoming good women: women who are "sensitive," "caring," women who would never "hurt anyone." They enter conventions of feminine goodness by cutting off the breath in their bodies, effectively disguising their feelings when they speak. These girls also silence themselves, deliberately choosing not to speak about what they know. This self-silencing, used at first as a political strategy of self-protection, slips over into a psychological resistance — the disconnection of one's own experience from consciousness (Gilligan, 1990a; Rogers et al., 1994). Then the silence or amnesia of the unconscious erases the memory of the struggle for voice and conscious knowledge. Although these girls convincingly appear to be doing quite well in schools — they report getting good grades, becoming less impulsive and more mature, and acquiring more "self-confidence" — they also report "losing weight," feeling "depressed" or "numb" or "out of touch." Moreover, at times they seem unable to know and name their feelings and thoughts clearly (see Brown & Gilligan, 1992; Rogers et al., 1994).

Girls who show this pattern are not simply victims of a society and a school system that undermine their belief in the reality of their own experience. These girls actively struggle to protect themselves. When they no longer feel welcomed as themselves in their relationships — with all their love, anger, and authenticity intact — then, in order to preserve some vital connection with themselves, the girls make a move to prevent a kind of self-murder. The "true I," the self who spoke a full range of feelings in detailed transparency, begins to see and hear double — to watch and listen to herself in her own terms, while at the same time comparing this knowledge of herself with what is named "reality" in her family and school. This fragmentation and muffling of voice means a loss of embodied feelings, the loss of a sense that courage can be quite ordinary. Yet the strategies that many girls growing into women adopt to live in androcentric culture are deeply self-preservative, for the deliberate move into hiding actually protects against the death of the "true I." The "true I" becomes an elusive, ephemeral, imprisoned self. Held away from public scrutiny, this hidden self speaks to the self who acts in the world. "But when the self speaks to the self, who is speaking?" Virginia Woolf asks. "The entombed soul, the spirit driven in, in, to the central catacomb; the self that took the veil and left the world — a coward perhaps, yet, somehow beautiful, as it flits with its lanterns restlessly up and down the dark corridors" (Woolf, 1921/1944, p. 19). From the "dark corridors" of women's diaries, dreams, and half-finished thoughts, the "true I" may potentially be recovered.

How is it possible, then, for adolescent girls and women who show this pattern of loss to recover voice and courage, to live whole, and to speak again in the world? This is a difficult process. The adolescent girls seemed to forget the memory of themselves as courageous and create another story, recalling themselves at ages from nine to twelve as "rude" or "inappropriate," "bad" or "disturbed." These are the very words some teachers and therapists also use to describe girls who stand outside the culture's conventions of the "good girl." But the process of recovering voice and courage involves remembering another story, recalling a girl-self who was in the oldest sense of the word courageous — able to "speak her mind by telling all her heart."

Beyond the bounds of childhood, many girls and women are also understandably reluctant to bring themselves authentically into their relationships. Their courage seems suddenly treacherous, transgressive, dangerous. But the "true I" lives on in an underground world, waiting and hoping for a sign that she may emerge, whole, and open herself again. This wish is nothing short of terrifying, for it reawakens the fear of another abandonment, another shattering loss. Girls, astute observers of their mothers and teachers, seem to know when women can and cannot face squarely into a struggle with them. Unfortunately, women's reluctance to experience another loss becomes a powerful psychological defense. When women cannot enter deeply into girls' struggles for a real relationship, women are effectively saying to girls, "No, I'll not risk being truthful with you; I will distance myself from you because I can't stay close to you any longer." Thus the defense — the story of inevitable loss and betrayal designed to protect from repeated losses — repeats itself generation after generation, handed down unconsciously from women to girls, from mothers to daughters.

But as difficult as it may be, I think that women can recover their courage with one another and find ways to preserve the courage of girls in the next generation. In my personal experience, this work has involved uncovering memories of myself in late childhood in relationships with older women and with girls. I have also seen women like Nora in the Intergenerational Women's Oral History Group recover voice and courage as they remember themselves at the edge of adolescence. Emily Hancock (1989) also found that women speaking to her about their lives spontaneously recalled themselves as young girls, and repeatedly uncovered memories of themselves as children. Through their "rediscovery of the true self" (p. 1), women found the touchstone of their adult identity, "the girl within." I have also seen teachers in another acting workshop designed specifically for teachers discover the power of their voices and come into vivid memories of themselves as girls.[10]

But what of the girls who are living in the world now as they are coming of age and facing a real crisis of courage? In my collaborative preventive and clinical work with girls, the hope of sustaining girls' courage is present moment by moment in the struggle for real relationship. This is what I call a practice of courage. This practice involves the art of being playful and outspoken, and of being a vulnerable and staunch fighter — someone who transgresses the conventions of feminine goodness. To engage in this practice would upset the structures of formal education that preserve the status quo of our society. If girls and women were to say in school what they know to be true, the inequities and the neglect of girls in our educational system would become much clearer, and also more poignant and disturbing.

Discovering this practice of courage is not a matter of good intentions. Instead, it seems to require a skilled listening, a way of listening now supported by empirical studies of girls' experiences. When I speak and listen to girls I am always seeking to get under the surface of what is being said — listening for the "true I," the voice of the girl who knows and describes her experience through a full range of feelings, who can tell the story of her life and her relationships in detailed transparency. This listening is difficult because a girl's voice may suddenly shift into indirect, coded speech that is hard to follow, or may get quickly covered over by conventions she wants to believe and may want me to believe too. When I ask a hard question or miss a critical point, she falls into an awkward silence. Sometimes she does not wish to reveal herself to me at all. To listen for courage then means to listen between sudden shifts in voice and silence, and to track my own feelings and responses in the moment-by-moment relationship. I find this activity, which is central to my research, teaching, and clinical work, frightening and exhilarating. To invite a girl to reveal herself in my presence, I have found it

[10] This workshop, funded by the National Endowment for the Humanities, brought teachers together for voice and acting training, so that they might be more effective teachers of Shakespeare. Beatrice Nelson, the project director, and Kristin Linklater asked me to attend and write an ethnography of this workshop.

necessary to make an opening for her courage through mine, revealing my-self as someone who struggles as she struggles, breaking conventions of standard teaching, research, and clinical practice to do so (see also Rogers, 1991a).

To learn this practice of courage with girls and women we need time and space to breathe freely, to be vulnerable, to speak honestly with one another. This means having time in the structure of our work as teachers or as psy-chologists to engage in this kind of relationship. It also means breaking traditional and time-honored conventions of feminine goodness to create a new order or logic of relationships between women and girls.

Engaging the artistic imagination and providing intergenerational inter-action between girls and women are two ways to reveal what girls and women know from their own experience. The three stories presented, which emerged respectively from the contexts of the Theater, Writing, and Outing Club, the Acting Workshop, and the Intergenerational Women's Oral His-tory Group attest to this possibility.

Central to my learning a practice of courage has been the continued presence of girls in my life and my deepening friendships and collaboration with women. These relationships have been a catalyst for remembering my-self as a girl. As I began to sift though these memories in relation to my clinical work and teaching and writing, I created a girl-woman, an amalgam of myself and the girls I have known. She is twelve years old, no longer entirely a child, not yet a woman. Finding strength in her presence, I look toward a practice of courage I hope will be useful to teachers and therapists, women and men, and to girls themselves.

Twelve

She perches on a flat rock in the rain
dances about on curled tongues of seaweed, barefoot,
careful of barnacles. She leaps down into warm waves, scoops
water, splashes, scoops and sprays warm salt water over
the rock to see if tiny white slits will open,
will tiny white mouths feed from her splashing hands?

She curls up in an old blue bathrobe, in a big wing
chair, balancing chocolate, diary, her tilting tea and doll.
Who would ever discern her courage, watching her?

Snow is falling. It's started. Each flake moves
upward in the night whispering about indirect questions
her mother's averted eyes. In her unblinking need to know
her heart can hear wicks sputtering golden words
the silver tongues of snow on every ledge.
No one will ever be able to translate this inscrutable
new language, the letters and characters
of an ingenious layered grammar
a whole and private music of her own tuned inside to
the air outside turns

the scrub oaks turn the cranberries turn red.
She bleeds but who will ever see this?
The time is coming
when she will turn tilting the world away
from diary and dolls poems and paintings.

But now she is still at home
still rock-leaping
she is of a whole
at the kitchen door listening out into love.
It is eight o'clock. It is still twilight and shore slapping
sounds travel about darkness innocent of grammar.

She comes back to me now with the story of how she forgot
her fossils and snake, left her mother without a kiss —
already she was homesick
when she climbed on the bus for summer camp, leaving
her mother's timeless scent and recent lap;
already she was homesick for all the lost collections.
The way I welcome her back she is in pieces
she etches images carefully if only it will stop somewhere
then crosshatches them out eye and ear and hand
cannot join the pieces now missing
depth will she slip off will she see the edge?

I am going back for her the way I remember her
standing on a rock in the rain, her head tilted back
rain pouring into her wide open mouth,
running down her upturned face.[11]

References

Bachelard, G. (1969). *The poetics of space.* Boston: Beacon Press. (Original work published 1958)

Baugh, C. (1963). *Chaucer's major poetry.* Engelwood Cliffs, NJ: Prentice-Hall.

Bernardez, T. (1965). The feminine role: Case report. *Bulletin of the Menninger Clinic, 29*(4), 204.

Block, J. (1990, October). Ego resilience through time: Antecedents and ramifications. In *Resilience and psychological health.* Symposium of the Boston Psychoanalytic Society, Boston.

Brown, L. (1989). *Narratives of relationship: The development of a care voice in girls ages 7 to 16* (Monograph No. 8). Cambridge, MA: Harvard Project on Women's Psychology and Girls' Development.

Brown, L. (1991a). A problem of vision: The development of relational voice in girls ages 7 to 16. *Women's Studies Quarterly, 19*(1/2), 52–71.

Brown, L. (1991b). Telling a girl's life: Self-authorization as a form of resistance. *Women and Therapy, 11*(3/4), 71–86.

Brown, L., Argyris, D., Attanucci, J., Bardige, B., Gilligan, C., Johnston, K., Miller, B., Osborne, D., Tappan, M., Ward, J., Wiggins, G., & Wilcox, D. (1988). *A guide to reading narratives of conflict and choice for self and relational voices* (Monograph No. 1). Cambridge, MA: Harvard Graduate School of Education, Center for Study of Gender, Education, and Human Development.

---

[11] This poem has also been published separately in a special issue of *Women's Studies Quarterly* (*19*, Nos. 1/2 [1991b], 29–30) on "Women, Girls, and the Culture of Education."

Brown, L., & Gilligan, C. (1990, August). Listening for self and relational voices: A responsive/resisting reader's guide. In M. Franklin (Chair), *Literary theory as a guide to psychological analysis.* Symposium conducted at the annual meeting of the American Psychological Association, Boston.

Brown, L., & Gilligan, C. (1992). *Meeting at the crossroads: Women's psychology and girls' development.* Cambridge, MA: Harvard University Press.

Brown, L., & Gilligan, C. (1993). Meeting at the crossroads: Women's psychology and girls' development. *Feminism and Psychology, 3*(1), 11–35.

Burks, B., Jensen, D., Terman, L., Leahy, A., Marshall, H., & Oden, M. (1930). *Genetic studies of genius: Vol. III. The promise of youth: Follow-up studies of a thousand gifted children.* Stanford, CA: Stanford University Press.

Collins, P. H. (1989). The social construction of black feminist thought. *Signs, 14,* 745–773.

Cook, J., & Fonow, M. (1990). Knowledge and women's interests: Issues of epistemology and methodology in feminist sociological research. In J. Nielsen (Ed.), *Feminist research methods: Exemplary readings in the social sciences* (pp. 69–93). Boulder, CO: Westview Press.

Debold, E. (1990, November). *The flesh becomes word.* Paper presented at the Conference on Diversity in Ways of Knowing, Association for Women in Psychology, Western Massachusetts and Vermont Region, Brattleboro, VT.

Ebata, A. (1987). *A longitudinal study of distress during early adolescence.* Unpublished doctoral dissertation, Pennsylvania State University, University Park.

Elder, G., Nguyen, T., & Caspi, A. (1985). Linking family hardship to children's lives. *Child Development, 56,* 361–375.

Gilligan, C. (1990a). Joining the resistance: Psychology, politics, girls and women. *Michigan Quarterly Review, 29,* 501–536.

Gilligan, C. (1990b). Teaching Shakespeare's sister: Notes from the underground of female adolescence. In C. Gilligan, N. Lyons, & T. Hanmer (Eds.), *Making connections: The relational worlds of adolescent girls at Emma Willard School* (pp. 6–29). Cambridge, MA: Harvard University Press.

Greenberg-Lake Analysis Group. (1991). *Shortchanging girls, shortchanging America: A nationwide poll to assess self esteem, educational experiences, interest in math and science, and career aspirations of girls and boys ages 9–15.* Washington, DC: American Association of University Women.

Hadas, P. (1987). Because it hath no bottom: Self, narrative and the power to die. In P. Young-Eisendrath & J. Hall (Eds.), *The book of the self: Person, pretext and process* (pp. 186–221). New York: New York University Press.

Hancock, E. (1989). *The girl within: A groundbreaking new approach to female identity.* New York: Fawcett Columbia.

Harding, S. (Ed.). (1987). *Feminism and methodology: Social science issues.* Bloomington: Indiana University Press.

Hoffman, L. (1975). Fear of success in males and females: 1965 and 1971. In M. Mednick, S. Tangri, & L. Hoffman (Eds.), *Women and achievement: Social and motivational analyses* (pp. 221–230). Washington, DC: Hemisphere.

Jordan, J. (1990). *Courage in connection: Conflict, compassion, creativity)* (Work in Progress, No. 45). Wellesley, MA: Stone Center Working Papers Series.

Krieger, S. (1991). *Social science and the self: Personal essays on an art form.* New Brunswick, NJ: Rutgers University Press.

Ladner, J. (1987). Introduction to tomorrow's tomorrow: The black woman. In S. Harding (Ed.), *Feminism and methodology* (pp. 74–83). Bloomington: Indiana University Press.

Langer, S. (1942). *Philosophy in a new key.* Cambridge, MA: Harvard University Press.

Linklater, K. (1976). *Freeing the natural voice.* New York: Drama Book.

Lueptow, L. (1980). Gender wording, sex, and response to items on achievement value. *Psychological Reports, 45*(1), 140–142.

Mazur, G. (1986). *The pose of happiness.* Boston: Godine.

Nielsen, J. (Ed.). (1990). *Feminist research methods: Exemplary readings in the social sciences.* Boulder, CO: Westview Press.

Petersen, A. (1988). Adolescent development. *Annual Review of Psychology, 39,* 583–607.

Petersen, A., & Ebata, A. (1987). Developmental transitions and adolescent problem behavior: Implications for prevention and intervention. In K. Hurrelmann, F. Kaufmann, & F. Losel (Eds.), *Social intervention: Potential and constraints* (pp. 167–184). Berlin: Walter de Gruyter.

Ponsot, M. (1988). *In the green dark.* New York: Alfred Knopf.

Reese, L., Wilkinson, J., & Koppelman, P. (1983). *I'm on my way running: Women speak on coming of age.* New York: Avon Books.

Rich, A. (1981). *A wild patience has taken me this far.* New York: Norton.

Rogers, A. (1990). *From the porch.* Unpublished poem.

Rogers, A. (1991a). A feminist poetics of psychotherapy. *Women and Therapy, 11*(3/4), 33–53.

Rogers, A. (1991b). Twelve. *Women's Studies Quarterly, 19*(1/2), 29–30.

Rogers, A. (1992). Marguerite Sechehaye and Renee: A feminist reading of two accounts of a treatment. *Qualitative Studies in Education, 5*(3), 245–251.

Rogers, A., Brown, L., & Tappan, M. (1994). Interpreting loss in ego development in girls: Regression or resistance? In R. Josselson & A. Lieblich (Eds.), *The narrative study of lives* (pp. 1–36). Newbury Park, CA: Sage.

Rogers, A., Fradin, D., Magee, V., & Sjostrom, L. (1992). *The Erikson Center: An ethnography of an intergenerational arts program.* Unpublished manuscript, Harvard Graduate School of Education, Cambridge, MA.

Rogers, A., & Gilligan, C. (1989). *Translating girls' voices: Two languages of development.* Unpublished manuscript, Harvard University, Project on Women's Psychology and Girls' Development, Cambridge, MA.

Rutter, M. (1986). The developmental psychopathy of depression: Issues and perspectives. In *Depression in young people: Developmental and clinical perspectives* (pp. 3–30). New York: Guilford.

Simpson, J., & Weiner, E. (1989). *The Oxford English dictionary* (2nd ed., vol. III). Oxford: Clarendon Press.

Webber, J. L., & Grumman, J. (1978). *Woman as writer.* Boston: Houghton Mifflin.

Wellesley College Center for Research on Women. (1992). *The AAUW report: How schools short-change girls.* Washington, DC: American Association of University Women and National Education Association.

Woolf, V. (1944). *A haunted house and other stories.* New York: Harcourt, Brace & World. (Original work published 1921)

Woolf, V. (1966). *Three guineas.* San Diego: Harcourt Brace Jovanovich. (Original work published 1938)

The research I draw upon in this article has been supported by Joan Lipsitz and the Lilly Endowment; by Lawrence Cremin, Marion Faldet, and Linda Fitzgerald and the Spencer Foundation; by Benjamin Barber and the Walt Whitman Center for Democracy; and by the American Association of University Women. I am grateful to Ginny Kahn, Dan Vorenberg, and Ted Mermin at the Atrium School, and to the Tobin School girls and their parents. My research and writing also draw from a feminist research collaborative, the Harvard Project on Women's Psychology and Girls' Development at the Harvard Graduate School of Education. The students who worked most closely with me — Kathleen Curtis, Kathryn Geismar, Amy Grillo, Heather Thompson, Sarah Ingersoll, and Kate O'Neill — listened and supported my interest in courage. Thank you to Kate O'Neill and to Sarah Hanson for help in editing and proofreading this article. I also want to acknowledge and thank Kathryn Geismar, Carla Rensenbrink, Sally Middlebrooks, and Gladys Capella Noya for working with me on behalf of the *Harvard Educational Review* Board. I have been inspired by the ongoing work of Lyn Mikel Brown and Carol Gilligan. A particular thanks to Carol Gilligan and Normi Noel, the women directly involved in the Theater, Writing, and Outing Club for Girls, and to the girls themselves.

Sexual Harassment in School: The Public Performance of Gendered Violence

NAN STEIN

In this chapter, Nan Stein argues that sexual harassment in schools is a form of gendered violence that often occurs in the public arena. She presents girls' and boys' experiences of sexual harassment in schools and finds parallels with cases documented in court records and depositions. While highly publicized lawsuits and civil rights cases may have increased public awareness of the issue, inconsistent findings have sent educators mixed messages about ways of dealing with peer-to-peer sexual harassment. The antecedents of harassment, Stein suggests, are found in teasing and bullying, behaviors tacitly accepted by parents and teachers. Stein makes a case for deliberate adult intervention and the inclusion of a curriculum in schools that builds awareness of these issues.

A sk Beth," the nationally syndicated teenage advice column, often includes letters from youngsters describing their experiences of sexual harassment at school. On February 3, 1994, the column in the Boston Globe contained this letter:

> Dear Beth: I am 11 years old and there's a boy in my class who just won't leave me alone. He chases after me and my best friend during recess. He hits and kicks me on the behind, stomach and legs. Once he slapped me so hard it brought tears to my eyes.
>   I try to tell my teacher, but she just laughs and tells him, "If you like her so much, ask her for her phone number." Is this sexual harassment? If it is, what should I do?
>
> HATES BEING HARASSED (Winship, 1994, p. 50)

When I read this letter aloud to middle school and high school students, from Maryland to Alaska, and ask them, "If these people were older, what might we call these behaviors?" I receive answers like "dating violence," "as-

Harvard Educational Review Vol. 65   No. 2   Summer 1995, 145–162

sault," "domestic violence," and "stalking." Yet, this teacher, this *woman* teacher, infantilized these assaultive behaviors, maybe perceiving them as flattery or as efforts from a youthful suitor. Do kids know something that adults don't want to know?

In this article on sexual harassment in schools I will document the allegations and the lawsuits; the surveys; the voices of adolescents and the panicked reactions from school personnel; and the popularization of the issue in the mainstream press. Although sexual harassment among K-12 students is now recognized as a form of sex discrimination and the rush to litigation has begun in earnest, sexual harassment is still not considered to be "violence" — not by most teachers or school administrators, not by most law enforcement or public health officials, and not by most nationally appointed or elected political leaders.

Seeing Is Not Believing

Thousands of preteen and teenage girls, responding to two open-ended questions in a self-report survey published in the September 1992 issue of *Seventeen* magazine (Stein, Marshall, & Tropp, 1993), revealed stories about the tenacity and pervasiveness of sexual harassment in schools. Letters by the thousands, with messages scribbled on envelopes — "Open," "Urgent," "Please Read," — and handwritten on lined notebook paper or perfumed stationary, all begged for attention, for answers, and, above all, for some type of acknowledgement and justice (Stein, 1992a). The following testimonials are girls' voluntary elaborations, which we received in response to the questions, "What do you think schools should do to prevent sexual harassment?" and "If you've been sexually harassed at school, how did it make you feel?":

> Of the times I was sexually harassed at school, one of them made me feel really bad. I was in class and the teacher was looking right at me when this guy grabbed my butt. The teacher saw it happen. I slapped the guy and told him not to do that. My teacher didn't say anything and looked away and went on with the lesson like nothing out of the ordinary had happened. It really confused me because I knew guys weren't supposed to do that, but the teacher didn't do anything. I felt like the teacher (who was a man) betrayed me and thought I was making a big deal out of nothing. But most of all, I felt really bad about myself because it made me feel slutty and cheap. It made me feel mad too because we shouldn't have to put up with that stuff, but no one will do anything to stop it. Now sexual harassment doesn't bother me as much because it happens so much it almost seems normal. I know that sounds awful, but the longer it goes on without anyone doing anything, the more I think of it as just one of those things that I have to put up with. (14 years old, White)[1]

> In my case there were 2 or 3 boys touching me, and trust me they were big boys. And I'd tell them to stop but they wouldn't! This went on for about 6

---

[1] Ethnic and racial descriptors that accompany the quotes are in the girls' own words.

months until finally I was in [one] of my classes in the back of the room minding my own business when all of them came back and backed me into a corner and started touching me all over. So I went running out of the room and the teacher yelled at me and I had to stay in my seat for the rest of the class. But after the class I told the principal, and him and the boys had a little talk. And after the talk was up, the boys came out laughing cause they got no punishment. (12 years old, Mexican American)

The guys would want you to let them touch you all over. But I was one of the girls that would not do that. Then one day they thought they would do it anyway. So I defended myself like you should. I kind of hurt him. The teacher caught me hitting him. And I got in trouble for hitting him. The teacher took him out of the room for his story and he lied and said he did nothing. My teacher wouldn't believe my story. I was the one getting in trouble. The school and the principal wouldn't listen to me. (13 years old, Mexican)

Sometimes, I would look at the teacher and think "help," but I was afraid to say anything because maybe it wasn't as bad as I thought it was. (15 years old, White)

These girls recognized that incidents of sexual harassment are often witnessed by adults, and expect the adults to see and feel these violations as they do. Yet, many girls cannot get confirmation of their experiences from school personnel because most of those adults do not name it as "sexual harassment" and do nothing to stop it (Stein, 1992b). These chilling stories and others like them reveal girls' repeated efforts to get adults to see and believe what is happening right before their eyes, and to do something about it. These young women begin to sound ominously like battered women who are not believed or helped by the authorities and who feel alone and abandoned. Listen again to the voices of students speaking about the public nature of sexual harassment:

At first I didn't really think of it because it was considered a "guy thing," but as the year went on, I started to regret going to school, especially my locker, because I knew if I went I was going to be cornered and be touched, or had some comment blurted out at me. I just felt really out of place and defenseless and there was nothing I could do. (14 years old, Black)

It was like fighting an invisible, invincible enemy alone. I didn't have a clue as to what to do to stop it, so I experimented with different approaches. Ignoring it only made it worse. It made it easier for them to do it, so they did it more. Laughing at the perpetrators during the assaults didn't dent the problem at all, and soon my friends became tired of doing this. They thought it was a game. Finally I wrote them threatening letters. This got me in trouble, but perhaps it did work. I told the school administrators what had been happening to me. They didn't seem to think it a big deal, but they did talk to the three biggest perpetrators. The boys ignored the administrators and it continued. And they were even worse. (14–15 years old, White)

I took a photography class, and the majority of the class was boys. A lot of the boys were my friends but three of them were after something different than friendship. On several occasions I was in the dark room developing pictures and they would come in and corner me. They would touch me, put their hands on my thighs and slide their hands up my shirt. They also often tried to put my hand down their pants. I often told my friends but no one believed me. One day I was in the room alone and one of the boys came in. When I went to leave he grabbed me and threw me down and grabbed my breast. I felt I was helpless but I punched him and he ran out. The teacher (who was a man) came in and yelled at me. When I tried to explain why I had hit him the teacher told me I deserved it because I wore short skirts. I was sent to the principal and I had to serve detention. I didn't want to tell the principal because I feared he would do the same and tell me it was my fault. I felt so alone. Everyday I had to go to class and face it. No girl should have to be uncomfortable because of what she wears or how she acts. (15 years old, White)

I have told teachers about this a number of times; each time nothing was done about it. Teachers would act as if I had done something to cause it. Once I told a guidance counselor, but was made to feel like a whore when she asked me questions like "do you like it?" and "they must be doing it for a reason. What did you do to make them do it?" (13 years old, White)

These stories illustrate injustices of considerable magnitude and suggest that schools may be training grounds for the insidious cycle of domestic violence. Girls are taught that they are on their own, that the adults and others around them will not believe or help them; in essence, they are trained to accept the battering and assault. Girls (and sometimes boys) who are the targets of sexual harassment find that when they report sexual harassment or assault, the events are trivialized while they, the targets, are simultaneously demeaned and/or interrogated. Boys, on the other hand, receive permission, even training to become batterers, because many of their assaults on girls are not interrupted or condemned by the adults in the school environment. Indeed, if school authorities sanction the students who sexually harass by not intervening, the schools may be encouraging a continued pattern of violence in relationships. This encouragement goes beyond those directly involved; it also conveys a message to those who observe these incidents that to engage in such behavior is acceptable. Other bystanders may receive the message that they may be the next to be harassed, and no one will do anything to prevent it (Stein, 1992b).

Sexual harassment, when it occurs in schools, is unwanted and unwelcomed behavior of a sexual nature that interferes with the right to receive an equal educational opportunity. It is a form of sex discrimination that is prohibited by Title IX, a federal civil rights in education law that addresses issues of sex discrimination and, by judicial precedent, sexual harassment.

Both the courts and the Office for Civil Rights (OCR) of the U.S. Department of Education recognize two forms of unlawful sexual harassment: 1) "quid pro quo" cases, where a person's entitlement to enjoyment of a particular benefit (such as an educational opportunity) is conditioned on sexual favors; and 2) "hostile environment" cases, where unwelcome conduct has the purpose or effect of unreasonably interfering with a person's right or benefit (such as education) by creating an intimidating, hostile, offensive environment. In school settings, particularly between students, allegations typically concern the hostile environment claim.

According to OCR memorandums:

> To find that a hostile environment exists, OCR must find that the alleged victim was subjected to verbal or physical conduct imposed because of the victim's gender, that the conduct was unwelcome, and that the conduct was sufficiently severe, persistent or pervasive as to alter the conditions of the victim's education and create an abusive environment. In cases of student-to-student harassment, an educational institution will be liable for hostile environment sexual harassment where an official of the institution knew, or reasonably should have known, of the harassment's occurrence and the institution failed to take appropriate steps to halt the conduct. (Nashoba, 1993)

In schools, harassment often happens while many people watch. This public enactment of sexual harassment may have more damaging ramifications than harassment that happens in private because of the potential for public humiliation, the damage to one's reputation, the rumors targets must fear and combat, and the strategies that the targets implement in an effort to reduce or avoid the encounters. When sexual harassment occurs in public and is not condemned, it becomes, with time, part of the social norm.

Teasing and Bullying, or Back to the Future

The antecedents of peer sexual harassment in schools may be found in "bullying" — behaviors children learn, practice, and experience beginning at a very young age. Children know what a bully is, and many boys as well as girls have been victims of bullying. Much of the bullying that takes place at this age is between members of the same sex (Kutner, 1993, 1994; Olweus, 1993; Slaby & Stringham, 1994; Whitney & Smith, 1993). Teachers and parents know about bullying, and many accept it as an unfortunate stage that some children go through on their way to adolescence and adulthood.

Despite its prevalence in U.S. culture, bullying remains an under-studied phenomenon in this country.[2] Public interest in bullying has been raised, however, by recent press accounts documenting horrific incidents in Japan that have ended in either suicide or murder (Nickerson, 1993; Pollack, 1994; Sanger, 1993). I was drawn to the problem of bullying through my work on sexual harassment in junior high and high schools, beginning in 1979. It became clear to me that, left unchecked and unchallenged, bullying might in fact serve as fertile practice ground for sexual harassment (Keise, 1992;

---

[2] Studies that have been done tend to focus on the sexually deviant child (Cunningham & MacFarlane, 1991) or on school violence (National Center for Education Statistics, 1988, and Search Institute, 1990, cited in Stepp, 1992). Most of the research on bullying has been conducted in Norway and Sweden (Olweus, 1993) and the United Kingdom (Keise, 1992; Whitney & Smith, 1993).

Stein, 1993). I began a search for appropriate strategies, interventions, and a conceptual framework that might help elementary educators bring this subject into their classrooms.

In late 1992, I received support from the Patrina Foundation, a private foundation located in New York, to conduct a small pilot project that involved seven classrooms in three elementary schools. Working with fourth- and fifth-grade teachers and their students in two schools for one year and in a third school for a period of more than two years, I developed and implemented eight to ten sequential classroom lessons, writing activities, reading assignments, and role plays that engaged children to think about the distinctions between "teasing" and "bullying." These activities helped the children focus on the boundaries between appropriate and inappropriate, hurtful behavior. In this unit, eventually named "Bullyproof," children gained a conceptual framework and a common vocabulary that allowed them to find their own links between teasing and bullying, and eventually sexual harassment.[3] The following reflections, written anonymously at the end of the unit by fifth-grade students between the ages of ten and eleven years, in a multiracial classroom, displayed new conceptual connections and insights about themselves and their classmates:

> Well, since we started this, people in my class and I learned a lot. Now they stopped doing mean things to each other. Like now that people know how I felt when they called me "shrimp" and "shorty" and other mean things they stopped doing that. Now we don't hurt other people's feelings and respect one another even if the person is short, tall or opposite sex. (male)

> I see a big difference in myself since we started discussing bullying, teasing and sexual harassment. Example: when it was my turn to be captain of the kickball game I picked x as a player. As soon as I picked x, he started to pick all the players and suddenly x was the captain. Not only that but x also picked who was pitcher and the batting order (all stuff a captain does). So, I stood up to x reminded him that I was captain (I would have never done that before). It made me feel good inside. (female)

> I do see a difference in the way that all of the boys in the class are treating the girls now. 1) they have mostly stopped teasing us and chasing us down the hallways while we are coming back from recess. 2) The boys have also mostly stopped insulting all of the girls and trying to dis us. I think that the girls have also mostly stopped teasing and bullying all of the shrimpy or short boys. (female)

> I really think sexual harassment can hurt because sometimes people may tease you about your body parts and it really hurts your feelings because you can't change them in any way. It can also interfere with your school work because all your thoughts are on your anger and then you can't concentrate. If I am harassed in the future, I will stand up for my rights and if a teacher doesn't care, I will pressure him or her to punish my harasser. (male)

---

[3] "Bullyproof" is copyrighted to Nan Stein (1996).

Bullying and its connections to sexual harassment in schools are of critical importance. This link is one that educators need to make explicit and public by deliberately discussing these subjects in age-appropriate ways with children (Stein, 1996). If educators and advocates pose and present the problem as "bullying" to young children, rather than labeling it immediately as "sexual harassment," we can engage children and universalize the phenomenon as one that boys as well as girls will understand and accept as problematic. Hopefully, such an approach will go a long way towards developing compassion and empathy in the students. Moreover, we can simultaneously avoid demonizing all little boys as potential harassers by initially presenting these hurtful and offensive behaviors as bullying.

The Surveys and the Lawsuits: From Many to One and Back Again

The media's attention to the problem of sexual harassment in schools has in large part been generated by lawsuits and surveys on sexual harassment in schools. Results from three recent national surveys on this topic illustrate its pernicious, persistent, and public nature, and demonstrate that it is a widespread, endemic phenomenon. The first survey, developed by the Wellesley College Center for Research on Women and cosponsored by the National Organization for Women's (NOW) Legal Defense and Education Fund, was published in the September 1992 issue of *Seventeen* magazine (the most widely read magazine for teenage girls in the country, with 1.9 million subscribers, and a "pass-along" circulation of 8 to 10 million girls). The results were compiled from a nonscientific, random sample of 2,000 girls aged nine to nineteen, selected from a total of 4,300 surveys received by the deadline of September 30, 1992. They were released in March 1993 (Stein, Marshall, & Tropp, 1993).

In two-thirds of the reports of incidents of sexual harassment in the *Seventeen* study, the girls reported that other people were present. The most frequently cited location of witnessed incidents was the classroom: 94 percent of the girls who indicated that others were present when harassment occurred reported that it occurred in the classroom; 76 percent of those who reported that other people were present during the harassment cited the hallway, and 69 percent cited the parking lot or the playing fields (note that respondents often cited more than one location).

The second survey, conducted by the Harris Poll, was commissioned by the American Association of University Women (AAUW) Foundation and released in June 1993 (AAUW, 1993). The study used a random sample of 1,600 boys and girls eight to eleven in seventy-nine public schools. The boys and girls sampled in the Harris poll painted a similar portrait of sexual harassment, one that included public incidents occurring throughout the school. Of the 81 percent of the students who reported some experience of sexual harassment in school, 66 percent said they had been harassed at least once in the hall; 55 percent reported the classroom as the site of their harassment; 43 percent happened outside the school, on school grounds (other than the parking lot); 39 percent reported harassment in the gym, playing field, or pool area; 34 percent were in the cafeteria; and 23 percent named the parking lot as the site of the harassment. Interestingly, students indicated that locker rooms (19%) and rest rooms (10%), presumably gender-segregated sites, were also locations for sexual harassment.

At least four important findings emerged from these surveys: 1) sexual harassment is pervasive in secondary schools (experienced by 85% of the girls in the Harris Poll/AAUW study and 89% of the girls in the *Seventeen* survey); 2) students consider sexual harassment a serious problem (75% from the Harris Poll/AAUW survey, 70% in the *Seventeen* survey); 3) the behavior occurs in public places (two-thirds of the situations reported in both studies); and 4) students have difficulty getting help, even though a majority in both surveys reported trying to talk to someone about the harassing behavior (Lee, Croninger, Linn, & Chen, 1996).

"In Our Own Backyard: Sexual Harassment in Connecticut's Public High Schools," a study of sexual harassment in the Connecticut public schools during the 1993–1994 school year, was released on January 26, 1995 (Permanent Commission, 1995).[4] In this survey, 78 percent of a random sample of high school students (308 girls and 235 boys) in grades ten through twelve reported experiencing at least one incident of sexual harassment in high school. The researchers found that girls were nearly twice as likely to report experiencing the problem as boys: 92 percent of the female students and 57 percent of the male students reported that they had been the targets of unwelcomed sexual conduct since they started high school.

The statistics that emerged from these three surveys might have dropped quickly into oblivion were it not for the complaints and lawsuits that girls and young women have been filing, and winning, in state and federal courts in the past few years. It takes only one influential case to change the landscape and the discourse about sexual harassment. Such a change occurred in February 1992 with the landmark 9-0 U.S. Supreme Court decision in *Franklin v. Gwinnett County (GA) Public Schools.* In this case, the Court decided that schools could be held liable for compensatory damages if they failed to provide an educational environment that was free from sex discrimination. This decision has caused school personnel to pay increased attention to the problem of sexual harassment and sex discrimination in schools.

---

[4] This report was published by the Permanent Commission on the Status of Women based upon research conducted by the University of Connecticut School of Social Work (research on incidents of sexual harassment) and the Connecticut Sexual Assault Crisis Services (research with Title IX coordinators).

Prototypical Lawsuits and Complaints: Sexual Harassment as Public Behavior

In one case that is often cited in popular magazines and teen literature and on television talk and news shows, Katy Lyle, a fifteen-year-old high school student in Duluth, Minnesota, was targeted through nasty graffiti that covered the walls of one stall in the boys' bathroom at her high school (*Lyle v. Independent School District #709,* 1991). Statements like "Katy does it with farm animals," "Katy is a slut," "Katy gives good head," and "Katy sucked my dick after she sucked my dog's dick" remained up on the walls for a period of sixteen months, despite repeated requests from Katy and her parents to the principal to have it removed. His responses included, "No one reads it anyhow," and "It'll make you a stronger person." He also claimed that his hands were tied by the custodians' union contract, which only makes provision for their painting the walls once every two years; since they had just completed a painting assignment, they could not paint over that graffiti. Boys would yell out across the hallways, "Hey, Katy, I took a leak in your stall today," and girls would wonder aloud what Katy had done to "deserve" this.[5] Katy was tormented daily on the school bus and as she entered the school. Finally, her older brother, home from college during a vacation, removed the graffiti in a matter of minutes. Although the physical evidence was removed, the taunting continued.

In a 1991 settlement with the Minnesota Department of Human Rights, Katy and her family were awarded $15,000, and the school district agreed to implement training programs for staff and students to develop and disseminate a sexual harassment policy. They also agreed to appoint an administrator to coordinate these efforts.

In another widely publicized case from Minnesota (*Mutziger v. Independent School District #272,* 1992), both the Minnesota Department of Human Rights and the Office for Civil Rights (OCR) of the U.S. Department of Education (Eden Prairie, 1993) found that six-year-old Cheltzie Hentz (and eventually several other girls) had been sexually harassed on the bus, on the school grounds, and in the classroom by boys who ranged in age from six to thirteen. The perpetrators were accused of making lewd remarks and sexual taunts, including references about girls' body parts and explicit suggestions about Cheltzie having oral sex with her father. This case became notable for the age of the target and the age of the perpetrators; Cheltzie was and remains the youngest child to file and win a sexual harassment complaint. In the stunning decision rendered by OCR, the "reasonable woman standard" was invoked to apply to six-year-olds:[6]

---

[5] Interviews with Carol and Katy Lyle conducted by Katie Couric, *The Today Show* (NBC, October 7, 1992); and Adrian LeBlanc (1992).

[6] "For both *quid pro quo* and *hostile environment* harassment, whether or not sexual harassment exists is to be judged from the perspective of the 'reasonable person.' That is, would a reasonable person

From the standpoint of a reasonable female student participating in district programs and activities, . . . the sexually offensive conduct was sufficiently frequent, severe, and/or protracted to impair significantly the educational services and benefits offered. . . . In this case, there is no question that even the youngest girls understood that the language and conduct being used were expressions of hostility toward them on the basis of their sex and, as a clear result, were offended and upset. (Eden Prairie, 1993, p. 12)

In Cheltzie's case, all of the events occurred around adults — either the bus driver or bus monitors, or the classroom teacher. As part of the investigation, other girls were interviewed about the same boys who were accused of harassing Cheltzie. According to the OCR finding:

During a social studies class, a seventh grade male student repeatedly made remarks of a sexual nature . . . touched the girls, and on one occasion, physically restrained one of them so that she could not escape his lewd remarks. According to the female students, the teacher witnessed the harassment, but was unresponsive to their requests for assistance. The teacher's response was to offer to change the boy's seat. According to the students, the boy's seat already had been changed numerous times as girls reported that he was bothering them. (p. 9)

Again, adults watched, students appealed for help, and adults offered only innocuous and insipid solutions.

The behavior of school personnel is mentioned in several lawsuits that have been filed in federal district courts. For example, in a 1992 lawsuit in Connecticut, Johana Mennone, a student at Amity Regional High School in Woodbridge, Connecticut, alleged that "in the presence of her teacher and a roomful of classmates, a male student grabbed her hair, legs, breasts, and buttocks nearly every day. He repeatedly made remarks about her breasts and told her that he was going to rape her" (Lawton, 1993). Again, a teacher watched while outright assaults took place in the classroom. Motions continue to be filed in this case. A case in Milford, Connecticut, with similar facts, but with middle school students as the plaintiff and defendants, is underway in another complaint filed in both federal district court and state court.[7] In federal court, the complaint draws on provisions included in Title IX; in state court, the suit is framed around tort actions of negligence on the part of the teacher, principal, and superintendent.

---

view the behavior complained of as sexual harassment? There is some uncertainty among federal courts and agencies as to whether the 'reasonable person' standard takes into account the circumstances of the victim, and if so, to what extent. Federal agencies, such as the EEOC and OCR, as well as several lower courts that have addressed the issue, have adopted a 'reasonable woman' or 'reasonable person in the victim's situation' standard that would appear to favor the complainant more than the 'reasonable person' perspective. . . . Moreover, in several Title IX Letters of Finding, OCR states that the existence of a sexually hostile environment is determined from the viewpoint of a reasonable person in the victim's situation" (Sneed & Woodruff, 1994, p. 10).

[7] The case is *Courtney Stern v. City of Milford (CT) Board of Education;* in Superior Court, Judicial District of Ansonia/Milford, filed January 29, 1993.

At least seven other federal Title IX actions involving student-to-student sexual harassment are pending in federal district courts in California, Georgia, Kansas, New York, and Texas (Lewin, 1994). Three more complaints have been filed in federal district courts in Iowa (Fuson, 1994).

Three contradictory rulings have emerged from three different federal court jurisdictions. In a case in Georgia, *Aurelia Davis v. Monroe County Board of Education,* U.S. District Judge Wilbur D. Owens Jr. of Macon ruled on August 29, 1994, that the school district was not liable for a fifth-grade student's alleged harassment of another student (*Aurelia Davis,* 1994). He dismissed the case on the grounds that the school did not have a special custodial relationship with its students and had no special duty to protect them from other students (Walsh, 1994). The complainant had alleged that school officials were slow to react to the harassing conduct by a boy who repeatedly tried to touch a girl's breasts, rubbed his body against hers, and used vulgar language. The complainant and her family have decided to appeal the decision.

However, an opposite decision was rendered in federal court in New York State. On November 15, 1994, Thomas J. McAvoy, Chief Federal Court Judge for the Northern District of New York in Albany, issued a ruling that held teachers and administrators liable and responsible for preventing student-to-student sexual harassment in schools. In this case, *Bruneau v. South Kortright (NY) Central School District,* the court ruled that a sixth- grade girl who was taunted with sexual comments ("prostitute," "dog-faced bitch," and "lesbo") and physically abused by boys in her class could sue her teacher and an assistant superintendent under Section 1983 of the Civil Rights Act of 1871 (*Bruneau,* 1994).[8] She was also able to bring a suit against the school district under Title IX and recover compensatory damages, punitive damages, and attorney fees. The school district was found liable in the New York case because teachers and administrators were alerted to the assaults, but took no action. In fact, when the girl's parents complained of the abusive behavior to their daughter's teacher, they were told "that their daughter was a beautiful child and they had nothing to worry about because boys would be all over her in a few years" (Jones, 1994). The parents requested assistance from the assistant superintendent of the school district following this meeting with the teacher, but again, no attempts to remedy the situation were made. When the parents asked that their daughter be allowed to transfer to

[8] Civil Rights Act of 1871, 42 U.S.C. section 1983:

Every person who, under color of any statute, ordinance, regulation, custom, usage, of any state or territory, subjects or causes to be subjected, any citizen of the United States or any person within the jurisdiction thereof to the deprivation of any rights, privileges, or immunities secured by the Constitution and laws, shall be liable to the party injured in an action at law, suit in equity, or other proper proceeding for redress.

Section 1983, which is a federal statute, provides an avenue of redress for individuals who have been deprived of their federal constitutional or statutory rights at the behest of state authority. Section 1983 provides redress for violation of explicit constitutional rights (e.g., the right to due process) and also of federal statutory rights passed pursuant to constitutional authority.

another class, their request was denied. At that point, the girl transferred to another school and the parents took legal action. The judge's ruling in this case provides that a plaintiff can proceed against a school district if the district's inaction (or insufficient action) in response to complaints of student-to-student sexual harassment is the result of an actual intent to discriminate against the student on the basis of sex (*Bruneau*, 1994).

Yet, in October 1994 in Utah, the U.S. Federal District Court refused to allow a locker room incident, directed at one football player by his fellow teammates, as an actionable case of hostile environment sexual harassment. In Judge Dee V. Benson's decision, the lawsuit against the Sky View High School and the Cache County (UT) School District was dismissed on the grounds that the boy failed to prove that he had been a victim of any concerted discriminatory effort (*Seamons v. Snow*, 1994).

By any stretch of the imagination, the facts of this case give one pause. After a football game, the young man, Brian Seamons, was restrained by four of his teammates and painfully taped naked to a towel rack after he left the shower area. He was humiliated further when a girl was involuntarily dragged in to view him (Brown, 1995; "Court Dismisses," 1994). Brian claimed that this team ritual was well-known to the coach and school officials.

The school authorities continued to either excuse the behavior as gender appropriate (i.e., "boys will be boys") or merely a case of team hazing; Brian was blamed for bringing the incident to the public's attention. The football coach reacted to Brian's complaints by first suspending and then dismissing him from the team. The next day, the superintendent canceled the remaining football games, prompting the coach, Douglas Snow, to demand that Brian apologize to the team for this course of action. Neither Snow nor any of the football players were disciplined for their behaviors in this incident. In fact, Snow stated publicly that "it was inappropriate to impose discipline on the other players for hazing." The judge in this case found no fault on the part of the coach or school administrators:

> It may have been wrong, or right, or ethical, or unethical, or noble, or ignoble, but no plausible treatment theory could construe it as an act intended to treat Brian negatively because he is a boy. . . . Because plaintiffs have not alleged that defendants' conduct was sexual in any way . . . [the] allegations are not sufficient to base a claim of sexual harassment. (*Seamons v. Snow*, 1994, p. 1118)

It is clear that if this incident had been directed at a female, not only would it have been viewed as sexual harassment, but there would also have been criminal assault charges pending against the perpetrators. The question remains: Why should the sex of the target make any difference when the behavior is publicly performed, seemingly school-approved, gendered violence?

Despite troubling and contradictory rulings from federal courts, students continue to file Title IX complaints with OCR. Although OCR cannot award compensatory damages, they can compel the school district to pay for costs incurred from counseling, tutoring, transportation, and tuition for the complainant. They can also require the district to provide training for staff and students on the subjects of sex discrimination and sexual harassment. Among the hundreds of districts that OCR has investigated, letters of findings and/or settlement agreements have been issued to school districts in Millis, Massachusetts; Petaluma, California; Meridian, Texas; Reno, Nevada; Sweet Home, Oregon; Mason City, Iowa; Albion, Michigan; and, Victorville, California.[9]

Notable among OCR's letters of findings are two in which the sexual harassment incidents involved students of the same sex. Both complaints involved high school girls who sexually harassed other girls, one case from San Jose, California, and the other from Bolton, Massachusetts. The facts in both cases are strikingly similar: a single girl at each site was subjected to verbal and written sexual harassment over a period of many months. The harassment consisted of sexually explicit taunts, graffiti, and rumors of the girl's alleged sexual behavior with male students. Both young women's grades fell, while one cut classes and altered her walking route to avoid further harassment (San Jose), and the other required private counseling (Bolton). In both cases, school officials had been informed of the harassment but failed to treat it as such. According to the letter of finding from OCR in the Massachusetts case,

> the student evidenced an extensive record of her numerous and repeated efforts to end the conduct. The student immediately reported the graffiti to her counselor upon discovering it in the bathroom. On her own initiative, the student weekly, and sometimes daily, reported new graffiti to the principal or her counselor, and she kept detailed notes of verbal harassment incidents. The student herself removed some of the graffiti from the bathrooms and walls. (Nashoba, 1993, p. 9)

The San Jose school staff had a different response and rationale; they assumed that sexual harassment could only occur "when a student approaches another student of the opposite sex and makes lewd gestures or asks for sexual favors" (East Side Union High School District, 1993, p. 5). Moreover, they did not consider the conduct between members of the same sex to be possible sexual harassment, especially since the target and her harassers had once been friends. For all of these reasons, the school district did not investigate the complaint.

In both of these complaints, OCR concluded that there had been pervasive, persistent, and severe sexual harassment in violation of Title IX, and that the school districts had inadequate grievance procedures for prompt and equitable resolution of complaints of sexual harassment.

---

[9] Office for Civil Rights' Letters of Findings and/or Settlement Agreements obtained through Freedom of Information Act (FOIA): Millis, MA (#01-93-1123, issued May 19, 1994); Petaluma, CA (#09-89-1050, May 5, 1989); Meridian, TX (#06-92-1145, July 29, 1992); Washoe County School District, Reno, NV (09-91-1220, March 27, 1993); Sweet Home, OR (#10-92-1088, November 15, 1991); Mason City, IA (#07-93-1095, March 28, 1994); Albion, MI (#15-94-1029, April 7, 1994); and Victor Valley Union High School District, Victorville, CA (09-90-1143, August 8, 1990).

Despite clear rulings in these two same-sex cases, another regional office of OCR refused to investigate a Minnesota third-grade student's claim that he was sexually harassed by other boys at school for several months. Jonathan Harms of the Sauk Rapids-Rice School District, who taped his verbal harassment by concealing a small tape recorder, was sexually taunted over a period of months by about a dozen of his male classmates in the third grade. The harassment escalated to an assault when his pants and underwear were pulled down to below his knees. Yet, OCR responded in June 1993 to the parents' complaint, stating that it found "no indication that the student was singled out for harassment because of his sex" (Sauk Rapids-Rice, 1993).[10]

Protests about OCR's decision came from expected and unexpected quarters. Jonathan's parents responded by saying that "their son's case sends a 'disturbing' message: while girls are protected from the sexual taunts of their male peers, boys are not" (Brown, 1994a). Minnesota Attorney General Hubert H. Humphrey III sent a letter on January 6, 1994, to U.S. Secretary of Education Richard Riley, seeking an explanation for OCR's decision not to investigate: "I would appreciate clarification of whether boys are covered under Title IX. I ask that the OCR reconsider its decision not to investigate the . . . case" (Brown, 1994a). In an October 17, 1994, letter to Senator Durenberger of Minnesota, Norma Cantu, the Assistant Secretary for Civil Rights of the U.S. Department of Education's Office for Civil Rights, indicated that the investigation might be reopened (Pitsch, 1994). This decision was undoubtedly influenced by the Minnesota Department of Human Rights September 1994 decision that found "probable cause" in the Harms case; the Department has decided to investigate Jonathan's claim as sexual harassment under Minnesota state law.

The outcomes in two California cases (Modesto City Schools, 1993, and Newark Unified School District, 1993) investigated by the Office for Civil Rights provide sharp contrast to the outcome in the Jonathan Harms complaint in Minnesota. In both of the California cases, OCR found against the schools and in favor of the complainants.

In the California cases, elementary school children were also involved, this time with boys as the alleged harassers and girls as the targets. The Modesto case began in January 1993, when several girls were restrained in chokeholds, pinched, tripped, and touched repeatedly on their chests, genitalia, and buttocks by some male classmates. The school officials treated the incidents as routine misbehavior and followed their standard disciplinary procedures without determining if a sexually hostile environment existed. Nor were the parents informed of their rights under federal law Title IX. In May 1993, a group of boys, some of whom had been involved in the earlier incidents, threw two girls to the ground, forcibly kissed and fondled them, made lewd

---

[10] Letter from Kenneth A. Mines, Regional Director of the Office for Civil Rights, U.S. Department of Education, Chicago office, to Mr. and Mrs. Harms (June 28, 1993), p. 1, re: case #05-93-1142, Sauk Rapids-Rice (MN) School District #47.

statements, and attempted to remove their clothing (Brown, 1994b). OCR's finding, issued on December 6, 1993, found that the school district had violated Title IX when it treated sexual harassment by elementary school students as a matter of misconduct and mischief rather than as a violation of federal anti-discrimination law.

The Newark case involved behavior classically viewed and typically dismissed as mutual, voluntary, and playful playground behavior. "Friday flip-up" days were an institution at this school: On Fridays, the boys in the first through third grades flipped up the dresses of their female classmates. OCR found that this practice subjected the girls to teasing and touching based on their gender, created different treatment for them, and limited their enjoyment of the educational program.

The California and Minnesota cases, which involve elementary school children, raise perplexing and disturbing questions: Are the ages of the targets and perpetrators the most salient factors that OCR considers when it decides to investigate a case? Or is it the sex of the target(s) and perpetrator(s)? Are incidents that involve children of the same sex ruled out if the students are in elementary school? What difference could the sex of the harassers or the target make when a student's clothes are pulled off? Are these acts not assaults, let alone sexual harassment? Or is it that gendered violence doesn't register with some federal and school officials as real violence?

Hopes, Actions, and Recommendations

As powerful and inspirational as legal decisions can be, we can't expect them to either enlighten educators or guarantee educational environments free from sex discrimination and sexual harassment. We need to promote non-litigious remedies and to transport the lessons of the lawsuits into the classroom. Lawsuits can be preempted through preventive and sensible measures employed in the schools.

Hope and impetus for change come from school-wide efforts to normalize the conversation about sexual harassment and other forms of gendered violence. This may best be achieved by inserting age-appropriate and sequential materials into class discussions and school curricula. The traditional practice of addressing sexual harassment only through disciplinary action has had little effect on the frequency of gendered violence. Recent attempts to enlist draconian prohibitions against hand-holding and other forms of affectionate behavior (Maroney, 1995) are also sure to fail.

Prior to initiating such classroom conversations, educators need to recognize sexual harassment in schools as a form of gendered violence that is often performed in public, sometimes in front of adults whose legal responsibility is to provide equal protection and equal educational opportunity. Sexual harassment can provide the impetus for opening the conversation about gendered violence.

Ultimately, a strategy to eliminate and prevent sexual harassment in schools needs to aim at a transformation of the broader school culture. Dealing effectively with sexual harassment is much easier if a school has committed itself to infuse a spirit of equity and a critique of injustice into its curriculum and pedagogy. On the other hand, harassment flourishes where children learn the art of doing nothing in the face of unjust treatment by others. When teachers subject children to an authoritarian pedagogy, they don't learn to think of themselves as moral subjects, capable of speaking out when they witness bullying or other forms of harassment. If youngsters have not been encouraged to critique the sexism of the curriculum, hidden and overt, then they are less likely to recognize it when they confront it in their midst. Too often, the entire school structure offers children no meaningful involvement in decision making about school policy, school climate, or other curriculum matters. Children rehearse being social spectators in their school lives (Stein, 1993).

We can make a difference in the classroom and beyond when we take up the subjects of teasing, bullying, and sexual harassment. When we frame the issue of sexual harassment as one of injustice and civil rights, and see the problem from the vantage points of the targets, the harassers, and the observers, we can teach empathy as we also teach children to emphasize and employ intervention strategies. In this way we teach children to see themselves as "justice makers" as opposed to social spectators (hooks, 1989).

I end this article in the same way I began, with the words of children. This time, however, we hear from boys who confirm the experiences of the girls cited at the beginning of this article — that sexual harassment is present and very public in schools.[11] Even for the boys who are observers, sexual harassment is sometimes scary, troubling, and certainly disruptive to the educational environment.

> Today, as usual, I observed sexist behavior in my art class. Boys taunting girls and girls taunting boys has become a real problem. I wish they would all stop yelling at each other so that for once I could have art class in peace. This is my daily list of words I heard today in art that could be taken as sexual harassment: bitch, hooker, pimp, whore.

> Today for the first time I was witness to sexual harassment in my gym class. A couple of girls came into the exercise room today and suddenly, almost like a reflex, some of the boys began to whistle at them and taunt them. I was surprised since I had never seen this kind of behavior from my gym class before. Some of the boys that I considered my friends even began to do it. It felt awful to watch, but if I said anything it would not stop them and would only hurt me.

---

[11] Selections are from the ethnographies that these White, middle-class, eighth grade students kept as part of a pilot curriculum development project. This pilot project, which involved approximately fifty Massachusetts classroom teachers in grades six through twelve in the fall of 1993, resulted in the publication, *Flirting or Hurting? A Teacher's Guide on Student-to-Student Sexual Harassment in Schools* (for grades six through twelve) by Nan Stein and Lisa Sjostrom (1994).

Today in class people reported their findings as ethnographers; that is, they told the class about the examples of sexual harassment they had witnessed. There were some pretty bad examples. It's amazing that this stuff goes on at our school. I think that part of the problem is that some kids don't know what sexual harassment is, so they don't know when they are doing it. One of the things that scared me was that no one said they had any trouble finding examples. Everybody had found at least one or two examples, and most people found many more. I found out that it happens everywhere: in the halls, the cafeteria, or even at basketball try-outs. It happens everywhere that teachers are not in direct supervision of students.

I think it's good that the eighth-graders are doing the curriculum at the same time, because then we can discuss it during lunch and stuff. I really do think that people are learning a lot from it. I mean, the person at our table at lunch who used to really be a sexual harasser has stopped and actually turned nice when all the girls at our table told him to stop or we would get [teacher] into it. I don't think he realized that what he was doing was really making us uncomfortable.

The sexual harassment [curriculum] is really doing the school some good. One of the harassers who has been always harassing any girl at all has stopped. X has stopped goosing and touching girls. I never thought I'd see the day — he no longer pinches girls and rubs up against them in the hall. Now I feel a lot more comfortable in art class. I have art with him, and now I don't have to always, literally, watch my back. And O has seen a lot of improvement. People are more conscious about what they say, and how they use words like gay, faggot, and lesbian. They realize that some people could really be offended by it.

These journal entries are hopeful in the way that they point out the impact that age-appropriate, deliberate, teacher-led conversations and curriculum can have on the lives of students. By creating a common classroom vocabulary and offering non-punitive and non-litigious ways to probe controversial and troubling subjects, educators and their students can confront and reduce sexual harassment and gendered violence in the schools. The first step is to recognize that sexual harassment is a common feature in children's school lives, and that the students — both boys and girls — recognize that most adults are sitting back, watching it happen. The next step is for the adults to name it as the kids see it, and to take it on — publicly, in the classroom, and throughout the whole school community.

References

American Association of University Women (AAUW). (1993). *Hostile hallways: The AAUW survey on sexual harassment in America's schools.* Washington, DC: Author.

Aurelia Davis v. Monroe County (GA) Board of Education, 862 F.Supp. 863 (M.D. GA, 1994)

Brown, A. (1994a, February). OCR declines to investigate male student's harassment claim. *Educator's Guide to Controlling Sexual Harassment, 5,* 1–2.

Brown, A. (1994b, May). Same-sex harassment by students proves a tough issue for U.S. enforcement agency. *Educator's Guide to Controlling Sexual Harassment, 8,* 1–3.

Brown, A. (1995, January). Hazing or sexual harassment? Football player appeals ruling. *Educator's Guide to Controlling Sexual Harassment, 2*, 5.

Bruneau v. South Kortright (NY) Central School District, 94-CV-864 (N.Dist. NY, November 15, 1994).

Court dismisses male student's Title IX harassment claim. (1994, November 18). *School Law News, 22*(23), 7.

Cunningham, C., & MacFarlane, K. (1991). *When children molest children: Group treatment strategies for young sexual abusers.* Orwell, VT: Safer Society Press.

East Side Union High School District, CA, No. 09-93-1293-I. Office for Civil Rights, U.S. Department of Education, San Francisco, CA (November 19, 1993).

Eden Prairie School District #272, MN, No. 05-92-1174. Office for Civil Rights, U.S. Department of Education, Chicago, IL (April 27, 1993).

Franklin v. Gwinnett County Public Schools, 112 S. Ct. 1028 (1992).

Fuson, K. (1994, August 5). Teens suing 3 schools over harassment. *Des Moines Register,* pp. 1, 3A.

Harms v. Independent School District #47 (Sauk Rapids-Rice), file #ED1990019, Minnesota Department of Human Rights, Minneapolis, MN (May 14, 1993).

hooks, b. (1989). *Talking back: Thinking feminist, thinking Black.* Boston: South End Press.

Jones, M. M. (1994, December 19). Student sues school for sexual harassment by other students. *Lawyer's Weekly USA, 94*(26), 1, 12–13.

Keise, C. (1992). *Sugar and spice? Bullying in single-sex schools.* Staffordshire, Eng.: Trentham Books.

Kutner, L. (1994, spring/summer). Everybody's teasing me. *Parent's Digest,* pp. 34–37.

Kutner, L. (1993, October 28). Bullying: A test of the limits of one's power and control. *New York Times,* p. C12.

Lawton, M. (1993, February 10). Sexual harassment of students target of district policies. *Education Week,* pp. 1, 15–16.

LeBlanc, A. (1992, September). Harassment in the halls. *Seventeen,* pp. 162–165, 170.

Lee, V. E., Croninger, R. G., Linn, E., & Chen, X. (1996). The culture of sexual harassment in secondary schools. *American Educational Research Journal, 33,* 383–418.

Lewin, T. (1994, July 15). Students seeking damages for sex bias. *New York Times,* p. B12.

Lyle v. Independent School District #709, file #ED341-GSS5-6N Minnesota Department of Human Rights, Minneapolis, MN (September 18, 1991).

Maroney, T. (1995, January 21). Coming unhinged over hand-holding ban. *Boston Globe,* pp. 1,9.

Modesto City Schools, CA, No. 09-93-1319. Office for Civil Rights, U.S. Department of Education, San Francisco, CA (December 10, 1993).

Mutziger v. Independent School District #272 (Eden Prairie), file #ED19920006, Minnesota Department of Human Rights, Minneapolis, MN (September 3, 1992).

Nashoba Regional School District, MA, No. 01-92-1327. Office for Civil Rights, U.S. Department of Education, Boston, MA (October 22, 1993).

Newark Unified School District, CA, No. 09-93-1113. Office for Civil Rights, U.S. Department of Education, San Francisco, CA (July 7, 1993).

Nickerson, C. (1993, January 24). In Japan, "different" is dangerous. Fatal attack in school casts light on bullying. *Boston Sunday Globe,* pp. 1, 19.

Olweus D. (1993). *Bullying at school: What we know and what we can do.* Oxford: Blackwell.

Permanent Commission (CT) on the Status of Women. (1995). *In our own backyard: Sexual harassment in Connecticut's public high schools.* Hartford, CT: Author.

Pitsch, M. (1994, November 9). O.C.R. stepping up civil-rights enforcement. *Education Week,* pp. 15, 20.

Pollack, A. (1994, December 18). Suicides by bullied students stir Japanese furor. *New York Times,* p. 20.

Sanger, D. E. (1993, April 3). Student's killing displays dark side of Japan schools. *New York Times,* pp. 1, 3.

Sauk Rapids-Rice School District #47, MN, no. 05-93-1142. Office for Civil Rights, U.S. Department of Education, Chicago, IL (June 23, 1993).

Seamons v. Snow, 864 F. Supp. 1111 (D. Utah, 1994).

Slaby, R., & Stringham, P. (1994). Prevention of peer and community violence: The pediatrician's role. *Pediatrics, 94*, 608–616.

Sneed, M., & Woodruff, K. (1994). *Sexual harassment: The complete guide for administrators.* Arlington, VA: American Association of School Administrotors.

Stein, N. (1992a, November 4). Sexual harassment — an update. *Education Week,* p. 37.

Stein, N. (1992b). *Secrets in public: Sexual harassment in public (and private) schools* (Working Paper No. 256). Wellesley, MA: Wellesley College Center for Research on Women.

Stein, N. (1993). No laughing matter: Sexual harassment in K-12 schools. In E. Buchwald, P. R. Fletcher, & M. Roth, *Transforming a rape culture* (pp. 311–331). Minneapolis: Milkweed Editions.

Stein, N. (1996). *Bullyproof.* Wellesley, MA: Wellesley College Center for Research on Women.

Stein, N., Marshall, N., & Tropp, L. (1993). *Secrets in public: Sexual harassment in our schools* (A report on the results of a *Seventeen* magazine survey). Wellesley, MA: Wellesley College Center for Research on Women.

Stein, N., & Sjostrom, L. (1994). *Flirting or hurting? A teacher's guide on student-to-student sexual harassment in schools.* Washington, DC: National Education Association.

Stepp, L. S. (1992, December 1). Getting tough with the big, bad bullies. *Washington Post,* p. C5

Study calls schools lax on sexual harassment. (1993, March 24). *Wall Street Journal,* p. 8.

Walsh, M. (1994, October 19). Harassment suit rejected. *Education Week,* p. 10.

Whitney, I., & Smith, P. K. (1993). A survey of the nature and extent of bullying in junior/middle and secondary schools. *Educational Research, 35*(1), 3–25.

Winship, B. (1994, February 3). Teacher is wrong to dismiss boy's actions as flirting. *Boston Globe,* p. 50.

The author would like to thank Susan Bailey, executive director of The Center for Research on Women at Wellesley College, for her editorial comments, many impromptu discussions, and a vibrant place from which to write. Helpful legal consultation and documents were provided by Kathryn Woodruff, Esq. of Hogan and Hartson, in Washington, DC; the New England regional office of the U.S. Department of Education Office for Civil Rights; and the National Women's Law Center in Washington, DC. Deb Tolman delivered inspiration; Theresa and Imani Perry offered support, ideas, challenges, and many shared meals; and Donaldo Macedo's friendship and loyalty lived beyond his many voice-mail messages. Finally, thanks to e-mail and fax, editorial comments came from David Leshtz from the University of Iowa, friend since high school, whose support and critical eye were invaluable, and who kept me laughing.

PART FOUR

History

"We Who Believe in Freedom Cannot Rest Until It's Done":
Two Dauntless Women of the Civil Rights Movement and the Education of a People

WILLIAM AYERS

In this chapter, William Ayers tells the story of two African American women educators in his review of the film Fundi: The Story of Ella Baker[1] *and the biography* Ready from Within: Septima Clark and the Civil Rights Movement. A First Person Narrative.[2] *Outlining two distinct yet convergent educational movements in the South — Freedom Schools, organized by the Student Nonviolent Coordinating Committee (SNCC), and Citizenship Schools, coordinated by older, more established civil rights groups — Ayers reviews the tributes of women whose stories, for the most part, have been lost to history. Baker, affiliated with the Freedom Schools, and Clark, affiliated with the Citizenship Schools, were part of a movement that "organized to teach basic literacy so that disenfranchised southern Blacks could register and vote, [but] the schools were also places of broader social and political empowerment" (p. 251). Ayers contextualizes the activism of each woman within the civil rights movement, noting their relative anonymity outside of that movement. By exploring the activism in each woman's life, he argues that present-day educators will find inspiration, hope, and a call to action in their stories.*

S tokely Carmichael taught classes in a Freedom School organized by the Student Nonviolent Coordinating Committee (SNCC) in Mississippi in the early 1960s. Freedom Schools grew out of the civil rights struggle, as a vehicle for community education and involvement, and Stokely was famous

---

[1] *Fundi: The Story of Ella Baker*, a film by Joanne Grant, dist. by First Run/Icarus Films, 1986.

[2] *Ready from Within: Septima Clark and the Civil Rights Movement. A First Person Narrative*, ed. Cynthia Stokes Brown (*Navarro, CA: Wild Trees Press, 1986*).

Harvard Educational Review Vol. 59 No. 4 November 1989, 520–528

as a Freedom School teacher in Mississippi long before he was nationally known as the leader who embodied the shift toward Black Power and greater militancy within the movement. Stokely's classes always began with some acknowledgement of what the students themselves knew, then traveled over new, often surprising terrain as students discovered, constructed, and connected with things not yet known. It was exciting to be in Stokely's classes; challenging, funny, sometimes troubling, always lively. One class began with Stokely writing several sentences opposite one another on the chalkboard:

I digs wine	I enjoy drinking cocktails
The peoples wants freedom	The people want freedom
I wants to reddish to vote	I want to register to vote[3]

Students laughed and teased as they watched him write. Stokely asked them what they thought of the two sets of sentences. One student said "peoples" didn't sound right. Stokely asked if they knew what "peoples" meant, if they knew anyone who said "peoples." Several students replied that everyone knew what it meant and that they knew many people, including themselves, who said "peoples" and often spoke sentences like those in the left column. But, added one, it isn't "correct English." Stokely then asked them who decides questions of correct and incorrect, and this exchange followed:

Stokely: You all say some people speak like on the left side of the board. Could they go anywhere and speak that way? Could they go to Harvard?

Class: Yes . . . No.

Stokely: Does Mr. Turnbow speak like on the left side?

Class: Yes.

Stokely: Could Mr. Turnbow go to Harvard and speak like that? "I wants to reddish to vote."

Class: Yes.

Stokely: Would he be embarrassed?

Class: Yes . . . No!

Zelma: He wouldn't be, but I would. It doesn't sound right.

Stokely: Suppose someone from Harvard came to Holmes County and said, "I want to register to vote?" Would they be embarrassed?

Zelma: No.

Stokely: Is it embarrassing at Harvard but not in Holmes county? The way you speak?[4]

The class stopped soon after for lunch, but not before Stokely asked the students to think about what constitutes a society and who makes the rules

---

[3] J. Stembridge, "Notes on a Class," in *Stokely Speaks: Black Power Back to Pan-Africanism*, Stokely Carmichael (New York: Vintage, 1971), pp. 3–4.

[4] Stembridge, "Notes," p. 5.

for society. Students noted that although most people spoke some form of "incorrect English," the "correct English" minority had a monopoly on jobs, money, and prestige. They left wrestling with important questions about language, culture, control, politics, and power. In this brief time in this class, these students were exposed to education at its best: their teacher treated them with respect and valued their knowledge, insight, and know-how as a starting place for a dialogue of learning; the students' knowledge was extended, connected, and compared as a framework for further discovering and knowing; and the students went away more thoughtful and more powerful than when they arrived.

Freedom Schools and Citizenship Schools grew up all over the South wherever the civil rights movement established itself as a serious force, and quickly became the grassroots base of the southernwide opposition to segregation. In general, Freedom Schools were organized by young militants from SNCC; Citizenship Schools by the older, more established civil rights groups. As the movement spread, the schools became in many places a spontaneous forum for action, and the character of each school was determined by local needs and the specific people who organized it. Usually organized to teach basic literacy so that disenfranchised southern Blacks could register and vote, the schools were also places of broader social and political empowerment.

Citizenship schools experienced dramatic growth in the 1960s. In 1962, a coalition of civil rights groups formed the Voter Education Project, and over the next four years this project prepared 10,000 teachers to organize Citizenship Schools and teach in them. Between 1957 and 1970, 897 Citizenship Schools were organized; in 1964 alone there were 195 functioning schools (p. 69). Often organized as a temporary forum for building voter education projects, the schools met in parks, in storefront offices, in people's kitchens, in tool sheds, and in fields under trees.

Citizenship Schools played a key role in breaking the back of Jim Crow voting laws in the South. Their success can be seen in the voter registration statistics for that period: in the early 1960s close to 700,000 new Black voters registered in the South, and in the years immediately after passage of the 1965 Voting Rights Act, another million Black persons registered to vote (p. 70). But these schools influenced more than voter registration: leaders like Fannie Lou Hamer and Hosea Williams were among their graduates. By 1972, the increase in Black political power was felt with the election of Andrew Young of Georgia (who himself taught in Citizenship Schools) and Barbara Jordan of Texas to the U.S. Congress — the first Black people so elected since Reconstruction.

This exercise in community education and empowerment was the result of imagination, grinding work, daily setbacks, and incredible courage. It was built on sacrifice, jail time, beatings, and death — on the often anonymous heroism of millions of people woven together into the fabric of a heroic community. It embodied private vision and public action. It was constructed from audacity, heart, intellectual courage, and generosity of spirit.

These last qualities describe two extraordinary women of action and principle, each of whom played a central role in the modern civil rights movement, and neither of whom was or is widely known outside that movement.

Ella Baker was an organizer and activist who held positions of leadership in the National Association for the Advancement of Colored People (NAACP) in the 1930s and 1940s, and was the first director of Martin Luther King's Southern Christian Leadership Conference (SCLC). She is widely regarded as the spiritual and intellectual inspiration for the creation of SNCC in the early 1960s, and was involved with Freedom Schools throughout the South. Septima Clark joined the NAACP in 1918 and was active in human- and civil-rights work for seventy years. She was a teacher for much of that time, beginning in a segregated rural school on Johns Island, South Carolina, in 1916. When the Supreme Court ruled in 1954 that racial segregation in the public schools was unconstitutional, South Carolina officials retaliated by requiring teachers to list all organizational affiliations. The following year, the legislature made public employees' membership in the NAACP illegal, so that in 1956, Septima Clark (along with 42 other teachers) was fired from her teaching job in Charleston. She then became director of workshops at the Highlander Folk School in Tennessee, a gathering place and political center for people committed to progressive social change through education. She was instrumental in the education of a generation of organizers and activists and in the creation of Citizenship Schools throughout the South.

With the making of *Fundi*, the powerful film account of Ella Baker's contribution, and the publication of *Ready from Within*, the autobiography of Septima Clark, the life stories of these two foremothers of action for freedom and justice are accessible to a wider audience. These accounts of their lives can enrich us immeasurably, adding depth and texture to our understanding of an important part of our past, inspiring us with examples of lives lived fully and purposefully. If we look closely we will find unfinished agendas, unfulfilled dreams, and guideposts for our own attempts to teach and to learn.

Our Objective Is Justice . . .

As a young teacher on Johns Island, Septima Clark discovered that the spoken language of the Carolina Sea Islands is a unique creation of the early slaves. While the Islanders understand English, their own language is Gullah, a mix of the languages native to the captured Africans, along with the various languages of the slave traders and imperialists.

Septima Clark was neither a bilingual teacher nor a special education teacher. She was simply a person who set out to teach students regardless of caste or condition. When she taught reading, for example, she "put down 'de' for 'the,' because that's the way they said 'the.'" She told her students that in books they would see the word "the": "You say 'de,' but in the book it's printed 'the'" (p. 106).

She taught beginning reading by creating homemade books based on the experiences of the Johns Islanders:

> I wrote their stories on the dry cleaner's bags, stories of their country right around them, where they walked to come to school, the things that grew around them, what they could see in the skies. They told them to me, and I wrote them on dry cleaner's bags and tacked them on the wall. (p. 106)

Later, after students could read stories of their own island, she brought in books and stories that could open them to a world beyond their experience. These "vicarious experiences" told of "great corn fields in the midwest where farmers made thousands of dollars" (p. 107), and of seals and mountains and cities. As a teacher, Septima Clark built on a foundation of what students knew and challenged them to move from the known to the unknown. She empowered her students in two ways: by affirming their life experiences and serving as a cultural and personal mirror for them; and by opening a wider world to them introducing them to the unknown and unexperienced through the various literacies that connected them to other people and other times.

The Citizenship Schools initiated by Septima Clark applied this fundamental lesson about teaching to the huge task of educating a whole community. As she recruited people to teach in the Citizenship Schools, Clark decided to begin with an understanding of the students, of how they experienced the world:

> We had a day-by-day plan, which started the first night with them talking, telling us what they would like to learn. The next morning we started off with asking them: "Do you have an employment office in your town? Where is it located? What hours is it open? Have you been there to get work?"
> The answers to those things we wrote down on dry cleaner's bags, so they could read them. . . .
> We were trying to make teachers out of people who could barely read and write. But they could teach. If they could read at all, we could teach them that c-o-n-s-t-i-t-u-t-i-o-n spells constitution. We'd have a long discussion all morning about what the constitution was. . . . (pp. 63–64)

The power of the lesson was in the content. People left the teacher education sessions to lead their own projects of voter registration and community education. In these projects they replicated the lessons learned: they discussed the problems and the needs of people in their own local communities; they posed questions ("How come the pavement stops where the Black section begins?"); and they organized a process that allowed for discovery and connection. The teachers listened and "let them know that we felt that they were right according to the kind of thing that they had in their mind, but according to living in this world there were other things they needed to know" (p. 53). The starting points for teaching were various and complex (how the local government functions, how the sharecropping system works, how to keep a bank account and avoid being cheated), but the goals were the same: affirmation, growth, power.

The Citizenship Schools and Freedom Schools are examples of community education as a process that opens doors, opens minds, opens possibilities — an education that enables people to surpass limitations. "Our objective is justice," Ella Baker argued. "Your life has been limited — both White and Black — by racism." The opening of possibilities in life, the healing and the transforming, begins with the identification of limitations and the willingness to act against them. "No human being relishes being sat upon," she insisted, and yet the natural human resistance to oppression must find an effective organized form: "Nobody will do for you what you have the power to do and fail to do." Education and freedom each requires self-activity, each requires the complex interplay of individual choice and assertion with collective action and interaction.

This kind of education opposed fear, ignorance, and helplessness by strengthening knowledge and ability. It enables people to question, to wonder, and to look critically. It requires teachers who are thoughtful, careful, and connected deeply to those they teach. This enabling education can be both the process by which people discover and develop various capacities as they locate themselves historically, and the vehicle for moving forward and breaking through the immutable facts, traditions, and objects of life as we find them. Its singular value is that it is education for freedom.

Learning to read in the South of Ella Baker and Septima Clark was a subversive activity, an activity that many thought could change the fundamental structure of the Jim Crow system. Like the slave owner who told Frederick Douglass that reading would "unfit him to be a slave," many in the South considered Black illiteracy a pillar of White supremacy. The Citizenship Schools, which paralleled the heroic efforts to educate ex-slaves during the radical period of Black Reconstruction immediately following the Civil War, challenged White supremacy by teaching basic literacy, encouraging people to vote, and providing alternatives and a sense of efficacy. The First Citizenship School organized at Johns Island was disguised as a grocery store "to fool white people" (p. 47). Reading represented power; for Black people it was the power to control and to change their destiny.

Education for freedom is always more a possibility than an accomplishment, more an achievement of people in action than a finished condition. It requires a continual identification of what is to be done, a constant process of unfolding and moving forward. The process of education, of discovery, of freedom, is seldom neat or logical or smooth or obvious in advance. It is more often messy, rough, unpredictable, and inconsistent. It can be halting and it can be slow, but it can also surprise with the suddenness and power of change. Ella Baker, reminiscing with an old friend who says with obvious good humor, "I never liked the SNCC people; they were so wild," notes: "Some of us were willing to forego manners to accomplish goals." She goes on to describe how good people can bog down in a single approach and thereby miss the point that requirements are always changing. At one point, she says, the freedom struggle was led by the NAACP, and an important part of that leadership was legal action through the courts. But when the NAACP became "tied to legalism," she claims, "they were stuck." Baker argues that people must "take what steps are necessary to move beyond a given spot — or you're stuck." Septima Clark reflected on this issue:

> You know, the measure of a person is how much they develop in their life. Some people slow down in their growth after they become adults. You can hardly tell they are changing at all. But you never know when a person's going to leap forward, or change around completely. Just think of how much Martin Luther King, Jr., grew in his life. That was the greatest thing about him. . . . I've seen growth like most people don't think is possible. I can even work with my enemies because I know from experience that they might have a change of heart any minute. (p. 103)

Ella Baker and Septima Clark were never stuck. They lived with visions and hopes and dreams that they were willing to work for. When the lives they led and the choices they made helped change conditions, they, too, were each willing to change, and to carry on in the transformed situation. New hopes and dreams emerged from the changes they helped to fashion, and those new hopes led to recreated requirements. And so on and on.

Septima Clark recalls joining the NAACP because a Black youth was arrested unjustly. Ella Baker remembers that "on the streets of Norfolk a little boy called me a nigger; I struck him back." This was the beginning. But, she argues, "it is not enough." Working in the movement for freedom requires organization, reaching out to others, and a "willingness to do what has to be done when it has to be done."

Organize!

Fundi is the Swahili word for a person who masters a craft and passes it on. The fundi is a storyteller, a leader, a teacher, whose strength and wisdom are embedded in a community. Ella Baker was called Fundi by the SNCC militants — people like Bernice Reagon, Bob Moses, Stokely Carmichael, Marion Barry, Eleanor Holmes Norton, Julian Bond, Dorie Ladner, James Foreman, Dorothy Zellner, John Lewis, Bob Zellner, Dorothy Cotton — whom she nourished, encouraged, inspired, and taught.

In Greensboro, North Carolina, 1960 was a decisive year in the southern civil rights movement. College students began a dramatic series of sit-ins at a segregated lunch counter, focusing the attention of the world on the degradation of life in the segregated south. Day after day a group of quiet, neatly dressed students walked into the store, sat at the lunch counter, and asked to be served. They were refused, as a howling racist crowd harassed them, spat on them, and threw food at them. Still they sat, and so they were threatened and pushed; sometimes beaten, always arrested. This went on for months.

"We were scared to death," one student said. "But we believed we were right." And so they sang to keep their spirits up, and they held onto one another. The issue, of course, was "bigger than a hamburger." These students challenged the structure of the social order and pushed the civil rights movement to a sense of greater urgency and action. Soon sit-ins at segregated public facilities were mushrooming throughout the South. "None of us who were older could fail to identify when the kids sat-in," Ella Baker said. "They acted as if they believed this was their right."

Ella Baker, who was then Executive Director of SCLC, suggested that those involved in the sit-ins hold a meeting to assess the situation and decide what needed to be done next. While she did not play a dominant role in the meeting, she set a tone of affirmation, connectedness, and purpose. She led by facilitating, by enabling others to speak and to act, by emanating a sense of groundedness and community. Her contribution was decisive, but it was mainly indirect. The one time she strongly asserted her own view was when she encouraged the young people to resist the pressure from the NAACP, CORE, and even SCLC to become an affiliated youth group. "The adults wanted to attach the young," she said later. "They wanted to claim this new and vital force." Ella Baker told the students that what they had was courageous and spontaneous. "Keep the special thing separate," she said. And so SNCC was founded in 1960.

Sometimes in looking back at events, we lose the sense of what it was like to take action without guarantees or certainties about outcomes. Looking back we can focus on the dramatic or the spontaneous as if that's all there was, as if there were no grinding hard work, no dead ends, and no confusion that built to courage and action. A lot of the work of SNCC was day-to-day, door-to-door, teaching and learning and organizing and building slowly, bit by bit, one piece at a time. The explosions, the leaps forward, the galvanizing moments were the visible peaks atop a mountain of human effort.

The story of Rosa Parks's role in the movement is instructive. Rosa Parks is a national hero because her simple refusal to move to the back of the bus in Montgomery, Alabama, on December 1, 1955, began the year-long bus boycott that began the modern civil rights movement and catapulted a young minister, Martin Luther King, Jr., to leadership and national fame. Rosa Parks's courage, dignity, and determination are rightly celebrated.

What is less known is that during the previous summer, Rosa Parks had participated in a leadership workshop led by Septima Clark at the Highlander Folk School. Parks had been the leader of the NAACP youth group in Montgomery and was well known as a local activist. She had organized a group of young Black people to attend a traveling exhibit from Washington, DC — the "Freedom Train" — that carried the original Constitution and Declaration of Independence. Whites didn't want to enter the exhibit side-by-side with Blacks, but the exhibit was integrated, and Rosa Parks made a point of exercising her right and the rights of the Black children to go right through the exhibit as equals. Afterward she became the target of abuse and harassment.

Rosa Parks attended the Highlander workshop and told her story. The workshops typically began by asking people what they needed to know, and they always ended with the question: "What are you going to do back home?" (p. 30). Parks noted that Montgomery was the "cradle of the Confederacy," and that little was possible because of how difficult conditions were and how hard it was for the Black people there to stick together. But she said she would continue her work with the young people, that they were the hope for the future, and that she would continue to teach them about their rights. She was given encouragement and pledges of support. Three months later she was arrested. When Septima Clark heard the news, she said, "Rosa? Rosa? She was so shy when she came to Highlander, but she got enough courage to do that" (p. 34).

Almost ten years later, in the summer of 1964, SNCC led the effort to open Mississippi, a state that typified the sanctioning of southern racism, by building a massive voter registration project. Mississippi Summer, as it was called, was a joint project of all of the civil rights organizations active in the South. It enlisted the efforts of hundreds of student volunteers, church people, and northern supporters. The organized White resistance, determined to stop the volunteers, kidnapped and murdered three civil rights workers — James Chaney, Andrew Goodman, and Micky Schwerner — as a warning to others preparing to work in the South. As word of the disappearance of the three young men spread, the response was the opposite of what the racists had hoped for: the news galvanized the determination, courage, and urgency of the forces for change. Mississippi was flooded with volunteers, and Mississippi Summer 1964 became one of the key moments in the civil rights movement.

At a memorial service Ella Baker's voice rang out in anger, echoing the sentiments of the families of the three murdered freedom workers: "Until the killing of Black mothers' sons becomes as important as the killing of a White mother's son, we who believe in freedom cannot rest." Her voice carried, too, a message of rededication, of recommitment and hope.

"I was difficult. . . . I could talk back."

Ella Baker and Septima Clark were women in male-led organizations, and they each noticed particular possibilities as well as the imposed limitations of that situation. Septima Clark notes that the history of the civil rights movement focuses on ministers, "but if you talk to the women who were there, you'll hear another story" (p. 83). She was an executive staff member of SCLC, "but the men on it didn't listen to me too well" (p. 77). Still she was heard. Ella Baker's self-assessment applies as well to Septima Clark: "I was difficult. . . . I could talk back."

What each of these leaders brought to her work was uncommon courage and common sense, abilities to make connections and empower others, and a strong sense of self that was grounded in a belief in community that demanded no fanfare, no adornment, no superficial hype. Each had a great sense of being important when helping others grow. "I didn't need to lead," says Ella Baker, and that single statement speaks volumes about the leader she was. Like a good teacher, she knew how to affirm and to challenge, how to step out in front when that was necessary, and how to watch and listen to the accomplishments of others when that was required. Both women's deepest goal was the strengthening of the community.

Septima Clark says: "Let me be modest and simple. This is the way I think I should be. . . ." She goes on:

> If I would sum up my life, I think of a little mischievous girl who would speak back to her mother, and her mother would flog her for doing just that. I would think of the young woman who dared to speak out in groups about the things that she thought were not right. . . . When I became a middle-aged woman, I think of the many dangers I had to go into, working in the eleven deep south states and five fringe states, and still these things did not make me feel afraid nor ashamed. And now in my old age I'm still working. . . .
>
> I think there will always be something that you're going to have to work on, always. That's why, when we have chaos and people say, "I'm scared. I'm scared. I'm concerned," I say, "Out of that will come something good. . . ." The only thing that's really worthwhile is change. It's coming. (pp. 125–126)

Ella Baker and Septima Clark were each activist community educators. They were workers in literacy and voting-rights projects, in community organizations and educational institutions. Their every work project was linked to a larger life project of community empowerment for liberation. Each was a teacher, then, in the largest and best sense: a dreamer, a builder, a creator of intellectual space and ethical action, an enabler of individuals, and a midwife of a new society. When history is being rewritten in the interest of a smoother, less troublesome tale, a story more tailored to an era of selfishness and perceived powerlessness, it is well to reaffirm the choices made in troubled times. Learning about these lives inspires us with what can be done and instructs us on what is yet to be done. Though there are periods of quiet and confusion, people always rise again. As Maya Angelou wrote: "You may write me down in history/With your bitter, twisted lies,/You may trod me in the very dirt/But still, like dust, I'll rise."[5]

People go on teaching, go on learning, go on hoping, toiling, troubling, and trying. Beaten down by racism, sexism, class exploitation, by the great White whale and the great White myth and the great White cultural emptiness, and also by fear of dying, fear of being different, fear of being impolite, still people rise. We rise because we perceive an alternative, we begin to identify the unacceptable. We find free voices that say "No!" and free minds that dare to dream of something different. We find then that our bodies move in new ways, that new freedoms demand new actions and together we reclaim our lives and begin to build our futures. This is perhaps the deepest

---

[5] Maya Angelou, *And Still I Rise* (New York: Random House, 1978), p. 41.

lesson in learning about the lives of these two women: dare to dream, dare to act. Like Septima Clark and Ella Baker, if we can become brave in our visions and in our actions, the rest will follow. We can perhaps contribute as builders of a new world, a world where people can care more, love more fully and more widely, touch each other more, think more clearly, solve more problems, laugh and cry more. This is worth our trouble.

Reconsidering a Classic:
Assessing the History of Women's Higher Education a Dozen Years after Barbara Solomon

LINDA EISENMANN

In this chapter, Linda Eisenmann examines the role and impact of Barbara Solomon's now classic 1985 text in women's educational history, In the Company of Educated Women: A History of Women in Higher Education in America. *Eisenmann analyzes how Solomon's book influenced, defined, and is some ways limited the field of women's educational history. She shows how current historical research — such as the study of normal schools and academies — grew out of Solomon's work. She points out where the book is innovative and indispensable and where it disappoints us as teachers and scholars in the 1990s. Eisenmann critiques Solomon for placing too much emphasis on women's access to higher education, thereby ignoring the importance of wider historical and educational influences such as economics, women's occupational choices, and the treatment of women in society at large. Finally, Eisenmann examines the state of subsequent research in women's higher educational history. She urges researchers to investigate beyond the areas defined by Solomon's work and to assess the impact of these neglected subjects on women's experiences in education.*

In 1985, Harvard University scholar Barbara Miller Solomon published a comprehensive historical study of women's higher education in the United States that became an instant classic. *In the Company of Educated Women: A History of Women and Higher Education in America* offered the first book-length synthesis of women's academic progress since Mabel Newcomer's 1959 effort, *A Century of Higher Education for American Women*, and was the first in its field to employ the new data, methods, and insights made available by the contemporary surge in women's history.[1]

Harvard Educational Review Vol. 67 No. 4 Winter 1997, 689–717

Benefiting from the expanded work of specialists in the new field of women's studies, Solomon synthesized secondary sources and reexamined primary materials, proclaiming women's higher education "an unfinished revolution" that continues to pose complexities for women.[2] Access constituted Solomon's major analytical theme, as she told the stories of successive generations of women pushing first for initial entry, and then struggling to make higher education meaningful to their sense of their own life opportunities. Cognizant of biases and omissions in earlier histories, Solomon's book included — more than any other single history of women's higher education — the stories of nontraditional institutions and students, adding sections on historically Black colleges, Catholic schools, and two-year institutions. She also included the stories of poor women and immigrants to those of middle-class and privileged students. Overall, she stressed that her book was not a history of institutions, but rather of generations of women. Thus, Solomon discussed successive eras in layers, detailing the institutions, curricula, clientele, job opportunities, and public debates surrounding women's education from the colonial era to the 1980s.

As the single most comprehensive and available historical study of women's higher education, Solomon's book appears widely in courses on women's history, higher education, and the history of education. It also constitutes the major source for nonhistorians seeking a solid and accessible discussion of women's higher education, and is consulted frequently by a wide range of readers. Now that *In the Company of Educated Women* has reigned as the strongest resource in the field for a dozen years, the time is right for assessing the book's role and impact as the classic source. The time is also propitious for examining the state of subsequent research in women's higher educational history that might supplement, or supersede, Solomon's ideas and for offering recommendations about future work. This article treats each of these issues in turn.

First, I outline briefly Solomon's approach and her analysis, suggesting where the book is innovative and indispensable, but also noting where it disappoints us as teachers and scholars in the 1990s. I argue, in terms of the book's legacy, that Solomon's framing of women's educational history as a story of access to traditional institutions, while vital, may actually have limited later historians' approach to questions and debates, encouraging them to focus their questions on these traditional settings. In the second part of this article I discuss new research that extends Solomon's work on the history of women's advanced education. Solomon urged her colleagues to consider the nineteenth-century normal schools and academies as appropriate components of higher education, to investigate the experience of a more diverse group of women, and to reevaluate the use women made of their education throughout successive eras.[3] Each of these areas has produced substantial work in the last dozen years, some building on Solomon and some going in entirely new directions. Finally, in the third section I explore some research areas that remain underdeveloped, suggesting that the field of women's higher education may not yet be ready for a new Solomonesque resynthesis.

The Solomon Legacy

In 1995, a panel of seven historians of higher education, convened to assess the legacy of Barbara Solomon's work, concluded unanimously that they "could not imagine teaching a history of education course without *In the Company of Educated Women*."[4] With its thorough presentation of American women's push for higher learning from colonial times through the post–World War II era, the book provides a basis for understanding women's education before colleges had opened for women and carries us through women's fight for equal access over subsequent generations. However, those same historians who lauded Solomon's work also admitted that the book cannot stand alone as the story of women's education; it requires heavy supplementing in the areas of racial, ethnic, geographic, economic, and intellectual history.

Until Solomon, no historian had tried to analyze the entire sweep of women's higher educational history since Mabel Newcomer's *A Century of Higher Education for American Women* in 1959. Newcomer, much as she tried to cover a wide variety of women's institutions, had fallen back on the environment she knew best as a Vassar professor: the eastern women's colleges. Even as she reminded her readers that three-quarters of all colleges were coeducational, Newcomer found women's experiences too diffuse in those larger institutions and turned instead to the separate women's colleges, where she could observe the particular arrangements that had been crafted for women in curriculum, residential life, and vocational guidance. Surprisingly few individuals appear in Newcomer's story: institutions rule the day and leaders control the institutions. Writing in a particularly dismal era for women's intellectual participation, Newcomer recognized the limiting effect that societal norms have on women's choices; focusing on women's actual efforts was the extent of her challenge to those limits.

Historian Patricia Palmieri has suggested that, just as Newcomer was as positive as the 1950s climate allowed, Solomon offered a type of scholarly challenge to the more pessimistic 1970s and 1980s view that colleges had failed women, at least in terms of their equal participation and performance. Solomon, Palmieri asserts, "restored a balance in the scholarly domain" by showing that women, over time, had asserted their place in higher education and had, in fact, repeatedly pushed colleges to accommodate their needs.[5] That is, a calculus that women remained far behind men in the 1980s should not overshadow the achievement women made in this educational arena.

Between Newcomer and Solomon came the resurgent women's movement and the first two decades of women's studies scholarship. Whereas Newcomer and her contemporaries had no language with which to analyze discrimination against women, Solomon could rely on scholarly explications of ways that economic and educational structures had inhibited women's advancement.[6] Solomon drew on older, factual material to document women's early efforts, including such works as Emilie J. Hutchinson's 1929 study, *Women and the Ph.D.*, and Jeanne Noble's 1956 work, *The Negro Woman's College*

Education, both of which outlined the early history of women's opportunities on a large scale.[7] Solomon also relied on dozens of institutional histories, biographies, novels, diaries, editorials, and newspaper articles to capture both the spirit and realities of earlier generations of women. By 1985, however, Solomon was also able to reinterpret this material with a feminist consciousness constructed by a new generation of historians and sociologists. Karen Blair's *The Clubwoman as Feminist,* for example, helped Solomon understand that women's clubs were more than safe opportunities for privileged women to share knowledge; rather, according to Blair, these clubs allowed women to claim power and influence in activities that men ceded to their authority, at the same time providing educational opportunities for many women unable to attend formal college.[8] Solomon could also use Nancy Cott's explanation of *The Bonds of Womanhood: "Woman's Sphere" in New England, 1780–1835* to understand that the limits of a designated female sphere of activity and influence could also develop as a center of power for women where religion, domesticity, and education were tailored to women's particular needs.[9] And, although access sustained a primary role as the organizing principle of Solomon's book, she did heed Jill Ker Conway's 1974 reminder that access alone never guaranteed women's full participation, using that caveat to look at issues for women once they had entered collegiate doors.[10]

In twelve chapters plus an "Afterthought," Solomon addressed three main eras of women's participation in higher education: the antebellum era (from the colonial period, with its few institutions, up to 1860), the growth period (1860 to 1920, the era of greatest proliferation of institutional types from women's colleges to land grant universities), and the modern period (1920 to the Second World War, which actually produced a decline in women's percentages of participation in higher education). One last chapter, entitled "The Promises of Liberal Education — Forgotten and Fulfilled," brought the story to the present, with a firm focus on the contemporary women's movement.

Solomon's approach is recursive. She describes the general conditions for women in a particular era, both in education and in society. In subsequent chapters, she swings back through that same time period to explain which women participated in higher education, what they studied, and how female students eventually used their education. Throughout her discussion, she tends to offer bits of women's lives to illustrate small points, but then does not develop those pieces into fuller stories. Instead she moves into other points, frustrating those readers who are seeking a more linear narrative. Because of her insistence on inclusivity, Solomon jumps among institutional types as well, sometimes leaving a dutiful but "tacked on" feeling to her discussion of Catholic colleges, historically Black institutions, and normal schools. In the chapters on women's use of their education, Solomon moves systematically through topics, treating teaching, the professions, marriage rates, and women's reflections on their college lives era by era.

Although offering a thorough discussion of women's collegiate participation, Solomon does not offer much additional context — another concern of those who would rely on the book for a thorough story. Economic history is woefully lacking in her explanation of women's occupational choices; intellectual history is limited to precise arguments about the usefulness of higher education; and except for the occasional connection to movements like suffrage and temperance, general U.S. history is altogether too absent from the discussion. This seeming neglect, however, results from Solomon's careful reliance on the extant secondary sources available to her to explain women's progress in collegiate life; she achieves a synthesis in her self-described "narrative," but never promises a new theoretical paradigm — particularly for a field where little theory existed.

Yet even with what appear now as limitations, the book advanced several categories of analysis — which Sally Schwager describes as Solomon's "sensibilities" — that were relatively new to the study of women's higher education in 1985 and that still ground our understanding. Extending work by David Allmendinger on poor students who attended college, Solomon looked at the economic standing of students, freshly examining the issues of financial aid and student self-support.[11] In turning the lens on women who needed help to attend college, she also promoted studying the role families played as sponsors for female students. Perhaps because of Solomon's earlier strong study of New England's immigrants, Schwager notes that Solomon was one of few historians to recognize the important role of immigrant parents who pushed their daughters into school.[12] Although the attention to historically Black and Catholic colleges seems forced and limited to a 1990s reader, Solomon's commitment to including those institutions and their students goes beyond the lip service of earlier studies. Even with little secondary work at her disposal, Solomon recognized the need to look at racial and ethnic diversity on predominantly White college campuses, perhaps laying groundwork for later comparative analyses.

Another advance by Solomon — a place where her focus on access is beneficial — was her resuscitation of the history of academies, and her claim that these pre-collegiate antebellum institutions were appropriate forerunners of higher education. By the turn of the twentieth century, high schools and colleges had developed into recognizable institutions, superseding the academies and female seminaries in influence and prominence. Relying on older work and a smattering of new sources, Solomon acknowledged the role that academies — many of them with all-female student bodies and headed by women — had played in offering both liberal and vocational opportunities to a range of nineteenth-century women. Finally, although her look at women's experiences after college, posed by many as the "after college what?" question, often ignores some of the influences women exerted outside traditional jobs and professions — such as their role in reform movements — Solomon tried to relate the purposes of women's education to actual results, going beyond scholars who had argued that women sought schooling primarily to expand their intellects.[13]

Overall, Solomon stressed that for women, "education evoked opposition" — thus the resistance to access.[14] Opposition sometimes occurred in students' own families, as daughters struggled for identity outside the family unit; it also developed from society, with educated women challenging expectations for female roles. On coeducational campuses, women were tolerated but rarely welcomed, finding barriers to their full participation and development. Across institutional settings, Solomon found that women learned as much from their female and male peers as they did in their classrooms, and her book attends to what Frederick Rudolph labeled "the extracurriculum" for its importance to students' lives.[15] With her themes of access, opposition, curriculum, and career development as guides, Solomon's story of female participation in higher education inevitably contains as many examples of frustrations and impediments as of successes and accomplishments.

Subsequent Historical Research

When a single book dominates and synthesizes a field of study, it also may shape the way subsequent scholars ask questions and frame debates in that field. Having waited twenty-five years for a synthesis like Solomon's, have historians of higher education been overly influenced by her approach, her data, and her paradigm? In what areas have Solomon's ideas held sway, and where have they sparked new approaches?[16]

Three of Solomon's constructs seem to have maintained primacy in the way that historians of women's education ask their questions, perhaps limiting the vitality of their investigations: first, her implicit hierarchy of women's colleges on top and others, especially the normal schools, arraying themselves toward the bottom; second, the dominance of access as an organizing principle; and third, the lack of attention to other agencies' influence on higher education, especially foundations, the government, and accrediting groups. In this section I discuss Solomon's impact on each of these areas and highlight recent work that is beginning to stretch her construction.

The Implicit Hierarchy

Solomon certainly succeeded better than Newcomer and others at attending to a range of institutional types in her story of women in higher education. Historian Patricia Albjerg Graham, in her 1975 call for future research, "So Much to Do: Guides for Historical Research on Women in Higher Education," lamented the continuing focus on women's colleges, highlighting a fact Newcomer herself had raised: by 1890, 70 percent of women attended coeducational institutions, a figure that continued to rise throughout the twentieth century.[17] Further, as Susan B. Carter asserted in her economic study of hiring patterns for female faculty, the land grant institutions were significant employers of women professors, even though far too many were shunted into teacher training departments and home economics.[18] Solomon unquestionably heeded Graham's challenge, noting that "the debate over the advantages of the separate college environment is largely anachronistic."[19] She included significant data on women in state universities, clarifying that, especially in the Midwest and West, coeducational state colleges and universities provided the primary collegiate experience for women students. Their access into these institutions hailed a major advance for women's education. Generally, the push to segregate women into separate settings was an eastern and southern phenomenon, one far outweighed by the number of women attending land grant and other public institutions. Solomon described fears about the "feminization" of the collegiate environment that appeared in the early part of the twentieth century, as women's presence at coeducational campuses and in the curriculum was growing. In fact, she expressed concern that an inherent class bias against these large, coeducational settings prompted both contemporary and modern preferences for the separate, all-female environments.

Nonetheless Solomon, somewhat like Newcomer, often fell back on the Seven Sisters and other women's colleges with their prominence and superior archives for filling out women's stories. This reliance is understandable since, in terms of traditional leadership, women's institutions provide the most data: many (but not all) of the female colleges hired women presidents and faculty, for example.[20] In addition, in the early years of these schools' existence, women students and professors proved the most self-conscious about their roles as pioneers. Thus, the women's colleges built stronger archives for both faculty and student experiences, and their women leaders recorded more of their own backgrounds and accomplishments. The ready availability of data for certain populations parallels the issue in writing any social history: how does the scholar uncover and honor the experience of less literate people or those whose traditions and opportunities do not favor recording their experience?

However, as both Patricia Palmieri and Margaret Rossiter have shown, women's institutions faltered in their commitment to female professors by the 1930s, when a male faculty was assumed to signal quality.[21] As women's overall participation slackened from its high in the 1920s, women's colleges may have maintained their commitment to female students, but not concomitantly to women faculty.[22] Solomon herself notes that "the assumption that women's colleges consistently offered female role models is an oversimplification."[23] Combined with the fact that women's colleges made up only 5–15 percent of institutions open to women from the 1940s to the 1980s, their seeming status as the most important setting for studying women should be challenged.

Only in the last decade or so, however, have historians of women's education begun serious efforts to rejuvenate the normal schools, the public institutions, and the female academies as worthy and important sites for studying women's participation. Perhaps the influence of social history needed time to affect the field, or perhaps women had too often fallen into the trap of trying to prove their equality with the elite men's institutions. Recent research provides correctives that were unavailable to Solomon in two important areas. First, historians of these more "marginal" institutions remind us that higher education — especially in the nineteenth century — was far more permeable as a system than a sense of hierarchy would suggest. Second, the normal schools and the female academies were frequently sources of both real access and power for women students and faculty.

In the last ten years, normal schools have attracted renewed attention, although not initially because of their role in educating a largely female population. Two book-length studies inaugurated a fresh look at the normal schools as providers of training for several generations of nineteenth- and early twentieth-century teachers. Jürgen Herbst, in *And Sadly Teach,* devoted keen attention to these institutions, tracing their theoretical lineage from German forebears who brought aspects of the normal model and of Pesta-lozzian pedagogy to the United States.[24] Although Herbst began with the birth of U.S. normal schools in Massachusetts, the intriguing part of his book was his demonstration that the normal school model, when transported to the public institutions of the Midwest and West, transmogrified into a new sort of "people's college" that served as basic higher education for men and women, whether or not their main goal was to prepare as teachers. Since most college graduates of the nineteenth century (and almost all of the women) became teachers, the normal schools played a vital role as they dotted the central part of the country with their new opportunities.[25]

A team of educational historians working with John Goodlad in his large study of teacher training in the United States also studied the normal schools, but as only one setting where teachers were taught. Whereas Herbst traced the legacy of the normal schools themselves, the Goodlad group stud-ied the range of places where teachers received training, examining the effects of training in normal schools, academies, land grant universities, and liberal arts colleges.[26] The Herbst and Goodlad books, along with Donald Warren's edited volume, *American Teachers: Histories of a Profession at Work,* focused a new lens on normal schools as both separate institutions and as elements within a system.[27]

The attention to normal schools in these works was seized upon by a new generation of scholars, who examined them specifically for the role they played for women. Christine A. Ogren, Laura Docter Thornburg, and Mary Alpern examined normal schools throughout the country, highlighting the degree to which women served as educational leaders. Thornburg studied the career of Julia Ann King, first "preceptress" of the Michigan normal school, examining King's influence as a practicing teacher and head of one of the primary teacher-training centers in that part of the Midwest. Ogren studied seven normal schools throughout the nation, finding similarities to women's colleges in students' involvement in academic and extracurricular activities, and those institutions' commitment to vocational preparation. She clarified ways that women used normal training as both teacher preparation and general education.[28] Mary Alpern's findings supported Ogren's sugges-tion of the normal schools' academic and career strengths. Alpern ques-tioned earlier assumptions that female "normalites" (a rejuvenation of an old term) were not serious students, citing others who had claimed that women students neither intended nor pursued lengthy careers as teachers and that they viewed teaching only as either a way station until marriage or a fallback in case of widowhood. Studying the Albany, New York, normal schools, Alpern traced 428 students, finding that women taught, on average, for 10.3 years and men 11.7. Of women who never married, the average tenure was twenty-two years. By examining social-class origins as well as subsequent careers, Alpern confirmed new findings that normal schools indeed strengthened women's educational and career options.

Ogren, Thornburg, and Alpern also highlighted the degree to which normal school graduates diffused their technical training beyond their local areas. The women's colleges, and the more famous female academies, such as Emma Willard's Troy Female Seminary, had long been recognized for their ability to "seed" like institutions. In her important 1979 article on "The Diffusion of Feminist Values" through Troy Seminary, Anne Firor Scott traced dozens of schools founded by graduates of Troy.[29] The women's colleges, too, were known to create "daughter schools" in the western part of the country. Margaret Nash recently studied the ecology of institutions for women in one part of Ohio, beginning with the Western Female Seminary in Oxford, a daughter school of Mount Holyoke College.[30] Looking, as Nash has, at the range of institutions serving women in a given area confirms the notion that "higher education" was in fact a flexible nineteenth-century concept depending on availability of institutions, funding, and stability.

Other new work on academies has begun to clarify the issues of student choice and its relationship to curriculum, markets, and vocational preparation. Nancy Beadie applied an economic analysis to student decisions on academy attendance, discovering that women's attendance, not men's, often directed the curricular emphases of these schools. Women paid for not only basic education, but also for science and music courses, encouraging academy founders to tailor curricula to female needs and expenditures.[31] Kimberley Tolley has traced women's curricular choice as well, focusing especially on their higher demand than men for science courses in both the nineteenth and early twentieth centuries. Her work, along with Beadie's, suggests that academies provided significant and advanced curricular opportunities for women who did not attend the now better known eastern women's colleges.[32]

None of this work on the variety of institutions that prepared women for their most populous profession was available to Solomon when writing *In the Company of Educated Women*. Her call for other sites of female leadership and academic success has been more fully realized with such subsequent illumination of these little-studied female institutions.

Access as the Organizing Principle

Women's history as a field came of age in an era when women were pushing for equal rights and equal access to men's institutions, careers, and opportunities. The "difference debate" of the 1980s and 1990s, in which some women claimed the right to differential treatment while others fought for the right to equal treatment, did not hold sway in the early years of the post-1960 women's movement. Instead, women focused on winning equal treatment and access to the same opportunities open to men.[33] Writing in 1985 from an institution that had long resisted granting women an equal place, Solomon focused steadily on the issue of women's hard-fought battle for access to collegiate life. She was not unaware of the complications that women faced once they arrived on college campuses; in fact, her focus on student life and the curriculum was dedicated to clarifying women's complicated maneuvering in a setting that rarely welcomed them. Because of her focus on access, however, she may have downplayed some other aspects of women's participation that indeed affected the development of higher education, such as their parallel involvement in non-educational settings, their treatment once they had achieved access, and the possible costs of women's educational entry points.

Work like Nancy Cott's and Karen Blair's, mentioned above, allowed historians to look for instances where women established authority without access to mainstream institutions. Cott looked at both religion and education as sites for women's power; Blair proclaimed the women's clubs as sources of education and influence for their all-female membership. Separatism as a conscious strategy by women was highlighted by Estelle Freedman, spurring historians to look for ways that women injected vitality into those areas ceded to them.[34] Linda Kerber furthered the construct of "separate spheres" as a potent organizing principle for historical investigations of women.[35]

In educational history, as in other areas of women's history, this notion of separate spheres of influence inspired scholars who were aware of barriers that had been erected to keep women in their separate institutions or in tributaries of the mainstream. Polly Kaufman, for example, offered a study of the Women's College at Brown University, showing how a parallel women's institution flourished alongside a reluctant male partner.[36] Lynn Gordon examined the women who coeducated the Universities of Chicago and California at Berkeley, exploring the different ways these schools welcomed women.[37] Carolyn Terry Bashaw and Jana Nidiffer explored the creation of the profession of dean of women as a formal recognition by university heads that women needed both tending and containing on coeducational campuses.[38] These fine educational studies build on Solomon's construction of women's educational history as a story of access sought or access denied, and fill out her presentation of women's participation in the mainstream.

Denial of women's full and equal participation prompted a different development, however, which Solomon addressed only occasionally. Lacking the opportunity to connect education with wider public life, women developed what Sally Schwager addresses as "counter-institutions" to the colleges where they could exert their influence, especially in the nineteenth century and in the Progressive Era.[39] Blair's recognition of the significance of women's clubs at the turn of the century signals one way women created offshoots from colleges and universities. Reform movements grabbed women's attention and their energies: temperance, suffrage, prison and moral reform, and any number of activist causes allowed women these opportunities for self-education and leadership. In the nineteenth century, these movements often took the place of absent collegiate education. Women like Elizabeth Cady Stanton, Frances Willard, Harriet Beecher Stowe, and Margaret Fuller preceded the era of widespread collegiate education, yet they established vital careers as informal educators through their writing and activism. In the Progressive Era, when women generally had experienced more formal education, the counter-institutions led to new careers and new agencies, such as the development of social work through women's efforts, the influence and reach of settlement houses, and the establishment of national government agencies like the Women's Bureau and the Children's Bureau.[40] In describing the pre-academy era, Solomon attends to some of these efforts. However, a full story of women's education might find these vibrant informal settings just as significant as the formal educational institutions where women were so long resisted.[41]

Geraldine Jonçich Clifford, who has studied both the history of teachers and of women in coeducational institutions, worried that writing women's history through the lens of access focuses historians too heavily on a story of victimization. She lamented a dedication to writing the history of the "education of women" and urged instead claiming the mainstream for women by writing the history of "women in education." Thus Clifford would ask, "How did the presence of women make a difference in colleges and universities? What did their presence pay for? speed up? permit?" She explained, for example, that the dominant historical paradigm of colleges developing into universities coincided with the growth of coeducation, yet the two phenomena are usually treated separately.[42] Lawrence Veysey and Roger Geiger, for example, wrote histories of the growth of research universities in which women seldom were mentioned; gender held little significance in their stories.[43] Coeducation, when attended to at all, usually appears in histories of women's education either as their push for access or their challenge to prevailing academic cultures.[44]

Clifford wondered how the story might change if the two were intertwined. She noted early challenges, especially in the Midwest and West, to using state funds for higher education when the elementary and grammar schools were still needy. The study of women's entry into teaching shows that women's consistent use of colleges to prepare as teachers ameliorated public sentiment about the use of tax money for collegiate training. Because of women's clear use of higher education as a road to teaching, that sector was able to assert its claim as a useful public benefit.[45]

Clifford also suggested that women influenced institutions they did not attend. Citing the sector of prestigious men's colleges that resisted the inclusion of women the longest, she explained that the Ivy League and other men's colleges were allowed to craft their own specialized education for men, "capturing a constituency" and becoming renowned as the most elite of educational sites until the final push for coeducation in the late 1960s brought women into their midst. Further, looking at the absence of women in southern colleges and universities might explain how those institutions lagged behind many of the larger public institutions when growth occurred in the decades after the Civil War. As both Clifford and historian of southern education Bashaw explained, southern institutions were among the only ones not to coeducate after the Civil War, clinging to their antebellum single-sex focus. Had they proceeded with coeducation, like the premier institutions in the Midwest, southern colleges might have grown more rapidly into the mainstream of higher education.[46]

This notion of women's influence even where they were physically absent challenges Solomon's focus on access, as does the development of counter-institutions outside the educational panoply. Generally, however, historians of women's higher education have tended to follow Solomon's lead, looking first to issues of access and only more rarely at a different way of reconceptualizing the history.

Influence of Outside Agencies

The lack of wider historical context in *In the Company of Educated Women* appears most strikingly in the absence of a discussion of how outside agencies — especially the federal government, foundations, and accrediting agencies — influenced the development of higher education. Perhaps focusing so tightly on the specific issues of women and their access to collegiate institutions steered Solomon away from examining some important other factors that affected the way institutions grew and oriented their missions, programs, and clientele. Although these agencies seldom targeted women's issues directly, they nonetheless affected women as a share of higher education participants. Solomon might have argued that her book never promised a full history of higher education, but her overlooking of governmental and nongovernmental influences has not encouraged historians of women to investigate these potent sources of influence.

The federal government played a fairly quiet role in higher education until after World War II, when the G.I. Bill of Rights, the expansion of federal financial aid, and the explosion of research dollars poured money into colleges and universities. Yet before 1945, both the Morrill Land Grant Acts (1862 and 1890) and the Smith-Hughes Act for vocational education (1917) provided new funds and new missions that shaped the development of many collegiate institutions. Solomon did note the importance of the land grant acts for creating large public institutions, and she mentions the struggles women had with opportunities for vocational education. But the real significance of the land grant institutions in the lives of women students and faculty members has been underestimated in traditional stories of higher education. As Clifford noted, the use of public money after the Civil War for widening the purview of higher education caused initial skepticism. Although Justin Morrill and his congressional colleagues had deemed colleges and universities an appropriate site for federal largesse to improve "the industrial, military, and mechanical arts," those institutions lagged well behind the federal funding in actually producing new scientific and agricultural research. Once the pump was primed, however, universities eventually expanded and began attending to the service needs of the nation. Although women took less advantage of some land grant university curricula (whether by choice or by force), they certainly flocked to both the home economics and teacher-training departments of these public institutions.

Likewise, the Smith-Hughes Act pumped money into vocational education, primarily at the secondary school level. Although generally an initiative that affected the schools, two facts about the use of federal vocational education funds bear on women's role in higher education. First, women pursued high school training more frequently than men, pushing especially into commercial education programs (and virtually ignoring attempts to "vocationalize" housework in the curriculum), increasing their overall access and participation in education. Second, the success of vocational education in the secondary schools prompted their growth into comprehensive high school institutions, which in turn allowed higher education to differentiate itself more clearly from high schooling and to offer more "tracks" of its own to increasing numbers of high school graduates. Since these developments affected the growth of colleges and universities (for instance, allowing them to eliminate their longstanding preparatory programs for ill-prepared entering students), it would appear that early federal influence in fact helped direct both the course of higher education and women's participation.[47]

Certainly, the more obvious governmental influences of the post–World War II era — the G.I. Bill, financial aid legislation, and research support — affected women both directly and indirectly, despite Solomon's relative inattention to these effects. The G.I. Bill was never intended as an educational effort; its primary concern was to ease the return of veterans into the job market and, secondarily, to reward them for wartime service. Women vets were equally eligible for provisions, and in fact used the bill in proportions equal to their military participation — about 3 percent.[48] However, the G.I. Bill produced an interesting unexpected consequence that reduced women's role on campuses. During the war, women's participation in higher education had soared, with so many college-age men in the service. The steady presence of women as students sustained many colleges that would otherwise have closed for lack of paying customers. Wartime women students also proved themselves capable of running campus organizations and providing academic leadership, both on the student and faculty levels. In fact, many restrictions against women that were relaxed during the pressures of wartime permanently opened doors after the crisis ended. At Harvard University, for example, wartime women students integrated classes with men for the first time; without these female students, numbers would have been too small to continue. After the war, Radcliffe women retained the right of shared classes, echoing a development on other campuses around the country. Hunter College, the largest women's college in the world in the 1930s, permanently adopted coeducation after experimenting with G.I. Bill male students. Yet, generally, women's high participation as students and their enhanced leadership roles diminished with the influx of male veterans, leading to a decade-long decline in women's participation as both students and faculty. In a nation eager to return to perceived normalcy, women's continued press for an enhanced presence in academe fell by the wayside.

The availability of financial aid and research dollars offers divergent stories of impact on women. Financial aid — especially in its consolidated form in the 1965 Higher Education Act — served women well, allowing their increased attendance at traditional colleges as well as in continuing education and community colleges. However, the increase in federal research dollars failed to enhance women's opportunities for advanced training, a story seldom told in the discussions of the growth of research universities. Research schools stand atop the academic hierarchy, but represent the very institutions where women have been least visible. Only with Rossiter's work on academic scientists in the United States have historians begun to look at how women were excluded or limited in the distribution of funds and fellowships that would have produced research scientists and scholars.[49]

Since the turn of the twentieth century, both private foundations and regional accrediting boards have affected the direction of higher education, yet the effect of their policies on women has hardly been studied. Here is a prominent area where, as Clifford suggested, the integrated involvement of women in higher education should be examined, rather than requiring a separate study of women's educational history. The Carnegie Foundation for the Advancement of Teaching, for example, affected higher education at several points. In the 1910s, their inducement of a large pension fund for penurious faculty members affected the way that various institutions planned and organized their curricula, their faculties, and their degree programs. Several institutions chose to abandon denominational affiliations in order to qualify for Carnegie funds; others enhanced library and curricular offerings in designated areas. Accrediting boards had the same effect later in the century, often pushing institutions seeking their imprimatur to develop research-oriented Ph.D. programs and to send more of their own faculty on for advanced training. With no governmental or system-wide force pushing on higher education, the foundations and accreditation agencies stepped in to exert a heavy hand on institutions, pushing and prodding them to upgrade facilities, curricula, and personnel.[50]

Women were seldom valued in these enhancements, and female institutions and programs either fell behind or were more clearly placed outside the increasingly obvious mainstream. One female organization, the American Association of University Women (AAUW), followed the accrediting boards' approach, using its own public list of approved colleges to exert the same push for upgraded facilities and training on some women's campuses. Later, the AAUW also tried to embarrass certain coeducational institutions by calling public attention to their low numbers of women faculty and trustees, although the effort produced only mild results.[51] Women, of course, were not the only population to suffer in the push for bigger and better resources. Black colleges and Catholic institutions faced the same pressures, with their leaders sometimes having to decide how to shunt money into developing only certain schools, knowing that others would fill a different, more generalist role.[52] The story of how foundations and agencies affected higher education's development has most often been told as a shining tale of producing a worthy elite; less frequently has it been examined for its overall effect on the system and its various populations.

New Areas for Research

Any discussion of the most promising or underdeveloped areas of historical research in women's higher education risks the same critique that we are applying to Solomon's work. That is, we ask here whether Solomon's conceptual framework may have directed research into certain paths and whether her lack of attention to other areas may have limited subsequent historians' inquiry. By singling out the following areas, I may be guilty of the same judgments for which I challenge her. Nonetheless, I would like to suggest three areas of historical research in women's higher education that seem particularly promising at this moment, especially for asking new questions of old issues and for focusing attention on women whose collegiate stories have been too long quiet. The three include: 1) as discussed above, a wider focus on institutions significant in women's educational development, especially the academies and normal schools; 2) attention to women's development as educated professionals, especially as academics; and 3) increased attention to marginalized populations of women and their participation in higher education, including African American, Latina, Asian American, and Native American women. Although this third area of racial and ethnic concerns should not be separated out from the wider study of women's higher education, doing so here provides an opportunity to focus appropriately on new work. Work in all these areas remains surprising small; in some the literature is growing; in others, the field remains relatively open.

Range of Institutions

In this article, I have already examined historians' recently expanded attention to normal schools and academies within the panoply of women's institutions. After a long period of neglect where historians assumed easy explanations for the role and clientele of these schools, scholars are now claiming them as significant players, rather than as aberrant non-colleges with little impact on higher education's long-term development. Perhaps because both institutions were frequently female dominated, normal schools and academies have been treated as stepsisters in most traditional educational histories. And, because these schools generally did not connect to the most prestigious women's colleges, educational histories of women have often ignored their influence as well.[53] Yet, if historians heed Clifford's call to integrate women's educational participation into the historical mainstream, these institutions will assume a more prominent role in the overall story. Ogren, Thornburg, Alpern, Beadie, Tolley, and Nash are beginning this work by regenerating interest in these institutions and also by examining the marginalized populations of women who turned to these less prestigious institutions for their advanced education.

By adding fuller discussions of both normal schools and academies, higher education can be studied more accurately as a flexible system or a set of options rather than a hierarchy. As Herbst showed, the midwestern version of normal schools assumed a very different form than the earliest versions in the Northeast. Likewise, from curricular and career standpoints, early academies and seminaries sometimes functioned more like colleges than many colleges did. By not integrating all these institutions into our studies, we stratify the system more than is necessary.[54]

Women as Academic Professionals

Barbara Solomon's book enriched the usual story of higher education by trying to connect women's post-collegiate lives to their collegiate preparation. The work draws criticism, however, for her lack of connecting women's professional pursuits to wider concerns of U.S. society. Although research on women as professionals is still young, some efforts are extending Solomon's ideas and providing a rich new base.[55] The strongest and most comprehensive — in many ways the model for such investigations — is Rossiter's two-volume study of women scientists in America. Exhaustively researched and carefully presented, Rossiter explores the history of science as an endeavor, as a curriculum, and as a career. While using women's experience as the organizing principle, she also investigates the fuller practice of science and compares men's and women's opportunities, preparation, and progress. Although it covers more than higher education, Rossiter's work belongs in higher education history for two reasons. First, she examines women's preparation for science careers within colleges, universities, and graduate schools, noting, for example, the difficulties experienced by women's colleges in supporting expensive laboratories. And, even when she traces women scientists in a host of non-academic job settings, Rossiter cites their collegiate preparation and experiences. Second, she devotes considerable and careful attention to women academic scientists, exploring the experience of women professors at small women's colleges as well as at large public institutions. She fulfills some of the promise that Solomon, Patricia Graham, and Susan Carter had hoped for by explicating the career issues for faculty women at coeducational universities. Overall, Rossiter concludes that women scientists were unable to capitalize on or sustain research and career opportunities over time; their advances in wartime, for example, were withdrawn or evaporated when men reasserted control of funding and research agendas.[56]

A new project that follows Rossiter's lead by studying the universe of women in one profession is Mary Ann Dzuback's focus on women academic social scientists from 1890 to 1940. Like Rossiter, Dzuback's self-created data base of faculty women allows her to study patterns of training, employment, career persistence, and accomplishment over time. Similar to Rossiter, who found enclaves of academic women who perpetuated their work by hiring their own students, Dzuback has observed how certain collegiate departments proved receptive and supportive to women social scientists, while many more continued to ostracize or ignore women academics. Dzuback's research in the economics department at Berkeley, for example, finds that the presence of one or two women faculty members, joined by the support of a few influential male colleagues, could sustain women's participation in the face of wider university ambivalence. Her research stresses ways in which women's activities "transgressed" the boundaries that had been assigned to them in academe, claiming "space" and access for their work.[57]

Palmieri, although drawing a tighter circle around the group she studies, has also presented an in-depth examination of a group of academic women, revealing strong connections between the work lives of one campus group and the wider society that affected women's opportunities. Palmieri's study of the female faculty community at Wellesley College between the 1880s and 1920 is noteworthy for its expansive coverage of these women's home lives, career preparation, and subsequent faculty work. Because Wellesley, more than some of the other women's colleges, challenged tradition by sustaining an all-female faculty, Palmieri is able to examine a women's setting that was both consciously separate from the mainstream and desirous of partaking in its scholarly opportunities. Palmieri succeeds especially well in demonstrating links between the faculty members' own training, their personal commitments to progressive causes, and their use of these commitments in their own classrooms.[58]

Rossiter, Dzuback, and Palmieri lead the present study of women academics' lives. Except for Rossiter, whose time period extends to 1972, little historical work has yet been produced on more recent faculty women (or, more generally, on women's higher education in the post–World War II era). My own ongoing study of various institutional efforts at gender equity in the 1950s and 1960s should fill a gap by looking at how advocates for women used philanthropy and special programs to build an array of structures to support women. The fellowship programs, research centers, and women's studies departments that these advocates created after 1960 sparked and later sustained women faculty's stronger movement into the academic mainstream.[59]

Much of the recent work that advances understanding of women as professionals appears via biography, both on women as faculty and as educational leaders. Biography, of course, has long been a staple of discussions on educated Americans' lives. However, feminist research and new approaches to writing women's biographies have generated thoughtful new work that expands our understanding of the role of education in women's lives.[60]

For example, in addition to work on women as faculty members and school leaders, scholars are beginning to examine women teachers' lives, finding a more complex picture of their career and leadership opportunities than previously assumed. Since the teaching profession long absorbed the bulk of women's college and normal school graduates, it deserves attention in studies of women's higher education. Yet teaching — numerically dominated by women but headed by influential men — was often judged a feminized "semi-profession" and suffered in attention when scholars turned to the more egregious fights for access to the traditional male fields of law, medicine, and business.

Recent work emphasizes teachers as actors in their own career decisions, rather than as functionaries subject to male leadership. Kathleen Weiler has investigated the range of career opportunities pursued by female teachers in California, reinvigorating the leadership role of county superintendent that allowed women considerable flexibility and autonomy in wide geographic and functional settings.[61] Kate Rousmaniere, whose interests include teachers' roles in union work, studies New York City teachers' preparation, activity, and progress.[62] Ruth Markowitz also focuses on New York teachers, with particular attention to how ethnicity influenced the lives of women teachers.[63] Turning to a particular type of teacher, Barbara Beatty explores how preschool teachers developed their profession from a vantage point outside the traditional school and college mainstream. In her examination of the development of preschool education, Beatty argues that over the course of the twentieth century, leaders of the kindergarten and preschool movements pushed colleges and normal schools to include child development and kindergarten training among the options available to women teachers.[64]

Jo Ann Preston's work on the feminization of the teaching profession connects the first two areas of new research: challenging the notion of an academic hierarchy and studying women as educated professionals. She examines the sites of women's preparation for teaching, comparing the preparation available at normal schools vs. academies. Preston suggests that academies and seminaries provided more liberal arts oriented training than did the normal schools, provoking her belief that subsequent teacher education (including its current organization) suffered from the direction sparked by the normal approach. Preston doubts that normals very often provided the kind of real advanced preparation that Ogren discovered, although she continues to find both settings dedicated to the needs of female students.[65]

These studies exemplify the connections of women's collegiate training to the wider sweep of social issues surrounding and sometimes limiting them. Whereas Solomon, and Newcomer before her, kept their lenses focused on women's lives within collegiate settings, recent authors are drawing parallels between what women students and leaders sought for female academic training, the actual career opportunities that faced women as graduates, and the structural issues that affected women's development.

Diverse Populations

Recent scholarship has begun to disaggregate the groups of women who participated in higher education, examining the specific experiences of racial, ethnic, and religious groups who sometimes formed separate institutions and sometimes pushed for a place within the mainstream. Historians have not yet, however, integrated this work into the overall story of women's higher education, causing it to remain a patchwork of secondary material awaiting a synthesis or broader framework, or appearing as appendages to wider histories in the way that Solomon wrote. Like the populations it discusses, this scholarship has too frequently been allowed by historians to sit at the periphery of traditional history.

Linda Perkins, whose work appears in this Symposium, stands as one of the most thorough scholars of African American women's role in higher education. Perkins's particular contribution lies in explicating the situation both for women at historically Black colleges, where they often competed with men, and at predominantly White institutions, where they were tolerated, but rarely welcomed. In earlier work, Perkins highlighted the dilemma faced by many African American women in the nineteenth century as they confronted the "cult of true womanhood" and its prescriptions for femininity. In the early to middle part of that century, "true womanhood" idealized women's purity and domesticity, generating a constellation of expectations that did not especially encourage women's pursuit of a useful education. Perkins explained how believers in such notions virtually omitted Black women because of strong racial prejudices that defied ever seeing these women as pure. Yet when African American women nonetheless persisted in their own Black colleges, their contributions were eventually downplayed by African American men, who needed to bolster their sense of men's contribution to "race uplift." Black women were doubly disadvantaged, then: they were excluded from White opportunities and devalued in Black settings where they had made initial progress.[66] As Perkins shows in her new study, African American women continued to navigate these difficult waters, slowly making inroads in the predominantly White settings and asserting their place in Black colleges.

Scholars are beginning to reassess Black women's role in the famous debate between Booker T. Washington and W.E.B. DuBois that frequently characterizes — and sometimes limits — the presentation of early twentieth-century African American educational history. Generally, historians assume that Black educational philosophy veered between the economic self-help focus of Washington (with its careful dependence on White philanthropy and its attendant demands) and the seemingly more virile declaration of DuBois's professional and classical training. Women were presumed to follow one or the other of these approaches, depending on predilection, opportunity, or connection to one of the major figures. Scholars have recently begun to look more deeply at the separate institutions created and sustained by female African American school founders, discovering that these women borrowed from both educational camps, depending on need and opportunity. Kathleen C. Berkeley and Ann S. Chirhart focus on Black southern school leaders, noting that when finances, curriculum, or other needs dictated, they could bend their missions to meet the needs of their clientele, sometimes professing vocational and classical training for women at the same time. These studies complicate the view not only of Black educational history, but also of women's role within it. As such, they serve as models of how adding women more purposefully into overall educational history clarifies the story.[67]

Women of other racial and ethnic groups have, as yet, received less concerted attention from historians of higher education. Developing work on Hispanic American, Asian American, and Native American women generally limits its focus to the schools where, arguably, the basics of the story need first to be investigated.[68]

Victoria-María MacDonald has surveyed educational historians' work on Hispanic Americans, noting three successive stages of analysis: pre-1960, characterized by use of anthropological perspectives on conditions of schooling; the 1960s and 1970s, featuring politically charged work responding to the Chicano movement, but which also benefited from a more sophisticated understanding of ethnic differences in uses of schooling; and the present, examining the political goals and activities of Hispanic American communities in their pursuit of self-efficacy.[69] Specific attention to women in these general histories is sporadic, however. As MacDonald explains: "The educational history of Hispanic American women occupies a nebulous position between the few works which examine the history of schooling for Hispanic Americans and the post-1970s flowering of scholarship on the history of women. Consequently, researchers . . . must seek information from widely scattered articles."[70] Looking specifically at higher education produces little from a historical perspective. Raymond Padilla and Rudolfo Chavez's *The Leaning Ivory Tower* and Felix Padilla's *The Struggle of Latino/a University Students* address Latinas in the higher education setting, but their work has a more contemporary than historical focus.[71]

Similar issues arise in the historical study of Asian American women. Work is beginning on Asian Americans in separate schools and "mixed" schools, but the majority of this work neither specifically extricates women's experience nor examines higher education. Historian Eileen Tamura has written on the experience of the Nisei generation of Japanese Americans in Hawaii, but once again the focus is on schooling rather than higher education. The same is true for Thomas James's *Exile Within: The Schooling of Japanese Americans 1942–1945*, a study of the educational experience in the World War II relocation camps.[72] As with Latinas, much prominent work on Asian American experiences in higher education considers current concerns, such as those gathered in the strong anthology by Don T. Nakanishi and Tina

Yamano Nishida.[73] As Sucheng Chan reminds us, the Chinese Exclusion Laws of the 1880s and other restrictive immigration quotas until 1943 eliminated most Asian women's early opportunities in the United States.[74] Asian women's participation in higher education was severely hampered by the long-term effects of these restrictions, perhaps explaining the focus on recent collegiate experience in much of the historical scholarship.

Native American women have received attention in recent years, both for their part in general educational histories of Native Americans and in a few separate studies on women. Scholars Ardy Bowker, David DeJong, Devon Mihesuah, David Wallace Adams, and Tsianina Lomawaima have examined the education of Indians, the last two from the perspective of the boarding school experience.[75] Adams, in his prize-winning study of how Indians were "educated for extinction," includes some attention to how cross-cultural gender expectations figured in the White leaders' plans for providing assimilative education to Native American girls and boys. Mihesuah's work offers the deepest focus on women in one actual institution. These works, however, treat pre-collegiate schooling, which was often the highest level available to most Native Americans; the tribal colleges that grew after the 1960s have yet to be the focus of much historical work.[76]

Catholic women reveal a long and influential history in higher education, with religious teaching orders responsible for founding scores of colleges for women beginning in 1895. Beyond institutional histories, the overall experience of Catholic collegiate women or religious teachers remains relatively unexamined by educational historians. A few works, including those by Eileen Mary Brewer, Barbara Misner, and Nikola Baumgarten, focus on religious women, emphasizing the opportunities for education, community-building, and leadership offered to Catholic women who chose convent life.[77] Generally, however, scholars are just beginning to examine the historical experience of Catholic collegians either in separate institutions or as contenders within mainstream higher education. Philip Gleason, for example, traces the ongoing Catholic effort to respond to changing collegiate missions, curricula, and values; Kathleen Mahoney studies Catholics who entered the collegiate mainstream. This tendency of Catholic youth to "drift" into nondenominational colleges caused great concern among Catholic leaders, who disagreed over the virtues of separatism or engagement for Catholics in American life, a theme explored by both Mahoney and Gleason.[78] Mary Oates's anthology of primary and secondary historical sources remains the single best work on Catholic collegiate women, but it does not assume an analytical focus, leaving this population awaiting fuller explication.[79]

Conclusion

In the twenty-five years that elapsed between Newcomer's and her own synthesis of women's higher education history, Barbara Solomon benefited from an explosion of educational studies. Lawrence Cremin led the way for seeing education as a whole array of learning opportunities beyond but in-cluding formal schooling where men, women, and children learned about life, scholarship, and culture.[80] Such an approach clearly created more room for women than in earlier, school-based histories. At the same time, histori-ans of women's lives began to look at how women used their "separate sphere" of influence in areas like religion, reform work, teaching, and do-mestic life.

Solomon infused her work with new scholarship from these areas, but it was the story of women's push for access into collegiate institutions that most captured her attention, perhaps because it best demonstrated women's con-certed work in claiming a place in one important part of mainstream U.S. culture. The story of access is clearly vital; we need a record of women's initial entry and subsequent participation in various fields and institutions. We also need, as Solomon recognized and provided as far as possible, a disaggregated record that shows how women of different racial, ethnic, re-ligious, and social-class backgrounds experienced and instigated the push for equal treatment.

In taking a long view, Solomon proposed a generational breakdown to understand how and where women pushed for educational equity. She di-vided her study among the antebellum era, the late-nineteenth and turn-of-the-twentieth centuries, and the post–World War II period, describing in-stitutions, clientele, curriculum, and purposes as they developed for the women of each era. Through this framework, Solomon could differentiate, for example, the experience of middle-class White women from that of Black women, finding a clear difference between available opportunities and ease of access. The discussion by era also enabled her to focus on institutions like the normal schools, academies, and women's colleges that established prece-dents and prospered in certain eras, only to be superseded by subsequent developments.

Some of Solomon's approaches and conclusions may, however, have nudged later historians into following her lead rather than asking different questions sooner about women's role and contributions in a wider array of settings. Although she likely did not intend such a focus, Solomon produced a book that gives prominence to women's colleges, even as she calls for more attention to normal schools and public institutions. She also underestimates the influence of outside agencies such as the government and accrediting bodies on the development of higher education. Most of these emphases, however, resulted from the lack of secondary material available to Solomon when she wrote a history designed to synthesize and organize the scholarship on women in higher education.

Current scholars can hope that, with unceasing attention to women's his-tory and to the histories of previously "marginal" groups, there will not be such a long wait for another re-crafting of the story of women's participation. However, higher education as a whole has been awaiting an equivalent syn-thesis for three decades. Most scholars continue to start with the 1960s his-tories created by Frederick Rudolph and Laurence Veysey for the fullest explications of how higher education developed from the colonial period to the present. Some recent and excellent work has studied particular segments of the collegiate enterprise, offering the new raw material for an updated historical synthesis. Roger Geiger has revised Veysey's story of the development of the research university, attending more to outside influences and research activities than to Veysey's more philosophical study. And, in a scheme reminiscent of Solomon's discussion of women, he has presented the history of higher education through "generational" characteristics produced in knowledge, constituents, and purposes.[81] David Levine has examined changes in higher education between the two World Wars, finding that interwar period to be a significant time for the growth of the business-college connection.[82] Ellen Schrecker has studied the effect of McCarthyism and its era on the collegiate enterprise.[83] Bruce Leslie has focused on changes in faculty life, including the impact of professionalization on prestige and pay.[84]

These studies, plus scores of smaller-scale monographs, have not yet produced a reworking of the American story of higher education, let alone one that includes the considerable strong work on women and diverse populations. Yet if ambitious historians heed Geraldine Clifford's call, the next synthesis will no longer find separate chapters on "the education of women" (à la Rudolph) or scattered index references to African American women or Hispanic Americans as students and faculty. These individual contributions seem not yet ready to cohere into a fuller story that blends the variety of populations, institutions, and purposes of U.S. higher education. One key to such a blending, however, may be to diminish the focus on separatism and access while still honoring the efforts of women and others to assert their place in traditional academe. Solomon's invitation to travel "in the company of educated women" may offer a guide for incorporating both new and familiar territories into a reconfigured map.

Notes

1. Barbara Miller Solomon, *In the Company of Educated Women: A History of Women and Higher Education in America* (New Haven: Yale University Press, 1985); Mabel Newcomer, *A Century of Higher Education for American Women* (New York: Harper, 1959). Barbara Miller Solomon, who died in 1992, was a senior lecturer in American history and literature at Harvard University for much of her career. Through her advocacy of women's history, which included directing the Radcliffe library now known as the Schlesinger Library on the History of Women in America, Solomon influenced the establishment of women's studies at Harvard. She also held posts as associate dean at Radcliffe and assistant dean at Harvard.

2. Solomon, *In the Company of Educated Women*, p. xvii.

3. Normal schools were institutions dedicated to teacher training that began in the United States in the late 1830s. Because they frequently offered students a review of elementary material before they extended a second or a third year of pedagogical training, these institutions have not always been considered "higher education." Similarly, academies and seminaries predated collegiate education in the eighteenth and nineteenth centuries. Many of these latter institutions arguably offered curricula equal to some of the early colleges.

4. The panel was convened by the author at the annual meeting of the American Educational Research Association in San Francisco in April 1995, as "Ten Years after a Classic: Historical

Research and Teaching on Women's Higher Education a Decade after Barbara Solomon." Panelists included Carolyn Terry Bashaw, Geraldine Jonçich Clifford, Patricia Palmieri, Linda Perkins, Sally Schwager, Linda Eisenmann, and Mary Ann Dzuback (chair). Although the present article had its genesis in the panel, it extends the discussion and, except where noted, represents my own thinking on Barbara Solomon's book and its impact on the writing of women's higher educational history.

5. Patricia Palmieri, comments made at "Ten Years after a Classic."

6. For a discussion of how women scholars of higher education in the 1950s failed to connect women's status with wider societal issues, see Margaret Rossiter, "Outmaneuvered Again — The Collapse of Academic Women's Strategy of Celibate Overachievement," Paper presented at the Berkshire Conference of Women's Historians, Vassar College, June 1993; and Linda Eisenmann, "Befuddling the 'Feminine Mystique': Academic Women and the Creation of the Radcliffe Institute, 1950–1965," *Educational Foundations, 10* (1996), 5–26.

7. Emilie J. Hutchinson, *Women and the Ph.D.: Facts from the Experiences of 1,025 Women Who Have Taken the Degree of Doctor of Philosophy Since 1877,* Institute of Women's Professional Relations, Bulletin No. 2 (Greensboro: North Carolina College for Women, 1929), and Jeanne L. Noble, *The Negro Woman's College Education* (New York: Teachers College Press, 1956).

8. Karen Blair, *The Clubwoman as Feminist: True Womanhood Redefined, 1868–1914* (New York: Holmes and Meier, 1980).

9. Nancy F. Cott, *The Bonds of Womanhood: "Woman's Sphere" in New England, 1780–1835* (New Haven: Yale University Press, 1977).

10. Jill Ker Conway, "Perspectives on the History of Women's Education in the United States," *History of Education Quarterly, 14,* No. 1 (1974), 1–12.

11. Allmendinger produced provocative work in the 1970s on poor students — both male and female — who used scholarships or other support to attend college. Interestingly, Solomon cites only Allmendinger's piece on women, ignoring his wider study of collegiate students. See David F. Allmendinger, *Paupers and Scholars: The Transformation of Student Life in Nineteenth-Century America* (New York: St. Martin's Press, 1975), and David F. Allmendinger, "Mount Holyoke Students Encounter the Need for Life-Planning, 1837–1850, *History of Education Quarterly, 19* (1979), 27–47.

12. Barbara Miller Solomon, *Ancestors and Immigrants: A Changing New England Tradition* (Cambridge, MA: Harvard University Press, 1956); Sally Schwager, "Ten Years after a Classic."

13. "After college what?" was a question asked by many individuals and authors as women and men considered their post-collegiate career and family opportunities, especially in the late nineteenth century. Helen Starrett encapsulated the concerns in her pamphlet "After College What? For Girls" in 1896. Joyce Antler used the notion to explore the competing senses of duty faced by college women graduates around the turn of the century; see "'After College What?' New Graduates and the Family Claim," *American Quarterly, 32* (1980), 409–435.

   For a discussion of the importance of studying differences between college students' "origins" and their "destinations," see Roger L. Geiger, "The Historical Matrix of American Higher Education," *History of Higher Education Annual, 12* (1992), 7–28.

14. Solomon, *In the Company of Educated Women,* p. xviii.

15. Frederick Rudolph, *The American College and University: A History* (New York: Vintage, 1962). Rudolph was the first educational historian to integrate residential life, athletics, and extracurricular activities into his discussion of collegiate effectiveness.

16. I am grateful to historian Harold Wechsler for raising this question of how to consider the legacy of Solomon's book.

17. Patricia Albjerg Graham, "So Much to Do: Guides for Historical Research on Women in Higher Education," *Teachers College Record, 76* (1975), 421–440. The figure for coeducation is cited in Newcomer, *A Century of Higher Education,* p. 49.

18. Susan B. Carter, "Academic Women Revisited: An Empirical Study of Changing Patterns in Women's Employment as College and University Faculty, 1890–1963," *Journal of Social History, 14* (1981), 675–699.

19. Solomon, *In the Company of Educated Women*, p. 208.
20. Several of the Seven Sister colleges supported women either as faculty or presidents. Among them, only Wellesley College sustained an all-female faculty and presidency for a substantial period of time. Vassar and Smith colleges, for example, both opened with male presidents.
21. Patricia A. Palmieri, *In Adamless Eden: The Community of Women Faculty at Wellesley* (New Haven, CT: Yale University Press, 1995); Margaret Rossiter, *Women Scientists in America: Struggles and Strategies to 1940* (Baltimore: Johns Hopkins University Press, 1982), and Margaret Rossiter, *Women Scientists in America: Before Affirmative Action, 1940–1972* (Baltimore: Johns Hopkins University Press, 1995).
22. Patricia Graham first called attention to the fact that women's participation in higher education had, in fact, peaked in the 1920s, only to fall over subsequent decades. Women's percentage of all undergraduates was 47 percent in 1920, 43 percent in 1930, 40 percent in 1940, and 31 percent in 1950. From there, the percentage began a slow climb. Women now constitute the majority in higher education. Patricia Albjerg Graham, "Expansion and Exclusion: A History of Women in American Higher Education," *Signs: Journal of Women in Culture and Society, 3* (1978), 759–773.
23. Solomon, *In the Company of Educated Women*, p. 208.
24. Johann Pestalozzi (1746–1827) was a Swiss-born educator whose ideas greatly influenced the early American normal schools. Pestalozzi believed in the power of love and nurturance as a way to influence children's behavior (thus eliminating the reliance on corporal punishment), and he advocated women as "natural" teachers of children. Much of his pedagogy replicated maternal instruction, suggesting the use of common household objects in his practical modes of teaching. Only after education of the senses could reason be exercised, he argued. See Jürgen Herbst, *And Sadly Teach: Teacher Education and Professionalization in American Culture* (Madison: University of Wisconsin Press, 1989) for a full discussion.
25. Herbst, *And Sadly Teach*.
26. John I. Goodlad, Roger Soder, and Kenneth A. Sirotnik, *Places Where Teachers Are Taught* (San Francisco: Jossey-Bass, 1990).
27. Donald R. Warren, *American Teachers: Histories of a Profession at Work* (New York: Macmillan, 1989).
28. Christine A. Ogren, "Where Coeds Were Coeducated: Normal Schools in Wisconsin, 1870–1920," *History of Education Quarterly, 35* (1995), 1–26; Christine A. Ogren, "Education for Women in the United States: The State Normal School Experience, 1870–1920," Diss., University of Wisconsin, 1996; Laura Docter Thornburg, "Rewriting the History of Teacher Education through the Life of the Woman Teacher: A Case of Julia Anne King and the Michigan State Normal School," Paper presented at the annual meeting of the History of Education Society, Toronto, Canada, October 1996; Mary Alpern, "A Successful Experiment in Teacher Education: The Founding and the Early Years of the Albany Normal School," Diss., Cornell University, 1996.
29. Anne Firor Scott, "The Ever-Widening Circle: The Diffusion of Feminist Values from the Troy Female Seminary, 1822–1872," *History of Education Quarterly, 19* (1979), 3–25.
30. Margaret A. Nash, "'A Salutary Rivalry': The Growth of Higher Education for Women in Oxford, Ohio, 1855–1867," *History of Higher Education Annual, 16* (1996), 21–37.
31. Nancy Beadie, "Defining the Public: Congregation, Commerce, and Social Economy in the Formation of the Educational System, 1790–1840," Diss., Syracuse University, 1989; Nancy Beadie, "Emma Willard's Idea Put to the Test: The Consequences of State Support of Female Education in New York, 1819–67," *History of Education Quarterly, 33*, No. 4 (1993), 543–562.
32. Kimberley Tolley, "The Science Education of American Girls, 1784-1932," Diss., University of California, Berkeley, 1996; Kimberley Tolley, "Science for Ladies, Classics for Gentlemen: A Comparative Analysis of Scientific Subjects in the Curricula of Boys' and Girls' Secondary Schools in the United States, 1794–1850," *History of Education Quarterly, 36* (1996), 129–154.
33. The issue of "difference" divided feminists early in the century and raises concerns among them now, as well. In the 1910s, in the struggles over the Equal Rights Amendment and

protective labor legislation, some feminists believed that women's differences should allow them differential treatment and protection, for example, for limits on the number of hours they could be forced to work or prohibitions against certain dangerous work settings. ERA advocates, on the other hand, pushed for equal treatment. The debate plays out among modern scholars, too, with some suggesting that women are different in their approach to morality or to learning, and other feminists concerned about the implications of such findings.

34. Estelle B. Freedman, "Separatism as Strategy: Female Institution Building and American Feminism, 1870–1930," *Feminist Studies*, 5 (1979), 512–529.

35. Linda K. Kerber, "Separate Spheres, Female World, Woman's Place: The Rhetoric of Women's History," *Journal of American History*, 75, No. 1 (1988), 9–37.

36. Polly Welts Kaufman, ed., *The Search for Equity: Women at Brown University, 1891–1991* (Hanover, NH: Brown University Press, 1991).

37. Lynn D. Gordon, "Coeducation on Two Campuses: Berkeley and Chicago, 1890–1912," in *Woman's Being, Woman's Place: Female Identity and Vocation in American History*, ed. Mary Kelly (Boston: G. K. Hall, 1979), pp. 294–317; Lynn D. Gordon, *Gender and Higher Education in the Progressive Era* (New Haven: Yale, 1990).

38. Carolyn Terry Bashaw, "We Who Live 'Off the Edges': Deans of Women at Southern Coeducational Institutions and Access to the Community of Higher Education," Diss., University of Georgia, 1992; Jana Nidiffer, "'More than a Wise and Pious Matron': The Professionalization of the Position of Dean of Women," Diss., Harvard University, 1994; Jana Nidiffer, "From Matron to Maven: A New Role and New Professional Identity for Deans of Women, 1892 to 1916," *Mid-Western Educational Researcher: Special Issue on Midwestern History* (1995), 17–24.

39. Sally Schwager, comments made at "Ten Years after a Classic."

40. For good general discussions of women's roles in these reform movements, see, for example, Gordon, *Gender and Higher Education in the Progressive Era;* Ellen F. Fitzpatrick, *Endless Crusade: Women Social Scientists and Progressive Reform* (New York: Oxford University Press, 1990); Kathryn Kish Sklar, *Florence Kelley and the Nation's Work* (New Haven, CT: Yale University Press, 1995).

41. In creating the *Historical Dictionary of Women's Education in the United States*, I included both formal and informal educational opportunities and organizations, arguing that "women's history has demonstrated that telling the full story of women's participation in American life involves traditional institutions as well as alternate routes" (p. 4). In preparing the dictionary's index, I observed that the informal educational connection appearing most often in all the entries was women's ties to the suffrage movement. Linda Eisenmann, ed., *Historical Dictionary of Women's Education in the United States* (Westport, CT: Greenwood Press, forthcoming).

42. Geraldine Jonçich Clifford, comments made at "Ten Years after a Classic." See also Geraldine Jonçich Clifford, *Equally in View: The University of California, Its Women, and the Schools* (Berkeley, CA: Center for Studies in Higher Education and Institute of Governmental Studies, 1995); and Geraldine Jonçich Clifford, "'Shaking Dangerous Questions from the Crease': Gender and American Higher Education," *Feminist Issues*, 2 (1983), 3–62.

43. Laurence Veysey, *The Emergence of the American University* (Chicago: University of Chicago Press, 1965); Roger Geiger, *To Advance Knowledge: The Growth of American Research Universities, 1900–1940* (New York: Oxford University Press, 1986); Roger Geiger, *Research and Relevant Knowledge: American Research Universities since World War II* (New York: Oxford University Press, 1993).

44. See, for example, Gordon, *Gender and Higher Education in the Progressive Era*.

45. Clifford, comments made at "Ten Years after a Classic."

46. Clifford and Carolyn Terry Bashaw, comments made at "Ten Years after a Classic."

47. For good discussions on the impact of vocational education on women (although they focus primarily on schools, not colleges), see John L. Rury, *Education and Women's Work: Female Schooling and the Division of Labor in Urban America, 1870–1930* (Albany: State University of

New York Press, 1991) and Jane Bernard Powers, *The "Girl Question" in Education: Vocational Education for Young Women in the Progressive Era* (London: Falmer Press, 1992).

48. Keith W. Olson, *The G.I Bill, the Veterans, and the College* (Lexington: University Press of Kentucky, 1974) remains the best source on the origins and impact of the bill.

49. Rossiter, *Women Scientists in America.*

50. On the Carnegie Foundation, see Ellen Condliffe Lagemann, *Private Power for the Public Good: A History of the Carnegie Foundation for the Advancement of Teaching* (Middletown, CT: Wesleyan University Press, 1983). For a good discussion of the effects of one accrediting organization, see Lester F. Goodchild, "The Turning Point in American Jesuit Higher Education: The Standardization Controversy between the Jesuits and the North Central Association, 1915–1940," *History of Higher Education Annual, 6* (1986), 81–116.

51. On the AAUW's role as accreditor, see Marion Talbot and Lois K. Mathews Rosenberry, *The History of the American Association of University Women* (Boston: Houghton Mifflin, 1931); and Susan Levine, *Degrees of Equality: The American Association of University Women and the Challenge of Twentieth-Century Feminism* (Philadelphia: Temple University Press, 1995).

52. For a thorough discussion of the effect of philanthropy on Black institutions, see James D. Anderson, *The Education of Blacks in the South, 1860–1935* (Chapel Hill: University of North Carolina Press, 1988).

53. In fact, some female academies did pave the way for elite women's colleges, although others phased out after decades of academy status. Mount Holyoke College, for example, began as Mount Holyoke Female Seminary in 1837. Interestingly, Mount Holyoke's push for collegiate status — although ultimately quite successful — made it among the last of the Seven Sisters to emerge as a college (1887). The others began as separate collegiate institutions or as "coordinate colleges" attached to older male institutions (e.g., Radcliffe as coordinate with Harvard, Barnard as coordinate with Columbia).

54. As early as Thomas Woody's classic, *A History of Women's Education in the United States,* (New York: Science Press, 1929), scholars recognized that the name of an institution did not always match our assumptions about its curriculum, clientele, or purpose.

55. Although this section primarily describes women as academic professionals, considerable new work is appearing on women in the professions. See, for example, Ellen Fitzpatrick, *Endless Crusade: Women Social Scientist's and Progressive Reform* (New York: Oxford University Press, 1990); Robyn Muncy, *Creating a Female Dominion in American Reform, 1890–1935* (New York: Oxford University Press, 1991); Virginia Drachman, *Women Lawyers and the Origins of Professional Identity in America: The Letters of the Equity Club, 1887 to 1890* (Ann Arbor: University of Michigan Press, 1993); Darlene Clark Hine, *Speak Truth to Power: Black Professional Class in United States History* (Brooklyn, NY: Carlson, 1996); Darlene Clark Hine, *Black Women in White: Racial Conflict and Cooperation in the Nursing Profession, 1890–1950* (Bloomington: Indiana University Press, 1989). For a general overview, see Linda Eisenmann, "Women, Higher Education, and Professionalism: Clarifying the View," *Harvard Educational Review, 66* (1996), 858–873.

56. Rossiter, *Struggles and Strategies* and *Women Scientists in America.*

57. Mary Ann Dzuback, "Women and Social Research at Bryn Mawr College, 1915–1940," *History of Education Quarterly, 33* (1993), 579–608; and Mary Ann Dzuback, "Joining the Ancient and Universal Company of Scholars: Women in Social Science Graduate Study, 1890–1940," Vice-Presidential Address at the annual meeting of the American Educational Research Association, Chicago, March 1997.

58. Palmieri, *In Adamless Eden.*

59. Linda Eisenmann, "Weathering 'A Climate of Unexpectation': Gender Equity and the Radcliffe Institute, 1960–1995," *Academe, 81,* No. 4 (1995), 21–25; and Eisenmann, "Befuddling the Feminine Mystique."

60. Ellen Condliffe Lagermann encouraged a wider approach to recognizing and assessing educational influences, especially in women's lives, with her *A Generation of Women: Education in the Lives of Progressive Reformers* (Cambridge, MA: Harvard University Press, 1979).

61. Kathleen Weiler, "Women and Rural School Reform: California, 1900–1940," *History of Education Quarterly, 34* (1994), 25–47.

62. Kate Rousmaniere, *City Teachers: Teaching and School Reform in Historical Perspective* (New York: Teachers College Press, 1997).

63. Ruth Jacknow Markowitz, *My Daughter, the Teacher: Jewish Teachers in the New York City Schools* (New Brunswick, NJ: Rutgers University Press, 1993).

64. Barbara Beatty, *Preschool Education in America: The Culture of Young Children from the Colonial Era to the Present* (New Haven, CT: Yale University Press, 1995).

65. Jo Anne Preston, "Gender and the Formation of a Women's Profession: The Case of Public School Teaching," in *Gender Inequality at Work,* ed. Jerry A. Jacobs (Thousand Oaks, CA: Sage, 1995); and Jo Anne Preston, "Gender and the Professionalization of School Teaching: An Investigation of Changes in Teacher Education in 19th Century New England," Paper presented at the annual meeting of the American Educational Research Association, Chicago, March 1997.

66. Linda Perkins, "The Impact of the 'Cult of True Womanhood' on the Education of Black Women," *Journal of Social Issues, 39* (1983), 17–28. See also Linda Perkins, "African-American Women and Hunter College, 1873–1945," *The Echo: Journal of the Hunter College Archives* (125th anniversary edition, 1995), 17–25.

67. Kathleen C. Berkeley, "The Sage of Sedalia: Education and Racial Uplift as Reflected in the Career of Charlotte Hawkins Brown, 1883–1961," and Ann S. Chirhart, "'The Rugged Pathway': Beulah Rucker, African American Education, and Modern Culture, 1920–1950," Papers presented at the annual meeting of the History of Education Society, Toronto, October 1996.

68. The terms "Hispanic American," "Asian American," and "American Indian" used here all are general terms for a wide array of people with varied cultural, linguistic, and educational histories. I use them here to represent the widest scope of historical studies.

69. Victoria-María MacDonald, "'Immigrants' or 'Minorities': Exploring the Complex Historiography of Hispanic American Education," Paper presented at the annual meeting of the History of Education Society, Toronto, October 1996.

70. Victoria María MacDonald, "Hispanic American Women's Education," in Eisenmann, *Historical Dictionary of Women's Education in the United States.*

71. Raymond Padilla and Rudolfo Chavez, *The Leaning Ivory Tower: Latino Professors in American Universities* (Albany: State University of New York Press, 1995); Felix M. Padilla, *The Struggle of Latino/a University Students: In Search of a Liberating Education* (New York: Routledge, 1997).

72. Eileen Tamura, "Gender, Schooling, and Teaching, and the Nisei in Hawaii: An Episode in American Immigration History, 1900–1940," *Journal of American Ethnic History, 14,* No. 4 (1995), 3–36; Eileen Tamura, *Americanization, Acculturation, and Ethnic Identity: The Nisei Generation in Hawaii* (Urbana: University of Illinois Press, 1994); Thomas James, *Exile Within: The Schooling of Japanese Americans, 1942–1945* (Cambridge, MA: Harvard University Press, 1987).

73. Don T. Nakanishi and Tina Yamano Nishida, eds., *The Asian American Educational Experience: A Source Book for Teachers and Students* (New York: Routledge, 1995). See, especially, the section "Higher Educational Issues and Experiences: Access, Representation, and Equity." The book offers a good historical section, but none of the four articles focuses on higher education or on women. See also, for current concerns, Joanne Faung and Gean Lee, *Asian American Experiences in the United States: Oral Histories of First to Fourth Generation Americans from China, the Philippines, Japan, Asian India, the Pacific Islands, Vietnam, and Cambodia* (Jefferson, NC: McFarland, 1991).

74. Sucheng Chan, "The Exclusion of Chinese Women," in *Entry Denied: Exclusion and the Chinese Community in America, 1882–1943,* ed. Sucheng Chan (Philadelphia: Temple University Press, 1991), pp. 94–146.

75. Ardy Bowker, *Sisters in the Blood: The Education of Women in Native America* (Bozeman: Montana State University, Center for Bilingual/Multicultural Education, 1993); David De-Jong, *Promises of the Past: A History of Indian Education in the United States* (Golden, CO: North

American Press, 1993); Devon Mihesuah, *Cultivating the Rosebuds: the Education of Women at the Cherokee Female Seminary, 1851–1909* (Urbana: University of Illinois, 1993); David Wallace Adams, *Education for Extinction: American Indians and the Boarding School Experience, 1875–1928* (Lawrence: University Press of Kansas, 1995); Tsianina Lomawaima, *They Called It Prairie Light: The Story of Chilocco Indian School* (Lincoln: University of Nebraska Press, 1994).

76. See, for example, the brief discussion by Michael A. Olivas, "Indian, Chicano, and Puerto Rican Colleges: Status and Issues," in *The History of Higher Education: ASHE Reader Series,* ed. Lester F. Goodchild and Harold S. Wechsler, 2nd ed. (Needham Heights, MA: Simon & Schuster, 1997), pp. 677–698.

77. Eileen Mary Brewer, *Nuns and the Education of American Catholic Women, 1860–1920* (Chicago: Loyola University Press, 1987); Barbara Misner, *Highly Respectable and Accomplished Ladies: Catholic Women Religious in America, 1790–1850* (New York: Garland, 1988); Nikola Baumgarten, "Beyond the Walls: Women Religious in American Life," *U.S. Catholic Historian, 14,* No. 1 (special issue, Winter 1996).

78. Philip Gleason, *Contending with Modernity: Catholic Higher Education in the Twentieth Century* (New York: Oxford University Press, 1995); Kathleen Mahoney, "Adrift: Catholics and American Higher Education," Paper presented at the Spencer Foundation Winter Forum, Cambridge, MA, February 1995. See also William Leahy, *Adapting to America: Catholics, Jesuits, and Higher Education in the Twentieth Century* (Washington, DC: Georgetown University Press, 1991).

79. Mary Oates, *Higher Education for Catholic Women: An Historical Anthology* (New York: Garland, 1987).

80. Lawrence Cremin reoriented the study of educational history through his monumental three-volume study of education in the United States. His now-familiar view of education expanded our previous school-based understanding to include those "agencies, formal and informal, [that] have shaped American thought, character, and sensibility over the years" (*American Education: The Colonial Experience,* p. xi). See his *American Education: The Colonial Experience, 1607–1783* (New York: Harper and Row, 1970), *American Education: The National Experience, 1783–1876* (New York: Harper and Row, 1980), and *American Education: The Metropolitan Experience, 1876–1980* (New York: Harper and Row, 1988).

81. Veysey, *The Emergence of the American University;* Geiger, *To Advance Knowledge* and *Research and Relevant Knowledge.* Roger Geiger, "The Historical Matrix of American Higher Education," *History of Higher Education Annual,* 12 (1992), 7–28.

82. David Levine, *The American College and the Culture of Aspiration* (Ithaca, NY: Cornell University Press, 1986).

83. Ellen Schrecker, *No Ivory Tower: McCarthyism and the Universities* (New York: Oxford University Press, 1986).

84. Bruce Leslie, *Gentlemen and Scholars: College and Community in "The Age of the University," 1865–1917* (University Park: Pennsylvania State University Press, 1992).

The African American Female Elite:

The Early History of African American Women in the Seven Sister Colleges, 1880–1960

LINDA M. PERKINS

The Seven Sister colleges are well known for educating some of the nation's most successful women. At the turn of the twentieth century, they were recognized as the leading institutions for elite White women. In this chapter, Linda Perkins outlines the historical experiences of African American women attending the Seven Sister colleges from the institutions' founding to the civil rights era of the 1960s, a period during which approximately five hundred Black women graduated from these institutions. Analyzing sources from university archives and alumnae bulletins and incorporating oral history testimony, Perkins shows that the Seven Sister colleges were not a monolithic entity: some admitted African American women as far back as the turn of the century, while others, grudgingly, and only under great pressure, admitted them decades later. Perkins outlines how the Seven Sister colleges mirrored the views of the larger society concerning race, and how issues of discrimination in admissions, housing, and financial aid in these institutions influenced and were influenced by the overall African American struggle for full participatory citizenship.

The seven private, elite northeastern women's colleges — Mount Holyoke, Vassar, Wellesley, Smith, Radcliffe, Bryn Mawr, and Barnard — commonly known as the Seven Sister colleges, are recognized for their academic excellence and distinguished alumnae. Founded in the nineteenth century in response to the leading private, elite male institutions' refusal to admit women, the Seven Sisters offered curricula of equal quality to these

Harvard Educational Review Vol. 67 No. 4 Winter 1997, 718–756

male institutions. Only Mount Holyoke was founded originally for the middle classes. By the turn of the century, Mount Holyoke and the other Seven Sisters became identified with the daughters of the White Anglo-Saxon Protestant of the middle and upper classes. The era of their founding was also one of much skepticism and hostility towards the higher learning of White women and of African American men and women, as both groups were believed to be intellectually inferior to White males. This article focuses on the history of African American women attending the Seven Sister colleges from the institutions' founding to the civil rights era of the 1960s, a period during which approximately five hundred Black[1] women graduated from these prestigious institutions. This exploration is important because these institutions are well known for producing some of the nation's professionally most successful women. The presence of African American women and their academic success in these institutions refuted the notion of Blacks' intellectual inferiority. Further, while these institutions did not explicitly prepare women for the world of work, the majority of the African American women who matriculated at the Seven Sisters did work, contributing their talents to both the Black community and the larger society.

By the 1890s, the Seven Sister colleges had evolved into institutions of academic excellence and were educating the daughters of the most wealthy and socially prominent citizens of the nation.[2] Although many histories and studies have been done on the Seven Sister colleges, none focuses on the presence (or absence) of African American women attending them.[3] This focus is nonetheless important, because the growth of these institutions paralleled the African American struggle to obtain full citizenship, as well as educational and economic rights. Exploring the experiences of African American women in these colleges will provide insight into the extent to which these institutions mirrored the views of the larger society concerning racial issues. As many White women sought parity in education and other aspects of American life, they in turn often denied the same to African American women. Black women found themselves unwanted and frequently barred from most White women's organizations and activities.[4] In a 1900 study conducted by African American scholar W.E.B. DuBois on Black college students, he noted that it was easier for a Black male to gain entrance into a White men's college than for a Black woman to enter a White women's college. DuBois noted that the White women's colleges were "unyielding" in their opposition to admitting African American women:[5]

> Negroes have graduated from northern institutions. In most of the larger universities they are welcome and have on the whole made good records. In nearly all the western colleges they are admitted freely and have done well in some cases, and poorly in others. In one of two larger institutions, and in many of the large women's colleges [referring to the Seven Sisters], Negroes while not exactly refused admissions are strongly advised not to apply.[6]

Yet, a small number of African American women did begin to attend the Seven Sister colleges in the late nineteenth century. As will be discussed, when photographs were not required with a college application and/or the applicant was light-skinned enough to be mistaken for a White person, these institutions sometimes unknowingly admitted African Americans; in other instances, they were admitted in token numbers. When DuBois became editor of *Crisis* magazine in 1910 (the publication of the National Association for the Advancement of Colored People [NAACP]), he tracked assiduously the status and treatment of Black students in U.S. higher education. Each year, DuBois contacted the presidents of all the nation's major White colleges and universities for an update on the status of African Americans in their institutions. In 1913, *Crisis* began publishing an annual issue on Blacks and higher education. By the 1920s, members of the NAACP began speaking on White college campuses to engender support for racial integration and equality from the students. As a result of these activities, along with the NAACP's continued legal efforts to integrate public education during the 1940s and 1950s and the heightened civil rights activities of the 1960s, the Seven Sister colleges began actively recruiting Black women by the 1960s.

This article outlines the historical experiences of African American women attending the Seven Sister colleges. First, I provide a general discussion of the historical context of African American women attending these colleges in the late nineteenth and early twentieth centuries. I address how these women differed from their African American counterparts at other types of institutions, as well as from their White classmates on their respective campuses. Second, I discuss how each of the Seven Sisters responded to the presence of African American women on their respective campuses and provide a look at the campus life of these students. I also explore why some institutions opened their doors to African American women while others kept theirs firmly closed.

The discussion of race and the presence of African Americans in these institutions becomes murky at times. Many of the African American women who attended the Seven Sisters were physically indistinguishable from White women, thus it is reasonable to assume that they passed as Whites and their actual race was not recorded or known. For example, Vassar, one of the last of the Seven Sisters to officially admit African American women, had a Black woman graduate in the class of 1897. However, the student appeared to be White, and Vassar discovered only shortly before commencement that she was, in fact, partially African American — or in their eyes, Black. This discussion centers around those African American women who self-identified as such and around the Seven Sister colleges' knowingly admitting them.

The number of African American women attending all the Seven Sisters combined was rarely more than one or two per class until the 1950s, and the information available on these women is uneven. The archives of the institutions that admitted African American women in more than token numbers — Smith, Radcliffe, Wellesley, and Mount Holyoke — are rich with biographical data, enrollment information, oral histories, and lists of these students. Barnard, Vassar, and Bryn Mawr, the last of the Seven Sisters to admit Black women, did not maintain such records and have less information on these students. When appropriate, oral interviews with some of these Black women supplement the written record.

The Black Elite[7]

Studies of Black communities in the nineteenth and early twentieth centuries acknowledge the existence of class differences. In his 1899 study, *The Philadelphia Negro,* DuBois noted the presence of what he defined as a small upper class of Blacks, which included caterers, government clerks, teachers, professionals, and small merchants. DuBois noted that many of these individuals had significant wealth, elite education, political influence, and connections.[8] Another study on the Black upper class at the turn of the century noted that this group was usually college educated, attended Episcopal or Presbyterian churches, and included community leaders. This group's wealth was not as great as its White counterpart's, and status stemmed primarily from occupation, education, and family background. The Black upper class included women who attended the Seven Sister colleges, and who came primarily from families in which both parents had a formal higher education.[9] This is not an insignificant fact, for as historian James Anderson found, until the mid-1930s, "almost all of the southern rural communities with significantly large Afro-American populations and more than half of the major southern cities failed to provide any public high schools for Black youth."[10]

By the late 1890s, the majority of African Americans resided in the South, where they suffered the economic, educational, legal, and social barriers of segregation. The *Plessy v. Ferguson* Supreme Court decision of 1896 established the "separate but equal" doctrine, which furthered legal restrictions on Blacks in the South, commonly known as "Jim Crow" laws. These laws suppressed any meaningful progress for African Americans in the South; even the Black middle class was subject to the same restrictions (e.g., segregated schools, public accommodations, etc.) as poorer African Americans. However, a different situation existed for those African Americans living in the North, at least those with money. DuBois observed that two classes existed among northern African Americans — "the descendants of the northern free Negroes and the free immigrants from the South."[11]

This group of elite northern African Americans lived in a self-contained, exclusive world of restrictive clubs, with memberships based on complexion, education, and wealth. Adelaide Cromwell Hill observed in her study of upper-class Boston Blacks that this group often preferred White tutors and servants because they believed "more gentility and culture would come from exposure to Whites." She noted further that this group gave "lavish and always tasteful entertainments, including catered dinners of many courses, dances with well-known orchestras, debutante balls, select musicales and literary gatherings. They were most often Episcopal and shunned denominations associated with emotionalism or lower-class African Americans." Their daughters were often well traveled and tended to spend their summers in such spots as Martha's Vineyard, Saratoga Springs, and Newport, Rhode Island.[12]

Willard B. Gatewood writes of these upper-class African Americans in *Aristocrats of Color: The Black Elite 1880–1920*. He notes the central role of higher education within the African American elite, stating, "No matter how significant family background, complexion and church affiliation might be as stratifiers, they were singly and collectively less important than the disciplined, cultivated mind produced by higher education."[13]

Higher education opportunities for African American women in the nineteenth century included a growing number of Black colleges in the South, which were mostly still of high school grade.[14] Even though they were called "colleges," in reality they were actually more like high schools. Outside of the South, African American women were admitted to some state universities, a few private White women's institutions, and teacher-training schools. Public sentiment during this period was often against educating African Americans of either gender on an equal basis with Whites. Thus, few White colleges admitted qualified African American women, and those institutions that did enroll them encountered hostile reactions. For example, when Prudence Crandall, a Quaker, attempted to enroll twenty-one Black girls at her Canterbury, Connecticut, Female Boarding School in 1833, local opposition to the notion that African American women should be educated similarly to White women was so great that Crandall's house was burned down, her well was poisoned, and she was ultimately driven out of town.

A 1979 study of the education of African Americans in New York State noted that, of the more than 150 academies and seminaries that existed in that state between 1840 and 1860, no more than eight admitted African Americans.[15] Throughout the northern and New England states, few White institutions during the antebellum period would admit Blacks; one exception was Oberlin College in Ohio. Oberlin, an institution founded by abolitionists, began admitting African Americans and women in 1833. Many African American families relocated to Oberlin so that their children could have an opportunity to obtain a higher education. From 1833 until 1910, more than four hundred African American women attended Oberlin College.[16] In sharp contrast, during the period addressed by this article — the 1890s through the 1960s — the Seven Sister colleges combined graduated approximately five hundred African American women.

By the turn of the century, the Seven Sisters were recognized as the leading institutions for elite White women. These institutions offered African American women from prominent families not only intellectual growth and stimulation, but also entrance into a world of White power and privilege. Most of the Black women who attended the Seven Sisters between the 1890s and 1960s were from these educated, solidly upper- and middle-class families. Education was expected to endow them with the refinement and culture essential for entry into the highest stratum of African American society.

Early History of Black Women in the Seven Sister Colleges

The early women's colleges were significant because they offered women a higher education degree equivalent to that of the leading men's colleges. Wellesley College in Wellesley, Massachusetts, and Smith College in Northampton, Massachusetts, were both founded in 1875. Radcliffe College (formerly known as the Harvard Annex) was founded in 1879. Although these three institutions are not the oldest of the Seven Sisters, they have the longest and most continuous history of Black women students and graduates. African American women began attending Wellesley, Radcliffe, and Smith in the mid-1880s in token, yet steady, numbers. Both Mount Holyoke, founded in 1837, and Vassar, founded in 1865, also had Black women students in the late nineteenth century; however, as will be discussed later in this article, these students were not known to be African Americans until after they arrived. Neither Barnard, founded in 1889, nor Bryn Mawr, founded in 1884, admitted African Americans until well into the twentieth century. Although the number of Black women who attended these institutions prior to 1960 was small (around five hundred), their influence within the African American community was significant. They went on to serve on faculties of African American high schools and colleges, and became prominent lawyers, physicians, and scientists.

Wellesley College

Wellesley College was founded in 1875 in Wellesley, Massachusetts, by Henry Durant, a Harvard graduate and successful lawyer. Durant, a trustee of Mount Holyoke Seminar and a devout Christian, sought to model Wellesley after the religious Mount Holyoke. Religion permeated the Wellesley campus with chapels, Bible classes, and questions to students concerning their religious condition. The college statute read, "The college was founded for the glory of God and the service of the Lord Jesus Christ, in and by the education and culture of women. . . . It is required that every Trustee, Teacher, and Officer, shall be a member of an Evangelical Church." According to Horowitz, Durant enforced these statutes literally.[17]

The first African American to graduate from Wellesley College was Harriett Alleyne Rice of Newport, Rhode Island. Rice, the daughter of a steward on the steamship "The Pilgrim," lived on campus in a single room, according to the campus directory.[18] After graduating in 1887, Rice earned a medical degree in 1893 from the Women's Medical School of the New York Infirmary. From all indications, Rice's experience at Wellesley was positive. She kept in touch with the college and returned there in 1920 to lecture on her experiences as a medical assistant in France during the First World War. Rice's services had been refused by the American Red Cross because of her race, and she worked instead for the French government.[19] In response to a

1937 alumnae questionnaire that asked, "Have you any handicap, physical or other, which has been a determining factor in your [professional] activity?" Rice replied, "Yes! I am colored which is worse than any crime in this God *blessed Christian* country! My country (100%) tis of *thee!*"[20]

While it appears that the African American women who attended Wellesley in the first two decades of the twentieth century did not articulate publicly any instances of discrimination at the institution, Jane Bolin, class of 1928, did. Bolin was from New York City and the daughter of a prominent lawyer who had attended Williams College, an elite men's college in western Massachusetts. She recalled that she and Ruth Brown, the only other Black woman admitted as a first-year student in 1924, were assigned to the same room in an apartment in which they were the only college students. Bolin notes a number of incidents that revolved around her race. For example, although African American women were allowed to eat in the dining hall, Southern students refused to sit with them; Bolin's roommate was asked to play the role of Aunt Jemima in a skit (including wearing a bandanna); and, although Bolin was an honors student, she was rejected from one of the sororities that claimed to be concerned with social problems. Her rejection letter was an unsigned note left under her door.

Bolin's "sharpest and ugliest" memory of Wellesley occurred during a mandatory conference with a guidance counselor in her senior year. Bolin wrote that the counselor was in shock when she heard that Bolin wanted to be an attorney. Bolin recalled, "She threw up her hands in disbelief and told me there was little opportunity in law for a woman and absolutely none for a 'colored' one. Surely I should consider teaching."[21] Despite this discouragement, Bolin had a distinguished career in law: after Wellesley she attended Yale Law School, earned an LL.B. in 1931, and in 1939, at the age of 31, was appointed the first Black woman judge in the United States by New York City Mayor Fiorello LaGuardia. Bolin recalled bitterly that, although her historic appointment was widely publicized and she received letters and telegrams from all over the world, "not a single note from teacher, president, dean, house mother" or anyone in an official capacity at Wellesley during her four years there acknowledged her achievement.[22]

However, from the perspective of a White southerner in the 1920s, Wellesley was extremely accommodating to African Americans. Virginia Foster Durr, Wellesley class of 1925, grew up in a prominent Birmingham, Alabama, family. A quintessential southern belle, Foster said that her family wanted her to be well married and that Wellesley was an investment in achieving that goal. After arriving at Wellesley in 1921, Foster met a southern woman in Cambridge whose Southern Club sponsored parties and dances for southerners. As a freshman she lived off campus in Wellesley village, as was customary; after her first year, she was able to live on campus. Of her first night in the dormitory, she wrote:

> I went to the dining room and a Negro girl was sitting at my table. My God, I nearly fell over dead. I couldn't believe it. I just absolutely couldn't believe it.

She wasn't very black, sort of pale, but she was sitting there eating at the table with me in college. I promptly got up, marched out of the room, went upstairs, and waited for the head of the house to come. She was a tall, thin, New England spinster. She wore glasses on her nose and she would cast her head down and look over them at us. I told her that I couldn't possibly eat at the table with a Negro girl. I was from Alabama and my father would have a fit. He came from Union Springs, Bullock County, and the idea of my eating with a Negro girl — well, he would die. I couldn't do it. She would have to move me immediately.[23]

According to Foster, the house mother informed her that Wellesley had rules, and that students had to eat at the table to which they had been assigned for a month, after which Foster could move. If she did not want to comply, she was told, she could withdraw from the college without penalty on her academic record. Foster said that when she presented her dilemma to her southern girlfriend, her friend convinced her of what was at stake. Foster was enjoying her college years: "I was having the time of my life at Wellesley. I was in love with a Harvard law student, the first captain of VMI, and life was just a bed of roses. But I had been taught that if I ate at the table of a Negro girl I would be committing a terrible sin against society."[24] Ultimately, Foster decided to stay and simply not mention to her father that she had to eat at the same table with a Black woman:

So I didn't tell Daddy and I stayed. But that was the first time I became aware that my attitude was considered foolish by some people and that Wellesley College wasn't going to stand for it. That experience had a tremendous effect on me. . . . There were other Southern girls at Wellesley. We were all a little ashamed of breaking the Southern taboos, and yet we didn't want to leave. I didn't know whether I had acted rightly or wrongly, whether I should have stood by Southern tradition and gone home or not. I only knew I had stayed because I didn't want to miss the good times I was having.[25]

Segregated housing remained an issue at Wellesley into the 1930s. The faculty in the Department of Biblical History addressed the problem in a letter to President Ellen F. Pendleton, protesting the college's policy of housing discrimination:

We wish cordially to express our recognition of the courtesy and kindness which the college administration has always shown to underprivileged groups at Wellesley, and our realization of the expenditure of time and effort in their behalf; but we feel that we must state our deep regret that the administration has felt it necessary to adopt a new policy — the definite ruling that students of different race [sic] may not room together.

Such a regulation made by the dominant group must inevitably be interpreted as an endorsement of race prejudice. Such an endorsement seems to us inconsistent with Wellesley's heritage, and with the teaching of Jesus as that teaching has been interpreted at Wellesley.

We therefore sincerely hope that the college will find it possible to modify its recent formulation of policy.[26]

There is no other correspondence concerning either the letter or the policy. College records make no further mention of segregated housing until 1948, when Dean of Residence Ruth H. Lindsay telegrammed a southern woman named Mary Chase to inform her: "It would be entirely contrary to the policy of the College to assign a white freshman and a negro freshman to [the] same room. Any rumor of such assignment is without slightest foundation."[27]

Three Black women attended Wellesley in the last two decades of the nineteenth century. Two of them earned baccalaureate degrees, one in 1887 and the other in 1888.[28] Only one other Black woman earned a degree from the school over the next twenty-five years. Portia Washington, daughter of prominent educator Booker T. Washington, attended for only one year. By 1960, seventy-five Black women had attended Wellesley; forty-five earned baccalaureate degrees, others were in graduate programs, and some attended without earning a degree.

Wellesley's first two Black alumnae were happy with their college experience. As noted above, Harriet Rice, Wellesley's first Black graduate, kept in touch with her alma mater. Ella Elbert Smith, who earned her degree in 1888, when asked in an alumni questionnaire about the weaknesses and strengths of Wellesley, wrote, "I think that one of Wellesley's finest characteristics now and from the beginning is that it makes no distinction as to race, color or creed."[29] When asked in 1952 to reflect on the most important aspect of her college experience, Smith noted, "personal contact and often fine and lasting friendships with members of the faculty. These were possible and priceless in the Wellesley of my day."[30] Upon Smith's death in 1955, her family requested that donations in her memory be sent to Wellesley College. In addition, Smith donated more than 1,300 books, pamphlets, and rare manuscripts related to slavery and the Civil War to Wellesley College.[31] As will be discussed later, most African Americans considered Wellesley, along with Smith College, to be the most welcoming of the Seven Sister colleges. The administration stood behind them when issues of racism arose, as was evidenced by Virginia Foster Durr's recollection. Although its housing was segregated in 1913, Wellesley was the only Seven Sister college that allowed Blacks to live on campus.

Radcliffe College

Originally known as the Harvard Annex, Radcliffe College was founded in 1879 in Cambridge, Massachusetts, by the Society for the Collegiate Instruction of Women. Women had to meet the same admission requirements as for Harvard. Radcliffe students were taught by Harvard faculty, and were awarded degrees and honors according to the same standards as Harvard.[32]

Radcliffe enrolled African American women continuously from the 1890s. Though barred from campus housing, they participated in all other aspects of campus life and extracurricular activities. The first Black Radcliffe graduate was Alberta Scott of Cambridge. Scott graduated from Cambridge Latin High School and entered Radcliffe in 1894. There, Scott was active in the Idler, a dramatics club, and in the German Club. She was also involved in music. After graduating in 1898, Scott went to Tuskegee Institute at the invitation of Booker T. Washington. She taught there until she became ill and had to return to Cambridge in 1900. She died in 1903 at the age of twenty-seven.[33]

Most of Radcliffe's earliest Black students were from Cambridge and the greater Boston area. Because African Americans could not live on campus, students from farther away had to find accommodations with members of Cambridge's Black community. As I describe later, the issue of discrimination in campus housing was revisited over and over by African American students, as well as by the NAACP. In 1913, Mary Gibson became the first African American from outside the Cambridge/Boston area to enroll in Radcliffe and was also the first student from a Black high school, Dunbar High School in Washington, DC. Her enrollment presented the first major racial problem for Radcliffe officials. Although Gibson was a brilliant student and had outstanding credentials, she needed financial aid. Her parents were both college educated. Her father had been a lawyer and her mother had taught at Tuskegee Institute, but her father's recent death had left them without financial resources.[34] Gibson's mother was eager for her daughter to receive a first-rate education, and they moved to Cambridge together to set up an apartment for Mary. Gibson had a recommendation from Roscoe Bruce, a prominent African American Harvard graduate. Bruce was assistant superintendent of the Washington, DC, Public Schools and a friend of Radcliffe President Lebarron Russell Briggs. Apparently the Gibsons felt confident that their connections through Bruce would give Mary an excellent chance for a scholarship, but this was not the case. Briggs told them that very few scholarships were awarded to first-year students.[35] Instead, Radcliffe Dean Bertha Boody found Mary a job doing domestic work. Her mother was outraged. She refused to allow her daughter to accept the position, saying the job offer was racist and insisting that Radcliffe could find scholarship monies or a job more suitable and less demeaning, such as working in the library.

President Briggs frantically attempted to raise money for Mary from outside supporters of Radcliffe. In the meantime, Mrs. Gibson refused to allow Mary to work and her tuition was not paid. The college hurriedly obtained a loan for Gibson. While Briggs worked intensely on Mary's behalf, Mary and her mother believed that her biggest obstacle at Radcliffe was Dean Boody. They believed Boody, a southerner, was racially prejudiced and under no circumstances wanted Gibson to be awarded a Radcliffe scholarship. Boody's influence was considerable, and she convinced Briggs that the Gibsons were ingrates and basically uppity Negroes.[36]

The Gibsons were from Washington, DC, where many prominent Black families had children attending Seven Sister and Ivy League colleges. Briggs was concerned about their interpretation of this problem, especially since Radcliffe had always been perceived as a liberal, welcoming institution to African American women. Mary Church Terrell was a prominent African American clubwoman, civil rights leader, and former educator (she had taught at Dunbar High School). In a letter to Terrell, who had spoken at

Radcliffe in 1912 on "The Progress of the Colored Women," Briggs apologetically explained the situation from his perspective:

> If you don't mind my saying so, there is, I suspect, a little difficulty in regards to Miss Gibson, a difficulty which probably comes from the fact that her mother has been a teacher and feels, naturally enough, a certain superiority in herself and in her daughter which makes her shrink from letting her daughter do certain kinds of honorable service. We have girls who have been with us a year or two, whom everyone respects who go as mothers' helpers or serve in any capacity whereby they may honorably help themselves along. . . . I suppose the fact that her daughter is a colored girl makes her the more cautious, so that she is unwilling that her daughter should do many things which the most earnest of our white girls do not hesitate for a moment to do and which everybody respects a self-respecting girl for doing.[37]

Mrs. Gibson secured employment in Boston and Mary found a part-time job selling magazine subscriptions, so they were able to support themselves during Mary's first year at Radcliffe. When Mary was refused a scholarship the second year, Mrs. Gibson went to prominent clergy in the Cambridge and Boston White communities to garner their support. Briggs admitted in a letter to one of the clergymen, the Reverend Dr. van Allen, that Radcliffe had not awarded Gibson a scholarship her second year because they did not want her to return to Radcliffe. However, he said that the question of the moment was "whether she will be saved by being forced out or by being kept here with uninterrupted college education, after which she can take care of herself and her mother too." Briggs ended his letter saying that Mary was an excellent student.[38]

Briggs always appeared torn about Radcliffe's treatment of Gibson, and his conscience ultimately haunted him. Within a month of his letter to van Allen, Briggs wrote in a confidential letter that he believed Radcliffe had been unjust in not awarding Mary a scholarship. He said that in spite of her financial difficulties and in the face of starvation and destitution, Mary had remained an outstanding student. He wrote: "The persistency with which she has done good work — even, as I have learned, at a time when she had insufficient food, is a mark of something which I believe should be encouraged."[39] He said that every visible avenue of help to Mary had been deliberately stopped. But, he now agreed, given Mary's academic record, it was reasonable for her to expect a scholarship. In fact, the person with whom she had tied for a scholarship in her second year came from a home of comfortable financial circumstances. With a change of heart and reason, Briggs said that he believed that Radcliffe's actions toward Mary were "harsh and unnatural," considering that the girl had no home or resources.[40] Dean Boody vehemently disagreed and said she would be "ashamed" if Radcliffe awarded anything to Gibson.[41] Boody's decision prevailed, but Briggs was able to secure a personal, interest-free loan from an anonymous donor for the remainder of Mary's stay at Radcliffe. After she graduated in 1918, she repaid the loan in full.[42]

Despite Mary's financial woes, she led an active, full life at Radcliffe. She was a member of the student government, the Science Club, and the Cosmopolitan Club; she was also class accompanist and wrote the Class Song for 1918. After graduating, she returned to Washington, DC, and taught at her alma mater, Dunbar High School, and sent many of her students to Radcliffe during the course of her years there. At her fiftieth Radcliffe reunion in 1968, Mary recalled with pleasure her years at Radcliffe, but stated, "the fly in the ointment was the dean from Baltimore, who demanded that I work as a domestic if I ever hoped to get her recommendation for a scholarship. In spite of her persistent persecution, I found consolation in the president, an ideal Yankee whom I adored."[43] Mary Gibson remained a loyal and devoted Radcliffe alumna throughout her life.

Black students had varying opinions about the discrimination they experienced. Margaret Perea McCane, who graduated from Radcliffe in 1927, recalled years later that

> it was fortunate that all of us lived at home, because in those days Black students could not live in the dormitories at Harvard or Radcliffe. It wasn't until my junior year in college that a Black girl was admitted to the dormitory at Radcliffe and it was a few years later that black boys at Harvard could live at college. But, McCane rationalized, those were some of the things that one took in one's stride then. I do not say that it was fair and that we should have been able to accept it. It was a situation [in] which one dealt with the problems that one had, with the handicaps that one met, and one did not let those things stand in the way of one's getting an education, a good education for that was why you were there. And you recognized the fact that your contacts and what you did and the record you made were going to influence other young black people who followed you. I think that always stood as a goal before all of us.[44]

Radcliffe's African American graduates contributed greatly to the education of their race at both historically Black colleges and Black public high schools. Beginning with the first, Alberta Scott, who taught at Tuskegee Institute in Alabama, all but one of Radcliffe's Black graduates during the first decades of the twentieth century taught at some point at Black education institutions.

By the second decade of the twentieth century, Radcliffe graduated more than one Black woman each year. By 1920, four Black women graduated in the same class. This was unheard of at the other Seven Sister colleges, where such numbers would not be achieved until the 1940s and 1950s. By 1950, Radcliffe had graduated fifty-six African American undergraduates and thirty-seven African American graduate students. It was by far the leader in the number of Black women graduates among the Seven Sister colleges.

Smith College

Smith College in Northampton, Massachusetts, was endowed by a wealthy single woman, Sophia Smith, in 1868. A devoutly religious woman, Smith sought to establish a college at which women could have an education equal to that offered by the leading men's colleges, but also wanted the college to be "pervaded by the spirit of evangelical Christian religion."[45] Thus, like its sister institutions of Mount Holyoke and Wellesley, religion was central to the life of Smith College.

The first African American woman to graduate from Smith was Otelia Cromwell of Washington, DC, who graduated in 1900. Her father, John Wesley Cromwell, was a prominent educator and, after earning a law degree, a chief examiner in the U.S. Post Office. Otelia Cromwell was a product of the segregated schools of Washington. She transferred to Smith College in 1898 from the all-Black Miner's Teachers College. As was the case at most White institutions, Cromwell was not allowed to live on campus and was housed in the home of a Smith College professor. Despite this, she apparently enjoyed her education; in a letter to her father in 1899, Cromwell expressed her happiness with Smith and her pleasure with classes and professors. She wrote, "I am having a very happy time of it this year." After graduating from Smith, Cromwell studied in Germany, earned a masters degree from Columbia University in 1910, and a Ph.D. in English from Yale University in 1926. She spent her life as an educator of Black youth in Washington, DC.

In 1913, Smith faced a situation that forced it to reconsider its discriminatory housing policy. The situation came to a head when Carrie Lee, the daughter of a letter carrier from New Bedford, Massachusetts, was admitted to Smith. Because photographs were not required for admission at the time, and because Lee was from a predominantly White high school, Smith officials were unaware of her race until she arrived on campus. Her race became an immediate problem because she had been assigned a room with a White student from Tennessee. When the White roommate protested, Smith told Lee to find accommodation within the approved housing of the Northampton community. The only approved housing available to Lee required that she be a servant and not use the main entrance of the house.

Insulted and outraged, Lee's parents contacted the NAACP. Minutes from an NAACP board meeting note that Dr. Joel. E. Spingarn, one of the organization's founders who served as chairman, treasurer, and president, met with Smith's president to discuss the matter. He told the school's dean that he would "unloose the dogs of war at Smith" if the situation was not resolved favorably.[46] In the face of such negative publicity, the college found housing for Lee in the home of a Smith professor, Julia Caverno, who had housed other African Americans. Although *Crisis* magazine did not name Smith College as the culprit, W.E.B. DuBois did cover the story. He reported that a "refined young girl of cultured parents who had won a scholarship in one of the large colleges" had been denied housing. He wrote that after the White student from Nashville complained,

> the colored girl was asked to leave and was unable to secure a room on the campus or anywhere in the college town. One of the teachers, a staunch friend,

took her in but was unable to solve more than the room problem. Then began the wary search for board which was finally only secured on condition that the young lady would act as waitress. Though she had never done work of this kind she pluckily determined to stay on the ground and fight out her battle. Meantime, the Association was working hard to reach the proper authorities. Fortunately, a friend of the colored people on the board of trustees of the college became interested and succeeded in getting the girl on the campus in a delightful room where she is entitled to all the privileges of the college, including, of course, the dining room. Best of all, she is becoming popular with her classmates and through her charming personality is winning friends for her race.[47]

Members of the NAACP board played a prominent role in changing Smith's housing policy. Moorfield Storey, a successful Boston lawyer and chairman of the NAACP board of trustees, wrote Smith's president, the Reverend Marion Burton, that if the story about Lee's housing dilemma was true, "I think it is the very greatest discredit to Smith College." Storey continued:

> For a Massachusetts College to so far forget the principles which have made Massachusetts what it is, and to weakly abandon the rights of colored people in order to conciliate Southern prejudice is to the last degree weak and discreditable. I sincerely hope that this statement I have received is not true, or that if it is true the policy will be abandoned. Otherwise I hope the facts will be published throughout the breadth and length of this state in order that the citizens of Massachusetts may understand how little regard the trustees of Smith College have for the principles of justice.[48]

Ruth Baldwin, an NAACP board member, Smith alumna, and the first woman to serve as a regular member on the Smith board of trustees, used her influence to have Smith's housing policy changed.[49] Baldwin discovered that Smith had no official policy about Blacks living on campus, but that this discriminatory practice was based on the individual decisions of college officials. Baldwin felt that the fact that Wellesley College allowed African American women to live on campus would influence Smith trustees who were sympathetic to the issue. The matter was resolved in October 1913, when the trustees affirmed the rights of African American women to live in Smith housing.[50]

The NAACP's influence at Smith widened with the appointment of William Allan Neilson as the college's third president in 1917. Neilson was a member of the national board of the NAACP. Walter White, a general secretary of the NAACP, recalled that Neilson "devoted a great portion of his extracurricular activity to service as a member of the board of directors of the NAACP."[51] White wrote:

> Thanks to Dr. Neilson and others on the Smith faculty, the college maintained leadership among American educational institutions in ignoring artificial lines of demarcation based on race, social position, wealth, or place of birth. Few colleges I have known have been more free from cant and hypocrisy or more ready to examine new ideas than Smith.[52]

He stated it was because of Neilson's and Smith's leadership that he and his wife decided to have their daughter Jane educated there.

The Lee incident led Smith officials to inquire about housing policies at the other Seven Sisters. Wellesley was the only institution that claimed not to discriminate in admissions or housing against African Americans. Mount Holyoke, which had graduated two African Americans in the late nineteenth century, did not admit Black women in 1913, nor did Barnard, Bryn Mawr, and Vassar admit African Americans that year.

After Otelia Cromwell, Smith consistently admitted African American women, usually one per year. It was not until 1925 that two Black women graduated in the same class. This was repeated in 1926, and then not again until 1934.[53] By 1964, sixty-nine Black women (including African women) had attended and/or graduated from Smith.

Mount Holyoke College

Mount Holyoke College in South Hadley, Massachusetts, is the oldest of the Seven Sisters. It was founded as a women's seminary in 1837 by Mary Lyon. Its mission was to train teachers, missionaries, and wives of missionaries, and did not achieve collegiate status until the 1890s.

In 1845, the Mount Holyoke trustees voted not to admit Black women. After the vote, Mary Lyon received a long letter from a White male resident of nearby Springfield. He protested the college's policy, which he believed was hypocritical, considering the Christian principles espoused by the school. He wrote that public sentiment was undergoing a rapid change, and that the events that occurred at Prudence Crandall's Canterbury Female Boarding School would not be repeated. He noted that Dartmouth College had recently decided to admit colored students, and concluded by stating, "I hope that the religious influence that goes out of the Mount Holyoke Seminary will no longer be contaminated with this hatred or that it will not *deliberately* decide to reject colored applicants."[54] Another letter to Lyon, from a former student, urged her to take a stand on the question of slavery, pointing out that while Mount Holyoke expressed interest in foreign missions, Black slaves in this country were ignored.[55] Lyon, who died in 1849, never took a public stand on slavery.

Mount Holyoke's earliest known African American graduate during its seminary years was Hortense Parker of Ripley, Ohio, in the class of 1883. The first Black to obtain a collegiate degree from Mount Holyoke was Martha Ralston of Worcester, Massachusetts, in the class of 1898. According to a letter from the dean of Mount Holyoke in 1913 to Ada Comstock, dean of Smith College, the race of both Ralston and Parker was a surprise to the officials of the college when they first arrived.[56] All students were required to live on campus at Mount Holyoke, and though records are missing for the years of Parker's matriculation, subsequent records indicate that African American students who were enrolled in the early years lived in single rooms in the Seminary Building.

Alumnae records state that Ralston's father was an Englishman and that her home "is located in one of the wealthiest sections of Worcester."[57] A musician whose education was financed by a patron, Ralston had planned to study in Europe, but the death of her patron in her senior year prevented her from being able to go abroad.[58] Ralston apparently made friends at Mount Holyoke. One of her White classmates wrote to her mother upon Ralston's arrival in 1894, "There is a colored girl here in the freshman class. She comes from Worcester, Mass. and the other girls who come from that place like her very much and say that she is of a very good family."[59]

Mount Holyoke's first African American graduate of the twentieth century was Francis Williams of St. Louis, Missouri. Until her death in 1992, Williams was the school's oldest living Black alumna. Like Otelia Cromwell, the first Black graduate of Smith College, Williams was a product of a Black segregated high school in the South. Her parents were college graduates, as were her three siblings. Her father was principal of the well-known Charles Sumner High School, a Black public school in St. Louis. After graduating as valedictorian from Sumner, Williams attended the University of Cincinnati for one year. She found the campus too large and impersonal, and decided to transfer. Her mother sent Williams's transcript to Mount Holyoke in 1916, and only after she had been accepted did her mother inform the college that Williams was African American. She received a letter from the college stating that they did not believe her daughter would be happy at Mount Holyoke, to which she responded that she wasn't sending her daughter to be happy, but to receive an education. Williams, who had a light complexion, recalled that many of her fellow students would not sit with her at meals, although some were not concerned about her race. Williams held a double major in chemistry and economics, and graduated Phi Beta Kappa in 1919. Her parents paid for her education at Mount Holyoke, but she received a fellowship from the college after graduation to attend the New York School of Social Work. After earning a certificate there, she earned a masters in political science from the University of Chicago. Williams spent her professional career working in the area of race relations for the National Young Women's Christian Association (YWCA) and various other civil rights organizations.[60]

More than the other Seven Sister colleges, Mount Holyoke attracted African American women from Black high schools and the South, including several from Atlanta, Georgia. There was one Black graduate in the Mount Holyoke class of 1926 from Wilmington, Delaware; the next five Black students at the school were from Atlanta and Washington, DC. Of this group, two were graduates of the prestigious all-Black Dunbar High School in Washington, which had a long history of sending its graduates to elite New England colleges. The other three were transfer students, two from Spelman College in Atlanta, and one from Atlanta University (an affiliate of Spelman).[61] The Atlanta connection was due to a prominent White alumna of the class of 1909, Florence Read. In 1927 Read was appointed president of the all-Black Spelman College, a women's college founded in 1881 and modeled in part after Mount Holyoke.[62]

Few African American women graduated from Mount Holyoke prior to the mid-1960s; by 1964, only thirty-nine had graduated since Hortense Parker in 1883. One African American graduated from Mount Holyoke during the twenties, six in the thirties, twelve during the forties (due to increased pressure from religious and civil rights groups), twelve during the fifties, and five from 1960 to 1964.[63]

Despite their small numbers, the African American women at Mount Holyoke participated fully in campus organizations and events. The institution and its environment nurtured the women intellectually and spiritually. The Black women who attended Mount Holyoke before the 1960s all said that they would attend the institution again.

Bryn Mawr College

Bryn Mawr College in Bryn Mawr, Pennsylvania, was founded in 1885 by Orthodox Quakers "for the advanced education and care of young women, or girls of the higher classes of society."[64] Bryn Mawr's mission, as interpreted by the institution's president, the formidable M. Carey Thomas, who reigned from 1893 to 1922, excluded Black women. Although Thomas explained the absence of Black students as being due to the "difficulty of the admissions examination and the fact that we do not admit on certificate of high school graduation," in reality it was her deeply held belief in the inferiority of African Americans that kept them out. Her bigotry, according to Thomas's biographer Helen Horowitz, was rooted in her Baltimore upbringing in which her only interactions with Blacks were with servants.[65]

In 1903, Jessie Fauset, an African American from Philadelphia, graduated at the top of her class at the city's Girls' High. It was customary that the school's top student would enter Bryn Mawr on scholarship, but when it was discovered that Fauset was Black, President Thomas raised money for Fauset to attend Cornell (Thomas's alma mater) rather than have a Black woman attend Bryn Mawr. In 1906, Thomas received an inquiry from M Street High School in Washington, DC, an important source of talented African American students to elite private colleges in the North, concerning the suitability of Bryn Mawr for its students. Thomas responded that their students should seek admissions to other New England colleges rather than Bryn Mawr, due to the large number of students those schools admitted from the middle and southern states. She reasoned:

> As I believe that a great part of the benefit of a college education is derived from intimate association with other students of the same age interested in the same intellectual pursuits, I should be inclined to advise such a student to seek admission to a college situated in one of the New England states where she would not be so apt to be deprived of this intellectual companionship because of the different composition of the student body.[66]

While Thomas implied that Bryn Mawr students would not feel comfortable with African American classmates, these sentiments actually reflected Thomas's own inhibitions.

In her opening address of the 1916 school year to the Bryn Mawr student body, Thomas expressed her belief in the intellectual superiority of the Anglo-Saxon race:

> If the present intellectual supremacy of the White races is maintained, as I hope that it will be for centuries to come, I believe it will be because they are the only races that have seriously begun to educate their women. . . .One thing we know beyond doubt and that is that certain races have never yet in the history of the world manifested any continuous mental activity nor any continuous power of government. Such are the pure negroes of Africa, the Indians, the Esquimaux, the South Sea Islanders, the Turks, etc. . . . These facts must be faced by a country like the United States which is fast becoming, if it has not already become, the melting pot of nations into which are cast at the rate of a million a year the backward people of Europe like the Czechs, the Slavs, and the south Italians. If the laws of heredity mean anything whatsoever, we are jeopardizing the intellectual heritage of the American people by this head-long intermixture of races. . . . If we tarnish our inheritance of racial power at the source, our nation will never again be the same. . . . Our early American stock is still very influential but this cannot continue indefinitely. For example, each year I ask each freshman class to tell me what countries their parents originally came from and for how many generations back their families have been on American soil. It is clear to me that almost all of our student body are early time Americans, that their ancestors have been here for generations, and that they are overwhelmingly English, Scotch, Irish, Welsh, and that of other admixtures, French, German, Dutch largely predominate. All other strains are negligible. Our Bryn Mawr college students therefore as a whole seem to belong by heredity to the dominant races. You, then, students of Bryn Mawr, have the best intellectual inheritance the world affords.[67]

Not surprisingly, given Thomas's views, no African American women attended Bryn Mawr while she was president, regardless of their qualifications.

Although Thomas retired as president of Bryn Mawr in 1922, she remained a director and member of the board of trustees for life. Thomas's successor was Marion Edwards Park, a former dean of Radcliffe College. Soon after Thomas's retirement, an African American student from New England enrolled at Bryn Mawr, but she left after one week. Her identity and circumstances, even the year she came, remain a mystery. College records indicate that this woman requested that her name never appear on any list concerning Bryn Mawr.[68]

In 1927, the Bryn Mawr board of directors voted to authorize President Park to reply to inquiries regarding the admission of African American women, but with the proviso that she make it clear that such students would be admitted "only as non-residential students." Board member Thomas's opposition to the admission of Black students was steadfast, but the college nevertheless moved forward in this regard.

Enid Cook entered Bryn Mawr in 1927. She majored in chemistry and biology, and in 1931 became the first African American woman to graduate from the college. Cook lived in the home of a Bryn Mawr professor her freshman year, and then with a Black family in the town during her remaining years. She earned a Ph.D. in bacteriology from the University of Chicago in 1937. The second Black woman to graduate from Bryn Mawr was Lillian Russell, in 1934. Russell, who was from Boston, was discouraged from attending Bryn Mawr by the Boston alumnae chapter. They did not believe it was a good place for a "coloured girl" and they felt she would not be happy. But Russell insisted that she wanted to attend, and was awarded the New England Regional scholarship. The Boston alumnae chapter was unable to have the housing restriction waived; thus Russell lived her first few weeks at the college with President Park, and subsequently with Black families in the area. She majored in chemistry and philosophy and was active in extracurricular activities. After graduating from Bryn Mawr, Russell did graduate study in physical chemistry at the Massachusetts Institute of Technology.

As mentioned earlier, M. Carey Thomas, while no longer president of Bryn Mawr after 1922, remained a trustee. Her biographer Helen Horowitz noted that after 1922, Thomas "kept her hand in Bryn Mawr," even to the point of interference.[69] In 1930, in the midst of Bryn Mawr's discussion of housing restrictions, Thomas wrote to Virginia Gildersleeves, dean of Barnard College, asking what Barnard's policy was on this matter.[70] Thomas confided to Gildersleeves her concern that, since Philadelphia had become a center for African Americans, she anticipated continued inquiries concerning admissions and housing from that community. Thomas expressed her concern about the presence of African American men if African American women were allowed to live on campus. She said that when four Black women were allowed to live on Bryn Mawr's campus during summer school, "whenever entertainments are given by the summer school a solid block of negro men from the neighborhood of Bryn Mawr appears in the audience, last summer I am told from twenty-five to thirty."[71] Gildersleeves responded that no African American woman had ever lived on campus at Barnard, but that they were allowed to live in graduate housing at Columbia.[72]

The debate on the admission of African American women and their right to be housed on campus clearly revealed that President Park, former dean at Radcliffe, was quite different from M. Carey Thomas. When a Bryn Mawr alumna wrote to the school's Alumnae Bulletin voicing her opposition to African American women living on campus, President Park responded:

> I agree with all the premises of your letter and arrive at the opposite conclusion as to Bryn Mawr's responsibility, but officially I shall not bring up the matter of the residence of negro students this year. There is much difference of opinion, I think, in all groups connected with the college . . . but I shall be unwilling to propose that a negro student should come into residence while there is strong undergraduate feeling against it, even although the feeling, as I believe it is, is actually on the part of a minority.[73]

Although a couple of Black women graduate students lived in the residence halls in the 1930s and early 1940s, the housing issue was not resolved until 1942, when the executive committee of the board of directors ended the restriction that Blacks could not live on campus. The board voted that "hereafter all students be admitted [and housed] according to the rules and regulations in force as adopted by the Faculty from time to time."[74] The first Black woman moved into unrestricted campus housing in 1946.

Even after African Americans were allowed to attend Bryn Mawr, beginning in 1927, few did. Considering the school's long history of discriminatory practices and attitudes towards African Americans, it took a courageous Black woman to seek admission to Bryn Mawr. By 1960, only nine African American women had graduated from the institution: two in the 1930s, one in 1948, one in each of the years from 1954 to 1960, except for 1956.

In a 1979 oral history, Evelyn Jones Rich, the African American graduate of the class of 1954, said that she felt she was graded harshly at Bryn Mawr and the marks she received did not fairly represent her work.[75] Rich, who later earned a Ph.D. from Columbia, believed that unjust grades prevented her from graduating cum laude. However, she also recalled that in her senior year, when she and a Black male friend were refused service at a restaurant in the town of Bryn Mawr, the Undergraduate Association, other students, and the college president pressured the restaurant to change its discriminatory policy. When the college lawyer found that the policy violated a Pennsylvania law, the restaurant owner stopped barring African Americans from eating at a booth.[76]

The 1958 Black Bryn Mawr graduate, Camilla Jones Tatem, became a doctor, but said she felt this was in spite of, and not because of, Bryn Mawr. She said she never felt a part of the biology department where she majored, and that the department members discouraged her academic pursuits.[77] In contrast, Christine Philpot Clark, a Black graduate of the class of 1960 who later earned a law degree at Yale, recalled that she liked Bryn Mawr and "even loved particular faculty." She said her Bryn Mawr years coincided with the Little Rock, Arkansas, push to integrate its Central High School, and that this created enormous guilt feelings in some of her White classmates.[78] She noted that two of the four Black women attending Bryn Mawr at that time (one per class) were elected class presidents. "I was approached by some classmates trying to enlist me to be the third," she recalled, "but I knew then the distorted motivations behind it all. I remember, too, the hate letters the two black presidents were receiving."[79]

Clearly, by the 1950s, when a few African American women began to attend Bryn Mawr, the other Seven Sister colleges offered more favorable options. Bryn Mawr and Vassar were the last of the Seven Sisters to admit African American women. For those few African American women who were the early graduates of these institutions, their greatest reward was the power of the degree to advance their career objectives and to demonstrate to the world their ability to compete with the majority members of society.

Vassar College

Vassar College was founded in Poughkeepsie, New York, in 1865, with the endowment of a wealthy brewer, Matthew Vassar. This was a significant event for women's higher education, as Vassar was established as a full-fledged liberal arts college from its inception. Vassar's academic reputation and its affluent alumnae probably account for its being the most resistant to the admission of African American students.[80] It was the last of the Seven Sister colleges to knowingly admit African American students.

The first known Black student at Vassar was Anita Florence Hemmings, from Boston. She enrolled in 1893 and graduated in 1897. A scandal erupted throughout New England when it was discovered that Hemmings, who was light-skinned and passed for White, was actually African American. The event drew significant press coverage. One headline read: "Negro Girl at Vassar: the handsomest girl there. Yale and Harvard Men among those who sought favor with the 'brunette beauty'"[81] Another article reported that "Vassar girls are agitated over the report that one of the students in the senior class of '97 is of Negro parentage. She did not disclose the fact until just before graduation when statements made to Hemmings' roommate led to an investigation."[82] The article said that Hemmings had been noticed as being very bright as a young child, and that her early education was financed by a wealthy White woman. Hemmings studied hard, passed the required examination, and entered Vassar. The article noted that "Vassar is noted for its exclusiveness, and every official of the college refuses to say aught regarding this girl graduate."[83] Another source reported that the faculty was debating whether Hemmings should be denied her diploma. "Never had a colored girl been a student at aristocratic Vassar, and professors were at a loss to foresee the effect upon the future if this one were allowed to be graduated."[84] In the end the faculty did consent to her graduation, reasoning that she was but a few days from commencement and, after this event, the girl would be gone and forgotten.

While at Vassar, Hemmings was active in the Debate Society, College Glee Club, and the Contemporary Club Literary Organization. After graduating she worked at the Boston Public Library in the foreign cataloguing division. She married a physician, and her daughter, Ellen Parker Love, graduated from Vassar in the class of 1927.[85] Presumably Love passed for White as well, since her application stated that she was English and French. Hemmings's husband's race was unknown.[86]

Vassar officials clearly felt that the presence of African American women, even those with a slight tinge of Black blood, would detract from the image it sought to project as an institution for the aristocratic and genteel woman. Historian Lynn Gordon points out that during this period, students from Vassar came almost exclusively from upper-middle-class families. By 1905, attendance at Vassar had become a tradition in many families and a Granddaughters Club was started for students whose mothers and aunts had attended the school.[87]

Continuing his pressure on White institutions, W.E.B. DuBois wrote Henry MacCracken, president of Vassar in 1930, to inquire into Vassar's policy on admitting African Americans. The letter read, "For many years the *Crisis* magazine has secured annually information concerning colored students in northern institutions. The answer from Vassar has always been that you have no colored students. I write to ask you if there has been any change in this rule recently. Are there any colored students in Vassar College today? If a properly equipped colored woman should apply, would you admit her?"[88] MacCracken returned a curt, two-sentence reply, saying that DuBois should read the statement in the Vassar catalogue that read, "No rules other than those there stated govern the admission of students."[89] Despite this response, the reality was that African Americans were neither admitted nor welcome at Vassar. In a 1932 issue of the *Crisis,* DuBois noted that "Vassar is the only first grade women's college in the North which still refuses to admit Negroes. Bryn Mawr and Mount Holyoke held out long but finally surrendered, although Bryn Mawr still keeps its dormitories lily White."[90]

A prominent African American minister from Harlem, the Reverend James Robinson, gave a lecture at Vassar in the late 1930s at a conference cosponsored by the college and the YWCA. In his lecture, Robinson challenged the White women students to improve race relations by getting Vassar to open its doors to Black women. When the students responded that they did not know any Blacks, Robinson offered to find a Black student for the college.[91]

Robinson's congregation included an outstanding student, Beatrix McCleary, the daughter of a physician and an extremely light-skinned Black woman who could have passed for White. "Beatty," as she was known, entered Vassar in the fall of 1940. McCleary excelled in her studies and was elected to Phi Beta Kappa. She was also the first Black to be a member of the Daisy Chain.[92] McCleary obtained the highest rank in zoology while at Vassar, and was awarded four Vassar College fellowships. McCleary went on to become the first African American woman graduate of the Yale University School of Medicine and went into the field of psychiatry.[93]

During the six years after McCleary's entrance into Vassar, six additional African American women were admitted. Separate dormitory rooms for the Black women were still required during this period. June Jackson, from Cambridge, Massachusetts, arrived at Vassar in 1941, the year after McCleary. Jackson had been an active member of the NAACP Youth Council in Cambridge, and had been accepted and awarded scholarships to both Vassar and Radcliffe. Her aunt, Geneva Jackson, had graduated cum laude from Radcliffe in 1919. Her aunt's accomplishments were a great source of pride in their family, and Jackson said she knew she would have to compete with her aunt's record. She said her parents were concerned about reports of snobbishness at Vassar, but after speaking with McCleary, whose views of Vassar were positive, Jackson decided to attend. Jackson noted in her housing request that she would like a roommate, but the president of the Boston Vassar

Club told her, in a "genteel but firm manner," that Jackson would be happier if she had a single room. The woman said further that the college had been courageous enough to increase the student body of African Americans by admitting Jackson and another Black woman that year, but that the school was not ready to integrate the dormitories.[94]

Jackson's recollections of Vassar differ from McCleary's, who wrote two years after her graduation that she felt she had been treated fairly at Vassar. Jackson, who was much darker than McCleary in complexion and appeared to have a more heightened consciousness about racial issues, said she was denied entrance into a Poughkeepsie skating rink where she had gone with a group of students because she was Black. She recalled that she could not find a room to rent for her freshman prom date, who was also visibly African American; in her sophomore year, a White roommate rented a room for her. Jackson said that a professor expressed surprise about a well-written paper she submitted, stating that "it didn't sound like a Negro's writing." Most of the White students' only previous interaction with African American women had been with their maids, and they repeatedly asked Jackson simplistic questions about race and told her she didn't talk like an African American. Their surprise at meeting an articulate, intelligent Black woman was symptomatic of the prevailing view of most Whites toward African Americans. As Jackson recalled, "Sometimes my personal pain at racist incidents was so deep that I could not share it with my new-found White friends until a greater sense of trust had developed." During Jackson's last years at Vassar, she lived in a cooperative house on campus where twenty women lived, studied, cooked, ate, and socialized together. Jackson was the only African American housemate, but she recalled that another woman of color lived in the house.[95]

Several other African American women were admitted to Vassar during World War II. These included Marie Lawrence, a day student from an old and prominent Poughkeepsie family who graduated in 1945 and later earned a masters degree in social work from Smith College; her sister, Stadella Lawrence, who graduated in 1947; and Olive Thurman, the daughter of renowned theologian Howard Thurman, then dean of the chapel at Howard University, who graduated in 1948. W.E.B. DuBois spoke at Vassar in 1942 and challenged the college of twelve hundred students to admit one hundred African American women, stating that the token number of African American women was ridiculously small, given the size of the student body. He pointed out that the acute racial problem in the United States caused most Blacks to be excluded from the best education, the best jobs, the best living accommodations, and everything that would allow them the opportunity to display their ability. DuBois noted that the cultural patterns of the United States, which continually upheld White superiority, must give way to the democratic ideals that were "preached much but practiced so little."[96]

But neither Vassar nor the United States was ready for true integration or the practice of democratic ideals. In the 1940s, only seven Black women graduated from Vassar. For nearly twenty-five years after McCleary was admitted in 1940, Vassar admitted no more than three African Americans in any given year. In some years, none were admitted.

Like its sister institution Bryn Mawr, Vassar had a long history of excluding African American women. Through the protests of people like the Reverend James Robinson and the work of the NAACP and other organizations, the doors of Vassar slowly opened to African American women. June Jackson writes that World War II and the heightened expectations of African Americans had created an activist spirit among Black women students in the 1940s. By the fifties, however, most Vassar students had become more apathetic about issues of race and social justice, and Black women students received a different message:

> Even though they were few in number, they were now expected to be there. It could be said that Vassar did admit Negroes. The implicit message was one that fostered assimilation and denial of differences, as expressed by "We don't see color," or "I never think of you as Black." This imposes a different burden, that of denying a part of your identity even though consciously acknowledging your race.[97]

By 1960 only twenty-three African American women had graduated from Vassar. These women were solidly middle to upper middle class, the daughters of professionals. They were the products of integrated high schools of New York and New England, and the renowned Dunbar High School of Washington, DC. These women excelled at Vassar, and most continued their education in graduate and professional schools. But, as June Jackson noted, despite their accomplishments, the early Black students at Vassar paid a huge personal cost:

> For the Black woman who entered Vassar during these early years, the lone Black student entered to live the demanding life of being the "one and only," a life many remember as lonely in an atmosphere which was unaccepting and, at times, hostile. Administrators and faculty who might have provided support and guidance or served as role models were lacking. For most of those early students, the college community did not provide a sense of being valued or belonging.[98]

Barnard College

Barnard College was founded in 1889 as the "sister" institution to the all-male Columbia. Given its New York City setting, Barnard should have provided a convenient location for college-bound African American women; however, this was not the case. Members of the Black community believed that Barnard discouraged applications from African American women and placed quotas on their numbers when it finally began to admit them.

Famed Harlem Renaissance writer Zora Neale Hurston enrolled at Barnard College as a transfer student in 1925. Hurston, who was the personal secretary of writer Fanny Hurst, had received a scholarship to Barnard after impressing one of its founders, Annie Nathan Meyer. Hurston was a day student and commuted from Harlem to the campus. Hurston was apparently the first African American woman to attend Barnard and was the only Black student during her three semesters there. A witty and eccentric personality, Hurston stated that she encountered no prejudice at Barnard. In fact, Hurston felt it gave White students status to say they had lunched with her. In her autobiography, *Dust Tracks on a Road: An Autobiography,* Hurston wrote:

> I have no lurid tales to tell of race discrimination at Barnard. I made few friends in the first few days. The Social Register crowd at Barnard soon took me up, and I soon became Barnard's sacred black cow.[99]

Hurston recognized the opportunity attending Barnard afforded her:

> I felt that I was highly privileged and determined to make the most of it. I did not resolve to be a grind, however, to show White folks that I had brains. I took it for granted that they knew that. Else, why was I at Barnard? . . . So, I set out to maintain a good average, take part in whatever went on, and just be a part of the college like everybody else. I graduated with a B record, and I am entirely satisfied.[100]

Hurston also expressed her indebtedness to Annie Nathan Meyer: "Mrs. Meyer, who was the moving spirit in founding the college and who is still a trustee, did nobly by me in getting me in. No matter what I might do for her, I would still be in her debt."[101]

Belle Tobias and Vera Joseph enrolled after Hurston's graduation in 1928. Tobias, a botany major, and Joseph, a chemistry major, had both attended New York City public schools. Tobias was the daughter of prominent civil rights and religious leader Channing Tobias, who was secretary of the Colored Department of the National Council of the Young Men's Christian Association, the first African American to serve as director of the Phelps-Stokes Fund, and a member of the board of the national NAACP. Belle Tobias graduated Phi Beta Kappa in the Barnard class of 1931, and went on to earn a masters degree from Wellesley College in 1932.[102]

Vera Joseph was an immigrant from Jamaica who had graduated from George Washington High School in Harlem. She had taken the commercial rather than the college preparatory curriculum in high school to prepare herself for the world of work, since her family had no financial resources for her education beyond high school. However, one of her teachers, Irene F. Gottesman, recognized Joseph's academic talents and insisted that she go to college. As a result, Joseph stayed an additional semester in high school to take the college preparatory courses that qualified her for admission to college. Joseph recalled that she had envisioned herself on a residential campus, but Barnard was the only college that her teachers suggested she consider. She enrolled in 1928 and graduated in 1932. Her first year at Barnard was financed by a scholarship from a group of African American businessmen and educators from Harlem, and by a Barnard scholarship; her subsequent years were financed through scholarships and jobs.[103] Joseph also graduated Phi Beta Kappa, entered Columbia Medical School in 1932, and later became a physician. Joseph, by now Dr. Peterson, said that she and Belle Tobias became good friends and recalled few slights or acts of discrimination at Barnard. As she recalled:

> I never looked for evidence of racial slights or discrimination, so if they occurred I may not have been aware of it. I was making great discoveries in my books and classes and was quite happy with my life at Barnard. It was not until my senior year when I discovered I was not being invited to join the Barnard Club in New York City after graduation that I recognized that I was being discriminated against, and resented it. But more important things than admission to a social club were happening in my life; I was going to medical school.[104]

Jeanne Blackwell transferred to Barnard in 1934 after spending three years at the University of Michigan. Blackwell had graduated in 1931 as valedictorian of her class from the segregated Douglass High School in Baltimore. She had wanted to attend a Seven Sister college, but her family could not afford the tuition. Thus, she enrolled in the University of Michigan, a public institution with an outstanding academic reputation. Blackwell's dream was to become a physician and she was a pre-med student at Michigan, where she also struggled for three years for the right to live on campus. Her mother became concerned about the amount of effort Blackwell was spending on the housing battle and felt she should transfer to another institution. Thus Blackwell transferred to Barnard, mistakenly believing the situation there would be better.

Barnard officials, unaware of Blackwell's race before she arrived, refused to allow her to live on campus. She instead lived in the nearby International House, which was integrated. Despite being refused permission to live on campus, Blackwell recalled her year at Barnard as positive. She recalled that one of her professors was quite embarrassed that Blackwell was refused dormitory housing and expressed her regret to her. Blackwell graduated in 1935, earned a B.S. from the Columbia School of Library Science the following year, and went on to become a prominent authority on Black literary and scholarly collections. In 1955 Blackwell was appointed curator of the renowned repository of African American collections, the Schomburg Center for Research in Black Culture of the New York Public Library.[105]

Throughout the 1930s and 1940s, the NAACP waged legal battles against discrimination against Blacks in higher education. With Black soldiers fighting and losing their lives in World War II, protests mounted against the discrimination and exclusion of African Americans in all aspects of U.S. life. When the Reverend James Robinson addressed an interfaith conference on the campus of Teachers College in February 1943, he spoke out again on the discrimination that talented African American women experienced in applying to certain Seven Sister colleges. Robinson said that it was well known that Barnard and Vassar had quotas for Black women, admitting no more than four every two years. Virginia Gildersleeves, dean of Barnard, issued a written response in the pages of the *Barnard Bulletin* vehemently denying Robinson's accusation:

Dear Mr. Robinson:

It has been reported to me that you stated in an address at the Teachers College Chapel yesterday that Barnard discriminated against Negro students and had a Negro quota which permitted the admission of four students every two years. This is quite untrue. We have no Negro quota. We never receive many applications for admission from Negroes. If we are going to have a quota, we certainly would not have such a foolish one as that reported in the strange rumor which seems to have reached you.

We always have some Negro students in Barnard. This year our most valuable graduate fellowship is held by a Negro, and one of our most distinguished alumnae is a Negro, of whom we are very proud.

I am anxious to do anything I can to further the solution of this serious race problem, and I shall be glad to discuss it with you, if you would like to call and see me. I regret you have such a bad opinion of us.[106]

An editorial in the same issue of the *Barnard Bulletin* commented that while the school might not have quotas for African American women, the issue of race should not die there, and that much should be done. While there were Black colleges for African Americans, the editorial continued, "there are, however, Negro students who are willing to sacrifice personal happiness in return for the opportunity of 'proving themselves' in the North." The editorial suggested that a certain number of scholarships should be earmarked for African American women students at Barnard.[107]

As a result of the editorial, a group of politically active White students established a Committee on the Investigation of Educational Opportunities for the Negro at Barnard. The committee concluded that two factors contributed to the dearth of Black women at Barnard. The first was financial, since most Black candidates could not afford to attend. Second, those who could afford to attend Barnard preferred to attend either a Black college in the South, or Radcliffe or Smith, which admitted more Blacks. The committee concluded that it should inform local high school counselors that Barnard did welcome African Americans and that no racial quotas existed.[108] However, since most of the Black students in the Seven Sister colleges paid their own tuition and many won scholarships after arriving on these campuses, this first explanation does not accurately reflect the reality of the situation. Barnard's location in New York, a city with a large Black population, made it accessible to a large pool of Black women who could have commuted to the campus. It appears that the primary reason Barnard had so few Black students was that Black women believed the school did not welcome them.

Charlotte Hanley was the immediate beneficiary of the effort to increase African American enrollment at Barnard. Hanley graduated from Yonkers High School in 1942 and planned to enroll in New York University, but she could not afford to attend. She moved to New York City to live with her maternal grandmother in hopes of attending the tuition-free Hunter College, which both her grandmother and aunt had attended. However, shortly after Robinson's lecture and the subsequent reaction, a social worker friend of Hanley's family informed them that Barnard was prepared to offer a full tuition scholarship to a deserving Black student. Hanley and her mother met with Reverend Robinson, after which she initiated the application process to Barnard, which she had always thought to be an expensive school available only to the daughters of the affluent. Barnard accepted Hanley and provided her with a full tuition scholarship (except for $50) to cover the entire period of her studies. She lived in Harlem with her godparents and worked in the community center of Reverend Robinson's church, to earn money for books and living expenses.[109]

Hanley entered Barnard as a mathematics major but changed to economics, which she felt would make her more employable. Hanley recalled her years at Barnard as being very enjoyable, and said that her degree meant a great deal in terms of social contacts and employment opportunities. She said that her professional success was due to a Barnard economics professor who offered her a job working as a researcher in the Department of Financial Research for the National Bureau of Economic Research. Several years later she became the first African American hired at the Federal Reserve Bank of Chicago as an economist, where in time she was appointed assistant vice president.[110]

Barnard did not maintain student rosters by race, and thus an exact count of African American women at the college prior to 1960 is not available. However, it is believed that Zora Neale Hurston was the first known African American graduate, and that she was followed by Black women graduates in the classes of 1931, 1932, and 1935. Both Hurston and Blackwell, who graduated in 1928 and 1935, respectively, said that there were no other African American women on campus while they were students. The publicity surrounding Reverend Robinson's challenge to Barnard increased the college's awareness and efforts to attract more African American women in the years after World War II. Charlotte Hanley pointed out that Barnard recruited Black women from New York City public schools who were not as socially or economically advantaged as many of the Black women at the other Seven Sister colleges.[111] The small number of African American women who attended Barnard in the middle of the century remember the classes and faculty fondly. Though Black students were barred from living on campus, the only other remembered racial slight was Vera Joseph's recollection stating that she was not invited to become a member of the Barnard Club of New York after graduation.[112] While all of the Black alumnae who commented on their Barnard years said they had made many friendships across racial lines, their primary concern at Barnard had been the value the degree gave them in their careers and professional growth.

Conclusion

In terms of policies related to race, the Seven Sister colleges are not a monolithic entity. Some admitted African American women as far back as the turn of the twentieth century, while others grudgingly, and only under great pressure, admitted them decades later. Discrimination in housing, however, was a constant problem for African American students at every Seven Sister institution. Even when they were finally allowed to live on campuses, they remained segregated within the dormitories. In 1927, Smith College's President Neilson informed a parent that "legally the College had no right to exclude colored girls . . . but we take care that a colored girl and a White girl never have to share the same room, and we advise colored girls for their own comfort to room outside the college."[113] Frances Monroe King, a Black Mount Holyoke graduate in 1942, recalled that "we did have a dean of residence who did not permit interracial rooming. I had a single room all four years, not always by choice."[114] In fact, White students' views on this issue often differed from the administration. King said that when a White and an African American student from the class of 1943 requested a room together, the college's rejection of their request caused an "outrage" on campus among students.[115]

Many White students joined the struggle for racial equality on the Seven Sister campuses. Interracial and Christian student groups, for example, were very active. June Jackson recalled that the early leaders of the Interracial Group at Vassar, many of whom were Jewish, were criticized for being "too interested in Negroes" — a charge tinged with anti-Semitism.[116] In 1937, the Student Christian Movement sent a letter to Radcliffe President Ada L. Comstock inquiring about the situation of "Negro" students: they asked how many had ever been admitted, whether quotas existed, what the school's housing policy was, and to what extent Blacks were allowed to participate in campus life.[117] Charlotte Hanley, a 1947 Barnard graduate, acknowledged that the efforts of certain White classmates made her scholarship possible:

> I celebrate Shirley Sexauer Harrison, Miriam Gore Ruff [member of the Committee on the Investigation of Educational Opportunities for the Negro at Barnard], the editors of the *Barnard Bulletin* for the editorial of March 4, 1943, and all the other Barnard women, who, along with Jim Robinson, caused Dean Gildersleeves to reflect on Barnard's student recruitment policies. Their strong commitment to the importance of having more Negro students at Barnard had lasting effects. Guidance counselors at high schools in Harlem and elsewhere thereafter were invited to locate promising candidates for admission. By the time of Dean Gildersleeves' retirement in 1947, the number of Negro students attending Barnard, as I recall, had risen to eight — the largest number in its history — an improvement, but still a small fraction of the 1,400 strong student body.[118]

Despite the resistance they faced, the small number of African American women who attended and graduated from the Seven Sister colleges overwhelmingly asserted that they would attend the same institution again. Many of their daughters and granddaughters have since attended these same institutions. Most of these women minimized any discrimination they experienced on these campuses, saying the pursuit of the degree was their primary goal. While they experienced discrimination, primarily in housing, these limitations did not paralyze them. Most were outstanding students, active in campus activities, and many formed lifelong friendships across racial lines during their years at the Seven Sisters.

Despite these positive feelings, however, not all Black alumnae from that era share the sentiments. For example, when some of Radcliffe's earliest Black graduates were asked to comment on their experience, one woman vehemently refused. The interviewer observed, "[Although] she had an interesting career . . . she is very, very bitter about Radcliffe because of her experience there. And she deeply resents Radcliffe's failure to recognize its early Black graduates and their accomplishments."[119]

The early Black graduates of the Seven Sister colleges were a privileged group, and they were aware of it. Their African American sisters in the South who attended Black colleges were often channeled into teacher-training, vocational, and home economics programs. While African American women who attended White coeducational institutions found themselves barred from many "male disciplines," the Seven Sister graduates were among the earliest Black women scientists, lawyers, and doctors: Harriet Rice, Wellesley's first Black graduate in 1887, became a physician; Jane Bolin, a 1928 graduate of Wellesley, became the first African American woman judge in the country; Eunice Hunter Carter, from Smith's class of 1921, became the first African American woman district attorney in the state of New York, whose work in the 1930s resulted in the biggest prosecution of organized crime in the nation; Evelyn Boyd, a 1945 Smith graduate, became one of the first Black women to earn a Ph.D. in mathematics (Yale, 1950). A 1988 study found that, of the twenty-eight living Black alumnae of Mount Holyoke, fourteen became prominent physicians and research scientists.[120]

Shirlee Taylor Haizlip, a 1959 graduate of Wellesley, noted that there were only two other Black women in her class and eight on the campus in total, but to her their small numbers did not matter. She said her closest friends were White, and that there was no consciousness concerning Blackness among the African American women at Wellesley, that they wanted to be viewed just like any other students. Haizlip explained that the thinking of the period was that "to be overly friendly with others of color would . . . set them too much apart," thus Black students deliberately avoided one another.[121] June Jackson recalled that in the 1940s at Vassar, African American women were expected to be assimilationist and integrationist, the unquestioned goals of most middle-class African Americans prior to the 1960s. She was told by college officials and faculty to think of herself as an American and not a Negro American.[122] Barbara P. Wright, Mount Holyoke class of 1943, also remembered that "there were few Black students [at Mount Holyoke], and although we were friends, we all went about our business."[123]

African American women appear to have preferred Wellesley and Smith, which were perceived as the most welcoming to Blacks of the Seven Sisters. In a letter to the dean of Radcliffe College in 1946, Mary Gibson Huntley, a 1918 graduate of Radcliffe, said that Smith and Wellesley were the fairest towards African American women in terms of scholarship awards and housing policy. She added that the alumnae clubs of these two institutions were more accepting of Black women.[124]

Early African American graduates of the Seven Sisters were frequently loyal alumnae. They attended reunions, were active in alumnae clubs, gave money to their alma maters, and served as trustees. Having earned degrees from these institutions gave these Black women unprecedented access to people of power and privilege. Fifty years after graduating from Radcliffe, Mary Gibson Huntley wrote: "The prestige of my degree brought contacts in emergency, when professional or racial problems arose."[125] Charlotte Leverett Smith Brown, a 1920 graduate of Radcliffe and the first Black woman at Radcliffe to graduate with a degree in science (chemistry), concurred with Huntley's assessment. Writing at age sixty-nine, Brown stated, "I always have been and always will be proud that I am a Radcliffe graduate, and find that when questioned the mention of Radcliffe seems to settle all arguments and discussions."[126] Frances M. King, Mount Holyoke class of 1942, agrees, "I continue to be grateful for having had the opportunity for a Mount Holyoke education. It stacks up well in the world and makes me proud to be an alumna."[127] Evelyn Rich, Bryn Mawr class of 1954, who did not enjoy her college experience and felt that she was given grades she didn't deserve, nevertheless stated in an interview, "I'm very supportive of the college now. . . . I give them money, and more importantly I give them time and my commitment because I feel . . . that the life I live now is largely a result of my Bryn Mawr experience."[128] In recent discussions, early Black Barnard College graduates shared the perspective that a degree from such a distinguished institution opened doors and provided invaluable contacts.[129]

While not every Black Seven Sister student was affluent — many worked to earn money while in college — the socioeconomic status and life experiences of most of them were far removed from those of the average African American. Wellesley graduate Shirley Taylor Haizlip, class of 1959, reflected on her fellow Black Seven Sisters:

> The hue of their skin barely distinguished them from other students. Like other young women in the Sister Colleges and men in the Ivy League schools, the Negroes generally came from life styles similar to that of the majority of the student body. More often than not, their parents were professionals, conservative in their politics, and moderate in their racial practices. . . . The Northern Negro student's identification with the economically and socially less fortunate of his brothers was tenuous at best. Although in each successful black family there were always some close familiar links with the poverty and the peculiar degradation of being black, strong attempts were made to ignore or avoid any contamination by association. These, and I, too, were blacks of a different color.[130]

The roster of Black Seven Sister graduates from the mid-1960s reads like a "who's who" of elite Black America. The daughters of doctors, religious and civil rights leaders, educators, and other professionals dominated. Jane White and Gladys White, the daughter and niece of NAACP President Walter

White, graduated from Smith in 1944 and 1942, respectively. Channing To-bias's daughter Belle graduated from Barnard in 1931; Black Nobel laureate Ralph Bunche's daughter Joan was a member of the Vassar class of 1953; Olive Thurman, the daughter of prominent Black theologian and dean of Howard University Divinity School Howard Thurman, was in the Vassar class of 1948; and Gail Lumet Buckley, daughter of actress Lena Horne, graduated from Radcliffe in 1959.

Many of these women were so light complected that they were easily mis-taken as White. June Jackson commented that her classmate at Vassar, Bea-trix McCleary, "was so light in complexion, and the student body so unused to the varied shades of Afro-Americans, that she was generally mistaken for any ethnic background other than Black."[131] Nevertheless, these women's high achievements often didn't change Whites' attitudes towards them, as they were viewed as atypical Blacks. For example, in 1914, when Radcliffe President Lebarron Russell Briggs attempted to help Mary Gibson get finan-cial aid, he repeatedly mentioned to donors that Gibson did not look African American. In one letter, he wrote, "this girl is almost White," and assured them that Gibson was extremely bright, and, although colored, that "she is a colored girl who would easily be taken for a Spanish girl."[132] However, these women's light skin did not prevent their schools from keeping them in seg-regated housing.

In many ways these African American women's Seven Sisters' education set them apart from most women of their race. It gave them the freedom, exposure, and opportunity to prove themselves intellectually on the same basis as Whites, and opened to them opportunities for a wider range of careers, including medicine, science, and law. In fact, Wellesley College alumnae records reported in 1964 that the number of African American alumnae who had earned graduate and professional degrees was "especially striking" and far exceeded that of the college population as a whole.[133] In contrast to many of their White classmates, who often married and stopped working outside the home, the early Seven Sisters' Black graduates over-whelmingly both married *and* maintained careers. These women knew that they were expected by other Blacks to be "a credit to the race," and that their success or failure had an impact not only on them as individuals, but on the African American race as a whole. They were race representatives regardless of how unrepresentative they were in other respects (e.g., social and familial backgrounds).

Mount Holyoke, Wellesley, and Smith, which were founded in part on Christian beliefs, were challenged when their policies and practices con-flicted with these beliefs. At Smith, the strong influence of the NAACP made the school popular among African American women. Radcliffe was a favorite among African American women for both undergraduate and graduate study. Radcliffe President Lebarron Russell Briggs was close friends with NAACP board members, and was considered a fair and liberal man by Afri-can American students. Vassar, Barnard, and Bryn Mawr were the most re-sistant to admitting African American women. As noted above, throughout the presidency of M. Carey Thomas, no African American woman attended Bryn Mawr. Her negative and stereotypical views of African Americans are a matter of record. Key personnel at the Seven Sisters made the difference in the treatment of African Americans and their ability to matriculate in these institutions. Historian Rosalind Rosenberg noted that Virginia Gildersleeves, dean of Barnard from 1911–1946, "welcomed Jewish students and faculty only so long as they were thoroughly assimilated, and she included African Americans only so long as they were well spoken and did not ask to live in the dormitories."[134]

In written and oral histories, early African American students at the Seven Sister colleges stated that these institutions had a quota of no more than two Blacks per class. Though there was in fact no written policy limiting the number of African American students at these colleges, there was an unwritten policy, like the one contested at Smith in 1913. Francis Monroe King, Mount Holyoke College class of 1942, recalled:

> When I was a freshman, the only other Negro was a senior. By my sophomore year there were two in the freshman class, thus shattering a long-standing unwritten quota among the Seven Sister colleges of "only two at a time on campus." When I was a senior, two more Negroes were freshmen, bringing our total to five![135]

Charlotte Hanley Scott, Barnard class of 1947, recalled that there were usually two women a year during her tenure. By the 1950s, more Blacks were being admitted. An article on Black students at Barnard noted that in the 1950s, when as many as three African Americans were admitted per class, Black women at the school referred to themselves as "The Holy Twelve" because there were never more than twelve Black women on campus in any given year.[136]

As noted above, the increased presence of African American women on the campuses of the Seven Sister colleges during the twentieth century was influenced greatly by the people in the leadership of those institutions and the protest efforts of the NAACP. Public condemnation and negative press also forced this issue to a head. Even with the most liberal of the Seven Sister colleges, the issue of social equality remained. The refusal to assign African American women rooms with Whites, regardless of their background or hue, clearly communicated to the Black community that in many ways these campuses reflected society's attitude towards them. In addition, the women were often viewed in racial terms. Letters of references from professors often noted that they were the brightest "colored or Negro" student. College student affairs records with comments like "well bred, deeply thoughtful, possible future leader of her race" reflected the bias and expectations that were envisioned for many of the Black women students.

It was sometimes believed by the administrators of these institutions that most of the African American women graduates would be employed in a Black setting. Mary Gibson recalled that Black women college graduates routinely faced discrimination in hiring and had little choice but to go South to teach in segregated high schools. She noted that a few also taught in New England schools and in New York City. While at Radcliffe, she relates,

in June, 1917, a rare opportunity made me the first colored bank clerk in Boston, where I worked two summers for the Tremont Trust Company on State Street. President Briggs had advised me to go back home and give my training to my people. That was the ideal of service for many decades. It was the hope of my widowed mother, a former Washington teacher. It had been the dream of my father, a Baltimore lawyer.[137]

Thus, despite the "rare opportunity," duty and service to her race prevailed. Gibson spent forty-five years teaching in public schools. She stated that this position brought "problems and sacrifices as well as many rewarding experiences."[138] Many graduates did break through racial barriers and had stellar careers outside of the African American community. However, some often reported limitations in their careers because of their race. Most of the women reported some active involvement with civil rights, community organizations, and interracial groups throughout their lives. As mentioned earlier, the expectation of the African American community was that those who had achieved academic and professional success would return and assist the community.

The Seven Sister colleges were certainly not utopias, but to many of the African American women who attended these institutions prior to the 1960s, it was an experience they valued enough to encourage the following generations of Black women to continue in their footsteps.

Notes

1. The terms "African American" and "Black" will be used interchangeably in this article.
2. Helen Lefkowitz Horowitz, *Alma Mater: Design and Experience in the Women's Colleges from Their Nineteenth-Century Beginnings to the 1930s* (Amherst: University of Massachusetts Press, 1993), p. 147.
3. See Arthur C. Cole, *A Hundred Years of Mount Holyoke College: The Evolution of an Educational Ideal* (New Haven, CT: Yale University Press, 1940); Cornelia Meigs, *What Makes a College? A History of Bryn Mawr* (New York: MacMillan, 1956); L. Clark Seelye, *The Early History of Smith College, 1871–1910* (Boston: Houghton, Mifflin, 1923); Florence Converse, *Wellesley College, a Chronicle of the Years, 1875–1938* (Wellesley, MA: Hathaway House Bookshop, 1939); Marian Churchill White, *A History of Barnard College* (New York: Columbia University Press, 1954); Horowitz, *Alma Mater*; Patricia Ann Palmieri, *In Adamless Eden: The Community of Women Faculty at Wellesley* (New Haven, CT: Yale University Press, 1995).
4. For a discussion of this, see Rosalyn Terborg-Penn's "Discrimination against Afro-American Women in the Women's Movement, 1830 to 1920," in *The Afro-American Woman: Struggles and Images*, ed. Sharon Harley and Rosalyn Terborg-Penn (New York: Kennikat, 1978); Linda M. Perkins, "The Impact of the 'Cult of True Womanhood' on the Education of Black Women," *Journal of Social Issues, 39*, No. 3 (1983), 17–28.
5. W.E.B. DuBois, "The College Bred Negro," in *Proceedings of the Fifth Conferences for the Study of the Negro Problems* (Atlanta, GA: Atlanta University Press, 1900).
6. W.E.B. DuBois, "The College Bred Negro," p. 30.
7. W.E.B. DuBois held a lifelong interest in the "talented tenth" of the race, those individuals who were formally educated. Beginning in the late nineteenth century, he surveyed and

kept data on the progress of African Americans in higher education. In his 1900 study, "The College Bred Negro," he summed up the progress of Blacks in gaining admission to White institutions.

8. W.E.B. DuBois, *The Philadelphia Negro: A Social Study* (New York: Schocken Books, 1970), p. 7.

9. See Adelaide M. Cromwell, *The Other Brahmins: Boston's Black Upper Class, 1750–1950* (Fayetteville: University of Arkansas Press, 1994), p. 10, and Willard Gatewood, *Aristocrats of Color: The Black Elite, 1880–1920.* (Fayetteville: University of Arkansas Press, 1990), pp. 247–271.

10. James D. Anderson, *The Education of Blacks in the South* (Chapel Hill: University of North Carolina Press, 1988), p. 186.

11. DuBois, *The Philadelphia Negro.*

12. Cromwell, *The Other Brahmins*, p. 139; Gatewood, *Aristocrats of Color*, p. 114.

13. Gatewood, *Aristocrats of Color*, p. 247.

14. For more on this topic see Anderson, *The Education of Blacks in the South.*

15. Carlton Mabee, *Black Education in New York State: From Colonial to Modern Times* (Syracuse, NY: Syracuse University Press, 1979), p. 104.

16. Roster of African American Women Students at Oberlin College, compiled in 1984 by Michon Boston, in History of Black Women at Oberlin Project. In possession of the author.

17. Quoted in Horowitz, *Alma Mater,* p. 54.

18. Wellesley College Directory of Students, Wellesley College Archives, Wellesley, MA, 1887–1888.

19. Harriett A. Rice, "On the Mountain Top," *Wellesley Magazine,* June 1943, p. 298.

20. Biographical records of Harriet A. Rice in Harriet A. Rice folder of Wellesley College Alumnae Association Records, Wellesley College Archives, Wellesley, MA.

21. Jane Bolin Offset, "Wellesley in My Life, " in *Wellesley After-Images: Reflection on Their College Years by Forty-Five Alumnae,* ed. Wellesley College Club of Los Angeles (Los Angeles: Wellesley College Club of Los Angles, 1974), p. 92.

22. Offset, "Wellesley in My Life," pp. 91–92.

23. Virginia Foster Durr, *Outside the Magic Circle: The Autobiography of Virginia Foster Durr,* ed. Hollander F. Barnard (University: University of Alabama Press, 1985), p. 56.

24. Durr, *Outside the Magic Circle,* p. 58.

25. Durr, *Outside the Magic Circle,* p. 58. In 1926, Virginia Foster married Clifford Durr. Durr was a former Rhodes scholar and prominent lawyer in Birmingham, Alabama. Despite Foster Durr's attitudes towards race while at Wellesley, by the 1950s she and her husband were living in Montgomery, Alabama, and had become active civil rights advocates. Her husband Clifford accompanied African American attorney E. D. Nixon when he bailed Rosa Parks out of jail after she was arrested for refusing to give up her bus seat to a White rider in 1955.

26. Letter from the Department of Biblical History to President Ellen Pendleton, Wellesley College, May 6, 1932, President's Office Papers, Residence Halls (1918–1967), Wellesley College Archives, Wellesley, MA.

27. Ruth H. Lindsay, Dean of Residence, Wellesley College, to Mary Chase, Charlotte, North Carolina, May 9, 1949, President's Office Papers, Residence Halls (1918–1967), Wellesley College Archives, Wellesley, MA.

28. As mentioned earlier, Mount Holyoke graduated a Black woman from its seminary in 1883.

29. Ella Elbert Smith, class of 1988, Alumnae Questionnaire of 1951, Wellesley Alumnae Records, Wellesley College Archives, Wellesley, MA.

30. Smith, Alumnae Questionnaire of 1951.

31. Ella Elbert Smith, class of 1988, biographical folder, Wellesley College Alumnae Records, Wellesley College Archives, Wellesley, MA.

32. Henry Parsons Dowse, *Radcliffe College* (Boston: H. B. Humphrey, 1913), n.p.

33. Alberta Scott biographical data sheet, Radcliffe College Collection of Biographical Data on African American Students, p. 1, Schlesinger Library, Radcliffe College, Cambridge, MA.

34. Mary Gibson Huntley, "Radcliffe in My Life," May 1968, Mary Gibson Huntley Papers, Box 10, folder 4, Schlesinger Library, Radcliffe College, Cambridge, MA.

35. Lebarron Russell Briggs to Mary Church Terrell, October 16, 1914, Briggs Papers, Box 7, folder 53, Schlesinger Library, Radcliffe College, Cambridge, MA.

36. See various correspondence on this issue in the Mary Gibson Huntley Papers, Schlesinger Library, Radcliffe College, Cambridge, MA.

37. Lebarron Russell Briggs to Mary Church Terrell, October 16, 1914, Briggs Papers, Box 7, folder 53, Schlesinger Library, Radcliffe College, Cambridge, MA.

38. Lebarron Russell Briggs to Rev. W. H. van Allen, October 21, 1916, Briggs Papers, Box 2, p. 677, Schlesinger Library, Radcliffe College, Cambridge, MA.

39. Lebarron Russell Briggs to Mrs. S. Burt Wolbach, November 7, 1916, Briggs Papers, Box 2, p. 713, Schlesinger Library, Radcliffe College, Cambridge, MA.

40. Lebarron Russell Briggs to Mrs. S. Burt Wolbach, November 7, 1916, Briggs Papers, Box 2, p. 714, Schlesinger Library, Radcliffe College, Cambridge, MA.

41. Lebarron Russell Briggs to Miss Elizabeth Hoar Storer, February 28, 1917, in Briggs Papers, Box 2, vol. 3, p. 829, Schlesinger Library, Radcliffe College, Cambridge, MA.

42. Lebarron Russell Briggs to Mary Gibson, March 5, 1920, Briggs Papers, Box 2, vol. 4, p. 573, Schlesinger Library, Radcliffe College, Cambridge, MA.

43. Gibson, "Radcliffe in My Life," p. 1.

44. Interview of Margaret McCane by her daughter Charlotte McCane on January 1, 1981, The Margaret McCane Papers, Box 1, folder 4, Schlesinger Library, Radcliffe College, Cambridge, MA.

45. Quoted in Horowitz, *Alma Mater,* p. 70.

46. Partial transcript of NAACP meeting [n.d.], "Discussion in re Carrie Lee," in Office of the President Files, Smith College Archives, Northampton, MA.

47. W.E.B. DuBois, "A College Girl," in *Crisis, 8* (1913), 293.

48. Moorfield Storey, Boston, Massachusetts, to Reverend Marion Lercy Burton, Smith College, October 14, 1913, in Carrie Lee folder, Individuals 1917, Box 1789, Smith College Archives, Northampton, MA.

49. Biographical Sheet, Faculty Records Bo-Br, Box 42, in Ruth Bowles folder, Smith College Archives, Northampton, MA.

50. Mary White Ovington, Brooklyn, New York, to Joel Spingarn, October 23, 1913, in Individuals 1917, Box 1789, Carrie Lee folder, Smith College Archives, Northampton, MA.

51. Walter White, *A Man Called White: The Autobiography of Walter White* (Bloomington: Indiana University Press, 1948), p. 336.

52. White, *A Man Called White,* p. 337.

53. Roster of Black Undergraduates Who Attended Smith College, 1900-1974, Admissions Office Records, Black students folder, Smith College Archives, Northampton, MA.

54. Jefferson Church, Springfield, Massachusetts, to Mary Lyon, November 17, 1845, Mary Lyon Collection, Series A, sub-series 2, Mount Holyoke College Archives, South Hadley, MA.

55. Francis Gillette, Bloomfield, Connecticut, to Mary Lyon, May 29, 1846, Mary Lyon Collection, Series A, sub-series 2, Archives and Special Collections, Mount Holyoke College, South Hadley, MA.

56. Florence Paringtow, Dean of Mount Holyoke College, South Hadley, MA, October 11, 1913, to Dean Ada Comstock, Smith College, Northampton, MA, in Individuals 1917, Box 1789, Carrie Lee folder, Smith College Archives, Northampton, MA.

57. History Department, Course Records for History 265, paper by Martha Ralston Perkins, Archives and Special Collection, Mount Holyoke College, South Hadley, MA.

58. Alumnae Biographical file for Hortense Parker, Class of 1883, Archives and Special Collections, Mount Holyoke College, South Hadley, MA.

59. Helen B. Calder Papers, Calder to "dear mamma," November 14, 1894, Archives and Special Collections, Mount Holyoke College, South Hadley, MA.

60. Interview with Frances H. Williams, October 31–November 1, 1977, Black Women Oral History Project, Schlesinger Library, Radcliffe College, Cambridge, MA; Interview with Frances William, October 9, 1991, Frances Williams, Class of 1919 Alumnae file, Archives and Special Collections, Mount Holyoke College, South Hadley, MA; (Massachusetts) *Transcript-Telegram,* February 2, 26, 1983.

61. Alumnae files of Alice Stubbs, 1926; Miriam Cunningham, 1932; Ida Miller, 1933; Laura Lee, 1936; Mabel Murphy, 1937; and Ruth Smith, 1937, Archives and Special Collections, Mount Holyoke College, South Hadley, MA; (Massachusetts) *Transcript-Telegram*, February 2, 26, 1983.

62. Beverly Guy-Sheftall and Jo Moore Stewart, eds., *Spelman: A Centennial Celebration, 1881– 1981* (Charlotte, NC: Delmar, 1981), p. 47.

63. History Department, Course Records for History 265, "Black and White Americans," Fall 1973, folder 1: Background Material, Archives and Special Collections, Mount Holyoke College, South Hadley, MA.

64. Quoted in Dean Karen Tidmarsh, Bryn Mawr College, "History of the Status of Minority Groups in the Bryn Mawr Student Body," p. 1, Collection 9JG, Bryn Mawr College Archives, Bryn Mawr, PA.

65. Helen Lefkowitz Horowitz, *The Power and Passion of M. Carey Thomas* (New York: Knopf, 1994).

66. M. Carey Thomas, Bryn Mawr College, to Georgiana R. Simpson, Washington, DC, May 2, 1906, M. Carey Thomas Papers, letter book 34, p. 320, Bryn Mawr College Archives, Bryn Mawr, PA.

67. M. Carey Thomas address to 1916 College Opening, reprinted in *The College News*, Bryn Mawr, October 11, 1916, p. 1.

68. Quoted in Dean Karen Tidmarsh, Bryn Mawr College, "History of the Status of Minority Groups in the Bryn Mawr Student Body," p. 3, Collection 9JG, Bryn Mawr College Archives, Bryn Mawr, PA.

69. Horowitz, *The Power and Passions of M. Carey Thomas*, p. 444.

70. M. Carey Thomas, Bryn Mawr, to Virginia Gildersleeves, Barnard College, New York City, December 12, 1930, Gildersleeves Papers, Barnard College Archives, New York, NY.

71. M. Carey Thomas, Bryn Mawr, to Virginia Gildersleeves, Barnard College, New York City, December 12, 1930, Gildersleeves Papers, Barnard College Archives, New York, New York.

72. Virginia Gildersleeves, Barnard College, to M. Carey Thomas, December 15, 1930, Gildersleeves Papers, Barnard College Archives, New York, NY.

73. Prue Smith Rockwell, Paris, France, February 7, 1931, to Marion Edwards Park, Bryn Mawr College, in *Bryn Mawr Alumnae Bulletin*, April 1931, p. 11; Marion Edwards Park to Prue Smith Rockwell, February 24, 1931, *Bryn Mawr Alumnae Bulletin*, April 1931, p. 11.

74. Karen Tidmarsh, "History of the Status of Minority Groups in the Bryn Mawr Students Body," 1988, Dean of the Faculty Papers, Bryn Mawr College Archives, Bryn Mawr, PA.

75. Evelyn Jones Rich, "Reflections on the Bryn Mawr Experience," July 24, 1979, audiotape, "Oral History Collection," Bryn Mawr College Archives, Bryn Mawr, PA.

76. Jones, "Reflections."

77. "Rediscovering Bryn Mawr — Past and Present, from a Black Perspective," conference held February 7 and 8, 1975, Summary 9, Bryn Mawr College Archives, Bryn Mawr, PA.

78. Christine Philpot Clark, "As It Was and As It Is," in *Bryn Mawr Alumnae Bulletin*, Spring 1969, p. 5.

79. Clark, "As It Was and As It Is," p. 5.

80. Based on statements made by June Jackson Christmas's recollection of Vassar and its reputation in the eyes of African Americans. See June Jackson Christmas's "A Historical Overview: The Black Experience at Vassar," in *Vassar Quarterly*, Spring 1988, p. 5.

81. Newspaper clipping, 1897, in Anita Florence Hemmings folder, Vassar College Archives, Poughkeepsie, NY.

82. Quoted in 1897 newspaper clipping, "Negress at Vassar," in Anita Florence Hemmings folder, Vassar College Archives, Poughkeepsie, NY.

83. Quoted in 1897 newspaper clipping, "Negress at Vassar," in Anita Florence Hemmings folder, Vassar College Archives, Poughkeepsie, NY.

84. Various newspaper clippings of the Hemmings affair, in Anita Florence Hemmings folder, Vassar College Archives, Poughkeepsie, NY.

85. Various newspaper clippings of the Hemmings affair, in Anita Florence Hemmings folder, Vassar College Archives, Poughkeepsie, NY.

86. Christmas, "A Historical Overview," p. 4.

87. Lynn D. Gordon, *Gender and Higher Education in the Progressive Era* (New Haven, CT: Yale University Press, 1990), p. 140. The club included students whose grandmothers, mothers, or aunts were alumnae.

88. W.E.B. DuBois to Dr. Henry MacCracken, May 15, 1930, in Presidential Papers, May 1930, Vassar College Archives, Poughkeepsie, NY.

89. Dr. Henry MacCracken to W.E.B. DuBois, May 17, 1930, in Presidential Papers, May 1930, Vassar College Archives, Poughkeepsie, NY.

90. W.E.B. DuBois, "Postcript," *Crisis,* August 1932, p. 266.

91. Christmas, "A Historical Overview," pp. 4–5.

92. The Daisy Chain was a prestigious Vassar commencement activity dating back to 1884. Vassar students were selected in their sophomore year based on leadership and willingness to assist seniors with commencement activities. Those chosen carried chains made of daisies.

93. Christmas, "A Historical Overview," pp. 4–5.

94. Christmas, "A Historical Overview," pp. 4–5.

95. Christmas, "A Historical Overview," pp. 4–5.

96. Quoted in article, "DuBois Suggests That Vassar Have 100 Negro Students," in *Vassar Miscellany News,* April 4, 1942, p. 1.

97. Christmas, "A Historical Overview," p. 8.

98. Christmas, "A Historical Overview," p. 3.

99. Zora Neale Hurston, *Dust Tracks on a Road: An Autobiography* (Urbana: University of Illinois Press, 1984), p. 169.

100. Hurston, *Dust Tracks on a Road,* p. 171

101. Hurston, *Dust Tracks on a Road,* p. 171.

102. Biographical entry on Channing Tobias in Rayford W. Logan and Michael R. Winston, eds., *Dictionary of American Negro Biography* (New York: W. W. Norton, 1982), pp. 593–595; Roster of Black Students, Publicity Office Files, Wellesley College Archives, Wellesley, MA.

103. Telephone interview with Vera Joseph Peterson, MD, and Linda M. Perkins, June 12, 1997, and comments in *Different Voices: The Experiences of Women of Color at Barnard* (New York: HEOP Office of Barnard College, 1996), pp. 11–12.

104. Vera Joseph Peterson, *Different Voices,* p. 12.

105. Interview with Jean Blackwell Hutson by Linda M. Perkins, New York, June 5, 1997.

106. Virginia Gildersleeves, Barnard College, to the Reverend James H. Robinson, n.d., reprinted in the *Barnard Bulletin,* March 1, 1943, p. 1.

107. Editorial, "Where Do We Go from Here?" in *Barnard Bulletin,* March 1, 1943, p. 2.

108. "Report on Educational Opportunities for Negroes," *Barnard Bulletin,* June 4, 1943, p. 1.

109. Statement written by Charlotte Hanley Scott to Caroline Niemczyk in Barnard College Archives, African American Student folder, New York, NY.

110. Telephone interview with Charlotte Hanley Scott by Linda M. Perkins, June 9, 1997.

111. Telephone interview with Charlotte Hanley Scott by Linda M. Perkins, June 9, 1997.

112. Vera Joseph Peterson, in *Different Voices,* p. 12.

113. Memo to file, President's Office, quoting President Neilson to parent, February 2, 1927, Black Students, 1929–1945, Neilson Papers, Smith College Archives, Southhampton, MA.

114. History Department, Course Records for History 265, Frances M. King Drue, Cleveland, Ohio, to Regina Elston, South Hadley, MA, November 26, 1973, in Regina Elston's student paper, folder 1, Archives and Special Collections, Mount Holyoke College, South Hadley, MA.

115. History Department, Course Records for History 265, Frances M. King Drue, Cleveland, Ohio, to Regina Elston, South Hadley, MA, November 26, 1973, in Regina Elston's student paper, folder 1, Archives and Special Collections, Mount Holyoke College, South Hadley, MA.

116. Christmas, "A Historical Overview," pp. 4–5, 7.

117. David Klugh, Chair, Interrace Group, to President Ada L. Comstock, January 8, 1937, Ada L. Comstock Papers, folder 217, Schlesinger Library, Radcliffe College, Cambridge, MA.

118. Charlotte Hanley Scott, class of 1947, letter to the editor of *Barnard Alumnae Magazine*, Winter 1996, p. 3.
119. Margaret P. McCane to Ellen Henle, January 9, 1982, in Margaret P. McCane Papers, folder 5, Schlesinger Library, Radcliffe College, Cambridge, MA.
120. Janet Novas, "Black Women in Science from Mount Holyoke: A Biographical Sketch of Two Mount Holyoke Alumnae," in History Department records, Series D, Course Records, Papers for History 381, Spring 1988, Archives and Special Collections, Mount Holyoke College, South Hadley, MA.
121. Shirlee Taylor Haizlip, "Only the Robes Were Black," *Wellesley Alumnae Magazine*, Fall 1985, pp. 10–11.
122. Christmas, "A Historical Overview," p. 8.
123. Quoted in Midge Nealon's history paper, "Barbara Penn Wright, class of 1943," in History Department, Course Records for History 265, "Black and White American," Fall 1973, folder 4, Archives and Special Collections, Mount Holyoke College, South Hadley, MA.
124. Mary G. Huntley to Dean Mildred P. Sherman, Radcliffe College, Cambridge, Massachusetts, April 8, 1946, in the Mary Huntley Papers, Box 4, folder 45, Schlesinger Library, Radcliffe College, Cambridge, MA.
125. Mary Gibson Huntley, "Radcliffe in My Life," Huntley Papers, Schlesinger Library, Radcliffe College, Cambridge, MA.
126. Charlotte Leverett Smith Brown biographical data in Radcliffe College of Biographical Data on African-American Students, p. 29, Schlesinger Library, Radcliffe College Archives, Cambridge, MA.
127. Frances L. Monroe King, History Department, Records Series D, Course Records, Papers for History 265, Fall 1973, Archives and Special Collections, Mount Holyoke College, South Hadley, MA.
128. Evelyn Jones Rich, "Reflections on the Bryn Mawr Experience," July 24, 1979, audiotape, "Oral History Collection," Bryn Mawr College Archives, Bryn Mawr, PA.
129. Interviews with Jean Blackwell Hutson and Charlotte Hanley Scott by Linda M. Perkins, June 5 and June 9, 1997 respectively.
130. Shirlee Taylor Haizlip, "Reflections," *Wellesley Alumnae Magazine*, Winter 1969, p. 45.
131. Christmas, "A Historical Overview," p. 5.
132. President Lebarron Russell Briggs, Radcliffe College, to Miss Harriet D. Buckingham, Bournedale, Massachusetts, August 4, 1914 in President Briggs Papers, Box 2, vol. 3, p. 91, Schlesinger Library, Radcliffe College, Cambridge, MA; President Lebarron Russell Briggs to Mrs. Storey, Bournedale, Massachusetts, August 4, 1915, Briggs Papers, Box 2, vol. 3, p. 93, Schlesinger Library, Radcliffe College, Cambridge, MA.
133. Negro Alumnae and Present Negro Students at Wellesley College list, June 1, 1964, Publicity Office, Black Students File, Wellesley College Archives, Wellesley, MA.
134. Rosalind Rosenberg, "The Legacy of Dean Gildersleeves," *Barnard Alumnae Bulletin*, Summer 1996, p. 21.
135. Francis L. Monroe King to Regina Elston, November 26,1973, in History Department Senior Papers, Francis L. King Paper, Archives and Special Collections, Mount Holyoke College, South Hadley, MA.
136. Andree L. Abecassis, "Black at Barnard: A Survey of Policy and Events," *Barnard Alumnae Journal*, Spring 1969, p. 4.
137. Huntley, "Radcliffe in My Life," p. 2.
138. Huntley, "Radcliffe in My Life," p. 2.

I would like to acknowledge the research assistance of Jane Lowenthal, Barnard College Archives; Jane Rittenhouse and Kathleen Whalen, Bryn Mawr Archives and Library; Joyce D. Miller, Office for Institutional Diversity, Bryn Mawr College; Patricia Albright, Mount Holyoke Archives and Special Collections; Jane Knowles, Schlesinger Library and Archives, Radcliffe College; Wilma Slaight, Wellesley College Archives; Nancy Mackechine, Vassar College Library; and the research support of the University of Illinois, Champaign-Urbana and the City University of New York.

The Hidden Half:
A History of Native American Women's Education

DEIRDRE A. ALMEIDA

*In this chapter, Deirdre Almeida presents an overview of Native American educa-
tion since the Europeans' arrival in the Americas with a focus on its effect on
Native American women in the United States from 1878 to the present. Until
recently the history of Native American women has only been touched upon, but
over the past decade, Native American women scholars have begun to present their
perspectives on the influence of both traditional learning and formal Western-based
educational programs on Native women. Almeida examines the educational experiences of Native American women resulting·from U.S. government policies, in
particular the off-reservation boarding school program of 1878–1928. Throughout
her overview, Almeida demonstrates how education was, and still is, connected to
the political power of Native American women. Traditional learning has been the
means by which Native American women have established and maintained their
voices and empowered themselves through gender roles. However, Western-based
education, under government control, has been used as an instrument to destroy
the traditional power of Native American women, through the shifting of gender
roles. The voices of the Native American women presented in this chapter illustrate
their resistance to the breakdown of traditional political standing and their use of
education to reclaim and protect it.*

I n their roles as missionaries, Indian agents, folklorists, and ethnographers, European and European American males have throughout history
been the ones to collect and interpret Native American narratives and
have established themselves as the "leading experts" on Native Americans,
including Native American women.[1] Even as we near the end of the twentieth

---

[1] The term "Native American" is used throughout this article instead of "American Indian" as it has
become the common term used in the northeastern region of the United States. The terms "Native"
and "American Indian" will also appear, with the latter being used primarily in quoted text.

Harvard Educational Review Vol. 67 No. 4 Winter 1997, 757–771

century, many European American students of Native American cultures still continue to present Native women as drudges of men and Native men as hardly distinguishable from lower animals. However, Native American scholars such as Paula Gunn Allen (1989), Rayna Green (1992), M. Annette Jaimes (1992), Haunani Kay Trask (1993), and Ward Churchill (1994) have developed a body of academic research that attacks the appropriation and exploitation of Native American and indigenous intellectual property rights.[2] The scholarship of these writers provides a critical historical and political analysis of the European American ownership of research focused on Native Americans. As Margo Thunderbird, an activist of the Shinnecock Nation of Long Island, New York, explains:

> They've (European Americans) come for the very last of our possessions; now they want our pride, our history, our spiritual traditions. They want to rewrite and remake these things, to claim them for themselves. The lies and thefts just never end. (Churchill, 1994, p. 216)

Oneida scholar Pam Colorado frames the issue this way:

> The process is ultimately intended to supplant Indians, even in areas of their own culture and spirituality. In the end, non-Indians will have complete power to define what is and what is not Indian, even for Indians. We are talking here about a complete ideological/conceptual subordination of Indian people in addition to the total physical subordination they already experience. When this happens, the last vestiges of real Indian society and Indian rights will disappear. Non-Natives will then claim to "own" our heritage and ideas as thoroughly as they now claim to own our land and resources. (Churchill, 1994, p. 216)

As a Native American educator, I embrace the views expressed by other indigenous scholars concerning ownership of our cultural research. As a Native American woman, I believe it is our responsibility and right to produce research that specifically relates to us as Native women. In their research, European Americans have continually portrayed Native Americans as a vanishing race. In addition, Native American women are virtually nonexistent in their writings. Allen (1989) states that there are a number of reasons why Native women's voices and stories have not always been heard, not all of which can be blamed on European American male chauvinism. Allen explains that, bolstered by the authority of long-standing customs, Native American men believe that Native women have their own mouths and can tell their own stories and should be allowed to do so. They simply do not feel qualified to tell about women's lives or activities, particularly to other men.

Native American women scholars are beginning to create our own research. Native American women activists and scholars, such as Zitkala-Sa

---

[2] "Indigenous intellectual property rights" refers to the rights claimed by an indigenous people over their traditional cultural knowledge (see Greaves, 1994).

(1921/1993), Beverly Hungry Wolf (1981), Ella Deloria (1988), Mary Crow Dog (1990), Winona LaDuke (Churchill & LaDuke, 1992), and Lilikala Kame' eleihiwa (1992) have all contributed to the development of a history of Native American women from a woman's perspective. This is a continuation of the practice of many Native American nations in which the women are responsible for keeping the oral traditions alive and passing them on to the future generations (Billson, 1995).

In this article I focus on the history of Native American women and education. Education has been a key factor in making Native women invisible and silencing our voices. A Native epistemology is needed, according to Hawaiian educator and scholar Manu Meyer (1997), because of the vast inequality between the diversity of knowledge structures and what is respected, assessed, and upheld in Native schools and society. Meyer describes cultural epistemology as a study of difference for its appeal to non-universal principles and because it challenges mainstream philosophical assumptions. This article contributes to the development of this epistemology by tracing both the positive and negative influences of education on the lives of Native American women.

Native Women's Marking of Time

Institutional racism was rampant in North American colonists' effort to educate Native Americans (Wright, 1992, p. 93). Educational institutions established by European colonists attempted to impose their beliefs and values on Native students, and their social, economic, and political structures onto Native American cultures and civilizations (Almeida, 1992, p. 2). Over the centuries, education has been misused to appropriate land, to destroy Native American languages and cultures, and to enslave nations of Indigenous peoples (Crow Dog, 1990; Trask, 1993). Spanish, French, and British missionary schools used education to disguise their efforts to eliminate Native American society. The U.S. government later established boarding schools that continued these efforts. Most importantly, education has been used to both justify and minimize first colonists' and later the federal government's involvement in these acts of genocide (Churchill, 1994, p. 45). This has been accomplished by eliminating any discussions of these facts from the U.S. history textbooks and from the U.S. educational system in general.

Immediately upon arrival, the first European explorers of Turtle Island in North America began recording their opinions of the "New World" (Jaimes & Halsey, 1992, p. 311) through written descriptions and drawings of the land and the Indigenous peoples encountered. These early records were often heavily influenced by European mythology and imagination rather than based on what the early explorers were actually observing. Prior to the mid-eighteenth century there was little research and scholarship that focused on Native American women; the non-Natives who documented history were usually male, and were primarily interested in war and diplomatic transactions (Green, 1992; Jaimes & Halsey, 1992). Today, European Americans continue to have a poor understanding of the historical significance of Native women. History highlights the accomplishments of Native American war heroes such as Geronimo, Sitting Bull, and Red Cloud, while the history of Native American women of significant importance is rarely acknowledged. Green's (1992) research shows that Native American women have primarily been represented as anonymous figures who prepare food, haul wood, tan hides, and take care of children.

Historical texts focus mainly on Native American men, especially those having a formal role such as chief, warrior, spiritual leader, or diplomat (Jaimes & Halsey, 1992, p. 315) even though Native American women held equally important roles in determining the sovereignty of their nations (Almeida, 1995, p. 2). Some examples include the clan mothers of many northeastern and southeastern Native American nations, and Native American women's societies of the Western Plains nations, such as the Cheyenne and Piegans (Billson, 1995, p. 14). The following observations reflect the leadership roles of Native American women:

> Though some observers saw women as drudges, LeJeune (Jesuit Priest) saw women as holding great power and having in every instance . . . the choice of plans. . . . The idea of Native American women actively participating in the decisions pertaining to the use of land and the governing of their community was widely accepted by Native American nations, however it would be an aspect of native cultures which European colonists could not comprehend and accept. (Jaimes & Halsey, 1992, p. 320)

Because it went against their cultural beliefs, as described by Jaimes and Halsey, European colonizers made it a priority to reduce the status of Native women within their nations. As a result, the economic, political, and social status of Native women suffered immeasurably (Green, 1992).

Education became a key component in the plan to eliminate Native American sovereignty (Churchill, 1994, p.139). Some of the most prestigious and enduring educational institutions, such as Harvard University and Dartmouth College, included the education of Native Americans in their charters (Wright, 1992, p. 93). Despite this history, Native American education still remains an overlooked and under-researched topic in education. The limited research that has been conducted on the history of Native American education has primarily been from non-Native scholars, the majority of whom are men (Allen, 1989; Green, 1989). Their focus has been on the development of educational systems for Native Americans and its impact on Native Americans in general, with emphasis on Native men.[3]

Over the past ten years, Native women historians and educators have begun to draw public attention to the history of Native American women, in-

---

[3] Examples of scholarship that has been produced with a focus on Native American men include La Flesche (1963), Alford (1936), and Rideout (1912).

cluding the influence of education on their lives and their roles within their nations. Scholars such as Rayna Green (1992), Ardy Bowker (1993), Paulette Molin (Hultgren & Molin, 1989), and K. Tsiania Lomawaima (1994) have provided a forum where Native American women — whom I call "the hidden half" — can be heard. Native American women scholars and other women seeking to preserve their Native culture have begun to document their lives and achievements in text, on film, and through oral histories.

Oral traditions and histories are an important source of information for and about Native Americans. These reflect how Native American women see themselves and how they are viewed and understood within their own culture by their own community, and must be valued as legitimate, relevant perspectives on Native women's history. However, non-Native scholars view Native American oral traditions as folklore and myths. Some examples would be the Haudenosaunnee and other nations of the Northeast who believe that the world rests on the back of a giant turtle and the first person to dwell on it was Sky Woman (Billson, 1995, p. 13). The Shawnee honor a spiritual holy woman named "Our grandmother," who received assistance from the "Great Spirit" in creating humankind; she gave the Shawnee life, as well as their code of ethics and most of their religious ceremonies (Allen, 1989, p. 7). Native scholars who utilize their oral traditions and indigenous knowledge find their research being labeled as nothing but a generalization and dismissed by self-appointed non-Native "experts" (Almeida, 1992, p. 4). Value and legitimacy has to be given to research and history from a Native American woman's perspective. Also, it is important when writing from a Native American point of view to present history in timeframes more relevant to Native American experiences.

Native American historians have identified five distinct periods since the European's arrival in the Americas: Creation (the beginning of time established in Native American stories of origin, prior to European contact in 1492); Contact with Europeans (1492–1800); The Removal Era (1800–1830); The Reservation Era (1830–1929); The Reform Era (1930–1969); and Contemporary Resistance (1970–1997). This article looks at the off-reservation boarding school education of young Native American women, with a focus on the Hampton Institute of Virginia during the mid-to-late Reservation Era, 1878–1929, and a brief discussion of the influence of off-reservation boarding schools on the lives of Native American women and their communities during the eras of Reform and Contemporary Resistance.

Native American Women's Education
Under the Indian Educational Reform Movement

The Native Americans' struggle to maintain our traditional lifestyles was increased with the Western invasion by European Americans onto Native American lands from the mid-1800s to the early 1900s. The eventual reduc-

tion of Native societies through systematic genocide,[4] warfare, broken trea-
ties, and the destruction of natural and food resources resulted in U.S. government control over Native American nations and the establishment of the
reservation system (Bowker, 1993; Green, 1992).

Confinement to reservations made Native American men unable to hunt
to supply their communities not only with food, but also with the materials
needed for clothing, housing, and other tools and implements. For Native
American women and men, the honor and respect that the hunt brought
them was also lost. Also at jeopardy was the traditional form of education for
Native American children. The tanning and quilling societies of the women
disappeared, because clothing made of hides was replaced by government-
distributed trade cloth. The training young Native American women had
traditionally received from their female elders was altered greatly; in time
they were forced to turn to another source for their education — the U.S.
government (Green, 1992; Standing Bear, 1975).

The reservation system thus led to the development of a major institution
of Native education, whose impact is still felt within contemporary times —
the off-reservation boarding school. These schools were viewed as a means
to speed up the assimilation process (Bowker, 1993, p. 24) in order to force
Native Americans into a European American lifestyle (Hultgren & Molin,
1989; Standing Bear, 1975). Non-native educators won federal support and
funding by promoting the idea that the best way to educate Native American
children was to remove them as soon as possible from their families and
communities and to place them where they only had contact with European
Americans.

Native children, young adults, and, in some cases, entire families were
transported from their communities to boarding schools, first in the East
and later to regional federal schools in the West. This formal education
system contributed enormously to the breakdown of Native families, including women's traditional roles, and led to the development of many of the
social ills that still affect Native nations today, such as dysfunctional families
and substance abuse (Almeida, 1992; Bowker, 1993; Green, 1989;
Lomawaima, 1994; Reyhner & Eder, 1994).[5] However, the off-reservation

---

[4] Systematic genocide is the deliberate destruction, in whole or in part, by a government or its
agents, of a racial, sexual, religious, tribal, ethnic, or political minority. It can involve not only mass
murder, but also starvation, forced deportation or removal, and political, economic, and biological
subjugation. For more information on genocide and systematic genocide, see Gioseffi (1993).

[5] Native American children were removed from their families and communities at very young ages.
Instead of being raised with their parents and extended family members, they grew up in an institutional setting. This resulted in the students' loss of knowledge of traditional parenting skills. Native
American students attending boarding schools were subjected to corporal punishment, and were
instructed to focus on the nuclear family instead of the extended family. When they became adults
and had families of their own, these boarding school students relied on the style of childrearing they
had experienced at boarding school, and passed it on to their children. Returning students also
experienced issues of trying to fit back into their communities, often with much difficulty and internal
conflicts. To cope with the frustration of a loss of identity, returning boarding school students often
turned to alcohol as a means of escape. The result was generations of substances abusers and domestic
violence. For more information on this, see, Bowker (1993).

boarding school was not a new concept in 1878. The idea that the best way to educate Native American youth was by removing them as far as possible from their home environment dates back to colonial times and Eleazer Wheelock Moor's Charity school.[6] These boarding schools flourished during the late nineteenth century, due to the increasing conflict over land and the U.S. government's misguided policies for "handling" Native Americans.

After the Civil War, many European Americans who had actively participated in the abolitionist movement sought a new cause to champion (Hultgren & Molin, 1989, p. 18). Those who chose the issue of Indian reform dedicated themselves to achieving the Americanization of Native Americans. With the end of the Native American wars at the close of the nineteenth century, new versions of containment policies for Native Americans sprang up in the belief that the United States would best serve Native Americans by assimilating them into European American society (Hultgren & Molin, 1989; Robbins, 1992; Standing Bear, 1975).

This Indian Reform movement was made up of politicians, ministers, educators, and lawyers. Most were men, but some of their wives were among the most active reformists. They established organizations such as the Friends of the American Indian and held conferences to discuss how they could assist with the reforms needed to help Native Americans become more assimilated or, in their words, "Americanized" (Reyhner & Eder, 1994, p. 46). The Indian reformists lobbied for the General Allotment Act, a bill sponsored by Senator Henry Dawes of Massachusetts. The Dawes Act, as it is also known, advocated for the breakup of Native American communal lands, to be replaced by allotted plots of land separately owned by Native families and individuals. Private ownership of land was one of the first strategies used to force Native Americans to assimilate into a European American value system (Noriega, 1992, p. 382). The other component of the Dawes Act dealt with providing educational training for both males and females so that Native Americans could be educated into becoming good, civilized Christians (Lomawaima, 1994, p. 2). The Indian Reform Movement also became known as the Indian Educational Reform Movement; the establishment of off-reservation boarding schools was one of its main projects (Reyhner & Eder, 1994, p. 46).

The first school to attempt to educate adult Native American students in the East was the Hampton Normal and Agricultural Institute in Virginia. Established in 1868 to educate African Americans following the Civil War, Hampton became the first boarding school to establish an Indian education program when, in April 1878, fifteen Native American adult male war hostages were admitted at the request of Captain Richard Pratt. Hampton's founder, General Samuel Armstrong, recognized the benefits to be gained from educating Native Americans (Almeida , 1992; Hultgren & Molin, 1989).

---

[6] The Moor's Charity School for Indians was established in 1760 by Eleazer Wheelock in Lebanon, Connecticut. Between 1761 and 1769, Wheelock enrolled approximately sixteen Native American girls at Moor's School. See Szasz (1988).

He expressed his reaction to the arrival at Hampton of the Native Americans in a letter to his wife:

> They are a new step ahead and make the school very strong and really, Kitty, they are a big card for the school and will diminish my gray hairs. There's money in them I tell you. (Samuel Chapman Armstrong to Emma Armstrong, April 19, 1878, in Williamsiana Collection)

In the late fall of 1878, Captain Pratt returned from the Dakota territories with the first group of Native American children to be educated in the off-reservation system. Included in this first group were nine girls, the first Native American females to undergo the "Americanization" process in an educational setting (Hultgren & Molin, 1989, p. 18). Pratt would eventually leave Hampton to establish the first government-sponsored, all-Native American boarding school, the Carlisle Indian Industrial School in Carlisle, Pennsylvania. By 1885, Hampton and Carlisle had served as models for 106 Native American boarding schools, many of which were established on abandoned military installations (Green, 1989, p. 12).

Native children were accustomed to being educated and taken care of by people other than their natural parents, but little had prepared them for the sheer strangeness of the boarding school, with its echoing halls and electric lighting, and a staff speaking an unintelligible language and taking unacceptable familiarities with them (Coleman, 1993, p. 79). In 1884, a Yankton female student named Gertrude Simmons, who would later become famous under her tribal name of Zitkala-Sa, entered the White's Manual Labor Institute in Wabash, Indiana. She later described her fearful arrival:

> Entering the house, I stood close against the wall. The strong glaring light in the whitewashed room dazzled my eyes. The noisy hurrying of hard shoes upon a bare wooded floor increased the whirring in my ears. My only safety seemed to be in keeping next to the wall. As I was wondering in which direction to escape from all this confusion, two warm hands grasped me firmly, and in the same motion I was tossed high in midair. A rosy-cheeked paleface woman caught me in her arms. I was both frightened and insulted by such trifling. I stared into her eyes, wishing her to let me stand on my own feet, but she jumped me up and down with increasing enthusiasm. My mother had never made a plaything of her wee daughter. Remembering this I began to cry aloud. (Zitkala-sa, 1921/1993, p. 225)

It was not unusual for Native children to be sent away to boarding school at the age of six or seven, and not to see their homes and families again until the age of seventeen or eighteen (Noriega, 1992, p. 381). The goals of these boarding schools were to teach Native American students how to speak English, to teach them basic academics, and to turn them into good, hard-working Christians. The education of female students at Hampton Institute was very general compared to the technical education of the male students. The girls' industrial curriculum included making and mending garments, crocheting and knitting, as well as learning to sew by hand and machine. Household training involved washing, ironing, cooking, and table duty, plus care

of their own dormitories. Beginning in 1886, female students also participated in the "Technical Round" established for male students, where they
learned skills like framing a window or building a set of shelves, which the
school administrators felt would be useful to them on the reservation (Hultgren & Molin, 1989, p. 28).

Another key component of the boarding schools was a work-study program known as the "outing system," which placed Native American students
in the homes of European Americans during the summer months so they
could be exposed to European American morals and manners and develop
their English-language skills. Hampton Institute placed its students on farms
and in households in western Massachusetts, where they provided cheap
labor, with the males working as farmhands and the females responsible for
domestic work.

Some of the female students wrote favorably of their placement, saying
that they were treated as a member of the family and provided opportunities
to expand their knowledge and coping skills needed for survival in European
American society. Lizzie Young, a Wyandotte from Oklahoma, was placed
with the Bryant family of Northampton, Massachusetts, in 1891. She shared
her experiences with her teachers back at Hampton Institute:

> I like my home very much, only once in awhile I get lonesome when it rains,
> for I do not know what to do with myself. Yesterday Mr. b. invited us down to
> see him play a scientific game of croquet. That was the first time I ever did see
> a game of that kind. . . . They are kind to me. There are just three of us in the
> family. . . . I do not do anything but the cooking. Another woman across the
> street does the washing. . . . I am learning to use the typewriter. Please excuse
> mistakes this time, for I am not an expert yet, but I hope I may be some day.
> (Letter from Lizzie Young published in *Southern Workman,* August, 1891, Indian
> Student files, Hampton University Archives)

However, most of the female students who went through the outing system
were not as fortunate as Lizzie Young. Their placements meant long days of
hard work with little time for themselves. One unidentified student wrote to
her friends at Hampton of her outing experience:

> I spent my summer in Westfield, Massachusetts. . . . I used to wash, iron, make
> beds and sweep the parlor and sitting room once a week, and keep the house
> when they all go away. When I came away they gave me $10.50. I never had a
> regular holiday, but once that was when we went to Sunday School picnic. I
> never went to visit any city or interesting place . . . (Letter from student
> published in *Southern Workman,* January, 1890, Indian Student files, Hampton
> University Archives)

The boarding school further destroyed the traditional roles of Native
American women, as the girls were expected to learn European American
techniques of childrearing, household maintenance, and food preparation.
The rationale for this instruction was not only to assist Native American
women in assimilating into mainstream culture, but also to limit their work
skills so that the only choices of work they had when they returned to the

reservation was to be a servant in a European American home. A few of those who returned to the reservation would be hired as maids in the federal Indian agent's home (Lomawaima, 1994, p. 81).

Native American women were discouraged by their teachers and school administrators from maintaining any knowledge of their traditional Native American lifestyle and brainwashed into looking down on anyone who still lived in a traditional manner. Except for the few Native women who integrated into mainstream European American society, the majority of the female boarding school students returned to their reservations and the same lifestyle they had left. However, they found that they had become disconnected from their traditional gender roles and from their communities. It was not always easy for them, as they had to prove themselves to regain the trust of their community members, many of whom were skeptical of returning students and viewed them as the new oppressor:

> The educated Indian does not hold the respect and admiration of the old people. . . . Instead, Indian alumni had to struggle to re-establish themselves in native communities, trying to gain acceptance while introducing changes resisted by family and friends. (*Indians' Education at Hampton Institute*, p. 19)

Returning students often accepted employment with federal Indian agencies, and many found employment as domestics in the same boarding schools that had trained them (Lomawaima, 1994, p. 81). Those who chose to assimilate into European American life changed not only their own lives, but also those of future generations, as it meant they would not pass on the traditional skills, culture, and social connections of their Native community. Attending boarding schools led many Native American women into situations of extreme isolation, and increased their dependency on the U.S. government.

In contrast, some Native American women used their boarding school education to help them lead their people to resist extinction. Armed with knowledge of European American ways and values, these women were among the central figures in the reform and resistance movements through which many Native nations, though virtual captives of the United States, would resist non-Native efforts to destroy their culture (Green, 1992, p. 69).

The boarding schools operated along these lines until 1928, when the U.S. government released the Meriam Report, which condemned the poor quality of services provided by the Bureau of Indian Affairs. It pointed out shocking conditions of boarding schools, recommended that elementary age children not be sent to boarding schools at all, and urged an increase in the number of day schools on the reservations (Reyhner & Eder, 1994, p. 50). The Meriam Report focused on educational reform within Western boarding schools, and called for improved nutrition and health care standards for Native American children attending these schools. It noted that "discipline of the schools were merely restrictive, not developmental, and did not encourage individual expression or responsibility" (Meriam, 1928, p. 11). It further suggested that Indian Services should devote its energies to social and economic advancements that would help Native Americans adapt to mainstream European American society, or to live on their own terms with at least a minimum standard of health and decency (Lomawaima, 1994, p. 31).

This policy of educational reform eventually lead to the Indian New Deal of 1934 and a reorganization of Native American government systems. Federal programs under the 1934 Johnson-O'Malley Act (JOM) were established to fund Native American educational programs. The Act allowed the federal government to pay states for educating Native American children in public schools (Reyhner & Eder, 1994, p. 50), and established two important concepts. First, it made it theoretically possible for Native American nations or organizations to contract for educational services with the Department of the Interior. Second, the Act reaffirmed the continuing legal responsibility of both the federal government and the states to provide education for Native Americans. These policies served to further support the boarding school approach, and during the period 1950–1975 the number of students attending off-reservation boarding schools increased. The Bureau of Indian Affairs maintained direct responsibility for the education of 52,000 Native American children. Of these, more than 35,000 were enrolled in boarding schools (Noriega, 1992, p. 385). Many of the older boarding schools were completely dilapidated and functioned more as holding pens than as schools, although a few, such as the Institute of American Indian Art in New Mexico, were very modern, having been recently constructed or refurbished (Bowker, 1993; Noriega, 1992). Despite continuous indications that the relocation experience was a disaster, for both the Native American individuals involved and their respective Native American nations, relocation programs were maintained up until 1980.

By 1980, ongoing federal pressure had resulted in the relocation to cities of slightly over half of all Native Americans, approximately 880,000 of the 1.6 million reflected in the 1980 census (Robbins, 1992, p. 99). Adjustment to urban living was often difficult for relocated Native Americans and their families, and created great pressures on women to deny their Native American identity. Many became alienated from their traditions and were rejected by Native Americans who remained on the reservation. Those who maintained contact with their relatives, both on reservations and those living in urban areas, were more successful in adjusting to a new way of life. Moreover, access to education and jobs meant that Native American women developed skills and independence that might have eluded them in the reservations' economic and social structures (Green, 1992, p. 87).

These relocation policies backfired on the U.S. government. Instead of creating a better atmosphere for assimilation, they produced a new population of educated Native American women who turned their newfound skills into tools for political and cultural activism (Green, 1992, p. 18). Nevertheless, the relocation presented Native American nations with new battles for survival. Native women met the challenge both on and off the reservations (Green, 1992; Jaimes & Halsey, p. 1992), though they had to make many personal sacrifices. For example, Menominee activist Ada Deer, who helped restore federal recognition to her nation, describes her experience:

> As a teenager, I saw the poverty of the people — poor housing, poor education, poor health. I thought, this isn't the way it should be. . . . I wanted to help the tribe in some way. . . . People said I was too young, too naive . . . so I dropped out of law school. That was the price I had to pay to get involved. . . . I spent six months in Washington influencing legislation and mobilizing the support of our people throughout the country. . . . The land was restored to trust status. . . . Where did the manpower and the woman power come to accomplish this? It came from the people. (Green, 1992, p. 88)

Coming Full Circle and Looking to the Grandmothers: Contemporary Native American Women and Education

During the late 1960s and the 1970s, Native American educators, along with Native political activists, became increasingly active in promoting the rights of Native Americans and calling for national attention to their plight (Bowker, 1993, p. 23). Native American activist groups such as the American Indian Movement (AIM) and Women of All Red Nations (WARN) grew out of the urban Native communities created by the relocation programs. These organizations and others encouraged Native Americans to stand up for their rights and to resist any further destruction of their cultures and land. AIM staged sit-ins and walk-outs in secondary and some elementary schools, where parents and students demanded greater curriculum relevance and increased Native involvement in school affairs. During this period of "Indian activism," a number of Native American educational organizations were established, including the National Indian Education Association and the Coalition of Indian Controlled School Boards (Bowker, 1993, p. 23).

The U.S. government, in another attempt to assimilate Native Americans through education, passed the 1975 Educational Assistance Act. This was the educational component of the Self-Determination Act, which was designed to provide Native American nations with more control over their reservations, including schools. The act was much criticized, especially by Native women connected to the alternative schools called "Survival Schools," who felt that the act was no more than another form of colonial domination. Through their work with the Survival Schools, this group of Native American women had come to believe the U.S. government wanted to train a selected group of Native American educators who would see themselves and their Native nations through the eyes of the colonizer. This would be the group from which the U.S. government would select Native American educators, place them in charge of Indian education, and have them carry out the 1975 Education and Self-Determination Acts (Bowker, 1993, p. 25). As Phyllis Young, an American Indian movement activist, explains:

Aside from some cosmetic alterations like the inclusion of beadwork, traditional dance, basket weaving and some language classes, the curriculum taught
in Indian schools remained exactly the same, reaching the same conclusions,
indoctrinating children with exactly the same values as when the schools were
staffed entirely by white people. . . . You've got to hand it to them in a way. It's
really a perfect system of colonization, convincing the colonized to colonize
each other in the name of "self-determination" and "liberation." (Noriega,
1992, p. 387)

Government policies under the Reagan and Bush administrations proposed that Native American students would succeed more if they attended
mainstream public schools. This led to a government effort to close all Bureau of Indian Affairs boarding schools and eventually reservation day
schools, regardless of their success rates, and mainstream Native American
students into public schools. Public schools have been a source of much
conflict and tension for both female and male Native American students.
Teachers, textbooks, and curriculum in public schools have been pro-
grammed to bring about the adoption of values such as competitiveness and
individualism. Native American students come from homes and communities
that value cooperation and positive interpersonal relationships. The results
of this conflict, especially for female Native American students, has been
high dropout rates, low achievement levels, and poor self-esteem. Public
schools have often become places of discomfort for Native American youth
(Bowker, 1993; DeJong, 1993).

Native American education has not been a major priority of the presidential administrations of the past two decades. Currently the majority of Native
American students are enrolled in public schools (Bowker, 1993, p. 28),
while federal funding for Native American education continues to suffer a
steady decline. At present there are 106 Bureau of Indian Affairs elementary
and secondary schools and sixty tribally controlled schools.

Native American women continue to play an important role in the education of their people. Many have come to understand and seek to preserve
the traditional roles women held in the past, and have sought out women
elders from their families and communities to instruct them in maintaining
that knowledge. Some, such as Beverly Hungry Wolf (Blackfeet) and Navajo
Ruth Roessel (1981) have become authors, thereby sharing their knowledge
of Native American women's traditions. Native American women have become involved with their nation's political affairs and have been elected to
leadership positions. Currently, approximately 12 percent of the five hundred or so federally recognized Native American and Alaskan Native nations
have female leadership (Green, 1992, p. 97).

Despite the changes in government education policy from the reservation
era to contemporary times, Native American women maintain their responsibilities as the keepers of their culture, working for the revitalization of the
languages, arts, and religious practices of their people, with the focus always
on future generations: "It was our grandmothers who held on to what they

could of our identity as a People. . . . Oftentimes the fire grew dim, but still our grandmothers persisted. We were taught that the time we are in is only borrowed from future generations" (Green, 1992, p. 93). Native women today draw on the same inner strength that sustained female Native students attending the off-reservation boarding schools of the late nineteenth and early twentieth centuries. A traditional Cheyenne saying reflects the reality of Native American women: "A people are not defeated until the hearts of its women are on the ground." As long as Native American women assert their traditional rights and assume their traditional responsibility of being the central voices of their communities, Native American nations will survive and their women's voices will remain loud and strong.

References

Alford, T. W. (1936). *Civilization: And the story of the absentee Shawnees.* Norman: University of Oklahoma Press.

Allen, P. G. (1989). Introduction. In P. G. Allen (Ed.), *Spider Woman's granddaughters* (pp. 1–21). Boston: Beacon Press.

Almeida, D. A. (1992). *The role of western Massachusetts in development of American Indian education reform through the Hampton Institute's summer outing program (1878–1921).* Unpublished doctoral dissertation, University of Massachusetts, Amherst.

Almeida, D. A. (1995). *An Indian summer: Surviving Disney's Pocahontas.* Unpublished manuscript.

Billson, J. M. (1995). *Keepers of the culture: The power of tradition in women's lives.* New York: Lexington Books.

Bowker, A. (1993). *Sisters in the blood: The education of women in Native America.* Newton, MA: WEEA.

Churchill, W. (1994). *Indians are us? Culture and genocide in Native North America.* Monroe, ME: Common Courage Press.

Churchill, W., & LaDuke, W. (1992). Native North America: The political economy of radioactive America. In M. A. Jaimes (Ed.), *The state of Native America: Genocide, colonization, and resistance* (pp. 241–266). Boston: South End Press.

Coleman, M. (1993). *American Indian children at school, 1850–1930.* Jackson: University Press of Mississippi.

Crow Dog, M. (1990). *Lakota woman.* New York: Harper Collins.

DeJong, D. H. (1993). *Promise of the past: A history of Indian education in the United States.* Golden, CO: North American Press.

Deloria, E. C. (1988). *Waterlily.* Lincoln: University of Nebraska Press.

Gioseffi, D. (Ed.) (1993). *On prejudice: A global perspective.* New York: Anchor Books.

Greaves, T. (Ed.) (1994). *Intellectual property rights for indigenous peoples: A source book.* Oklahoma City: Society for Applied Anthropology.

Green, R. (1989). "Kill the Indian and save the man": Indian education in the United States. In P. F. Molin & M. L. Hultgren (Eds.), *To lead and to serve: American Indian education at Hampton Institute 1878–1923* (pp. 9–13). Virginia Beach, VA: Virginia Foundation for the Humanities and Public Policy.

Green, R. (1992). *Women in American Indian society.* New York: Chelsea House.

Hampton University Archives, Special Collections, Hampton Normal and Agricultural Institute, Indian Education Collection, Administration and Indian Student Files (1878–1928). Hampton, VA: Hampton University.

Hultgren, M. L., & Molin, P. F. (1989). *To lead and to serve: American Indian education at Hampton Institute, 1878–1923.* Virginia Beach, VA: Virginia Foundation for the Humanities and Public Policy.

Hungry Wolf, B. (1981). *The ways of my grandmothers.* New York: Morrow.

Indians' Education at Hampton Institute: Report of the Principal to Virginia Superintendent of Public Instruction. Hampton University Archives, Special Collections, Hampton Normal and Agricultural Institute, Indian Education Collection, Administration and Indian Student Files (1878–1928). Hampton, VA: Hampton University

Jaimes, M. A., & Halsey, T. (1992). American Indian women: At the center of indigenous resistance in North America. In M. A. Jaimes (Ed.), *The state of Native America: Genocide, colonization, and resistance* (pp. 311–344). Boston: South End Press.

Kame' eleihiwa, L. (1992). *Native lands, foreign desires.* Honolulu: Bishop Museum Press.

La Flesche, F. (1963). *The middle five: Indian school boys of the Omaha tribe.* Lincoln: University of Nebraska Press.

Lomawaima, K. T. (1994). *They call it prairie light: The story of Chilocco Indian School.* Lincoln: University of Nebraska Press.

Meriam, L. (1928). *The problem of Indian administration: Institute for Government Research.* Baltimore: Johns Hopkins University Press.

Meyer, M. (1997). *Native Hawaiian epistemology: A case study of other intellectualism.* Unpublished manuscript.

Noriega, J. (1992). American Indian education in the United States: Indoctrination for subordination to colonization. In M. A. Jaimes (Ed.), *The state of Native America: Genocide, colonization and resistance* (pp. 371–402). Boston: South End Press.

Reyhner, J., & Eder, J. E. (1994). A history of Indian education. In J. Reyhner (Ed.), *Teaching American Indian students* (pp. 33–58). Norman: University of Oklahoma Press.

Rideout, H. M. (1912). *Williams Jones: Indian cowboy, American scholar, and anthropologist in the field.* New York: Frederick A. Stokes.

Robbins, R. L. (1992). Self-determination and subordination: The past, present, and future of American Indian governance. In M. A. Jaimes (Ed.), *The state of Native America: Genocide, colonization, and resistance* (pp. 87–121). Boston: South End Press.

Roessel, R. (1981). *Women in Navajo society.* Rough Rock, AZ: Navajo Resource Center.

Standing Bear, L. (1975). *My people the Sioux.* Lincoln: University of Nebraska Press. (Original work published 1933)

Szasz, M. C. (1988). *Indian education in the American colonies, 1607–1783.* Albuquerque: University of New Mexico Press.

Trask, H. K. (1993). *From a native daughter: Colonialism and sovereignty in Hawaii.* Monroe, ME: Common Courage Press.

Williamsiana Collection, Williams College Archives and Special Collections. Williams, MA: Williams College.

Wright, B. (1992). American Indian and Alaska Native higher education: Towards a new century of academic achievement and cultural integrity. In P. Cahape & C. B. Howley (Eds.), *Indian nations at risk: Listening to the people* (pp. 93–96). Charleston, WV: ERIC Clearinghouse on Rural Education and Small Schools.

Zitkala-Sa (Bonnin, G.). (1993). American Indian stories. In W. G. Regier (Ed.), *Masterpieces of American Indian literature* (pp. 193–238). New York: MJF Books. (Original work published 1921)

Reflections on
Writing a History of
Women Teachers

KATHLEEN WEILER

In this chapter, Kathleen Weiler reflects on the historiography of Country Schoolwomen, *her recent study of women teachers in rural California. Using a broad
definition of feminist research, Weiler summarizes some of the most salient issues
currently under debate among feminist scholars. She raises questions about the
nature of knowledge, the influence of language in the social construction of gender,
and the importance of an awareness of subjectivity in the production of historical
evidence. Using several cases from* Country Schoolwomen, *Weiler discusses the
importance of considering the conditions under which testimony is given, both in
terms of the dominant issues of the day — for example, the way womanliness or
teaching is presented in the authoritative discourse — and the relationship between
speaker and audience. She concludes that a feminist history that begins with a
concern with the constructed quality of evidence moves uneasily between historical
narrative and a self-conscious analysis of texts.*

For many years, the history of women teachers was ignored by education historians. In the last two decades, as the significance of gender has increasingly been acknowledged, the lives and work of women teachers have begun to be addressed, primarily by women historians influenced by feminist scholarship. Generally, feminist historians have argued that gender needs to be made a major category of analysis in historical research, but the implication of a feminist approach is a matter of continued discussion. There is, after all, no authoritative feminism; fundamental differences exist among those of us who consider ourselves feminists, and the relationship between the political stance of feminism — that is, a concern with seeking a more just and equal society for all women and men — and scholarly research is by

Harvard Educational Review Vol. 67 No. 4 Winter 1997, 635–657

no means settled. Shulamit Reinharz has recently argued that feminism should be considered a perspective, not a methodology.[1]

Like Reinharz, I accept a broad definition of feminist research, including research that is concerned with recovering women's lives; with documenting sexist and patriarchal practices; and with considering the ways in which language and culture organize our lives and experience through the prism of gender. My own historical research is concerned with all of these issues. And like many others, I have been particularly influenced by debates within feminist theory about methodology and the kinds of claims that can be made about women in the past. In this article, I consider some of the underlying epistemological concerns that have guided my attempt to write a history of women teachers, issues that are common both to the enterprise of writing history and the project of feminism. I then discuss some examples from my own ongoing research, not to provide definitive answers or guidelines, but to illustrate theoretical debates and to raise questions.

Recently I completed a local history of rural women teachers in one area of the western United States, California's Tulare and Kings counties, during the period 1850–1950.[2] My choice to write this particular history emerged from my own history and desires.[3] In writing this history, in a sense I explored my own past, since I was born and raised in a small town in California, the daughter and niece of women teachers in country schools. The idea that history is a narrative construct shaped by the interests of the historian has been widely discussed in recent years, but it is feminist historians who have emphasized the importance of the stance of the historian, not only in terms of intellectual and political beliefs, but in terms of personal history as well.[4]

I have previously written about contemporary women teachers and about questions of feminist pedagogy.[5] As I completed my first book, my mother, who had been a teacher in country schools, died of heart failure at the age of seventy-eight. Motivated by a sense of loss, I began to reflect on what teaching might have meant for my mother, for my aunt, and for my great-aunt, all teachers in early twentieth-century rural schools in California. In my memory, they were respected figures in their communities, women who lived in the public world. And unlike many other women in these communities, women teachers earned their own money. At the same time, their work was the care of children, otherwise seen as a private and unremarkable matter. They worked in the public world of the school while maintaining the domestic world of their families and households. Although teaching was one of the few choices available to them in terms of waged work, the women teachers I knew growing up seemed proud of their positions; if they felt constrained or demeaned by this work, they showed no public sign of it.

When I undertook this history, I held the unexamined belief that I could come to understand the lives of these women and that in writing their history I would provide witness to their valuable and unrecognized work. But when I began formal research into this world through interviewing retired teachers and reading local school records and state documents, these guiding assumptions became less sure. I came to see more clearly that the social and cultural world of my mother and other teachers was built on assumptions of White and Protestant hegemony. And what I saw as autonomy and pride in their work coexisted uneasily with evidence of increasing state control and community surveillance. The more I explored this history, the more complex it became.

In time it became clear to me that my attempt to understand the meaning of teaching for women in California was part of an ongoing history of women teachers that is being written as a collective exploration in a wide range of settings throughout the world and from a number of perspectives.[6] The scholarly work of other historians provided me with categories and theories with which to understand this world. Like many others, I am interested in how the conception of "woman" is constructed in dominant discourse and the ways individual women have made sense of their experiences through the concepts and language available to them. But I also believe that focusing on the construction of meanings as contested should not preclude the analysis of other kinds of evidence. Scholars have explored the history of women teachers using a wide range of sources and approaches. They have used quantitative data to determine who taught, for how long, and who held positions of administrative power; to analyze teaching as a segmented labor market; and to explore questions of the length of teachers' careers, wage differentials for men and women, and shifting patterns of men and women teachers and administrators in both rural and urban settings. All of these approaches — analyzing the ideological construction of the woman teacher in the authoritative discourse of the powerful; examining the quantitative data that remain; analyzing the construction of selves through memory and narratives — are important in coming to understand the lives of women teachers. In my exploration of the history of these country women teachers I used all of these methods. But at the same time, I have been increasingly influenced by debates within women's history and feminism about the nature of evidence and representations of social reality.

Feminist Theory and Women's History

Both feminist theory and women's history have produced rich and original work over the past three decades. In the second wave of the women's movement in the late 1960s, feminists began to explore the lives of women who had been "hidden from history." The focus of these histories was on the oppressions of patriarchy. But very quickly, feminist historians shifted their focus to include studies of women's resistance to the dominant order. These two approaches of either documenting patriarchal oppression or celebrating women's resistance continue to shape feminist history and the history of women teachers, even as historians have moved to more complex levels of analysis of women teachers' work in relation to the state and economy or of the language constructions within which women teachers imagined themselves or were imagined. Perhaps inevitably, as feminist historians have produced an extensive and impressive corpus of work, conflicts over interpretation and approach have emerged.[7] These conflicts reflect debates among feminist scholars and within history as a discipline, as poststructuralism and deconstruction have challenged the traditional approach of historians.[8]

The debate among historians about the process of writing history and the nature of textual evidence echoes parallel concerns of ethnographers and sociologists. Within the last decade, a number of ethnographers, for example, have begun to theorize the process of their research (sometimes almost to a point of paralysis). Clifford Geertz has commented:

> The basic problem is neither the moral uncertainty involved in telling stories about how other people live nor the epistemological one involved in casting those stories in scholarly genres — both of which are real enough, are always there, and go with the territory. The problem is that now that such matters are coming to be discussed in the open, rather than covered over with a professional mystique, the burden of authorship seems suddenly heavier.[9]

In arguing as he does that ethnography is ultimately "an act of the imagination," Geertz doesn't mean it is a fantasy, but that it is a creative work by an author, who gives order and meaning to what she has found out. It is not "reality," but it is not a myth or a poem either. In response to these concerns, ethnographers have experimented with innovative approaches, attempting to reveal the complexity of both their own constructed accounts and the lives of those they try to understand. Such ethnographers attempt, as Dorinne Kondo comments, to "decenter and de-essentialize selves, focusing on the ways people construct themselves and their lives — in all their complexity, contradiction, and irony — within discursive fields of power and meaning, in specific situations, at specific historical moments."[10] This kind of emphasis on the construction of meaning through discursive fields also marks the recent work of feminist historians.

In the United States in recent years, feminist historians influenced by poststructuralism have introduced the concerns of literary and critical theory to women's history.[11] This approach has encouraged a critical questioning of the claim that historians were simply describing reality "out there" and has suggested instead that historians are deeply implicated in the kinds of truth they uncover. Historiographers, such as Dominick LaCapra and Hayden White, and feminist poststructuralist historians, most notably Denise Riley and Joan Scott, have argued that history is an imaginative construction resting on certain rhetorical effects, but unlike these male theorists, feminists such as Riley and Scott have emphasized as well that it has been deeply gendered.[12] As is true of many other feminists who are attempting to write about women in the past, I have been influenced both by the ongoing political commitment of feminist historians and by recent poststructuralist theory and historiography.

Here I want to articulate some of my own developing theoretical concerns, particularly my understanding of three key concepts that have come to shape my own reading and approach. These are the interrelated concepts of knowledge, language, and subjectivity. By knowledge I refer to the debate about universal versus particular truth claims and the nature of historical evidence, the question of what exactly are our sources of understanding the past; by language, the question of discourse and its relationship to experience as the source of our knowledge of the past; and by subjectivity, the question of essence and identity. While I hardly have space to enter fully into a discussion of these complicated issues, I want to discuss my understanding of these concepts at least briefly here, to explain why I have approached the history of women teachers as I have.

First, there is the question of historical knowledge, the nature of the evidence about the past and the kinds of truth claims that can be made about it. As is true of many other feminists, I write from a situated and conditional perspective, emphasizing my own reading and partial perspective in presenting what I read as important and true. Feminist theorists from a number of disciplines have challenged the conception of a universal perspective on truth, arguing that terms like "universal" and "human" in fact have referred to the experiences and reality of a small number of White privileged men.[13] Feminist theory in many respects begins with a critique of the empirical tradition in European science and political theory. Feminist theorists argue that the essential flaw not only in philosophical empiricism as it emerged in the seventeenth century, but also in the movement of modernism at the turn of the twentieth century, was to assume a single "human" interest or essence. They argue that the universal concept of humanity in fact referred to White bourgeois men; the poor, workers, women, people of color, and the colonized were invisible in this paradigm. The feminist critique both of humanism (assuming a universal human identity) and modernism is similar to other poststructuralist analyses in emphasizing that the world is in fact made up of deeply conflicting, opposing groups and discourses and that a universal perspective smoothes out tensions among competing forms of power and knowledge held by these groups. I think it is ironic that the work of Michel Foucault, a theorist who showed little interest in women's lives, has been so influential in feminist theory.[14] Foucault's critique of truth, his connecting of knowledge and power, strikes a powerful chord for feminist theorists who are suspicious of claims of a pristine, universal truth imagined outside of history.

It is typical of feminist theorists to view knowledge as both contextual and historical. This is particularly true of socialist or materialist feminists, who have incorporated a materialist analysis of oppression and a dialectical method deeply influenced by Marxism into their feminist analysis of gender. Feminist materialist theorists like Rosemary Hennessy and Anna Yeatman have built upon the earlier work of such theorists as Nancy Hartsock, Sandra Harding, and Dorothy Smith to emphasize the material and practical life experiences and activities of women as the source for their knowledge of the world.[15] Just as Hegel argued for the privileged perspective of the slave or Marx for the privileged perspective of the worker, these feminist theorists have argued that women have a particular epistemological standpoint because of their oppression. In a similar vein, Patricia Hill Collins has argued for the importance of seeing knowledge as emerging from practical life experiences defined by race as well as by gender and class.[16] Such theorists argue that women's differing experiences of oppression, like the experiences of Hegel's slave or Marx's worker, provide a knowledge or standpoint that is in some sense "truer." Truer in that it reveals more of power relationships than does the hegemonic knowledge of those who control and exploit them and who seek to obscure that control. This is similar to what Ruth Pierson calls the "epistemic privilege of the oppressed."[17] For me, the strength of feminist standpoint epistemology is that it ties knowledge to power. But while I continue to believe that this approach has much to teach us, it also seems important to consider not only women's "life activities," as Hartsock suggests, but also the ways in which different women are positioned as subordinate or "other" in discourse, and to consider that everyone, including the "oppressed," understands experience through language.

As is true for other epistemologies of difference, feminist standpoint epistemology rests upon the recovery of outlawed or denigrated knowledge. In history that knowledge has meant stories of the experiences of women. An emphasis on the situated nature of truth claims and a recognition of those who have been overlooked or excluded seems essential to a feminist history. But recovering and celebrating hidden knowledge, what Foucault has called "dangerous memories," can lead to an acceptance of memory and experience as sources of a "true past." Poststructural feminist historians such as Catherine Hall, Joan Scott, and Denise Riley have argued that the category of "experience" itself is one that needs to be carefully examined. As Scott argues:

> When experience is taken as the origin of knowledge, the vision of the individual subject (the person who had the experience or the historian who recounts it) becomes the bedrock of evidence upon which explanation is built. Questions about the constructed nature of experience, about how subjects are constituted as different in the first place, about how one's vision is structured — about language (or discourse) and history — are left aside.[18]

Thus for Scott the object of historical inquiry shifts from an empirical documenting of the facts of the past to an analysis of the way meaning is created through language. As Scott says, "To do this a change of object seems to be required, one which takes the emergence of concepts and identities as historical events in need of explanation."[19] This kind of historical epistemology takes as the object of study not only knowledge, but also the processes by which people make sense of their lives. Scott and Riley argue that rather than documenting the narratives of experience of historical actors, historians should analyze the "historical processes that, through discourse, position subjects and produce their experiences."[20] This is similar to Kimberle Crenshaw's comment that "one important way social power is mediated in American society is through the contestation between the many narrative structures through which reality might be perceived and talked about."[21]

Theorists such as Scott, Riley, and Crenshaw are concerned with language as a way of ordering and evaluating what becomes "experience" and of understanding the past as constantly contested and constructed through competing discourses.

The argument about language is in many ways an argument about texts, about what texts can tell us. The most extreme "linguistic" perspective seems to imply that we can only understand the past through the workings of written language, that the past is available only through texts and, thus, the focus of historical analysis must be textual. Although this position has made a valuable intervention in making historians more cautious about their claims of knowing the "true past," it has also raised dangers of its own — of slighting other kinds of evidence and failing to raise questions other than those of the workings of written language. Linda Gordon, for example, argues that while the analysis of representations can help us understand the ways language works to justify power, this analysis of language does not mean that the material past — economic and political developments — did not exist and should not be explored.[22] Thus to become sensitive to the linguistic turn makes the historian less innocent, but does not, I think, necessarily erase a concern with understanding the material past.

It is the sensitivity to the constructed quality of memory and experience that has led feminist theorists in a number of disciplines to suggest the use of the term "subjectivity." Subjectivity has been employed to try to capture this quality of the social construction of the self: it implies the struggle and contest over identity; the ways in which selves are unstable, shifting, constructed through both dominant conceptions and resistance to those conceptions; and suggests the incomplete and sometimes contradictory quality of our lives both in the present and as we construct our pasts through memory. Emphasizing the constructed quality of subjectivity also implies the constructed nature of gender. The belief in the social construction of gender is central to feminist thought. As Jane Flax has commented: "The single most important advance in feminist theory is that the existence of gender relations has been problematized. Gender can no longer be taken as a simple, natural fact."[23] By insisting on the artificial nature of historically defined aspects of gender, feminist theorists point to the instability and contradictions in these socially constructed gender roles and the possibilities for individual manipulation and resistance to them. People are not simply defined by ideological constructs of what they should be, but negotiate expectations, both external and internalized in their own consciousness, in the context of material need and desire through competing discourses. In this sense they engage in the construction of their own gendered subjectivities — in Teresa deLauretis's terms, "within the context of existing practices, discourses, and institutions."[24]

Along with considerations of the nature of experience and the evidence of texts, feminist historians have taken up the debate about the meaning of the concept "woman." Is there an "essential" womanliness that all women share across race, ethnicity, culture, class, sexuality, and time? How do individual women come to identify themselves and make sense of their lives? A number of feminist theorists have argued that both "woman" and "women" are contested terms. Judith Butler points out: "In a sense, what women signify has been taken for granted for too long, and what has been fixed as the 'referent' of the term has been 'fixed,' normalized, immobilized, paralyzed in positions of subordination."[25] This line of analysis, deeply influenced by the critiques of lesbians and Black, Asian, and Latina women, has pointed to the complexity of socially given identities. African American women's historians have called on feminist historians to take into account what Elizabeth Higginbotham calls the "metalanguage of race" in their study of women's history.[26] Like postcolonial theorists, Higginbotham points out that the coherent identity "woman" obscures the significance of race, class, age, or other descriptors that might be used to differentiate some as deviant from a mythical norm. These theoretical developments have led to a questioning of the concept of a coherent subject moving through history with a single identity and instead suggest the constant creation and negotiation of selves emerging from competing and contradictory discourses within structures of material constraint.[27] The construction of gendered subjectivities through discourse, the contradictions of our various ways of categorizing and understanding what happens in our lives and who we are, naming ourselves, becomes the point of entry for historical analysis.

Women Teachers' Narratives

Women teachers' narratives and the descriptions of their lives by contemporary observers both draw upon existing representations of what it means to be a teacher and what it means to be a woman. The outside observers' descriptions tend to draw on dominant representations to give meaning and shape to the lives they describe, while in their own accounts women teachers represent themselves both through the dominant discourses and through counter-memories that resist the expectations of the dominant discourse. Although they make sense of their lives through the categories of dominant discourse, at other moments oppositional and alternative meanings emerge. These oppositional meanings recall Carolyn Steedman's comment that "personal interpretations of past time — the stories that people tell themselves in order to explain how they got to the place they currently inhabit — are often in deep and ambiguous conflict with the official interpretative devices of a culture."[28] A theoretical reading of the narratives of women teachers raises questions about the complexity of the construction of meaning and identity through discourse. But a feminist approach addresses not only the contradictions of competing discourses, but also the context and the relationships of power in which narratives are produced.[29] This approach raises a number of questions for researchers: What kinds of knowledge do narrative texts provide? How can we read them? How are we as researchers implicated in the creation of social knowledge? A recognition of the situated quality of narratives demands that the historian be conscious of her own assumptions as she collects "evidence," but also that she consider the context in which such evidence (as texts or narratives) is produced. Ruth Pierson cautions: "As collectors and recorders of the stories of others, therefore, we cannot accept a woman's recollection uncritically, that is, as unmediated by cultural/historical context. Instead, we need to contextualise women's narratives, for to be understood they have 'to be thoughtfully situated in time and place.'"[30]

To illustrate the ways in which these theoretical concerns shape a feminist history, I turn now to some examples of narratives — published texts and oral testimony — from my recent study of women teachers in California. In my analysis, I have been influenced by the theoretical approaches outlined above that suggest ways of reading these narratives of teachers' lives critically as discursive constructions produced in specific historical contexts.[31] Although I made use of other documentary evidence, such as the U.S. manuscript census (an actual record of names collected available after 70 years) and county and state school records, my major sources for trying to understand the meaning of teaching for women were first-person accounts and life-history narratives. I used a variety of sources, among them privately printed autobiographies, newspaper accounts of teachers and schools, narratives written by retired teachers for retired teachers' newsletters and journals, accounts of school visits by state officials, as well as twenty-five oral histories I collected between 1988 and 1993. But as has become increasingly clear to me, these sources do not provide a transparent picture of past lives; each kind of evidence needs to be read for the context and conditions of its production and with a consciousness that my own location as a White feminist seeking to "recover" the lost lives of women has led me to select certain texts as significant and to highlight certain themes within them. The texts of women teachers' lives are contradictory and fragmented. Representations of gender in fact profoundly shape the lives of these teachers, but these discursive categories are so fundamental to their construction of themselves that they usually are not remarked upon. The same is true of the categories of race and class.[32] As a contemporary reader of historical texts and an oral historian eliciting life-history narratives, I have attempted to draw out these contradictions and highlight the workings of power in their production. In the following discussion, I explore the different kinds of evidence provided by different kinds of texts.

Reading Narratives of African American Women Teachers

As a White feminist scholar writing in the late 1990s, I am concerned with race as well as class and gender. My concern with race implies not only a focus on the lives of women of color, but also an acknowledgement of Whiteness as a racial construct shaping White women's lives. California education was profoundly defined by racial categories from its founding. For Black women teachers, race shaped their lives much more overtly than did gender. White women teachers were constrained by their gender, but their race privilege was accepted as natural and was not even mentioned in the White teachers' narratives I have collected. By 1900, segregated schooling for African Americans had taken on its familiar form as a de facto but no longer de jure practice. But faculties in the formally integrated schools, even when the majority of students were children of color, continued to be almost exclusively White. In 1900, the U.S. Census listed only two teachers in the category "Indian, Negro or Mongolian" for the entire state of California;[33] in 1910, sixteen "Negro" and twenty "Indian, Chinese or Japanese" teachers are listed.[34] African American teachers had taught in the segregated colored schools in the nineteenth century, but when the separate colored schools were closed, the possibilities of employment for Black teachers disappeared. The evidence of the lives of these early African American teachers is scanty, and is often found primarily in descriptions by contemporary White observers. In seeking to know the lives of Black women teachers, we frequently know more about the ways White observers constructed them within racist and patriarchal discourse than we do about their own consciousness or life experience.

In my research on the women teachers of California's Tulare and Kings counties, I have found some evidence of the lives of a handful of African American women teachers. But this evidence itself needs to be interrogated. For example, consider the example of two African American women teachers, Mary Dickson and Margaret Prince Hubert. The kind of historical understanding we have of the lives of these two women is constrained by the nature of the sources available to us. Darlene Clark Hine has pointed out that even when we have the autobiographies or letters of nineteenth- or early twentieth-century African American women, we need to read them with an understanding of the conditions of their production. Hine argues that given the realities of racism and of sexual violence, African American women tended to conceal their inner selves from a hostile world: "Because of the interplay of racial animosity, class tensions, gender role differentiation, and regional economic variations, Black women, as a rule, developed and adhered to a cult of secrecy, a culture of dissemblance, to protect the sanctity of inner aspects of their lives."[35] Hine goes on to argue that this culture of dissemblance developed not only in the face of the threat of physical violence, but in response to the "negative social and sexual image of their womanhood" as well. But as she points out, while hiding or misrepresenting the inner self may have been an understandable strategy for survival, it presents the historian with serious difficulties in trying to understand the lives of Black women. In the case of Mary Dickson and Margaret Prince Hubert, the historian is dependent on quite different sources — that is, the observation of a White observer in the 1880s and the words of a Black woman solicited in an oral history interview with a Black scholar in the 1970s. The context in which these two texts were produced has shaped the evidence in very different ways; these texts reveal as much about the workings of culture and ideology as they do of specific material conditions.

According to Tulare County school records, Mary Dickson taught in the Visalia Colored School between 1881 and 1884. The Visalia Colored School had been founded two years before by an African American farmer to provide schooling for his own children and for other children of the Black community who were denied entrance to the local public schools. The school had since been taken over by the town, and was small and poorly supported. In this period, teachers who did not have a Normal School certificate were required to take and pass the county teachers' examination. In December 1881, fourteen prospective teachers took the Tulare County teachers' examination in Visalia. Six passed, but only one received a first-grade certificate. This was Mary Dickson, an African American woman, "about twenty three," who had come to Visalia from the Colored School in Vallejo. Besides the presence of her name on the county list, the only other evidence I have found of Dickson is in an article from the *Visalia Delta* describing the teachers' examination of 1881. This article, entitled "Successful Candidates," in fact is what the unnamed (and I assume male) journalist calls "a pen portrait" of Dickson. The teachers' examination included both written and oral components; the oral section of the 1881 examination was open to the public and the *Delta* journalist was present. Dickson received the highest mark on the examination, but the journalist does not speculate on where she might be sent to teach or indicate that she would be sent to the Visalia Colored School, by other reports a shabby one-room school on the outskirts of town, rather than to the town's new graded grammar school. Writing in 1881, he seems to take for granted that Dickson would teach in a segregated school, no matter what her performance on the examination.

Instead he provides his "pen portrait," a detailed description of Dickson's body and manner. He is fascinated with her beauty and accomplishments, precisely because, as he says, "she belongs to the race properly called 'colored.'" She is for him the exotic "other," subject to what literary critics have called the gaze of the dominant observer, in this case not just the male gaze, but the White gaze as well.[36] Although the journalist mentions her intellectual accomplishments, his main concern is her body:

> She belongs to the race properly termed "colored" and this fact adds interest to the subject in view of her remarkable success. She has the medium height of women; her form is full, straight, rounded and symmetrical, and as near perfect as the form of a handsome woman can well be; her hands and feet are narrow, and her fingers denote artistic taste, her hair is remarkably abundant, is straight with occasional graceful waves, and of course is black as night.

In this description, Dickson is presented as the object of the journalist's desire, using terms such as "full, straight, rounded," "perfect," "handsome," "artistic," "abundant" to describe her, and then emphasizing the contradictions between these "Caucasian" qualities and her identity as a member of the "race properly termed 'colored'" by his description of her hair: "of course . . . black as night." It is almost as though she represents to him a White woman trapped inside a Black body. He goes on to describe her:

> [She has] large, black, intelligent eyes, and more expressive than which there are none. Negatively, the cheek-bones have not the prominence noticeable in the black race, and the chin, though prominent, betrays no evidence of African blood. Her mouth is almost faultless, the lips inclining to fullness, but only agreeably. The tout ensemble of the face is a slight rounding of the cheeks and the elongation that belongs to the Caucasian race; and perhaps handsomer features, altogether, are not to be found in California.

Dickson's intelligence and manner impressed the journalist, but he emphasizes not only her intelligence and beauty, but also her delicacy in not presuming familiarity with the "white ladies" present:

> The most strongly marked feature of her deportment during the examination was her retiring modesty, as she seemed to fear that voluntary intercourse with the white ladies present would be looked upon as intrusion, on account of her color. She is an unusually good reader, having a clear strong voice that denotes the complete physical woman. She has an extensive knowledge of general literature, and is what may be termed a bright and ready conversationalist. She employs the choicest language, which is free from those numerous violations of grammar that daily custom almost sanctions. She is fluent and animated, though reserved in manner.[37]

It is important historically to know of the Visalia Colored School, of Dickson, and of her intellectual accomplishments. Her life expands our knowledge of the work and achievements of nineteenth-century African American woman teachers. And the article in the *Visalia Delta* describing her reveals a great deal about the intersection of exoticism, sexuality, and racism characteristic of White discourse. But it tells us nothing about Dickson's inner life. Darlene Clark Hine has discussed the ways in which African American women protected themselves by failing to reveal their inner thoughts in their written work in this period. In the case of Dickson, we do not even have her own words. She exists for us through the imagination of the *Visalia Delta* journalist as exotic, fascinating, desirable, and other. We know nothing of her thoughts or feelings, or the condition of her work or life. After 1884, she left the Visalia Colored School. I have found no further evidence of her. What kind of claim of knowing her can we make?

A different kind of knowing is possible for the life of Margaret Prince Hubert, an African American teacher who taught at the all-Black school at Allensworth in Tulare County between 1914 and 1919. In this case, we have Hubert's own account of her life, solicited by a Black scholar, Eleanor Ramsay, who conducted an interview with Hubert while Ramsay was a student in anthropology at Berkeley for her Ph.D. dissertation on Allensworth.[38] The interview seems to have taken place in the early or mid-1970s. In her narrative, Hubert frames her life as a struggle to obtain an education and decent work in a racist society. Hubert grew up in Pasadena, California, in what she describes as a loving and supportive family. She was the only Black graduate of Pasadena High School in 1911 and went on to be one of two Black students at the California State Normal School in Los Angeles, which later became UCLA. Hubert was committed to teaching, but she describes the loneliness and isolation of her years at Normal School: "Often now I think about times and remember moments when I got so lonesome that I wished I would die."[39] Once she graduated, she faced the racist realities of California education, in which only White teachers would be hired except in segregated Black schools:

> Here is where I had my first real setback, for I rudely discovered that my ability to control and direct my professional career virtually ended with the completion of my formal training. . . . At the time, the only Los Angeles school hiring Black teachers, Home Street School, had only two staff positions. The school served Furlong Tract, the Black section located just outside Los Angeles City Limits. Home Street School certainly did not offer serious employment opportunities for the many Black teachers resident in the Los Angeles area.[40]

But in the summer of 1914, William Payne, the principal of the Black school at Allensworth and a friend of Hubert's family, offered her the position of primary school teacher at Allensworth. Allensworth was a colony of African American settlers that had been established in the arid southern San Joaquin Valley a few years earlier. Although the Allensworth School was a public school and was not formally segregated, all the children were African American.

Allensworth was marked by idealism and hopes for a better future.[41] For the African Americans who settled there, the school was in many ways the key to these hopes. But for Margaret Prince Hubert, it was also a choice that was no choice at all. As she told her story to Eleanor Ramsay in the 1970s, she remembered her move to Allensworth in the context of her family's history of forced choices and limited opportunities. She recalled the life of her grandmother, who had been forced to work as a maid, traveling with rich White families and separated from her own children and family:

> My parents too well knew that the only employment locally available to our people was in the service industry. Thus, they quietly accepted the fact I would be separated from the family nest. As I now remember my parents' beaming faces at my graduation — twenty strong in the fourth row in the Pasadena High School auditorium — they must have known then about my destiny. For their own reasons, my parents chose not to tell me then, that to break the occupational pattern of the Prince family, I would have to leave home, just as my grandmother had done twenty-six years before. Continuously though, they reminded me, "To have an education is to be somebody."[42]

Remembering her life in the 1970s, Hubert frames her identity as an African American teacher through a consciousness of the long African American struggle for education in the United States. She documents racist practices and presents the attitude of her family as one of quiet determination ("they must have known about my destiny. . . "). In reading her testimony it is also important to consider the circumstances and historical moment that framed

Hubert's narrative. She was interviewed by an African American woman scholar at a time in which Black students were first admitted to White-dominated institutions like the anthropology department at Berkeley. A major focus of the research of these students was documenting the rich history of the African American freedom struggle. While Mary Dickson was constructed as a mute exotic Other by the White journalist in 1881, Margaret Prince Hubert speaks as a powerful and committed woman in her interchange with a Black researcher.

The Autobiographical Narrative of a White Christian Teacher

As an example of the impact of audience and historical moment, consider the evidence of the autobiography of Grace Canon Pogue, published in the early 1950s, a deeply conservative time in the United States in which the language of feminism had essentially been lost in everyday discourse. Pogue was a White Protestant teacher in the country schools of Tulare County. Her narrative is framed by the conventional theme of sacrifice and caring for others.[43] This representation, recalling the nurturing "true woman" of the common school movement, constructs and gives meaning to lives in memory; but it also often reveals a pattern of caring and responsibility that frequently mark women teachers' narratives. Pogue's narrative calls forth the convention of moral guardianship, speaking out for the good of the community from a position of ethical guide. This theme can be found in other accounts of women principals and community leaders, who were often active church members and associated with the temperance movement; Pogue was an active member of the Presbyterian Church in Woodlake and staunchly opposed to drinking.

Pogue's narrative also reveals the hidden workings of class.[44] Teachers, particularly women teachers, are difficult to place within conventional conceptions of class. In rural California, teachers were seen as "respectable," and although they did not control wealth or exercise political power, they often, like Pogue, represented themselves as the defenders of the moral order, as middle class. Nonetheless, as was true for Pogue, teaching was in fact a necessary source of livelihood for many women teachers, and their wages were equivalent to those of semi-skilled male laborers. Pogue's autobiography is written through a discourse of the nurturing and morally upright woman teacher, but it also reveals the material needs of a struggling family dependent on her teacher's salary.

Pogue's family settled in Tulare County in the late 1880s. Her father was a farmer, and the family seemed to be on the margin of making a living. When she reached high school age, her parents rented out their farm and moved into town so Pogue could attend high school, a common practice among farming families. Pogue was an outstanding student in high school, winning an essay contest on "The California Fruit Ranch" and graduating as valedictorian. But once she graduated, Pogue was faced with the realities of her class and gender:

> A period of mental adjustment followed High School graduation. For four years, dreams of Stanford University had taken shape. A girl needed more units to enter Stanford than were required of a boy. I had the units. Also my recommendation said, "Rank in class, distinguished." But . . . the idea of working my way through college didn't appeal to my family.[45]

In this passage, Pogue describes barriers of both gender and class, but in her presentation she does not denounce these barriers as unjust. For example, she uses the phrase "mental adjustment" to describe her emotions, which surely must have included deep disappointment if not anger at not being able to attend college. She describes Stanford's different entrance requirements for boys and girls without comment. And although she met the higher requirements for girls and was accepted at Stanford, she concedes to her family's decision that as a girl she should not work her way through school. Instead, once she graduated from high school, she went to work in a cannery, a common practice among girls from farming families in rural California at this time.

But Pogue did not remain a cannery worker. At the age of nineteen, she passed the county teacher's examination and was immediately offered a position in the mountains at the one-room school at Yokohl. Mountain schools like this one tended to hire young women, often still teenagers, as teachers. Commonly they would board with local families. But Pogue's parents, who had moved into town so she could attend high school, now moved with her to the mountains, whether to protect and support her or to be supported is not clear. The economic benefits of the job suggest that the family needed Pogue's salary; she was paid $70 a month for an eight-month term and rented a vacant house about a half mile from the school for $8 a month. In her description of this first job, however, she does not mention her need to earn money, but presents this position as the fulfillment of her life's ambition:

> It was decided that Sister and Mother and Dad and I would live at Yokohl and Sister would be one of my pupils. My ambition to teach was about to be realized. When I was a little girl, I had declared my intention to be a matron of an orphans' home; then came a dream of being a missionary. But my love for children and my yearning for an opportunity to guide them in the right paths could be realized in the teaching profession. And so, by the time I reached my teens, I was determined that a teaching career was what I wanted.[46]

Here Pogue ignores her earlier ambition to attend Stanford and instead presents as her deepest desire (from the time she was a little girl) the opportunity to serve others as a moral guide (matron of an orphans' home, missionary, teacher). This presentation of herself as moral guide simply ignores the material conditions and limitations she describes in the earlier passage. Her family could not afford to send her to Stanford; because she was a girl they wouldn't allow her to work her way through college. In taking a job in a one-room mountain school, she supported her parents and her sister. Later in her narrative she marries and, in hard economic times, supports her husband and son with her teacher's salary. Throughout her narrative she presents these material realities without comment; when she reflects on her inner life or the meaning of her choices, she employs the representation of a moral Christian woman.

Her narrative also ignores the themes of adventure or coming of age, themes that appear in many other teachers' narratives, particularly in their depictions of "the first school" or "the first car," which mark the transition from childhood to adulthood. The first teaching job often was the first time away from home for these young women and offered them their first opportunity to earn real wages. Accounts of the first year of teaching in one-room country or mountain schools are often filled with descriptions of physical dangers overcome. In the narratives of California teachers, for example, rattlesnakes often appear, and the teacher typically dispatches the snake as a mark of her competence and courage. In their reminiscences, women who taught in California in the 1920s and 1930s frequently and similarly describe their first car as a symbol of their power and personal independence. Teaching made it possible for these young women to buy cars and thus to escape the scrutiny of their communities. Accounts of the responsibilities and dangers of the first school or the pleasure and freedom of the first car are presented without reference to authoritative images of nurturing or self-sacrificing womanhood. Instead they recall the discourse of the "new woman," or of the flapper, or of earlier nineteenth-century narratives of women travelers as brave adventuresses. All of these images counter Pogue's vision of the maternal and self-sacrificing "true woman."

In reading autobiographical accounts, particularly those of "ordinary" women like Pogue, whose lives would otherwise be unknown, it is a temptation to accept their self-presentation as both transparent and representative. But as Marjorie Theobald has argued, the representation of women teachers as morally upright, self-sacrificing, and heroic needs to be read as precisely that: as a representation of social reality, not necessarily the truth for all women, or even for any single woman. Theobald notes that the depiction of teaching in the novels and memoirs of women who went on to become writers is quite different. In the work of such writers as Janet Frame and Christina Steed, teaching is presented as a trap, intellectually barren and filled with frustration and cruelty.[47] These accounts of women who left teaching are the mirror image of Pogue's. And, of course, it is also important to remember the conditions of the production of Pogue's text. Her autobiography was privately published, and would have been circulated among members of the community in which she still lived and of which she was a respected member. She wrote in the early 1950s, in the revival of "true woman" ideology and repressive politics in the United States. This was not a moment in which expressions of a woman's anger or her criticism of patriarchal practices would be welcomed. Pogue's narrative thus not only reflects conventional representations of the woman teacher; in another sense it also reproduces them and keeps them alive in the virulently sexist 1950s, when her book was published.

Oral History Narratives of Country Teachers

As a final example of the ways women teachers' lives are represented and may be read, consider the following excerpts from a series of oral history interviews I conducted in Tulare and Kings counties between 1988 and 1992. In oral history, women's narratives are elicited by the historian; this raises further questions about the ways subjectivities are presented and become historical evidence. The question of responsibility and the nature of the interaction between feminist researcher and woman narrator has been addressed in recent years by a number of feminist scholars.[48] In a recent study of women teachers, Kathleen Casey argues that a feminist researcher must respect her "subject" as a subject — that is, a human being with the right to define the meaning of her own life.[49] She enjoins us as feminists to avoid a moralistic judgment of the narratives we have requested and have been generously given, and to try to demystify the production of these narratives by acknowledging the relationship between researcher and researched, which, as Sue Middleton points out, is "almost always bracketed out or rendered invisible in the written analysis."[50] My own experience exemplifies the ways oral accounts are shaped by the setting and relationship between researcher and narrator. As the interviewer, I asked for the gift of these country women's stories and established the context in which these stories were produced. In my case, I was uneasily positioned as an urban university professor, a distant and possibly judgmental figure; women told me their stories with a wary consciousness of who I might be and how I might receive these stories.

The following excerpts are taken from a series of interviews in which I was exploring the nature of the married women teachers' bar during the Depression. The stricture that women teachers could not be married was never officially made law in California, as it was, for example, in Pennsylvania, but the bar was widely enforced in California. In Tulare and Kings counties, the bar against married teachers varied from place to place. In the 1920s, the practice was still enforced in many towns, but smaller districts would hire married women or allow women teachers who were already employed and who were well known in the district to continue teaching after marriage. The retired teachers I interviewed all mentioned the existence of the marriage bar. Ellen A., for example, recalled a married woman she knew who was teaching in a school near hers: "She told me, 'Don't call me by name.' I don't know whether she went by her maiden name or her married name. I never did find out. I just called her by her first name." When I asked Ellen A. why she thought school boards refused to hire married women, she said, "They just wanted to be dictatorial. Husbands were supposed to provide for you." Miriam J. mentioned that she quit teaching when she married. When I asked why, she said:

> It was the thing to do in those days. When you got married you weren't supposed to have a career, you were supposed to stay home and keep house. I guess you know that. I suppose you can become interested in keeping house. It's just a little boring. I persuaded my husband to let me go back and teach.

In these comments, Ellen A. and Miriam J. described common practices of discrimination against married women teachers and ways individuals resisted them. But they also framed their comments in ways that showed their disapproval of these practices: Ellen A. says school boards wanted to be "dictatorial," and Miriam J. describes housework as "just a little boring." In both cases, they may well have been influenced by their perception of who I was, an outsider, a woman professor, and therefore probably critical of the marriage bar.

In another example, however, Ruth G. provided a more ambivalent account. Ruth G. also left teaching during the Depression when she married. In the interview, the following interchange took place:

> *Ruth G.:* I got married and they weren't hiring married teachers. But I didn't want to teach then anyways.
>
> *K.W.:* That's interesting too. Once you got married at Thermal they wouldn't have kept you on?
>
> *Ruth G.:* No, they wouldn't have over at Oakland Colony either, that's the school out by Tulare. The principal was married, but she had been there quite a while. A woman. Well, she taught it as a one-teacher school. But they wouldn't hire married teachers after that. There weren't enough jobs really.
>
> *K.W.:* Did they give reasons?
>
> *Ruth G.:* No, except there were, there was a surplus of teachers, and that was one way of not hiring. Married teachers, their husbands could support them. Other than that I don't know.
>
> *K.W.:* Wasn't that kind of hard on you, to give up your job in the Depression?
>
> *Ruth G.:* Well, he was working. He made enough. Ninety-eight dollars a month, and it was ample compared to now. I subbed some, quite a bit. No, that amount seemed to go as far as, a great deal more than now-a-days. I can remember, on our honeymoon, in September, and we'd drive by these schools with people in them and I'd sit there and cry and he'd say, this is a heck of a honeymoon.
>
> *K.W.:* You were crying because. . .
>
> *Ruth G.:* I wanted to teach.

Ruth G.'s account contains striking contradictions and breaks. At the beginning of this interchange, she says she didn't want to teach after she was married; the story of crying when she passed a school on her honeymoon seems to escape from her narrative. While discussing living on $98 a month ("that amount seemed to go as far as, a great deal more than now-a-days"), she then begins a seemingly unrelated story: "I can remember, on our honeymoon. . ." Consider as well the circumstances under which this story was told. I conducted this interview in the summer of 1990. I was a professor from "back East." Even though I was born in the valley and had grown up there, by leaving, and particularly by going as far as Massachusetts (not to a more familiar place like Texas or Kansas, which are also known as "back East"), I was identified as an Easterner, probably a liberal, and possibly, since I was a woman professor, a feminist. Ruth G. had married into a well-known conservative family of early settlers to the valley. When I looked at her, I saw a Republican! My relationship with Ruth G., while polite on both sides, was wary. Throughout her narrative, Ruth G. presented to me a past in which things turned out all right, in which the authorities acted wisely, and traditional values were upheld. Like all of us in recalling our pasts, she was constructing a story for the circumstances of the telling.

Conclusion

Accounts of women teachers' lives, their own memories, the ways they frame the choices they made, the way they are viewed by observers, all need to be examined as constructs produced at specific historical moments, under particular circumstances, with different audiences in mind. As Sandra Harding points out, people are not simply defined by an ideological construct of what they should be, but negotiate conflicting discourses in the context of their own life activities and desires. It is important to consider the conditions under which testimony is given, both in terms of the dominant issues of the day — the way womanliness or teaching is presented in the authoritative discourse, for example — but also the relationship between speaker and audience. Think of the differences between a written text like Grace Canon Pogue's (privately published, and thus almost certainly to be circulated among members of the community in which she lived), an account of an observer like the Visalia journalist fascinated with Mary Dickson as the exotic Other, and the interchange between researcher and subject in an oral history interview when both are positioned "on the same side," or see one another as potentially hostile, on opposite sides.

A feminist history that begins with a concern with the constructed quality of evidence moves uneasily between historical narrative and a self-conscious analysis of texts. There is the seductive attraction of narrative, to write the past as a coherent story or plot, framed by implicit or explicit judgments and perceived as a moral lesson. On the other hand, there is the analysis of representations, a critical suspicion of the evidence of written texts or the oral accounts produced through questioning, and a concern with the contemporary biases of the historian/critic/narrator. Giovanni Levi has recently argued for a history in which "the historian is not simply concerned with the interpretation of meanings but rather with defining the ambiguities of the symbolic world, the plurality of possible interpretations of it and the struggle which takes place over symbolic as much as over material resources."[51] This is similar to Roland Barthes's comment that history would be less "mytho-logical" if it were presented in modes that "overtly called attention to their own process of production and indicated the 'constituted' rather than 'found' nature of their referents."[52] In writing the history of these women teachers' lives, I was trying to consider the ways in which they construct their pasts through the discursive categories available to them, while acknow-ledging that my own questions and categories "constitute" a story, in Barthes's term. Carolyn Steedman wrote:

> Visions change, once any story is told; ways of seeing are altered. The point of a story is to present itself momentarily as complete, so that it can be said, it does for now, it will do; it is an account that will last for a while. Its point is briefly to make an audience connive in the telling, so that they might say: yes, that's how it was; or, that's how it might have been.[53]

As is true of any historian, I can only analyze and understand the evidence of lives through discursive categories while recognizing and acknowledging my complicity in the narratives I call forth and the narrative I construct. In my history, I hope to present both a story and a meditation on what it means to be a teacher and a woman and to try to capture what, in Steedman's words, "might have been."

Notes

1. Shulamit Reinharz, *Feminist Methods in Social Research* (New York: Oxford University Press, 1992).
2. Kathleen Weiler, *Country Schoolwomen: Teaching in the California Countryside, 1850–1950* (Stanford, CA: Stanford University Press, in press). This study of the lives and work of women teachers moves from a general discussion of competing representations of the woman teacher to a history of the development of educational state policy in California to a local study of women teachers in two rural counties. The women teachers in this study taught in isolated one- and two-room schools, in migrant schools during the Depression, and lived through the rapid changes of the First and Second World Wars. The book draws upon a wide range of approaches, bringing feminist and critical theory to an analysis of both written and oral life history narratives, while also analyzing manuscript census data, materials from state and local archives, and state publications.
    This study challenges a number of common assumptions about the lives and work of women teachers. For example, it is often assumed that men have always controlled the work of women in schools. *Country Schoolwomen* supports the view of a number of historians of women's education that teaching has been a source of power for women, offering them respect, autonomy, and money. The work of these women puts forth a vision of classroom teaching as valuable and intellectually challenging.
3. Shulamit Reinharz notes that feminist research is often motivated by what she calls "an intellectual question and a personal trouble." See Reinharz, *Feminist Methods*, p. 260. See also Carolyn Steedman, "Culture, Cultural Studies and the Historians," in *Cultural Studies*, ed. Lawrence Grossberg, Cary Nelson, and Paula Treichler (New York: Routledge, 1992), pp. 613–622.
4. See Hayden White, *The Content of Form* (Baltimore: Johns Hopkins University Press, 1987) for a theoretical discussion of the structure of historical narratives.

5. Kathleen Weiler, *Women Teaching for Change* (South Hadley, MA: Bergin & Garvey, 1988).

6. I have been most influenced by the work of feminist historians in the United States and Canada. I have discussed some of this work in "Women's History and the History of Women Teachers," *Journal of Education, 171,* No. 3 (1989), 9–30. For a comparative discussion of the emerging tradition of studies on women teachers in these English-speaking nations, see Alison Prentice and Marjorie Theobald, "The Historiography of Women Teachers," in *Women Who Taught: Perspectives on the History of Women Teaching,* ed. Alison Prentice and Marjorie Theobald (Toronto: University of Toronto Press, 1991), pp. 3–36. Other examples of this work are: Geraldine Clifford, "Eve: Redeemed by Education and Teaching School," *History of Education Quarterly, 21* (1981), 479–492; Geraldine Clifford, "Man/Woman/ Teacher: Gender, Family and Career in American Educational History," in *America's Teachers,* ed. Donald Warren (New York: Macmillan, 1989), pp. 293–343; Geraldine Clifford, "Lady Teachers and the Politics of Teaching in the United States 1850–1930," in *Teachers: The Culture and Politics of Work,* ed. Martin Lawn and Gerald Grace (London: Falmer Press, 1987), pp. 3–30; Geraldine Clifford, "Marry, Stitch, Die or Do Worse," in *Work, Youth and Schooling,* ed. Harvey Kantor and David Tyack (Stanford, CA: Stanford University Press, 1982), pp. 223–268; Mary Cordier, *Schoolwomen of the Prairies and Plains* (Albuquerque: University of New Mexico Press, 1992); Marta Danylewycz and Alison Prentice, "Teachers, Gender and Bureaucratizing School Systems in Nineteenth Century Montreal and Toronto," *History of Education Quarterly, 24,* No. 1 (1984), 75–99; Marta Danylewycz and Alison Prentice, "Teachers Work: Changing Patterns and Perceptions in the Emerging School Systems of Nineteenth- and Early Twentieth-Century Central Canada," in Prentice and Theobald, *Women Who Taught,* pp. 136–159; Nancy Hoffman, *Woman's 'True' Profession* (Old Westbury, NY: Feminist Press, 1981); Polly Kaufman, *Women Teachers on the Frontier* (New Haven: Yale University Press, 1984); Alison Oram, *Women Teachers and Feminist Politics* (Manchester, Eng.: Manchester University Press, 1996); Linda Perkins, *Fannie Jackson Coppin and the Institute for Colored Youth* (New York: Garland Press, 1987); Alison Prentice, "The Feminization of Teaching in British North America and Canada 1845–1875," *Social History/Histoire Social, 8* (1975), 5–20; Jo Anne Preston, "Female Aspiration and Male Ideology: School-teaching in Nineteenth Century New England," in *Current Issues in Women's History,* ed. Arina Angerman, Geerte Binnema, Annemieke Keunen, Vefie Poels, and Jacqueline Zirksee (New York: Routledge, 1990), pp. 171–182; Myra Strober and David Tyack, "Why Do Women Teach and Men Manage?" *Signs, 5* (1980), 494–503; Marjorie Theobald, *Knowing Women* (Cambridge, Eng.: Cambridge University Press, 1996); Courtney Vaughn-Robeson, "Having a Purpose in Life: Western Women in the Twentieth Century," in *The Teacher's Voice,* ed. Richard Altenbaugh (London: Falmer Press, 1992), pp. 13–25; Sally Schwager, "Educating Women in America," *Signs, 12,* No. 2 (1987), 333–372.

7. See, for example, the exchange between Linda Gordon ("Response to Scott") and Joan Scott ("Response to Gordon"), *Signs, 15* (1990), 848–859; also the earlier discussion over women's culture and resistance among Ellen DuBois, Mary Jo Buhle, Temma Kaplan, and Carroll Smith-Rosenberg, "Politics and Culture in Women's History," *Feminist Studies, 6* (1980), 28–36.

8. Judith Newton, "History as Usual? Feminism and the New Historicism," in *The New Historicism,* ed. H. Adam Veeser (New York: Routledge, 1989), p. 152.

9. Clifford Geertz, *Works and Lives: The Anthropologist as Author* (Stanford, CA: Stanford University Press, 1988), p. 138.

10. Dorinne Kondo, *Crafting Selves* (Chicago: University of Chicago Press, 1990), p. 43.

11. See, for example, Catherine Hall, "Missionary Stories: Gender and Ethnicity in England in the 1830s and 1840s," in Grossberg, Nelson, and Treichler, *Cultural Studies,* pp. 240–276; Ruth Roach Pierson, "Experience, Difference, Dominance and Voice in the Writing of Canadian Women's History," in *Writing Women's History: International Perspectives,* ed. Karen Offen, Ruth Roach Pierson, and Jane Rendall (Bloomington: Indiana University Press, 1991), pp. 79–106; Denise Riley, *Am I That Name?* (Minneapolis: University of Minnesota Press, 1989); Joan Scott, *Gender and the Politics of History* (New York: Columbia University Press, 1989); Ann-Louise Shapiro, ed., *History and Feminist Theory* (Middletown, CT:

Wesleyan University Press, 1992); Carolyn Steedman, "Culture, Cultural Studies and the Historians," in Grossberg, Nelson, and Treichler, *Cultural Studies*, pp. 613–622.

12. Hayden White, *The Content of Form: Narrative Discourse and Historical Representation* (Baltimore: Johns Hopkins University Press, 1987); Riley, *Am I That Name?*; Scott, *Gender and the Politics of History;* Dominick LaCapra, *History and Criticism* (Ithaca, NY: Cornell University Press, 1985). See also Ann-Louise Shapiro, "Introduction: History and Feminist Theory, or Talking Back to the Beadle," in Shapiro, *History and Feminist Theory*, pp. 1–23.

13. For an accessible discussion of the phallocentric basis of Western thought, see Elizabeth Minnich, *Transforming Knowledge* (Philadelphia: Temple University Press, 1990).

14. See, for example, Lois McNay, *Foucault and Feminism: Power, Gender and the Self* (Boston: Northeastern University Press, 1983).

15. Nancy Hartsock, "The Feminist Standpoint: Developing the Ground for a Specifically Feminist Historical Materialism," in *Discovering Reality: Feminist Perspectives on Epistemology, Metaphysics, Methodology and Philosophy of Science,* ed. Sandra Harding and Merrill B. Hintikka (Boston: D. Reidel, 1983), pp. 283–310; Sandra Harding, *The Science Question in Feminism* (Ithaca, NY: Cornell University Press, 1986); Rosemary Hennessy, *Materialist Feminism and the Politics of Discourse* (New York: Routledge, 1993); Dorothy Smith, *The Everyday World as Problematic* (Boston: Northeastern University Press, 1987); Anna Yeatman, *Postmodern Revisionings of the Political* (New York: Routledge, 1994).

16. Patricia Hill Collins, *Black Feminist Thought* (Boston: Unwin Hyman, 1990).

17. Ruth Pierson, "Experience, Difference, Dominance and Voice in the Writing of Canadian Women's History," p. 84.

18. Joan Scott, "Experience," in *Feminists Theorize the Political*, ed. Judith Butler and Joan Scott (New York: Routledge, 1992), p. 25.

19. Scott, "Experience," p. 33.

20. Scott, "Experience," p. 25.

21. Kimberle Crenshaw, "Whose Story Is It Anyway?" in *Racing Justice, Engendering Power*, ed. Toni Morrison (New York: Pantheon Books, 1992), pp. 22–41.

22. See Gordon, "Response to Scott."

23. Jane Flax, "Postmodernism and Gender Relations in Feminist Theory," in *Feminism/Postmodernism*, ed. Linda Nicholson (New York: Routledge, 1990), p. 44.

24. Teresa deLauretis, *Alice Doesn't* (Bloomington: Indiana University Press, 1984), p. 159.

25. Judith Butler, "Contingent Foundations: Feminism and the Question of Postmodernism," in Butler and Scott, *Feminists Theorize the Political*, p. 16.

26. Elizabeth Higginbotham, "African-American Women's History and the Metalanguage of Race," in *Feminism and History*, ed. Joan Scott (Oxford, Eng.: Oxford University Press, 1996), pp. 183–208.

27. Donna Harraway calls all claims to a womanly essentialism into question: "With the hardwon recognition of their social and historical constitution, gender, race, and class cannot provide the basis for belief in 'essential' unity: There is nothing about being 'female' that naturally binds women. There is not even such a state as 'being' female, itself a highly complex category constructed in contested sexual discourses and other social practices. Gender, race, or class consciousness is an achievement forced on us by the terrible historical experience of the contradictory social realities of patriarchy, colonialism, and capitalism." Donna Harraway, "A Manifesto for Cyborgs," *Socialist Review, 80* (1985), 18. See also Jennifer Terry, "Theorizing Deviant Historiography," in *Feminists Revision History*, ed. Ann-Louise Shapiro (Middletown, CT: Wesleyan University Press, 1994), pp. 276–304.

28. Carolyn Steedman, *Landscape for a Good Woman* (New Brunswick, NJ: Rutgers University Press, 1987), p. 6.

29. I have discussed some of these questions in "Remembering and Representing Life Choices: Retired Teachers' Oral History Narratives," *International Journal of Qualitative Research in Education, 5*, No. 1 (1992), 39–50. See also Margaret Nelson, "Using Oral Histories to Reconstruct the Experiences of Women Teachers in Vermont," in *Studying Teachers' Lives*, ed. Ivor Goodson (New York: Teachers College Press, 1992), pp. 78–89; Luisa Passerini, *Fascism in Popular Memory: The Cultural Experience of the Turin Working Class* (Cambridge, Eng.:

Cambridge University Press, 1987); Popular Memory Group, "Popular Memory: Theory, Politics, Method," in *Making Histories*, ed. Richard Johnson, Gregor McLennon, Bill Swartz, and David Sutton (Minneapolis: University of Minnesota Press, 1982), pp. 205–252; Rafael Samuel, "Myth and History: A First Reading," *Oral History, 16,* No. 1 (1988), 10–17.

30. Pierson, "Experience, Difference, Dominance and Voice," p. 91.

31. Susan Frieden, "Transformative Subjectivity in the Writings of Christa Wolf," in *Interpreting Women's Lives*, ed. Personal Narratives Group (Bloomington: Indiana University Press, 1989), pp. 172–188; Frigga Haug, *Female Sexualization: A Collective Work of Memory* (London: Verso Press, 1987); Nancy Osterud, "American Autobiographies," *Gender and History, 2,* No. 1 (1990), 80–85; Luisa Passerini, "Women's Personal Narratives: Myths, Experiences, and Emotions," in *Interpreting Women's Lives,* ed. Personal Narratives Group (Bloomington: Indiana University Press, 1989).

32. See Peggy Pascoe, "The Challenge of Writing Multicultural Women's History," *Frontiers, 12,* No. 1 (1991), 1–4. Pascoe argues that it is important not only to seek the history of women who have been excluded from history, but also to "mark as race and class specific the history of white middle class women who have so frequently been used by historians to stand in for all women" (p. 2).

33. U.S. Bureau of the Census, *Statistics of Women and Work* (Washington, DC: Government Printing Office, 1907), p. 111.

34. U.S. Bureau of the Census, *Thirteenth Census of the United States 1910: Vol. 4. Population, Occupation Statistics* (Washington, DC: Government Printing Office, 1914) p. 440.

35. Darlene Clark Hine, "Rape and the Inner Lives of Black Women in the Middle West," in *Unequal Sisters,* ed. Vicki Ruiz and Ellen DuBois, 2nd ed. (New York: Routledge, 1994), p. 344.

36. This description recalls the "orientalizing" described by Said in his discussion of the representation of the exotic Other. Edward Said, *Orientalism* (New York: Vintage Books, 1979).

37. "Successful Candidates," *Weekly Delta,* December 30, 1881, p. 1.

38. Eleanor Mason Ramsay, "Allensworth: A Study in Social Change," Diss., University of California at Berkeley, 1977.

39. Margaret Prince Hubert as cited in Ramsay, "Allensworth," p. 149.

40. Margaret Prince Hubert as cited in Ramsay, "Allensworth," p. 148.

41. For a more extensive discussion of the role of education in the Allensworth colony, see Kathleen Weiler, "The School at Allensworth," *Journal of Education, 17,* No. 3 (1990), 9–38.

42. Margaret Prince Hubert as cited in Ramsay, "Allensworth," p. 146.

43. See, for example, Jane Roland Martin, *Homeschool* (Cambridge, MA: Harvard University Press, 1992); Madeleine Grumet, *Bitter Milk* (Albany: State University of New York Press, 1988); Carol Gilligan, *In a Different Voice* (Cambridge, MA: Harvard University Press, 1982).

44. For an interesting discussion of the question of teachers' class location see Marta Danylewycz and Alison Prentice, "Teachers' Work," in Prentice and Theobald, *Women Who Taught.*

45. Pogue, *The Swift Seasons,* p. 29.

46. Pogue, *The Swift Seasons,* p. 32.

47. Marjorie Theobald, "Teachers, Memory, and Oral History," in *Telling Women's Lives,* ed. Sue Middleton and Kathleen Weiler (London: Open University Press, forthcoming).

48. See in particular Sherna Berger Gluck and Daphne Patai, *Women's Words* (New York: Routledge, 1991) and Gwendolyn Etter-Lewis and Michele Foster, *Unrelated Kin* (New York: Routledge, 1996).

49. Kathleen Casey, *I Answer with My Life* (New York: Routledge, 1993).

50. Sue Middleton, *Educating Feminists* (New York: Teachers College Press, 1993), p. 66.

51. Giovanni Levi, "On Microhistory," in *New Perspectives on Historical Writing,* ed. Peter Burke (University Park: Pennsylvania State University Press, 1992), p. 95.

52. As quoted by Hayden White, *The Content of Form* (Baltimore: Johns Hopkins University Press, 1987), p. 35.

53. Carolyn Steedman, *Landscape for a Good Woman* (New Brunswick, NJ: Rutgers University Press, 1987), p. 22.

PART FIVE

Identity

How We Find Ourselves:
Identity Development and
Two-Spirit People

ALEX WILSON

Psychological theorists have typically treated sexual and racial identity as discrete and independent developmental pathways. While this simplifying division may make it easier to generate theory, it may also make it less likely that the resulting theory will describe peoples' real-life developmental experiences. In this chapter, Alex Wilson examines identity development from an Indigenous American perspective, grounded in the understanding that all aspects of identity (including sexuality, race, and gender) are interconnected. Many lesbian, gay, and bisexual Indigenous Americans use the term "two-spirit" to describe themselves, a term drawn from the experience of their culture and community. How can this self-awareness and re-visioning of identity inform developmental theory? The author offers her personal story as a step toward reconstructing and strengthening our understanding of identity.

The interconnectedness of sexual identity and ethnicity contributes to the complex nature of the process of identity development. As educators, we must acknowledge that fact in the supports and services we offer to our students. Although the research on lesbian, gay, and bisexual Indigenous Americans is extensive, these inquiries are typically from an anthropological perspective.[1] Much of this research is based on the rereading and reinterpretation of early field notes, testimony, and biographical sketches, twice removed from Indigenous American experiences, and twice filtered through non-Indigenous eyes (C. McHale, personal communication, March

---

[1] The term "Indigenous American" in this article refers to Canadian First Nations and Native American peoples. I acknowledge that, in a sense, this term presents our diverse cultures and communities as monolithic. However, my use of the term here is an appeal to the commonality of our origins and colonial/post-colonial experiences.

Harvard Educational Review Vol. 66 No. 2 Summer 1996, 303–317

21, 1996). Anthropologists and historians such as Evelyn Blackwood (1984), Beatrice Medicine (1983), Harriet Whitehead (1981), Walter Williams (1986), and Will Roscoe (1988, 1991) have contributed to a body of work that describes and documents the construction of sexuality and gender in Indigenous American communities. Their work provides a critique of Western assumptions about sexuality and gender, but generally fails to recognize the existence of and to acknowledge the contributions of "two-spirit" Indigenous Americans today.[2] From my perspective as a two-spirit Swampy Cree woman, I will critically assess current theory in identity development through reflection on my life and identity development.[3] This reassessment has implications for developmental theorists, counselors, and educators who engage with two-spirit people.

I have chosen the terms "two-spirit" and "Indigenous American" carefully. Until recently, anthropologists claimed authority to name two-spirit people by labeling them the *berdache* (Blackwood, 1984; Jacobs & Cromwell, 1992; Jacobs & Thomas, 1994; Weston, 1993). *Berdache* described anthropological subjects who did not fit neatly into European American gender and sex role categories, meaning a category of (gendered and sexual) "other." The term was imported to North America by Europeans who borrowed it from the Arabic language. Its use, to describe an "effeminate" (Blackwood, 1984, p. 27) or "morphological male who does not fill a society's standard man's role, who has a non-masculine character" (Williams, 1986, p. 2), spoke articulately about European assumptions about gender roles and sexuality (Weston, 1993). The metaphoric power of the term grew over time; the role of *berdache* acquired, at least within gay history and storytelling, considerable spiritual power. In Tom Spanbauer's (1991) revisionist story of the American West, his narrator explains:

> Berdache is what the Indian word for it is. . . . I don't know if berdache is a Bannock word or a Shoshone word or just Indian. Heard tell it was a French word but I don't know French so I'm not the one to say.
> What's important is that's the word: Berdache. "B . E . R . D . A . C . H . E . means holy man who fucks with men." (Spanbauer, 1991, p. 5)

Because of the historical and spiritual connotations that had been vested in the term, some members of Indigenous American communities embraced it as their self-descriptor (Roscoe, 1988). More recently, in recognition of the poor fit of the term *berdache*, we have looked for language that more accurately describes our historic and present-day realities.

---

[2] The term "two-spirit" will be used in this article to describe lesbian, gay, and bisexual Indigenous Americans.

[3] The Cree Nation spreads in a wide swath across central Canada, from Quebec in the East, west through Ontario and Manitoba along the James and Hudson Bays, across Saskatchewan to the plains of Alberta, and South from there into northern Montana. Most of these communities are located in remote areas. I am from the Opaskwayak Cree Nation, located five hundred miles north of the border between the United States and Canada. The Cree Nations form one of the largest groups of Indigenous people in North America. There are over twenty-three Cree dialects.

The growing acceptance of the term two-spirit as a self-descriptor among lesbian, gay, and bisexual Indigenous American peoples proclaims a sexuality deeply rooted in our own cultures (Brant, 1995; Fife, 1993). Two-spirit identity affirms the interrelatedness of all aspects of identity, including sexuality, gender, culture, community, and spirituality. That is, the sexuality of two-spirit people cannot be considered as separate from the rest of an individual's identity (Jacobs & Thomas, 1994). Two-spirit connects us to our past by offering a link that had previously been severed by government policies and actions.

Pueblo psychologist and educator Terry Tafoya (1990) states that there have been "direct attempts [by] the federal government to regulate, control, and destroy Native American behavior patterns. . . . There are more than 2,000 laws and regulations that only apply to American Indians and Alaskan Natives and not to other American Citizens" (p. 281). The religious freedom of Indigenous peoples in the United States was not legally supported until 1978 (Tafoya, 1990). The Canadian federal government made a similar effort to separate Indigenous peoples from their cultural traditions (York, 1990). Two-spirit reconstitutes an identity that, although misstated by anthropologists, had been based on the recognition of people with alternative genders and/or sexualities as contributing members of traditional communities. In contemporary European American culture, sexuality is perceived as a discrete aspect of identity, constructed on the basis of sexual object choice (Almaguer, 1993; Whitehead, 1981). This conception stands in sharp contrast to two-spirit identity.

There are over five hundred Nations (tribes) in the United States and Canada. In spite of the vast physical distances between the autochthonous people of North America, few ideological barriers exist between these Nations (Sioui, 1992). Each of our traditional worldviews recognizes the deep interdependency between humans and nature, that our origin is in the soil of the land, and that we are bound to each other in an intimately spiritual way. This shared understanding of the world shapes the life experiences of North America's Indigenous peoples and, in turn, their identity development.

The existence and value of two-spirit people's difference is recognized in most Indigenous American cultures, oral histories, and traditions. In some cultures, two-spirit people were thought to be born "in balance," which may be understood as androgyny, a balance of masculine and feminine qualities, of male and female spirits. In many Indigenous American cultures, two-spirit people had (have) specific spiritual roles and responsibilities within their community. They are often seen as "bridge makers" between male and female, the spiritual and the material, between Indigenous American and non-Indigenous American. The term two-spirit encompasses the wide variety of social meanings that are attributed to sexuality and gender roles across Indigenous American cultures. Many gay historians, anthropologists, and other researchers have struggled with the "epistemological differences in Native American concepts of gender and sexual behaviors" (Tafoya, 1990, p. 287) and veered into dangerous generalizations about the specialness and spiritual power of two-spirit people. Today, academics argue over whether or not two-spirit people had a "special" role or were special people in Native societies. In my community, the act of declaring some people special threatens to separate them from their community and creates an imbalance. Traditionally, two-spirit people were simply a part of the entire community; as we reclaim our identity with this name, we are returning to our communities.

Since European contact with the Americas, many of these Indigenous American traditions have been misrepresented and misinterpreted. Within an imposed construct based on eighteenth-century European values, difference became deviance (D'Emilio & Freedman, 1988; Jacobs & Cromwell, 1992; Tafoya, 1990; Williams, 1986). It is difficult to understand the concept of two-spirit from these perspectives. Within the European American perspective, the male and female genders are the only two acknowledged. Transsexuals who surgically alter their bodies to become physically the "opposite" sex, individuals who choose to dress in clothing thought to be only appropriate for the "opposite" gender, or those who choose not to adhere to either of the dichotomous gender types are seen as abnormal and, therefore, as deviant.

Cartesian definitions of gender, which impose dual roles defining the respective "acceptable behaviors" for women and men, have procreation as their ultimate goal (Jacobs & Cromwell, 1992). These notions of gender categorization have been misapplied to Indigenous Americans. For European explorers, philosophers, and anthropologists, too many Indigenous American people did not fit into the two categories found in Cartesian theories.

The anthropologist Sue-Ellen Jacobs has reconstructed her own notions about gender and sexual identity. In her ethnographic observations of Tewa Pueblo people, she observed a number of gender categories reflecting an individual's "sexuality, sexual identity and sociocultural roles" (Jacobs & Cromwell, 1992, p. 48). This conception of gender reflects a fluid understanding of sexual identity that has persisted for many present-day Indigenous Americans who consider themselves bisexual, rather than strictly lesbian or gay (Tafoya, 1990).

Traditional teachings, however, have also been influenced by events that have altered the construction of sexual identity in contemporary Indigenous American communities. In an attempt to assimilate Indigenous Americans, government policy has been directly involved in the destruction of many aspects of Indigenous American life (Ross, 1992; York, 1990). For almost one hundred years it was illegal to practice traditional religion in both the United States (Deloria, 1969) and Canada (Cardinal, 1969; Miller, 1989). Generations of children were forcibly removed from their families and placed in residential schools, where they were punished for speaking their own language, for practicing their own religion, or for any other expressions of their "Indian-ness" (Berkhofer, 1978; Ing, 1991; York, 1990). In spite of these assaults on traditional values, they still shape the lives and communities of Indigenous American people. Today, most leaders in Indigenous communities express a commitment to traditional spirituality and an Indigenous worldview.

Indigenous Ethics

Our worldviews are shaped by our values, our ideologies, theories, and assumptions about the world. They circumscribe our encounters with the world, creating and re-creating our cultures and our epistemologies, pedagogies, psychologies, and experiences. How are Indigenous American worldviews constructed?

The Mohawk psychiatrist Clare Brant, in his work with Iroquois, Ojibway, and Swampy Cree people, has identified five ethics that, he believes, underpin these Indigenous peoples' worldview (1990). These cultural ethics and rules of behavior include: an Ethic of Non-Interference, an Ethic That Anger Not Be Shown, an Ethic Respecting Praise and Gratitude, the Conservation-Withdrawal Tactic, and the Notion That Time Must Be Right. As Brant himself points out, these Ethics cannot be assumed to describe all Indigenous American people. At the same time, these Ethics resonate deeply with me and describe the emotional substance of much of my own experiences in the Cree community. Although Indigenous American cultures have changed since first contact with Europeans, and continue to change, it is important to realize that these traditionally based Ethics exist in some form today and will persist in some form into the future. Brant's Ethics are further developed by Rupert Ross (1992) in his book *Dancing with a Ghost: Exploring Indian Reality,* which includes an important reminder:

> Until we realize that Native people have a highly developed, formal, but radically different set of cultural imperatives, we are likely to continue misinterpreting their acts, misperceiving the real problems they face, and imposing, through government policies, potentially harmful "remedies." (p. 42)

These Ethics shape our worldview and direct our behavior. The Ethic of Non-Interference refers to the expectation that Indigenous Americans should not interfere in any way with another person. This has shaped culturally distinctive childrearing practices in Indigenous American communities. Generally, children are allowed to explore the world without the limitations of punishment and praise, or of privileges withheld and rewards promised by members of the community. Children are taught through the patient practice of modeling, by stories, and by example. There are unwritten rules against giving advice or telling someone what to do (Ross, 1992; B. Wilson, personal communication, ongoing).

The Ethic That Anger Not Be Shown is demonstrated by the absence of emphasis on or displays of emotions in speech and other forms of communication by Indigenous American people. Implicit in this ethic is a prohibition against showing grief and sorrow. Ross goes so far as to say that it is not acceptable even to *think* about one's own confusion and turmoil; in this way, one does not "burden" others with one's own personal emotional stress. The Ethic Respecting Praise and Gratitude may appear as a lack of affect to a non-Indigenous observer. Rather than vocally expressing gratitude to someone, a person might simply ask the other to continue their contribution, because voicing appreciation may be taken by an Indigenous American as creating an embarrassing scene. Because the idea of community is inherent in the Indigenous American philosophy and existence, an egalitarian notion of place within a society exists. To call attention to one person is to single them out and to imply that they have done better or are better in some way or at something than others are.

The Conservation-Withdrawal Tactic emphasizes the need to prepare mentally before choosing to act. Thinking things through before trying them or thinking thoughts through before voicing them is seen as a well-calculated preservation of physical and psychic energy. According to Ross (1992), the more unfamiliar the new context, the more pronounced a withdrawal into stillness, silence, and consideration may become. This concern that time should be taken to reflect on the possible outcomes of a particular action and to prepare emotionally and spiritually for a chosen course of action is reflected in the Notion That Time Must Be Right. Attention to the spiritual world gives a person the opportunity to examine her or his state of mind before initiating or participating in the task at hand (Ross, 1992).

Additionally, an important part of Indigenous American traditional spirituality is paying respect to our ancestors, to those who died tens of thousands of years ago as well as those who have just recently entered the spirit world. The land that we live on today is made up of our ancestors; the food that we eat (for the most part) is grown from the soil that our ancestors went back to when they died; and the animals and plants in our world have also grown out of and been nourished by this soil. We thank the spirits of animals, minerals, and plants, and turn to them for strength and continuity. This gratitude helps to maintain or regain the balance that is necessary to be a healthy and complete person. We understand that the spiritual, physical, emotional, and intellectual parts of ourselves are equally important and interrelated. When one aspect of a person is unhealthy, the entire person is affected. This too is true for the entire community; when one aspect of the community is missing, the entire community will suffer in some way.

Some Current Models of Sexual Identity and Development

Within the context of these basic principles, identity development can be examined. How do these ethics become incorporated into who we are or whom we identify as? What impact do they have on our responses to experiences? How do they shape our identities? For Indigenous American Nations now in contact with European American culture, racism and homophobia are inevitably present to some degree. Currently, the way some Indigenous

Americans deal with homophobia and racism and the way that they construct their sexual and racial identity is framed by an Indigenous American spirituality and worldview.

This traditional Indigenous worldview can inform current theories of sexual and racial identity development for theorists and educators. I will examine three developmental theories, one of which addresses sexual identity, another racial identity, and a third sexual and/or racial identity. Sexual identity formation is typically presented in stage theory models. In her book *Psychotherapy with Lesbian Clients: Theory into Practice*, psychologist Kristine Falco (1991) presents a review of theory on lesbian identity formation.[4] Finding many similarities in the five models she examines, Falco sketches a generalized model for the sexual identity development of lesbians by combining and summarizing others' models. In the first stage, a person is aware of being different and begins to wonder why. In the second phase, she begins to acknowledge her homosexual feelings and may tell others. Sexual experimentation marks the next stage, as the person explores relationships while seeking a supportive community. She then begins to learn to function in a same-sex relationship, establishing her place in the lesbian subculture while passing as heterosexual when needed. In the final stage, she integrates her private and social identities.

Racial identity development theory examines the psychological implications of membership in a racial group and the resultant ideologies. William Cross's Black Racial Identity Development model is often assumed to represent the racial identity formation experience of people of color in general (Tatum, 1992, 1993). Cross's model representing the racial identity formation experience of people of color in general doesn't hold for Indigenous Americans. In the Pre-encounter stage, which is described in the model as the initial point, an individual is unaware or denies that race plays any part in the definition of who they are. Thereafter, they move through a predictable series of stages: Encounter, after a sequence of events forces them to realize that racism does affect their life; Immersion/Emmersion, as they respond by immersing themselves in their culture, and reject with anger the values of the dominant culture; Internalization, as they develop security in their identity as a person of color; and Internalization/Commitment, when they have acquired a positive sense of racial identity (Cross, Parham, & Helms, 1991; Tatum, 1992, 1993).

Susan Barrett (1990) offers a developmental theory that attempts to encompass the experiences of all "others," including those of us who have been "othered" because of racial and sexual identity. This is the five-stage Minority Identity Development Model, which Barrett suggests can be applied to anyone who is not part of the dominant European American male heterosexual

---

[4] I choose Falco because lesbian identity formation theory is the most appropriate focus for the use of my own narrative as a critique of contemporary developmental theory. Theorists who describe the developmental stages of gay men's sexual identity use similarly structured models (e.g., Coleman, 1982).

culture. In the Conformity stage, a person is ashamed of her membership in a minority culture, and accepts the devaluing judgments of the dominant culture. In the Dissonance stage, she wants to express her membership in a minority culture, but is still restricted by discomfort with it. She then moves into a Resistance and Immersion stage, as she becomes aware of the positive value of her membership in a minority culture and rejects the dominant culture. Following immersion in her minority culture, she enters an Introspective period, as she realizes that she cannot express herself fully within the constraints of an isolated minority identity. Finally, in the stage Barrett calls Synergetic Articulation and Awareness, she finds self-fulfillment when she integrates her minority identity into all aspects of her life.

Each of the above identity development models was constructed in an attempt to fill some gaps in developmental psychology. They attempt to recognize the diversity of human experience by describing the developmental sequences that occur in response to the experience and context of homophobia or racism. They do not, however, describe the effects of the *simultaneous* experience of homophobia and racism. These models assume an availability of supportive experiences that provide the means for an individual to progress from one stage to the next. Although each of these models is claimed to be nonlinear and nonhierarchic, each posits a final stage that represents a developmental peak of mental health. In this self-actualized stage, a person's sexual identity is no longer problematic and their bicultural adaptation (comfortably being the "other" within the dominant culture) has become a source of empowerment. Therefore, the underlying assumption is that a supportive bicultural experience is available to all "others." We (two-spirits) become self-actualized when we become what we've always been, empowered by our location in our communities (versus the micro-management of an individuated identity).

Indigenous American Perspectives on Sexual and Racial Identity

Despite the reationship between sexual and racial identity development presented in European American models, for Indigenous American lesbian, gay, or bisexual people, the effects of racism and homophobia cannot be separated from each other or from the rest of their experiences. The emphasis of the Indigenous American worldview on the interconnectedness of all aspects of an individual's life challenges the compartmentalized structure of developmental stage models. As Pueblo psychologist and educator Terry Tafoya states, "[D]etermination of an individual's identity on the basis of sexual behavior makes no conceptual sense to many American Indians" (1989, p. 288). That is, any presentation of sexual and racial identity development as two distinct phenomena and any analysis proceeding from that assumption cannot adequately describe the experiences of Indigenous American people.

Furthermore, Indigenous Americans may respond to homophobia and racism in markedly different ways than people from other cultures. For example, if she respects the Ethic That Anger Not Be Shown, she may appear not to react to the "isms" that affect her. If she uses the Conservation-Withdrawal Tactic or the Notion That Time Must Be Right in her response, the strength of her resistance might not be recognized. Also, the Ethic of Non-Interference would require her friends and family to respect and trust the choices she makes.

Two-Spirit Identity Formation

Because there is limited research and few case studies available on the developmental experiences of gay and lesbian Indigenous Americans, in the following section I will use my life experiences to illustrate both the impact of racism and homophobia (including sexism) on identity development, and the ill fit between current identity development theory and an Indigenous American reality.[5]

I grew up in northern Canada in a very small, isolated Cree community that could only be reached by boat in the summer or by plane in the winter. After I was born, as was the custom, elders came to visit, bringing gifts and blessing me as the newest member of their community. We returned to my father's home community, a reserve on the edge of a pulp mill town, before I was five. Some of my first memories of that town are of racism, although at the time I did not have a name for the meanness I experienced. I knew that unfair things were happening to me because I was an Indian, but I couldn't make the conceptual leap required to understand that racism meant, for example, that I was not allowed to play inside the homes of some of my White school friends. My family was a place of strength and support, where we spoke, listened, and answered with respect. I was never made to feel wrong there. As I grew older, I dreamt of hockey and minibikes. I preferred to play with "boy's toys," so my parents sensibly brought me Hotwheels instead of Barbies. Later, I was allowed to hunt with a gun, and *moosum,* my grandfather, taught me and my brothers how to make snares to trap ermines and rabbits on the frozen creek behind our house. In my family, I was taught what I wanted to learn.

I remember dancing at a gathering when I was ten or eleven. Everyone was dancing around and around the reserve hall to the powwow music that was piped in over the bingo loudspeaker system. Back then the dance was an ordinary thing. Some people wore bits of regalia. Most of us, though, just wore jeans and sweatshirts. I was really enjoying myself, dancing the way that I wanted to. I was picking up my feet and even taking spinning steps at times. The old people were watching from the chairs on the side in encouraging

---

[5] Sexism, when directed at children, is often a homophobic attempt to regulate or direct the development of their sexual identities.

silence, clapping their knees and smiling, inviting us to continue. Everything seemed so natural. I was learning new steps by watching what others were doing and learning the Cree songs in my head.

Then a friend danced up along side of me and told me to quit dancing like a boy. Confused, wondering how I could dance the wrong steps, I stopped. After that evening, I became self-conscious about the toys I wanted to play with. Knowing became not knowing, and the sureness of my experience was replaced by a growing certainty that I could not be the girl that was wanted outside of my family. Being "different" was no longer a gift, and my self-consciousness led me to learn ways to pretend and ways to hide myself. I would play sports with my younger brothers and their friends but was wary around kids my own age. When I was fourteen, I was given the hockey skates I wanted, but when we had skating at school, rather than showing up in "boy's" skates, I pretended that I didn't have any. By that age, I understood that sexist judgments directed at me had a homophobic subtext, but I did not grasp the extent of their effect on me. I sat alone on the sideline benches that winter.

As I grew older, racism continued to erode my self-confidence and pride. Eventually I refused to identify as Cree, acknowledging only my Scottish heritage, although everyone in our small community knew my family. When I was in town I would avoid my relatives. I would even pass right by *moosum* without saying hi, acknowledging him only out of the corner of my eye. He knew what was going on: I was embarrassed to be related to him. At the same time as I struggled with my Cree identity, I was beginning to realize that I was a lesbian. The combination of racism and homophobia, much of it internalized, was very devastating for me; I didn't finish high school. I moved to the nearest city, in part to get away from the racism of the small town that surrounded our community, and in part to explore my new-found sexuality in a more anonymous way. I was looking for the idealized gay world that I had caught sight of in movies, in books, and on television. Somehow, I had lost my place in my own community as a result of the move, combined with how I felt.

In the city, I began a pre-medical study program at a university by enrolling as a mature student.[6] There were twelve Indigenous students in the program; six of us were two-spirit. However, we did not acknowledge it, and it was only when most of us had quit university that we realized we had experienced the same struggles at the same time. The "coming out" process was not easy for any of us. For example, as an Indigenous woman, I could not find a positive place for myself in the predominantly White, gay scene. I looked there for support in my lesbian identity, and instead found another articulation of racism. Although a large number of gay and lesbian Indigenous people live in the city, the Indigenous community remains segregated from the mainstream, non-Indigenous gay and lesbian community.

---

[6]"Mature student" is a category similar to "nontraditional," referring to students who have been out of high school for a few years before entering university.

Immersion in the White, gay party scene became a way to numb a growing depression. I remember the excitement of getting ready to go out for the evening. I studied the culture: the way people danced, dressed, talked, moved, and even the way everyone greeted each other with a hug. This was all new to me, and I dove into that culture with anthropological zeal, hoping to uncover the secrets of it strangeness. I cut my hair, as though proclaiming a new identity was enough to make me belong in the lesbian and gay community. I know that, in Cree tradition, we cut our hair when we are in mourning. When someone we are related to or someone we love dies, a part of ourselves dies. It is a personal ceremony. The hair, usually a braid, is buried in a quiet safe place where no people or animals can step on it or disturb it. There I was with a flattop, shaved on the sides and short, spiky, and flat on the top. My hair was everywhere on the floor of the flashy salon of a new-found friend. People were stepping on it, walking through it, and eventually it just ended up in the garbage along with everyone else's. A connection with my community was buried in that garbage can.

The support of my family, culture, and spiritual traditions helped me through this period. When I "came out" to my parents, they were not shocked by my confession and told me that they already knew. This puzzled me. How could they know and I didn't? I understand now that they respected me enough not to interfere, and enough to be confident that I would come to understand my sexuality when the time was right. Throughout my life, my family had acknowledged and accepted me without interference: my grandfather gave me hunting lessons and my parents brought me the toys that I would enjoy. As I was told by another child that I danced the "wrong" dance, the elders of my community smiled and clapped, quietly inviting me to continue. My development has obviously been shaped by a traditional Indigenous worldview.

I came to be empowered by who I was, rather than disempowered by who I wasn't. In the context of Native spirituality, I learned about the traditions of two-spirit people. I acquired strength from elders and leaders who were able to explain that as an Indigenous woman who is also a lesbian, I needed to use the gifts of my difference wisely.

Even my "maladaptive" responses to homophobia and racism can be understood as at least in part shaped by traditional values. The Conservation-Withdrawal Tactic and the Ethic That Anger Not Be Shown are both resistive responses that can easily be misread as passive acceptance. In Cree culture, "Silence" does not equal "Death," and to "Act Up" should not lead us to remove ourselves from our community. If it does, we seem most often to quietly find our way back home.[7] When confronted with racism and homophobia, I had internalized many of the devaluing judgments of the dominant culture. As I struggled with my racial and sexual identity, I had looked for affirmation by immersing myself in the minority cultures to which I be-

[7] In last year's "Indian Days" celebration at a reserve neighboring my own, the community celebration included a drag show by two-spirit people in traditional clothing.

longed. Most significant, though, is the fact that when I sought support in the mainstream lesbian and gay community, it simply was not there.

This struggle is very typical of the "coming out" experiences of Indigenous people. As I reflect on the lives of my Indigenous friends, I realize that those of us who are happy have achieved our presence within the Indigenous American community. Two-spirit identity is rarely recognized in the mainstream lesbian and gay community unless it is accompanied by romantic notions that linger from the concept of the *berdache*. We are either Spanbauer's "holy man who fucks" or "just a fuckin' Indian."[8]

What this means, then, is that the positive bicultural adaptation that sexual and racial identity development models prize is simply not available to most of us. Although elements of my life could be neatly arranged into these identity models, this partial fit does not mean that a model expresses a life story, or even a simple developmental sequence.

It is possible for psychological theory to illuminate our understanding of the identity development of two-spirit people. Unlike the three theories discussed earlier, Robinson and Ward's (1991) work with African American adolescent girls uncovered an important distinction between strategies for survival and strategies for liberation. While survival strategies move the girls further from their true selves, liberation strategies strengthen their voices because they are "alternative avenues to personal empowerment and positive change" (p. 96). Robinson and Ward place the girls' experiences within a worldview that emphasizes an identity that is strengthened by a sense of interconnectedness with others.

This extended sense of self that Robinson and Ward offer is similar to an Indigenous worldview and includes a sort of timelessness, one that includes not only those of us here now, but also those who have come before us and those who will follow. Within this worldview, the girls' strategies are forms of resistance. Within Robinson and Ward's construct, the choices I made throughout my adolescence and early adulthood could be seen as short-term survival strategies. For two-spirit people, this can emerge from a commitment to community and collective experience, to creative and courageous action, and to an intimately spiritual worldview. This is how I have negotiated my own identity in the distance that stretches between the values of my culture and the values of Western culture.

Gloria Anzaldua (1990), in the introduction to her collection of writing by women of color, calls such survival strategies "making face," the way that we must become "like a chameleon, to change color when the dangers are many and the options few" (p. xv). Quick fixes, like wishing away my skates, dropping out of school, and walking past *moosum*, were strategies that pushed me away from my sense of self and my sense of community. Did racism force me out of my home town, or did I choose to distance myself from my community? When confronted with racism and homophobia, I internalized many

---

[8] These words were hurled at me by a lesbian who had been, I thought, one of my closest friends for ten years.

of the devaluing judgments of the dominant culture. Leaving my home community was an attempt to leave behind my devalued status, to become "race-less." However, it removed me from the strength and support I found in my community. I was even more of an "other" in the city than I was at home, even farther from a place where my self could be found.

Returning Practice to Theory

Last summer, I was part of a gathering of two-spirit people. When I first arrived, I was cautious. Everyone seemed cautious, as though we were all unsure of how we should act. On the wall of the main cabin a sign was posted; it said, "pow-wow, Saturday night." When I read it, I felt dizzy, overwhelmed by my imagining what the dance might be. Two-spirit people dancing. I have lived with dreams of dancing, dreams where I spin around, picking up my feet. I have many feathers on my arms and my body and I know all the steps. I turn into an eagle. Arms extended, I lift off the ground and begin to fly around in big circles. Would this be my chance?

For the rest of the week I listened for tidbits about the pow-wow. I learned that a local drum group would be singing. I heard about a woman who was collecting her regalia — "Her regalia . . . " — and wondered, did that mean men's? I waited patiently for Saturday night to come. Listening.

When the drumming started, I was sitting still, listening and watching. The first people to dance were women. They had their shawls with them. Next, some men came in; they were from different Nations, but still danced in distinctively male styles. I watched with disappointment in my heart but said to myself that I would still enjoy the pow-wow. And then a blur flew by me and landed inside the circle of dancers that had formed. It was a man in a jingle dress. He was beautiful and he knew how to dance and he danced as a woman. It was a two-spirit dancing as it should be. After that, more two-spirits drifted into the circle. I sat and watched, my eyes edged with tears. I knew my ancestors were with me; I had invited them. We sat and watched all night, proud of our sisters and brothers, yet jealous of their bravery. The time for the last song came. Everybody had to dance. I entered the circle, feeling the drumbeat in my heart. The songs came back to me. I circled the dance area, in my most humble moment, with the permission of my ancestors, my eleven-year-old two-spirit steps returned to me.

The aspect of my own experience (and that of my two-spirit friends) that current sexual and racial identity development models cannot encompass is that my strength and identity, along with the strength and identity of my peers, is inseparable from our culture. Educators and school counselors need to acknowledge that this is the reality for our community. This means that we need to stop assuming that all lesbian and gay people can find support in mainstream gay culture, and that we make a point of creating opportunities for two-spirit indigenous people to find their place in their traditional communities. There has been little research done on the developmental experiences of Indigenous American people, and there is almost no research on the experiences of two-spirit people, despite grim statistics that reveal the urgency of addressing the needs of these groups. Gay and lesbian youth are two to six times more likely to attempt suicide than heterosexual teens (Kroll & Warneke, 1995), and Indigenous Canadians have the highest suicide rate of any racial group in the world (York, 1990).

Whenever possible, we need to ensure that two-spirit youth have access to the history and unwritten knowledge of their community, and that it is available to them in a culturally congruous way. Educators can also easily access written texts by important Indigenous American leaders, such as Beatrice Medicine (1983), Terry Tafoya (1989, 1990), Chrystos (1988, 1991, 1993), Connie Fife (1992, 1993), and Beth Brant (1985, 1988, 1991, 1993, 1995). These authors ground their work in their identities as Indigenous Americans, and they offer insight into the historic and present-day realities of two-spirit people. Tafoya's work as a psychologist and educator has made invaluable contributions to an effective approach to AIDS education for Indigenous American people. Two-spirit writers such as Chrystos, Connie Fife, and Beth Brant provide stories and narrative texts that record the contemporary life of two-spirit people. Their body of work is a rich resource for identity development theorists, and an invaluable affirmation for two-spirit youth.

Educators and developmental theorists need to study the resistance, strength, and liberation strategies two-spirit people employ as part of their development of an empowered identity. By examining the meaning of these strategies relative to an Indigenous American worldview, educators and theorists can increase their awareness in a way that will inevitably have a spill-over effect. They will learn to look beyond the limits inscribed by mainstream lesbian and gay culture and into the lives of the women, men, and children who are lesbian, gay, and two-spirit. We, whether educators, Indigenous Americans, or two-spirit people, must abandon the assumptions of a European American worldview in order to understand the identity development of two-spirit Native American and Canadian First Nations people, and to develop our theory and practice from within that understanding.

References

Almaguer, T. (1993). Chicano men: A cartography of homosexual identity and behavior. In H. Abelove, M. Barale, & O. Halperin (Eds.), *The lesbian and gay studies reader* (pp. 225–273). New York: Routledge.

Anzaldua, G. (1990). *Haciendo caras, una entrada. Making face, making soul.* San Francisco: Aunt Lute.

Barrett, S. E. (1990). Paths toward diversity: An intrapsychic perspective. In L. S. Brown & M. P. P. Root (Eds.), *Diversity and complexity in feminist therapy* (pp. 41–52). New York: Harrington Park Press.

Berkhofer, R. F. Jr. (1978). *The White man's Indian.* New York: Vintage Books.

Blackwood, E. (1984). Sexuality and gender in certain Native American tribes: The case of cross-gender females. *Signs: Journal of Women in Culture and Society, 10,* 27–42.

Brant, B. (1985). *Mohawk trail*. Ithaca, NY: Firebrand Books.

Brant, B. (Ed.) (1988). *A gathering of spirit: A collection by North American Indian Women*. Ithaca, NY: Firebrand Books.

Brant, B. (1991). *Food and spirits*. Ithaca, NY: Firebrand Books.

Brant, B. (1993, Summer). Giveaway: Native lesbian writers. *Signs: Journal of Women in Culture and Society, 18*, 944–947.

Brant, B. (1995). Lesbian writers. *Aboriginal Voices, 2*(4), 42–42.

Brant, C. (1990). Native ethics and rules of behavior. *Canadian Journal of Psychiatry, 35*, 534–539.

Cardinal, H. (1969). *The unjust society: The tragedy of Canada's Indians*. Edmonton: M. G. Hurtig.

Chrystos. (1988). *Not vanishing*. Vancouver: Press Gang.

Chrystos. (1991). *Dream on*. Vancouver: Press Gang.

Chrystos. (1993). *In her I am*. Vancouver: Press Gang.

Coleman, E. (1982). Developmental stages of the coming-out process. In W. Paul, J. Weinrich, J. Gonsiorels, & M. Hotvedt (Eds.), *Homosexuality: Social, psychological, and biological issues* (pp. 149–158). Beverly Hills: Sage.

Cross, W. E., Parham, T, & Helms, J. (1991). The stages of Black identity development: Nigrescence models. In R. Jones (Ed.), *Black psychology* (pp. 319–338). Berkeley: Cobb & Henry.

Deloria, V. Jr. (1969). *Custer died for your sins: An Indian manifesto*. Norman: University of Oklahoma Press.

D'Emilio, J., & Freedman, E. B. (1988). *Intimate matters: The history of sexuality in America*. New York: Vintage Press.

Falco, K. (1991). *Psychotherapy with lesbian clients: Theory into practice*. New York: Brunner/Mazel.

Fife, C. (1992). *Beneath the naked sun*. Toronto: Sister Vision Press.

Fife, C. (Ed.) (1993). *The colour of resistance*. Toronto: Sister Vision Press.

Ing, N. R. (1991). The effects of residential schooling on Native child rearing practices. *Canadian Journal of Native Education, 18*(Supplement), 65–118.

Jacobs, S., & Cromwell, J. (1992). Visions and revisions of reality: Reflections on sex, sexuality, gender, and gender variance. *Journal of Homosexuality, 23*, 43–69.

Jacobs, S., & Thomas, W. (1994, November 8), Native-American two-spirits. *Anthropology Newsletter, 7*. Arlington, VA: American Anthropological Association.

Kroll, I., & Warneke, L. (1995, June). *The dynamics of sexual orientation and adolescent suicide: A comprehensive review and developmental perspective*. Calgary, Canada: University of Calgary.

Medicine, B. (1983). "Warrior women": Sex role alternatives for Plains Indian women. In P. Albers & B. Medicine (Eds.), *The hidden half: Studies of Plains Indian women* (pp. 267–280). Lanham, MD: University Press of America.

Miller, J. R. (1989). *Skyscrapers hide the heavens: A history of Indian-White relations in Canada*. Toronto: University of Toronto Press.

Robinson, T., & Ward, J. V. (1991). "A belief in self far greater than anyone's disbelief": Cultivating resistance among African American female adolescents. In C. Gilligan, A. Rogers, & D. Tolman (Eds.), *Women, girls and psychotherapy: Reframing resistance* (pp. 87–103). New York: Harrington Park Press.

Roscoe, W. (Ed.). (1988). *Living the spirit: A gay American Indian anthology*. New York: St. Martin's Press.

Roscoe, W. (1991). *The Zuni man-woman*. Albuquerque: University of New Mexico Press.

Ross, R. (1992). *Dancing with a ghost: Exploring Indian reality*. Markham, Ontario: Octopus.

Sioui, G. (1992). *For an Amerindian autohistory: An essay on the foundations of a social ethic*. Buffalo, NY: McGill-Queen's University Press.

Spanbauer, T. (1991). *The man who fell in love with the moon*. New York: Harper Perennial.

Tafoya, T. (1989). Dancing with Dash-Kayah. In D. M. Dooling & P. Jordan-Smith (Eds.), *I become part of it: Sacred dimensions in Native American life* (pp. 92–100). New York: Parabola Books.

Tafoya, T. (1990). Pulling coyote's tail: Native American sexuality and AIDS. In V. Mays (Ed.), *Primary prevention issues in AIDS* (pp. 280–289) Washington, DC: American Psychological Association.

Tatum, B. (1992). Talking about race, learning about racism: The application of racial identity development theory in the classroom. *Harvard Educational Review, 62*, 1–24.

Tatum, B. (1993). *Racial identity development and relational theory: The case of Black women in White communities* (Work in Progress Series). Wellesley, MA: Stone Center for Research on Women.

Weston, K. (1993). Lesbian/gay studies in the house of anthropology. *Annual Review of Anthropology, 22,* 339–367.

Whitehead, H. (1981). The bow and the burden strap: A new look at institutionalized homosexuality in Native North America. In S. B. Ortner & H. Whitehead (Eds.), *Sexual meanings* (pp. 80–115). Cambridge, Eng.: Cambridge University Press.

Williams, W. L. (1986). *The spirit and the flesh: Sexual diversity in American Indian culture.* Boston: Beacon Press.

York, J. (1990). *The dispossessed: Life and death in Native Canada.* Boston: Little, Brown.

I would like to acknowledge and thank my family, my partner Janet, and my two-spirit brothers and sisters for their help and support.

The Colonizer/Colonized Chicana Ethnographer:
Identity, Marginalization, and Co-optation in the Field

SOFIA VILLENAS

In this chapter, Sofia Villenas describes being caught in the midst of oppressive discourses of "othering" during her work as a Chicana ethnographer in a rural North Carolina Latino community. While focusing on how to reform her relationship with the Latino community as a "privileged" ethnographer, Villenas missed the process by which she was being co-opted by the dominant English-speaking community to legitimate their discourse of Latino family education and child-rearing practices as "problem." By engaging in this discourse, she found herself complicit in the manipulation of her own identities and participating in her own colonization and marginalization. Through her story, Villenas recontextualizes theories about the multiplicity of identities of the researcher. She problematizes the "we" in the literature of qualitative researchers who analyze their race, class, and gender privileges. Villenas challenges the dominant-culture education ethnographers to move beyond the researcher-as-colonizer position and to call upon their own histories of complicity and marginalization in order to move toward new identities and discourses. Similarly, she calls upon ethnographers from marginalized cultures to recognize their position as border crossers and realize that they are their own voices of activism.

> It is not easy to name our pain, to theorize from that location.
> (hooks, 1994, p. 74)

> Like a "mojado" [wetback] ethnographer, I attempt to cross the artificial orders into occupied academic territories, searching for a "coyote" [smuggler] to secure a safe passage.
> (E. G. Murillo Jr., personal communication, 1995)

Harvard Educational Review Vol. 66 No. 4 Winter 1996, 711–731

What happens when members of low-status and marginalized groups become university-sanctioned "native" ethnographers of their own communities? How is this "native" ethnographer positioned vis-à-vis her own community, the majority culture, the research setting, and the academy? While qualitative researchers in the field of education theorize about their own privilege in relation to their research participants, the "native" ethnographer must deal with her own marginalizing experiences and identities in relation to dominant society. This "native" ethnographer is potentially both the colonizer, in her university cloak, and the colonized, as a member of the very community that is made "other" in her research.

I am this "native" ethnographer in the field of education, a first-generation Chicana born in Los Angeles of immigrant parents from Ecuador. Geographically, politically, and economically, I have lived under the same yoke of colonization as the Chicano communities I study, experiencing the same discrimination and alienation from mainstream society that comes from being a member of a caste "minority."[1] I share the same ethnic consciousness and regional and linguistic experiences. The commonly used terms "Hispanic" and "Latino" do not adequately describe who I am.[2] Racially and ethnically I am *indigena*, a detribalized Native American woman, descendant of the Quechua-speaking people of the South American Andes. Politically I am a Chicana, born and raised in the American Southwest, in the legendary territories of Aztlan.[3] This story is about how these identities came into play in the process of conducting research with an emerging Latino community located in the U.S. South.

The Colonizer/Colonized Dilemma

Rethinking the political and personal subjectivities of researcher and ethnographer has in recent times pushed the boundaries of theorizing about the multiple identities of the researcher within the research context of privi-

---

[1] "Chicano" and "Chicana" are self-identified terms used by peoples of Mexican origin. They are political terms of self-determination and solidarity that originated in the Chicano liberation movement of the 1960s.

[2] "Hispanic" is a U.S. government term used to classify Spanish-speaking peoples of Latin America living in the United States. "Latino" refers to a collective community of Latin Americans. "Latino" is my chosen term, which I use interchangeably with the emic term "Hispano." I use "Latino" to refer to the very diverse Spanish-speaking community of Hope City (a pseudonym), North Carolina. "Latino" also refers to male members of the community, while "Latina" refers to the women. Members of the Latino community in Hope City usually refer to themselves in national terms: Mexican, Salvadoran, Guatemalan, etc. However, they have also adopted the term "Hispanos" to refer to themselves collectively as a community. It is also important to note that people self-identify differently. For this reason, when I refer to my friends, I use the various terms with which they identify themselves. Also, an "Indigenista" or "Mesocentric" (Godina, 1996) perspective has spurred interest among Latinos and peoples of indigenous ancestry between themselves and tribal Native Americans. In essence, through this movement we (including myself) are saying that we *are* Native American people.

[3] "Aztlan" refers to the mythical origins and ancient homelands of the Aztec civilization. Over the last thirty years, Aztlan has been popularized by the Chicano liberation movement and is linked to the vast northern territories of Mexico that were invaded and annexed by the United States in 1848.

lege and power. Qualitative researchers in education have called for a reexamination of the raced, gendered, aged, and classed positions of the researcher with respect to the research participants (Fine, 1994; Lather, 1991; Roman & Apple, 1990). These researchers are also recognizing that they are and have been implicated in imperialist agendas (Pratt, 1986; Rosaldo, 1989) by participating in "othering" (Fine, 1994) and in the exploitation and domination of their research subjects (Roman & Apple, 1990).[4]

In the last decade, ethnographers and qualitative researchers have illuminated the ways in which the researched are colonized and exploited. By objectifying the subjectivities of the researched, by assuming authority, and by not questioning their own privileged positions (Crapanzano, 1986; Fine, 1994; Rosaldo, 1989; Van Galen & Eaker, 1995), ethnographers have participated as colonizers of the researched. Rosaldo (1989) uses the image of the "Lone Ethnographer" who once upon a time "rode off into the sunset in search of his 'natives'" (p. 30). After undergoing arduous fieldwork as his rite of passage, the Lone Ethnographer "returned home to write a 'true' account of the culture" (p. 30). In the texts of classic anthropology, people were depicted as "members of a harmonious, internally homogenous and unchanging culture" (p. 31), and written about in a way that "normalizes life by describing social activities as if they were always repeated in the same manner by everyone in the group" (p. 42). Rosaldo reminds us that this manner of objectifying people's lives has been the classic norm of ethnography, and that researchers have rarely asked what the researched think about how their lives are being interpreted and described in text.

Researchers are also implicated as colonizers when they claim authenticity of interpretation and description under the guise of authority. In a critique of Geertz's description of the Balinese cockfight, Crapanzano (1986) exposes the ways in which the event described is subverted and sacrificed to "a literary discourse that is far removed from the indigenous discourse of their occurrence" (p. 76). This discourse, according to Crapanzano, is ultimately masked by the authority of the author, "who at least in much ethnography, stands above and behind those whose experiences he purports to describe" (p. 76).

As ethnographers, we are also like colonizers when we fail to question our own identities and privileged positions, and in the ways in which our writings perpetuate "othering." As Fine (1994) explains:

> When we write essays about subjugated Others as if *they* were a homogeneous mass (of vice or virtue), free-floating and severed from contexts of oppression, and as if we were neutral transmitters of voices and stories, we tilt toward a narrative strategy that reproduces Othering on, despite, or even "for." (1994, p. 74)

Moreover, we are like colonizers when, as Van Galen and Eaker (1995) point out, the professional and intellectual gatekeeping structures (e.g., university

---

[4] "Othering" refers to objectifying people who are different than the Western White self in a manner that renders them inferior.

admissions to graduate studies, journal publication referees) from which we gain our legitimacy and privilege remain "highly inaccessible to those on whose behalf we claim to write" (p. 114).

For example, women teachers of working-class backgrounds are expected to consume a body of literature that emanates from elite universities from which they are excluded, and that thus excludes them from the production of material used for the teaching profession and their own training. Fine (1994) and Van Galen and Eaker (1995) urge ethnographers to probe the nature of their relationship to those they write about.

While we continue to push the borders of the multiple, decentered, and politicized self as researcher, we continue to analyze and write about *ourselves* in a unidirectional manner as imperialist researchers (Rosaldo, 1989) and colonizers (Fine, 1994) in relation to the research participants. Yet, what about the researcher as colonizer *and* colonized? Here is my own dilemma: as a Chicana graduate student in a White institution and an educational ethnographer of Latino communities, I am both, as well as in between the two. I am the coloniz*ed* in relation to the greater society, to the institution of higher learning, and to the dominant majority culture in the research setting. I am the coloniz*er* because I am the educated, "marginalized" researcher, recruited and sanctioned by privileged dominant institutions to write for and about Latino communities. I am a walking contradiction with a foot in both worlds — in the dominant privileged institutions *and* in the marginalized communities. Yet, I possess my own agency and will to promote my own and the collective agendas of particular Latino communities. I did not even consider the multiplicity of self and identity and the nuances of what such consideration meant until I had to confront my own marginality as a Chicana researcher in relation to the dominant majority culture in the research setting. In the research context of power and domination, I encountered what it means to examine closely within myself the intersectedness of race, class, gender, and other conceptual notions of identity.

I am a Chicana doctoral student, and have been conducting research in a small rural community in North Carolina, which I have named Hope City. My research project involved the educational life histories of Latina mothers who were recent immigrants to Hope City. In the telling of their stories, the women defined education — how they experienced it in their lives as learners and teachers in families, communities, and schools, and how they constructed educational models for raising their own children. I spent over two years in Hope City, teaching English as a Second Language (ESL) at the local community college and in an after-school tutorial program for elementary-school-age Spanish-speaking children. I participated in family social gatherings, and in community and church events and meetings. I also had a lot of contact with the English-speaking community of professionals who were servicing Latino families in health care and education, joining them in meetings and informal gatherings. These professionals were also formally interviewed by other colleagues involved in the Hope City project. As a team, we were funded by a child development center to investigate the beliefs about education held by the agencies and schools serving the Hope City Latino community, and by the diverse Latino community members themselves. In my own research, I systematically analyzed the public sphere and the organization of relations of power in Hope City. Through a historiographic analysis of the town's newspaper and through my observations and participant observations within the community of school and agency professionals, I found that the Latino community in Hope City was being framed as a "problem."

At the beginning of the research project, I was aware of the politics and privilege of my researcher role and my relation to the research participants. I was eager to experience the process of constructing meaning with the research participants. By talking with these Latina mothers about their beliefs and philosophies of child-rearing and education, as well as my own, I hoped to engage them in conversations about how they could create a dignified space for themselves and their families in a previously biracial community that was not accustomed to Latinos. I had vague ideas about community projects that I hoped would emerge from the research participants themselves. When I reflected later, these notions seemed arrogant, as if I thought I knew the hopes and aspirations of this Latino community. I realized I had to question all my assumptions about this southern Latino community, such as defining as problems certain aspects of their lives that, to them, were not problematic at all. I was certainly ready to learn from this Latino community, but in the process of seeking to reform my relationship with them, I failed to notice that I was being repositioned and co-opted by the dominant English-speaking community to legitimate their discourse of "Latinos as problem." In the course of working with Hope City's non-Latino school and service professionals, I discovered that while I engaged in a rethinking of my own politics and the processes of empowerment within the Latino community, I was hiding my own marginality in relation to the majority culture. I did not know then that I would have to scrutinize my own lived experiences as a Chicana daughter, mother, wife, and student in confronting the dominant community's discourses of "othering" and of difference.

In this article, I attempt to heed Fine's words in "unearthing the blurred boundaries between Self and Other" (1994, p. 72). Weis (1995) summarizes the discourse on colonialism, which takes as its central point the idea that the colonial "other" and the self (read the "Western White" self) are simultaneously co-constructed, the first being judged against the latter. Furthermore, Weis notes, "this process of 'othering' is key to understanding relations of domination and subordination, historically and currently" (p. 18). This article, then, speaks to the discourses of "othering" that jolted me out of my perceived unproblematic identity and role as a Chicana researcher in education, and into a co-construction of the "Western" self and the Chicana "other." This ongoing story involves my confrontation with my contradictory identities — as a Chicana researcher in the power structures of the dominant discourse of "other," and as a Chicana working with this marginalized Latino community. Through this story, I hope to recontextualize the ways in which qualitative researchers in education have theorized about identity and privilege to include the repositioning and manipulation of identities that can occur, particularly with native ethnographers. This recontextualization problematizes the ways in which qualitative researchers who seek to analyze privilege and the "situatedness" of each ethnographer fail to note that we as ethnographers of education are not all the same "We" in the literature of privileged ethnographers. My standpoint as a Chicana and my historical relation to Latino communities mediate and complicate my "privilege." Unveiling the ways in which the ethnographer is situated in oppressive structures is a critical task for qualitative researchers in the field of education. Even in new positions of privilege, the Chicana ethnographer cannot escape a history of her own marginalization nor her guilt of complicity.

Personal History

My encounter with discourses of difference and of "othering" as a child in Los Angeles neighborhoods and schools intensified my scrutinization of my own identity and role as a Chicana in academia. Growing up in Los Angeles, I was aware of racism. As a child, I acted out the effects of colonization, refusing to speak Spanish, emphasizing that I was South American and not Mexican, as Mexicans were relegated to second-class citizenship. I grew up knowing that my culture and language were not valued, but I did not suffer direct, blatant racism. I found safety in numbers, as there were many other Latinas, Chicanas, and Mexicans with whom I could hang out.

As I grew older, our peer group continually created and celebrated our Chicano/Latino cultures and languages. As an adult, I thought I had overcome the loss of self that comes with second-class relegation of the Spanish language and Latino cultures, and that I did not speak with the voice of a colonized person, one whose culture and language were devalued. Yet I was not as prepared for Eurocentric academia as I thought I was. In community, I had learned to manipulate my identities successfully and did not expect them to be manipulated by others. But such a manipulation is precisely what occurred when I began my professional university training in ethnographic research. At the university, I experienced the dilemma of creating my identity as a Chicana researcher in the midst of Eurocentric discourses of "other." Being an ethnographer made my contradictory position more obvious, complex, and ironic. I recognize this contradiction now, but at the university, the discourse of "othering" did not begin with my research study.

An awakening of sorts occurred for me when I attended a seminar on topics in education. On that particular day, the topic was whether public single-population schools should exist. The readings for that week centered on public and private schools for women only, for gays and lesbians, and schools based on Afrocentric or Chicano-centric curriculum. Most of my fellow classmates argued that people should not be separated, reasoning that students should be integrated so that everybody could come together to talk about societal inequities and find solutions together. They argued that single population schools promoted separatism, and that through integrated schools, the Eurocentric curricula would be challenged. While I agreed that all people need to dialogue about oppression and work together to bring about social justice, and therefore was in favor of integrated schools, I did not agree that Afrocentric or Chicano-centric curricula and schools promoted separatism. In trying to engage in the discussion, however, I began to feel uncomfortable. I tried to explain why I felt that disenfranchised groups had the right to these curricula if they wanted them and, furthermore, why I felt they were important and necessary. I argued that people who have been stripped of their cultures through public schooling need to come together and reclaim their cultures, histories, and languages, but although I believed this, I was nevertheless buying into the discourse of fear of separatism, saying that we needed to have separate spaces before coming together to be a part of the larger group. Of course, implicit in this argument was the idea that as people of color, we were going "to come together" to join the dominant culture and integrate ourselves within it, rather than challenge the notion of a single common culture.

The discourse of this group of fellow students and friends was so powerful that it disabled me. I explained my stance apologetically, acquiescing to the notion that we would have to come back and join a mainstream culture and society rather than challenge it. Everyone else was speaking as if they were detached and removed from the topic, rationalizing the logic of their arguments, but it was different for me. The topic was personal and deeply embedded in my experiences. In this conversation, I was not the subject anymore but the object, the "other." Using Cornell West's words, hooks (1990) writes that people often engage in debates that "highlight notions of difference, marginality, and 'otherness' in such a way that it further marginalizes actual people of difference and otherness" (p. 125). hooks likens these debates to reinscribing patterns of colonization: "When this happens . . . the 'Other' is always made object, appropriated, interpreted, taken over by those in power, by those who dominate" (1990, p. 125).

In this same manner, I felt that my experiences as a Latina going through the Eurocentric curriculum of public schools was being objectified and appropriated through a rationalized logical argument against Chicano- or Afrocentric schools. In the rational, logical arguments in that seminar, no space existed for my deeply passionate personal experience and voice, for me to argue for the right to choose to be with Latinas/os, for us to be educated together and to center our curriculum in our diverse roots and history, to find out about ourselves and to claim ourselves in our own terms. My classmates and I talked against oppressed groups coming together to form their own schools in a way that ignored the existence of race, class, and gender privileges among the class participants. In this discussion, an aura of disinterested, detached, scientific rationalism existed that rendered me voiceless and silenced. Ellsworth (1989) describes the oppression of rational argument as putting as its opposite the irrational "other" — for example, women and people of color. In schools, she said, the rational argument has become the "vehicle for regulating conflict and the power to speak" (p. 303).

After the group dispersed, I was left feeling stripped of my identity and angry with myself for betraying my own voice. I had fallen into the trap of the dominant discourse, trying to convince the group not to worry, that we would eventually come around to integrating ourselves. But into what? I did not know, but it was implied that we would integrate ourselves into some core set of shared social and cultural ideals and belief systems, a core that evidently was the White, middle-class lifestyle. I was reminded again of Ellsworth's (1989) critique of critical pedagogy. She argues that the dialogue emphasized in critical pedagogy assumes that we could all engage in dialogue equally as if we were not raced, gendered, and classed persons with vested interests and different experiences. The seminar participants (including myself) failed to see how, in the process of discussing people of color, we silenced and marginalized the very voices of those who were supposed to have been the subjects and authors of their experiences — the voices of fellow Chicana and African American classmates.

I now realize that something else also occurred that afternoon in our seminar. The topic, as well as the disinterested, detached way in which the discussion was carried out, fueled what I wanted so desperately to express, but could not. I was the only Chicana there, and had to think and speak individualistically rather than collectively. I was without my Latino friends from home who shared the power of our activism in defying the colonization of our identities and of our people. In the absence of that collectivity, I changed my commitment and orientation from the visions my friends and I had shared. Cut off from those who collectively sustained them, I lost those visions of activism and self-determination. Deep inside, I wanted to voice what I was experiencing at that moment — the disempowerment that comes from being cut off from your own. Perez (1991), a Chicana feminist, writes what I wanted to express at that time:

> You attempt to "penetrate" the place I speak from with my Chicana\Latina hermanas. I have rights to my space. I have boundaries. . . . At times, I must separate from you, from your invasion. So call me a separatist, but to me this is not about separatism. It is about survival. I think of myself as one who must separate to my space and language of women to revitalize, to nurture and be nurtured. Then, I can resurface to build the coalitions that we must build to make the true revolution — all of us together acting the ideal, making alliance without a hierarchy of oppression. (p. 178)

Only now, as I am writing these words, do I realize what was happening. It hit me and it hurt me. I felt it in my bones, but I could not articulate it until now. The coalitions referred to by Perez imply groups of empowered and self-identified peoples who do not have to pack neatly and put away their languages and cultures in order to comply with a "standard" way of being. To be Chicanas in the myriad and infinite ways there are of being, to come as we are, poses a threat to integrated schools and to mainstream society. In the absence of collectivity in my graduate seminar, I could not be true to my vision of a Chicana.

Revealing Tension in My Identity as a Chicana Researcher

As I look back, describe, and theorize about my seminar experience, I can articulate the elements that constituted my marginalization and my complicity in the discourses of difference and "othering." The power of the dominant discourse of "other," the objectification of my experiences as the "other" through detached, rational argumentation, and the severing of a collective vision and memory that disabled me and rendered me voiceless, all constituted marginalization and complicity. These elements resurfaced when I started the process of conducting qualitative research with the Latino community in Hope City, North Carolina. There, my dilemma of being a Chicana and a researcher became problematic in ways similar to my experiences in the seminar, that is, as an accomplice to the marginalization and objectification of my identity and experiences as a Chicana, which became embedded in the power structure of the dominant and the disenfranchised.

Going into the field, my intent was to gain access to the Hope City Latino community so that I could interview Latina mothers about their beliefs on child-rearing and education, particularly as their narratives played out in the context of a changing rural southern town. Yet I did not want only to take their stories and leave. I also wanted to become involved in some way with their Latino community, either through bilingual tutoring for children with their mothers or through English as a Second Language (ESL) instruction. As I sought to gain access to the community, I had to speak with numerous English-speaking institutional representatives, including educators in the elementary school, community college, and health department. From the beginning, I felt uncomfortable in my conversations with these community leaders and with their cultural views of Latino families, and of the women in particular. They constructed Latino families as "problems" tending towards violence, sexism, machismo, and low educational aspirations. In their meetings, well-meaning providers talked about showing Latina mothers models of proper child-rearing. A Hope City newspaper headline read, "Program Teaches Hispanics How to Be Better Mothers." Other articles about Latino families carried headlines such as "Literacy Void." Again, the dominant discourse concerning the "other" was powerful and overwhelming — so much so that I found myself, as in the seminar, participating in it as an accomplice. I began to talk the talk.

I remember accompanying an ESL instructor from the community college to the trailer park where he gave classes. We stood in the grassy area in the middle of the park, looking out at the individual trailers, some with children and families outside them. The instructor was giving me the rundown on their living conditions and other problems. I was nodding my head, all the while gazing at the people who looked back at us. I remember ducking my head, painfully aware of my awkward position. Whose side was I on? In participating in this manner with the instructor, I was, as hooks (1989) says, "one with them in a fellowship of the chosen and superior, [it was] a gesture of inclusion in 'whiteness'" (p. 68), affirming that I had been assimilated. I felt uncomfortable, yet I participated, as in the graduate seminar, by betraying my anger and remaining silent, and by not challenging the discourse. In conversations with Hope City professionals, I had to choose my alignment in the power structure of the community — either with the leaders who were in positions to make policy, or with the disenfranchised Latino community.

Choosing to align myself with the dominant English-speaking leaders entailed sharing the same discourse and language to talk about the Latino community. To do this, I had to distance myself from the Latino community and the experiences I shared with them, and speak as the subject about the object. I could do this in the eyes of the dominant English-speaking community because I was formally educated and spoke English as well as they.

In this southern community, there were no other Chicanas/os in leadership positions. I had no one with whom to share a collective vision for the empowerment of "our" community. The ESL instructor and I spoke in a detached manner about the problems of "these people," as if I had not been socialized in a Latino family and immigrant community. I spoke as if Latino families and friends had not been the most important people in my private life. I silenced myself so that I could have further conversations with the community leaders who were the key to my accessing the educational institutions of the community. By participating in their discourse, I had to disengage myself from my experiences as an intimate participant in Latino families and communities. The dominant discourse of difference was powerful, and my experiences were again nullified through my participation in detached and rational discussions of the problems of the "other."

My uncomfortable feelings soon turned to outrage and hurt. One particular discussion with a school principal startled me out of my perceived unproblematic role as a Chicana researcher. My advisor and I went to speak with the principal about my starting a mother/child class to teach children how to read and write in Spanish. The principal, who held blatantly racist views of Latino families, told us he would play the devil's advocate and point out some problems — for example, how were we going to get mothers to come? He went on to say that we had to understand the Hispanic family. The man, he said, dictates, and the woman is subservient: "The man will not let her out of the house. They do not care about education and so it's hard to get the mothers to come to the school." An ESL teacher who was also in the room explained that these were poor people, blue-collar workers who did not have education themselves. I later responded angrily in my field notes:

> How dare you say this to me. How is it that you are telling me what Latino families are like. I was so insulted. They were talking about my "raza" so negatively as if I were not Latina myself. This goes to show how easily I can "pass" and that in certain contexts, I am not identified as one of "them." With

this conversation as in others, I have felt that I have had to put on a different persona in order to play along with well meaning racist discourse. I have felt very uncomfortable talking to benevolent people about the "other," the exotic poor people who need our help. "Our" referring to my complicity as researcher. (Field notes, March 1994)

After that incident, I began to question my identity and my role as a Chicana researcher. It was evident that the dominant English-speaking community did not consider me a Latina, like the women we were discussing, but a middle-class, educated woman of Spanish descent. How was I to relate to this dominant discourse of difference and "othering?"

I looked to recent works on the researcher's role in disenfranchised communities in which the researcher shares the same cultural background as the research participants. Delgado-Gaitan (1993) and Delgado-Gaitan and Trueba (1991) write about an ethnography of empowerment, a framework that "provides a broad sociocultural premise and possible strategy for studying the process of disempowerment and empowerment of disenfranchised communities" (p. 391). This kind of ethnography is based on a Freirian notion of self-awareness of the social and cultural context of the nature of oppression suffered by disempowered people (Delgado-Gaitan & Trueba, 1991). Such a framework calls for "the construction of knowledge through the social interaction between researcher and researched with the fundamental purpose of improving the living conditions of the communities being researched" (Delgado-Gaitan & Trueba, 1991, p. 392). Delgado-Gaitan (1993) emphasizes that the researcher shapes the research participants and their environment while, at the same time, the researcher is also shaped by the participants and the dynamics of their interactions. Delgado-Gaitan's (1993) own provocative story is of the transformation of her role with respect to her work on literacy practices in the homes and schools of a Latino community. As the parents mobilized to effect changes in the school, Delgado-Gaitan redefined her role as researcher to become involved as facilitator and informant in the process of community empowerment. As a result of her own unique experiences, Delgado-Gaitan, a Latina herself, built upon the notion of making problematic her relationship with Latino communities. By doing so, she put into practice qualitative researchers' call for the reexamination of one's identity and place within the research context of privilege and power.

My story extends this notion by problematizing the relationship between the marginalized researcher and the majority culture. The internalization of oppressive discourses relating to one's own people, especially as a product of institutionalized education and university training, can lead to a disempowerment of the researcher and the research process. The analysis can be extended then to include the empowerment of the researcher and the role of the ethnographer's culture, self-identity, and her/his raced, classed, and gendered experiences in the research process. In my case, while I naively looked for ways in which I could help Latina mothers "empower" themselves (see Le Compte & de Marrais, 1992, for a critique on the discourse on empowerment), I failed to realize that I needed to help myself become empowered vis-à-vis the dominant, English-speaking community. I needed to examine my own identity in the particular cultural arena that formed the context for my research study. Not having done so, I could not engage in the process of constructing knowledge with the research participants. I needed first to ask myself, How am I, as a Chicana researcher, damaged by my own marginality? Furthermore, how am I complicit in the manipulation of my identities such that I participate in my own colonization and marginalization and, by extension, that of my own people — those with whom I feel a cultural and collective connectedness and commitment?

For these reasons, researchers must examine how their subjectivities and perceptions are negotiated and changed, not only in relation to the disenfranchised community as research participants, but also through interactions with the majority culture. In most cases, the latter are the people who espouse the dominant discourse of difference and "other," that is, the cultural views of Latino families as a "problem" — poor, disadvantaged, and language deficient. In Hope City, Latina mothers are constructed as "at risk" in the discourse of the dominant community (i.e., professionals in education, health, and social services) so that the ways in which they raise and educate their children are devalued (Swadener & Lubeck, 1995). It is this "at risk" and "problem" discourse that I was being pushed hard to legitimate in Hope City. Yet this discourse concerned my own rearing, my own family, my own mother, and my own beliefs and those of my community. Through my engagement in the majority culture's "Latinos as problem" discourse, I was further marginalized and encircled in my own guilt of complicity.

Identity, Tension and Power: Interpreting My Insider/Outsider Perspective

I find it useful to appropriate Delgado-Gaitan's (1993) insider/outsider concept and apply it in a different manner to my emerging and changing identity as a Chicana researcher. In the process of conducting her study, Delgado-Gaitan (1993) learned that a researcher initially could only be an outsider to the community of research participants, but that with insight, the researcher could foster relational and reflective processes with their participants and in time become an insider. What are the particular behaviors and/or characteristics of the researcher that can make her/him an insider to the community of research participants? In a general sense, it is the sharing of collective experiences and a collective space with the research participants, such that the researcher is gradually accepted as a member of that particular community. As researchers, we can be insiders and outsiders to a particular community of research participants at many different levels and at different times.

In my case, I had two layers of communities to penetrate, at least on different terms. From my perspective at the time, the irony was that I was becoming an insider to the "wrong" community — the dominant, English-speaking community of leaders with whom I felt no familial, historical, or intimate relation. I was, in fact, the outsider to the Latino community of this town, since I was not *of* their community and did not share in their everyday experiences (I did not live in Hope City). Further, I was being recruited by the institutional representatives to become an insider in the legitimization of the dominant discourse of Latinos as "problem" and "victim." The effects on me of participating in the dominant discourse in a detached manner through rational dialogue were powerful. Consequently, I had to step back and negotiate internally the ongoing recruiting efforts of the dominant, English-speaking community leaders to their discourses of difference.

I began my fieldwork on site at the beginning of the spring semester of the academic year. I discussed with my advisor how the White community might be cautious in talking with me about the Latino community, since I might be perceived as a member of this community. As I stated earlier, my advisor and I were soon proven wrong. The White community leaders were eager to talk to me about their perceptions of Latino families.

I had worked hard all semester to gain access to the Hope City Latino community and to find a niche in which to practice my profession of "maestra" (teacher), and to do research as well. My diligence paid off in that many opportunities were opened for me by English-speaking community leaders. I had received invitations to teach ESL and literacy in the churches (both the Catholic and Methodist churches), the elementary school, the community college, and the health department.

I decided to dedicate my time to teaching ESL to adults at the community college, a job in which I not only had experience but that I also thoroughly enjoyed. At the end of the semester, I looked to see what my story in terms of my research had been thus far. I had written in my field notes about my uneasy and uncomfortable feelings as I had conversations with English-speaking community leaders. Interestingly, I had also recorded my feelings of awkwardness when I talked to Latinas/os as a researcher researching "them." I was unconsciously documenting the power relations that defined the research context of which I, the dominant community leaders, and the Latino immigrant community each formed a part. Roman and Apple (1990) emphasize that a crucial task for the ethnographer should be the "elaboration of the structural power relations that formed the basis for conducting the field research and the study" (p. 60). The documentation of my feelings of anger and awkwardness formed the basis for the elaboration of my identity as a Chicana researcher in the community's power structure.

The power play in the recruitment efforts of the White power structure, and later in their efforts to appropriate me, was clearly evident. To recruit me to their discourse and narratives of difference, the community leaders had to view me as equal with them in the power structure. They appropriated my persona and appeared, at least initially, to welcome me as an equal.

I later understood this welcome to be a form of colonizing. They appropriated my persona by presuming shared assumptions of a body of experiences. For example, a community college instructor warned me about the dangers of the trailer park, implying that I shared his fear of poor people and of people of color. The community leaders also treated me as an equal by talking about Latinos as the "other" and including me in the distanced and detached conversations about the "problems of Latinos." Sharing our detached, rational observations of Latinos made me seem objective and scientific, and seemed to put us on equal footing with each other and in a superior position to the Latino community.

I felt powerful because I could discuss "their" problems. I was even in a position to negotiate power with the elementary school principal when I proposed Spanish tutoring classes for young children and their mothers. Not only did my credentials give me leverage in these negotiations, but my professional identity and language also met the criteria for inclusion and commonality with the institutional representatives. In more ways than one, I found it easier to be an insider to the community of dominant English-speaking leaders than to the Latino community.

The powerholders' recruiting efforts were intense precisely because they had a lot at stake in interpreting, structuring, and legitimating their cultural constructions of difference and diversity. The schools and agencies were interpreting Latino "cultures" and child-rearing practices. They were structuring the relationships between the Latino and English-speaking communities through the mediating force of agency bureaucracies (see Adkins, Givens, McKinney, Murillo, & Villenas, 1995). And, they were legitimating the "at risk" and "problem" discourses.

Undoubtedly, as a "Hispanic" professional, I served to legitimate the "at risk" discourse and the definition of Latino child-rearing as a "problem." Sleeter (1995) argues that "the discourse over 'children at risk' can be understood as a struggle for power over how to define children, families, and communities who are poor, of color, and/or native speakers of languages other than English" (p. ix).

In later months, community leaders called on me to speak about and for the Latino community. In their eyes, I was the "expert" on the educational experiences of Latino families, not because I had begun talking with Latina mothers and could possibly articulate their points of view, but because I was seen as the professional who possessed formal education, teaching experience, and spoke both Spanish and English. Indeed, they would introduce me not only by name, but also by my academic credentials and past teaching experience. On one occasion, I was asked to speak to a group of community leaders from various social service agencies about Latino families and their educational needs. I chose to speak about the strengths of language and literacy socialization in Latino families. On another occasion, I was asked to translate for and represent the Latinas from my ESL class at a meeting to organize a county chapter of a council for women. At yet another meeting, called by the county migrant education office, about one hundred Latino parents met in the elementary school cafeteria where I spoke to them about strategies to help their children in school. On all of these occasions, I was serving as the broker for and the link to the Latino community for the professional community leaders. They called on me to participate in meetings and to give presentations. The stakeholders of this community clearly felt an urgent need to co-opt certain people, such as myself and other English-speaking town leaders, to represent the Latino community. It was as if in doing so, they did not have to handle the raw material. The Latino community was too foreign, too different, too working class, too brown; so they appropriated me, Sofia, the preprocessed package, wrapped in formal education and labeled in English.

Of course I did not want to be associated with the dominating power structure in the eyes of the Latino community. I had qualms about being perceived as the imperialist researcher. I felt tension with the Latino community when I was in my role as researcher, and when they saw me in company and complicity with the community leaders. I am reminded of two situations in which I felt these tensions most acutely.

It felt normal and comfortable, for example, when I visited Tienda Adrian (Adrian's Store), a Latino food store, with my husband and children. We spoke with the store owners in Spanish, asking about the town. However, the following week I felt uncomfortable when I revisited Tienda Adrian with my advisor and approached the store owners cloaked in my university researcher role to ask about the town. Similarly, I felt the tension of power in my researcher role when I began formal interviews with the women in the Latino community. The interviewing situation was uncomfortable for me, in contrast to the times we had engaged in informal talks about raising and educating children in Hope City.

I felt the tension of power and complicity even more directly when I engaged in social interaction with an English-speaking institutional representative and a Latina client at the same time. I felt this more acutely when service agency providers used English to talk about Latina clients in their presence. The Latina clients, who, for the most part, were new arrivals in Hope City, could not speak English. One particular service provider had the habit of introducing me to a Latina client and then giving me her personal life history right in front of her. In these situations, power was wielded through language, and English became the language of exclusion. The women's personal lives were presented to me like an open book in a language that they did not understand. In having to respond in English to the service provider, I was self-conscious and awkward about the exploitation and "othering" of the women. I did not want to be complicit with the "colonial administrator," but I was unaware that this was how I was being positioned.

My feelings of complicity and guilt, however, led me to engage in small spontaneous subversive strategies and acts of resistance. Any time a community leader spoke in English about a Latina client in her presence, I translated. Sometimes I would change the meanings somewhat so as not to cause embarrassment or hurt. On one occasion, for example, I said, "He's saying that you had gone through some rough times," even though the service agency provider said that she had had a nervous breakdown and had psychological problems. I began to translate into Spanish everything I said to community leaders when Latinos were present.

I also brought politics and subversion to the meetings at which I spoke for the community leaders. I did not always say what they wanted to hear, stirring controversy at one meeting and causing some Whites to react defensively at another. At one meeting at the elementary school, I disrupted the discourse of dominance by not accepting the seat they had saved for me in the front of the room facing the Latino audience. Instead, I took a seat among some Latino friends.

As an ESL instructor, a "maestra," in the Latino community, I am more active in dialogue and discussions with my Latino students than with the community of school and agency professionals. In being able to name and identify the situatedness of my identities, I am beginning to react to my positioning and act towards a transformation of my identity and role as a Chicana educational researcher in a Latino community.

Negotiating Identities: Toward New Discourses

I am in the process of my own learning, and it is not my goal to arrive at a final resolution. Rather, I am in continual discovery. Identity and self are multiple and continually remade, reconstructed, reconstituted, and renewed in each new context and situation (Stone, 1992). When I left Los Angeles to attend graduate school in the South, I also left behind identities formed against the backdrop of a segregated city and against a historical context of the racial subordination and conquest of Native and Mexican peoples. In my limited and segregated experiences, I only knew Whites as living the middle-class lifestyle, and rarely as working-class people. I defined myself and was defined by this historical relationship.

In North Carolina, at first I believed I had encountered a place where a historically embedded antagonism did not exist between Mexicans and European Americans, as it exists in the Southwest. There is no territorial Alamo to remember, nor a U.S.-Mexico treaty that appropriated one-third of Mexico's land. I seemed to have forgotten the history of the genocide of American Indians and of the slavery and segregation of African Americans. Nevertheless, I believed space existed in which I could enter into new relationships with the majority culture and define new grounds and new terms. Because of this belief, I found it painful to go into the town where I was to conduct my research project, a town where a new immigrant community of Latinos were the objects of oppressive discourses. The old relationships and identities formed against these discourses were being re-inscribed in me. In confronting these oppressive discourses of difference, I experienced domination and oppression, and was a party to the exercising of them.

This story demonstrates that some Chicanas/os do not move from marginalization to new positions of privilege associated with university affiliation, as if switching from one seat to another on the bus. We do not suddenly become powerful in our new identities and roles as university researchers. We do not leave one to get to the other. As Chicanas/os and ethnographers of color, we carry our baggage with us — a baggage of marginalization, complicity, and resentment, as well as *orgullo* (pride) and celebration. These are not easily cast away. No doubt it is not too difficult to embrace whole-heartedly the privileges of upward mobility, but to many of us the costs are great. Just as becoming raceless was a strategy for Black adolescents who, in Fordham's (1988) study, had to unlearn their racial identities and cultural behaviors in order to make it through high school and beyond, so must some Chicanas/os do the same. As bilingual, tricultural peoples, we "continually walk out of one culture and into another" (Anzaldúa, 1987, p. 77). In Anzaldúa's images, we are straddling multiple worlds, trying to break from colonized identities formed against White supremacy and male dominance and to form a new consciousness: "I am in all cultures, at the same time" (p. 77). We learn to tolerate contradictions and ambiguities of identities and to "seek new images of identities, new beliefs about ourselves" (p. 87).

While I recognize that part of my ongoing process is seeking, forging, and negotiating new images and identities, I am also raging against postmodern renderings of the White middle-class "discovery" that politically and socially situate the ethnographer as synonymous with colonizer, imperialist, and privileged researcher. In this view, it does not matter whether we are Chicanas/os or middle-class White male ethnographers. In the name of a post-modern understanding of identity and privilege, I am led to believe that I am now the same "researcher as colonizer," that I am now privileged, and that I share the same guilt for the same exploitation of the less privileged research participants. In a sense, I was not only being recruited to legitimate the majority culture's discourse of "Latinos as problem," but I am also sym-bolically being co-opted to legitimate academia's declaration of the postmod-ern ethnographer as the socially and politically privileged colonizer. In both instances, I am being co-opted to be like the colonizer, the oppressor, in ways that ignore my own struggle as a Chicana against subjugation and mar-ginalization.

Thus, while I recognize my contradictory position and privilege (that come from university affiliation), and while I would gladly serve as a facili-tator and translator for the voices of the Latina mothers of a small rural town in North Carolina (if they would have me), I must also see myself as going beyond the role of facilitator. I must see my own historical being and space. I must know that I will not "mimic the colonizers" (Perez, 1991, p. 177) and call myself the ethnographer/colonizer, for this insults my gendered, racial memory.

As I look back on my experience in the graduate seminar, I know that in the future I will not be silent, just as I could not be silent any more in the face of the dominant community's attempts to recruit me to their discourses about the Latino population in Hope City. I cannot continue to pretend that as a qualitative researcher in education, I am distanced from intimacy, hope, anger, and a historical collectivity with Latino communities. For these reasons, I cannot be neutral in the field, because to be so is to continue to be complicit in my own subjugation and that of the Latino communities. To take on only the role of facilitator is to deny my own activism. I must recognize that my own liberation and emancipation in relationship with my community are at stake, and that continued marginalization and subjugation are the perils.

I did not seek these confrontations and realizations. They came upon me while I was turned the other way, disengaging myself from the intimacy of Latina sisterhood. They came upon me as I convinced myself that I had to be careful because I was the privileged and thus the colonizer. I was attuned to seeking to reform my relationship with the research participants and to promote their empowerment, without realizing that *I* was being worked on and commodified, that *I* needed to be empowered. I suddenly found myself complicit in my own subjugation, vis-à-vis the dominant public discourse.

In the meantime, I find hope in Fine's (1994) narrative of the way her Latina niece, who was adopted into her middle-class Jewish family, moved in and out of identities as she fought a criminal case for sexual assault. Fine writes:

> Jackie mingled her autobiography with our surveilled borders on her Self and the raced and gendered legal interpretations of her Other by which she was surrounded. She braided them into her story, her deposition. . . . She slid from victim to survivor, from naive to coy, from deeply experienced young woman to child. In her deposition she dismantled the very categories I so worried we had constructed as sediment pillars around her, and she wandered among them, pivoting her identity, her self representations, and, therefore, her audiences. (1994, p. 71)

Herein I find the key: to resist "othering" and marginalization is to use our multiplicity of identities in order to tolerate and welcome the contradictions and ambiguities, as Anzaldúa (1987) writes, so that in our quest for liberation, we also dismantle the categories and the conquering language of the colonizer. In this manner, we "work the hyphen between Self and Other," as Fine (1994, p. 72) challenges us to do, yet we work from within ourselves as the Self/Other, Colonizer/Colonized ethnographer.

Thus, it is important to continue theorizing on the researchers' multiplicity of identities and the implications of this for qualitative research in education. As members of marginalized groups assume more privileged positions in the educational socioeconomic structures of hierarchy, people who were once merely the exotic objects of inquiry are now the inquirers — the ones formulating and asking the questions. As some enter the ranks of teachers, administrators, and scholars, we are becoming the enforcers and legitimators as well as the creators of official knowledge. Hence, as qualitative researchers in the field of education, we need to explore and understand the dilemmas created for Chicanas/os, African Americans, Native Americans, and scholars from other disenfranchised groups vis-à-vis the majority culture. We scholars/activists of color need to understand the ways in which we manipulate our multiple, fluid, clashing, and colonized identities and how our identities are manipulated and marginalized in the midst of oppressive discourses. Luke and Luke (1995) argue, "Only by describing and understanding how power works in oppressive social formations, how identity is shaped both through contestation and collusion with oppressive regimes of control, is it possible to lay down a systematic knowledge of marginal identities" (p. 376).

Further studies are also needed that capture the intricacies of marginalized teachers and scholars who are teaching and researching their own communities. Watson-Gegeo (1994) introduces a collection of articles that illuminate important questions dealing with "minority" teachers teaching "minority" students.[5] These excellent studies encourage further probing of the questions of resisting, negotiating, and tolerating identities in a context of power and privilege — in other words, to pay close attention to how we manipulate our identities and how our identities are manipulated by others. We need to see how Latino ethnographers, for example, become commodified in the process of research. At the same time, we also need to examine the gender, race, and class dynamics created in the university setting, where for example women of color, who are professors, and middle-class White students come together (see Vargas, 1996). These are critical questions that need further exploration.

Conclusion

This story is an attempt to untangle my own multiplicity of identities played out in the terrains of privilege and power in ethnographic research. With the new generation of "native" ethnographers, including myself, increasingly working within and writing about our own communities, we are beginning to question how our histories and identities are entangled in the workings of domination as we engage the oppressive discourses of "othering." In my case, while researching in a rural town in North Carolina, I had to confront both my own marginalization and my complicity in "othering" myself and my community, as I encountered the discourse that identified Latino family education and child-rearing practices as "problem" and "lacking."

At a time when qualitative researchers in education are questioning their own privilege in relation to the research participants, the "we" in the literature needs to be re-theorized. My identity/role as a Chicana ethnographer cannot be collapsed in terms of "privileged" researcher in the same manner that other ethnographers are privileged in their relationships with their research participants. In failing to address the ways in which the ethnographer

---

[5] This edited collection includes articles by Foster (1994) on the views of African American teachers who counter prevailing hegemonic beliefs about African American children in reform efforts to improve their achievement in schools; Watson-Gegeo and Gegeo (1994) on the ways in which a history of colonization and modernization in the Solomon Islands serves to keep teachers' cultural knowledge out of the classroom; and Lipka (1994), who examined how Yup'ik Eskimo teachers in Alaska face administrative barriers when working to include their language and culture in their classrooms.

can be damaged by her/his own marginalization in the larger society, the literature has created a "we" that does not include my experience in the field as a Chicana ethnographer.

What might this story teach majority-culture ethnographers of education so that they too move beyond the "researcher as privileged" dilemma? I believe they also can confront their own multiplicities of identity and histories of complicity and mark the points of their own marginalization. Rosaldo (1989) and Patai (1991) write that ethnographers cannot escape their complicity in exploiting the "researched," yet I still need to ask, What is the nature of the space that I have found, and what are the possibilities for the Latino community in Hope City, North Carolina? My space is a fluid space of crossing borders and, as such, a contradictory one of collusion and oppositionality, complicity and subversion. For "Hispanos" in Hope City, surrounded by a historically violent and entrenched biracial society in which one is either Black or White, emancipatory possibilities lie in the creation of a dignified public space where they can negotiate new identities and break down the biraciality. Likewise, my challenge to majority-culture ethnographers is that they call upon their own marginalizing experiences and find a space for the emergence of new identities and discourses in the practice of solidarity with marginalized peoples.

My own journey moves me towards new transcendent discourses that are transformative and emancipatory. I hope to be, in Olson and Shopes's words, a "citizen-scholar-activist(s) rooted in the community" (cited in Van Galen & Eaker, 1995, p. 120). Recognizing our multidimensional identities as colonizers, colonized, neither, and in-between, we *camaradas* in struggle must work from within and facilitate a process where Latinas/os become the subjects and the creators of knowledge. My answer to the ethnographer-as-colonizer dilemma is that I will not stop at being the public translator and facilitator for my communities, but that I am my own voice, an activist seeking liberation from my own historical oppression in relation to my communities. We *mojado* ethnographers look anxiously to learn about the rich diversity of Latino communities in the U.S., and in doing so, create our own rich diversity of models, paradigms, and languages as we cross between our communities and "the artificial borders into occupied academic territories" (E. G. Murillo Jr., personal communication, 1995).

References

Adkins, A., Givens, G., McKinney, M., Murillo, E., & Villenas, S. (1995, November). *Contested childrearing: The social construction of Latino childrearing.* Paper presented at the meeting of the American Educational Studies Association, Cleveland, OH.

Anzaldúa, G. (1987). *Borderlands/La frontera.* San Francisco: Aunt Lute Books.

Crapanzano, V. (1986). Hermes' dilemma: The masking of subversion in ethnographic description. In J. Clifford & G. Marcus (Eds.), *Writing culture* (pp. 51–76). Berkeley: University of California Press.

Delgado-Gaitan, C. (1993). Researching change and changing the researcher. *Harvard Educational Review, 63,* 389–411.

Delgado-Gaitan, C., & Trueba, H. (1991). *Crossing cultural borders: Education for immigrant families in America.* London: Falmer Press.

Ellsworth, E. (1989). Why doesn't this feel empowering: Working through the myths of critical pedagogy. *Harvard Educational Review, 59,* 297–324.

Fine, M. (1994). Working the hyphens: Reinventing self and other in qualitative research. In N. Denzin & Y. Lincoln (Eds.), *Handbook of qualitative research* (pp. 70–82). Thousand Oaks, CA: Sage.

Fordham, S. (1988). Racelessness as a factor in Black students' school success: Pragmatic strategy or pyrrhic victory? *Harvard Educational Review, 58,* 54–84.

Foster, M. (1994). The role of community and culture in school reform efforts: Examining the views of African American teachers. *Educational Foundations, 8*(2), 5–26.

Godina, H. (1996, April). *Mesocentrism: Teaching indigenous Mexican culture in the classroom.* Paper presented at the annual meeting of the American Educational Research Association, New York.

hooks, b. (1989). *Talking back: Thinking feminist, thinking Black.* Boston: South End Press.

hooks, b. (1990). *Yearning.* Boston: South End Press.

hooks, b. (1994). *Teaching to transgress: Education as the practice of freedom.* New York: Routledge.

Lather, P. (1991). *Getting smart: Feminist research and pedagogy with/in the postmodern.* New York: Routledge.

LeCompte, M., & de Marrais, K. (1992). The disempowering of empowerment: Out of the revolution and into the classroom. *Educational Foundations, 6*(13), 5–31.

Lipka, J. (1994). Schools failing minority teachers: Problems and suggestions. *Educational Foundations, 8*(2), 57–80.

Luke, C., & Luke, A. (1995). Just naming? Educational discourses and the politics of identity. In W. Pink & G. Noblit (Eds.), *Continuity and contradiction: The futures of the sociology of education* (pp. 357–380). Cresskill, NJ: Hampton Press.

Patai, D. (1991). U.S. academics and third world women: Is ethical research possible? In S. Gluck & D. Patai (Eds.), *Women's words: The feminist practice of oral history* (pp. 137–153). New York: Routledge.

Perez, E. (1991). Sexuality and discourse: Notes from a Chicana survivor. In C. Trujillo (Ed.), *Chicana lesbians: The girls our mothers warned us about* (pp. 158–184). Berkeley, CA: Third Woman Press.

Pratt, M. (1986). Fieldwork in common places. In J. Clifford & G. Marcus (Eds.), *Writing culture* (pp. 27–50). Berkeley: University of California Press.

Roman, L., & Apple, M. (1990). Is naturalism a move away from positivism? Materialist and feminist approaches to subjectivity in ethnographic research. In E. Eisner & A. Peshkin (Eds.), *Qualitative inquiry in education: The continuing debate* (pp. 38–73). New York: Teachers College Press.

Rosaldo, R. (1989). *Culture and truth: The remaking of social analysis.* Boston: Beacon Press.

Sleeter, C. (1995). Foreword. In B. Swadener & S. Lubeck (Eds.), *Children and families "at promise"* (pp. ix–xi). Albany: State University of New York Press.

Stone, L. (1992). The essentialist tension in reflective teacher education. In L. Valli (Ed.), *Reflective teacher education: Cases and critiques* (pp. 198–211). Albany: State University of New York Press.

Swadener, B., & Lubeck, S. (Eds.). (1995). *Children and families "at promise."* Albany: State University of New York Press.

Van Galen, J., & Eaker, D. (1995). Beyond settling for scholarship: On defining the beginning and ending points of postmodern research. In W. Pink & G. Noblit (Eds.), *Continuity and contradiction: The futures of the sociology of education* (pp. 113–131). Cresskill, NJ: Hampton Press.

Vargas, L. (1996, April). *When the other is the teacher: Implications for teacher diversity in higher education.* Paper presented at the annual meeting of the Eastern Communication Association, New York City.

Watson-Gegeo, K. (1994). Introduction: What's culture got to do with it? Minority teachers teaching minority students. *Educational Foundations, 8*(2), 3–4.

Watson-Gegeo, K., & Gegeo, D., (1994). Keeping culture out of the classroom in rural Solomon Islands schools: A critical analysis. *Educational Foundations, 8*(2), 27–55.

Weis, L. (1995). Identity formation and the process of "othering": Unraveling sexual threads. *Educational Foundations, 9*(1), 17–33.

I am indebted to George Noblit for the conversations that enabled me to tell this story. I also wish to thank Amee Adkins and Lynda Stone for their insights on the manuscript and to Bernardo Gallegos for his encouragement. The research project in Hope City was funded by the Frank Porter Graham Child Development Center, with partial funding by the North Carolina Humanities Council.

Learning in the Dark:
How Assumptions of Whiteness
Shape Classroom Knowledge

FRANCES A. MAHER
MARY KAY THOMPSON TETREAULT

In this chapter, Frances Maher and Mary Kay Thompson Tetreault revisit data presented in their book, The Feminist Classroom. *In their book, they located their analysis in a traditionally feminist position of marginality, where they saw themselves allied with women of color in resisting a patriarchal academy. Subsequent discussions with colleagues and the proliferation of literature on Whiteness led them to realize that their own Whiteness, and the effects of Whiteness itself, remained uninterrogated in their original work. In this reanalysis of data from their book, they examine how assumptions of Whiteness shape the construction of knowledge as it is produced and resisted in the classroom. Drawing on classroom and interview data, they investigate how students' constructions of gender, class, ethnicity, and race are informed by unacknowledged assumptions of Whiteness.*

> So when they met, first in those chocolate halls (of Garfield Primary School) and next through the ropes of the swing, they felt the ease and comfort of old friends. Because each had discovered years before that they were neither White nor male, and that all freedom and triumph was forbidden to them, they had set about creating something else to be.[1]

This quotation from Toni Morrison's novel *Sula* opened one of the chapters in our recent book, *The Feminist Classroom,* a study of learning and teaching in six colleges and universities across the country.[2] We chose this quote because it captured one of the central interpretive frames of our research, which explored how feminist professors and their students "set about creating something else to be" by choosing to study the histories, experiences, and aspirations of women, people of color, and other groups

Harvard Educational Review Vol. 67 No. 2 Summer 1997, 321–349

previously ignored or trivialized by the academy. As we gathered our observations, audiotaped classes, conducted in-depth interviews with selected students and seventeen of the teachers, and constructed a portrait of each professor's teaching, we engaged in a process of bringing their perspectives to light and explored the implications of these perspectives for the social construction of classroom knowledge.

In our self-defined role as champions of suppressed voices, we missed Morrison's invitation to Whites to examine what it means to be "White." Instead, we considered ourselves feminist researchers sharing a common perspective with the women of color that we studied, all of us being feminists resisting a male-centered academy. While we sought to acknowledge and understand our own position as White researchers, we did not fully interrogate our social position of privilege, which made us, vis à vis our subjects, oppressors as well as feminist allies.

Our original analysis of this data resulted in our book, *The Feminist Classroom,* which was organized around four themes: mastery, voice, authority, and positionality. In our subsequent reanalysis of our *Feminist Classroom* data, we found that exploring the theme of positionality became the most salient theme in understanding our own Whiteness. Positionality is the concept advanced by postmodern and other feminist thinkers that validates knowledge only when it includes attention to the knower's position in any specific context.[3] While position is always defined by gender, race, class, and other significant dimensions of societal domination and oppression, it is also always evolving, context dependent, and relational, in the sense that constructs of "female" create and depend on constructs of "male"; "Black" and the term "of color" are articulated against ideas of "White." Thus peoples' locations within these networks are susceptible to critique and change when they are explored rather than ignored, individualized, or universalized.

We ended *The Feminist Classroom* with a call for "pedagogies of positionality," for approaches to teaching in which these complex dynamics of difference and inequality could be named and examined. What we ignored, however, were the persisting powers of the *dominant* voices that continue to "call the tune" — that is, to maintain the conceptual and ideological frameworks through which suppressed voices were distorted or not fully heard. We did not see the ways in which a thorough "pedagogy of positionality" must entail an excavation of Whiteness in its many dimensions and complexities.

One reason for our omission is that we lacked the interpretive frameworks to examine Whiteness, which the proliferation of recent literature on the topic has since given us.[4] Much feminist theory has come from examining certain types of marginality; we, like other White feminists, focused on the situations and experiences of women as victims of gender oppression, leaving the positions of racial domination unexplored.[5] To explore Whiteness would have meant examining and reframing our own positions vis à vis our informants, particularly our informants of color.

In Toni Morrison's *Playing in the Dark: Whiteness and the Literary Imagination,* she invites us to go beyond looking at racism in terms of its effects on the victim and to consider, through works of American literature, "the impact of racism on those who perpetuate it. It seems both poignant and striking how avoided and unanalyzed is the effect of racist inflection on the subject."[6] Morrison's proposal drew us back to a quote we used in our book to show the complex ways in which students from the dominant White culture began to learn about themselves from these newly emerging voices:

> Never in my life have I ever been ashamed of being an upper-class white male. . . . I don't have anything to gain by having Black and White equal. I feel like if it happens, I'll still have a good life, a profitable life. And if women stay home or not, you know like men want them to . . . I can gain, like mankind gains, or womankind, but personally I don't have to deal with that. I'm an upper-class White male; I'm the boss. . . . If you're born and you could have your choice of what you wanted to be, White male would probably be the choice, because that's the best thing to be.[7]

This student's construction of his identity was bound up with, and expressive of, a deep-rooted sense of entitlement based on gender and class, as well as race. Reflecting on the importance of taking a course that addressed both sexism and racism, he went into great detail about being a minority in a class composed of a majority of African Americans, both female and male, and a small group of White women.[8]

This student, Mark, was from a privileged Atlanta family and had attended high school at both an exclusive private day school and a local magnet school for the performing arts, which was 60 percent African American.[9] In both places he had friendly acquaintances with Black students. His father owned an art gallery specializing in African art, and he had taken several African American history classes, which he had loved, at his historically White research university. Characterizing himself in an interview as not being brought up "typically Southern," he placed great store in learning about Black culture and history as an antidote to racism. Mark was in a class on "Women and Literature" taught by an African American woman, which emphasized texts by women of color. When we saw that learning about the lives and works of African American women left Mark's own racial and gender positions intact and unexplored, we were initially taken aback. We did not examine our assumption that by learning about African American lives, Mark and others would be more aware of the pernicious effects of racism on everyone, and thus more conscious of the standpoint from which he, and many other Whites, look at the world. Could a different emphasis in this class have made Mark more conscious and reflective about his position of privilege in a network of relations of dominance?

We began to wonder how to address the implications of ingrained assumptions of White privilege amid the persistence of racial oppression and the growing racial alienation of our society. Among the most powerful mechanisms maintaining the superiority of dominant voices is the failure to acknowledge and understand how assumptions of Whiteness shape and even dictate the limits of discourse, in the classroom as elsewhere.[10] Assumptions of Whiteness gain much of their power by passing as "normal," "an invisible package of unearned assets" that Whites "can count on cashing in on each day, but about which they were meant to remain oblivious."[11]

As we became increasingly aware of these issues in our own professional and personal lives, and as we decided to return to our classroom data, we were drawn to new literature on the ideology and practices of Whiteness. Writers and scholars such as Toni Morrison, David Roediger, Elizabeth Ellsworth, Andrew Hacker, and Karen Sacks have recently focused on the cultural construction of the categories "White" and "Black," or "White" and "of color," attacking the assumption that racial differences are "natural states" deducible from physical characteristics. These writers assert, as the concept of positionality implies, that these categories of race depend on each other for their elaboration as meaningful entities, as well as for the multiple (and changing) significance attached to them.[12] Whiteness, like maleness, becomes the norm for "human"; it is the often silent and invisible basis against which other racial and cultural identities are named as "other," and are measured and marginalized.

Whiteness operates at different levels simultaneously. Authors such as Becky Thompson and her colleagues have distinguished among "Whiteness as description," referring to the assignment of racial categories to physical features, "Whiteness as experience," referring to the daily benefits of being White in our society, and finally, "Whiteness as ideology," referring to the beliefs, policies, and practices that enable Whites to maintain social power and control.[13] By the institutionalization of physical appearance as social status, all Whites gain special advantage over those marked "Black" or "people of color." Whiteness thus becomes a marker for location of social privilege, as well as individual identity. To understand Whiteness as a social position is to assign everyone, not only people of color, differentiated places in complex and shifting relations of racialized and gendered hierarchies.

Whiteness may be further defined, in Elizabeth Ellsworth's recent work, as "instead of a fixed, locatable identity, or even social positioning, . . . a dynamic of cultural production and interrelation."[14] In the college classrooms we studied, as in other settings, Whiteness was both assumed and continually in need of assertion, always being constituted as it was simultaneously being challenged and resisted.

David Roediger, Karen Sacks, and Andrew Hacker all show how notions of Whiteness change over time. To become White has often been constructed as synonymous with becoming truly American. Roediger explores ways in which nineteenth-century White workers learned to depend for their self-definition on their sense of themselves as White by defining themselves against Black slaves and freedmen.[15] The concept of who was White also changed to include successive groups of European immigrants, just as immigrants themselves changed to fit into some concept of Whiteness. America's larger systems of racial formation often confounded religion and race as well. For example, Hacker observes that Irish-Catholic immigrants took longer to shed an alien identity because Catholics were not regarded as

altogether White, and Jews were kept at the margin of White America because they were not Christians.[16] Further, Sacks shows how this concept of
Whiteness evolved as Jews "became White folks" following World War II.
Roediger says that "the central implication of the insight that race is socially
constructed is the specific need to attack *Whiteness* as a destructive ideology
rather than to attack the concept of race abstractly."[17]

What new questions, therefore, do we need to ask as teachers and classroom researchers in order to expose Mark's and others' classroom experiences as complex reflections of and reactions to the racialized power relations of our society? How firmly, for example, are assumptions of Whiteness
lodged in the academy's ideological frameworks, in its exercise of intellectual domination, and how do they work to shape classroom knowledge? How
is Whiteness produced and resisted as a function of the ongoing production
of classroom meanings, and what role does it play in the students' construction of their own places within racial, as well as class and gender, hierarchies?
Given the practice of understanding racialism only in terms of its effect on
people of color, how do people of color construct the role of Whiteness as
they go about "imagining something else to be?"

A necessary part of perceiving how the assumption of Whiteness shapes
the construction of classroom knowledge is understanding its centrality to
the academy's practices of intellectual domination, namely, the imposition
of certain ways of constructing the world through the lenses of traditional
disciplines. Such domination is often couched in the language of detach-
ment and universality, wherein the class, race, and gender position of the
"knower" is ignored or presumed irrelevant. By evoking the academic mirror's assumptions of Whiteness as well as maleness, Adrienne Rich named
two major attributes of the universalized perspective that scholarly pursuits
both depart from and aim for:

> When those who have the power to name and to socially construct reality
> choose not to see you or hear you, whether you are dark-skinned, old, disabled,
> female, or speak with a different accent or dialect than theirs, when someone
> with the authority of a teacher, say, describes the world and you are not in it,
> there is a moment of psychic disequilibrium, as if you looked into a mirror and
> saw nothing.[18]

Our use throughout *The Feminist Classroom* of a "methodology of positionality," one in which we continually revisited our work and our own position
with perspectives gained from new experiences and insights, allows us now
to write a new "last chapter" as both an extension and a reversal of how we
initially looked at race in our book. We can now use theories of Whiteness
as lenses to reexamine some of our classroom portraits, to see how Whiteness
was constructed, and how that construction shaped the discourse. By comparing our original analysis with this new perspective, we can also see our
own positions as researchers anew.[19]

In undertaking this reanalysis of our data, now from the acknowledged
position of our own Whiteness, we have to ask ourselves why we are revisiting

these classrooms. As Ellsworth points out, academic writing on Whiteness, by Whites, often makes us again into "experts" on race, reifying the same relations of oppression that we wish to contest.[20] With these warnings in mind, we want to reexamine several classroom vignettes, not to produce the White experts' last word on them, but to illuminate some ways of rereading the students' production of "White," "Black," and other racialized positions and identities. We stress the particularity of these rereadings, not only as being contingent on our present take on our own positions, but as presentations of unique situations, "not the one but the one among many," and as "responses to historically specific encounters with particular racisms." We want to portray some of "the context-specific responses made possible when Whiteness is related to the other social positioning that people live out and live through" — in these cases, not only gender and class, but the specific dynamics produced by the teacher and student composition of these different classrooms as well.[21]

Our first few examples will reflect class discussions in which Whiteness is assumed as a normal condition of life rather than a privileged position within networks of power. It appears to be a safe, well-marked path, powerful because it is an invisible one to Whites, which allows discussions of race to slide effortlessly forward as notations of features of "the other." Specifically, we look at the dynamics of White racial formations in enactments of gender and class.

Next we turn to a situation where Whiteness began to come into focus as a position. The path of discussion becomes bumpy and painful, but the critique of the relationships of oppression necessary to a positional understanding of Whiteness becomes possible through these interactions. Finally, we look at one class, in which the teacher and the majority of participants were people of color. In this class, Whiteness had to be named and actively resisted in order for participants to proceed with the construction of knowledge on their own terms.

Constructing Social Class as White and Male

We look first at the ways White males construct their masculinity and class positions, using the assumption of Whiteness as part of their guiding ideological framework. The first case we look at is a senior seminar in literary theory at a small liberal arts college. Nine students were enrolled, five males and four females, all White, several of whom were in their late twenties to mid-thirties. One of us was always present in the classroom as an observer, in this case, Mary Kay Tetreault. All discussions were taped and later transcribed and edited. This discussion, from which the following excerpt is drawn, concerned the ideas of a prominent French feminist, Julia Kristeva, as analyzed in Toril Moi's book *Sexual/Textual Politics*.[22] The initial focus on Kristeva was "derailed" when the professor, who is White, used "class" to show how the same term can have different meanings.

Her comment led to an extended argument about whether women could be seen as a class; two males fought vigorously against the idea, and one female defended it. Ralph, who referred to himself as a "former SDSer,"[23] began this debate by saying, "I'm rejecting sexes as defined as classes; I think classes are defined by economics." Jane replied, "Right, and economics are defined by gender." Ralph's next remarks — that "gender is defined by economics," that "it has less to do with . . . sexual oppression in itself as it does [with] power, or acquisition, or ownership" — made Jane bristle. She responded, "That seems so irrelevant to this — you argue that it's power and acquisition, but the fact of the matter is a high majority of women are making less money [than men]." Ned came to Ralph's defense, asserting at one point that "if you look at gender, you will see all women as being oppressed," implying that not all women are oppressed in economic terms.

These students did not mention race at all as being part of their discussion of class analysis, but we can examine how assumptions about race and gender drove the discussion. Ralph, for example, drew class divisions along both gender and racial lines, unconsciously constructing class as both White and male while simultaneously claiming class as the primary oppression. In this discussion, sex belonged only to women; males' gender was not named. Therefore, Jane's introduction of gender into the analysis was treated by Ralph and Ned as an introduction of women. When Ralph said, "it has less to do with sexual oppression than power or ownership," he was resisting the introduction of women's oppression into the equation because it muddied the water and because class oppression has no gender (i.e., it is assumed to be male against male). Jane's earlier comment about working-class women's lower wages (when compared to working-class men's wages) led only to a stalemate about whether gender or class is the primary type of oppression. That stalemate continually reinforces and normalizes the idea that the working class (and the ruling class, too, presumably) is male.

But were these students constructing the working class as White, as well as male? After a while the teacher introduced the concept of positionality to move the discussion forward:

What we need is a description that is not based on categories but on positionality, on relations. No group is in and of itself oppressed or marginal. It's only in relation to something else. So that women, we can say, are marginal compared to men. But Black women are marginal compared to White, middle-class women.

What is perceived as marginal at any given time depends on the position one occupies. You have to see centrality and marginality, oppression, oppressor and oppressed as relational concepts. That is, they are marked by difference, not by any positive kind of thing. [So] you have to keep the whole thing moving.

Feminism posits itself as a counter to patriarchy. It argues that patriarchy is central and women are marginal. The working class has been fairly ignored in the feminist movement. . . . Black women's struggles have been marginal to the feminist movement. The feminist movement in this country, by and large, has been White and middle class. So, already they have reinscribed that same center-margin dichotomy within itself.

Ralph then asked his teacher, "What determines White and middle class? I still have problems with this." The teacher responded, "Well, again you have to see it as relational, not a positive kind of term." Ralph then replied, "Well, that is different, then. It is negative, you know."

In our original analysis of this class, we worried that women's oppression could be ignored in the relativism of such an approach. We observed gender oppression being given a back seat to the males' assertion that economic class was the main oppression, which we thought enabled them to ignore the issue of male privilege. We saw male dominance enacted, not only in their vocal domination of the discussion, but also in the way Ned and Ralph collaborated in opposing Jane. Even though we noted that their own position was not critiqued or made visible by either the professor or the students, we also inadvertently equated gender primarily with women.

What we did not see were the powerful ways in which the students and teacher were constructing maleness and Whiteness as the norm, both for economic classes and for people in general. While the teacher's use of positionality challenged the students to break out of the categories they were debating and to see them all in relation to each other, race and gender were still presented as sets of complementary opposites and exclusions (women compared to men, Black women compared to White women). While the professor called centrality and marginality into question as shifting and relational concepts "marked by difference, not by any positive kind of thing," she failed to articulate (nor did we pick up) the power relationships that produce these forms of centrality and marginality in the first place, namely Whiteness and maleness.

Ralph's class analysis may have been his way of expressing a covert identity politics, one whose central figure is not working people in general, but the working-class White male. If Ralph were to include the perspectives of women and Blacks in his construction of working class, this might challenge the primacy of class oppression, and make the interrelations of class, gender, and race oppression more complex. In a subsequent interview, Ralph reaffirmed his view of the importance of class while continuing to construct it as White and male. He wondered if it would ever be possible to "quantify human needs," and thought that paying attention to gender detracted from human needs. "Once you consider gender issues, you're immediately led to the sword of economic theory . . . and I haven't seen any fundamental change in the level of suffering among women." Again, "gender" is "women." Ned told us he preferred Kristeva's call to deconstruct the hierarchies over "feminism's idea of a feminist self," which he viewed as "a limitation on the human self." Better to erase all differences than risk the reversal of the hierarchies that a feminist self implied. Both men wished that the whole notion of gender would go away, because White males, in their formulation, have no gender (and perhaps no race) themselves.

Despite the professor's assertion that "what we need is a description that is not based on categories," this discussion of race presupposed the categories Black and White as a binary opposition, rather than exploring the ways in which these categories (as well as the categories "woman" and "man") actively produce each other. Race only entered the discussion when the professor began speaking about positionality. But Whiteness, like maleness, had been central to the identity of the working class in the discussion all along. In short, this whole discussion, in which the students resisted the inclusion of race and gender, was profoundly "racialized" and "genderized."

Constructing Whiteness in Individualized Terms

In reexamining much of our original research data, we found that the students in other classes tended to construct social class in implicitly White and male terms as well. Moreover, in one case where Whiteness was acknowledged, its treatment as an aspect of individual identity masked its operations on deeper social and ideological levels.

Our next example comes from an honors freshman writing class of five male and five female White students at a large comprehensive university, which, as a state institution, draws upon a less affluent, predominantly White student body.[24] This discussion treated issues of social class in much more concrete terms than the previous example, perhaps due to the participants' location nearer the bottom of the class hierarchy. In our book, we described the discussion as reflecting many White students' typical attitudes towards social class, where middle-class status is assumed for all White people, leaving the category "poor" as a marker for Blacks and avoiding exploration of the wide class differences among White people themselves.

As an introduction to *The Women of Brewster Place*, Gloria Naylor's novel about working-class Black women in an urban setting, the professor, a middle-class White female, wanted the students to look at the structural elements of class, race, and gender oppression, and see how they are interrelated. In response to her question, "Have any of you read any books that talked about social class?" the male students (no females spoke) described class in anecdotal terms, telling stories of financial upward mobility. One student contrasted rich people who "can afford to do what they want . . ." with those who have only a moderate amount of money, who "cannot just go crazy; they are saving up and investing."

While agreeing with the students that "income is a major determinant of class," the instructor pushed them towards more structural issues, asking, "Is there class mobility?" Most students answered, "Sure," but several males noted underlying class rigidities. For example, one said,

> A lot of snobbery exists between old money and new money. I could become rich tomorrow, but because I don't come from a rich family I couldn't be in that upper class. Class isn't what I determine myself to be, but what someone else makes it. That's the problem.

A few minutes after the above remarks, she asked, "What about racism?" and a few minutes later, "What about Affirmative Action? Does that help [to fight racism]?" Based on an equation of Blacks with the underclass, and extending to other minorities as well, the students assumed that those who get ahead are a priori lacking the proper qualifications:

> It's really like a slap in the face. You've got the jobs just because you're Black or Asian, they're not saying you got the job because you're better or more qualified, [but that] we need your minority groups because our supervisor is going to come down on us.

When the teacher later sought to turn the discussion back to race, we saw one of the rare instances in our data where the construct of race included the idea of Whiteness:

> The consciousness level in the United States has been raised, where we're much more highly aware of gender issues. Whereas race, White people don't often think of racial identity in terms of their own identity, what it means to be a White person. . . . The minority races are much more conscious of who they are. That's not true for Whites in America, that the first thing you identify with as "Who are you?" is White.

Our original analysis in *The Feminist Classroom* characterized this comment as showing how the teacher "helped her students confront racial issues," and we still associated "race" with African Americans, not Whites. Upon further reflection, we see this remark, and indeed this whole discussion, as a vivid example of the extreme individualism in mainstream culture. While the students assert that class position is determined by individual upward mobility, the students also seem to be unconsciously noting structural factors, such as snobbery: "class is what someone else makes it." However, these factors are always experienced in individual terms, "I could not be upper class." This perspective is carried over to their dismissal of Affirmative Action policies as unfair acts of favoritism, a personalized "slap in the face." But again, this "slap" is read as coming from "your minority groups"; Blacks are seen not as individuals, but as a group. Yet, because of the White student's construction of Affirmative Action as a threat to his individual mobility rather than a response to a group history of discrimination, he spouted the worst stereotypes about unqualified people getting jobs.

These students tell a familiar narrative of discrimination in which they feel simultaneously victimized as individuals by groups from above and below. However, only the latter group is racialized and seen as "the other." Whiteness is unconsciously constructed and relied upon here as the social glue normalizing their connection to other, "higher-up" Whites, thus stabilizing an inherently unstable situation. The professor could not get her White students to understand the position of Blacks because they didn't understand their own position as Whites. Although they understood something of class privilege, through their lack of it, they could not see themselves as privileged within the social relations of race.

We now see that even the teacher's insightful last remark about White racial identity, while ahead of our own thinking at the time, still casts Whiteness in individualized rather than structural terms — as an issue of "what it means to be a White person." Indeed, this excerpt illustrates that the acknowledgment of Whiteness as an individual attribute does not automatically lead to an expanded understanding of its social structural relations, or of its ideological power; rather, people may acknowledge their Whiteness simply as a self-justifying or self-excusing marker of relative personal privilege, and no more. That Whiteness is a social construction organizing people into social relations of dominance and oppression, through which some individuals benefit, eluded us at the time as well. Moreover, we now wonder if, among the students who spoke, their exploration of their class and race resentments assumed maleness as another unmarked attribute of their identity, an assumption that would have accounted for the female students' silence in that discussion. Assumptions of Whiteness took another form in our next example, however, as women students explored issues of femininity and beauty from different, but no less complex, racial positions.

Whiteness, Sexuality, and Femininity

In her novel *The Bluest Eye,* Toni Morrison offers an illustration of the ways in which dichotomizing White as the norm and Black as different shapes notions of beauty in the African American world. In the relationships among Pecola, a powerless girl, and the other characters in the novel, Morrison shows how the others construct themselves through demonizing her:

> All of us felt so wholesome after we cleaned ourselves on her. We were so beautiful when we stood astride her ugliness. Her simplicity decorated us, her guilt sanctified us, her pain made us glow with health. . . . Her inarticulateness made us believe we were eloquent. Her poverty kept us generous. Even her waking dreams we used, to silence our own nightmares.[25]

Remembering this insight prompted us to examine the racialization of femininity and sexual attractiveness in classes in *The Feminist Classroom.* One of the most telling examples of this theme took place in a course entitled "Women Writers since 1800." The class was composed of seventeen women and five men, ranging from freshmen to seniors, and was taught at the same liberal arts college as our first excerpt. The teacher began one class by asking if anyone had written in their journal about Emily Dickinson in response to the discussion of her poetry in the previous class. Nancy, a Japanese American woman who sat at the edge of the room and had not spoken during our previous observations, nodded, and began to read from her journal entry. She based part of her entry on a poem that begins, "I'm Nobody! Who are you?"

> I'm Nobody! Who are you?
> Are you — Nobody — Too?
> Then there's a pair of us?
> Don't tell! They'd advertise —
> you know!

How dreary — to be — Somebody!
How public — like a frog —
To tell one's name — the live-
long June
to an admiring Bog![26]

I couldn't help thinking of the idea of a mute culture within a dominant culture. A "nobody" knowing she's different from the dominant culture keeps silent and is surprised to find out there are others who share this feeling. But they speak only to each other and hide otherwise. This is what it must have been like being a woman and thinking against the grain. But don't tell! At least if you are silent and no one knows, you can continue to live your inner life as you wish, your thoughts at least still belong to you. If "they," the somebodies, find out, they'll advertise and you'll have to become one of them.

Nancy then turned to some comments about Poem 327:

Before I got my eye put out
I liked as well to see —
As other Creatures, that have
Eyes
And know no other way —

But were it told to me — Today —
That I might have the sky
For mine — I tell you that my
heart
Would split, for size of me —

The Meadows — mine —
The Mountains — mine —
All Forests — Stintless Stars —
As much of Noon as I could
take
Between my finite eyes —

The Motions of the Dipping
Birds
The Morning's Amber Road —
for mine — to look at when I
liked —
The News would strike me dead —

So safer — guess — with must my
soul
Upon the Window pane —
Where other Creatures put their eyes —
Incautious — of the Sun —[27]

But looking at poem 327 it's problematic, there is a price to pay, and it isn't always voluntary. Infinite vision seems to come from suffering through enforced pain. "Before I got my eyes put out I liked as well to see — As other Creatures, that have Eyes and know no other way." You can run around in ignorant bliss until something breaks through this level of illusion, takes out the "eye" that makes it possible for you to view the world this way and once you see through it, you can't go back, trying to face yourself backwards would "strike you dead." I'm not articulating this well but it's like growing awareness.

A silly example: It's like watching a Walt Disney movie as a child where Hayley Mills and these other girls dance and primp before a party singing "Femininity" how being a woman is all about looking pretty and smiling pretty and acting stupid to attract men. As a child I ate it up, at least it seemed benign, at the most I eagerly studied it. But once your eye gets put out and you realize how this vision has warped you, it would split your heart to try and believe that again, it would strike you dead.

In our interpretation of this class, we concluded that Nancy was rejecting her earlier attempt to model herself on Hayley Mills, a prototypical White teenager of the 1960s, and embarking on a second rite of passage in which she recognized the harm of modeling herself on such a trite stereotype of American femininity. In the invocations of both Emily Dickinson's poetry and of Hayley Mills, who is young and blond, Nancy's images of femininity and of womanhood are not only images of superficial physical characteristics associated with Whiteness, but of female sexuality as well. Neither in the class discussion nor in our original interpretation was this point taken up. By concentrating on her evocation of gender oppression, we allowed Nancy's recognition of the harm of modeling herself on a stereotype of White femininity to pass us by. We also did not see that Hayley Mills's "beauty" depended on Nancy's "otherness" for its intensity. This oversight reveals the extent to which we too had internalized the complex interplay of physical beauty and sexuality that on the one hand primarily constructs femininity as White, and on the other hand fails to understand the extent to which women of color also carry around a White norm of beauty.

Nancy's musings underscore the physical and visual power of race as part of imagining one's appearance to others, and therefore one's effect on others. How does one read and internalize messages of beauty and ugliness, visibility and invisibility, as inscribed on one's body? Feminist theorists have long since taught us the importance of understanding the ways in which women internalize "the male gaze," learning how to see themselves as objects of others' viewpoints rather than subjects of their own construction. We have learned from Nancy the extent to which physical racial identification confers instant ascribed identity, and with it, social status. However, since we as White women are not often conscious of our race, we do not experience our bodies as "raced" as many women of color do.

A subsequent interview with Nancy, who grew up in a Japanese American family in a small Finnish community in the Northwest, "where there were three Japanese families that lived down our little road," leads us to wonder now about how much Nancy had in fact internalized White images. As a young Asian American, did she after all identify as "White" most of the time?

We were the only Japanese family that went to school in a Finnish community. [If] you look at my yearbook, everyone is blond and tall and then there is us.

We grew up in this community where we're obviously very different physically, but since we grew up there we didn't really perceive ourselves as very different. Whenever we were among a lot of other Japanese, we would notice that and feel, "Oh, look, everybody's Japanese!"

We are now also struck by the complexity of Nancy's racial identification — "We're obviously very different physically, but we didn't really perceive ourselves as very different." Writers on Whiteness like Andrew Hacker, Neil Gotanda, and others have pointed out that one of the most pernicious aspects of American racism has been its rigid construction of anything "non-White" as Black. The confusion caused by these dichotomies has left some Asian Americans, for example, identifying as White and others as junior versions of Blacks.[28]

The impact of the ideal of "pretty and blond" on Nancy's sense of herself as a woman, and the cost of "living in the roles" of the dominant culture, meant that Nancy had to see herself in terms of Hayley Mills, or *not* Hayley Mills, before she could construct an alternative vision of who she was. But who "was" she, in terms of "Black" and "White"? What are the fault lines and discontinuities that emerge when the category of "Whiteness" as description offers up only mixed messages to an Asian American woman? The vivid, visual nature of the lesson Nancy learned about Whiteness is shown in the language she used to name the end of innocence — "how this vision has warped you."

Mirrors are also metaphors for showing us how others see us, and therefore for the imposition of ideology and culture onto our multilayered consciousness of self. The earlier quote from Adrienne Rich describes the pain of looking into a mirror, and the impossibility of merging the way you see yourself with the ways the outer world experiences you. By contrast, a professor we worked with at a historically Black women's college told her African American students how to use a mirror to reclaim their bodies against the Whiteness of the "beauty myth":

So I tell my students, the way I look at the "beauty myth" is about trying to look into a mirror and trying to see yourself. In a very systematic way thinking about those sociocultural corporate entities that keep you from seeing and appreciating who you are — your face, your breasts, everything. And then we move on from there to how to wipe the mirror clean. Not with Windex, which involves buying something already packaged, but with vinegar and water, which is something that your mother told you will cut through the dirt in a real special way.[29]

When Toni Morrison made "our" beauty contingent on Pecola's ugliness, she too was emphasizing the ideological and cultural freight carried by White standards of beauty, its association with virtue and truth, the "normal" against which the "other" is demonized, or disappears. To reconceptualize the assumptions that construct beauty, as did Nancy, is to claim the possibility and necessity of conscious resistance. As Nancy wrote: "Once you see through it, you can't go back, trying to face yourself backwards would 'strike you dead.'"

Whiteness and the Resistance to Intellectual Domination

The professor who helped us to see most clearly how intellectual domination is tied to Whiteness, as well as to issues of classroom processes and power relations, taught history and gender studies at the liberal arts college Nancy attended.[30] Worrying about a gender studies class, Feminism in Historical Perspective/Feminist Theory, in which thirty students were enrolled (including three people of color — a man and two women) the professor found that about half the students were silent. The professor, a White woman, assumed at first that the quieter students just needed time to become equal participants. She did not realize that they felt unprepared to join a discussion that presumed so much prior knowledge and experience of feminist theory and practice. She viewed part of the problem as her own emphasis on the academic discipline: "My engagement with the subject matter interfered with my performance as a teacher."

But her use of democratic classroom processes, in enabling some students to become authorities for each other, also meant that a few students who were more outspoken were dominating the others. She observed that it was common for the student majority from the dominant White culture, in exploring their own experiences, to end up avoiding and resisting the experiences of others. She reported in a paper:

> The culture of our gender studies program validates personal experiences and suppresses the expression of differences that challenge other peoples' perspectives. People feel empowered to speak of their own experiences, and construct theory on that basis, and that is good. But they do not feel impelled to include other peoples' experience in their explanatory frameworks, . . . and when the other people insist that their experiences too must be taken into account, they respond with barely concealed hostility.[31]

To illustrate these problems, and their relation to Whiteness, we turn to the professor's course, in which a small number of theoretically minded seniors were taking over class discussions. Their distinctive discourse, which drew heavily on the post-structural language they had learned in literary theory courses, was incomprehensible to the rest of the students.[32] This pattern was broken by Amy Santos, a quiet student who described herself as "mixed Latina and Native American." Her frustration with these seniors led her to a critique of the "academic realm" as one of domination and subordination, one in which "you can be in the 'not knowing' position or you can be in the 'knowing.'" Academic discourse constricts "what we really mean and puts a real limitation on how we communicate." She said, "Sometimes I go to class thinking, that was a bunch of theory, and feeling like the more abstract people are looking down on me, which I think is a product of their own insecurity and insensitivity."

While the students themselves came up with a solution together about their own responsibility for the class,[33] we now believe that this earlier revolt.

against a few seniors created a climate for some of the formerly quieter students to bring issues of racial and gender oppression and invisibility into the classroom. The discussion we take up next, led by the three students of color, concerned the absence of a discussion of race in feminist theory and their own need for the creation of explicit racial and ethnic identities. While part of it was in the book, we missed the continuing assumptions of Whiteness that framed the discourse.

We now want to reconsider this class by looking at how the White students' construction of gender and racial oppression worked to mask the naming of Whiteness as a social position and as an oppressive aspect of feminist theory. We also want to illustrate the ways the students of color challenged the White students by insisting on exploring the need to name themselves, to give themselves identities, and how the pervasiveness of Whiteness as a dominating conceptual apparatus frustrated their efforts. We can see here how Whiteness is actively constructed and maintained even as it is resisted.

The discussion began with some observations by Sharon, a Filipino American, about the absence of women of color in Sheila Rowbotham's book, *Woman's Consciousness, Man's World,* because discussions of the Black movement focus on men and discussions of women focus on White women. "Most of the feminist literature that I've come across doesn't say a lot about racism," she commented.

Ned, a White male student who also took the literary theory course discussed earlier, responded by pointing out that the problem lay in the connections between experience and theory; specifically Rowbotham's "extolling of individual experience" and "looking for too generalized similarities between us . . . which overlooks problems like race." He then added, "If she never had to entertain race and it never crossed her mind once, I would indict her methodology, her starting from personal experience," implying that Rowbotham went wrong because she started from personal experience, which does not include her race because she is White. To his mind, to take up race would be to consider women of color.

The frequent reaction of the White female students who spoke to these points was to push for a general theory of gender that would unite all women across their different experiences, without having to pay attention to particular forms of oppression and dominance, namely Whiteness and White racism, that would disrupt that unity and cast them into oppressor roles. One White female student, for example, wanted to know "how you can maintain the diversity but still get some kind of unity." Another resisted the loss of women as a "distinct" group, saying, "[When] women's issues are intermixed with racial issues and oppression . . . women (i.e., White women) get lost in the shuffle."

But Ned continued to worry about both the necessities and the perils of beginning with individual experiences. He believed that theory ought to broaden out by connecting "personal experiences" of oppression by giving groups a "common battle to fight," or "linking up with someone who is similarly oppressed and slog through the bog." He worried that "increasingly narrow experiences" would result, as if combining all the different oppressions cancels out each one:

> I think my question about women's consciousness earlier was, is this an attempt to erode class [unity]? I think you can just assume it was answered yes and was also an attempt to erode racial barriers — but what comes out of [talking about gender and race] is an increasingly narrow experience.

Ned seemed to understand that individual experiences in and of themselves are at best a starting point of analysis, and he was reaching for a more structural analysis. However, he overlooked the complex relations of oppression and dominance hidden by Whiteness and maleness that are not being marked as social positions; only the "oppressed" position is marked.

Thus the feminism of all these White students, based on assumptions of Whiteness, did not include any consciousness of being White. Race was seen as an exclusive (and obstructive) property of Black women only. Indeed, for Ned and Ralph, gender, belonging only to women, is also an obstruction to unity. Moreover, while they were able to construct Black women as members of a social group, not as individuals, the White students could not see that White people, too, were not simply individuals with common personal experiences, but differentially placed members of an unequal social order. But there was another discussion going on, led particularly by Sharon and Ron, an African American male, where the prevailing assumptions of Whiteness operated not only as unacknowledged social location, but also as active ideology — where Whiteness was a key feature of a normalized and unmarked "center" of intellectual discourse. In later interviews, both Sharon and Ron acknowledged that they were very aware of working to raise the White students' consciousness around issues of race. In response to comments like those from Ned and the White female students earlier in the discussion, Sharon tried to show how looking at people of color exposed the intellectual dominance of the White academy, and its distance from the real world:

> It makes me wonder if we're not being too theoretical and abstract when we don't consider those things. It makes me wonder if this isn't just a bunch of you know intellectual masturbation and what action is going to come out of it, if we're not going to be diverse about what we're going to be concerned about and be realistic about it.

She went on:

> Ya, but if I weren't here to voice these concerns — we are not Black people in this class and I keep thinking to myself I'm a surburban kid, I'm not an urban kid. And I think, this is all great but how do we apply it?

Sharon attributed the lack of attention to racism to the culture of the campus. She said in an interview, "I've been at this college for a long time and it's predominantly White. People aren't really dealing with the issue of racism." Her comment that "we are not Black people in this class" was perhaps about the impossibility of encountering layers of "Blackness" in a context where the complexities and varieties of other cultures are erased by the Black/White duality imposed by the dominant discourse. "Black" could only be apprehended as "not White," where both White and Black are defined on White terms.

Later, Ron tried another tack, addressing the need to construct identities outside the margin:

> In a way, to get at the center you have rings of light to bring to light what is marginal and spread [it]. And the only way to do that being a woman or being a Black person whose experience is marginalized, you've got to talk about that experience, you have to establish some kind of identity.

He was trying to push gently at the limits of the White students' under-standings, to help them look at identities relationally, as situated positions implicating both Whites and people of color in the social construction of gender and race. But his quote illustrates the silent workings of Whiteness, in that "the center" is not named. The White students continued to insist on marking race as a concern only for Blacks, so that unity could only occur either through transcending race, or "doing it for them," as one White female student remarked:

> *Ned:* Or we never have a common battle to fight? If we're not all suburbanites together then we can't fight the same battle?
>
> *Laurie:* If a White person defines Black struggles, that's not an answer, so somehow we have to, if we're White or if we're privileged or if we're male or whatever . . . people have to somehow empower others to do it instead of doing it for them.

As the discussion proceeded, Sharon and Ron, joined by Amy, made com-ments that suggest that they were also continuing to struggle specifically against Whiteness as a form of intellectual domination. Because they could not identify the center of knowledge production as White, they could not fully articulate a language of their own to produce a different knowledge:

> *Sharon:* But [oppressed groups] all have to form an identity first . . . in a lot of ways it doesn't exist, in that it is so *threatened* given — (italics are authors')
>
> *Ron:* I think it's *dangerous* to form, the question of whether we have the where-withal to form groups without first knowing who you are.
>
> *Sharon:* You know just part of it is the individual knowing his or her cultural experience, historical experience.
>
> . . .
>
> *Amy:* I think one thing interesting about learning *political language that the mainstream culture understands* [is] so that you can, as an oppressed group, be validated [sic]. But once you learn how to communicate then I think it is necessary to go back to your own language, your own identity, your own culture and I guess they, we, the marginal people face sort of a problem on the one

hand to be autonomous and form an identity and reevaluate it, on the other hand, be able to communicate to —

Ron: So there will always be a double consciousness, sisters under the veil.

Sharon then made the point that most feminist theory is written by White women, "with their ideologies and values," to which Ron replied,

> But that's the whole point, that's how language is used to oppress people. People close the doors and talk about all this stuff, and I'm saying that theory provides a key to that door — it also presents a way of changing meaning, changing the way things are.

As a muted challenge to the fixed path of assumed Whiteness, this conversation was halting, rocky, uncomfortable, representing a "'teeth-gritting' and often contradictory intersection of voices constituted by gender, race, class, ability, ethnicity, sexual orientation, [and] ideology," in Elizabeth Ellsworth's words.[34] In the face of unspoken assumptions about Whiteness as the norm, the students of color struggled to "get at the center." If the center could be named and positioned as White, then the processes of "forming groups," of knowing one's "cultural and historical experience," would be shared by all groups and would not be only the task of the marginalized. A language exposing the positional operations of power relations could be developed, by which all "cultures" could be constructed and deconstructed relationally. The key is undertaking a conscious discourse of Whiteness, theorizing Whiteness, and thus "changing language" in order to change meaning, and "changing the way things are."

It was not that the students of color did not understand what they were up against. Ron clearly understood that the oppressor has a position. He said in an interview:

> The position of the oppressor is the most inflexible. A person who is in an oppressed position will idealize what is above him. [The oppressor] objectifies everything. I just think that oppressed people . . . are better at ripping apart the disguises than creating them. The oppressors are greater at creating them.

Amy and Sharon also saw the problem as tied to Whiteness. The numerical and intellectual dominance of White students on campus contributed to Sharon's wish that "we would try to imagine ourselves to be something other than White, upper-class people." Amy too felt "cultural alienation on campus because the majority of students in the class are White and . . . over-looking a lot, a lot of things that are conscious but can't be formed into academic lingo and come out in weird ways or don't come out."

In the book we noted that, according to the professor, "the White students [avoided] confronting their own position as Whites, [as] they repeatedly objectified, generalized about, and posited the unknowability of the 'other.'" We pointed out that "White students' resistance to theorizing their 'Whiteness' — to being caught in the racial matrix — hampered the students of color in their aim of articulating their ethnic identities."[35] We were helped to these insights by the professor herself, who saw her class as reflecting deep societal inequalities because of assumptions of Whiteness as the norm, on the one hand, and individuals' unawareness of that on the other. She left the college in 1988 in part because she could not accept these limitations to her teaching, limits "rooted in the fundamental nature, social location, and ideology of this institution."[36] While the emphasis on student perspectives in the gender studies program "passed as feminist because it seemed to be supportive and sisterly, in practice it reinforced the exclusion and subordination of people of color." After our initial positive analysis of her class, this teacher wrote:

> I may have done better around authority than around race, but sharing authority with students who are predominantly White and who are unwilling to recognize their position and the different positions of other, or unable to develop a systemic analysis of racial inequality, leaves crucial problems unsolved.[37]

In our tentative grasp of these issues, however, we underestimated the power of Whiteness as ideology, as the assumed basis of a governing intellectual framework, in part precisely because it was not confronted or named directly; we have returned to read between the lines. Indeed, it was only in situations where people of color were a majority, as in the class below, that issues of Whiteness were explicitly taken up in class discussions.

Resisting Intellectual Domination: A White Author and Black Audience

What problems are caused for people of color because the crucial problem of Whiteness is left unnamed and unresolved? To answer this question, we turn to a class where the majority of students, and the teacher, were people of color. In classes like these we can more fully see the effects of unanalyzed Whiteness on the ways in which people of color framed their own views, in resistance to, and outside of, the worldviews accorded them by the dominant White culture. African American students at the historically Black college mentioned above, for example, affirmed the value of constructing knowledge from their own standpoint, against "truths" of White social scientists who claimed they were "deviant" and "pathological." They complained about being prevented by White stereotypes from living the normal, complex lives of "ordinary" middle-class people. One said:

> I always hear people talk about NBC as the Negro Broadcasting Company, (laughter) because they always tend to try, well this is a stereotype, they try to cater to Black struggles, but it's not necessarily that realistic, because we go from "Good Times" to "Cosby," and there is no middle.

When the teacher at this college urged her students to understand the culture's "beauty myth," it was the ideology of Whiteness that kept them from seeing and appreciating who they were. Until they saw the loaded meaning and value behind those categories, they could not reconstruct the world and their place in it.

When we wrote about her classroom in our book, we emphasized the participants' struggles to forge their own knowledge. But, in emphasizing this new knowledge, we minimized the role of Whiteness. These teachers and students, in essence, had to come to terms with Whiteness, almost before they could go about "creating something else to be."

The following classroom discussion explored the ways in which a White author used an African American figure for his own critique of White society. This was a class at a large, elite, predominantly White southern university in which the teacher, a visiting African American female literature professor, was teaching "Images of Women in Literature" to a group mixed by both race and gender. The twenty-six students included thirteen African American women, seven African American men, four White women, and two White men. The teacher made a point of consciously exposing the racial and gender stereotypes embedded in the dominant culture's views of Black and White women. One day she gave a summary of the learning process she wanted them to go through, stressing the importance of revealing what is on one's mind so that stereotypical assumptions can be named and confronted:

> The problem is that the culture tells you these things again and again and you internalize them, and you make an effort to find the cases that support what you've been programmed to believe. Liberation is liberation of the mind. You liberate your mind. Then you change society. But you can't liberate your mind until you examine honestly what has been put in your mind.[38]

In *The Feminist Classroom* we noted that this setting, in looking at White privilege, may have simply made the few White students in the class, like Mark, who was quoted in the introduction, appreciate their positions more.[39] The following discussion, centering on Dilsey, the mammy figure in William Faulkner's *The Sound and the Fury*, shows the students beginning with an analysis of an African American central character, a victim of racial oppression, and then shifting to a focus on the perpetuators, in this case Faulkner himself. In the course of uncovering the meanings in the book, the students discovered that Faulkner, while critiquing White society, was not writing for or to African Americans, but for White people. Paradoxically, they found, in a literary treatment that explores White racism, African American readers are shut out.

The way into Faulkner's view of Dilsey had been paved by lengthy observations, directed by the teacher, into the many ways that Faulkner emphasizes, subverts, and ultimately exposes the toxic effects of racism on a decaying White southern culture. For example, in an echo of Toni Morrison's point from *The Bluest Eye* about beauty and ugliness offsetting each other, she had a student read aloud a passage where the family son, Quentin, goes north to Harvard, and reflects on his changed views of African Americans:

> When I first came East I kept thinking You've got to remember to think of them as colored people, not niggers. . . . And if it hadn't happened that I wasn't

431

thrown with many of them, I'd have wasted a lot of time before I learned that the best way to take all people, Black or White, is to take them for what they think they are, then leave them alone. That was when I realized that a nigger is not a person so much as a form of behavior; a sort of obverse reflection of the White people he lives among.

The professor initiated the following discussion by soliciting the students' reactions to the stereotype of the mammy figure. She asked them, "What do you want to say to Dilsey?" Immediately Stacy, a Black female, spoke up, expressing the point of view of a Black child whose mother had to take care of Whites: "It doesn't seem she cares about her own children as much as she does about Quentin [the White family's son]." The next students to speak were Edgar, Kathy, Michael, and James, African Americans whose "explanations" for Dilsey's failure to nurture her own children ranged from fear that Whites might take them away to the idea that her role as nanny meant she had to ignore her children in favor of the White children:

Kathy: Maybe she doesn't want to get too attached, maybe they'll get rid of her kids. She still has this mindset not very different from slavery. . . .

Edgar: I agree — even though it was the 1920s, she did have that mindset that . . . goes from generation to generation, so the time we are dealing with is something like slavery. Look at what it did to African American lives! You really can't put a time limit on that. But she totally forgot about the nurturing of her children.

Michael: I felt that she didn't love her children, in fact I would go as far as to say that she more or less did not give them a stable beginning whatsoever, she criticized everything they did. . . .

Kathy: It's not her fault that she has to take care of those other children!

Edgar: Regardless of what the social constraints are or whatever, she's a Mom, and she could nurture them in some way. It is obvious that she has the capability to nurture. Why couldn't she do it with her own children!?

Mark (White male): It seems like it's more of a job though, isn't it? Wouldn't it be her job to do that? It would be like any other job, when the job's over you're not like what you were on the job.

James: But that's the thing — it's not just a job!

More discussion of Dilsey's relationship with Quentin's family ensued, during which the professor pointed out that Faulkner made Dilsey "the moral conscience of the novel," and that "she is also a stereotype":

Edgar: I think that Faulkner thinks Dilsey's positive, but she's positive for White people. And that really upsets me, that I get the impression that Faulkner thinks he's doing us a favor by showing a positive image — when she's not really being positive for us! I wish she could be positive for us, not for them, because they have their own family — their mother and their daddy.

432

Professor: She's positive — I mean, be honest. The negative images are the images of the White people! I mean give Faulkner credit. . . . She's the moral conscience of this novel, and we, the readers, are supposed to say this is positive.

In our analysis of this class in our book, we focused on the African American students' identification with Dilsey's children and concluded that Dilsey was so objectionable to them:

> Not so much because her portrayal in the novel seemed to them to contradict stereotypic notions of women as nurturing; rather, it was because of the whole history of the merging of femaleness and racial identification in slavery.[40]

Could the Black students' anger have also been focused on the unspoken racialized assumptions of the White students — namely, their unproblematic location of Dilsey in the servant role, leaving "normal" mothers as White women taking care of their own children?

However, despite the attempts by the White students to locate Dilsey unproblematically in her servant role, the students of color were able to uncover "literary Whiteness" — to position Faulkner as a writer not for a universal, normative, and unnamed audience, but specifically for White readers. We now see also that these students were resisting the connection of a certain kind of motherhood with Black racial identity, namely that Blacks "mother" Whites, not their own children. More broadly, they were displaying the resentment they felt that once again, both in the way Dilsey acted and in the way Faulkner appropriated the figure of a Black woman to be the conscience of a White family, Blacks were being made to live for Whites and not on their own terms. As Edgar put it, Faulkner made Dilsey positive for White people, "who already have their own family — their mother and their daddy." The African American students' discussion of Dilsey reveals their struggle to perceive themselves as "normal," as children with all the expectations of American children in middle-class nuclear families in the late twentieth century. It was important to confront Faulkner's "universal appeal," his hiding assumptions of Whiteness as the center of his normative universe, in order to reconsider these issues in their own lives.

Conclusion

In this reanalysis of some of the classroom vignettes we used in writing *The Feminist Classroom,* we have returned to our themes of "pedagogies" and "methodologies" of positionality, using the construct of "Whiteness" to examine positions of dominance, rather than marginalities as we did in our book. We have focused here on largely unacknowledged assumptions of Whiteness as a key aspect of the dominant culture, and how these assumptions interact with constructions of gender, class, ethnicity, and race to shape the construction of classroom knowledge. We have seen Whiteness operate both differentially and simultaneously, as "always more than one thing"; it has been physical description, individual identity, social position, ideology, and, throughout, a "dynamic of cultural production and interrelation" operating "within a particular time period and place, and within particular relations of power."[41]

Thus for Nancy, "breaking through illusion" was necessary to confront Whiteness both as physical description and feminine ideal. To her, as to the students in the Images of Women in Literature class, the ideology of appropriate gender roles, all the way from "looking stupid to attract men" to being a good mother, was derived from White stereotypes that needed to be named and deconstructed. For the students in the literary theory course and the honors freshman writing course, it was maleness as well as Whiteness that was assumed in their discussions of working-class unity and middle-class mobility. From the unacknowledged perspective of the dominant position, both "race" and "gender" were properties of the "other."

While in the honors freshman writing class, Whiteness was constructed primarily as a matter of individual identity, in the literary theory class the White students fretted about the ways in which "race," and to a lesser extent "gender," interrupted the theoretical unity of the oppressed that they were seeking within feminist theory. Based on physical description as marker for social location, both groups of students assigned "race" to minorities, especially to Blacks, while staying oblivious to their own position as Whites.

Thinking about Whiteness as ideology as well, we can see how the conceptualization of race as a bipolar construct, with Black and White as the two poles, operated to make all "difference" oppositional in nature, so that Black lives could not be normal, but only the obverse or the exception to those of Whites — whether in *The Bluest Eye,* Faulkner, a Hayley Mills movie, or *The Cosby Show.* Also caught in this dualism, the Asian, Filipina, and Hispanic students lacked any appropriate "mirror" for their identities. Finally, the pervasive power of Whiteness as a feature of the intellectual dominance of the academy, wherein the universalized knower and known are always assumed to be White, can probably be seen everywhere in these discussions; however, only in the Images of Women in Literature class, and to some extent in Feminism in Historical Perspective, was it actively named and resisted. Each discussion probably reveals Whiteness operating at many more levels than we have captured here, through layers of personal, political, and ideological constructions and assumptions, and through discourses of gender and class as well as race.

We have also to come to terms with the fact that we now "see" dynamics in our data hidden from us before. Yet to "recognize" (or "re-see") those dynamics positions us partly as expert-detectives who want to "get it right" this time around. We see more clearly the importance of continuing to learn about ourselves, to interrogate our own social positions of privilege and to use that knowledge to inform our research, our teaching, and our professional practice. As White scholar-activists committed to anti-racist work, we are always, to quote Ellsworth again, "simultaneously ignorant and knowledgeable, resistant and implicated, committed and forgetful, ambivalent, tired, enjoying the pleasures and safety of privilege; effective in one arena and ineffective in another."[42]

We also see again the value of the community of feminist scholars that we and others have created. It was in a final interview with Angela Davis that we first learned about the whole field of scholarship on Whiteness, in the form of Ruth Frankenberg's work examining the constructions of race in White women's life narratives.[43] Grey Osterud's observations that we had treated positionality only as it arises from marginality, thus concealing the dominant position, became another nagging issue that would not go away.[44] The last-minute arrival of articles, some pre-publication, by Neil Gotanda, Elizabeth Ellsworth, and Sandra Lawrence gave us new insights into this work.[45]

Finally, beginning to be able to understand and "track" Whiteness in these ways, as constructed socially and historically, allows us to think about the possibilities of revealing its various operations so as to challenge and rene-gotiate its meanings — "to change language, change meaning, and change the way things are," as Roy put it above. Because we, having lived through and participated in the civil rights and women's movements, know that some of our generation have begun to examine their dominant positions, we be-lieve that many more Whites now can do the same. We also know from our students and our own children that one aspect of our positionality is genera-tional; that our children, growing up in a much more diverse society than we did, have different relations and constructions of gender and race than we. We have seen how, for example, several Latinos and Asian American students have begun to push up against the bipolar construction of Black and White that we ourselves experienced.

While classrooms often not only reflect, but also impose, the dominant culture's ideological frameworks, they may also function as somewhat shel-tered laboratories where those frameworks may be exposed and interro-gated. One hope thus lies in students (and professors) becoming authorities for each other as they are explicit about themselves as positioned subjects with respect to an issue or a text. As this article has shown, however, many of the steps towards these kinds of awareness are tentative. They are often undertaken, at some risk, by people occupying the subordinate positions. Students of color in the Feminist in Historical Perspective class speak of danger and threat in looking at their own identities.

In relation to Whiteness in particular, however, increasing numbers of teachers have begun to use the literature on Whiteness with students, both Whites and students of color, to help them see themselves and each other differently: not as individuals, whose relations to racism must be either "in-nocent" or "guilty," but as participants in social and ideological networks. While these networks are not of their own making, they can nevertheless come to understand and challenge them. Indeed, some writers have de-scribed Whiteness as not only a social position, but also as a set of ways of thinking and acting in the world. Whiteness, in this sense, can be about making choices.[46] Teachers such as Ellsworth, Beverly Tatum, and Sandra

Lawrence, among others, have written about work with students in this regard.[47] In the course of working on this article over the 1995–1996 academic year, Maher has used the work on Whiteness by Tatum, McIntosh, Roediger, and Morrison described in this article with various groups of students to help them understand the workings of Whiteness in their own lives, as well as "cultural mapping exercises" to help students find themselves in a variety of different and simultaneously overlapping social positions. In so doing, she has not "solved" the problem, but has continually located, dislocated and relocated herself in terms of the students' sometimes uncomfortable, sometimes resentful, but always interested growth in awareness of these issues. As one of our professor-informants once told us, "They don't live their Whiteness, I don't live my Whiteness. I'm working hard to see how to do that."

A glimmer of hope in the direction we would like to proceed may lie in a final comment by Mark, the White male student we quoted at the beginning of this article. Mentioning that an older African American woman student in the class had become an authority for him, he told us that:

> [the professor] seems like she's teaching on more than one level. She's teaching me just to open my eyes, but with Blanche it's totally different because she has open eyes. Blanche is ten steps ahead of me in understanding all this. . . .

> This class could easily have ended up all Black women, but it's important for me to be in there because I have to understand it. I can't understand it when I am in a nice little fraternity house, predominantly White men from North and South. It's good for me and maybe if I take something from this and go home and sit with my roommates and talk about it and open it up there, rather than keep it in the classroom . . . it seems like we need it for us. We need it and [other] White males and females probably need it just as much.

One teacher in our study, an African American woman, left us with a message, one that we now see exhorts Whites to understand our Whiteness and to work from that position: "Black women need to understand how special they are. For Whites, you need to understand what you can do working as a White American, one who can make a difference."

Notes

1. Toni Morrison, *Sula* (New York: Alfred A. Knopf, 1974), p. 52.
2. Frances A. Maher and Mary Kay Tetreault, *The Feminist Classroom: An Inside Look at How Professors and Students Are Transforming Higher Education for a Diverse Society* (New York: Basic Books, 1994). In this article, we include excerpts from five classes at three different institutions. The first one is from a seminar in literary theory at Lewis and Clark College. The second is from an honors freshman writing course at Towson State University. The third is from a course on women writers since 1800, and the fourth is from a course entitled "Feminism in Historical Perspective/Feminist Theory"; both of these courses were also at Lewis and Clark College. The fifth is from a class, "Images of Women in Literature," taught at Emory University.
3. Maher and Tetreault, *The Feminist Classroom*, chapter one.

4. See, among other works, the following: Ruth Frankenberg, *White Women, Race Matters: The Social Construction of Whiteness* (Minneapolis: University of Minnesota Press, 1993), and Ruth Frankenberg, "Whiteness and Americanness: Examining Constructions of Race, Culture and Nation in White Women's Life Narratives," in *Race*, ed. Steven Gregory and Roger Sanjek (New Brunswick, NJ: Rutgers University Press, 1994), pp. 62–77; Peggy McIntosh, "White Privilege and Male Privilege: A Personal Account of Coming to See Correspondences Through Work in Women's Studies," in *Race, Class and Gender: An Anthology*, ed. Margaret Andersen and Patricia Hill Collins (Belmont, CA: Wadsworth, 1992); Toni Morrison, *Playing in the Dark: Whiteness and the Literary Imagination* (New York: Vintage, 1993); David Roediger, *The Wages of Whiteness: Race and the Making of the American Working Class* (New York: Verso, 1991), and David Roediger, *Towards the Abolition of Whiteness: Essays on Race, Politics and Working Class History* (New York: Verso, 1994); Karen Brodkin Sacks, "How Did Jews Become White Folks?" in Gregory and Sanjek, *Race*, pp. 78–102; Beverly Daniel Tatum, "Talking about Race, Learning about Racism: The Application of Racial Identity Development Theory in the Classroom," *Harvard Educational Review, 62* (1992), 1–24.

5. Grey Osterud made this point to us in a telephone conversation with Mary Kay Tetreault on October 22, 1993.

6. Morrison, *Playing in the Dark*, p. 11.

7. Maher and Tetreault, *The Feminist Classroom*, p. 196.

8. There was only one other White male in the class; he rarely attended.

9. We use pseudonyms for all the students in this article.

10. Privileges accorded people because they are middle or upper class, male, and heterosexual are also often unacknowledged, and operate in similar ways. In this essay we focus on Whiteness, while noting ways that Whiteness intersects with other forms of privilege in the different vignettes that we explore.

11. McIntosh, "White Privilege," p. 71.

12. Morrison, *Playing in the Dark*; Roediger, *Towards the Abolition of Whiteness*; Elizabeth Ellsworth, "Double Binds of Whiteness," in *Off-White, Readings on Society, Race and Culture*, ed. Michelle Fine, Lois Weis, Linda C. Powell, and Mun Wong (New York: Routledge, 1997), pp. 259–269; and Elizabeth Ellsworth, "Working Difference in Education," *Curriculum Inquiry*, forthcoming; Andrew Hacker, *Two Nations, Black and White, Separate, Hostile, Unequal* (New York: Ballantine Books, 1995); Sacks, "How Did Jews Become White Folks?"

13. Becky Thompson and White Women Challenging Racism, "Home Work: Anti-Racism Activism and the Meaning of Whiteness," in Fine et al., *Off-White*, pp. 354–366.

14. See Ellsworth, "Double Binds of Whiteness," p. 260.

15. Sacks, "How Did Jews Become White Folks?"; Roediger, *Towards the Abolition of Whiteness*, pp. 13–14.

16. Hacker, *Two Nations*, p. 8.

17. Roediger, *Towards the Abolition of Whiteness*, p. 3.

18. We first saw this quote from Adrienne Rich in a paper by Renato Rosaldo, entitled "Symbolic Violence: A Battle Raging in Academe," presented at the American Anthropological Association Annual Meeting, Phoenix, Arizona, 1988.

19. Maher and Tetreault, *The Feminist Classroom*, chapter seven.

20. Ellsworth, "Double Binds of Whiteness," p. 265.

21. All quotes in this paragraph from Ellsworth, "Double Binds of Whiteness."

22. Toril Moi, *Sexual/Textual Politics: Feminist Literary Theory* (London: Methuen, 1985). See Maher and Tetreault, *The Feminist Classroom*, pp. 72–76, for a discussion of this class. The quotes in this essay are not always fully quoted in the book; we returned to the data to reexamine it for other issues. The data for the classroom vignettes and analyses in *The Feminist Classroom* were gathered over a period of at least three weeks through classroom visits and taping of class discussions. Class discussion data were supplemented by interviews with the professor and four or five selected students. Based on this material, we wrote detailed case studies of each professor's teaching, and shared them with our informants. Based on informants' comments and our own further research, we revised these case

studies, and finally used them as the basis for the vignettes and analyses in the book, which were organized around four themes: "Mastery," "Voice," "Authority," and "Positionality."

23. SDS, Students for a Democratic Society, was a student movement in the 1960s that opposed the war in Vietnam and worked for civil rights.

24. Maher and Tetreault, *The Feminist Classroom*, pp.178–185.

25. Toni Morrison, *The Bluest Eye* (New York: Pocket Books, 1972), p. 159.

26. Thomas H. Johnson, ed., *Complete Poems of Emily Dickinson* (New York: Macmillan, 1967), Poem 288, p. 133.

27. Johnson, *Complete Poems*, Poem 327, p. 155.

28. Hacker, *Two Nations*, pp. 18–19. Neil Gotanda spoke of these issues at a presentation, "Reconstructing Whiteness: Color Blindness, Asian Americans, and the New Ethnicity," at California State University, Fullerton, April 16, 1996.

29. Interview with a teacher at Spelman College, April 1993.

30. The college is known for its strong Gender Studies program and an institutional pedagogy focused on student perspectives as learners. A hallmark of their pedagogy is the practice of beginning with the students' questions rather than the common approach of beginning with the teachers' questions.

31. Nancy Grey Osterud, "Teaching and Learning about Race at Lewis and Clark College," Unpublished manuscript, 1987.

32. There were other issues present that beset many feminist classrooms: how to attend to theory by getting students to think theoretically without separating it from the their personal experience and feminist practice; how to enable the students to set their own agenda; and how to deal with the disparate discourses in a class that arise from, in the professor's words, "that real separation, the gap between inside the classroom and the real world of personal experience out there . . ."

33. The students agreed that they had to take collective responsibility for the class as a whole and changed some of their classroom processes. Students met in small groups for part of the class and then as the full group of thirty students. They agreed to select report topics for the small groups and the subsequent agenda for the large one, and to choose a student to chair the large-group discussion each day.

34. Elizabeth Ellsworth, "Why Doesn't This Feel Empowering? Working through the Repressive Myths of Critical Pedagogy," *Harvard Educational Review*, 59 (1989), 297–324.

35. Maher and Tetreault, *The Feminist Classroom*, pp. 112–113.

36. Maher and Tetreault, *The Feminist Classroom*, p. 39.

37. Maher and Tetreault, *The Feminist Classroom*, p. 160.

38. Maher and Tetreault, *The Feminist Classroom*, p. 178.

39. Maher and Tetreault, *The Feminist Classroom*, pp. 172–178; 191–197.

40. Maher and Tetreault, *The Feminist Classroom*, p. 194.

41. Ellsworth, "Double Binds of Whiteness," pp. 260–261.

42. Ellsworth, "Working Difference," p. 14.

43. Frankenberg, *White Women*.

44. Maher and Tetreault, *The Feminist Classroom*, p. 112.

45. Ellsworth, "Working Difference"; Lawrence, "White Educators"; Gotanda, "Reconstructing Whiteness."

46. Anoop Nayak, "Tales from the Dark Side: Negotiating Whiteness in School Arenas," Unpublished manuscript, University of Newcastle, UK.

47. Ellsworth, "Working Difference"; Lawrence, "White Educators"; Tatum, "Talking about Race."

Thanks to all our participants, especially those included in this article, whose contributions in the form of classroom dialogues in some cases go back ten years. Thanks also to Gloria Wade-Gayles, K. Edgington, Joyce Canaan, and Ellen Junn for commenting on this article.

The Road to College:
Hmong American Women's Pursuit
of Higher Education

STACEY J. LEE

In this chapter, Stacey Lee examines the phenomenon of low educational partici-
pation and achievement among Hmong American women. She argues that the
focus on cultural differences as the sole explanation for this fact ignores the exist-
ence of economic, racial, and other structural barriers to Hmong American
women's educational persistence and success. Lee shares the stories of several
Hmong American women who are pursuing or have completed higher education
in the United States, investigating the factors — economic, racial, and cultural
— that helped or hindered their decisions to continue their education. These women
are part of a movement within the Hmong community that questions traditional
expectations for women and girls, in particular early marriage and motherhood.
Lee illustrates how these women's experiences are also shaped by environmental
factors such as welfare policies and racism. Their stories demonstrate that cultural
transformation is neither a smooth nor unambiguous process.

Since the first Hmong refugees arrived in the United States from South-east Asia more than twenty years ago, journalists and scholars have writ-ten extensively on this Asian American ethnic group's adjustment expe-riences. Many of these works have stressed the differences between Hmong culture — described as rural, clan-based, preliterate, and traditional — and mainstream American culture. In describing the Hmong, one U.S. policy analyst wrote, "This country has rarely, if ever, welcomed a group of immi-grants so culturally distant from the native social and economic mainstream" (Fass, 1991, p. 1).

The differences between Hmong and American culture are often de-scribed as differences between a premodern and a modern society. In an article in *National Geographic*, for example, the Hmong's adjustment difficul-

Harvard Educational Review Vol. 67 No. 4 Winter 1997, 803–826

ties are portrayed as almost inevitable, given that they are "unfamiliar with locked doors, light switches, [and] modern plumbing" (Sherman, 1988, p. 592). Journalists and scholars have suggested that the social and economic problems faced by the Hmong (e.g., welfare dependence, gang involvement, inter-generational conflict, high school dropout rates, depression, etc.) are due entirely to these enormous cultural differences (Hirayama & Hirayama, 1988; Sherman, 1988; Tapp, 1988).

Several scholars have noted the particularly stark contrast between the roles of women and girls in U.S. and Hmong culture (Donnelly, 1994; Goldstein, 1985; Scott, 1988; Walker-Moffat, 1995). Stories of bride theft and early marriage, for instance, provide vivid examples of how Hmong attitudes towards women's roles clash with mainstream U.S. ideas (Goldstein, 1986; Scott, 1988). These and other cultural traditions that Hmong girls and women face are of particular interest to researchers in the field of education (Goldstein, 1985; Rumbaut & Ima, 1988; Walker-Moffat, 1995). These researchers link Hmong values regarding women's roles to the relatively high dropout rates among Hmong female students. In her research on Hmong American adolescents, Goldstein discovered that "girls who dropped out for domestic reasons won community approval by moving into valued gender roles" (1985, p. 276). Rumbaut and Ima assert that the high dropout rates and low achievement levels of Hmong girls are connected to the "patrilineal and patriarchal norms that tend to devalue females among the Hmong" (1988, p. xiv).

Anthropological research on the Hmong has done a great deal to illuminate the culture that Hmong refugees bring with them to the United States. Educational research on cultural differences has revealed the particular pressure that Hmong American girls face within their communities to marry and begin having children during their teens. Cultural differences, and issues that arise out of these differences, are often characterized as private concerns. For example, in their study on the relationship between stress and the social support systems of Hmong refugees, Hirayama and Hirayama labeled problems such as "homesickness, child rearing, automobile breakdowns, and family finance" as "private matters" (1988, p. 104).

The sole focus on cultural obstacles, however, has in effect ignored the existence of economic, racial, and other structural barriers to Hmong American women's educational achievement and persistence. By relegating cultural and family issues to the "private" sphere, the "public" sphere is freed from any responsibility (Fine, 1991). According to this position, if Hmong American girls drop out of school to get married and have children, or if few Hmong American women pursue higher education, the reasons lie entirely within the Hmong community. Although an understanding of culture is important, an exclusive focus on culture conceals the impact of racism on Hmong American women's opportunities and on their self-perceptions. In short, by focusing solely on cultural differences, the inequalities in power and interests are silenced (Lutz & Collins, 1993).

The implicit assumption behind much of the focus on cultural differences is that Hmong culture is static and unchanging, which fails to recognize that all cultures are dynamic, constantly in the process of being created and re-created. Cultures are not only transmitted from generation to generation, they are also created within current history (Erickson, 1997). The assumption of a static Hmong culture ignores the history of accommodation, resistance, and transformation that the Hmong have undergone as an ethnic minority, first in China, then in Laos, and now in the United States (Dunnigan, 1986; Fish, 1991; Hendricks, 1986). In recent history alone, Hmong culture has been transformed by war, migration, life in refugee camps, and resettlement in the United States. Despite these historical realities, the Hmong are often portrayed as people without a history who arrived in the United States in a natural and unchanged state (Wolf, 1982). Within this framework, Europeans and European Americans depict non-Europeans as timeless and primitive peoples who are the passive victims of the changes imposed on them by modern, dynamic, and postcultural European societies. With respect to the Hmong, Hendricks asserts that this type of thinking "leads some to think in terms of before and after, that there was a traditional almost unchanging way of Hmong living that has been severely altered by the events of the period of flight and subsequent resettlement" (1986, p. 3). Thus the Hmong, like other non-European cultures, are exoticized and essentialized at the same time that European cultures are normalized and often made invisible.

During this current historical period, the practice of focusing solely on cultural differences supports existing political, economic, and social inequalities (Balibar, 1991; Harrison, 1995; Razack, 1995). Citing Said's (1978) work on orientalism, Erickson observes that "when more powerful nations or interest groups identify some Other as exotic and different there can be a tendency for the more powerful to project their own flaws, contradictions, and hostilities on the constructed Other" (1997, p. 45). Within today's anti-immigrant rhetoric in the United States, cultural differences are used as evidence of immigrants' unfitness to be "real Americans" (Suarez-Orozco, 1996). In this discourse and associated public policy, the exclusive focus on cultural difference and the concomitant denial of the mainstream group's relative power leads to victim blaming. In describing the current anti-immigrant sentiment, Suarez-Orozco writes:

> Discourse on immigration has taken a decidedly post-utopian tone. Gone are the romantic fantasies of poor immigrant peasants pulling themselves up by their bootstraps to become proud and loyal Americans. The dominant image in the public space now is that of unstoppable waves of parasitic "aliens" set on (ab)using our social services, refusing to "assimilate," and adding to the crime and social pathologies of the American urban landscape. (1996, p. 153)

In this article, I examine the cultural, economic, and racial factors that affect Hmong American women's pursuit of higher education, with a focus

on the experiences of those who are pursuing or have completed higher
education in the United States. I chose to focus on Hmong women who
pursued higher education because I was interested in the experiences of
women who actively challenged existing cultural norms. Attention to the
experiences of these pioneer women will contribute to an understanding of
minority student achievement, and of cultural transformation among refugee groups in the United States. The overarching questions considered in
this article include: What motivates some Hmong American women to pursue higher education? What obstacles do they face in this pursuit? How are
these women transforming Hmong culture? How are their families responding to their changing roles and expectations of women?

The twenty-one women in my study range in age from eighteen to thirty-
two. All are first generation in the United States, and all are either pursuing
or have completed four-year college degrees. Far from being a monolithic
group of traditional, subservient, and docile women, as often described by
the popular press, the Hmong women in my study vary in their personal
experiences and in their social and political perspectives. Some of the
women identify as feminists, while others shun the term. Some of the women
live at home while attending college, others attend colleges halfway across
the country from their families. Some of the women are more comfortable
speaking English, and others are more comfortable with Hmong. Some of
the women married and had children as teenagers and are now returning
to school, while others have postponed marriage in order to pursue their
education.

I selected my participants from a variety of sources. I met my first informant by chance when she called to find out more about my research on Asian
American students. During our conversation she spoke about her own experiences as an educated Hmong woman, and thus the seeds for this study were
sown. I met a few informants at a national Hmong American student conference, some I met through Hmong American student organizations, and others I recruited through referrals.

My primary means of data collection was in-depth, open-ended interviews.
Throughout the research process I made efforts to be sensitive to issues of
power and identity raised by feminist researchers (Fine, 1994; Oakley, 1981;
Reinharz, 1992). Based on my belief that women are the experts on their
own lives, and in the spirit of collaboration, I solicited each informant's help
in locating other potential informants and asked them to suggest additional
interview questions and topics. I also encouraged the women to ask me questions about myself and my research. Although only a few of the women asked
about the research, many expressed interest in my ethnic background. The
women asked questions such as "What is your ethnicity?" and "Where were
you born?" As a third-generation Chinese American who conducts research
in Asian American communities, I have come to expect and welcome such
questions (Lee, 1996). Researchers who share ethnic, racial, cultural, or
other similarities with their informants are often scrutinized for signs of
authenticity (Aguilar, 1981; Foster, 1994; Kondo, 1990). Upon meeting me,

the women immediately recognized that I was not a Hmong woman (i.e., not one of them), but they were interested in whether or not we shared any cultural similarities. They were particularly interested in my relationship with my family. When I told them, for example, that my ninety-year-old grandmother, who has lived in the United States for nearly seventy years, insists that I speak Chinese to her, the women nodded in understanding. When I recalled my mother's strict rules regarding dating when I was a teenager, the women and I shared a laugh. I even commiserated with one of the women about feeling "short" in the company of non-Asians. Most of the women determined that although I am not an "insider," the fact that I share race, gender, and certain cultural characteristics with them means that I am not completely an "outsider" either. This "in-between" status, sometimes called the "halfie" status, enabled me to use my experiences to invite more open and honest conversation (Abu-Lughod, 1991).

The interviews were one-and-a-half to seven hours long and took place in one to three sessions. During the initial phase of the interview, I invited the women to tell me their life histories. My approach was purposely non-directive in this phase in order to encourage the women to tell the stories that they deemed important. In subsequent phases of the interview, I asked more focused questions with an eye to uncovering information about the women's educational histories, the nature of their family life, the nature of their relationship with the larger Hmong community, their reasons for pursuing higher education, and their experiences in college. Their stories communicate what they face at home, in school, and in the larger society in their struggle to pursue higher education, as well as how their aspirations are transforming Hmong culture. The women's words reveal some of the ways in which culture, intergenerational relationships, racism, and economic conditions affect their choices and options.

In addition to the interviews, I reviewed a number of Asian American and Hmong American community newspapers and newsletters, and conducted limited participant observation in some of the women's homes and at Hmong American college student events, including a national Hmong American student conference.[1] In order to preserve the spirit of the women's voices, the quotations used in this article are verbatim transcriptions. All names are pseudonyms.

The next section focuses on cultural issues, both the cultural obstacles that Hmong women face and the ways in which they are reinventing Hmong culture through their hopes, dreams, and actions. I then focus on how the current political, economic, and social climate in the United States is affecting Hmong American women's ability to achieve their dreams. I look at how

[1] Newspapers and newsletters included the following: *Asian American Press*, St. Paul, MN: Asian Business & Community Publishing. *Asian Week: The Voice of Asian America*, San Francisco: Pan Asian Venture Capital Corporation. *The Hmong Free Press*, Minneapolis, MN: Sai Publishing. *Hmong Women Pursuing Education: A Newsletter Compiled by the Hmong Women Students at UW-Stout*, Menomonie, WI: Academic Skills Center, University of Wisconsin-Stout. *Wisconsin Hmong Life: A Monthly Publication of News and Events Concerning Hmong People*, Madison, WI: Hmong Refugee Committee, Bayview Center.

economic issues, including current proposals for welfare reform, may affect Hmong American women's pursuit of higher education, and consider how racial and ethnic stereotypes affect these women's self-perceptions.

Hmong American College Women: Agents of Cultural Transformation

As noted earlier, researchers and journalists have written a great deal about the ways in which Hmong cultural ideas clash with mainstream American ideas regarding appropriate gender roles for girls and women. As newcomers to the United States in the late 1970s and 1980s, Hmong families often found themselves in conflict with the U.S. legal system over their marriage customs (Scott, 1988). Researchers interested in gender issues singled out the practices of early marriage and childbearing as the biggest obstacles to school achievement and persistence among Hmong adolescent girls (Donnelly, 1994; Rumbaut & Ima, 1988; Walker-Moffat, 1995). Walker-Moffat, for example, notes that due to cultural practices, "Hmong girls who continue to study beyond puberty are exceptional" (1995, p. xiv). The assumption behind much of this work is that the practice of early marriage is simply a reflection of Hmong cultural traditions, as opposed to an adaptation to being in the United States.

Some research, however, suggests that the push for early marriage in Hmong communities may be a response to the perceived threat of the dominant U.S. culture. For example, Rumbaut and Ima (1988) argue that early marriage among Hmong girls is less a cultural expression than a reflection of parents' attempts to prevent their daughters from assimilating into the dominant culture. Hmong elders are particularly fearful about American pressure to assimilate. They fear the loss of a distinct Hmong identity, and have responded by reasserting gender and age hierarchies (Donnelly, 1994; Walker-Moffat, 1995). This research suggests that contact with outsiders (i.e., non-Hmongs) forces the Hmong to reevaluate their cultural practices and identities. As active makers of their culture, the Hmong do not simply passively accept imposed change, but evaluate their situations and respond according to what they believe is in their best interest. Thus young Hmong American women, for example, are likely to respond to life in the United States differently from elderly Hmong men.

Economic forces and conditions in the United States and the Hmong's evaluation of these forces have also altered their culture. Adult Hmong males who were once the unquestioned center of family authority have found themselves economically dependent on their wives, children, and the government (Donnelly, 1994). One response to these economic conditions has been an increased emphasis on formal education for the younger generation. Goldstein (1985), for example, found that Hmong parents encourage both their sons and daughters to work hard in school in order to achieve economic security. However, despite their belief in the instrumental purposes of education, Hmong parents continue to hold higher expectations for their sons than for their daughters (Goldstein, 1985; Walker-Moffat, 1995).

For their part, the women in my study are motivated by economic forces to pursue higher education. Economic conditions have also led Hmong women to transform *paj ndau* (i.e., the art of Hmong needlework) from a folk art to a source of income. In Laos, subgroups of Hmong differentiated by dialect wore clothes decorated with distinct needlework patterns that served as ethnic markers (Koltyk, 1993; Peterson, 1988). In the United States, many Hmong women make these needlework pieces for the consumer market. They have formed needlework cooperatives, and the profits from sales help to support their families (Donnelly, 1994). The actual style of needlework produced here has also changed. While the needlework was previously based largely on geometric designs, pictorial narratives in the form of story clothes now dominate (Koltyk, 1993). Peterson (1988) argues that Hmong women are aware that the story clothes represent their culture to non-Hmongs, and they purposely control the content of the story clothes in an attempt to control the image of their people. Thus, subjects such as the cultivation of opium poppy are excluded from the story clothes.

The Hmong American college women in my study understand that Hmong culture is in the process of significant change, and they see themselves as central agents of that change. They identify themselves as pioneers who are leading the Hmong people into the next generation. In the interviews, several women proudly asserted that they were among the "first" new generation of Hmong American college women. As pioneers, these women hope to affect their own lives and the lives of other Hmong women. They are motivated to pursue higher education by economic interests and by a desire for increased independence. A number of them stressed the importance of postponing marriage in order to pursue higher education; some of them also asserted that Hmong women should have smaller families. It is critical to point out that while these women are re-creating and transforming their role within their culture, they continue to assert a distinct ethnic identity as Hmong people. That is, while they describe themselves as "less traditional," they do not see themselves as being "less Hmong" than their elders.

Although proud and excited, the women are quick to point out that it is often difficult to be pioneers. Because different members of a culture may have different interests and goals, the possibility for internal struggle is endless. These women's struggles are evidence that cultural transformation is neither a linear nor a smooth process. Their ideas of cultural transformation are often at odds with those of their elders, who emphasize the importance of a strict gender hierarchy in which men are on top. Some of the women say that while the older males mourn what they believe is the loss of male power, many Hmong women of all ages embrace what they perceive to be the increased opportunities for freedom offered by life in the United States. Donnelly (1994) found that middle-aged Hmong American men often joked that if they had the opportunity to return to Laos, the first thing they would do upon their return would be to beat up on the women. By contrast, Donnelly notes that "no Hmong woman has ever told me she wanted to live in Laos again" (p. 74). The women in Donnelly's study and in mine see greater gender equality and freedom in the United States. My informants cited both U.S. cultural norms and laws as being favorable to women.

My informants assert that internal cultural struggles often center around whether women should marry early or postpone marriage in favor of pursuing higher education. They report that early marriage and childbearing continue to be the biggest obstacles to Hmong women's pursuit of higher education. All of the women who are over twenty-five years old report that their families pressured them to get married when they were adolescents. Some of these women married and remain married, some married and divorced, and a few were successfully able to resist family pressures to marry. It should be noted that while divorce is becoming more common in Hmong American communities, it is still viewed as a last resort (Donnelly, 1994; Vang, 1981). Although most of my younger informants have postponed marriage in order to pursue their education, they still cite early marriage as one of the biggest obstacles to Hmong American women's pursuit of higher education.

Pioneers

The first time I met Joua she referred to herself as a pioneer. At thirty-one, Joua has never been married. She works for the state government, is a leader in the Hmong American community at local and national levels, and is a part-time graduate student in social work. Active in women's issues, she attended the 1996 International Women's Conference in Beijing with the Hmong women's delegation. As a pioneer, Joua is committed to encouraging Hmong women to stay in school. Reflecting on her role in the transformation of Hmong culture, Joua says:

> Culture changes every day, and I look at myself as changing the culture in my family and in my community. When you decide to stick with education and realize that education is important and really decide to go forward, that's when you . . . you change it.

Although Joua sees herself as an agent of Hmong cultural transformation, she is against cultural assimilation. Her deep commitment to maintaining a distinct Hmong identity is reflected in her interest in Hmong folk arts, the Hmong language, and her continuing work on behalf of the Hmong community.

Several of my younger (i.e., twenty-four and under) informants mention that they looked up to Joua as a role model. Blia, a twenty-one-year-old in her second year at a large midwestern university, describes Joua as a mentor who encouraged her to pursue education while reminding her that she should be proud of her Hmong background. Blia speaks of Joua's influence on her life and about Joua's status within the Hmong community:

All of the Hmong adults in the Hmong community, they trust her and they respected her, and if she wanted to take us places, like for [Hmong] dance competitions, our parents were very okay with it. She always stressed individuality, and to pursue whatever you wanted without a spouse. And I think part of, part of my dreams and goals came from her, too, 'cause I saw what she was doing and I thought that, that's something that, that I would want to do, too.

Joua's success in gaining the confidence of Hmong elders has likely been because she fosters the preservation of certain cultural traditions (e.g., Hmong folk dancing), and encourages young people to maintain a separate Hmong identity. Blia recalls that, as an adolescent, she and some of her Hmong peers considered changing their names to "American" names, and that Joua lectured them about the importance of keeping their ethnic identities.

Reflecting on her life history, Joua notes that she has always been "different," and that this has not always made her life easy. She remembers that when she was an adolescent, Hmong girls were expected to get married and leave school. Most of the Hmong girls she knew followed this pattern. During the time Joua and her family were in the Thai refugee camps, her family arranged for her to marry a Hmong man who was living in the United States. Joua was thirteen years old and had no interest in marriage: "That time I was young. I didn't know what to say or to really argue the point, but I did just cry and say, 'I don't want to marry him.'" After she had cried for three days, one of her male relatives interceded and the marriage was called off:

And so, finally, one of our relatives came. He was a key man, and he said [to my father], "Let me see your girl. Why do you make such a big deal out of this thing? Let me go and talk to her and see your girl." And so he came in and he said, "My gosh! Your daughter is such a little kid. She is just a girl. Why do you make such a big deal out of this arranged marriage? Why don't you just say to them [the prospective groom's family] that we'll wait until [we] get to the U.S. Then if the girl and the boy like each other, then they can initiate their own and go on with the marriage." . . . So that was that. But, I mean, that experience has, I think, taught me to be, has taught me to stick with what I believe.

As a high school student, Joua faced the skepticism of Hmong adults who questioned whether any girl had the ability or disposition to persist in school. She recalls that one of her male relatives bet her and her female cousin that they would not be able to finish high school:

And so we were talking about the subject of education versus marriage. And so he said, "Well, if you think, if you think that you're tough, and you really want me to believe, then I make a bet that if you finish high school, then I give you both a hundred dollars each. But if you don't finish high school, then you pay back those two hundred dollars to me."

Joua laughs when she recalls this, and asserts that although her male relative never did pay her the hundred dollars he owes her, he has also never again questioned her abilities.

447

After graduating from high school in 1984, Joua and her female cousin attended the local community college. Joua studied secretarial science and her cousin pursued food management. During this time she and her cousin were the only two Hmong women she knew of who were pursuing postsecondary educations. After earning her associate's degree, Joua worked as a secretary, but she wanted to go back to school because she believed that more education would offer her more opportunities. Joua enrolled at a small liberal arts college where she was the first Hmong student. As a college student, Joua once again faced the criticism of the larger Hmong community. She recalls what some of her relatives said about her during this period:

> "God, why doesn't she get married? What's wrong with her?" And the general feeling is that girls go to school only because they want a husband, you know, to attract husband. They won't have a career. They won't go through with it. They won't succeed.

Since the college was a long drive from her family's home, Joua lived in the dorms. She explains that living away from home was yet another departure from Hmong tradition that brought her further criticism from the Hmong community.

Moua, a twenty-seven-year-old bilingual education teacher, is another pioneer. As one of the first Hmong public school teachers in her state, Moua believes that it is her obligation to help Hmong students. In addition to her teaching job, Moua is active in the Hmong community in her city. She and her husband chaperoned a group of students to the Hmong Youth Conference in Washington, DC, where I met her. Reflecting on her role in the Hmong community, Moua states proudly:

> I am the only lady, Hmong lady, on the executive board for the Hmong community in my city. Parents, community leaders respect me and see that I have potential to lead the Hmong into better things in the future.

Although Moua's parents are very proud of her now, they were ambivalent about her educational aspirations when she began college. As a high school student she was pressured by them into marrying a relative, and was divorced less than three months later. Moua talks about her experience with early marriage:

> I guess I'm one of those statistic cases. I was pressured into an early marriage to my Aunt and Uncle's son when I just finished my junior year in high school. We were together for two-and-a-half months. It didn't last because we didn't love each other and had never been with each other since we were in Laos. And that was twelve years ago.

After her divorce, Moua finished high school and went on to pursue a bachelor's degree at a small four-year college. Like Joua, Moua talks about the discouragement and ridicule she faced as one of the first Hmong American women to go to college in her family's network:

When I went away to college and stayed in the dorms and hardly came home, there was a lot of rumors about me . . . [that] I was dating American (White) guys, [that] that's why I hardly came home, [that] I would never make it or finish because I'll probably get pregnant and drop out soon, and that I was too old and had wanted to wear the pants in the family.

Moua got married a few months after her college graduation. Although this time she was able to marry the man of her choice, she still feels that she married sooner than she would have liked because of community pressures.

"Getting Ahead in the United States": Economic Motivations for Pursuing Higher Education

Despite all of the intergenerational conflicts, Joua and Moua persisted in school because they believed that a college education would lead to economic security and independence. These women's faith in the power of education is so strong, in fact, that they maintain it is difficult, if not impossible, to get ahead in the United States without an education. Moua's and Joua's ideas regarding the connection between education and economic self-sufficiency reflect the dominant society's philosophy regarding the purpose of education. Their ideas were confirmed by their experiences growing up in families that struggled to make ends meet in their new country. When I asked Moua about her motivation for pursuing higher education, she reflected on her childhood:

I think [I was motivated] by seeing my parents suffering and their lack of education. It was hard for my parents to make a living in the U.S. without an education and having to wait for the welfare check or getting minimum wage at $3.50 per hour and hardly make ends meet.

Moua's belief in the importance of education has led her to pursue her master's degree. Although she is often overwhelmed by her various responsibilities as a mother, wife, graduate student, and full-time teacher, she continues to go to school because she believes that further education will translate into greater financial security for her family, and will also make her a better teacher.

The belief that education will lead to financial security was echoed by all of my informants. They all maintain that one of the primary reasons they pursued higher education was to achieve social mobility and financial security. They consider access to free public education and the opportunities associated with education to be among the greatest advantages of life in the United States. Thus, like the voluntary immigrant minorities described by Ogbu (1987, 1991), my informants are motivated by folk theories of achievement that link education to success. According to Ogbu, voluntary immigrants hold a folk theory of getting ahead that leads them "to believe that in the United States they, too, can get ahead through hard work, school success, and individual ability" (1987, p. 325).

Like Moua and Joua, the younger women's ideas regarding the purpose of education are based on their family experiences. Many speak at length about their parents' struggles to survive in the United States without formal education and/or skills that could be translated into jobs. Public assistance and low-paying jobs were often the only options open to their parents, and memories of financial hardships motivated the women to persist in school. May, a nineteen-year-old in her third year at a large midwestern university, describes the impact of her family's experiences on her attitudes towards schooling:

> Well, I guess, my family, we weren't too rich. We didn't have a lot of money. So, I mean, I want money. I want to be success — successful. And I wanted to support, like have enough money to have children and take care of them, too, you know. So I mean, well you know in this society you really need money if you want to go anywhere. We knew that we can get money through you know, good education . . .

The women's belief in the connection between education and economic self-sufficiency is often shared by their parents. Some of their parents impressed upon them, as children, the importance of getting an education for economic survival in the United States. Since childhood, Mai, a twenty-year-old in her second year at a large midwestern university, was encouraged by her mother to go to college. Discussing her mother's interest in her education, Mai explains:

> [Getting an education,] that's the only way to survive here in America. And, she [Mai's mother] wants to see us [Mai and her siblings] succeed, you know? She doesn't want us — to see us struggle like, the way she had to, you know, to raise us in America.

"Becoming More Equal": Breaking Free of Hmong Gender Norms

In addition to a belief in the link between education and economic security, all of the women speak about the link between education and freedom from male domination. Their talk centers around the idea that education leads to independence and self-empowerment. Although the women vary in their attitudes towards feminism, they all agree that men and women should be, in their own words, "more equal" than in "traditional" Hmong families. The women point to the fact that male children are more valued than female children and the fact that men have more power than women within marriages as examples of the gender inequality in Hmong families. They believe that through education they will be able to achieve the gender equality within their families that their mothers and grandmothers did not have. The women reason that college degrees will lead them to good jobs, which in turn will make them equal economic partners in their marriages. Reflecting on her motivation for pursuing an education, one woman simply states: "I

450

don't wanna ever be in [a situation] to be so dependent on a guy, on a man." They also believe that the process of education will empower them to speak up for their own interests.

Several of the younger women assert that Hmong women are better, more assertive, and more active college students than Hmong men. My observations of Hmong college student events and my reviews of Hmong American community newspapers support the women's perceptions of themselves as being more active students than Hmong men. For example, I learned that Hmong women, and not Hmong men, were the organizers of the two national conferences directed at young Hmong adults during the 1995–1996 academic year.

The women in my study explain that Hmong college women are motivated to do well in college by their desire to break free of the traditional Hmong gender norms. They maintain that while Hmong men have power and get respect with or without an education, Hmong women need to get educated in order to gain freedom. They suggest that their experiences in and out of school have taught them that they have to be assertive if they want to succeed. Ploa, a twenty-two-year-old recent graduate of an Ivy League university, states that she and her Hmong female college friends work hard in school because they have a lot to gain by getting a college education, and a lot to lose if they don't succeed in college. In the following passage, Ploa compares Hmong men's experiences with those of Hmong women:

> We are in a patriarchal culture and men get the support, men get the respect, just, they get a lot more of things upon birth than the women, the women do. And I think a lot of us feel that, many of us have to sort of prove ourselves in a lot of ways in that . . . a lot of us have to speak up because if we don't speak up for ourselves, no one's gonna speak up for us . . .

Although Ploa and other Hmong women are proud of their own academic accomplishments, they argue that they are the exceptions within the Hmong community. All the women relate stories of Hmong girls who never made it to college because they dropped out of high school to get married, and several women tell stories of Hmong women who matriculated in college and then dropped out.

The women's understanding of gender roles within Hmong families and their hopes for their own futures come from what their own mothers taught them and from what they have observed. The women state explicitly that they do not want to live their mothers' lives. Several women report that their mothers and/or older sisters warned them about how hard it is to be a woman within Hmong families and said that life in the United States offers greater gender equality than life in Laos. Their mothers and sisters taught them that they could escape male domination by obtaining a college education. Joua explains that her older sister encouraged her to go to school and take advantage of the educational opportunities in the United States, reminding her of the lack of educational opportunities for women in Laos. Remembering her sister's influence, Joua says:

My oldest sister is, I think, the key person who really has, I mean, deserve[s] all the credits for getting me through school. Because she['s] older and my mom and dad didn't let her go to school. They let my brother go to school but they needed her help in the house. So she always regret[ted] that she never got a chance to go to school. So when we got here, she wanted to make sure that I get educated and all that. And so she would be the one that really keep a close eye on me.

Joua recalls that her older sister made it clear that she did not want Joua to "live a life like hers." Joua laughs and adds that this has meant that she has had the pressure of living both her own life and her older sister's dream life.

Lia, a twenty-one-year-old undergraduate at a large midwestern university, says that her mother always encouraged her to go to school in order to ensure her independence:

My mother has always told me — she says it's hard being a Hmong wife because you always have to feel like . . . you always depend on someone else and you don't have your own identity. She would never want us to feel that way. She wants us to be our own individual. The only way to do that is that you go to college, you get a good job. She has always said to me to go.

Lia asserts that because of her mother's support she "can't imagine not going to college."

The mothers who seem most straightforward in their discussions about the difficulties faced by women in traditional Hmong families are often those who have experienced marital difficulties or are widowed. The fact that some Hmong mothers encourage their daughters to go to college in order to change the nature of gender relations within their families suggests that cultural transformation is not solely the purview of the younger generation. At times these women went against their husbands in encouraging their daughters to be more independent. This intragenerational disagreement between fathers and mothers over appropriate gender roles for their daughters further demonstrates that cultures are not monolithic and static. In this case, people within the same generation are viewing their culture from gendered positions.

Other women assert that, while their mothers never spoke about the difficulties of being Hmong women, they reached this conclusion by observing gender roles within their own families. Ploa reports that her ideas about being an independent and self-sufficient woman are based on witnessing her mother's marital problems. During Ploa's senior year in high school, her father had an affair with a woman he planned to take as a second wife, a plan rooted in his desire to have more sons. Although Ploa's maternal grandfather was able to put a stop to these plans, Ploa has not forgiven her father. Furthermore, Ploa is angered by the Hmong tradition that makes Hmong women dependent upon men for support. Within traditional Hmong practices, marriage represents the union of two men's families, and thus the negotiation of marital problems must be done by men (Donnelly, 1994). Reflecting on how her father's actions have influenced her ideas, Ploa says:

> That's exactly like what I don't wanna ever be in, is to be so dependent on a guy, on a man, and to like, that he would do something like that to you without even thinking about your feelings.

Ploa asserts that while she was always an exemplary student, this event motivated her to work even harder in school.

Interestingly, despite their refugee status, the women in my study share many attitudes with the voluntary immigrants described by Ogbu (1987, 1991). Ogbu argues that voluntary immigrants are motivated by a dual frame of reference, whereby they compare their life in the United States with life in their native country and conclude that things are better in their new country. It is important to point out that, as refugees, the women in my study do not match Ogbu's definition of voluntary immigrants. However, like Ogbu's voluntary immigrants, the women in my study hold folk theories of achievement that link education to socioeconomic mobility. Like voluntary immigrants, the Hmong women have a dual frame of reference, which also, in this case, is directly related to their understanding of gender and gender dynamics. Specifically, these Hmong American women compare the position of women in the United States to what they believe to be the position of women in Laos, and conclude that there is greater gender equality in the United States.

Cultural Change and Resistance to Change

The women's desire for economic security, personal independence, and gender equality motivates them to pursue college educations. Their actions and desires are changing not only their own lives; they are also beginning to alter Hmong culture. Today, women like Moua and Joua are viewed as role models both by younger Hmong women and by older members of the Hmong community, who turn to Moua and Joua for advice and assistance. Joua and Moua work between and within the Hmong and mainstream communities. The very fact that Moua and Joua are seen as role models and leaders suggests that cultural expectations among the Hmong regarding the education of women are changing. According to the 1990 U.S. Census, over one-third of the Hmong who have bachelor's degrees and nearly one-half of those with master's degrees are women.

Another indicator of cultural change is the fact that many Hmong women who interrupted their studies in order to follow traditional marriage patterns are now returning to school in increasing numbers (Fass, 1991). Several of my informants follow this pattern. Like the women in my study who are postponing marriage in order to pursue higher education, the married women are enrolling in college because they believe that education will lead to economic security. Returning to school after following traditional marriage patterns, these informants struggle to balance their family responsibilities and expectations with their school work. Family support for their pursuit of higher education varies. While some women report that their families encourage their decision to pursue higher education, others report being criticized by parents and in-laws for straying from their traditional roles as wives and mothers.

The women in my study who are mothers face the difficulty of finding safe and affordable child care for their children while they are at school. Those from more supportive families are often able to enlist the help of family members, but women who live far from their families or have unsupportive families are forced to turn to paid child care (e.g., baby-sitters, daycare centers, nursery schools). Many Hmong women find that child-care costs, which are roughly the same for families from all social-class backgrounds, are beyond their economic reach. Ironically, all of the women report that one of the primary reasons they decided to return to school was to improve economic conditions for their families, but they often find it difficult to improve their situations because the cost of child care is prohibitive.

Mao, a twenty-four-year-old who recently graduated from a small college with a degree in nursing, is one of these returning women. During her senior year in high school Mao eloped with a Hmong man ten years her senior. Although her husband followed the Hmong cultural practice and "captured" her in the middle of the night, Mao is quick to assert that this was a marriage of choice, not a forced marriage.[2] After graduating from high school, Mao settled into a life as a wife and mother. Two years after she had the first of her three children, Mao decided that she wanted to go to college in order to get a better job:

> Right after I finished high school, I didn't want to go on, you know? I just wanted to work and just, you know, earn money. But then I guess you can't earn money just, you know, not a lot of money anyway, just straight from high school anyway. So that's why I decided that, you know, I need to go back to school and get a degree . . . get more education.

Her greatest challenge as a student has been finding child care. Mao considers herself fortunate in that her husband, who does not have a college education, is very supportive of her pursuit of education. Although he does help with the children, he is often busy with his job for Head Start. Fortunately, during most of her college career, Mao has been able to arrange child care with other young Hmong mothers who live in her low-income housing complex. Two of the women with whom she shares child care most frequently are also pursuing their college degrees.

Bla, a twenty-two-year-old in her second year in college, is another returning student. Bla married her boyfriend during her junior year in high school in order to escape community rumors that she was "bad." After getting married, Bla transferred to a high school in the city where her new husband was attending college. Although she got pregnant during her senior year, Bla

---

[2] In an elopement, the man kidnaps or captures the woman, and after three days and three nights the couple returns to the home of the woman's parents and marriage is negotiated. Mao points out that she decided to run away with her future husband. For more on Hmong marriage customs, see Donnelly (1994), Meredith and Rowe (1986), and Vang (1981).

managed to graduate with her class. Two years after graduating from high school, Bla and her husband decided that they would have better economic opportunities if she returned to school to earn a college degree. Their dream is to move out of the low-income apartment in which they currently live and buy their own home. They believe that if they both earn college degrees and get good jobs, they will be able to achieve that dream.

Bla initially attempted to go to school full time, but has had to drop down to one or two courses per term because of difficulties finding safe and affordable child care for her two-year-old daughter. Pregnant with her second child, Bla is worried because she knows that affordable infant care is very difficult to find. Like Mao, Bla has shared child care with other young mothers in her housing complex, but her schedule often conflicts with the other mothers' schedules. Bla's mother has been particularly supportive of her return to school and has tried to provide child-care assistance, but she lives almost two hours away. Bla experimented with leaving her daughter at her mother's house during the week, but she has not done this recently because she finds the separation from her daughter too painful. When I asked Bla whether her in-laws ever help with child care, she shook her head and said that her husband's family does not believe that women should go to college.

Bla has also attempted to find paid child care for her daughter, but has found that to be too expensive. The university where Bla and her husband are students has a program that provides student-parents with up to $750 per semester to help cover the expense of child care. The amount given is based on financial need. During the 1995–1996 school year, Bla and her husband received $375 per semester, an amount too small to cover the cost of daycare centers in her area. Ironically, Bla works part-time at a day care center to help with the family finances, but she and her husband can't afford the cost of that center. Bla's difficulty finding child care has led her to conclude that she should have no more than two children. This decision to have a small family is a move away from the Hmong cultural norm of large families (Donnelly, 1994).

Although the number of Hmong American women who pursue higher education has grown, the women in my study continue to face many of the cultural barriers to education described by previous researchers (Donnelly, 1994; Rumbaut & Ima, 1988; Walker-Moffat, 1995). These women assert that they are concerned that the majority of Hmong girls and women still marry early and do not pursue four-year college degrees. At the Hmong Youth Conference in Washington, DC, the issue of early marriage came up in several student-led workshops. The women attending these workshops, in particular, expressed concern that Hmong girls are still marrying "too young," and that going to college is still the exception. These college women argued that early marriage among their peers will negatively affect the married women's economic and emotional lives.

In interviews and informal conversations with college women at the Hmong Youth Conference, I was told that while some girls are forced into early marriage by their families, many girls choose to marry early in order to escape parental control. The women in my study report that many of their friends see marriage as the only way to circumvent their parents' strict ideas about dating. In families that don't allow unchaperoned dating, for example, some Hmong girls find that marriage is the only culturally acceptable way to spend time alone with a boyfriend. One woman attending the Hmong Youth Conference said that she got married when she was in high school because she could not figure out another way to spend time with her boyfriend, that she had been "young and in love" and had "traditional parents who didn't understand." Lia talks about a friend who married early to escape her parents' authority:

> They got married because her parents wouldn't let them go out with each other and . . . [because] she always felt that she was doing things at home. She didn't have any freedom and she thought they just should get married.

According to Lia, this friend had imagined that marriage would give her freedom and independence, but has found out that marriage is not easy. Lia, who says her friend warns her not to make the same mistake, uses her friend's experiences to bolster her confidence in her decision to postpone marriage and to make her college education a priority in her life.

Another factor that leads to early marriage among Hmong girls and women is the fear that if they postpone marriage until after they graduate from college, Hmong men will consider them to be too old and undesirable. These fears are based on their understanding that Hmong men prefer young wives, a preference that has been documented by several scholars (Donnelly, 1994; Goldstein, 1985). In fact, Donnelly (1994) found that Hmong parents push their sons to marry young girls. The women in my study stated that their relatives often warn them that they will not find husbands unless they marry while they are still young.

Several women asserted that Hmong men's preference for young wives is connected to their preference for quiet, passive, and submissive wives whom they can control. The women have found that even college-educated Hmong men prefer to marry teenage Hmong girls. Several of my informants said they believe that most Hmong men view college-educated women as being too assertive and that they purposely choose young wives they can "boss around." Some women in my study argue that most Hmong men are insecure about losing their authority. According to Moua, Hmong men "are scared because they think all college women want to wear the pants in the family."

Hmong men's preference for younger wives concerns even women who are satisfied with their decision to postpone marriage. Lia, for example, is concerned that she might not be able to find a Hmong husband who will be interested in her and who will respect her:

> The thing, too, is that guys my age don't marry women — Hmong women my age. They marry younger women, and I don't really have that much. . . . I get worried every now and then. Am I gonna find a Hmong husband when I'm twenty-five? Guys who are twenty-five aren't gonna want to marry me. They'll want to marry someone younger.

Lia would ideally like to marry a Hmong husband, but like other college-educated Hmong women, she says that it is more important for her to find a husband who will respect her as an equal partner than to marry someone Hmong. She plans to look for a Hmong man to marry, but is open to marrying a non-Hmong. Sao, a twenty-five-year-old graduate student who is engaged to marry a Chinese immigrant from Taiwan, explained that she realized two years ago that she would not be able to find a Hmong man who would respect her. Like other women in my study, Sao believes that Hmong men prefer young women because they want passive wives. Sao maintains that once she accepted the fact that most Hmong men are sexist, she was open to marrying a non-Hmong. She says that marrying out of her ethnic group is a way to escape what she perceives as Hmong patriarchy. Similar research on out-marriage among Japanese American and Chinese American women suggests that some women out-marry in order to escape Asian patriarchy (Fong & Yung, 1995/1996). It is important to point out, however, that although Sao plans to out-marry, she insists that she will continue to assert a distinct ethnic identity as a Hmong person.

Blaming the Victim: Anti-Immigrant Rhetoric and Welfare Reform

In addition to the cultural obstacles these women face, it is crucial to point out that their ability to achieve their educational dreams is also influenced by larger social, economic, and political factors. In the 1990s, anti-immigrant sentiment and welfare bashing have created a hostile climate for Asian American and Latino immigrants and refugees (Suarez-Orozco, 1996), who are perceived to be a drain on the economy. They are simultaneously accused of taking jobs away from "real Americans" and living off the government (e.g., public assistance), which puts them in a no-win situation. Within this anti-immigrant rhetoric, the Hmong have been targeted and stereotyped as "lazy welfare recipients." In this section I focus on how the current social, political, and economic situation in the United States affects Hmong women's self-perceptions and their ability to reach their educational goals.

Responding to Racism

My informants all spoke about the negative impact of racial and ethnic stereotypes on them and other members of the Hmong community. The women complained that the media characterized all Hmong as "lazy," "stupid," "backwards," and "foreign."[3] They were particularly upset by the stereotype that "all Hmong are on welfare." Many of these women have been tar-

---

[3] For more on the stereotyping of Southeast Asians, see DuBois (1993).

gets of racist taunts. Mao, for example, recalls that as a teenager she was confronted by an elderly White woman one day on her way home from school:

> This lady say, "Why the Hmong . . . like why they on welfare?" So then she said, "Oh those Hmong just have a lot of kids, just stay home, you know, they have a lot of . . . just keeps having children, and just stay home, receiving aid, receiving all those benefits, just stay home, just keep on having kids. Why don't they — don't they just move back to their country?"

Such racist attacks ring in the ears of these women and remind them that some Americans don't want them to be here.

Some of my informants suggested that the Hmong should respond to these stereotypes by working hard to educate Americans about the history and accomplishments of Hmong Americans, a view shared by prominent Hmong American organizations. The Hmong American Partnership in Minnesota, for example, published a report that sought to "challenge the misconceptions of the Hmong and provide the public with a greater understanding of our complex situation" (Yang & Murphy, 1993, p. 1). Similarly, male and female students at the Hmong Youth Conference in Washington, DC, suggested that Hmong people need to do more "to educate Americans about the Hmong [situation]."

Some of my informants, however, assert more directly that the stereotypes of the Hmong are racist, ignorant, and unwarranted. Sao, for example, is particularly angry about what she sees as the dominant society's ignorance about welfare and the Hmong community. Although she believes in the value of educating Americans about the Hmong, she maintains that they need not be apologetic for being in this country or for receiving public assistance. Sao defends the Hmong people's right to receive public assistance, since they were U.S. allies during the Vietnam War:

> I think in this case the Hmong have every right to use the welfare system. . . . We fought along with the Americans. You know? We were on their side and we fought the communists for so long. . . . Thirty percent of us died. . . . When they came here they have no money, nothing. Only the clothes on their back, and so of course you have to start somewhere and so it is only right the government, since they make the promise, it is only right that they help these people start something.[4]

Sao is angry at politicians who claim that welfare perpetuates dependence. She is quick to point out that many Hmong people, like her own family, have successfully used public assistance to help them get started:

> Government needs to talk to people who benefit from welfare. The policymakers, they don't understand the impact of the rules and regulations that they make. I wish that the policymaker will walk in shoes of a poor person for one

---

[4] According to many Hmong refugees, the CIA promised that the United States would help and protect the Hmong in return for their help in the war. For a brief discussion of the role of the Hmong in the war in Laos, see Chan (1994).

day. . . . The system works! I mean, look at — look at me! Look at my family. We aren't on welfare [anymore] — all my brothers and sisters all work and it only took us less than seven years. . . . We started off on welfare and now we are off welfare.

Furthermore, Sao asserts, far from being a drain on society, the Hmong are becoming business and property owners who contribute to the economic growth of American communities.

Some of these women seem to have internalized the racism of the dominant society, questioning their own self-worth and worrying about what non-Hmong Americans think about them. In school, the self-doubt leads them to withdraw and remain silent in class. Blia, for example, explains that she is afraid to speak out in her college classes because she fears that all the non-Asians are judging her:

College is really intimidating. I think I really feel, um, the fact that I'm a minority here. And I think that I'm inferior, I don't know as much. I don't have the cultural background. I don't have the economic upbringing to perhaps know something.

Such insecurity and the internalization of racism appear to be more common among the younger women in my study who came to the United States as very young children. These women have few memories of life before coming to the United States, and many seem confused about the details of the Hmong involvement in the war in Vietnam. At the Hmong Youth Conference, for example, young men and women expressed confusion over the role of Hmong soldiers in the war. In their efforts to get "the facts about the war," the organizers of the Hmong Youth Conference invited Hmong elders and former members of the CIA to speak on a panel.

I would argue that the younger women's confusion regarding the Hmong involvement in the war and their uncertainty about the circumstances surrounding their arrival in the United States make it difficult for them to resist racist stereotypes. It is important to point out, however, that their naiveté about the Hmong experience is not simply a reflection of their age, but also a reflection of their education. When I asked my informants whether they had been taught in school about the role Hmong soldiers played during the war, most looked at me blankly. One stated that she remembered reading a bit about the Vietnam War in a textbook, but did not get any information about the Hmong. As is true of other minority groups, the absence of a culturally relevant pedagogy that teaches about the Hmong American experience and about the Hmong involvement in the war alienates Hmong students from their history (Ladson-Billings, 1995). I am not simply referring to a curriculum that includes information about minority culture and history. While it is certainly important to teach students about their history and culture, I would argue that it is also important to help them develop the critical skills necessary to challenge racism and other forms of inequality. In describing culturally relevant pedagogy, Ladson-Billings states: "Not only must teachers encourage academic success and cultural competence, they must help students to recognize, understand, and critique current social inequalities" (1995, p. 476). A culturally relevant practice that encourages critical thinking would help empower these Hmong students to resist racism.

Impact of Welfare Reform

Policymakers, politicians, journalists, social workers, and members of the Hmong community have expressed concern over high levels of poverty and large numbers dependent upon public assistance among Hmong Americans (Fass, 1991; Rumbaut & Ima, 1988; Yang & Murphy, 1993). According to the 1990 Census, 61.8 percent of Hmong families in the United States lived below the poverty level in 1989, and 9,946 out of the 14,815 Hmong households in the United States (67.1%) received some form of public assistance. Despite room for concern, a closer look at the statistics provides some reason for optimism. For example, according to the 1990 Census, although two-thirds of all Hmong households in Minnesota receive some form of public assistance, more than a third of these households are made up of people who came to the United States after 1987 (Yang & Murphy, 1993). This may suggest that newcomers use public assistance to help them get established and move off of assistance once they are able to secure work, a view supported by my study, as most of my informants were raised in families in which public assistance was used as a transitional form of support. In general, these families depended on welfare until they were able to establish themselves financially, although those women raised by single mothers relied on public assistance long term.

Because of the relatively high numbers of Hmong Americans dependent on some form of public assistance, the current welfare reforms across the country will no doubt have an impact on the Hmong American community. The focus in the new welfare reform is to move people into the work force as quickly as possible. Many states will require recipients to work in order to receive support and will also limit the period for which support can be received (Haveman, 1996). The reforms are based on the assumptions that welfare discourages self-sufficiency and encourages dependence.

The state of Wisconsin, for example, which has one of the country's largest Hmong populations, has proposed a radical welfare reform plan (Wisconsin Works, or W-2). W-2 proposes that all assistance be time-limited and tied to work or other W-2 approved activities, not including training or education (Corbett, 1996). This work requirement will likely have a significant effect on Hmong families in Wisconsin who currently receive public assistance. Hmong adults with limited English-language skills may face serious barriers to employment. Language barriers are, in fact, a reality for a quarter of all welfare recipients (Haveman, 1996). The fact that W-2 payments do not include adjustments for the number of children in a family are potentially problematic for Hmong families, which are on the average larger than other American families (Rumbaut & Weeks, 1986).

For Hmong American women who are mothers and on public assistance, the full-time, year-round work requirement will create child-care concerns. Research shows that women with child-care problems are less likely to achieve self-sufficiency (Folk, 1996). Furthermore, researchers have found that for low-income mothers, child-care subsidies are crucial to becoming and remaining employed. Under W-2, families at or below 165 percent of poverty level who also meet all W-2 requirements are eligible for child-care subsidies for children under thirteen years of age. While these subsidies will help pay for child care, it is still unclear whether the supply of child care will be sufficient. Finally, it is crucial to point out that since child-care subsidies will only be provided for children under age thirteen, older children will run the risk of having no adult supervision after school hours and/or during the summer months.

Sao is particularly critical of the new welfare regulations that require work. In the following passage, she discusses the possible impact of welfare reform on Hmong who are single mothers and on their children:

> Now because of welfare reform or whatever they call it, I can see a lot of trouble already. A lot of the Hmong women that are here in America — a lot of them are single parent. You force women to go to work and the kids are left at home — Who are going to take care of their kids? . . . And then when they have no adult supervision they stay after school and they get involved with gangs.

Sao points out that single motherhood is a reality for many Hmong American women, a situation created not only by the death of a spouse or divorce, but also by the collision of the Hmong cultural practice of polygamy with U.S. laws. In Laos, the practice of polygamy meant that some Hmong men had more than one wife, as did the fathers of several of my informants. Because of the laws and cultural sanctions against polygamy in the United States, many women who are second or third wives of Hmong men raise their children as single mothers. Sao explained that her father had three wives in Laos, but after the war he officially separated from her mother. Thus, Sao's mother came to this country as the single mother of eleven dependent children. With eleven children, few marketable skills, and limited English-language ability, Sao's mother found it necessary to rely on public assistance. Sao maintains that this allowed her mother to be at home to provide the necessary guidance for her and her siblings, which she credits for the fact that she and all her siblings have been able to successfully finish some form of postsecondary education and find their way off public assistance and into jobs. Without adult supervision, Sao believes that both Hmong girls and boys will be drawn to gang involvement and all its attendant problems.

I would argue that the advent of W-2 could have a particularly harsh impact on Hmong daughters. With mothers having to "choose" work in order to receive public assistance, and with the prohibitive cost of child care, daughters in Hmong families are likely to be relegated to their traditional roles as the caretakers of younger siblings. Having to juggle such responsibilities with their school work may inhibit school persistence and achievement among these girls, making it more difficult for them to go to college.

Finally, the emphasis on work under W-2 and other welfare reform programs means that women will not be able to pursue higher education on a full-time basis while receiving public assistance. In my study, two women reported receiving some form of public assistance while attending college. Like the others in my study, these women see a college education as a way to get off welfare. Furthermore, the fact that child-care subsidies under W-2 are tied to work will mean that mothers will not be able to receive child-care subsidies to attend school, thereby inhibiting and most likely preventing any efforts on their part to educate themselves and become financially self-sufficient. And, given the Hmong cultural tradition of early marriage and motherhood, women who adhere most closely to the cultural norms will be most negatively affected by programs such as W-2, in that they will find it increasingly difficult to return to school once they have become mothers.

Conclusions

These women's stories demonstrate the complexity and texture of the lives of Hmong American women, even as journalists and scholars reduce their situation to one of pure cultural difference or symbolic exoticism. The culture in which Hmong American college women live is not simply a static entity, but rather a dynamic, shifting "work-in-progress" in which Hmong American college women act as agents of change through the expression of their hopes, dreams, and achievements, and through their adjustment to external political, economic, and social factors. Not only do the experiences of these women affect their own and future generations, they also have an impact on the older generations. However, despite evidence of cultural transformation that encourages school persistence, Hmong women still face cultural barriers to the pursuit of higher education demonstrating that cultural transformation is not a smooth process, but is fraught with tension and struggle.

In addition to ongoing cultural struggles, Hmong women face economic and racial barriers in their pursuit of higher education. With the prospect of welfare reform, such as Wisconsin's W-2, economic barriers to their pursuit of higher education could become even greater. I would argue that, although it is too early to say with any certainty, W-2 may be especially threatening to the educational aspirations of low-income Hmong American women who have followed the traditional Hmong practice of early marriage and motherhood.

The experiences of Hmong American college women illustrate the connection between cultural/private and structural/public concerns. In the face of structural limitations, any cultural change is limited in its potential to provide members of a minority group with the ability to fully pursue their dreams and transform the conditions of their lives.

References

Abu-Lughod, L. (1991). Writing against culture. In R. G. Fox (Ed.), *Recapturing anthropology: Working in the present* (pp. 137–162). Santa Fe, NM: School of American Research Press.

Aguilar, J. (1981). Insider research: An ethnography of a debate. In D. A. Messerschmidt (Ed.), *Anthropologists at home in North America: Methods and issues in the study of one's own society* (pp. 15–26). Cambridge, Eng.: Cambridge University Press.

Balibar, E. (1991). Preface. In E. Balibar & I. Wallerstein (Eds.), *Race, nation, class* (pp. 1–13). New York: Verso.

Chan, S. (1994). *Hmong means free: Life in Laos and America.* Philadelphia: Temple University Press.

Corbett, T. (1996). Understanding Wisconsin Works (W-2). *Focus, 18*(1), 53–54.

Donnelly, N. (1994). *Changing lives of refugee Hmong women.* Seattle: University of Washington Press.

Dubois, T. (1993). Constructions construed: The representation of Southeast Asian refugees in academic, popular, and adolescent discourse. *Amerasia, 19*(3), 1–25.

Dunnigan, T. (1986). Processes of identity maintenance in Hmong society. In G. Hendricks, B. Downing, & A. Deinard (Eds.), *The Hmong in transition* (pp. 41–53). New York: Center for Migration Studies.

Erickson, F. (1997). Culture in society and in educational practices. In J. Banks & C. Banks (Eds.), *Multicultural education: Issues and perspectives* (3rd ed., pp. 32–60). Boston: Allyn & Bacon.

Fass, S. (1991). *The Hmong in Wisconsin: On the road to self-sufficiency.* Milwaukee: Wisconsin Policy Research Institute.

Fine, M. (1991). *Framing dropouts: Notes on the politics of an urban high school.* Albany: State University of New York Press.

Fine, M. (1994). Dis-stance and other stances: Negotiations of power inside feminist research. In A. Gitlin (Ed.), *Power and method: Political activism and educational research* (pp. 13–35). New York: Routledge.

Fish, A. (1991). *The Hmong of St. Paul, Minnesota: The effects of culture, gender, and family networks on adolescents' plans for the future.* Unpublished master's thesis, University of Minnesota.

Folk, K. (1996). The W-2 child care plan. *Focus, 18*(1), 66–68.

Fong, C., & Yung, J. (1995/1996). In search of the right spouse: Interracial marriage among Chinese and Japanese Americans. *Amerasia, 21*(3), 77–98.

Foster, M. (1994). The power to know one thing is never the power to know all things: Methodological notes on two studies of Black American teachers. In A. Gitlin (Ed.), *Power and method: Political activism and educational research* (pp. 129–146). New York: Routledge.

Goldstein, B. (1985). *Schooling for cultural transitions: Hmong girls and boys in American high schools.* Unpublished doctoral dissertation, University of Wisconsin-Madison.

Goldstein, B. (1986). Resolving sexual assault: Hmong and the American legal system. In G. Hendricks, B. Downing, & A. Deinard (Eds.), *The Hmong in transition* (pp. 135–143). New York: Center for Migration Studies.

Harrison, F. (1995). The persistent power of "race" in the cultural and political economy of racism. *Annual Review of Anthropology, 24*, 47–74.

Haveman, R. (1996). From welfare to work: Problems and pitfalls. *Focus, 18*(1), 21–24.

Hendricks, G. (1986). Introduction. In G. Hendricks, B. Downing, & A. Deinard (Eds.), *The Hmong in transition* (pp. 3–5). New York: Center for Migration Studies.

Hirayama, K., & Hirayama, H. (1988). Stress, social supports, and adaptational patterns in Hmong refugee families. *Amerasia, 14*(1), 93–108.

Koltyk, J. (1993). Telling narratives through home videos: Hmong refugees and self documentation of life in the old and new country. *Journal of American Folklore, 106*, 435–449.

Kondo, D. (1990). *Crafting selves: Power, gender, and discourses of identity in a Japanese workplace.* Chicago: University of Chicago Press.

Ladson-Billings, G. (1995). Toward a theory of culturally relevant pedagogy. *American Educational Research Journal, 32*, 465–491.

Lee, S. J. (1996). *Unraveling the "model-minority" stereotype: Listening to Asian American youth.* New York: Teachers College Press.

Lutz, C., & Collins, J. (1993). *Reading National Geographic.* Chicago: University of Chicago Press.

Meredith, W., & Rowe, G. (1986). Changes in Hmong refugee marital attitudes in America. In G. Hendricks, B. Downing, & A. Deinard (Eds.), *The Hmong in transition* (pp. 121–131). New York: Center for Migration Studies.

Oakley, A. (1981). Interviewing women: A contradiction in terms. In H. Roberts (Ed.), *Doing feminist research* (pp. 30–61). London: Routledge & Kegan Paul.

Ogbu, J. U. (1987). Variability in minority school performance: A problem in search of an explanation. *Anthropology and Education Quarterly, 18,* 312–334.

Ogbu, J. U. (1991) Immigrant and involuntary minorities in comparative perspective. In M. Gibson & J. U. Ogbu (Eds.), *Minority status and schooling: A comparative study of immigrant and involuntary minorities* (pp. 3–33). New York: Garland Press.

Peterson, S. (1988). Translating experience and the reading of a story cloth. *Journal of American Folklore, 101,* 6–22.

Razack, S. (1995). The perils of talking about culture: Schooling research on South and East Asian students. *Race, Gender, and Class, 2*(3), 67–82.

Reinharz, S. (1992). *Feminist methods in social research.* New York: Oxford University Press.

Rumbaut, R., & Ima, K. (1988). *The adaptation of Southeast Asian refugee youth: A comparative study.* Washington, DC: Office of Refugee Resettlement.

Rumbaut, R., & Weeks, J. (1986). Fertility and adaptation: Indochinese refugees in the United States. *International Migration Review, 20,* 428–465.

Said, E. (1978). *Orientalism.* New York: Random House.

Scott, G. (1988). To catch or not to catch a thief: A case of bride theft among the Lao Hmong refugees of southern California. *Ethnic Groups, 7,* 137–151.

Sherman, S. (1988). The Hmong: Laotian refugees in the "Land of the Giants." *National Geographic, 174,* 586–610.

Suarez-Orozco, M. (1996). California dreaming: Proposition 187 and cultural psychology of racial and ethnic exclusion. *Anthropology and Education Quarterly, 27,* 151–167.

Tapp, N. (1988). The reformation of culture: Hmong refugees from Laos. *Journal of Refugee Studies, 1*(1), 20–37.

Vang, K. (1981). Hmong marriage customs: A current assessment. In B. Downing & D. Olney (Eds.), *The Hmong in the West: Observations and reports* (pp. 29–45). Minneapolis: University of Minnesota, Southeast Asian Refugee Studies Project and Center for Urban and Regional Affairs.

Walker-Moffat, W. (1995). *The other side of the Asian American success story.* San Francisco: Jossey Bass.

Wolf, E. (1982). *Europe and the people without history.* Berkeley: University of California Press.

Yang, P., & Murphy, N. (1993). *Hmong in the 90's: Stepping towards the future.* St. Paul, MN: Hmong American Partnership.

About the Contributors

DEIRDRE A. ALMEIDA is Assistant Professor of Education at the University of Massachusetts, Amherst. Her professional interests center around curriculum and learning, with a focus on Native American and indigenous education reform. She is author of "Introduction to Campus Tensions in Massachusetts" in *Equity and Excellence in Education* (1993), and *Detecting Anti-Indian Bias in Instructional Material* (1996).

WILLIAM AYERS is a Professor of Education and senior university scholar at the University of Illinois at Chicago. His primary area of professional interest is teaching for social justice. He is author of *A Kind and Just Parent: The Children of Juvenile Court* (1997).

JOY CAIRES is an English major at Smith College in Northampton, Massachusetts.

YELENA DYNNIKOV is a student at Queens College, City University of New York, in Flushing. She is interested in teaching and writing. Her article, "Under a Rap Attack," has appeared in *New York Newsday* (1993).

LINDA EISENMANN is Assistant Professor of Education in the Graduate College of Education at the University of Massachusetts, Boston. Her current research interests focus on the history of women in education, in particular on institutional efforts at gender equity in the 1950s and 1960s. She is author of "Befuddling the Feminine Mystique: Academic Women and the Creation of Educational Foundations" in *Educational Foundations* (1996), and editor of the *Historical Dictionary of Women's Education in the United States* (in press).

MICHELLE FINE, Professor of Psychology at the Graduate Center of the City University of New York, also works nationally as a consultant on issues of school reform. Her recent books include *Chartering Urban School Reform: Reflections on Public High School in the Midst of Change* (1994) and *Becoming Gentlemen: Women, Law School, and Institutional Change* (coauthored with L. Guinier and J. Balin, 1997). She was the 1994 recipient of the Janet Helms Distinguished Scholar Award.

CAROL GILLIGAN is Patricia Albjerg Graham Professor of Gender Studies at Harvard Graduate School of Education. Her recent books include *Meeting at the Crossroads: Women's Psychology and Girls' Development* (coauthored with L. M. Brown, 1992), and *Between Voice and Silence: Women and Girls, Race and Relationship* (coauthored with J. M. Taylor and A. M. Sullivan, 1995).

KARI LARSEN, a sophomore at the Pilot School in Rindge and Latin High School in Cambridge, Massachusetts, was born in Qui Nhon, Vietnam. She is a member of a lively family that includes her adoptive parents and five brothers and sisters who represent many different nationalities and cultures. (Editors' note: This information is from 1988, when we originally published her work. No more recent information is available.)

RACHEL LIBERATORE is a first-year student at Grinnell College in Grinnell, Iowa, where she is considering a degree in English education. Her poem "The River" appeared in *The Twelfth Annual High School Poetry Anthology*.

STACEY J. LEE. Associate Professor in the Educational Policy Studies Department of the University of Wisconsin-Madison, is interested in the ethnic identity and school achievement of Asian American students. Her previous publications include *Unraveling the "Model Minority" Stereotype: Listening to Asian American Youth* (1996).

FRANCES A. MAHER is a Professor in the Education Department of Wheaton College, Norton, Massachusetts. Her research interests focus on feminist pedagogy and women's studies. Her published works include *The Feminist Classroom: An Inside Look at How Professors and Students Are Transforming Higher Education for a Diverse Society* (coauthored with M. K. Tetreault, 1994), and *"Women's Ways of Knowing* in Women's Studies, Feminist Pedagogies and Feminist Theory" in *Knowledge, Difference and Power, Essays Inspired by Women's Ways of Knowing* (1996).

JANE ROLAND MARTIN is Professor of Philosophy Emerita at the University of Massachusetts, Boston. She is author of *Reclaiming a Conversation* (1985), *The Schoolhome* (1992), and *Changing the Educational Landscape* (1994).

MARIWILDA PADILLA-DIAZ is a Consultant at the Department of Health of Puerto Rico in San Juan. Her professional interests focus on Latina Women's preventive health and social policy, with a particular expertise in women's empowerment issues. She is author of several articles on women's health for community newspapers, women's organizations' newsletters, and adult literacy magazines.

LINDA M. PERKINS. Associate Professor in the Department of Education at Hunter College, City University of New York, is interested in the history of U.S. higher education. Her publications include *Fanny Jackson Coppin and the Institute for Colored Youth, 1837–1902* (1987), and "For the Good of the Race: A Historical Perspective on African American Academic Couples" in *Academic Couples: Problems and Promises,* edited by M. A. Ferber and J. W. Loeb (1997).

IMANI PERRY is presently pursuing a joint J.D.-Ph.D. program at Harvard University. Her dissertation addresses the issue of race in American law and literature between 1870 and 1910. She is author of "Toasts, Jam and Libation: Or, How We Place Malcolm in the Folk Tradition" in *Teaching Malcolm X* (edited by T. Perry, 1996), and *A Nation on No Map: The Politics and Poetics of Hip Hop* (forthcoming).

ANNIE G. ROGERS is Associate Professor in Human Development and Psychology at Harvard Graduate School of Education. Her research focuses on the psychology of girls and women, gender and trauma, ego development theory, and feminist qualitative research methods. Her published works include *Women, Girls and Psychotherapy: Reframing Resistance* (coedited with C. Gilligan and D. Tolman, 1991), and *A Shining Affliction: A Story of Harm and Healing in Psychotherapy* (1995).

MARILYN R. SCHUSTER. Professor of French and Women's Studies at Smith College in Northampton, Massachusetts, is interested in women's studies, feminist literary criticism, and women's literature and queer studies. She is coeditor of *Women's Place in the Academy: Transforming the Liberal Arts Curriculum* (with S. R. Van Dyne, 1985), and *Marguerite Duras Revisited* (1993).

NAN STEIN is a Senior Research Scientist at the Center for Research on Women in Wellesley, Massachusetts. Her professional interests include gender violence, sexual harassment in K-12 schools, and curriculum development. She is author of *Bullyproof: A Teacher's Guide on Teasing and Bullying for Use with Fourth and Fifth Grade Students* (coauthored with L. Sjostrom, 1996), and *Between the Lines: Sexual Harassment in K-12 Schools* (forthcoming).

MARY KAY THOMPSON TETREAULT is Vice President of Academic Affairs at California State University, Fullerton. Her professional interests center around feminist pedagogy, social constructions of Whiteness, and the epistemology of knowing and learning. She is coauthor of *The Feminist Classroom: An Inside Look at How Professors and Students Are Transforming Higher Education for a Diverse Society* (with F. A. Maher, 1994), and author of "'They Got the Paradigm and Painted It White': Higher Education Classrooms and Legal Discourse" in *Duke Journal of Gender Law and Policy* (1997).

SUSAN VAN DYNE is Professor of Women's Studies and English, and Director of the Women's Studies Program at Smith College, Northampton, Massachusetts. She is interested in contemporary American women poets. Her publications include *Women's Place in the Academy: Transforming the Liberal Arts Curriculum* (coedited with M. R. Schuster, 1985), and *Revising Life: Sylvia Plath's Ariel Poems* (1993).

SOFIA VILLENAS is Assistant Professor in Educational Studies and Ethnic Studies at the University of Utah. Her present areas of interest include anthropology of education, educational issues of Latino communities, and multicultural and bilingual/bicultural education.

JANIE VICTORIA WARD. Associate Professor of Education and Human Services at Simmons College in Boston, Massachusetts, is interested in adolescent development, racial identity development, and racial socialization. She is coeditor of *Mapping the Moral Domain: A Contribution of Woman's Thinking to Psychological Theory and Education* (with C. Gilligan and J. Taylor, 1989) and *Black Adolescent Portraits* (with A. Garrod and T. Robinson, forthcoming).

KATHLEEN WEILER. Associate Professor of Education at Tufts University, Medford, Massachusetts, is interested in the history of women in education. Her published works include *Women Teaching for Change* (1988), *Feminism and Social Justice in Education* (coedited with M. Arnot, 1993), and *Country Schoolwomen: Teaching in the California Countryside, 1850–1950* (in press).

ALEX WILSON is a doctoral candidate in Human Development and Psychology at the Harvard Graduate School of Education. Her research centers around the psychologies of indigenous peoples.

EVA YOUNG. a facilitator and consultant, works in the areas of community development, children's educational achievement, and diversity dialogues and linkages. She is author of *Inside Images* (1990), *Pelo Bueno/Pelo Malo—Good Hair/Bad Hair* (1994), and *Cultura Es Vida (Culture Is Life)* (1996).

About the Editors

HOLLY S. GELFOND is a doctoral candidate in Human Development and Psychology at the Harvard Graduate School of Education. She is also a therapist at the Trauma Center, Arbour-HRI Hospital in Brookline, Massachusetts. As a rehabilitation therapist at McLean Hospital in Belmont, Massachusetts, she designed therapeutic programs using the arts to foster resiliency in children and adolescents. Her current research interests include the relationship between Eye Movement Desensitization Reprocessing (EMDR) and the biophysiological effects of neglect and trauma on psychological development.

CHRISTINE A. WOYSHNER is a teacher educator and doctoral candidate at the Harvard Graduate School of Education. Her dissertation is a study of the origins of the Parent Teacher Association. Her other research interests include the history of teacher education and the educational experiences of women in nineteenth-century civic voluntary organizations, such as the National Congress of Mothers and the Women's Christian Temperance Union. She previously taught second and third grade.